The Record
of the
First Presbyterian Church
—of—
Morristown, New Jersey

Containing

First:

Volumes I and II, Jan., 1880–Dec., 1881
Conducted by Rev. Rufus S. Green
Pages 1–240

with

Supplement, pages 145, 152 (241–248)
being Report of the Church and
Roll of Members, 1884

Second:

Volumes III, IV and V, Jan., 1883–Dec., 1885
Conducted by Rev. William Durant
Pages 1–192

HERITAGE BOOKS
2018

HERITAGE BOOKS

AN IMPRINT OF HERITAGE BOOKS, INC.

Books, CDs, and more—Worldwide

For our listing of thousands of titles see our website
at
www.HeritageBooks.com

A Facsimile Reprint
Published 2018 by
HERITAGE BOOKS, INC.
Publishing Division
5810 Ruatan Street
Berwyn Heights, Md. 20740

Originally published
Morristown, New Jersey
First Presbyterian Church
1885

International Standard Book Numbers
Paperbound: 978-0-7884-4747-1
Clothbound: 978-0-7884-6235-1

NOTE.

The Minutes of the Trustees have been reprinted, forming Part I of the "History of the First Presbyterian Church, Morristown, N. J."

The Baptisms, Marriages, List of Members and Burials have been included in Part II, forming the Combined Registers.

THE RECORD.

FIRST PRESBYTERIAN CHURCH, MORRISTOWN, N. J.

"This shall be Written for the Generation to Come."—Psalms 102 : 18.

VOL. I.	JANUARY. 1880,	NO. I.

(Printed with the approval of Session.)

PROSPECTUS.

THE RECORD will be published monthly during the year 1880. Terms, 50 cents in advance ; 75 cents after June. As it is not expected that the subscriptions will be sufficient to meet the necessary expenses of publication, THE RECORD is commended to the generosity of all interested in the early history of the town. . Should more money be received than is needed for actual expenses it will be placed to the credit of the Benevolent Fund of the Session. THE RECORD desires to secure anything pertaining to the history of the town and county of Morris and its early settlers— old papers, pamphlets, sermons and lectures, books, family histories and genealogies, printed or in MS., or copied (*carefully*) from old Bibles and records, &c., &c. ; also, all marriages during the pastorate of Dr. McDowell, from 1814 to 1825, and marriages of members of the congregation by ministers not pastors of this church. Items with reference to any named in the various lists will be thankfully received and preserved for future use. We especially desire our readers to aid us in supplying all omissions and correcting all mistakes on our rolls.

Subscriptions will be received at the book-stores of Messrs. Runyon and Emmell, or through the mail. ALL COMMUNICATIONS should be addressed to

THE RECORD,

Morristown, N. J.

Lock box 44.

CHURCH DIRECTORY.

:o:

Pastor.—RUFUS S. GREEN.

RULING ELDERS.

ENOCH T. CASKEY, WM. W. STONE,
JOEL DAVIS, LEBBEUS B. WARD.
H. M. DALRYMPLE, JOS. H. VAN DOREN.
THEODORE LITTLE, Clerk,

DEACONS.

VICTOR FLEURY, HENRY M. OLMSTED.

TRUSTEES.

A. B. HULL, President.

| H. C. PITNEY, | } Committee on Buildings and Grounds. |
| EDWARD PIERSON. | |

| WM. E. CHURCH, | } Committee on Seats, Music, etc. |
| WAYL'D SPAULDING | |

| THOS. C. BUSHNELL, | } Committee on Finance. |
| J. H. VAN DOREN, | |

J. H. VAN DOREN, Clerk.

The President is *ex officio* member of each Committee.

A. B. HULL, Treasurer of Parish.
JAS. R. VOORHEES, Clerk of Parish.
FRANCIS L. WHITEHEAD, Sexton.

THE OBJECT

Of THE Record is such as to lead to the belief that many will gladly give it their encouragement. It desires especially to gather and preserve much that is fading of the early history of the town and county, to perfect our Church rolls, and to awaken an interest in the important events and noble men and women of the past. The history of the First Church prior to the year 1800 is largely the history of the town. The statement will doubtless surprise all that *prior to the year 1800 over 10,000 names appear upon our records.* We deem it of the greatest importance that these names should be put, by means of the printed page, beyond all danger of destruction. THE RECORD refuses to make any money, but *it must pay expenses,* or cease publication at the end of the year, and before it has had the time to fulfil its mission. We therefore ask the aid of all who appreciate the importance of our work, and will be especially thankful to the press for any kind words which will make THE RECORD known to the thousands in our land descended from those whose names we hope to print.

NEW YORK, January 9, 1880.

Rev. Rufus S. Green.:

DEAR BROTHER.—I congratulate you and the good people of Morristown on the issue of the first number of your church paper. In the ancient records of the old Morristown church, as I have had occasion during the past Summer to ascertain, are found statements of facts and registries of events of no little interest to the old families of your town and its immediate neighborhood.

It must be of interest to know who were the founders of these old families; who were their wives—when they were married; who were their children—when they were born and baptized; and whom and when they, too, married. So, too, it is desirable to know when they connected themselves with the church, under whose ministrations, and whether by profession of faith or by certificate from other churches. Nor less to know when, and at what age, and of what disease, these forefathers and fore-mothers of the hamlet died. The story of that populous cemetery in the rear of the old church is told in part in the two editions of your *Bill of Mortality* from 1768 to 1812, a period of more than forty-three years. But the book itself belongs to the past; it is rarely to be found except in public libraries or in the collection of the antiquarian. Your paper will help to make its treasures the common property of the people. And then, what of the dead who preceded 1768, and passed away since 1812?

A medium of communication between the pulpit and the pew is very desirable; the pastor has many things to say, many inquiries to make, much information to communicate, for which a monthly or bi-monthly is better adapted than the pulpit. The history of the time-honored church over which Johnes and Richards and Fisher and Mc-Dowell and Barnes, noble and illustrious men all, presided with so much credit to themselves and profit to the people, is worthy of a permanent record. The materials are ample; many of them are scattered about among the unpublished letters and diaries of the generations gone by, and in the unwritten traditions of the past. What a thrilling episode was the repeated wintering of Washington and his Generals with their regiments in and about Morristown! What vivid and thrilling recollections may still be gathered up and put on record for unborn generations, of the great revivals of other days! The humble periodical, the first number of which now goes forth in promise of many more to come, may properly be made the medium of gathering these and a thousand other precious memories of the past to aid the historian in his work.

And the people, too, have inquiries to make, information to gain, long-sought but in vain, respecting their ancestry, their kindred, their former neighbors. Here is a vehicle by which they may seek to gratify long-cherished desires.

The uses to which such an humble periodical may be put are too many to be enumerated in the brief space allotted to this article. Let the means for keeping it up not be wanting; it is a good design; a blessing is in it. With God's favor it will surely prosper.

Yours truly,

EDWIN F. HATFIELD.

LIST OF PASTORS.

1. *Rev. Timothy Johnes, D.D.*
   Began Aug. 13, 1742; ordained Feb. 9, 1743; died Sept. 17, 1794.

2. *Rev. Aaron C. Collins.*
   Settled Jan. 6, 1791; dismissed Sept. 2, 1793.

3. *Rev. James Richards, D.D.*
   Settled May 1, 1795; dis. Apr. 26, 1809.

4. *Rev. Samuel Fisher, D.D.*
   Settled July or Aug. 1809; dis. Apr. 27, 1814.

5. *Rev. Wm. A. McDowell, D.D.*
   Settled Dec. 13, 1814; dis. Oct. 23, 1823. *(8m 1/2 1. 24 3)*

6. *Rev. Albert Barnes.*
   Ordained and installed Feb. 8, 1825; dis. June 8, 1830.

7. *Rev. Charles Hoover.*
   Settled Feb. 8, 1832; dis. March 10, 1836.

8. *Rev. Orlando L. Kirtland.*
   Settled March 23, 1837; dis. Aug. 26, 1840.

9. *Rev. A. Henry Dumont.*
   Settled Jan. 20, 1841; dis. July 9, 1845.

10. *Rev. Alexander R. Thompson.*
    Ord. and inst. Jan. 14, 1846; dis. July 28, 1847.

11. *Rev. James R. Richards, D.D.*
    Settled Dec. 28, 1847; dis. April 15, 1851.

12. *Rev. John H. Townley.*
    Settled Dec. 27, 1851; died Feb. 5, 1855.

13. *Rev. David Irving, D.D.*
    Settled Nov. 5, 1855; dis. May 10, 1865.

14. *Rev. Gavin Langmuir.*
    Settled July 17, 1866; dis. Sept. 9, 1868.

15. *Rev. John Abbott French.*
    Settled Dec. 21, 1868; dis. Jan. 31, 1877.

16. *Rev. Rufus Smith Green.*
    Began June 17, 1877; inst. July 18, 1877.

——:o:——

Before the settlement of Dr. Johnes the church was ministered to by the Rev. John Cleverly, of whose work no record is left. He was buried in the First Church yard Dec. 31, 1776.

A CHARTER FOR THE PRESBYTERIAN CHURCH IN MORRISTOWN.

George the Second, by the Grace of God, of Great Britain, France and Ireland, King, Defender of the Faith. To all to whom these presents shall come, GREETING:

WHEREAS, the advancement of true Religion and virtue is absolutely necessary for the promotion of Peace, order and prosperity of the State,

AND WHEREAS, it is the duty of all Christian princes and Governors by the law of God, to do all they can for the encouragement thereof;

AND WHEREAS, Sundry of our loving Subjects of the Presbyterian Persuasion Inhaabitants of an about the Township of Morris, within our Colony of New Jersey, by their humble petition presented to our Trusty and well beloved Jonathan Belcher, Esq., our Captain General and Commander in Chief of our Province of New Jersey and Vice Admiral in the same, shewing that the petitioners and others of the same persuasion Inhabitants, in and about the Township of Morris aforesaid, do make up a verly large and considerable congregation, that the most advantageous support of religion among them necessarily requires that some persons should be incorporated as Trustees for the community that they may take grants of lands and chattels thereby, to enable the Petitioners to erect and repair public buildings for the Worship of God, and the use of the Ministry and School Houses and Alms Houses, and suitably to support the Ministry and the Poor of their church, and to do and perform other acts of Piety and Charity, and that the same Trustees may have power to let and grant the same under a Publick Seal for the uses aforesaid, And that the same Trustees may plead and be impleaded in any suit touching the premises and have perpetual succession; that also the known Loyalty of the Petitioners and the Presbyterians in General to us, their firm affection to our person and Government, and the Protestant succession in our Royal House, gave the Petitioners hopes of reasonable Indulgence and favour within the same Colony where the Religious rites of Mankind are so happily preserved, and where our equal Grace and

Bounty to all our Protestant faithful Subjects however differing in opinion about lesser matters has hitherto been so sensibly felt and enjoyed, the said Petitioners therefore most humbly prayed our Grant of an Incorporation to the Petitioners by the name of the Trustees of the Presbyterian Church in Morris Town, with all such powers, capacities and privileges as might be effectual in law for the purposes aforesaid, and that Benjamin Hatheway, Charles Howell, Henry Primrose, Benjamin Bayles, Thomas Kent, Benjamin Coe and Samuel Roberts might be the first Trustees, which petition signed with the names of a great number of our faithful and loving subjects, Inhabitants in and about the said Town, we being willing to Grant ——

KNOW YE, that we of our especial Grace, certain knowledge and meer motion, have willed and ordained, constituted, given and granted, and for us, our heirs and successors by these presents, Do, will, ordain, constitute, give and grant, that Benjamin Hathaway, Charles Howell, Henry Primrose, Benjamin Bayles, Thomas Kent, Benjamin Coe and Samuel Roberts, from henceforth and their successors forever hereafter, shall be and remain one body politick and corporate, in deed, fact and name, by the name of the Trustees of the Presbyterian Church in Morris Town, and them and their successors by the name of the Trustees of the Presbyterian Church in Morris Town one body body corporate and politick, in deed, fact and name, really and fully. We do for us, our heirs and successors, erect, make, ordain constitute, declare and create by these presents, and by that name they shall and may have perpetual succession.

AND ALSO, that they and their successors, by the name of the Trustees of the Presbyterian Church in Morris Town, be and forever hereafter, shall be persons able in law, to purchase, take, hold, receive and enjoy any messuages, Houses, Buildings, Lands, Tenements, rents, possessions and other heriditaments and real estate, in fee simple or otherwise, so as the yearly clear value of the same does not exceed the sum of Two hundred pounds sterling, the statute of Mortmain or any other law to the contrary notwithstanding, and also goods, chattels and all other things of what kind or quality soever.

AND ALSO, that they or their successors, by the name of the Trustees of the Presbyterian Church in Morris Town, shall and may give, grant and demise, assign, sell or otherwise dispose of all or any of their messuages, houses, lands, tenements, rents, possessions and other hereditaments and real estate, and all their goods, chattels and other things aforesaid as to them shall seem meet. And also, that they and their successors, by the name of the Trustees of the Presbyterian Church in Morris Town, be and forever hereafter, shall be persons able in law and capable to sue and be sued, implead or be impleaded, answer or be answered, defend or be defended in all Courts of Judicature whatever. And also, that the said Trustees of the Presbyterian Church in Morris Town for the time being, and their successors shall and may forever hereafter, have and use a common seal with such device or devices as they shall think proper for sealing all and singular deeds, grants, conveyances, contracts, Bonds, Articles of Agreement, assignments, powers, authorities and singular, their affairs and things touching or concerning the said Corporation. And also, that the said Trustees and their successors forever, may as oft as they see fit break change and new make the same or any other their common seal. And further, we do of our especial Grace certain knowledge and mere motion for us, our heirs and successors by these presents, Will, ordain, constitute, give and grant, that upon any vacancy among the Trustees of the said Presbyterian Church in Morris Town, by death, removal or other Incapacity whatsoever, that the Minister or Ministers, Elders and Deacons for the time being of the said Presbyterian Church in Morris Town, shall and may meet together at Morris Town aforesaid, and then and there elect and choose such person or persons out of the Congregation of said Church as they think proper to supply the vacancy of such Trustee or Trustees, caused by death, removal or other Incapacity as aforesaid. And also, that at any and all times whatsoever, when the said Minister or Ministers, Elders and Deacons of the Church afores'd or the majority of them for the time being, shall and may meet together at Morris Town aforesaid, and are hereby sufficiently authorized then and there to displace and to remove from the office of Trustee and such Trustee or Trustees, and in their room and stead to elect and choose out of the Congregation of said Church, any person or persons to supply the place or places of such Trustee or Trustees so displaced, and, removed, provided always that the number of the said Trustees exceed not seven, and every Trustee so elected & appointed as aforesaid, shall by virtue of these presents and of such election and appointment be vested with all the power and privileges which any of the other Trustees has or has had. And we do further, will and Ordain, give and grant that the Trustees of the said Presbyterian Church in Morris Town and their successors for the time being, shall from time to time have power to choose their President out of the Trustees for the time being, who shall have the custody of the publick seal of the said corporation, and all the Books, Charters, Deeds and Writings anyways relating to the said corporation, and shall have power from time to time and at all times hereafter, as occasion shall require to call a meeting of the said Trustees at Morris Town aforesaid, for the election of all or any of the powers hereby given and granted; and in case of sickness, absence or death of the President, all the powers by these presents granted to the President shall be and remain in the Eldest Trustee upon record until the recovery or return of the President, or until a new President be chosen as aforesaid. And we do further Will, ordain, give and grant that all and every act and order of four of the said Trustees (but not of any lesser number) consented and agreed to at such meeting of the Trustees aforesaid, shall be good, valid and effectual to all intents and purposes as if the whole number of the said Trustees had consented and agreed thereto. And we do further Will and Ordain, that all the acts of the said Trustees, shall from time to time be fairly entered in a Book or Books to be kept for that purpose by the President of the Trustees for the time being, which book or books together with the Seal of the said Corporation and all charters, deeds and writings

whatsoever belonging any ways to the said Corporation, shall be delivered over by the former President to the President of the said Trustees newly elected for the time being, as such President shall hereafter from time to time successively be chosen.

And Lastly, we do of our especial Grace certain knowlege and mere motion for us, our heirs and successors by these presents, give and grant unto the said Trustees of the Presbyterian Church in Morris Town and their successors forever, that these our Letters Patent on the Enrollment thereof, shall be good and effectual in the law to all intents and purposes against us, our heirs and successors without any other License, Grant or Confirmation from us, our heirs and successors hereafter by the said Trustees of the said Presbyterian Church in Morris Town, to be had or obtained notwithstanding the not reciting or misrecital, or not naming or misnaming of the aforesaid offices, franchises, privileges, immunities or other, the premises or any of them, and notwithstanding the Writ of Ad Quod Damnum hath not issued forth to enquire of the premises or any of them before ensealing hereof, any Statute, act, ordinance or provision, or any other matter or thing to the contrary notwithstanding.

To have, hold and enjoy all and singular, the privileges, advantages, liberties, immunities and all other the premises herein, and hereby granted and given or which are meant, mentioned or intended to be herein given and granted unto them, the said Trustees of the Presbyterian Church in Morris Town and to their successors forever.

In Testimony Whereof, we have caused these our Letters to be made Patent, and the Great Seal of our said Province of New Jersey to be hereunto affixed.

Witness, our Trusty and well beloved Jonathan Belcher, Esquire, Governor and Commander in Chief of our said Province of New Jersey, this Eighth day of September, in the Thirtieth year of our reign, and in the year of our Lord one thousand Seven hundred fifty and Six.

CHARLES READ, Secr'y.

I have perused the above charter and find nothing therein contained inconsistent with the honor and interest of the Crown. September 17th, 1756.

C. SKINNER, Att'y Gen'l.

Let the Great Seal of the Province

(GREAT) be hereunto affixed.
(SEAL) J. BELCHER.
(OF) To the Secretary of New
(NEW JERSEY.) Jersey.

Recorded at Trenton, Oct. 5, 1774, in Book C, 3, of Commissions, page 7, &c.

BAPTISMS.

" The Names & number of the Children I have baptized with the time of their Baptism."

TIMOTHY JOHNES.

1743.
Feb. 19 Benjamin Bayley's child William.
Feb. 19. John Perkhurst's ch. Mary.
" 27. Stephen Mahurin's ch. Ebenezer.
Mrch. 5. Benj. Conger's ch. Noah.
" 27. Joseph Prudden's negro's ch. Violet.
Apr. 3. John Lindley, Jun., His ch. Silenus.
" " Sam'l Ford's ch. Eunice.
" 29. Joseph Tichenor's ch. Moses.
Jun. 29. John Stiles' ch. Enos.
" 12. Abraham Johnson, of Rockaway, ch. Esther.
" 19. Joseph Edmister, of Roxitcus, ch. Daniel.
" " Mary, wf. of Hur Orsborn, ch. Thomas.
" 26. Jacob Ford, his ch. Elizabeth.
" " Susanna, wf. of Caleb Tichenor, ch. Susanna.
Aug. 28. Jacob Cusat of Succasunny, ch. Lea.
Aug. 28 Jonah Austin, ch. Moses.
Sept. 18. Job Allen, of Rockaway, ch. Elizabeth.
" " John Clark, ch. Joseph.
" 25. Eleanor, wf. of Richard Easton, children William and Sarah.
" " Elizabeth, wf. of Benjamin Hains, ch. Amariah.
Oct. 30. Matthew Fairchild, ch. Caleb.
" " Wm. Losey, ch. Zebulun.
Nov. 6. Stephen Ogden, of Basking Ridge, ch. Jonathan.
" " Tabitha, wf. of Dan'l Frost, ch. Mary.
" " Benj. Hathaway, ch. Benoni.
" " John Holloway, ch. Lois.
Dec. 23. Benj. Coe, ch. Phebe.
" " Benj. Perkhurst, ch. Mary.
1744.
Jan. 15. Joseph Prudden's negro's ch. Oliver.
Feb. 5. Samuel Day's Household, Silas, and twins Ezekiel & Phebe.
" " Benj. Pierson & wf., ch. Patience.
" " Sam'l Lindley, ch. Kezia.
" 24. James Tompkins, adult.

Feb. 24. Sarah, wf. of Richard Woods, adult.
Feb. 26. Timothy Peck, ch. Abigail.
Mrch. 7. Abigail, wf. of John Johnson, Jr., ch. Gershom.
" 11. Philip Cundit, ch. Mary.
" 25. Samuel Bailey, ch. John.
" " Catharine, wf. of Peter Stagg, ch. William.
" " Mary, wf. of Isaac Clark, ch. Phebe.
Apr. 8. Peter Cundit, ch. Peter.
" " Joseph Howard, ch. Sarah.
" 15. Cornelius Austin, ch. Peter.
" " Zophar Gildersleeve, ch. Susanna.
May 20. James Cole, ch. Elizabeth.
" 27. James Tompkins, twins, Thomas & Mary.
" " Gilbard Heady, ch. Elisha.
" " John Perkhurst, ch. Sarah.
July 1. Timothy Mills, ch. Jedidiah.
Aug. 12. Benj. Conger, ch. David.
" 26. Richard Minthorn, child Rachel.
" " Seth Hall, ch. Jane.
" " Thomas Allerton's Household, Sarah, (on own account), John, Charity & David.
Sept. 30. Matthew Fairchild, ch. Ruth.
Oct. 7. Jonah Austin, ch. Mary.
" " William Frost, ch. Abigail.
" 14. Stephen Mahurin, ch. Silas.
Oct. 28. Benj. Freeman, ch. Benas. (?).
" " Joseph Moore, ch. Rachel.
Nov. 4. Zachariah Fairchild, ch. Abiel.
" 18. Uriah Cutler, ch. Bathiah.
1745.
Jan. 11. Bathiah, wf. of Nathan'l Wheler, Household, Joseph, Miriam, Jemima & Rachel.
" 13. Dan'l Lindley, ch. Zenas.
" 27. Bois John Prudden, ch. Amos.
Feb. 24. Sarah, wf. of Richard Wood, ch. Hopestill.
Mrch. 24. Joseph Stiles, ch. Silas.
" " Dan'l Freman, ch. Chloe.
" " Sarah, wf. of Wm. Smallpeace, ch. Elizabeth.
Apr. 14. John Losey, ch. Timothy.
" " Sam'l Fford, ch. Demas.
June 2. Abner Beach, ch. Benjamin.
" " Wm. Minthorn, ch. Sarah.
" 5. Jacob Allerton, " Jacob.
May 19. Ame, wf. of Elijah Davis, ch. Ame.
June 16. David Day, of Turkey, ch. Jemimah.

(Continued on page 18.)

MARRIAGES.

"A Register of my Marriages with ye time,
names of ye Persons & their Places of
abode.

N. B. Those yt Belong to ye town are not
Registered."

TIMOTHY JOHNES.

1743.

Mrch. 9. John Eston, of Roxbury, & Sarah Muchmore, of Turkey.

Apr. 12. Eliphalet Luis & Elizabeth Cusat, of Blackriver.

Apr. 13. David Moor & Elizabeth Buff (?)

" 19. Thomas Young & Thankful Robarts.

Nov. 9. Sam'l Munson & Elizabeth Potter.

Apr. 20. Peter Stagg, of Hanover, & Catharine Primrose.

Dec. 15. Uriah Cutler & Rachel Campfield.

" 21. Sam'l Ludlum & Abigail Hathaway.

" 22. Abraham Stagg & Jemima Cole.

1744.

Mrch.11. Jonathan Orsborn & Mary Hopkins, of Roxbury.

" 14. Benj. Hathaway & Elizabeth Crosman, wido.

Apr. 1. Daniel Gobil & Priscilla Cook.

" 8. Thomas Gilbard, of Rockaway, & Abigail Corey.

May 3. Seth Croel & Else Eddy, of Woodbridge.

" 29. Moses Tomkins, of Roxbury, & Hannah Tompkins.

June 17. Jonathan Reeve & Elizabeth Arnold.

Aug. 15. Simon Kent, of Rockaway, & Penelope Carter, of Rockaway.

Dec. 24. Sam'l Muckelroy, foreigner, & Elizabeth Jones.

1745.

Jan. 21. John Aber & Mary Hulbard.

Feb. 6. Joseph Wigget & Desire Cranmer.

Mrch. 4. Peter Norris & Mary Mahurin.

" 10. Isaac Potter & Sarah Munson.

Apr. 4. Hajadiah Sampson & Rachel Catterlin.

" 25. Timo. Dunnin & Elizabeth Smith.

June 20. Creed Ludlum & Elizabeth Carl.

Aug. 8. Daniel Howard & Rachel Latiner.

Oct. 9. Sam'l Munson, wid'r, & Mary Allen.

" 10. James Watkins & Mary Primrose.

Oct. 20. Peter Dickerson & Ruth Coe.

" 24. James Sheperd (?) & Elizabeth Tasley, (?).

Dec. 23. Joseph Wood & Hannah Lindley.

1746.

Jan. 16. Benj. Hathaway & Hannah Bailey.

Feb. 2. Joik'm Brown & Jane Fanger.

Apr. 9. Abraham Orsborn & Mary Harris.

May 16. Ezekiel Younglove, of Reddis Town, & Mary Lyon.

Sept. 15. Stephen Lindley & Phebe Dickerson, wido.

Nov. 12. Benj. Hathaway & Mary Fairchild.

Dec. 15. Isaac Tuttle, of Hanover, & Sarah Lindley.

Dec. 24. Ichabod Tompkins, of Hanover, & Hannah Gobil.

1747.

Jan. 16. Benj. Halsey & Sarah Prudden.

Feb. 19. Joseph Edmister & Abigail Beman.

Apr. 20. Sam'l Sweasy, Justice of Roxbury, & Susanna Huntington, wido.

July 5. Isaac Daton & Ann Herimon, of Hanover.

July 23. Zeb. Harison, of Augusta Co., Va., & Margaret Primrose.

" 27. David Gauden & Hopefull Wood.

Sept. 14. John Glover, Southold, Long Is., & Martha Lyon.

Sept. 17. David Cranford, of Elizabeth Town, & Prescott Primrose.

Oct. 21. John Johnson & Jane Doty, of Succasunny.

Nov. 18. Benj. Lyon & Mary Lum, of Lyons Farm.

1748.

Jan. 14. Jonathan Cory, of Hanover, & Rachel Merrit, of . "

" 27. Caleb Leonard, of Roxiticus & Jemima Minthorn.

Mrch.20. John Fford & Penelope Gennings.

" 29. Henry Primrose & Rebecca Stites.

May 2d. Gershom Hough, of Roxbury, & Hannah Walker, wido., of Hanover.

May 14. Henry Gardiner & Rachel Coe.

" 18. William Tuttle & Abigail Hulbard.

" 25. William Miller & Catherine (?) Mabon (?)

" 26. Nathaniel Stilwell & Mary Cole.

Sept. 7. Richard Easton & Saran Lyon, of Lyon Farms.

Oct. 16. Sam'l Arnold & Phebe Fford.

(Continued on page 14.)

WHO CAN TELL?

1. The exact date of the settlement of Rev. Samuel Fisher?

2. Who can fill any of the blanks in the list of Elders?

3. In contemporary papers the following entries appear; Elder Caleb Munson died at New Vernon, Feb. 25, 1815, aged 80.

Caleb Munson died at Green Village, April 8, 1822, aged 84.

Which, if either, was the Elder upon our list?

4. The name of Abner Beach occurs upon the roll of church in Parsippany in 1773. Was he our Elder Abner Beach?

5. The "Bill of Mortality" begins its record of burials July 3rd, 1768. During the remaining part of that year there were 21 burials; in 1769, 27 burials; in 1770, 30 burials, &c. We have recovered 55 names of persons buried in the old cemetery previous to July 3rd, 1768. This as we see from the above figures is but a small part of those who before this date must have been interred there. As this was the only cemetery in the vicinity, all interments must have been in it. We begin next month the Record of Burials. That this record may be made as complete as possible, we request our readers kindly to search in their old Bibles, family records, &c., for deaths previous to July 3rd, 1768, and send them (with date of death, age or date of birth, &c.,) as soon as possible to THE RECORD.

6. Two very important books are missing from our safe:

1st. The first volume of Records, kept by the Parish Clerk, previous to the year 1831.

2nd. The Trustee's Record from 1831 to 1838.

Who can find these important books and return them to the safe?

NEW YORK CITY, Aug. 14, 1879.

Rev. and Dear Sir:

Early in the present century, Mrs. Phebe Scribner, with her daughters Esther, Elizabeth, and Anna Scribner, established and successfully conducted a young ladies boarding school at Morristown, and it is to be presumed they were members of the church over which you are now settled. Mrs. Scribner was the widow of Captain Nathaniel Scribner, an officer in the American Revolution. They were my maternal great-grand-parents. Whilst the family were at Morristown, my great-uncles (sons of Mrs. Scribner,) went West as pioneers, and bought and laid out, what is now New Albany, Ind.

After the sons had sufficiently subdued the forest, they persuaded their mother and sisters to relinquish the school at Morristown, and add their capital to the development of the new enterprise at the West, and in 1814, I think, the family emigrated West.

There they established society on the same basis as at the East, and the First Presbyterian Church at New Albany was organized in the first house (not a log-cabin) ever built there, for the home of Mrs. Scribner, and with but four members—Mrs. Scribner, her daughter Esther Scribner, and her sons, Joel and James Scribner. Consequently the pioneer history of New Albany and the church, is the history of my mother's ancestors. I am very desirous of getting all the additional information I can to enrich our family history, and of procuring any papers, autographs, or anything that will enable me eventually to put the early family history of the Scribners in suitable form for preservation and perpetuation. It has occurred to me that there might be some aged persons in your church, or in Morristown, who would remember something concerning them. The building is still standing in which the school was conducted, and the records of your church and town ought to furnish valuable dates.

I am most desirous of obtaining the autograph of my great-aunt, Esther Scribner, and I hope to learn of an old paper, letter, or my best chance, perhaps, would be to find in the possession of some old lady who went to school to them, an old book with her name, Esther Scribner, written on the fly-leaf. Will you not have the kindness to make such enquiries for me as your residence and acquaintance at Morristown would give you an especial advantage in doing. My address is at the *New York Observer* office, 37 Park Row.

I remain, dear sir.

Yours, very truly,

MOREY H. BARTOW.

Rev. Rufus S. Green, Morristown, N. J.

THE RECORD.

FIRST PRESBYTERIAN CHURCH, MORRISTOWN, N. J.

"This shall be Written for the Generation to Come."—Psalms 102 : 18.

VOL. 1.   FEBRUARY, 1880.   NO. 2.

(Printed with the approval of Session.)

PROSPECTUS.

The Record will be printed and published monthly at Morristown, N. J. Terms, 50 cents per annum in advance ; 75 cents after June.

Subscriptions will be received at the book-stores of Messrs. Runyon and Emmell, or through the mail. All communications should be addressed to the

EDITOR OF THE RECORD.

Lock box 44.   Morristown, N. J.

As it is not expected that the subscription price of this periodical will be sufficient to meet the necessary expenses of publication, The Record is commended to the generosity of all interested in the early history of the town. Should more money be received than is needed for actual expenses it will be placed to the credit of the Benevolent Fund of the Session. The Record desires to secure anything pertaining to the history of the town and county of Morris and its early settlers—old papers, pamphlets, sermons and lectures, books, family histories and genealogies, printed or in MS., or copied (*carefully*) from old Bibles and records, &c., &c.; also, all marriages during the pastorate of Dr. McDowell, from 1814 to 1825, and marriages of members of the congregation by ministers not pastors of this church. Items with reference to any named in the various lists will be thankfully received and preserved for future use. We especially desire our readers to aid us in supplying all omissions and correcting all mistakes on our rolls.

WHO CAN TELL?

In the list of the members of the church, the names are copied as found upon the old record. The date of death is added, when it could be ascertained, by the RECORD. We would be glad if our friends would aid in filling out all of these blanks. Some of the old members moved away. Where did they go? and when? Who can give the date of death of any not given in THE RECORD?

Among other fruitful sources of trouble in perfecting our roll of members is the fact that many women have been dismissed who united with the church before marriage, and whose maiden name therefore is the only one upon the roll.

Who can tell the maiden name

Of Mrs. Emma Beach, dismissed to 1st Ch. Orange, Sept. 5, 1856?

Of Mrs. Boune, dis. June 5, 1857 to Ref, D. Ch. Newark?

Of Maria, w. of Chas. Burnet, dis. June 8, 1841, to So. St. Ch.?

Of Mrs. Chas. Burnet, dis. May 3, 1816 to N. Y. city?

Of Widow Harriet H. Coburn, dis. June 8, 1811, to So. St. Ch.?

Of Sarah A., wf. of Wm. L. Crowell, dis. same time and place?

Of Roda, wf. of Wm. S. Cook, dis. Apr. 20, 1829, to Hanover?

Of Phebe Ann, wf. of Dr. Silas L. Condit, dis. Dec. 13, 1846, to 1st Ch.. N. Y.?

Of Mrs. Caleb Campbell, dis. May 16, 1819, to 1st Ch. Newark?

Of Mrs. Edwin Ford, dis. Sept 6, 1842, to So. St. Ch.?

Of Mrs. Catharine A. Fewsmith, dis. Oct. 10, 1853, to Camden?

Of Mrs. Chas. Foster, dis. Feb 27, 1857?

Of Joanna, wf. of Ashbel U. Guerin, dis. Nov. 9, 1831, to New Foundland?

Of Maria C., wf., of Rob't Godden, dis. Sept. 9, 1836, to Indiana?

Of Widow Gaston, dis. June 12, 1811, to Elizabeth Town?

Of Mary, wf. of George Haun, or Hann, dis. Feb. 13, 1829, to Chatham?

Of Hannah, wf. of Elias Howel, dis. Nov. 1, 1811, to Bapt. Ch.?

Of Mrs. Jabez T. Johnson, dis. May 27, 1841?

Of Mrs. Caroline P. James, dis. Sept. 5, 1856, to Mt. Olive.

WANTED.

The Bill of Mortality.

The Bible printed by Jacob Mann.

The Catechisms printed by P. A. Johnson.

The pictures of former pastors and of the old Session House.

In the (about) 3300 members which the First Church has had since its origin the name of

Pierson occurs		100	times,
Johnson	"	94	"
Prudden	"	63	"
Condict	"	58	"
Lindsly	"	58	"
Freeman	"	50	"
Stiles	"	35	"
Byram	"	33	"
Smith	"	30	"
Burnett	"	30	"
Whitehead	"	29	"
Beers	"	24	"
Day	"	23	"
Conklin	"	22	"
Canfield	"	22	"
Cutler	"	22	"
Young	"	21	"

THE RECORD must not be held responsible for the orthography of the old documents which it may reproduce. A number of mistakes occur in the Charter given last month and still more in the Trustees' record in this issue—which are, however, the exact reproductions of the originals. In this connection it should also be said that the names in our various lists are printed as found upon the old records.

In the Jan. RECORD the "N. B.," of Dr. Johnes at the head of the list of marriages needs explanation. The residence of those only who lived out of town is registered. Where no residence is given, the persons thus unregistered were Morristown people.

"Clark of Trustees," Samuel Roberts, it will be observed, is not accurate in the date he assigns to the granting of the charter. A reference to that document shows that it was granted the eighth, and not the eighteenth, of Sept. 1756, in the thirtieth instead of the twenty-ninth year of the reign of King George the Second.

Extract from a Historical Sketch of the Presbyterian Church of Hanover, by Rev. J. A. Ferguson, Pastor.

In the year 1718, a successful effort was made to erect a building for divine worship, on the site of the present cemetery in Whippany. This land was donated to the village. The ancient deed reads as follows: " I, John Richards, of Whippanong, in the county of Hunterdon, Schoolmaster, for and in consideration of the love and affection that I have for my Christian friends and neighbors in Whippanong, and for a desire to promote the public interest, and especially for those who shall covenant and agree to erect a suitable meeting house for the public worship of God, give 3 1-2 acres of land situate and being in the township of Whippanong, on that part called Percipponong, on the Northwestward side of Whippanong river; only for public use, improvement and benefit, for a meeting-house, school-house, burying yard and training field, and such like uses and no other." This was probably the starting point of the church. This old deed is dated Sept. 2d, 1718; and, if the actual organization of the church did not take place before the death of Mr. Richards in December, it could not have been delayed long after. The church building was small and stood on the northwest corner of the lot.

The first pastor was the Rev. Nathaniel Hubbel from Massachusetts, and a graduate of Yale College. The probable date of his dismissal was about 1730; and the reason, mentioned by Mr. Green in his brief sketch, was, "some uneasiness between him and the people." It was during Mr. Hubbel's pastorate that the village of Whippany received the name of Hanover, although it continued to be "most commonly known by the Indian name Whippanong."

In perhaps 1730, the Rev. John Nutman, grandson of the Rev. John Prudden, pastor of the church at Newark, was "ordained pastor of the church in Hanover." He also was a graduate of Yale College, and a man of fine scholarship. His congregation extended over a wide range of country, embracing "the territory now covered by Hanover, Whippany, Chatham, Madison, Parsippany, Morristown," and even reaching beyond the limits of these congregations. Not long after his settlement, as the meeting house was old and dilapidated, a sharp contention arose among the people of the different sections concerning the location of the new building, should one be erected. The people coming from Madison were very desirous of having it located nearer them, while those from Morristown were determined that, if the site were changed, it should be in their favor. Strange as it may seem, it was at length determined to decide the matter by "casting the lot," all parties agreeing to abide by such decision. We are told that, "with much solemnity, the appeal was thus made to God to determine in this way the question in dispute." When the lot was taken, it was against the Morristown section, and in favor of continuing on the old site. This should have settled the difficulty; but this faction, notwithstanding their previous agreement to abide by the decision of the lot, withdrew and, afterwards, formed the first Presbyterian church of Morristown. This secession left the congregation so diminished that it could not raise the salary of the pastor; and Mr. Nutman felt called upon to represent the difficulty to the Synod and to ask its aid in seeking an adjustment between the church and the Morristown faction. "The Synod referred the matter to the Presbytery of East New Jersey to travail with the people of West Hanover (now Morristown), and East Hanover, in order to prevail with them to agree upon conditions of re-union, at least for a while, until they be better able to subsist apart. In case the effort failed, then the Presbytery was directed to grant Mr. Nutman a dismission from the congregation." This, however, was not the end of the matter. The same case came up again the following year in Synod; and, at no less than "six separate sessions, that body considered it." All this long consideration did not result in the reconciliation of the Morristown people. They refused to return to the old church; and, in 1735, they asked the installation of John Cleverly, a graduate of Harvard, as their pastor. This aroused an intense opposition on the part of the Hanover church. They determined, if possible, to prevent the installation of Mr. Cleverly; and the reason they urged against it was, that the Morristown people were not able "to support the institutions of religion." Mr. Cleverly was not ordained, but continued to preach for three years or more. The difficulty was finally settled in July, 1738.

MEMBERS.

—:o:—

*" The Number and Names of the Persons that
were in full communion when the ch. was
first collected and founded, together with
the number of those that came since from
other churches with their Removal."*

TIMOTHY JOHNES.

John Lindley, died Mrch. 9, 1750, aetas 56.
Elizabeth Lindley, his wife, buried Apr. 21,
1772, aet. 91, 1.
John Lindley, Jun. d. Sept. 10, 1784, aet. 56.
Sarah Lindley, his wf.
Jacob Fford, d. Jan. 19, 1777, born Apr. 13,
1704.
Hannah Fford, his wf., b. July 31, 1777, aet.
76.
Joseph Prudden, b. Sept. 27, 1776, aet. 84.
Joanna Prudden, his wf.
Caleb Fairchild, b. May 3, 1777, aet. 84.
Ann Fairchild, his wf., b. Apr. 8, 1777, aet.
86.
Joseph Coe.
Judith Coe, his wf.
Joseph Coe, Jun.
Esther Coe, his wf.
Solomon Munson, b. Feb. 8, 1803, aet. 78.
Tamar Munson, his wf., b. Jan. 28, 1779,
aet. 79.
Benjamin Pierson, d. Aug. 2, 1783, aet. 81,
9, 26.
Patience Pierson, his wf., d. Jan. 7, 1785, aet.
77.
Stephen Freman, b. Aug. 2, 1771, aet. 84.
Hannah Freman, his wf., b. July 22, 1779,
aet. 85.
Matthew Lum, b. May 21, 1777, aet. 70.
Susanna Lum, his wife., d. May 23, 1758,
aet. 63.
Peter Cundit, b. July 11, 1768, aet. 69.
Phebe Cundit, his wf., b. July 26, 1768,
aet. 65.
Philip Cundit, d. Dec. 23, 1801, aet. 92, 8.
Mary Cundit, his wf., b. Sept. 30, 1784,
aet. 72.
Joseph Howard.
Mary Howard, his wf., b. Jan. 30, 1782,
aet. 79.
Sarah, wf. of Samuel Ford.
Benjamin Bailey, b. Mrch. 20, 1783, aet. 83.
Letitia Bailey, his wf., b. Aug. 11, 1781, aet.
78.
Samuel Nutman.

Abigail Nutman, his wf.
James Cole.
Phebe Cole, his wf.
Benjamin Coe.
Rachel Coe, his wf., b. Dec. 20, 1776, aet. 58.
Thomas Kent.
Ebenezer Mahurin.
wf. of Eben. Mahurin.
Uriah Cutler, b. Feb. 5, 1795, aet. 86.
Timo. Mills., d. Mrch. 4, 1803, aet. 85.
Job Allen, of Rockaway.
John Clark.
Abigail Clark, his wife.
Benjamin Beach, of Rockaway.   Suspended
May 26, 1756.
Abner Beach, of Rockaway. Sus. May 8,1752.
Jonah Arstin.
Arstin, his wf.
Zeruiah, wf. of Isaiah Wines, "now of Capt.
Samuel Day," b. Dec. 21, 1776, aet. 56.
Sarah, wf. of Isaac Price.
Martha, wf. of Cornelius Arstin.
Susanna, wf. of Caleb Tichenor.
Sarah, wf. of James Frost.
Mary, wf. of Isaac Clark.
Elizabeth, wf. of David More.
Ann, wf. of Alexander Robards.
Ann Allen, wido.
Sarah, wf. of Abraham Hathaway.
Bethiah, wf. of Thomas Wood, b. Nov. 7,
1773, aet. 74.
Experience, wf. of Benj. Conger, b. Sept.
30, 1784, aet. 73.
Charity, wf. of Benj. Shipman.
Phebe, wf. of Shadrach Hathaway.
wf. of John Jonson.
Catharine, wf. of Peter Stagg.
wf. of Eliacam Suerd.
Mary Burt.
Comfort, wf. of Joseph Stiles, d. June 17,
1785, aet. 76.
Joanna, wf. of Peter Prudden.
Sam'l Sweasy.
Susanna Sweasy his wf., b. Nov. 5, 1776,
aet. 80.
Joseph Fowler's wf. Hannah.
Hannah, wf. of Jeremiah Johnson.
Martha, wf. of John Fford.
Abigail, wf. of Jonathan Conklin,
now of Sam'l Bayles.
Charles Howell, d. June 18, 1759, aet. 38.
Deborah, wf. of Charles Howell, d. Dec. 19,
1765, aet. 43.

(Continued on page 20.)

(Continued from page 6.)

BAPTISMS.

——:o:——

July 6, Joseph Tichenor, ch. Joshua.
" " Wm. Bates, of Hanover, ch. Ephraim.
" 13, John Kitchel, of Hanover, ch. Mary.
Aug.14. ⎧ Abner Beach, ch. Isaac.
At ⎪ Adam Blackman, twins James &
Rock- ⎨ Adam.
away ⎩ Ebenezer Holiberd, ch. Mary.
Oct. 25. John Burrel, ch. Jehoiden.
" " Thomas Gilbard, ch. John.
" " Catharine, wf. of Peter Stagg, ch. John.
Sept. 1. Mary, wf. of Hur Orsborn, ch. Phebe.
" 8. Dan'l Lum, of Hanover, ch. Squire.
" 16. Zachariah Blackman, adult.
" " Stephen Freman, ch. Hezekiah.
" " Ann, wt. of David Ogden, Household, John, David, Abigail, Mary.
" 22. Benj. Bailey & wf., ch. Mary.
" 25. Zachariah Blackman, Household, Hannah & Patience.
Oct. 13. Matthias Burnet & wf., child Matthias.
" " John Clark & wf., ch. Phebe.
" " Susanna, wf. of Caleb Tichenor, ch. Mary.
Nov. 10. Thomas Bridge, Household, David, Elizabeth, John, Rafe. (?)
Dec. 8. Bathiah, wf. of Mat. Wheler, ch. Abiel.
" " John Stiles, ch? Phebe.
" 25. Abraham Johnson, of Rockaway, ch. ——.
" 29. Benj. Coe, ch. Patience.
" " Sam'l Day, ch. David.
1746.
Jan. 26. John Perkhurst, ch. Hanna.
Feb. 2. Uriah Cutler, ch. Hanna.
Mar. 3. Mary, wf. of Isaac Clark, ch. Reuben.
" 3. Abigail, wf. of John Johnson, Jr., ch. Joseph.
" 9. Alexander Jonson, wf. accompt., ch. Phebe.
" 23. Isaiah Wines & wf. ch. Abigail.
Apr. 2. Joseph Winget, adult, and his ch. Benjamin.

Apr. 2. Timo. Mils, ch. John.
" 2. Sarah. wf. of Matthew Fairchild, ch. Ann.
" 20. Samuel Bailey, ch. Zephaniah.
May 11. Philip Cundit & wf., ch. Rebecca.
" 11. Zophar Gildersleve, ch. Rachel.
" 18. Joseph Howard & wf., ch. Matthias.
July 6. Gilbard Heady, ch. Abigail.
" 6. Peter Norris, ch. Peter.
" 6. Sarah Woods, wf. of Richard ch. Abijah.
" 6. I with my wife, stood ingaged for negro child, name John ; born April, 1743.
" 27. Joseph Coe & wf., stood ingaged for negro ch. Margaret.
Aug. 10. Elizabeth, wf. of David Moor, ch.
——.
" 17. Job Allen, of Rockaway, ch. Deborah.
" 17. Benjamin Conger & wf., ch. Lydia.
" 17. Thomas Bridge, ch. Thomas.
" 17. Peter Dickenson & wf., ch. Mary.
" 17. Tabitha, wf. of of Daniel Frost, ch. Jedidiah.
Sept. 14. Seth Hall, ch. Jacob.
Oct. 6. Benjamin Hathaway & wf., ch. Abigail & her (?) 2 children Theophilus & Betty.
" 12. Benjamin Freman, ch. Rachel.
Nov. 17. Benjamin Pierson & wf., ch. Aaron.
" 17. Thomas Cole, child'n Enos & Joanna.
" 30. Stephen Mahurin & wf., ch. Bathshua.
1747.
Jan. 11. William Frost & wf., ch. Ebenezer.
Jan. 11. Daniel Freman, ch. Charity.
Feb. 15. Joseph Mure & wf., ch. |Azubah.
Apr. 10. Joseph Prudden & wf. stood ingaged for negro ch. Titus.
" 19. Daniel Lindley, ch. Elizabeth.
" 26. Joseph Wood & wf., ch. Phebe.
" 26. Abner Beach, of Rockaway, ch. Ann.
" 26. William Losey, ch. Cornelus.
June 7. Benjamin Coe & wf., ch. Usual.
" 28. Daniel Wick, oh. Ann.
July 12. Jonah Arstin & wf., ch. Jesse.

(Continued on page 21.)

(Continued from page 7.)

MARRIAGES.

——:o:——

Nov. 7. Thomas Hermon & Mary Ludlum.
  "   14. Daniel Potter, of Turkey, and
         Mary Losy,   "   "
Dec. 22. John Gobil, of ye town & Elizabeth
         Burrel, of Newark.
1749.
Feb. 7. Edward Riggs, of Roxitcus, & Jane
         Buckley, of New England.
Mrch. 6. Ebenezer Perry & one Stagg, of
         Rockaway.
Feb. 23. Simeon Gobil & Abigail Conger.
May   8. Simon Ely, of ye Borough of Eliz-
         abeth, and Abigail Halsey, of
         Southampton.
June 1. Shadrach Howard & Sarah Con-
         duit.
  "   20. Joseph Tompkins & Eleanor
         Homes.
July 12. Sam'l Peck, of Basking Ridge, &
         Jane White-ker-neack.
Aug. 16. John Lose, Jr., & Hannah Hol-
         bord.
  "   20. John Keney, of Hanover, & Sarah
         Fford, of ye town.
Sept. 6. David Osborn & Anna Hains, of
         Elizabethtown.
  "   11. Isaac Wessels & Mary Jones.
  "   12. Elijah Jones, of Basking Ridge, &
         Jane Doty,   "   "
Nov. 2. Job Lorain & Sarah Stanborough.
  "   9 David Clark, of Mendham, &
         Sarah Pratt, "   "
1750.
Jan. 31. John Hermon & Sarah Price.
March 1. Moses Crane, of Hanover, &
         Susanna Brant.
  "   8. Benj. Leonard, of Mendham, &
         Martha Hains, of ye town.
  "   12. Junia Lindsly & Charity Hains,
         of Mendham.
Apr. 10. Josiah Hand, of Hanover, & Ann
         Burnet,   "   "
June 21. Nathaniel Morris, of Basking
         Ridge, & Rebecca Bailey, of ye
         town.
Aug.   Ebenezer Fairchild & Salome
         Gobil.
Oct. 16. Solomon Munson & Mary Pierson.
  "   18. James Lose & Mary Selee.
Nov. 28. Aaron Allen, S. Hanover, & Abi-
         gail Bonel, of Turkey.

Nov. 28. Nathaniel Bonel, of Turkey, &
         Elizabeth Allen, of S. Hanover.
Dec.   5. Zophar Freman & Phebe Wood.
1751.
Jan. 15. Jacob Allen, of S. Hanover, &
         George Day wido., at River.
  "   20. John Fford & Martha Raighnor,
         of S. Hampton.
Feb. 17. Josiah Stanborow, of Mendham,
         & Sarah Wood.
         Daniel Gobil & Rhoda Doud (?)
May   1. Sam'l Munson & Sarah Prudden,
         wido. -
  "   2. John Lindly & Joanna Hudson.
July   3. Benj. Day & Abi- ⎫
         gail Darling.   ⎪ All belong-
                           ⎬ ing to S. Han-
         David Sampson &   ⎪ over Society.
         Deborah Day.   ⎭
Aug.   6. John Allen & Tabitha Lyon, wido.,
         of Mendham.
Oct.   6. Sam'l Howard & Ann Clark, Rock-
         away.
  "   9. Abram Scisco & Ungeneche Kent,
         Rockaway.
  "   24. Essacar Huntington & Phebe
         Burrel, of Newark.
Nov. 3. Samuel Tuthel, Doc. & Sarah
         Kenny.
  "   28. James Pitney & Desire Tomp-
         son, both of Mendham.
  "   28. Benjamin Pitney & Abigail
         Tompson, wido, both of
         Mendham.
         These four "stood up together."
  "   28. Ephraim Burwell & Mary Her-
         mon.
  "   28. John Whitehead & Mary Rose,
         of Mendham.
         These four " stood up together."
Dec. 23. Jacob Smith, of Mendham, &
         Ruth Whitehead.
  "   27. Jacob Low & Diadema.
1752.
Jan.   3. Nehemiah Holloway & Lea Jones.
  "   19. Stephen Wiggins & Sarah White,
         widow.
  "   30. Jonah Allen & Sarah Muir.
Feb.   9. Thomas Demoss & Abia Beach.
Aug. 28. Nathaniel Haden & Zervia Sut-
         ten, both of Baskingridge.
Aug. 31. Edward Luis & Elenor Rooker(?)
         both of Baskingridge.

(Continued on page 22.)

BURIALS IN THE FIRST CHURCH YARD.

——:o:——

The following is a list of the names, so far as we have been able to recover them, of those buried in the First Church Cemetery, previous to July 3rd, 1768, the date of the first entry in the "Bill of Mortality:"

DIED.

Jan. 2, 1731, Martha, wife of Abraham Parson, aet. about 23.

Mrch. 6, 1740, Wm. Halluck, aet. 19 y. 6 mos.

Oct. 17, 1742. Abigail, w. of — Goble, aet. 62.

Apr. 24, 1746, Samuel Potter, Jr., aet. 47, o, 14.

June 12, " George, aet. 4, 3. ⎫ Children of Joseph and Comfort Stilles.
" 13, " Silas, aet. 16, 7. ⎭

Sept. 19, 1748, Elizabeth, w. of Rev. Timothy Johnes, aet. 31.

Oct. 18, " Penelope, w. of John Ford, aet. —.

Jan. 16, 1749, Sarah, w. of Richard Woods, aet. 22, 3.

Jan. 3, 1750, Sarah, w. of John Lindsley, Esq., aet. 52.

" 6, " Sarah, w. of Matthew Fairchild, aet. 32, 10.

March 9, " John Lindsley, Esq., aet. 56.

March, 1751, Mary, w. of Benj. Hatheway, aet. 24, 7, 8.

Sept. 18, " Ephraim Nuttman, aet. 30.

June 13, 1752, Charity, w. of Junia Lindsley, aet. 21, 6, 29.

Aug. 11, " Samuel Ford, aet. 42, 10.

1754, Stephen Arnold, Letter of Administration granted to Rachael, his wife, Feb. 16, 1754.

June 3, 1755, Hannah, da. of Samuel and Phebe Ford Arnold; born July 22, 1754.

Nov. 14, 1756, John Primrose, aet. 88, 6.

Dec. 14, " John, s. of Sam'l & Phebe F. Arnold ; born Nov. 19, 1752.

Apr. 13, 1757, Dabriat, w. of Zechariah Fairchild, aet. 50.

Aug. 30, " Phebe, w. of Timothy Peck, aet. 53, 0, 14.

Sept. 14, " Shadrach, s. of Philip Hatheway, aet. 2.

Oct. 3, " Isaiah Winds, aet. —.

May 23, 1758, Susanna, w. of Dea. Matthew Lum, aet. 63.

Nov. 15, " Jonathan Stiles, aet. 80.

June 18, 1759, Charles Howell, aet. 38.

Nov. 23, 1760, Samuel, s. of Sam'l & Phebe Ford Arnold ; born July 8, 1757.

Apr. 22, 1761, Elizabeth, w. of Capt. Samuel Day, aet. 46.

1762.

Feb. 12, Abigail, w. of Gilburd Ludlam, aet. 24.

" " Sarah, da. of Joseph & Hannah Wood, aet. 14.

Mrch. 2, Samuel Loree, aet. 33.

" 22, Isaac Pain " —.

" 24, Benjamin Shipman, aet. 69.

Apr. 9, William Brown, " 41.

" 21, Benjamin Harthway, Esq., aet. 63.

July 16, Phebe, w. of Silas Condict, " 18, 11, 22.

Aug. 14, Sarah, w. of Nathan'l Condict, aet. 22, 7, 14.

Sept. 10, Wm., s. of Wm. & Jane Brown, aet. 15, 9, 15.

1763.

Feb. 10, Ruth, w. of Peter Dickerson, aet. 34, 4, 20.

Mrch. 31, Silas Day, aet. 24, 3, 14.

Aug. 18, Hannah, da. of Mattaniah & Mary Lyon, aet. 5m.

1764.

Feb. 2, Prudence, w. of Joseph King, aet. 25.

Mrch. 1, Abigail, da. of Henry & Rebeca Primrose, aet. 8.

June 9, Jacob Allen, " 26.

Oct. 3, Samuel Arnold, aet. 37, 11, 2.

1765.

Oct. 25, Anna, w. of Jonas Phillips, aet. 19.

Dec. 19, Deborah, wid. of Chas. Howell, aet. 43.

1766.

Mrch. 13, Martha, w. of —— Warman, aet. 77, 10.

Dec. 10, Afa, s. of Isaac & Rhoda Pierson, aet. 2, 2, 13.

1767.

Feb. 14, John Ford, Esq., eld. s. of Jacob, born, Apr. 5, 1728.

Mrch. 13, Sarah, w. of Joseph Young, aet. 37.

Apr. 1, Zophar Halsey, aet. 31.

Dec. 17, Augustine More, Esq., aet. 44.

1768.

Mrch. 12, Elizabeth Reeve, aet. 46.

April 5, Samuel Stevens, s. of Rev. Timothy Johnes, aet. 24.

(Continued on page 28.)

TRUSTEES' BOOK.

A Record of the Transactions of the Trustees in and for the Presbyterian Chh & Congregation at morristown, in Vertue of a Charter granted to the said Chh. & Congregation by his Excellency Jonathan Belcher, Esqr., Captain General and Governor in Cheif in and over his majesties Province of Nova Cesarea or New jersey and territories thereon Depending in America Chancellor and Vice admiral in the same, &c., which Charter was granted the eighteenth of September, in the twenty ninth year of his majesties Reign 1756, the Expence of which Charter being about seven Pound Proc. was Raised by Publick Contribution Excepting the writing of Sd Charter, which was Generously done by Ezekiel Cheever, member of Sd Society

The Incorperated Trustees, Viz.: messiurs. Benjamin Hatheway, President ; Benjamin Bayles, Thomas Kent, Benjamin Coe, Charls Howell, Sam'l Robarts & henry Primrose, on the Receiving the Charter at the ministers hous from the hands of Mr. Johnes, who had Been Desiered and was Principally Concerned in obtaining the Sd Charter, the Trustees by a Vote did then and there appoint Saml' Robarts the Corporation Clark

The President according to Charter appointed a meeting of the trustees at his own hous January 18, 1758, all the members being Present it was agreed that as the President had heretofore given a Deed for the Parsonage to mess. mathew Lum, thomas Cleverly & Timothy mills that it might now fall under the Priviledges of the Charter, and it was agreed that Sd Parsonage Land by a Quit Claim be Conveyed to the President that Sd Lands by the President might be Directly Conveyed to the trustees it was also agreed to take a Quit Claim Deed for the meeting hous Land which is now in the hands of Joseph Prudden & the Heirs of John Lindsley Deseased Both of the town of morris

apriel 2 1759 the trustes met at ye Presidents hous acording to the appointment All Present Except Benj Bayles at which time the President Received his Quit Claim of Said mathew Lum timothy mills and Thomas Cleaverly and acordingly Gave a warrantee Deed to the trustees

apriel the 9 1759 the Clark by appoint-

ment of the Trustees Received a Quit Claim Deed for the meeting hous Land of Joseph Prudden

apriel 16 1759 at a meating of the trustees by Appointment Benjn Hatheway & Thomas Kent being absent Carls Howell was Chosen President and Wee Enquired into the over Plus money of mr Johnes Rates including the year 1757 when it was found that of all Past Rates only £14 13 0 was due to him and after his demands was answered and the Assessor Colector from Sd Rats the Remainder Should be Lodged in the trustees hands

Novem 8 1759 the Elders of the Chh in morris town met Present messrs Jacob Ford Joseph Prudden mathew Lum Joseph Coe Daniel Lindsley and Timothy Johnes moderator and after Prayers acording to. the Charter they Proseded to the Choice of a Trustee in the Room of our worthy Brother Charls Howell Deceased and acordingly they Chose Capt Joseph Stiles to Succeed him.

may the 1 1761 the Trustees met on the Green But Capt Stiles absent and agread to Lay out into Lots and Sell Som Part of the Pairsonag Land Lying before the meeting hous Dore.

June the 8 1761 the Trustees met at the Court hous and agreed upon a Price for three Lots the first which they then Conveyed to Joseph King was Sixteen Pound taen Shilling and Seald the Conveyance with the Shape of a mans head and the Second or midle Lot is Likewise Sixteen Pound taen Shilling the third or corner Lot twenty Five Pound which two Lots remain yet not Sold

august 26 1761 the trustees met at Doctor tuthills and Conveyed the Second Lot to Daniel Cooper Sealed with the Shape of a mans head.

apriel the 6 1762 the trustees met at Doct hatheways and Conveyed the third Lot to Isaac Bobet for twenty five Pound and Sealed it with the Seign of a Sheaf and that same Day Agread and Bought that Same Seal for the use of the Charter

October 14 1762 the Elders met and maid Choice of Stephen Conklin for a trustee in the Room of our worthy Brother & President Benjamin hatheway.

(Continued on page 24.)

THE RECORD.

FIRST PRESBYTERIAN CHURCH, MORRISTOWN, N. J.

"This shall be Written for the Generation to Come."—Psalms 102 : 18.

VOL. 1.   MARCH, 1880.   NO. 3.

(Printed with the approval of Session.)

THE RECORD

Will be printed and published monthly at Morristown, N. J. Terms, 50 cents per annum in advance; 75 cents after June.

Subscriptions will be received at the book-stores of Messrs. Runyon and Emmell, or through the mail. ALL COMMUNICATIONS should be addressed to the

EDITOR OF THE RECORD,

Lock box 44.   Morristown, N. J.

Entered at the Post Office at Morristown, N. J., as second class matter.

WANTED.—Anything either in print or in MS. pertaining to the history of Morristown and county, and their early inhabitants.

Mr. S. C. Burnet has called our attention to an important error on page 3 in the Jan. RECORD. The date for the ordination and installation of Rev. Albert Barnes should be Feb. 8, 1825 instead of 1824. Our error was due, strange as it may seem, *to the manual of the church prepared by Albert Barnes himself*, where the date is given as found in THE RECORD of January. That 1825 is the true date appears beyond doubt from the Sessional Records. The meetings of Session are in chronological order through 1824; then in 1825 there are entries under dates of Jan. 7, Jan. 21, Jan. 24, and on Feb. 8th a record of the ordination and installation of Rev. Albert Barnes. This finishes the book. Mr. Barnes procured a new Session Book, and the first entry in it, in his own hand writing, is " Rev. Albert Barnes was ordained and installed pastor of the First Presbyterian Church and Congregation in Morris Town, by the Presbytery of Elizabeth-Town, Feb'y 8, 1825. The Rev. David Magie presided and gave the charge to the minister; the Rev. John McDowell, D.D., preached the sermon from 2 Thes.

v. 12 & 13: the Rev. Wm. Barton gave the charge to the people."

The minutes of Session continue in chronological order thereafter. These facts place beyond doubt the date as given above, Feb. 8th, 1825, as the day of Mr. Barnes' ordination and installation.

The wrong date, copied from Mr. B's own manual, has found its way into quite general acceptance.

Mr. Burnet noticed the error because he was married by Mr. Barnes in less than a month after the latter's ordination and hence remembered the year perfectly, especially as his was the first marriage at which the young minister officiated. The original entry is March 2, 1825, married, Samuel Crane Burnet to Sarah Elizabeth Mills, both of Morris Town, county of Morris.

The first Presbytery in the United States was that of Philadelphia, which was formed in 1705 or 1706. The first leaf of the Records is lost, which fact leaves it uncertain which of the above dates is the correct one. The Presbytery consisted at its formation of seven ministers, viz: Francis MaKemie, John Hampton, George Macnish, Samuel Davis, John Wilson, Jedediah Andrews, and Nathaniel Taylor.

THE FIRST SYNOD.

By the year 1717, the original Presbytery had so increased in numbers, that it was deemed expedient to divide it into four Presbyteries, viz: Philadelphia, New Castle, Snow-Hill and Long Island.

These four Presbyteries were consequently erected into a Synod, dating from 1717, and called the Synod of Philadelphia. It is from the minutes of this body that the extract on page 18 is made. The General Assembly was not constituted until 1789.

EXTRACT FROM THE MINUTES OF THE SYNOD OF PHILADELPHIA.

Sept. 20th, 1733.

The affair of Hanover coming under consideration, and many papers being read to give light to the Synod in that affair, it was agreed that the committee bring in an overture on said business at our next *sederunt.*

Sept. 21st, 1733.

The committee having spent much time in reasoning on the affair of Hanover committed to them, at length agreed upon an overture on it in the following articles, viz : First, That the Synod look upon the practice of submitting of congregational affairs to the decision of a lot, though accompanied with sacred solemnity, to be unwarrantable, inasmuch as lots are only warrantably used to decide matters that can't be otherwise determined in a rational way ; particularly by applying to higher judicatories.

Secondly, The Synod do think that in their present circumstances of poverty & weakness, it might be very advisable for the people of West Hanover, at least for some time, to join themselves with the congregations of East Hanover and Basking Ridge, as may be most convenient, until they, as well as the said neighbouring congregations, be more able to subsist of themselves separately. Yet in the meantime, as the case now stands with that people, if re-union between East and West Hanover be found impracticable, according to our above advice, the Synod judge that the people of West Hanover be left to their liberty to erect themselves into a separate congregation. Withal we earnestly obtest and beseech, that nothing be done in that affair that may have a tendency to hurt the interest of religion in those places, so far as in them lies.

The above overture being read was approven by a great majority of votes.

Sept. 24th, 1733.

Mr. Nutman representing to the Synod, the great dificulties he is falled under, as to his continuing pastor of the congregation of East-Hanover, by reason of the division and discord between them and the people of West-Hanover ; they, viz : of West-Hanover being allowed by this Synod, to erect themselves into a separate congregation (in case, as per minutes of the Synod) the

Synod considering the same, do earnestly recommend it to the Presbytery of East-New-Jersey to travail with the people of West-Hanover and East-Hanover, in order to prevail with them to agree upon conditions of re-union, at least for a while, until they be better able to subsist apart. But if the Presbytery's endeavors to this purpose should not have effect, it is this Synod's judgment, that a dismission may be granted to Mr. Nutman from the people of East-Hanover, by the said Presbytery, upon his application for the same.

Sept. 19th, 1734, 10 A. M.

Ordered that the last year's minutes with relation to Mr. Nutman and the people of Hanover, be further considered.

4 P. M.

The affair of Mr. Nutman and Hanover continued.

Sept. 20th, 1734, 10 A. M.

The affair of Mr. Nutman further considered.

3 P. M.

The affair of Mr. Nutman continued.

Sept. 21st, 1734, 9 A. M.

The affair of Mr. Nutman—yet continued.

4 P. M.

Mr. Nutman's affair still continued.

Sept. 23rd, 1734, 10 A. M.

Resolved, That the affair of Mr. Nutman, from time to time continued, be first considered the next *sederunt.*

3 P. M.

The affair of Mr. Nutman and the people of Hanover resumed, and after reading our last year's minutes, and Mr. Dickinson proposing a difficulty concerning the obligation of the determination by the lot mentioned in said minutes, whether the obligation of the said determination yet remains binding upon said people, the Synod after much discourse and reasoning about that matter, at length came to a judgment in the following propositions :

1. That the Synod look upon the obligation of a determination of a difference by a lot, to be sacred and binding upon the conscience, if the matter so determined be lawful and practicable, and consequently to act contrary thereunto must be a very great sin.

2. That as the foundation upon which a lot is cast may cease, and the practicableness of acting according to the determina-

tion thereof may, in time, cease also,(though for a time it may continue practicable,) in such a case we judge that the obligation thereof doth cease also, because it can never be designed that such an obligation should remain after the design thereof becomes either impossible or hath been fully obtained.

3. Our determination last year relating to the people of Hanover did wholly go upon this supposition, that the affairs of that people and their circumstances were so far altered, upon representations then made to us, that we supposed the foundation of said lot, and of the people's acting upon it were ceased, which, whether it be certainly so or not, we do not peremptorily determine, but leave parties to judge thereof as in conscience they can.

4. That however, as in our minutes last Synod, we disapprove of the use of lots, without necesity, yet we are afraid, upon representation, that there hath been much sin committed by many, if not all that people, in their profane disregard of said lot in time past, and therefore excite them to reflect upon their past practices in reference thereunto, in order to their repentance.

(*To be Continued.*)

WABASH COLLEGE,
CRAWFORDSVILLE, IND.,
Feb. 5, 1880.

Rev. Rufus S. Green:

MY DEAR SIR :—I have received and read with great interest the first number of THE RECORD. It is worthy of the old historic church, of which you are pastor, to preserve the history of itself and the community in which it has been a light so long. I congratulate you on your pluck in the undertaking, and wish you great success.

I have spent so many pleasant hours in this examination of what you are now taking in hand and have paid out so many dollars in the unremunerative but pleasant work, that I am glad it has attractions for a younger man.

I find the enclosed scrap which I think you will be glad to get. It was handed me years ago by H. A. Ford, Esq.

The Col. Ford spoken of is Col. Ford, Sr., the ancestor of many descendants. Hon. Gabriel H. Ford was his grand-son, as also a grand-son of Rev. Timothy Johnes, D.D.,

the greatly admired and beloved pastor of the First Church from 1743 to 1794.

Very truly yours,
JOSEPH F. TUTTLE.

Extract from the Diary of the Hon. Gabriel H. Ford, dec'd.

THURSDAY, 21st June, 1849.

A census was taken in the years 1771 and 1772, in the British Provinces of America and deposited after the revolution, as public archives, at Washington ; but their room becoming much wanted, those of each province were delivered to the members of Congress from it, to cull what they chose, preparatory to a burning of the rest ; Gen. Mahlon Dickerson then a member from New Jersey, selected some from the county of *Morris,* and sent me yesterday a copy verbatim of one entry as follows : " *Widow Elizabeth Lindsley, mother of Col. Jacob Ford, was born in the city of Axford, in old England, came into Philadelphia when there was but one house in it—and into this Province when she was but one year and a half old. Deceased April 21st, 1772, aged 91 years and one month.*"

I always understood in the family by tradition from her (whose short stature, and slender, bent person, I clearly recall, having lived in the same house with her, and with my parents in my grand-father's family at her death and before it), that her father fled from England when there was a universal dread of returning Popery and persecution, 3 years before the death of Charles the Second, A. D., 1682, and two years before the accession of James the Second in 1684. That while landing his goods at Philadelphia he fell from a plank into the Delaware river and was drowned between the ship and the shore, leaving a family of young children in the wilderness. That she had several children by her first husband whose name was Ford, but none by her second husband whose name was Lindsley ; at whose death she was taken into the family of her son, Col. Jacob Ford, Sen., and treated with filial tenderness the remaining years of her life which were many. I am in the 85th year (since January last) of my age, being born in 1765, and was 7 years old at her death.

[Charles II. died Feb. 6th, 1685 ; James II. succeeded immediately to the throne.—Ed.]

(*Continued from page* 12.)
MEMBERS.

——:o:——

Daughter (?) of Chas. Howell.
Doc. Elijah Jillet.
Jane, wf of Doc. Jillet.
Elder Morris, of Basking Ridge.
Mary, his wife.
Abraham Campfield's wife (Sarah), buried July 22, 1783.
Phebe, Joshua Ball's wife.
Elizabeth Kermicle, wido.
Nathan Ward's wife.
Jemima, wf. of Dea. Matthew Lum.
Samuel Baldwin, of Mendham.
Rebecca, ——, Fairchild's wife.
Elizabeth, Cap. Clark's wife.
Wf. of Sam'l Mills (Sarah), bur. Jan. 15, 1785, aet. 61.
Elizabeth, w. of David Gauden.
Mattaniah Lyon, died Feb. 2, 1794, aet. 69, —— his wife.
Alexander Johnson's wife.
Silas Halsey.
Abigail, his wf., bur. March 26, 1777, aet. 60.
Bathiah, Benj. Halsey's wf., died Jan. 23, 1785, aet. 62.
John Mac Feran, bur. Nov. 22, 1778, aet. 80, —— his wife (Elizabeth), bur. Sept. 13, 1778, aet. 77.
Nathan Price.
Peter Prudden, bur. April 21, 1777, aet. 55.
Aug. 18, 1765, Naomi, wf. of John Laporte, turned from the anabaptists and received on ye foot of her being a member of that ch. in good standing.
1766—Robert or Hobart Hinds.
Amos Prudden & wf. returned. He died Sept. 22, 1799, aet. 54.
Thaddeus Dodd.
John Lyon, & his wife (Esther.)
Amos Burrol.
Sarah, wf. of Abel Lyon.
Lydia Guinny.
Demas Ford, excom. July 1, 1796.
Rebecca, wf. of Jno. Allen.
Wido. Mary Armstrong.
Dan. Morris, Jun.
Henry Primrose, bur. Oct. 20, 1780, aet. 70.
Mary Clark.
Elizabeth, wf. of Samuel Robarts, bur. July 18, 1795, aet. 71.

Cornelus Woodruff & —— his wife.
Elkanah Babbet.
Abigail, wf. of Joseph Wood.
Wido. Isabel Drake, bur. March 1, 1777, aet. 67.
Wido. Eleanor Woodruff.
Phebe, wf. of Ichabod Cooper, bur. Apr. 30, 1777, aet. 32.
Hannah, wf. of Isaac Prudden.
Hannah, wf. of Joseph Riggs.
Edward Jones.
Eli Anderson & Mary, his wife.
Elizabeth Dubois, widow.
Esther, wf. of Joseph Prudden, Jun.
Peter, servant of Samuel Robarts, "diped by Baptists."
Deborah, wf. of Howell Orsborn.
Temperance, wf. of Joshua Whitehead.
John Cole & —— his wife.
David Rattan, bur. Feb. 8, 1775, aet. 75.
Thomas Lee, bur. Jan. 9, 1805, aet. 76.
Dinah, his wife.
Peter Hill, bur. Jan. 20, 1787, aet. 66.
(Anne Margaret), his wife, bur. Jan. 20, 1782, aet. 52.
Nathan Howell, bur. Mrch. 21, 1830, aet. 74.
John Hill, & Anne Christian, his wf.
Abigail, wf. of John Pierson.
1774.
Paul Ferber, & Mary, his wife.
Josiah Broadwell & Abigail, his wife.
Susanna, wf. of Philip Castenor, bur. July 17, 1778, aet. 51.
Zeruiah, Richard Kenny's wife.
Mary, wf. of John Hunt.
Abigail, wf. of Stephen Conkling.
Stephen Burnet & —— wife.
Miriam, wf. of Nicholas Comesau, susp. Aug. 12, 1800, bur. June 20, 1809, aet. 80.
Sarah, wf. of John Pitney.
Mrs. —— Dow. school-madam.
Doritheah Cooper, school-madam.
Phebe, wf. of Zophar Freeman, bur. Feb. 17, 1779, aet. 54.
Anne, wf. of Samuel Day.

(*Continued on page* 28.)

(*Continued from page* 13.)

BAPTISMS.

—:0:—

1747.

July 12. Gideon Rigs & wf., child Abigail.
" 26. John Clark & wf., ch. Ebenezer.
" " Thomas Wilkerson & wf., ch. John.
" " Joseph Potter & wf., ch. Elizabeth.
Aug. 9. James Cole & wf., ch. Abigail.
" 16. Stephen Lindsley & wf., ch. Benjamin.
Sept.13. Bathiah, wf. of Nath'l Wheler, ch. Nathaniel.
" 20. John Losey, ch. Elizabeth.
" " Thomas Allerton & wf., ch. Benjamin.
" 25. Elizabeth, wf. of Ebenezer Mott, ch. Sarah.
" 27. Ezekiel Younglove, his wf. adult & ye ch. Dorcas.
" " Mary, wf. of Hur Orsborn, ch. Abraham.
Oct. 11. Benjamin Hathaway; Doc'r son & wf., ch. Isaac:
" " Josiah Crain & wf., ch. Samuel.
" 18. Peter Dickerson & wf., ch. Jonathan.
Nov. 1. Simeon Hathaway & wf., Household, Elijah, Chloe, Samuel, Anna.
Nov. 8. John Perkhurst & wf., ch. Martha.
" " Benjamin Hathaway; Capn. son & wf., ch. Rebecca.
" 22. Benjamin Hathaway & wf., ch, Zephaniah.
" 25. Abraham Johnson & wf., of Roc'y, ch. —.
" " Zachariah Plackman, of Rock'y, ch. —.
Nov.29. Uriah Cutler, ch. Abijah.
Dec. 13. Sarah, wf. of Mat. Fairchild, ch. Sarah.
" 27. Isaac & Ann Daton his wf., ch. Jemimah.

1748.

Jan. 31. Benjamin Halsey & wf., ch. Deborah.
" " Tabitha, wf. ot Daniel Frost, ch. Elizabeth.
Feb. 14. Samuel Fford & wf., ch. James, born Nov. 21, 1747.
" " Joseph Stiles & wf., ch. George.
" " Eliacam Suard & wf., ch. Sarah.
" 15. Phebe, Amos Cilborn's wf., adult.

Feb. 28. Samuel Day & wf., ch. Jeduthan.
" " Abigail, wf. of John Johnson, Jun., ch. Abigail.
Mar. 20. Richard Wood, ch. Samuel.
Apr. 3. Mary, wf. of Isaac Clark, ch. Moses.
" " Joseph Wood & wf., ch. Sarah.
" 17. Daniel Howard & wf., Household, Phebe & Benjamin.
May 15. Samuel Bailey & wf., ch. Nathaniel.
" " David Gauden, ch, Mary.
" 29. Joseph Edmister, ch. Hannah.
June 5. Benjamin Hathaway, wf. own (?) ch. Joshua.
" " Thomas Bridge, ch. Sarah,
" 12. Zophar Gildersleve & wf., ch. Silas.
" " Joseph Winget & wf., ch. Hanna.
" 19. Samuel Munson & wf., chn. Ruth, Elizah (?).
July 10. Job Allen & wf., ch. Lois.
" 31. Stephen Mahurin, & wf., ch. Samhaul.
Aug. 6. Shadrack Hathaway & wf., ch. Sarah.
" 10. Adam Blackman & wf., ch. —.
" " David Herimon & wf., ch. Martha.
Sept.11. William Smith & wf., ch. Sarah.
" 25. Stephen Freman. Jun. & wf., ch. Elijah.
Oct. 16. Benjamin Hathaway; Capn. son & wf., ch. Abraham.
Nov. 6. Benjamin Coe & wf., ch. Benjamin.
" 27. Benjamin Hathaway & wf., ch. Job.
Dec. 25. John Slater & wf., ch. Benjamin.
" " Henry Gardiner & wf., ch. Jemima.

1749.

Jan. 1. Timothy Conner's wf., on her account, ch. Mary.
" 5. William Frost & wf., ch. Elizabeth.
" 15. Abigail, John Robord's wf., Abigail. At same time Household Phebe & Peter.
" 22. Samuel Lyon, Household, Daniel, David, Rachel, Ezekiel.
" 29. Ebenezer Mott's wf., ch. Abigail.
Feb. 5. William Brown & wf., ch. William.
" 19. Joseph Potter & wf., ch. Mary.
Apr. 16. Henry Primrose, ch. Thankfull.
" " Matthew Fairchild & wf., ch. Stephen.
" 21. Benjamin Freman & wf., ch. Sarah.
" 23. Timothy Mils & wf., ch. Nehemiah.
" " Daniel Freman, ch. Nelle.
" 30. Samuel & Lydia Shipman, chn. Lois & Benjamin.

(*Continued on page* 29.)

(Continued from page 14.)

MARRIAGES.

—:o:—

Oct. 2. Henry Stagg & Tabitha Beach, both of Rockaway.

" 2. Benjamin Hathaway & Hanah Hopkins.

" 5. —— Leverage & Cloe Penne, of Mendham.

" 13. Juniah Lindsley& Hannah Nuttman

" 14. David Manele & Agnes Hull, of Mendham.

" 19. John Oharrah, of Somerset co., & Sarah Armstrong.

1753.

Jan. 2. Ephraim Leonard & Hanna Hinds, of Mendham.

" 18. John Brown, of Somerset, & Margaret Akeman, of Morris co.

Apr. 8. David Gauden & Elizabeth Stanborough.

" 11. Jonathan Burt & Mary Howard.

May 21. Azariah Dunham, of Piscatua, & Mary Fford.

" 24. John Hinds & Hannah Sutten.

Sept.27. Job Foster & Abigail Johnes, both of Newark.

" 30. John Allen & Sarah Fford, wido.

Nov. 1. Thomas Troop & Abigail Clark.

" 15. Joseph Hathaway & Sarah Lyon.

1754.

Jan. 15. Thomas Tuthel & Mehitabel Fairchild.

" 17. Elijah Pierson & Jane Aimstrong.

" " John Ayres of Baskingridge & Sarah Bailey.

June 20. Joseph Hains & Priscilla Whiternack.

Oct. 25. Lodewick Wortman & Elizabeth Maxwell.

Dec. 18. John Allerton & Hannah Kent.

1755.

Jan. 2. John Pitney & Sarah Leonard,

" 23. Demas Lindley & Joanna Prudden.

" 30. Nathaniel Beach & Sarah Peck.

Feb. 8. Stephen Munson & Letitia Ludlam.

" 20. Samuel Oliver & Sarah Primrose.

" " Philip Hathaway & Catura Fairchild.

Mar. 19. Waitstill Munson & Mary Wade.

" 23. Christopher Wood & Phebe Freeman.

Aug.10. Adam Weaver Ros & Royena Crozenor.

Oct. 26. Jonathan Wilkerson & Elizabeth Freeman,

" 29. Daniel Dikins & Phebe Cole.

Nov.27. Eliphalet Whitaker & Ruth Bailes,

Dec. 4. John Lindly & Sarah Rainer.

1756.

Jan. 29. Ezeziel Soulguard & Mary Crane.

Feb. 29. Israel Aber & Dorithea Leapord.

Apr. 1. Benjamin Bailes & Deborah Austin.

June 16. John Hunterdon & Elizabeth Heady

" " John Rogers & Hannah Mack.

Nov. 3. Benjamin Pierson & Phebe Raynor.

Dec. 1. Benjamin Woodruff & Mary Cross.

" 8. William Akeman and Letitia Bailees

" 15. Moses Tuttle & Jane Fford.

" 31. Shubaal Pitney & Charity Stiles.

1757.

Jan. 11. Ezra Fairchild & Priscilla Burt.

Mar. 3. Benjamin Gobil & Elizabeth Conger.

" 7. Samuel Bailes & Abigail Conkling, wido.

" 10. Nathaniel Cundit & Sarah Coe.

" 21. Jedidiah Gregory & Rhoda Fairchild.

Apr. 5. Matthew Fairchild & Rebecca Lyon.

June 10. John Pierson & Ruth Howell.

Aug.12. Zach. Fairchild & wido. Lidia Hathaway.

Nov. 9. David Fairchild & Catharine Gregory.

Dec. 1. Daniel Morris & Hannah Armstrong.

1758.

Jan. 2. Robert Plumb, of Newark, & Ester Pierson.

" 18. Gershom Gard & Phebe Huntington.

Feb. 23. Caleb Rude, of Rockaway, & Ann Wade.

Mar. 2. Ralph Tucker & Thankful Hathaway.

" 15. Timothy Peck & Sarah Ball.

Jan. John Vandine & Naomi Moore.

Apr. 23. David Core & Eunice Allen.

May 2. Samuel Hull & Glover's daughter.

" 4. Joseph Beach & Kezia Johnson.

June19. Ebenezer Blechly, Doc., & Mary Wick.

" 22. Caleb Munson & Susanna Ludlam.

Aug.23. Thomas Millage & Sarah Stagg.

Oct. 4. William Jackson & Mahitable Woods.

Nov. 16. David Kilpatrick & Ann Bayles.

Dec. 7. Constant Cooper & Abigail Kenny.

(Continued on page 30.)

BILL OF MORTALITY,

——:0:——

(*Title Page.*)

Being a Register of all the Deaths which have occurred in the Presbyterian and Baptist congregations of Morris-Town, New-Jersey, for Thirty-Eight Years past.—Containing (with but few exceptions) the cause of every decease.—This register, for the first twenty-two years, was kept by the Rev. Doctor Johnes, since which time, by William Cherry, the present Sexton of the Presbyterian Church at Morris-Town.—" *Time brushes off our lives with sweeping wings.*"—*Hervey.*

Morris-Town, Printed by Jacob Mann, 1806.

NOTE.—Those marked thus * were Church Members—thus † Baptists—thus *† Baptist Church Members.

1768.

Cecelia, widow of Tomothy Tuttle, Esqr., aet. 68, decay of nature, buried July 3.

Noah, son of Robert Hinds, July 5.

Moses Pierson, aet. 29, consumption, July 8.

Peter Condict,* aet. 69, fever, July 11.

A young woman, aet. 21, child-bed, July 16.

Phœbe, widow of Peter Condict,* aet. 65, fever, July 26.

Rose, servant of Joseph Wood, fever, August 26.

John Robinson, September 17.

Malatiah, wife of Deacon Jonas Goble,*† aet. 66, September 24.

Child of Ichabod Carmichael, September 29.

Hannah, wife of Joseph Wood,* aet. 49, dysentery, October 3.

Elizabeth, daughter of E'.phalet Clark, October 8.

Widow Clark, aet. 50, October 13.

Abigail, wife of Samuel Lyon, aet. 55, consumption, October 22.

John Axtell, November 15.

David Trowbridge,† aet. 59, fever, November 16.

Child of David Godden, November 25.

Francis Casterline, aet. 96, old age, December 12.

Child of Hooks Roy, December 13.

An illegitimate child, December 13.

Abraham Howell, aet. 26, consumption, December 20.

1769.

Henry, son of John Lindsly, January 9.

Byram, son of Ebenezer Condict, aet. 5, whooping cough, January 17.

Child of Joseph Youngs, Jan. 26.

Peter Berry, aet. 30, accidental, February 12.

Phœbe, wife of Joseph Youngs, aet. 34, child bed, February 14.

David Corey, aet. 45, accidental, February 19.

Abel Hathaway, aet. 32, fever February 20.

Samuel Reeve, aet. 21, consumption, March 16.

John Clark, aet. 80, apoplexy, March 19.

Child of Edward Byram, sudden, March 23.

Sarah, wife of Robert Hinds, aet. 27, consumption, April 18.

Child of Ezekiel Brown, April 18.

Servant child of widow Moore, April 20.

Widow Dikins,* aet. 70, old age, May 20.

Lydia, wife of Zachariah Fairchild, aet. 45, Measles, May 22.

Child of Henry Gardner, May 22.

Child of James Loree, June 6.

Child of John Hathaway, June 14.

Child of Jonas Goble,† June 20.

Anne, wife of James Loree, aet. 22, child bed, June 25.

Child of Paul Farber, July 16.

Sarah, daughter of Phineas Fairchild, aet 11, drowned, September 9.

Child of James M'Bride, September 20.

Child of Ebenezer Coe, October 10.

Walter Irvin, son of James M'Bride, aet. 3, drowned, October 20.

Elizabeth, daughter of Jabez Beers, aet. 3, a swelling, October 29.

Timothy, son of Alexander Johnson, November 20.

1770.

Jacob, son of Isaac Pierson, aet. 9, diabetes, January 5.

Hannah, widow of James Rodgers, aet 73, pleurisy, January 28.

Jemima, daughter of Job Loree, aet. 3, Mortification, February 7.

Eunice, daughter of Abraham Pierson, aet. 10, diabetes, February 17.

Child of Jonathan Starke, March 25.

Mabel, wife of Israel Jennings, aet. 23, diabetes, April 1.

Junia Lindsly, aet. 45, pleurisy, April 2.

Joanna, wife of Isaac Ayres,* aet. 24, consumption, April 12.

Nathaniel, son of Jonathan Hathaway, aet. 9, asthma, April 22.

Martha, wife of Uzal Tompkins,† aet. 19, consumption, April 24.

Peter Indian, ulcer in his thigh, April 26.

(*Continued on page 81.*)

(*Continued from page 16.*)

TRUSTEES' BOOK.

October 22 1762 the trustees met and chose henry Primrose President who now sucseads our worthy Brother Benjamin hatheway Decesd

November 18 1762 the Elders and trustees met Being Leagely warned &c. Mr. Kent one of the trustees being infirm by Reason of Age was Dismissed from being a trustee by the Elders and Samuel tuthill of Morris Town Esq. was maid choice of in the Roome of Mr. Kent and then the trustees Proseaded Samuel tuthill absent By the advice and consent of the Elders and Drew a Subscription to Rais a Sum of money in order to purtchas a Peas of Land for the Benefit of the minister of morris town

Septem 19 1763 the Trustees met at Doctor tuthills and all agreed that Gideon Allwood might set his shop on the meeting hous Land below the hill near freanans Store and Remain for Seven yeaıs and also gave there consent that the society might Build a Steple to the meeting house Mr. Conklin absent

January 24 1764 the Elders and Trustees Being Leagely called met at Doctor tuthills and agreed that Colonel Ford should have the care management and over Site of Building the Steple and acordingly he consented to the Same

January 24 1766 the Trustees Being Called and met at Doctor tuthills and Gave Consent that the Burieng Ground should be fenced Samuel Robarts absent

January 12 1767 the trustees Being called and met at the School hous henry. Primrose Joseph Stiles and Benjamin Coe absent Proseaded and chose Benjamin Bayle President and Gave Lieve that a school hous might be Built on the Green Near whair the old hous Now Standeth

May 17 1770 the trustees being Duely Called and met at the county (?) hous and agreed to Convey a Part of the meating hous Land to the freeholders of the County of morris for the Benefit of the Court hous

June 7 1770 the trustees met & Gave a Deed for one acre of Land on which the Court hous Standeth to three majestrets and the Freeholders of the County of morris

Octob 7 1771 the trustees met at Doct tuthills Esq. Sam Robarts absent and agreed that the money that Mr. Watt (or Walt. Ed.) Left to the town Should be Laid out towards Purtchasing utensils for the comunian Table also that the school hous now on Peter Mackees Land be Removed onto the Parsonage Land and there to Remain During the Pleashure of the trustees and then Lyable to be Removed.

october 19 1772 the Elders met at Mr. Jones and made Choyce of Silas Cundict for a Trustee in the Roome of Samuel Robarts

December 10 1772. The Trustees Met at Samuel Robarts and chose Silas Condict Clerk of this corporation & the said Trustees ordered the said Clerk to settle with Mr. Robarts accordingly the sd Clerk settled with Mr. Roberts & the sd Roberts gave the sd clk. Sundry Notes to the amount of fifty Seven pounds five Shillings & four pence, which The Trustees accepted as payment for so much money & the sd clk. gave Receipt for the same, and the Trustees appointed Henry Primrose & Silas Condict as a committee to settle with Mr. Timothy Johnes.

January 8, 1773. Henry Primrose & Silas Condict (as appointed by the Trustees) Met at Mr. Timothy Johnes' and settled with the sd. Mr. Johnes, (Respecting his salary) from a former Settlement made in A.D 1757 for the Several Years Since until and including the Year 1769 and made an even ballance in the whole.

(*Continued on page 32.*)

In answer to the inquiry in the January RECORD concerning Mrs. Scribner and her daughters, our records show the following : Mrs. Phebe Scribner (widow) united with this church Dec. 27th. 1809, by certificate from the Cedar street Presbyterian Church of New York city. Esther and Ann Scribner joined July 3, 1812, and Elizabeth Scribner Dec. 25, 1812—all by profession. Ann Scribner died Jan. 18, 1814. (born Oct. 16, 1785.) The mother and two other daughters were dismissed Apr. 22, 1814, to "Indiana Territory." Who can furnish Mr. Bartow with the autograph of Esther Scribner ?

Morris County was formed by act of Assembly, March 15th, 1738-9, from the county of Hunterdon.

THE RECORD.

FIRST PRESBYTERIAN CHURCH, MORRISTOWN, N. J.

"This shall be Written for the Generation to Come."—Psalms 102 : 18.

VOL. I.   APRIL, 1880.   NO. 4.

(Printed with the approval of Session.)

THE RECORD

Will be printed and published monthly at Morristown, N. J. Terms, 50 cents per annum in advance; 75 cents after June.

Subscriptions will be received at the book-stores of Messrs. Runyon and Emmell, or through the mail. ALL COMMUNICATIONS should be addressed to the
EDITOR OF THE RECORD,
Lock box 44.   Morristown, N. J.

Entered at the Post Office at Morristown, N. J., as second class matter.

The annual meeting of the Parish was held the 16th of March. The old Board of Trustees was re-elected. The Committees remain as already given on the first page of the January RECORD.

Sunday, March 21st, 1880—Aaron D. Whitehead, James R. Voorhees, William D. Johnson and Wayland Spaulding were by unanimous vote of the members of this church elected to the office of Ruling Elder. Sunday, April 4th, they were solemnly ordained to their sacred office, and assisted in the celebration of the Lord's Supper. With these brethren this church has been served by sixty-six Elders, most of whom have fallen asleep in Jesus. The next number of THE RECORD will contain the complete list.

We call the attention of our readers, who may be interested in the Tuthill and Kent families, to the offer which THE RECORD through the kindness of Mr. Wm. S. Auchincloss, of Philadelphia, is able to make them. Mr. A. by the aid of the old records of this church has made a genealogical chart of the two families above mentioned. Any desiring it may have this valuable chart by sending stamp to the editor of THE RECORD.

A very generous donation by an unknown friend "for defraying the expenses of publishing the history of the church" was found in the collection of the first Sunday of this month. The treasurer of the church has put it into the hands of the editor of this paper. We suppose it was intended for THE RECORD, in answer to our appeal for such encouragement, and we desire heartily to thank the donor. If this supposition be incorrect, we shall expect to be so informed by the giver.

We take this occasion to thank the many who have shown an interest in our work. In addition to the above gift about one hundred more subscribers are needed to meet expenses for the year.

The First Church makes the following report to Presbytery for the year ending April 1st, 1880 :

Added on examination,	9
" " certificate,	17
Total No. of communicants,	575
No. of adults baptized,	3
" infants "	9
Sunday school membership,	456

FUND CONTRIBUTED.

To Home Missions,	$1,058 00
" Foreign "	1,287 00
" Education,	836 00
" Publication,	40 00
" Church Erection,	230 00
" Relief Fund,	185 00
" Freedmen,	104 00
" Sustentation,	80 00
" General Assembly,	51 66
" Miscellaneous Causes,	1,218 00
" Congregational Expenses,	6,400 00

Aside from the above and not reported to Presbytery, $2,000 have been privately contributed to weak churches in our own State.

The Presbytery of Morris and Orange will meet the 13th inst. at Succasunna. This church will be represented by Elder H. M. Dalrymple.

PLAN FOR COLLECTING.

The Current Expenses and Funds for Benevolence of the First Presbyterian Church of Morristown, N. J. Originally Adopted at a Parish Meeting held March 6, 1873, and Modified at a Similar Meeting held March 13, 1877.

MARCH, 1880.

1st. At each annual Parish Meeting the Trustees will submit for the approval of the Parish an *estimate* of the *probable expenses of our home work* for the ensuing year, and immediately after such meeting each pew holder and adult member of the church will be called on, either by a committee appointed by the Parish meeting or in such mode as the Trustees may deem advisable, to pledge such amount as he or she may be able to pay *monthly or quarterly towards such expenses.* Each payment to be inclosed in an envelope furnished by the Treasurer and returned on the *second Sabbath* of each month, with the name of the person making payment and the number of the pew.

2d. At the Parish meeting recently held a committee of two was appointed who, in connection with the Treasurer, were directed to prepare a schedule of the pews of the church and *an estimate of the minimum amount which each pew should yield to produce in the aggregate the current expenses of the church.*

In cases where the sum pledged for any pew *which is owned by the church* shall be less than the aforesaid minimum amount, the *Trustees have the right,* whenever there shall be a demand for pews, to inform the occupant of such pew of the fact, and either to arrange with such occupant for the payment of at least such minimum sum or for a removal to some other pew.

Where, in similar cases, the occupants of pews are the owners of them, they are also to be notified of such discrepancy and requested to pay at least such minimum sum, and if they fail to do so the matter is to be reported to the Session.

3d. A collection will be taken up as heretofore on each Sabbath. The amount collected on the first Sabbath of each month, unless otherwise directed by the donor, will be appropriated as follows:

First Sabbath of April—Board of Sustentation.

May—The Bible Society.

June—Freedmen.

First Sabbath of July—Foreign Missions.

August—Church Erection.

September—Home Missions.

October—Cause to be designated by the Session.

November—Education.

December—Poor of the Church.

January—Publication.

February—Disabled Ministers.

March—Cause to be designated by the Session.

All other moneys received from the Sabbath collections or from any other source are paid to the Treasurer, elected at the annual Parish meeting, who is required to render a statement of his receipts and disbursements quarterly to both the Trustees and Session, and to present also a full report for the year at each annual Parish meeting.

4th. The Treasurer is required to forward promptly all moneys which may be *contributed for any specific object.*

Out of the other moneys received by him he is required, first, to pay on the orders of the Trustees, which are to be drawn so far as practicable monthly, all the *expenses necessary for our home work,* (which now includes the support of the Sabbath School); which payments, however, are in no case to exceed the amount designated by the Parish meeting.

Of the balance of such moneys the Treasurer pays eight-twelfths to the eight Boards of our Church, in quarterly payments, in the proportion recommended by the General Assembly, and four-twelfths constitute the contingent fund of the Session, to be paid on their order, and used for the support of the poor of the church and matters of a similar kind.

5th. If during any year the current expenses of our home work, should from any cause, exceed the estimate of the Parish meeting, the Trustees are to provide for such excess, if possible, by special application to the members of the congregation; and if such effort fails, such excess is to be included in the estimate and paid out of the collection of the next year. THE ESTIMATE FOR THIS YEAR IS $6,500.

The fixing of a minimum sum which each

pew should yield in order to raise our current expenses, is not intended as any intimation of the amount which each pew holder or church member ought in conscience to pay. It is fully believed that the duty of supporting the Gospel at home and abroad rests on each individual, not according to the location of his pew, but in proportion to his ability.

The voluntary system was never intended to furnish an excuse for any one paying less than under the old system of assessment, but to awaken the conscience of all, and induce each one, if possible, to pay more than before, and to give conscientiously as God may give ability.

[The following letter in addition to what is said on the first page of the March RECORD, will settle beyond all possible doubt the date of the ordination and installation of the Rev. Albert Barnes.—Ed.]

MORRISTOWN, Feb. 8th, 1825,
Eleven o'clock A.M.

The Presbytery of Elizabethtown met at the call of the Moderator, and was opened with prayer.

Present, David Magie, Mod., etc., etc.

The Moderator informed the Presbytery that he had called them together for the purpose of ordaining Mr. Albert Barnes to the work of the gospel ministry, and installing him pastor of the congregation of Morristown; also, etc., etc., (other matters.)

On inquiry it appeared that the Presbytery had been duly called.

The Presbytery proceeded to the ordination of Mr. Albert Barnes, to the work of the gospel ministry, and his installation as pastor of the congregation of Morristown. Dr. M'Dowell preached the sermon from 1st Thes. 5: 12, 13. Mr. Magie presided, made the ordaining prayer, and gave the charge to the people, and Mr. Barnes was solemnly ordained to the work of the gospel ministry, by prayer and imposition of hands, and installed pastor of the congregation of Morristown. After which Mr. Barnes took his seat as a member of the Presbytery."

The above is a true extract from the minutes of the Presbytery of Elizabethtown.

Baskingridge, N. J., March 9, 1880.

JOHN C. RANKIN, *Stated Clerk.*

(*Continued from page 19.*)

SEPTEMBER 24th, 1735.

The West part of Hanover having applied to the Synod for the ordination of Mr. Cleverly, the Synod do order it to be left to the Presbytery of Philadelphia.

MAY, 29th, 1738.

Upon the affair of West Hanover, overtured as follows. Upon Mr. Budd's representation of the affair of Hanover: Overtured, That, however in a former minute relating to West Hanover, we have granted, that solemn obligations by lot or otherwise may cease, when by any turn of Providence what is engaged unto becomes impossible or impracticable, or the end thereof is otherwise fully and completely answered; yet it appearing doubtful to us whether this be the case of said people in respect of the obligation laid upon them to unite or join with the people of East Hanover, by a lot or solemn engagement to submit to the judgment of the committee of the Presbytery of East Jersey, who were called to judge in that affair; the Synod does judge that the safest way to come to a final determination of that affair is, that a committee be appointed to meet in that place in order to make as exact inquiry as they can into the circumstances of that people, whether there really be such a change in their case as to cause the above obligation to cease, and either give their judgment of this matter, or else represent it as it shall appear to them to the Synod at our next meeting, which they shall judge most meet, and that Messrs. Gilbert Tennent, William Tennent Junior, Samuel Blair, David Cowell, Eleazar Wales, Jedediah Andrews, Aaron Burr, John Cross and Richard Treat, be a committee to meet at Hanover the last Wednesday of July next, upon the affair, at eleven of the clock *ante meridiem.* Approved *nemine contradicente.*

(*To be continued.*)

Inquiry is made for "the name of the father of Miss Aruba C. Condict of Morristown, who was married Dec. 12, 1843, to Rev. D. O. Allen." Answer may be sent to editor of THE RECORD.

(Continued from page 90.)

MEMBERS.

——:0:——

1774.
Joanna, John Ayrs' wife.
Phebe, Silvanus Arnold's wife.
Samuel Morison, susp. June 27, 1800 d. Dec. 30, 1805, aet. 52.
Abigail, wf. of Aaron Riggs, dis. June 12, 1811 to "the Western Country."
Donald Morison.
Kezia, wf. of Gilbert Thornton.
Elizabeth, wid. of John Davis.
Wido. of Ezra Fairchild.
Wf. of John Enslee, (Phebe).
Nathaniel Mather.
Thankful Cory or Cary.
Latta, wf. of Tunis Bocard.
Mary, wf. of Cap. Jed. Mills.
Wido. Margaret Steal.
Anna, wf. of Jeduthan Day.
Martha Lyon, from Mendham.
Henry Young's wife.

*

" *The names and Number of Persons that have renewed their Cov. or taken their Baptismal Vows upon themselves.*"

TIMO. JOHNES.

——

1743.
Apr. 24. Joseph Tichenor.
June 10. Sarah Fairchild, daughter of Caleb.
Oct. 30. Matthew Fairchild & his wife.
Nov. 20. John Holloway & his wife.
1744.
Feb. 5. Samuel Day & his wf.
Feb. 24. Sarah, wf. of Richard Wood.
" 25. Thomas Allerton & wf. & daughter Sarah.
Aug. 28. Benjamin Freman.
1745.
Jan. 11. Bathia, Nathaniel Wheler's wf.
Mar. 24. Stephen Freman.
Aug. 25. John Burrel & wf.
" " Thomas Gilbard & wf.
Sept. 16. Zachariah Blackman, Daniel Freman, Ann, wf. of David Ogden.
Oct. 13. Matthias Burnet, of Hanover, & wf.
Nov. 10. Thomas Bridge.
1746.
Feb. 16. Peter Prudden.
Apr. 2. Joseph Winget.
Aug. 17. Peter Dickerson & wf.

Oct. 6. Benjamin Hathaway & wf. Elizabeth.
Nov. 17. Thomas Coe.
1747.
July 26. Joseph Potter & wf.
Aug. 16. Stephen Lindsley.
Sept. 26. Ezekiel Younglove Renewed & wf., entered Cov. & was Bap.
Oct. 11. Benjamin Hathaway, Jr., & wf., & Joanna, Josiah Cranes' wf.
Nov. 1. Simeon Hathaway & wf.
" 8. Benjamin Hathaway & Capt. Son, & wf.
Dec. 27. Isaac Daton & wf.
1748.
Jan. 31. Benjamin Halsey & wf.
Feb. 15. Phebe, Amos Cilborn's wf.
Mar. 20. Richard Wood.
Apr. 17. Daniel Howard & wf.
June 12. Desire, Zophar Gildersleeve's wf.
" 19. Samuel Munson & wf.
Aug. 6. Shadrack Hathaway.
Nov. 6. Mary, wf. of Peter Norris.
Dec. 25. John Slater & Henry Gardiner & wf.
1749.
Jan. 15. John Robard & wf., entered Cov. & was Bap.
" 22. Samuel Lyon's wf.
Feb. 5. William Brown & his wf.
Apr. 30. Samuel & Lidia Shipman his wf.
June 25. Nathaniel Stilwell & Mary his wf.
July 30. Wido. Ann Dillane.
Aug. 30. Sarah Price.
" 27. Solomon Stanborough.
1750.
June 20. Jesse Reeve, of Rockaway.
Nov. — David Orsborn.
1751.
Feb. 10. Jabish Bears.
Mar. 30. Abraham Hathaway.
Apr. 21. John Johnson, Jr.
May 12. Jemima Stuard's wife.
June 30. Sarah, Joseph Whitehead's wife.
" " Ruth, John Whitehead's daughter.
Oct. 27. Hannah, John Lose, Jr.'s wife.
Nov. 1. Suse Jones, wf. of Joseph Jones.
1752.
Apr. 5. Zophar Freman & his wf.
May 9. Shadrach Howard & his wf.
July 7. Lindsley. Junia
" " John Lindsley & his wf.
Sept. 24. Elizabeth, wf. of Jonathan Reve.

(To be Continued.)

(*Continued from page* 21.)

BAPTISMS.

—:o:—

1749.

Apt. 30. Benjamin Hathaway, Jun., child Lois.

June 18. John Perkhurst & wf., ch. David.

" 25. Nathaniel Stilwell & wf., ch. Phebe.

" " Dea. Prudden & wf., for negro ch. Luis.

July 23. Peter Dickenson & wf., ch. Jesse.

" 30. Daniel Lindley & wf., ch. Susanna.

" " John Burrel & wf., ch. Susanna.

" " Ann Dillane, wido., ch. Nansey.

Aug. 6. Joseph Mead(?) & wf., ch. Joseph Stevens.

" " Daniel Wick & wf., ch. Jane.

" " Uriah Glover's wf. ch. Charles.

" " William Brown & wf., ch. Richard.

" 27. Solomon Stanborough's wf., adult.

Sept. 10. Philip Condict & wf., ch. Abner.

" " William Lose & wf., ch. Peter.

" " John Robords & wf., ch. ———

" 24. Hur Osborns' & wf., ch. Jedidiah.

Oct. 29. Gideon Rigs & wf., ch. Phebe.

Nov. 5. John Clark & wf., ch. Isaac Baker.

" 8. Simeon Hathaway & wf., ch. Silas.

" " Peter Norris & wf., ch. Walter.

Dec. 17. Benjamin Halsey & wf., ch. Joseph.

" " Daniel Howard & wf., ch. William.

1750.

Jan. 15. Daniel Frost's wf., ch. ———

Feb. 25. Uriah Cutler & wf., ch. Bathia.

" " Isaiah Wines & wf., ch. Phebe.

Mar. 11. Isaac Daton & wf., ch. Rachel.

" " Thomas Gilbard & wf., ch. Elizabeth.

" 25. David Gauden, ch. Samuel.

" " Samuel Shipman & wf., ch. Azel.

Apr. 15. Thomas Bridge, ch. Benjamin.

" 22. Joseph Fowler's wf., ch. Susanna.

May 20. Stephen Mahurin & wf., ch. Lucretia.

" " Robard Arnold & wf., ch. Robard.

" " Wido., wf. of Isaac Clark, ch. Mary.

" 27. Benjamin Pierson & wf., ch. Daniel.

" " Eliacam Suard & wf., ch. Anna.

June 3. Joseph Stiles & wf., ch. Silas.

" " John Lose, ch. Philip.

" 20. Jesse Reeve, of Rockaway, ch. ——

July 8. John Brookfield, ch. Phebe.

" " John Marsh, ch. Sarah.

" 15. Zophar Gildersleeve & wf., ch. Hanna.

Aug. 5. Samuel Day & wf., ch. Robard.

" " Jeremiah Johnson's wf., accompt., ch. Jeremiah.

Sept. 2. Stephen Freeman & wf., ch. Silas.

" 10. Gilbard Heady, ch. Jacob.

" 16. Henry Gardiner, ch. Hanna.

Oct. 7. Benjamin Coe & wf., ch. Moses.

" 14. Thomas Coe, ch. Ursula.

" " Thomas Wilkerson & wf., ch. Aaron.

Nov. 11. David Orsborn, ch. Mary.

Dec. 2. David Ogden's ch. wf. accompt., Stephen.

" 16. Benjamin Hathaway & wf., ch. Kezia.

1751.

Jan. 20. Matthew Fairchild & wf., ch. Asher.

Feb. 10. Jabish Bears & wf., ch. Joseph.

Mar. 3. Benjamin Hathaway, Jun., & wf., Capn. son, ch. Sarah.

" 31. Abraham Hathaway, Jun., Household—Miriam, William, Nathan, Rhoda and Joanna.

" " Peter Dickerson & wf. ch. Phebe.

Apr. 21. John Johnson & wf., ch. Jacob.

" " Richard Wood, ch. Sarah.

" 29. Joseph Edmister, ch. David.

May 12. Stephen Ogden, ch. Elizabeth.

" " William Hay's wf. on her accompt., ch. Joseph.

" " Jemima Stuards, ch. David.

" 19. Elizabeth Mott, ch. Abigail.

May 24. at Rockaway. { Zachariah Blackman, ch. ——— David Herimon, ch. ——— Adam Blackman, ch. ——— Abraham Johnson, ch. ———

June 9. John Perkhurst & wf., ch. Ezekiel.

" 15. Henry Primrose, ch. Sarah.

" 21. Sarah Relict of Bois John Prudden, chn. John, Sarah.

" " Benjamin Halsey & wf., ch. Joanna.

" " Deacon Joseph Prudden & wf., Servant's ch. Daniel.

" 30. Joseph Whitehead, children, wf. accompt., Joseph, Rhoda.

" " Nathaniel Stillwell & wf., ch. Nicholas.

" " Sarah Whitehead & Ruth Whitehead, adults.

Aug. 11. Samuel Bailey & wf., ch. Daniel.

" 14. Job Allen on wf. accompt., ch. Job.

" 18. Shadrack Hathaway & wf., ch. Abner.

" " Abel Lyon on wf. accompt. ch. Joanna.

(*To be continued.*)

(Continued from page 22.)
MARRIAGES.
—:o:—

1759.
Jan. 14. William Loid, Soldier, & Elizabeth Ward.
"   " Alexander Kermicle & Elizabeth Ogden.
"   15. Abraham Kitchel, of Hanover, & Charity Fford.
"   24. Abraham Pierson & Affia Crane, of Hanover.
"   " Aaron Tompkins & Hannah Campfield.
"   25. Henry Clark, of Medham, & Massey Fanger.
"   26. Samuel Whitehead & Jemima Vandine, of Rockaway.
Feb. 26. Christian Aber & Anna Margaret Battleren.
"   28. Augustin Bayles & Kezia Pierson.
Mar. 1. Abel Hathaway & Mary Orsborn.
"   8. Samuel Kitchel, of Hanover,& Sarah Lum.
Apr. 1. Joshua Crossman & Elizabeth Cleverly.
"   5. Isaac Losey & Miriam Hathaway.
"   12. George Bockoven & Mary Whitekernek.
"   " Joseph Morris & Hannah Fford.
"   17. Peter Snyder & Catrena Temont, of Pequanack.
"   30. John Riddel & Margaret Scisco.
May 31. John Faugerson & Phebe Cathcart.
June 27. Silas Day & Phebe Condict.
July 4. John Primrose & Abigail Coe.
Oct. 3. Samuel McCollum & Hannah Freman.
Nov. 4. Isaac Person & Rhode Crain.
"   18. Ezekel Mulford & Charity Ludlum.
Dec. 20. Jonathan Hathaway & Lydia Peck.
"   24. Benjamin Daves & Priscilla Palmer, both of Mendham.
"   26. Wm. Throgmorton & Sarah Gillet.
"   27. Daniel Drake & Phebe Extel.
1760.
Jan. 16. Elijah Holloway & Hannah Smith.
"   31. Joseph Stiles & Phebe Ann Wilkison.
Feb. 7. Henry Wick & Elizabeth Cooper.
"   21. James Macke & Susanna Garrigas.
Mar. 2. William Gobil & Sarah Conger.
"   19. Moses Lindsley & Trane (?) Raynor.
Apr. 9. Benjamin Price & Sarah Lyon.
"   10. Silas Condict & Phebe Day.

Sep. 7. Joshua Bald & wido. Martha Tompkins.
"   11. Josiah Beeman & Huldah Wines.
Dec. 10. Job Bacorn & Rhoda Wheler.
"   " Thomas Pierson & Elizabeth Hunterton.
"   18. Jonathan Johnson & Phebe Perkhurst.
1761.
Jan. 8. Jesse Muire & Hannah Leonard.
"   16. Doctor David Gould & Catharine Budd.
"   29. Samuel Perkhurst & Sarah Gard.
Feb. 11. Mathew McCollester & Elizabeth Fanger. & ?3
Mar. 1. Hur Orsborn & Wido. Rebecca Cady
"   " John Denton, of Jemaica, & Eliz. Wisnor, of Goshen.
Apr. 21. Stephen More & Eunice Ford.
June 26. William Walton & Phebe Muir.
"   30. Samuel Ward & Hannah Johnson.
July 15. Doctor Barnabus Budd & Phebe Wheler.
"   26. Isaac Vanduyn & Phebe Cole.
Sep. 17. Ebenezar Coe & Eunice Jaggar.
Oct. 12. Capt. Samuel Day & Zervia Wines, wido.
Nov. 27. Peter Meterr, a Frenchman, & Mary Roggers.
1762.
Jan. 27. Jacob Ford & Theodosia Johnes.
Feb. 3. Moses Pierson & Anne Wick.
Mar. 17. John Primrose & Eunice Morris.
Apr. 15. Soloman Southard & Mary Frost.
May 17. Joseph Smith, of Newark Mountains & Abigail Condict.
June 2. Ephraim Gard & Mary Pierson.
"   6. Amos Sutherd & Jane Simson.
July 4. Benjamin Pool & Jem.ma Burt.
"   15. Edward Byram & Phebe Coe.
Aug 26. John Ogden & Phebe Howard.
Sep. 12. Joseph Coe & Abigail More, of Rockaway.
"   26. Elisha Johnson & Hannah Lyon, wido.
Oct. 14. Daniel Kermicael & Bathsheba Clark.
Nov. 14. Jeremiah Gard & Elizabeth Moor, wido.
"   " Enoch Conger & Susanna Whitehead.
"   23 Frederic King & Mary Ayrs.
"   28. Jacob Plow & Dinah Tompkins.
Dec. 1. Jas. Chadwick & Anne Holloway.
(To be Continued.)

(*Continued from page 18.*)

BILL OF MORTALITY,

——:o:——

1770.
May 10. Child of Philip Hathaway.
" 13. Child of Ebenezer Stiles.
‹ " Jared, son of Uzal Tompkins†, consumption.
June 2. Samuel Lyon, aet. 56, dysentery.
" 21. Child of Alexander Carmichael,
" 28. Child of David Godden.
" " Child of Alexander Johnson.
July 15. Abigail, wife of John Sutten, aet. 20, childbirth.
" 17. Simon Huntington, aet. 74, dropsy.
" 25. Child of Coonrod, scalded.
Aug. 6. Timothy, son of Jonathan Hathaway, aet. 5, ulcer in his head.
" " Child of Nathan Wilkerson, aet. 2.
" 20. Child of Benoni Hathaway.
" 24. Rev. Mr. John Pierson*, aet. 82, old age.
Sept.20. Child of John Ogden.
" 27. Abraham, son of John Ogden, aet. 3, drowned.
Oct. 1. Rev. Mr. John Walton,† * aet. 35, small pox.
" 15. Widow Lyon, aet. 84, dysentery.
Nov. 30. Samuel Godden, aet. 73, old age.
1771.
Jan. 2. Susanna, wife of John Wheeler, aet. 21.
" 5. John Pierson, aet. 39, small pox.
" 15. Hannah, daughter of Joshua Ball, aet. 15, white swelling.
" 22. Perkins Byram, aet. 23, small pox.
" " Child of Frederick King.
Feb. 1. Jonathan Clark, aet. 18.
" 21. Child of Philip Hathaway, small pox.
" 25. Addi Serjant, small pox.
Mar. 25. Silas, son of David Fairchild, aet. 2, scald.
" " Sarah, wife of Ebenezer Howell, aet. 60, small pox.
" 26. David Watt, aet. 87, old age.
Apr. 3. Child of Joseph King.
May 8. Samuel, son of Jonas Philips, aet. 1, teething.
" 15. Mary, widow of Ebenezer Gregory, aet. 64, old age.
June 19. Silas Flint, aet. 24, ulcers in his hip and thigh.
July 11. Abigail, wife of Constant Cooper, aet. 28, decay.

July 24. Child of widow Flint.
Aug. 2. Stephen Freeman* aet. 84, sudden.
Sept. 2. Mary Cheever, aet. 16, consumption.
Oct. 1. Mary, daughter of Benoni Hathaway, aet 6, putrid fever.
" 5. Thomas Cheever, aet. 24, consumption.
" 25. Ruth, daughter of John Mills, sprew.
Nov. 6. Josephus, son of Daniel Gard,† aet 2, worms.
" — Solomon Bates, aet. 100, old age.
" — Child of John Bridge.
Dec. 27. Child of Isaac Ayres.
1772.
Jan. 1. Phœbe, daughter of Ezekiel Day, aet. 6, fever.
" 10. Child of Elijah Pierson.
Feb. 10. Child of Silas Moore.
" 20. Thomas Wood, aet. 77, old age.
" 27. Child of John Arnold.
" " Moses, son of Thomas Miller, aet. 2, worms.
Mar. 26. Child of Nathaniel Lhomedieu.
" 30. Child of Philip Hathaway.
Apr. 17. Richard Easton. aet. 92, old age.
" 21. Elizabeth, widow of John Lindsley,* aet. 91. old age.
May — A child of Trowbridges.†
June 1. Child of James Kearney.
" 24. Mary, daughter of John Losey.
July — Child of Nathaniel Thompson.
Aug.28. John, son of Jedediah Gregory, aet. 14, drowned.
Sept. 5. Child of Nicholas Carter.
" 6. Twins of Isaac Morris.
" 21. Child of Doct. Samuel Tuthill.
" 28. Hephzibah, daughter of Joseph Pierson, aet. 7, cholic.
Oct. — Child of Patrick M'Gill.
" 26. Abijah Cheever, aet. 20, consumption.
" 29. Rebekah wife of Nathan Hathaway, aet. 25.
" — Child of Epenetus Beach.
" 30. Samuel Loree, aet 23, bleeding at the lungs.
Nov. — Child of Jonathan Starke, aet. 6.
" 27. Child of Phinehas Fairchild.
Dec. — Child of Isaac Morris.
1773.
Jan. 4. Child of Abraham Hathaway.
" 11. Ruth, daughter of Capt. Peter Dickerson, fever.

(*To be Continued.*)

(Continued from page 24.)

TRUSTEES' BOOK.

——:o:——

March 9, 1773, the Trustees met at Doc't Tuthill's; all present but Mr. Coe. agreed this Messr. Primrose, Tuthill, Baleys and Stiles be a committee to view a certain tract of land of Shadrach Hayward's and if they think proper to agree for and purchase the same for the use and benefit of our community and make Report at the next meeting of the Trustees, and further agreed to pay to Coll. Jacob Ford the Sum of Twenty one pounds Sixteen Shillings and eight pence, Light money being the full of his Demand for moneys Expended and service done at & upon a certain Gully near the Courthouse and that the Said Sum be paid out of the moneys now in bank.

April 24, 1773, the Trustees met at Doc't Tuthill's; all present; the committe appointed at the last meeting Reported that they had Viewed the Lands proposed to be purchased of Shadrach Hayward and that they had agreed for the Same, being Sixty one Acres, & Seventy two hundreths of an acre, at three pounds pr. acre, then the Trustees proceeded & confirmed the Said purchase by taking Deed of sd. Hayward which is Dated April 2d, 1773, in consideration of the sum of one hundred & eighty five pounds three Shillings & two pence, containing the sd. quantity of 61 acres & 72 hundredths strict measure, and gave two Bonds to sd. Hayward, one for the payment of £139,, 3,, 2, and the other for the payment of the sum of £46,, 0,. 0.

Total, £185,, 3,, 2

Further agreed that Silas Condict draw a copy of the old Subscription and present the Same to Such as have not Subscribed, towards purchasing a Parsonage in order that they may have opportunity to subscribe, & also to call upon the Inhabitants to discharge their Several Subscriptions formerly subscribed, &c.

Oct. 18, 1773, the Trustees met at Cap't Dickersons; present Mess. Primrose, Coe, Stiles & Condict; agreed that Silas Condict again Request the Inhabitants who Subscribed on the old subscription for the purchasing a parsonage to' discharge the same or confess a judgment to the trustees for the same before Robert Goble, Esq.

June 13, 1774, the Trustees met at the Courthouse; all present but Mr. Coe; agreed that Sam'l Tuthill, Esq., draw a subscription and present it to Such Persons as he shall think proper in order to Raise moneys to purchase a Tract of Land of Thomas Kenny, Esq., to enlarge and accommodate the Public Parade, &c.

August 22, 1774, the Trustees met at the Courthouse all present but Mess. Bayles & Stiles; agreed that Silas Condict (at the expence of the Society) goe to Perth Amboy and get the Charter Recorded, and also *That he,* the sd. Silas, Draw a copy of the sd. Charter & keep for common Perusal to save the original, &c.

Also agreed that the Society may Enlarge the Meeting House at their discretion. Also appointed Mess. Henry Primrose, Sam'l Tuthill & Silas Condict a committee to meet and settle several Lines of the Parsonage & meeting house Tracts of Land.

March 12, 1776, the Trustees met at Mr. Johnes's; present Mess. Baleys, Conklin, Stiles, Tuthill &|Condict; absent Mess. Primrose & Coe. Mr. Johnes made application to the Trustees to purchase a small parcel of Land of the East Corner of the parsonage adjoining the Road; the determination whereof was deferred to the next meeting; adjourned to fryday, 22 Int. at Mr. Primrose, to meet at nine o'clock.

March 22, the Trustees meet according to adjournment at Mr. Primrose; all present & took into consideration the Request of Mr. Johns which was Referred to this meetand determined not to sell any of the Parsonage Land at present; then took into consideration the matter Respecting the house built on the Parish Land by Mr. Huntington & determined that the property of sd. House from the time of the Death of sd. Huntington & his wife belongs to the Trustees in behalf of the parish. agreed that the profits that have arisen since the death of sd. Huntington & wife may be appropriated to discharge the Just Debts of sd. Huntington So far as it shall Extend there unto in such manner as shall appear Equitable to this Board and that for the future the profits that may arise therefrom be at the disposal of the Trustees.

(To be Continued.)

THE RECORD.

FIRST PRESBYTERIAN CHURCH, MORRISTOWN, N. J.

"This shall be Written for the Generation to Come."—Psalm 102 : 18.

VOL. 1.   MAY, 1880.   NO. 5.

(Printed with the approval of Session.)

THE RECORD

Will be printed and published monthly at Morristown, N. J. Terms, 50 cents per annum in advance; 75 cents after June.

Subscriptions will be received at the book-stores of Messrs. Runyon and Emmell; or through the mail, and may begin with the first number. ALL COMMUNICATIONS should be addressed to the

EDITOR OF THE RECORD,

Lock box 44.   Morristown, N. J.

Entered at the Post Office at Morristown, N. J., as second class matter.

— We call attention to the inquiry of Rev. Dr. Hatfield on the last page of this number of the RECORD.

Can any one give us the date of the death or removal from town of any of the Elders marked * in the list printed this month ?

WHO CAN TELL.

The date of the death or removal from town of the following persons :

NAME.	DATE OF JOINING CHURCH.
Samuel Bailey,	June 26, 1743.
John Dorkis,	" "
Mary, wf. of Benj. Perkis,	" "
Hannah, da. of John Lindsley, Jr.,	" "
Elizabeth, wf. of Thomas Headley,	Dec. 28, "
James Tompkins,	Feb. 24, 1744.
Peter Norris,	Aug. 31, "
Jude, serv. of Dea. Prudden,	" " "
Deborah, wf. of Thomas Allerton,	Nov. 2, "
Sarah, wf. of Stephen Freeman,	Jan. 11, 1745.
Jacob Allerton,	May 10, "
David Chitester,	July 15, "

Abigail, sister of David Chitester,	July 15, 1745.
Rachael, wf. of John Stiles,	" " "
Rachel, wf. of Sam'l Samson,	Sept. 6, "
David Gauden,	March 7, 1746.
Susanna, wf. of Jno. Frost,	Oct. 24 "
Phebe, wf. of Sam'l Bailey,	May 1, 1747.
Elizabeth, wf. of Ebenezer Mott,	Sept. 25, "
Joseph Wood,	Apr. 3, 1748.
Joseph Tichenor,	Sept. 2, 1749.
Ame Holloway,	" " "
Samuel Hudson,	May 25, 1750.
Mrs. Samuel Hudson,	" "
Hannah, wf. of Thos. Wilkerson,	Oct. 6, 1751.

(Continued from page 27.)

SYNOD OF PHILADELPHIA.

——:o:——

MAY, 24th, 1739.

The committee appointed to go to Hanover and help the people there in their difficulties, made report to the Synod of their compliance, and brought in the minutes of their proceedings, which being read were approved and ordered to be inserted in their minutes, and are as follows, viz.: At a committee of the Synod met at Hanover, July 26th, 1738, according to appointment of Synod, *ubi post preces sederunt* Messrs. Jedediah Andrews, Gilbert Tennent, William Tennent, Jun'r, John Cross, David Cowell and Richard Treat. Ministers of the Committee absent : Messrs. Samuel Blair, Eleazer Wales and Aaron Burr; Mr. Andrews chosen Moderator; Mr. Treat, Clerk; Mr. Gilbert Tennent opened the committee by a sermon, Ezek. xi, 19. The committee in order to lay a clear foundation to go upon, thought proper to read a schedule sider the minutes of the Synod in relation to the affairs, and after that was done the Moderator proceeded to inquire into the matter they were come about, and asked the people of West Hanover; whether their circumstances were altered for the better since the casting of the lot, and it was answered by some of them in the hearing and behalf of the whole that they were much increased as to numbers of persons in their society, and that they were near one-half abler than they were. Which representation was not contradicted nor disproved by any, and plainly appeared to the committee to be the truth of their case. A paper was also brought in by Mr. Kitchell and some others, in behalf of the eastern part, as their committee, setting forth their weakness and expressing their desire of an union with their western brethren, if it could be had upon reasonable terms. Upon which, that the committee might come to understand the real truth with respect to said eastern people, the Moderator proceeded to interrogate Mr. Kitchell, and others of said eastern part about their affairs and they informed the committee that they were much stronger than when the lot was cast, that though it was hard with them for the present to fulfil their obligations to Mr. Nutman, yet they cannot but acknowledge they are in growing circumstances, and able to support of themselves, adding withal, that it is their mind and the mind of this society, not to have an union with the whole of the western society but with a part only, and that if the committee should judge them to unite upon any of the former terms, covenants and agreement, it would be the destruction of the whole, and be prejudicial to the interest of religion among them. Whereupon the committee came unanimously to form their judgment after the following manner, viz., That according as things are represented to them and as they appear, they cannot but judge,

1. That the former obligations of said people, by virtue of the lot formerly cast among them, are now impracticable.

2. That the end of the said lot will be much better answered by their being two separate societies, than by being united into one as formerly was desired and proposed.

3. That therefore we judge said western people may be a separate society by themselves. Furthermore, to prevent any disputes or difficulties between said western society and Basking-Ridge, it was proposed and agreed to, mutually by said people, that whosoever were desirous of going from the congregation where they belonged to the other, shall have liberty so to do, provided they pay off all their respective debts to the society to which they have belonged.

———

The above determinations of the committee were published to the aforesaid people, and all parties expressed their entire satisfaction therein. Concluded with prayer.

———:O:———

LIST OF RULING ELDERS OF THE FIRST CHURCH.

———:0:———

	IN OFFICE	
Joseph Prudden,	1747,	Buried Sept. 27, 1776, aet. 84.
Matthew Lum,	"	" May 21, 1777, aet. 70.
John Lindsley,	"	Died March 9, 1750, aet. 56.
Joseph Coe,	"	*Nov. 8, 1759.
Jacob Ford,	"	Died Jan. 19, 1777, aet. 73.
Abner Beach,	1752,	Suspended May 8, 1752.
Solomon Munson,	1754,	Buried Feb. 8, 1803, aet. 78.
Daniel Lindsley,	"	Died Aug. 14, 1777, aet. 76½.
Daniel Morris,	Nov. 6, 1761,	*Aug. 20, 1767.
Timothy Mills,	" "	Resigned Aug. 25, 1775.
Matthias Burnet,	" "	Res. Oct. 31, 1782,& bur. Oct. 18, 1783, aet. 60.

*Met with Session for the last time.

John Ayres, Esq.,	June 20, 1769,	Died Apr. 29, 1777, aet. 57, 11, 5.
John Lindsley, Jr.,	" "	" Sept. 10, 1784, aet. 56.
Ezra Halsey,	Nov. 2, 1770,	Buried Oct. 23, 1775, aet. 48.
Joseph Lindsley,	July 31, 1777,	Died Oct. 8, 1822, aet. 87.
Gilbert Allen,	Sept. 12, 1777,	" Jan. 6, 1816, aet. 80.
Philip Condict,	" "	" Dec. 23. 1801, aet. 92, 8,
Jonas Phillips,	" "	" Dec. 26. 1813, aet. 78, 9, 13.
Joseph Prudden, Jr.,	1785,	" April 20 or 24, 1816, aet. 87.
Caleb Munson,	July 2, 1785,	" Feb. 25, 1815, aet. 80.
Philip Lindsley,	" "	*July 2, 1789.
Ezra Halsey,	" "	*Dec. 27, 1830.
Isaac Prudden,	1792,	Bur. June 22, 1798, aet. 60.
Samuel Freeman,	"	Died Sept. 16, 1833, aet. 80., 7,, 25.
Jesse Cutler,	"	" Sept. 4, 1827, aet. 70,, 6,, 14.
Mathias Crane,	"	Dis. to Union Town Pa., Jan. 7, 1825.
Henry Vail,	Sept. 11, 1805,	Died Nov. 12, 1832, aet. 79,
David Lindsley,	" "	*Dec. 11, 1832.
Zophar Freeman,	" "	Dis. to Chatham, Aug. 26, 1825.
James Stevenson,	" "	Died Oct. 1842, aet. 82.
Stephen Young,	May 14, 1812,	Died Feb. 10, 1867, aet. 92,, 2,, 13.
Jacob Pierson,	" "	Suspended Dec. 16, 1816.
Lewis Mills,	" "	Resigned Sept. 1, 1839.
Peter A. Johnson,	" "	Died Feb. 12, 1854, aet. 71,; 7,, 14.
Timothy Tucker,	Oct. 1, 1826,	Died Dec. 8, 1839, aet. 70,, 4,, 1.
William Enslee,	" "	" Sept. 17, 1860, aet. 83,, 6.
George K. Drake,	" "	Bur. May 8, 1837, aet. 48.
Frederick King,	" "	Died Aug. 13, 1874, aet. 81,, 11,, 2.
Jonathan Thompson,	" "	Resigned March 30, 1836.
Jonathan Oliver,	" "	*May 23, 1833.
Stephen A. Prudden,	Sept. 9, 1832,	Died Dec. 29, 1869, aet. 85.
Jonathan D. Marvin,	" "	Resigned Dec. 15, 1870.
John B. Johnes, M. D.,	" "	" March 30, 1836.
John R. Freeman	" "	Died Nov. 25, 1859, aet. 73,, 7,, 19.
Jonathan Pierson,	" "	*Nov. 15, 1832.
Sylvester R. Whitehead,	" "	*May 30, 1856.
John W. Cortelyou,	" "	*Feb. 20, 1834.
Ezra Mills,	Sept. 21, 1843,	Died May 1, 1872, aet. 72,, 7,, 15.
Ira Condict Whitehead Esq.,	May 3, 1846,	" Aug. 27. 1867, aet. 69.
David Olyphant,	June 28, 1857,	Dis to N. Y. City, Jan. 6, 1875.
Richard W. Stevenson, M. D.,	" "	Resigned Aug. 3, 1870.
Joel Davis,	March 27, 1859,	
Theodore Little, Esq.,	" "	
Henry M. Dalrymple,	Jan. 2, 1870,	
James D. Stevenson, Esq.,	" "	Dis. to San Antonio, Texas, Oct. 4, 1878.
Lebbeus B. Ward,	Dec. 17, 1871,	
Austin Requa,	" "	Died Aug. 4, 1872, aet. —
William W. Stone,	" "	
Enoch T. Caskey,	" "	
Joseph H. Van Doren,	" "	
William G. Anderson,	" "	Resigned Nov. 13, 1879.
Aaron D. Whitehead,	April 4, 1880.	
James Richards Voorhees,	" "	
William D. Johnson,	" "	
Wayland Spaulding,	" "	

(*Continued from page 28.*)

HALF-WAY MEMBERS.

1753.
May 14. Solloman & Mary Munson, his wf.
Sept.23. Philip Hathaway entered Cov.
Nov. 2. John Fford.
1754.
Feb. 24. Samuel Arnold entered Cov.
" 24. Phebe " his wf. Renewed Cov.
" 24. Mary, Samuel Hudson's wf.
Apr. 1. Samuel Tuttle. Doc.
" 1. Sarah, wf. of Doc. Tuttle.
July 6. Phebe Cole.
Dec. 30. Joseph Pierson & wf.
1755.
Jan. 3. Jonathan and Joanna Stiles.
Mar. 9. John Cole and his wf.
May 10. Margaret Sorden Entered Cov.
June 8. Humi Whitehead " "
" 15. Phineas Fairchild.
" 15. Sarah " wf.
Aug. 3. Mary Shipman.
1756.
Apr. 4. Elijah Pierson & his wf.
" 4. Demas Lindsley & his wf.
" 26. John Pitney & Sarah his wf.
" 26. Christopher Wood & Phebe his wf.
May 16. Catura, Philip Hathaway's wf.
June 20. Jemima Burt.
Aug. 1. Moses Prudden & his wf. Mary.
" 15. Sarah, Daniel Freman's wf.
Sept.19. Rebecca Woods, Wido.
Oct. 3. David Beeman & his wf.
Dec. 5. Sarah, John Lindsley's wf.
1757.
May 1. Benjamin Prudden & his wf.
" " " Bailey, Jr, & wf.
" " Stephen Hedges & his wf.
July 3. Thomas Tuttle & his wf.
" 10. Adoniram Prudden & his wf.
1758.
Jan. 1. Benjamin Pierson & his wf. Phebe.
" " Ebenezer Hathaway & his wf. Abigail.
Mar. 19. Wido. Sarah Allen.
July 10. Seth Mahurin & his wf.
Aug.13. Sarah, wife of William Goodwin.
" 12. William Akeman & wf. Letitia.
1759.
Feb. 18. Abigail, wf. of Constant Cooper, Entered Cov. & Bap., Adult.
" " Phebe Wheler, Entered Covenant & Bap., Adult.

Mar. 25. Moses Johnson & his wf.
Apr. 22. Samuel Bayles & Elizabeth his wf.
May 8. Daniel Morris & Hannah, his wf.
June 10. Joshua Gearing & wf. Susannah.
July 29. John Hunterdon & his wf. Elizabeth.
Aug.12. John Pierson & wf. Ruth.
Nov.25. Samuel Lorain & wf. Sibilli.
" " Mary, James Lose's (?) wf.
1760.
Feb. 10. Benjamin Lindley & Sarah his wf.
May 25. Rhoda Wheeler Bap. adult, ⎱ Sisters
" 25. Sarah " " " ⎰
June 22. Elizabeth, wf. of Thomas Kenny, Bap. Adult. ●
" " Hannah, wf. of Joseph Morris.
" 29. Elizabeth, wf. of William Loyd.
July 20. David Fairchild & Catharine his wf.
Aug.10. Daniel Coe and his wf.
" " Bette Lyon, Wido.
Sept. 5. Philip Price & Sarah his wf.
1761.
Jan. 18. Silas Day & Phebe his wife.
" 25. Eleazar Lindsly and his wf. Mary.
Feb. 8. Alexander Kermicle & his wf. Mary.
Apr. 19. Joseph Stiles & his wf. Hannah.
June 21. Jonathan Hathaway & his wf. Lydia.
July 17. Gibard Allen & Elizabeth entered Cov.
" " Joseph Cundict & Rhoda his wf.
" " Nathaniel Cundict & Sarah his wf.
July 26. Gilbard Ludlum & Abigail his wf.
Aug.18. Dan. McKenne.
" " John Loder.
Dec. 6. James McKey.
1762.
Jan. 17. Stephen Norris & his wf. Rebecca.
" " Sarah Nicholl & Bap. adult.
Apr. 11. Catharine, Doc'r Goold's wf.
May 23. Jeremiah Gard & his 3 chn.. John, Phebe & Rebecca.
June 13. Moses Lindsly & Trane (?) his wf.
" 27. Hannah & Mary Garrigus, Bap. adults.
" " Josiah Beman & Huldah his wf.
July 25. Sarah, Ephraim Howard's wf.
Sept.19. Silas Condict.
" 26. Charity Pitney.
Nov. 7. Letitia, Stephen Munson's wf., Bap. adult.
" " Susannah, Caleb Munson's wf., Bap. adult.
(*To be continued.*)

(Continued from page 29.)

BAPTISMS.

—:o:—

1751.

Sept. 22. William Nanne, child Rachel.

Oct. 6. William Lose & wf., twins, Susanna & Jane.

" 6. Peter Stagg 'on wf's. accompt., ch. Sar..h.

" 20. Hur Orsborn on wf's. accompt., ch. —

" 27. John Lose, Jun'r. on wf's. accompt., ch. Phebe.

Nov. 11. Suse, wf. of Joseph Johnes, chn. Bap., Named, I think, Joseph, William & John.

" 14. Jesse Reves at Rockaway, Daughter, name Denson,

" 18, Daniel Wick & wf., ch. Jane.

Dec. 15, Philip Condit & wf., ch. Ezekiel.

1752.

Jan. 19. Daniel Frost, child, wf's. accompt., Named Susanna.

" " Joshua Whitehead, child, wf's. accompt., Named Caleb.

Mar. 8. John Robards, ch. —

" 15. Thomas Wilkerson & wf., ch. Miriam.

" 19. Gideon Rigs & wf., ch. —

Apr. 2. Eliacam Sicard & wf., ch. Sarah.

" 5. Zophar Freeman & wf., ch. Joanna.

" 12. Simeon Hathaway & wf., ch. Miriam.

May 9. Thomas Bridge & wf., ch. Pamela.

" " Shadrack Howard & wf., chn. Rhode & Isaac.

" 24. Benjamin Freman & wf., ch. Sarah.

" " Uriah Cutler & wf., ch. Phebe.

June 13. Stephen Mahurin & wf., ch. Phebe.

" 13. Peter Norris & wf., ch. Kezia.

" 24. William Brown & wf., ch. Ezra.

July 7. Junia Lindley, ch. Charity.

" " John Lindley & wf., Joanna, ch. Hanah.

Sept. 24. Jonathan Reve, Household—wf. Elizabeth, chn. Samuel, Martha, Nathan, John.

" " Robard Arnolds on wf's. accompt., ch. Elizabeth.

Oct. 14. Isaia Wines & wf., ch. Ebenezar.

" " Abraham Hathaway, Jun., ch. Martha.

" " Jeremiah Johnson on wf's. accompt., ch. Comfort.

" " Zophar Gildersleeve & wf., ch. Ezekiel.

Oct. 14. John Burrel, ch. Unice.

Nov. 5. Ruth, wf. of Jacob Smith, ch. Huml.

" 26. Thomas Coe, ch. Mary.

Dec. 3. Caleb Lindsley, ch. John.

" 10. Matthew Fairchild, and wf. ch. Jonathan.

1753.

Jan. 14. Richard Wood, ch. Richard.

" 21. Capt. Joseph Stiles & wf., ch. Comfort.

" " Benjamin Coe & wf., ch. Peter.

" " Henry Gardiner & wf., ch. Joanna.

Feb. 18. Jabish Bears & wf., ch. Daniel.

" 25. David Ogden on wf's. accompt., ch. —

Apr. 8. Samuel Day, twins, Samuel & Abraham.

May 14. Solloman Munson & wf., ch. Martha.

June 17. Philip Cundit & wf. ch. Philip.

" 17. John Allen & wf., ch. Daniel,

" " Benjamin Halsey & wf., ch. Ezra.

" " Joseph Tompkins on wf's. accompt., ch. —

July 8. John Perkhurst & wf., ch. John.

" 29. Jude is Servant of Deacon Prudden, ch. Tabitha.

Aug. 25. Eliacam Suads wf., ch. Samuel.

" 29. Sarah, wf. of James Frost, son John & 2 Servants chn., Peg & Ame.

Sept. 9. Gideon Riggs & wf., ch. Gideon.

" " Benj. Pierson & wf. had ye negro chn. bap. Peg & Lewis.

" 23. Philip Hathaway, Adult.

" 30. Peter Dickerson & wf., ch. Jesse.

" 30. Abel Lion on wf's. accompt., ch. Jacob.

Oct. 21. Jonathan Reeve & wf., ch. Mary.

" 27. William Nanne & wf., ch. Daniel.

Nov. 2. John Fford & wf., chn. Penelope & Jacob.

" " Junia Lindley, ch. Ephraim.

" 18. Nathaniel Stilwell, Jun. & wf., ch. Martha.

Dec. 29. Henery Primrose & wf., ch. Phebe.

1754.

Jan. 20. Abraham Hathaway, ch. Richad.

" " Jonathan Woods on wf's. accompt., ch. Samuel.

" " Joshua Whitehead on wf's. accompt., ch. Timothy.

" 27. Samuel Munson, ch. Elizabeth.

" " Stephen Conklin & wf., ch. Ruth.

Feb. 24. Samuel Arnold, Adult; & his chn. Jacob & John.

(To be continued.)

(Continued from page 30.)
MARRIAGES.

1763.

Jan. 5. Solloman Boyle & Sarah Alling, wido.
" 9. Ebenezar Haultbut,& Sarah Nichol.
Feb. 6. Peter Prudden & Rhoda Cundict.
" 8. Philip Lindsley & Mary McFeran.
Mar. 16. Silas Condict & Abigail Byram.
" 20. Eliphalet Clark & Wido. Rebecca Stockbridge.
" 23. Nicholas Carter & Sarah Easton.
" " Boys Prudden & Elizabeth Baldwin.
" 24. Benoni Thomas & Wido. Elizabeth Bates.
" 31. Jacob Faugerson & Abigail Mills.
Apr. 3. Amos Wade & Elizabeth Jewel, both of Connecticut Farmes.
" 17. Abraham Drake & Anne Young, both of Succasunny.
" " Uriah Cutler & Wido. Sarah Whitehead.
July 13. Abial Fairchild & Esther Gard.
Aug. 18. Henry Clark, Jun., Widower & Sibbel Loring, wido.
" 24. Nathaniel Morris & Hopestill Wood
Sep. 11. John Cooper & Magdalen Boyle.
Nov. 6. John Hathaway & Jemima Extell.
" 7. Peter Dickerson & Wido., Sarah Oharrow,
" 9. Larence Cumming & Lea Hall.
Nov.23. Jacob Frase, of New Providence, & Elizabeth McFeran.
Dec. 19. Gilman Freman & Mary Nicholl.
" 20. Caleb Fairchild & Phebe Gard.
" 22. Seth Babbit & Jemima Lindsley.
" " David Case, of Roxbury & Mary Dickerson.
" 29. Benj'n Silvester & Hannah Stillwell, both of Mendham.

1764.
Jan. 5. Libeus Dod & Mary Baldwin.
" " Ebenzer Cook & Elizabeth Dod, all of Mendham stood up together.
"Now married 284 couple."
" 8. Alexander Aikman & Elizabeth Lewis,
" 12. John Roy & Abigail Morris.
" " Thomas Miller & Bathiah Post.
" 18. Ebenezer Byram & Lydia Guiring.
" " Joseph Lefollet & Lydia Carter, all of Mendham.

Feb. 9. Charles Milton & Abigail Davis, both of Mendham.
Mar. 7. Thomas Kent & Wido. Sarah Fanger.
" 21. Nathaniel Peck & Mary Condict.
" 26. Moses Wilkerson & Phebe Orsborn.
Apr. 8. Ephriam Lyon & Hannah Morris.-
May 29. Zephaniah Burt & Hannah Axtel.
June 13. John Laporte & Naomi Day.
" 26. Jabish Baldwin & Eunice Carter, both of Mendham.
Aug. 14 Nehemiah Stanborough & Mary Minthorn.
" 22. Isaac Woodruff & Mary Leohard, both of Mendham.
Sept.23. Josiah Hall & Abigail Johnson.
Oct. 3. Hugh Catter & Elizabeth Southard.
" 4. Daniel Trowbridge & Sarah Ludlum.
" 18. Nathaniel Cundict & Abigail Wines.
" 23. Joseph Clark & Mary Baldwin.
" 31. Onessimus Whitehead & Rebecca Cundict.
Dec. 6. Abel Tompkins & Elizabeth Bridge.
" 13. Joseph Winget & Wido. Sarah Freman.
" 20. Zebedee Wood & Mary Carson.

1765.
Jan. 19. David Lewis & Mary Rude, both of Ringwood.
" 22. Benoni Hathaway & Ruth Ludlam.
Feb. 3. Ephraim Hayward & Jehoaddan Burrell.
Mar. 28. Icabod Cermichael & Phebe Clark.
Apr. 15. Robart Hinds & Sarah Lindsley.
May 14. Jonathan Stark & Margaret Ball.
June 10. John Redman & Hannah Cutler.
Sept. 1. Zenas Cundit & Phebe Johnson.
Oct. 10. James Brookfield & Deborah Rayner.
" 25. Nathaniel Mather & Mary Whitehead.
Nov.19. Henry Dow Trip & Zerujah Kenny
Dec. 3. Shubael Trowbridge & Mary Bayle
" 4. Andrew Wade & Martha Riggs.
" 10. Jonas Gobill & Ruth Fairchild.
" 11. Henry Gobill & Lydia Conger.
" 22. Samuel Wright & Mary Walker.
" 24. Nathaniel Armstrong & Racha Lyon.

(To be Continued.)

(Continued from page 81.)

BILL OF MORTALITY.

——:o:——

1773.

Jan. 16. Elizabeth, daughter of Stephen Arnold, aet. 1, Putrid sore throat.
" 17. Ezekiel, son of Stephen - Arnold, aet. 2, Putrid sore throat.
" 20. Elizabeth, daughter of Widow Case, aet. 2.
" 25. Rhoda Casterline, aet. 20, Phrenzy.
" 25. Child of Robert Youngs, jun., aet. 4.
Feb. 1. Rebekah, wife of William Verguson,* aet. 30, Consumption.
" 2. Solomon Southard, aet. 37, Consumption.
" 10. Child of John Arnold,
" 11. Shadrach, son of Daniel Howard, aet. 10, Consumption.
" 17. Rachel, wife of Abraham Ludlow, aet. 29, Consumption.
" 18. Joshua Ball, aet. 50, Consumption.
" 22. Child of Ichabod Blacklidge, aet. 4.
" 23. Charles, son of Silas Howell, aet. 1.
" 26. Flora, servant of Col. Ford,
Mar. 9. John Bridge, aet. 30, Consumption.
Apr. Child of William Hulberts, aet. 11.
June Child of Barnabas Winds.
" Dol, Servant of Deacon Burnet, aet. 9, Mortification in her hip.
" Child of Carter.
July 13. Abijah, son of Widow Cheever, aet. 1, Consumption.
" 18. Rachel, daughter of Jacob Ball, aet 1, Worms.
" 25. Child of Ralph Bridge,
" 26. Child of John Gard, aet. 1.
Aug. Child of Amariah Parker.
Sept. 6. Child of Jonathan Benjamin.
" 17. David Reynolds,
" 24. Elizabeth, daughter of Gilbert Ludlow, aet. 1.
" 28. Hannah, Widow of Daniel Smith, aet. 58, Consumption.
Oct. 29. John, son of William Cherry, † aet 3, Inflammatory Fever.
Nov. 7. Child of Mockridge.
" 7. Bethiah, Widow of Thomas Wood,* aet. 74, Old age.
Dec. 1. Matthias Hoppen, aet. 68, Fever.
" 14. Rhoda, daughter of Peter Prudden, aet. 8, Putrid sore throat.

1774.

Jan. 7. Edward Griffin, son of Timothy Mills, jun., aet. 3, Fever.
" 14. Mary, Wife of Ezekiel Day, aet. 29, Consumption.
Feb. 7. William, son of David Youngs, aet. 2.
Mar. 12. Sally, daughter of Frederick King, aet. 6, Fever.
Apr. 11. Samuel Rolfe, aet. 70, Asthma.
" 11. Child of Elisha Johnson,†
" 15. Creed Ludlow, aet. 53, Small-Pox.
" 24. Nathan, son of Peter Norris, jun., aet. 2, Hives.
" 25. Thankful, wife of Joseph Cathcart, aet. 66, Decay of Nature.
" 28. Stephen Arnold, aet. 14, Consumption.
May 14. Anna, daughter of Joseph Lindsley, aet. 3, Fever.
" 28. John, son of Aaron Pierson and Mary, aet. 28, Accidental.
" 30. Servant boy of Ebenezer Howell, aet. 15, Drowned.
" 30. Lydia, daughter of Hezekiah Stibbens, aet. 4, Fever.
July 14. Peter Condict, aet. 30, Sudden.
" 24. Child of David Douglass, Fever.
Aug 24. Kezia Ball,* aet. 27, Consumption.
" 25. Deborah, wife of Stephen Conkling, aet. 49, Rupture.
Sept. Child of Reeves Lozaw,
" 21. Mary, widow of John Johnson,* aet. 91, Old-age.
" 14. Mary, wife of William Arnold, aet. 38, Consumption.
" 26. Rachel, wife of Benjamin Freeman, aet. 60, Epilepsy.
" 27. A child of George Phillips,
Oct. 16. A child of Dennis Combs,
" 24. Anne, wife of Joseph Benway, aet. 30, Consumption.
Nov. 5. Benjamin, son of widow Southard, aet. 2, Sore throat.
" 9. A child of Abraham Talmage.
" 14. James, son of James Brookfield, aet. 4, Inflammatory fever.
" 27. A child of Peter Hill.

1775.

Jan. 15. A child of Elijah Holloway.
" A child of Benjamin Prudden.
Feb. 8. David Rattan,* aet. 75, Old-age.
" A child of Zerah Rolfe.

(To be continued.)

(Continued from page 82.)

TRUSTEES' BOOK.

The Trustees appointed Stephen Conklin & Samuel Tuthill, Esq., a committee to hire out the sd. House for the year ensuing & to Repair the fence round the Burying yard ——— agreed that Silas Condite take the further trouble to call on such of the Inhabitants as have hitherto neglected to discharge their subscription for a Parsonage to pay the same or give their notes for the same & also to require such as are Indebted by note &c. to pay their Interests that are due or Renew their obligation & to make Return of the names of such as may Refuse to comply herewith at the next meeting the Trustees agree to accept a note of £5,, 10, from Deacon Lum against Thomas Coe & discharge his subscription & settle with sd. Lum the over plus that the sd. note is more than sd. subscription at a future time.

September 16, 1777, the Trustees met (and being Informed by the Rev'd. Mr. Johnes that upon the Death of Joseph Stiles, Esq., one of the Trustees, Jonathan Stiles, Esq. was elected in his Room, & that Benjamin Lindsley, Esq., & Jonathan Ford were Elected in the Room of Henry Primrose & Benjamin Baleys who had resigned on account of Infirmity & that John Mills was Elected instead of Benjamin Coe who had removed out of the Parish) present, Mr. Conklin, Mr. Tuthill, Mr. Stiles, Mr. Mills.

Agreed that a copy of the Charter be made out & delivered to the Elders of the church. Also agreed that Mr. Conklin, Mr. Tuthill, Mr. Lindsly & Mr. Stiles or any two of them wait upon some of the Docts. of the Hospital in Morristown & apply for a resignation of the meeting house and if obtained then to apply to the Commanding Officer at this post to remove the troops thence & at their discretion to proceed further in cleansing and refiting the House for Public Worship & to make report of their progress in the premises at their next meeting.

April 27, 1778, the Trustees met at Mr. Johnes, present Mr. Conklin, Mr. Lindsly, Mr. Stiles, Mr. Ford, Mr. Mills & Mr. Condict. The former president Mr. Primrose, having Resigned the Board proceeded to the choyce of another when Silas Condict was duly Elected president.

Agreed that the Rever'd Mr. Johnes be requested to employ some persons who understands the Business to alter the method of Ringing the Bell from that in which it now swings to that of setting it up in Ringing and that the Board will defray the expenses thereof.

Agreed that Mr. Stiles, Mr. Mills & Mr. Ford be a committee to complete the parsonage fence & to collect the subscript'n therefor & Report to the Board at their next meeting.

Agreed that Mr. Stiles do by writing or otherways call on such of the Inhabitants who have not paid their subscrip'n for purchasing a Parsonage, and to acquaint them that a further neglect of paying the same will be deemed a refusal to pay.

Agreed that Mr. Tuthill & Mr. Condict or either of them do Settle accounts with the Rev'd Mr. Johnes, & make Report to the Board at the meeting.

July 13th, 1778, the Trustees met at Docr. Tuthills, present, Mr. Conklin, Mr. Tuthill, Mr. Stiles, Mr. Lindsley, Mr. Mills & the President agreed that Mr. Tuthill, Mr. Stiles & Mr. Mills be a committee to wait on Doct. Draper & inform him of the Law of this State Relative to Billeting of Soldiers, & that the committee or either of them be Impowered to prosecute such Person or Persons who may take possession of the meeting house or other property of the Trustees contrary to the said Law, & that they make report what they have done in the premises to this Board at their next meeting.

Mr. Condict Reported that he had settled accounts with Mr. Johnes Respecting his Salary from a former Settlement in the year 1769 untill the year 1775 inclusive and made an even Ballance.

(To be continued.)

WANTED.—To learn the parentage of Mr. THOMAS MILLER, and of MARGARET, his wife. They resided at New Vernon, Morris county and were the parents of James, John, Thomas, & Isaac Miller. Their son Isaac married 1768, Joanna, daughter of Benjamin Halsey, and was the father of Halsey, Joseph and Silas Miller, and of Mr. Jacob Mann & Mrs. Kimball Bridge. E. F. H.

THE RECORD.

FIRST PRESBYTERIAN CHURCH, MORRISTOWN, N. J.

"This shall be Written for the Generation to Come."—Psalms 102 : 18.

VOL. I.   JUNE, 1880.   NO. 6.

(*Printed with the approval of Session.*)

THE RECORD

Will be printed and published monthly at Morristown, N. J. Terms, 50 cents per annum in advance; 75 cents after June.

Subscriptions will be received at the book-stores of Messrs. Runyon and Emmell, or through the mail, and may begin with the first number. ALL COMMUNICATIONS should be addressed to the

EDITOR OF THE RECORD,

Lock box 44.   Morristown, N. J. Entered at the Post Office at Morristown, N. J., as second class matter.

——:o:——

(The following articles are taken from the Feb. and Dec., 1851, Nos. of *The Presbyterian Magazine*, edited by C. VanRensselaer. —Editor of RECORD.)

WASHINGTON AT THE COMMUNION TABLE IN MORRISTOWN, NEW JERSEY.

The Rev. Dr. Cox, of Brooklyn, New York, first gave to the public the circumstances attending this interesting event, which he received from Dr. Hillyer, who had it from the lips of Rev. Dr. Timothy Johnes himself; the latter being the pastor of the church at Morristown at the time.

"While the American army under the command of Washington, lay encamped in the environs of Morristown, New Jersey, it occurred that the service of the communion, then observed semi-annually only, was to be administered in the Presbyterian church of that village. In a morning of the previous week, the General, after his accustomed inspection of the camp, visited the house of the Rev. Dr. Johnes, then pastor of that church, and after the usual preliminaries, thus accosted him : " Doctor, I understand that the Lord's Supper is to be celebrated

with you next Sunday. I would learn if it accords with the canons of your church to admit communicants of another denomination ?" The Doctor rejoined, "most certainly; ours is not the Presbyterian table. General, but the Lord's Table; and we hence give the Lord's invitation to all his followers, of whatever name.' The General replied, 'I am glad of it ; that is as it ought to be; but as I was not quite sure of the fact,I thought I would ascertain it from yourself, as I propose to join with you on that occasion. Though a member of the Church of England, I have no exclusive partialities.'

The Doctor reassured him of a cordial welcome, and the General was found seated with the communicants the next Sabbath."†

†Having been recently at Morristown, we obtained additional evidence of the truth of Dr. Cox's anecdote. The Rev. James Richards, D.D., the present pastor of the 1st Presbyterian church, and son of the venerable Dr. Richards who succeeded Dr. Johnes in 1794, says that he has often heard his father relate the circumstance, who had himself heard it from Dr. Johnes. The Rev. Albert Barnes, formerly pastor of the same church, also says that he has never had any doubt on the subject. We may give the evidence in detail hereafter.

In the February number of the Presbyterian Magazine we gave some historical incidents connecting the memory of Washington, in a somewhat interesting manner, with the Presbyterian church. Among the incidents mentioned, was the fact that the only time Washington was known to partake of the Lord's Supper, after the commencement of his public career, was in the Presbyterian Church, in Morristown, N. J. Shortly after the publication of the article referred to, we received a letter from our friend, the Rev. *Nicholas Chevalier*, of Christianburgh, Va., who stated that in a visit at Dr. Johnes at Morristown, some years since, he was informed by that venerable man, who was a son of the *Rev.* Dr. Johnes, that he had often heard his father say, that the religious services of the Church were held, not in the *meeting-house,* but in *an orchard* not far from the parsonage. In order to ascertain more fully the facts of the case, we addressed a letter to the Rev. O. L. Kirtland, pastor of the Second Presbyterian Church, at Morristown, who was the more competent to answer the inquiries, from the circumstance that he had himself married into the family of the Rev. Dr. Johnes. The following is Mr. Kirtland's reply:

Rev, and Dear Brother:

* * * *. Touching the religious services in the orchard, and the communion there attended by Washington, the information which you speak of as received from the Rev. Mr. Chevalier was substantially correct. The father of Mrs. Kirtland was the son of the Rev. Dr. Timothy Johnes —lived with him, and took care of him in his old age, and till his death—remained in the homestead of his father, and died there in his 83d year, Nov. 1836. Mrs. Kirtland was born in the same house, and never had her home elsewhere till a short time since. She recollects very distinctly that she was accustomed to hear her father speak of the fact that the religious services of the congregation *were conducted in the orchard, in the rear of the house,* whilst Washington was here during the Revolutionary War. This was one of the familiar facts often repeated during her early years. She has no doubt, that a part of the familiar subject of the conversation of her father with the family, and with visitors, was, that the communion which General Washington attended was held in the orchard.

In the orchard there is a natural basin several feet deep, and a few rods in diameter. The basin was formerly considerably deeper than at present, having been partly filled in the process of tilling ever since the Revolution. Mrs. Kirtland recollects that her father used to say, that when the people assembled for worship, they occupied the bottom of that basin for their place of meeting. The minister stood on one side

of the basin, so as to be elevated above his congregation. The whole field inclines towards the morning and mid-day sun. The rising grounds in the rear would, to a great extent, shield the congregation from the usual winds of winter. Indeed, the basin was formerly so deep, that the wind from any direction, would mainly pass over them.

A brother of Mrs. Kirtland, several years older than herself, and other members of the family, tell me that their recollections are distinct, and in harmony with hers, touching the meetings in the orchard, the communion, and the presence of Washington there.

John B. Johnes, M. D., now living in this place, and over sixty years of age, grandson of the old minister, and cousin of Mrs. Kirtland, recollects it as the familiar talk of his father, and also of his uncle, Mrs. Kirtland's father, that the religious services, whilst Washington was here, were in that orchard.

Mrs. Scofield, wife of one of our lawyers, and grand-daughter of a Mrs. Ford, whose name has been handed down to us fragrant with piety, informs me that her grandmother used to tell her about attending the meetings in the orchard. On one occasion, when the old lady was present, *Washington was there sitting in his camp chair, brought in for the occasion. During the service, a woman came into the congregation with a child in her arms ; Washington arose from his chair and gave it to the woman with the child.*

I think a large amount of similar testimony may be obtained, making the proof of the meetings in the orchard, of the communion, and of the attendance of Washington there, about as strong as tradition could make it.

You wished to know *why* they should and *how* they could meet in the open air in the winter. Tradition says that there was a vast amount of sickness and suffering in the army, that the small-pox prevailed fearfully, and that the *Presbyterian* and Baptist churches, and court-house were occupied as *hospitals*—the father of Mrs. Kirtland having, the latter part of the time, the supervision of the hospitals—so that there was no place for the meeting of the congregation, except in the open air.

We should not forget that the soldiers of the Revolution, and the good people who lived here at that time, were more hardy than this generation. Trembling, as they were, all winter, with the fear of an attack from the British, their house of worship occupied with poor, sick, dying and dead men, (for tradition says that numbers of dead men would be found under the seats in the morning *i. e.* before the arrangements for their care had been perfected by my wife's father) it is by no means incredible that the pious souls of such a race should meet in such a basin as Providence had made for them, to pay their homage to the Most High, and to commemorate the love of the Redeemer, even in winter, We forget the character of the people, and of the times, if we suppose that there were not those who would think very little of the cold, if they could, in such circumstances, enjoy a season of religious worship, even in the open air. Those now living here, who have heard their fathers and grandfathers describe, as eye-witnesses of, and partners in, the sufferings of the times, would think that a season of worship in such circumstances, must have been sought as a relief from sufferings, to which many of them were constantly subject.

You will excuse me for departing from the subject of your inquiries to state a fact. Soon after I came to Morristown, in 1837, I think, I visited my native place, and met there an old man, bowed down with age, leaning tremblingly upon the top of his staff. His name was Cook. In my early childhood, he had been the physician in my father's family. As the old man met me, he said, "You are located in Morristown, are you?" "Yes sir." "I was there too," said the Doctor, "once; I was under Washington in the Army of the Revolution. It was hard times then—hard times. There was a time when all our rations were but a single *gill of wheat a day.* Washington used to come round and look into our tents, and he looked so *kind,* and he said so tenderly, 'Men, can you bear it?' 'Yes, General, yes, we can,' was the reply; 'If you wish us to *act,* give us the word, and we are ready.'"

This single fact has done more to reveal to me the secret of that power, by which Washington maintained such influence over the army, and kept them together through such severe and protracted sufferings, than anything else that I have known. "He came to our tents, and looked so kind," &c.

I fancy that he felt the influence of those meetings in the orchard, when he went to sympathize with his men—perhaps had lately been at the communion-table, when he made such an impression upon the old Doctor of my native place.

Your inquiries have pushed me out on a train of inquiry, for which I am much obliged to you. I don't know but the results will render me as loquacious about matters appertaining to the Revolution, as the old soldiers to whom I listened in my boyhood.

Very respectfully yours,
O. L. KIRTLAND.

DATES IN OUR EARLY CHURCH HISTORY WORTH REMEMBERING.

——:o:——

Sept. 21, 1733.—Permission granted by the Synod of Philadelphia "to erect themselves into a separate congregation." The separation from the church in Hanover had *already* taken place. The appeal had been to the "lot," and although the lot had fallen out against the people of West Hanover (Morristown), they would not abide by it, and so withdrew to form a separate church.

Sept. 24, 1735.—Application made to the Synod for the ministerial services of Mr. John Cleverly, who however was never installed. He ministered to the church for a time but no record of his labors was left.

May 29, 1738.—The trouble with the mother church at Hanover finally settled by a commission of Synod.

Aug. 13, 1742.—Rev. Timothy Johnes began work.

Feb. 9, 1743.—He was installed.

Sept. 17, 1794.—He died, his pastorate covering a period of 52 years.

————

Special attention is called to extracts from the Trustees' Book in this number of the RECORD and in that for May. They will be found to contain valuable historical data relating to the presence of the Revolutionary army in Morristown,

(Continued from page 36.)

HALF-WAY MEMBERS.

----:o:----

1762.

Nov. 7. Dorcas, Zebede Brown's wife.
" 14. Isaac Pierson & Rhoda his wf. Bap. adult.
" " Wilby Clark & Sarah his Wf.
Dec. 26. Prudence, Joseph King's wf.

1763.

Feb. 13. Jacob Ford, Junr. & Theodosia his wf.
Mar. 12. Ebenezer Coe & Eunice his wf.
May 1. Joseph Lindsley & Anne his wf.
" 8. Edward Byram & Phebe his wf.
July 10. Ebenezar Condict & Huldah his wf.

1764.

July 1. Dan'l Cermicael & Huldah his wf.
" 22. Thomas Millar & Bathiah his wf.
" 29. Nathan Turner & Phebe his wf.
Aug. 5. Rhoda, Peter Prudden's wf.
" " Mary, wf. of Soln. Southard.
" " Boys Prudden & Elizabeth his wf.
" 31. Larence Cummin & Leah his wf.
Sept. 16. Augustin Bayles & Kezia his wf.
" 23. Jarzel Turner & Sarah his wf.
Oct. 19. Wickey Ludlamb.
" 27. Elizabeth Bridge.
" " Susannah Tichenor.
" " Anne Freman.
Nov. 1. Peter Price, adult.
" " Hannah, wf. of John Roggers.
" 4. Josiah Crane, adult.
" 15. Joshua Whitehead.
Apr. 14. Sam. Allwood & —— his wf.

1766.

Feb. 23. Frederick King & Mary King his wf.
Mar. 10. Phebe, wf. of Jabish Cundict.
" 23. Jabez Campfield, Docr. & Sarah his wf.
June 22. Phebe, wf. of Zenas Cundict.
Nov. 9. Ruth, wf. of Benoni Hathaway, Bap. and both renewed ye covenant.

1767.

Feb. 1. John Mintonye & Susanna his wf.
Mar. 8. Hannah, wf. of John Hathaway.
" 15. Mary, wf. of David Ogden.
Aug. 16. Moses Pierson & Anne his wf.
Sept. 6. Mary, wf. of Ezek. Day.
Dec. 6. Rachel, Malcolm McCourry's wf.

1768.

Mar. 9. Sam'l S. Johnes & Sarah his wife, my children.
July 26. Eunice, Jon. Ford's wf.
" " Phebe, Sam. Hain's wf.
Aug. 28. Silas Howell & Hannah his wf.

1769.

June 25. Rebekah, wf. of Jonathan Tichenor.
" 29. Kezia, wf. of Josh. Winget.

1770.

Jan. 22. Perkins Byram & Hannah his wf.
Feb. 11. Peter Cundict & Anne his wf.
May 4. Lindsley Burnet & Elizabeth his wf.
" 6. Martha, wf. of Richard Johnson.
" " Phebe, wf. of Jacob Palmer.
Nov. 29. David Wheeler, entered covenant & Bap. & Hannah his wf.

1771.

May 3. Joseph Pierson, Junr. & Mercy his wf.
July 5. Abraham Talmadge & Phebe his wf. Bap. & entered covenant.
" 14. Rhoda. wf. of Daniel Kenny.
" 21. Kezia Ball.
" " Rachael, wf. of Jabish Ropes (?).
Aug. 4. Catharine, wf. of Wm. Walton.
" 11. John Millar & Mary his wf.
" 25. Wm. Gray & Hannah his wf.
May 5. Sam'l Pierson & Rebecah his wf.
Sept. 3. Martha, wf. of Shadrach Hathaway.
" 22. Mary Chever, Bap. adult. on sick bed.
Oct. 6. Thom. Lashly & wf. by certificate.

1772.

Feb. 21. John Bridge & Hannah his wf.
" 23. David Youngs & Jane his wf.
Apr. 26. Silas Stiles & Sarah his wf.
May 3. James Smith & Mehitabel his wf.
June 14. James Gillespie & Jane his wf.
Aug. 23. Usual Coe & Mary his wf.
" 30. Matthias Burnet, Junr. and Phebe his wf.
Sept. 4. William Charlot & Sarah his wf.
Oct. 15. Abijah Chever & Sarah his wf.
Nov. 15. Esther, wf. of John Jacks.
" 20. Abraham Ludlam, Bap. adult & Rachael his wf., renewed covenant.

(To be continued.)

(*Continued from page 87.*)
BAPTISMS.

—:o:—

1754.

Feb. 24. Mary, wf. of Samuel Hudson, Jun., chn. Zervia & Abraham.

Apr. 1. Deacon Samuel Tuttle & wf., ch. Elizabeth.

" " Shadrack Halward & wf., ch. Eunice.

" 14. Samuel Bailey & wf., ch. Jonah.

" " Shadrack-Hathaway & wf.,ch. Bette.

" 21. John Marsh & wf., ch. John.

May 5. Solloman Munson & wf., twins Abraham & Sarah.

June 9. John Losey, Jun., on wf's Accompt, ch. Elizabeth.

July 5. Phebe Cole, ch. Adoniram.

" 21. Joseph Edmister & wf., ch Ledia.

Aug. 4. Junia Lindley, ch. Sarah.

" " David Gauden & wf., ch., Jeremiah.

" 10. Benj. Freeman & wf., ch. Benjamin.

" 25. Sam'l Arnold & wf., ch. Hannah.

" " John Robards & wf., ch Eunice.

Sept. 1. Benj. Hathaway, Jun., ch. Letitia.

" 22. Robard Arnold & wf., ch. Nathan, born Aug. 17, 1754.

Nov. 3. Daniel Freeman, on wf. accompt, ch. Daniel.

" " Isaiah Wines & wf., ch. Deborah.

" " Thomas Coe & wf., ch Sarah.

" 10. Joseph Whitehead, on wf's accompt, ch. Deborah.

" 17. Richard Wood, ch. Hannah.

Dec. 1. John Fford & wf., ch. Hannah.

" 22. Daniel Howard & wf., ch. Abigail.

" 30. Josiah Pierson & wf., Household of chn., Mary, Joseph, David, Jonathan.

1755.

Jan. 3. Jonathan Stiles & wf. Joanna, ch. Timothy.

" 5. Stephen Mahurin & wf., ch. Priscilla.

" 19. Uriah Cutler & wf., ch. Phebe.

" 28. Zophar Gildersleeve & wf., ch. Asa.

Feb. 9. Gideon Riggs & wf., ch. Junia.

" 16. Jeremiah Johnson, on wf. accompt, ch. Ruth.

" " Jemima Stuard, ch. John.

" 29. Benj. Coe & wf., ch. Patience.

Mar. 9. John Cole, Bap. and with his wf. had ye household, viz., John, Joseph, Phebe & Hannah.

Mar. 16. Samuel Day & wf., ch. Jarerd.

" 23. Timothy Mills & wf., ch. Mary.

" " Benj. Halsey & wf., ch. Joseph.

" " Peter Norris & wf., ch. John.

" 30. Matthew Fairchild & wf., ch. Theodosia.

Apr. 6. Flora, my negro ch., born March 12, 1755.

" 21. Peter Dikerson & wf., ch. John.

" " James Frost & wf., ch. Sarah.

" " her negro ch. at ye same time, Hanna.

May 4. Samuel Hudson's wido., ch. Samuel.

" 12. Margaret Sorden, Bap. & her ch. Susanna.

June 1. Daniel Wick & wf., had ye negro chn., bap., Jo & Luis.

" 8. Humi Whitehead, adult.

" 15. Jabish Bears & wf., ch. ——

" " Phineas Fairchild & wf., chn., Stephen, born Nov. 30, 1753, Abigail, born Dec. 24, 1754.

" 22. John Jonson & wf., ch. Lidia.

" " Henry Gardiner & wf., ch. Daniel.

" 29. Isaac Tuttle, on wf. accompt, ch. Cissel.

Aug. 3. Abraham Hathaway & wf., ch. Abraham.

" " Mary Shipman, 2 chn., —— & Mary.

" 10. Susanna, Joseph Johnes' wf., ch. Sarah.

" 30. John Lose, ch. Jane.

Sept 14. Jonathan Reeve & wf., ch. Jonathan.

" 28. Jemima Stuard, ch. Mary.

Oct. 13. John Perkhurst & wf., twins, Jemima & Eunice.

" 19. Daniel Wick & wf., ch. John.

" 26. Jonathan Stiles & wf., ch. Jonathan.

" " Ellizabeth, Ebenezar Mott's wf., ch. Sarah.

Nov. 2. William Brown, ch. Zuba.

" " David Ogden, on wf. accompt, ch. Eunice.

" 9. Charles Howell & wf., ch. John.

Dec. 1. Jonathan Wood, ch. Joanna.

" 15. John Marsh & wf., ch. Joseph.

1756.

Jan. 18. Solloman Munson & wl., ch. Usual.

" 25. Junia Lindley & wf., ch. Mary.

" " Benj. Shipman & wf., ch. Charity.

" " Hur Orsborn's wf., on her own accompt, ch. Abraham.

Feb. 15. Samuel Munson & wf.,ch.Catharine,

(*To be continued.*)

(*Continued from page* 88.)

MARRIAGES.

——:o:——

1766.
Jan. 7. David Gardiner & Abigail Peck.
" 29. Gershom Johnson & Mary Ann Trobridge.
Feb. 20. Abrm Lyon & Phebe Ede, both of Mendham,
Apr. 6. Peter Marserau & Rebecah Lake of Staten Island.
Aug. 14. Daniel Bishop & Lois Burnet.
" 31. Samuel Martin & Hannah Moor.
Sept. 17. Hezekiah Stibins & Susanna Tichenor.
Nov. 19. Joseph Lyon & Rachael Crane of Lyon's Farms.
" 25. Aaron Pierson & Mary Howell.
Dec. 3. John Cole & Nelle Freeman.
" " Jotham Burt & Phebe Cole.
" 4. Richard Edwards & Rachel Gildersleeve.
" 14. Enos Ward & Mehitabel Burnet.
" 21. Daniel Talmadge, Baskingridge, & Lois Allen, Rockaway.
" " Macolm McCoury & Rachael Freman.
" 24. Jonas Philips & Phebe Arnold.
1767.
Jan. 1. Robart Young & Elizabeth Morris.
" 7. Henry Axtil & Phebe Day.
" 8. Nathan Hathaway & Rebeccah Gard.
" 15. John Wortman, of German Town, & Sarah Howard.
" 21. Artemas Day of Mendham, & Bethany Axtel.
Mar. 3. Thomas Riggs of Baskingridge, & Rhoda Tuttle of this town.
" 23. Samuel Stevens Johnes & Sarah Wheeler.
May 6. Benj. Forger of Sussex, & Anna Mather.
" 11. John Leferty & Elizabeth Johnes.
June 4. Jonathan Tichenor & Rebeccah Stratten.
" 15. Timothy Loce & Hannah Moore.
July 29. Richard Rigens & Lois Jillet.
Dec. 24. John Clutter & Ruth Wade, Mendum.
1768.
Jan. 19. Thomas Barlow & Rebecca Davis, Sucasunney,

" 21. Sam. Robarts & Elizabeth Ogden, wido.
"_ " Docr. Oliver Barnet & Elizabeth Ogden, all of Barnards Town.
Feb. 18. Nathan Reeve & Ruth Goble.
Mar. 28. Josiah Crane & Abigail Hathaway.
" 29. Usual Kitchel & Hannah Tuttle, both of Hanover.
Apr. 10. William Farguson & Rebeccah Stockbridge.
" 26. Icabod Blacklidge & Susanna Woodruff.
May 11. Isaac Morris & Rebecca Hathaway.
Aug. 4. Robart Cirk-Patrick & Elizabeth Guiering, Mendum.
" 11. Matthias Howard & Lois Hathaway.
" 22. Silas Tompkins & Rachel Chever.
Sept. 14. Joshua Winget & Kezia Hall.
" 20. Joseph Sanderson & Hannah Loree.
" 21. Isaac Miller & Joannah Halsey.
Oct. 12. Jonathan Dickerson & Mary Coe.
" 13. Thomas McCullion & Anne Johnson.
Nov. 3. Squire Lum & Phebe Ward.
" 10. John Mills & Cleo Wines.
" " James Loree & Anne Armstrong.
" 24. John Youngs & Hannah Mitchel.
" " Aaron Willis & Joannah Lyon.
" 30. Jacob Parmer & Phebe Lyon.
Dec. 1. Silas Stiles & Sarah Ayres.
" 6. Abraham Talmadge & Phebe Fairchild.
" 14. Lewis Core & Jane Drake.
" 21. Abraham Davenport & Eve Sneider, both of Pequannock.
" 26. William Laine & Kezia Mather.
1769.
Jan. 19. Usual Tompkins & Martha Reeve.
" 24. Jonathan Benjamin & Elizabeth Hinds.
" 25. Allexander Drake & Phebe Cook, Mendham.
" 30. John Breis, Jun. & Hannah Gildersleeve.
Feb. 8. Isaac Ayres & Joannah Coe.
" 14. Caleb Chadwick & Susannah Loey(?)
" 15. Azariah Breis & Susannah Gildersleeve.
" 16. Peter Norris & Phebe Ludlum.
Mar. 8. Perkins Byram & Hannah Raynor.
" Richard Johnson & Martha Raynor, Married up to this date 392.

(*To be continued.*)

(*Continued from page* 39.)

BILL OF MORTALITY,

1775.
Mar. 5. Wife of James M'Bride, aet. 32, consumption.
" 16. Isaac Whitehead, aet. 16, Pleurisy,
" 22. A child of Doct. Timothy Johnes, Epileptic-fits.
" 30. Widow of Samuel Godden, aet. 73, old age.
Apr. 17. —— Hamilton, executed.
" 21. Widow Brown, aet. 80, old age.
" 22. John Loree, aet. 63, pleurisy.
" 23. Child of Nathan Turner.
May 3. Ezekiel Cheever, aet. 64, consumption.
" 8. David Wheeler, aet. 27, pleurisy.
" 9. Child of David Treadwell.
" 11. Joannah, wife of Abraham Gilbert, aet. 24, consumption.
" 26. Thomas Bridge, aet. 29, consumption.
June 11. Thomas Cleverly, aet. 65, consumption.
" " Mary, daughter of Peter Norris, Jun., aet. 1, consumption.
July " Matthew, son of Moses Lindsly.
" " Joseph, son of Samuel Allwood, aet. 2, rheumatism.
" " Child of Abraham Hathaway.
" 27. Elizabeth, wife of William Hamilton, aet. 18, child bed.
" " Child of William Hamilton, still born.
Aug. 10. Matthew Ball's wife's child.
" 18. Sarah, daughter of Jacob Whitehead, convulsion fits.
" " Child of Abraham Day.
" 20. Cornelius, son of Reuben Holloway,† aet. 16, drowned.
" 27. Child of William Leonard.
Sept. 1. Child of Abraham Canfield.
" " Child of David Douglass, still born.
" 3. Mabel, daughter of David Fairchild, aet. 1, fits.
" 10. Child of Matthias Howard.
" 16. Child of Matthias Howard.
" 18. Child of Nathaniel Armstrong, still born.
" 20. Mary, daughter of Nathaniel Lhomedieu, aet. 1.
" 24. Rhoda Woodrdff, aet. 10, fever.
" 26. Child of Jonathan Starke.
" " Child of Seudars.
" 29. Child of John Bloomfield, aet. 4.

Oct. 4. Phebe, wf. of Samuel Bayles, aet 45
" 11. Philip, son of Philip Hathaway, aet. 2.
" 23. Elder Ezra Hallsey,* aet. 48, putrid fever.
" 26. Child of Matthias Howard.
Nov. 8. John, son of John Pool, whooping-cough.
" 20. Simeon Hathaway, son of Joseph Beers, fits.
" " Robert Tompkins,† aet. 18, nervous fever.
" 22. Huldah Griffin, aet. 32.
" 26. Ezra, son of John Pool, aet. 7, inflammatory fever.
" 27. Phœbe, daughter of Nathaniel Armstrong, aet. 2, whooping cough.
Dec. 20. Child of Stephen Arnold, hives.
" 22. Lydia Seward,* aet. 40, consumption.
1776.
Jan. 8. Catharine, wife of Daniel Tichenor,* aet. 40, consumptiou.
" 15. Euphemia, wife of William Cherry,*† aet. 27, consumption.
Feb. 7. James M'Bride, aet. 35, apoplexy.
" " Child of Elijah Holloway.
" " Child of David Fairchild.
" " Mrs. Farber, aet. 104, old age.
" 26. Sarah, daughter of Daniel Tichenor, aet. 19, consumption.
Mar. — Child of Caleb Munson.
" — David Treadwell, aet. 30, accidental.
" — Phœbe, daughter of Peter Prudden, aet. 3, epileptic fits.
Apr. — Eunice, wife of Joseph King, Jun., aet. 30, intermittent Fever.
" 9. Nathaniel, son of Daniel Carmichael, worms.
" 15. Abraham, son of Joseph Pierson, aet. 18, consumption.
" 23. Ezra, son of John Mills, inflammatory fever.
" 24. Oliver, son of Doc. Timothy Johnes, epileptic fits.
May 4. John Johnson, aet. 70, inflammation in his head.
" — Wife of Foster Williams, aet. 45, fever.
July 2. Child of David Gardner.
" 7. Joseph, son of Henry Gardner, aet. 19, drowned.

(*To be Continued.*)

(*Continued from page 40.*)

TRUSTEES' BOOK.

—:o:—

August 31, 1779, the Trustees met at Mr. Alexander Carmichael's; present Mr. Stiles, Mr. Lindsley, Mr. Mills and the president. Moore Furman, Esq., D. Q. M. G. of this State applied to the Board for liberty to erect a Store house for the use of the continent on the Parsonage lot betwen Mr. Carmichaels and Doct. Tuthills, the Board having considered the proposal made by Mr. Furman agreed thereto, and agreed that the President in behalf of the Board of Trustees do enter into and sign an article of agreement with Joseph Lewis or the assistant Q. M. at this post for the time being discribing the land to be occupied by the said D.Q.M.G. for the use of continent and the conditions on which the same is let, agreed that Mr. Carmichael be employed to hire the manure made and left on the green or commons near the meetinghouse property heaped up in order to be removed onto the parsonage lot.

April 16, 1781, the Trustees met at the request of the president at his House, all present but Doct. Tuthill, and agreed that Mr. Timothy Johnes be requested by the president to employ some proper person to clean out the Ditches in the parsonage meadow and that the Board will defray the expense thereof. The Trustees then proceeded to settle accounts with Mr. Condict as Clerk and Treasurer of the Board, and found a balance due to Board of one hundred and forty pounds, the most of which appeared to have been received by the said Mr. Condict in continental Money in its depreciated State and was by him Loaned to the continent the first day of March, 1780, the Loaning of which the Board approved of and agreed not to call for or demand the same until it is paid by the Continental Loan office and the certificate which includes the same with other monies be and remain in the hands of Mr. Condict at the risk of the Board he paying the interest as often as the same is Received from the Loan office.

The Trustees then settled accounts, Mr. Stiles for his expence and time in going to Philadelphia by order of the Board and found due to him the sum of three pounds, thirteen shilling and three pence.

The Trustees agreed to draw a petition to the surveyors of the Roads to meet at William Templetons on Tuesday the 8th day of may next, to in order to Lay out a Road to the parsonage wood Lot.

the Board adjourned to fryday next, two o'clock, to meet at Capt. Arnolds.

April 20, 1781, The Trustees met persuant to adjournment at Captn. Arnolds, all present but Mr. Ford. In persuance of a former agreement the Trustees executed a deed of conveyance to Alexander Carmichael for a small lot of land adjoining to the sd. Carmichaels, one acre Lot whereon he now dwells dated the 15th of May, 1776. The consideration money paid by the said Carmichael £3., 12,, 0. John Huntington applied to the Board to discharge a debt of £7 principal said to be due from Simon Huntington, Deceased, to Samuel Huntington, and also a debt said to be due from the sd. Simon to to Sarah Winters of the sum of £3., 10,, 0. After deliberating on the matter the Board agreed to discharge on the same being proven to be Justly due and that as soon as a sufficiency of money shall be Received for the use or Rent of a certain House which was built by the said Simon Huntington on the parish Lands.

(*To be continued.*)

THE LOT.

One of the first acts of the young pastor Johnes was to remind his people of the sin they had committed in the matter of the lot cast a few years before. This "accompt" is the first in a list embracing nearly two hundred names of those who "confessed" for very various sins during his pastorate.

We copy as follows: "*An accompt for Public Confession.* A public confession at the settlement of the ch. for a transgression Relating to a Lot Cast with Reference to the Setling of a house for Public Worship between Hanover & this town. Ye Persons that confessed are Joseph Coe, John Lindley, Jun., Joseph Prudden, Matthew Lum, Uriah Cutler, Stephen Freman, Peter Cundit, Jacob Fford, Joseph Howard, Benj. Bailey, Philip Cundit, Benjamin Coe, Ebenezar Mahurin, Samuel Nutman, Timothy Peck, Cornelius Arstin, Solomon Munson, Caleb Fairchild, Joseph Coe, Zachariah Fairchild, Joseph Tichenor."

THE RECORD.

FIRST PRESBYTERIAN CHURCH, MORRISTOWN, N. J.

"This shall be Written for the Generation to Come."—Psalms 102 : 18.

| VOL. 1. | JULY, 1880. | NO. 7. |

(*Printed with the approval of Session.*)

THE RECORD

Will be printed and published monthly at Morristown, N. J. Terms, 50 cents per annum in advance; 75 cents after June.

Subscriptions will be received at the book-stores of Messrs. Runyon and Emmell, or through the mail, and may begin with the first number. ALL COMMUNICATIONS should be addressed to the

EDITOR OF THE RECORD,

Lock box 44. Morristown, N. J.

Entered at the Post Office at Morristown, N. J., as second class matter.

——:o:——

(The following is the thirteenth of a series of articles entitled *Glances at the Past*, written for *The Presbyterian*, and appearing in that paper Oct 3, 1846. No one now in the office of *The Presbyterian* is able to say who K. H., the author, is.—Ed. of RECORD.)

GLANCES AT THE PAST.—NO. XIII.

Whippanny, New Jersey, was formed into a township in 1700, and included Hanover. It was settled about 1685 from East Hampton, Long Island, and from old England and New England. Forges were established at an early period, and among the active settlers were the Tuttles from England, near Tweed, Joseph and Abraham Kitchel and Francis Lindsly, also from England. The congregation originally included Morristown, Madison, Parsippany, Hanover and Chatham. Three acres and a half were given by John Richards, a schoolmaster, on which, in 1718, a meeting house was built, and which is now used for a grave yard.

The first minister was the Rev. Nathaniel Hubbel, who graduated at Yale in 1723, and was settled as pastor of Hanover and Westfield in 1727. He retained the pastoral charge of Westfield till 1746, when he was succeeded by the Rev. Nathaniel Tucker, a native of Milton, Massachusetts, and a graduate of Harvard University. He was ordained by New York Presbytery April 9, 1747, and died in December, 1748. He was succeeded by the Rev. John Grant, who died in 1759.

In 1730, the Rev. John Nutman settled at Hanover. He graduated at Yale in 1727, and he appeared in Synod in 1733, to seek relief, his congregation having divided into East and West Hanover. West Hanover desired to stand by itself, and a resort had been had to the casting of lots to decide their action. The Synod heard all the papers in the case, and resolved that West Hanover ought to unite, at least for a time, either with Baskingridge or East Hanover; they also disapproved of the casting of lots. Mr. Nutman represented that he could not remain, if the breach were not healed, and the Synod therefore exhorted the Presbytery of East Jersey to travail with the two parties to effect a reconciliation. They had leave to dismiss Mr. Nutman if there were no other way of bringing them together. The next year President Dickinson brought up the affair again, inquiring whether they, having cast the lot, and so appealed to God for a decision, were not bound to abide by the issue of the lot. By the *lot*, it was decided they should remain united, and the Synod blamed them for their profane disregard of the ordering of the Lord in the fall of the lot; and declared that they were bound to abide by the *lot*, however presumptuous they had been in using it. All measures were unavailing; united they would not be, and Mr. Nutman remained pastor of East Hanover until 1745.

In September, 1735, West Hanover applied to the Synod to ordain Mr. Cleverly, and the Synod referred the business to the Presbytery of Philadelphia. In May, 1736, the people opposed the Presbytery to proceed, and the were erected to appoint a day, and give the Presbytery notice that they might on the spot, attend properly to the business. In August, 1737, the congregation were excused for having made no appointment, and the Presbytery resolved to set out the next day for West Hanover. On their journey, the brethren stopped at Captain Hart's, in Hopewell, New Jersey, and took on trials as a candidate "a young man, John Guild, who had offered in April." At West Hanover, objections were made to Mr. Cleverly, but the Presbytery did not judge him unfit for the ministry ; nevertheless, they would not ordain him in opposition to a part of the people, and they gave him leave to go and seek some other field of labour. They then wrote to the rector of Yale College to send on a minister, giving as a reason, that "they knew no other way to supply them."

In May, 1738, the Synod finding the difficulties still existing, appointed a large committee to meet and make a final adjustment. On the 26th of July, Andrews of Philadelphia, Gilbert Tennent of New Brunswick, William Tennent, of Freehold, John Cross, of Baskingridge, Cowell of Trenton, and Treat of Abington, met, and Gilbert Tennent preached from Ezek. xi. 19, "I will give them one heart." The result was, that Hanover and Mr. Nutman acknowledged they did not need the help of West Hanover in maintaining the gospel, and the two congregations expressed their entire satisfaction in the judgment of the committee that no further attempts should be made to merge them in one.

The Rev. Jacob Green was born at Malden, Massachusetts, January 22, 1722, and was educated at Harvard University. He was converted under the ministry of Gilbert Tennent, during his journey through New England ; he came with Whitefield to New Jersey, and studied divinity with President Dickinson. He was installed by the Presbytery of New York, pastor of Hanover in November, 1746. In 1755, the old meeting house was deserted, and one built at Hanover Neck, and one at Parsippany. In 1757, Mr. Green gave up the charge of Parsippany. Previously, in 1748, a portion of the congregation separated and formed the

church of South Hanover ; they dropped that name for Bottle Hill, and now, the name is Madison. Mr. Green was elected Vice-President of New Jersey College in 1758, and for a season was at the head of that Institution. He was also a member of the Provincial Congress during the trying times of the revolution, and is said to have prepared an able series of papers on the currency. Toward the close of his life, he with several other ministers of New York Presbytery, withdrew and formed Morris County Presbytery—one reason for this was their unwillingness to refuse admission to the ministry to those who had not enjoyed a liberal education.

There were three revivals at Hanover under his ministry ; there was a remarkable one in 1790, in the midst of which he died on the 24th of May. This was so noiseless that the neighboring ministers did not know of it till they came to his funeral, and so powerful that after his death, thirty persons the gleaning of the harvest, came to his son to seek spiritual direction and to lament that they had not turned at their pastor's reproof while he was yet with them. His death was so sudden, that his son, then settled over the Second Presbyterian church, Philadelphia, did not receive the tidings in time to attend the funeral. When preaching, after this mournful bereavement, Dr. Green addressed the younger members of the congregation, the men of his own age, most unexpectedly to him they rose in their seats and stood up to receive the word of life.

Mr. Green married the daughter of the Rev. John Pierson, of Woodbridge, New Jersey. He was an active, devout man, and did much to enstamp on the community a high moral and religious character. His venerable son has occupied a distinguished place in the history of our church for nearly sixty years, and one of his grandsons is the respected and useful pastor at Bedford, New York.

The West Hanover congregation is now Morristown. The first pastor was the Rev. Timothy Johnes, who graduated at Yale in 1737, and commenced his labors at Morristown in August, 1742. He was ordained by the Presbytery of New York, February 9, 1743, and he died September 15, 1794. He was born May 24, 1717, but in what country does not appear.[*] Few men laboured more zealously or more successfully than Dr. Johnes. He was asked by Gen. Washington on the approach of a sacramental season, if the rules of the Presbyterian Church admitted of such a thing as receiving to the Lord's table a pious person of the Episcopal persuasion. The General assigned as a reason for the inquiry, his desire to partake of the ordinance with Dr. Johnes's congregation. He was assured that the word of God was the rule of the Presbyterian church, and that therefore every pious person was heartily invited and welcomed to join in obedience to the Saviour's command. The army then lay in the neighborhood; disease, want and death prevailed in the camp, and there was a recklessness about the soldiery that was truly horrible. Washington turned from these things, so mournful and discouraging, and sought comfort under his responsibilities and anxieties at the foot of the cross.

The South Hanover congregation had for their first pastor the Rev. Azariah Horton, a native of New England, but whose parents removed in his childhood to New Jersey. He graduated at Yale in 1735, and on being licensed, received a call to a promising parish in Long Island. Dickinson, Burr and Pemberton had been appointed by the Scottish Society for the Propagation of the Gospel, to select missionaries, and to direct their labors among the heathen. They selected Mr. Horton, and prevailed on him to relinquish the call, and devote himself to the Indians on the east of Long Island.

He was ordained by New York Presbytery in 1740 or '41, and his labours at the outset were greatly blessed, and he soon baptized thirty-five Indians. He had little or no success during the remainder of his stay, being sadly annoyed by the Separates. He abandoned the mission in 1752, but the fruits of his labours remain to this day in two Indian churches, one at Poosepatuck, three miles south-west of Moriches, and a larger one at Shinnecock, two miles west of Southampton. These churches are independent in their organization, and had, until 1812, a succession of Indian pastors in the Rev. Samson Occum, a Mohegan, Peter, John and Paul Cuffee, of the Shinnecock tribe. Mr. Horton was the pastor of South Hanover from 1752 till his death, March 27, 1777, at the age of 62.

South Hanover was supplied till the close of the war by the Rev. Aaron Richards, who had been obliged to remove, on account of the nearness of the British army, from his charge at Rahway. The Rev. Ebenezer Bradford graduated at Nassau Hall in 1773, and was licensed by New York Presbytery in 1775. A request was made to the Synod by his Presbytery in 1775, for leave to ordain him as an evangelist, and the Synod left the matter to the discretion of the Presbytery. He was ordained before 1777, probably as pastor of South Hanover. He was settled there in 1781, when he withdrew with his father-in-law, the Rev. Jacob Grear, t. and Messrs. Tuttle and Grover, and formed Morris County Presbytery. He left New Jersey before 1784, and settled at Rowley, Massachusetts, where he died. Two of his sons entered the ministry, the Rev. Dr. John M. Bradford, of Albany, and the Rev. James Bradford, of Sheffield, Massachusetts. The late Judge Ebenezer G. Bradford, of York and Lancaster, was also his son.

The Rev. Alexander Miller was his successor at South Hanover. He graduated at Nassau Hall in 1764, was licensed by New York Presbytery in 1768, and was ordained in 1771. He was directed to spend six or eight Sabbaths among the settlements on the Hudson, and we find him applying for aid for the church in Schenectady, and the Synod directed him to supply every fifth Sabbath among the vacancies around that city. Tradition reports him to have been a frequent supply at Albany, and to have made himself sadly unpopular by stopping the clerk in the midst of the psalm, with an intimation that *a little of such singing was enough ;* the said veritable authority avouching that there was abundance of reason from the style of the singing to justify Mr. Miller in his opinion of it. He was installed pastor of South Hanover in 1784, and in 1794 was principal of Hackensack Academy. He presided at the opening of Albany Presbytery in 1802, when the Presbyteries of Columbia and Oneida had been set off, and he appears to have resided without charge in Columbia Presbytery from 1809 to 1819.   K. H.

[*Born at Southampton, L. I.—ED RECORD.]

[t" Green"—ED. RECORD.]

(*Continued from page 44*).
HALF-WAY MEMBERS.
——:o:——

1773.
Jan. 10. Hannah, wf. of David Phillips.
" 24. Silas Ayrs & Mary his wf.
Feb. 28. Deborah, David Day's wf.
Apr. 1. Joseph Bears & Miriam his wf.
June 27. John Gwinnup & Rachel his wf.
July 18. Joseph Lewis & Anne his wf.
" " David Moor & Bathiah his wf.
" " Calvin Extel & Mary his wf.
" " Hannah, wf. of Timo. Loce.
Dec. 14. Elizabeth, wf. of Jacob Arnold.
1774.
Jan. 2. Mary, wf. of Isaac (?) Ayrs.
Feb. 6. Timo. Mills, Junr. & Anne his wf.
May 22. Jno. Milborn & Mary his wf.
June 16. Aaron Pierson & Mary his wf.
" " James Humes & Agnish or Ann his wf.
July 17. Elias Hedges & Mary his wf.
Aug. 14. David Dalglish & Jane his wf.
" 28. Abraham Gilbard & Joanna his wf.
Sept. 18. Isaac (?) Morris & Rebecca his wf.
" " Elizabeth, Rob't Young's wf., on her accomt.
Dec. 27. Abigail, wf. of David Garrigus.
1775.
Jan. 10. Ezek. Crane. Bap. Eunice his, re-new cov.
" " Sam'l Baldwin & Rhoda his wf.
" 15. Daniel Smith & Joanna his wf.
June 29. Abel Tompkins.
" " Rachel, wf. of Uriah Allen.
July 9. Mary, wf. of Demas Ford.
" " Sarah Chever, adult.
" 20. Abrham Day & Sarah his wf.
" 30. Docr. Bern Budd.
Aug. 3. Eunice, wf. of Jno Primrose.
" " Hannah, wf. of Ephrain Lyon.
" 31. Mary, Matt. Ball's wf.
" " Joseph Cook & Kezia his wf.
May 4. Jonathan Ogden & Abigail his wf.
" 4. Sam Freeman & Sarah his wf.
1776.
Feb. 11. Nathan Guiering & Abigail his wf.
" 18. Zippora Conger & Bap.
Mar. 24. Jabez Beach & Anne his wf.
Apr. 14. Robert Rolfe, Bap. adult.
" " Mary, wf. of David Hoppen.
May 5. Mary, wf. of Moses Wick & Bap.
June 2. Jonathan & Mary Hallick of South-old.
" 23. Elizabeth, wf. of Thomas Pierson.

June 30. Phebe, wf. of James Bullen.
July 28. Phebe, wf. of Abr. Hathaway.
" " Lidia, wido. of Will Crane.
Aug. 11. Elizabeth, wf. of Barzillai Orsborn.
Nov. 3. Phebe, wf. of Jeduthan Day.
1777.
Aug. 28. Ezra Halsey & Sarah his wf.
Sept. 21. John Beach consort of Sarah Chever in cov. before.
Oct. 19. Sarah, wf. of Silas Gildersleeve.
" 30. Nathaniel Thompson & his sister.
" " Phebe, wf. of Jno. McCaulin.
Nov. 6. Mary, wido. of Abraham Hathaway.
Dec. 21. Leah, wido. of John Sutten.
1778.
Apr. 5. Abijah Cutler & Dinah his wf.
" 26. John Arnold & his wf.
May 10. Abigail, wf. of Jedediah Osborn.
Aug. 2. Mary, wf. of Daniel Freeman, Junr.
Nov. 15. Esther, wido. of Rob. Day.
1779.
Apr. 25. Luther Extel & wf.
Oct. 17. Abner Condict.
" " John Lyon & wf. Rachel.
Nov. 25. Timo. Stiles & Damaris his wf.
Feb. 13. Phebe, wf. of John Kenny.
June 25. Nathaniel Broadwell & wf. Joanna.
Aug. 13. Stephen Conkling, Junr., his wf. Rachel.
Sept. 10. Mary, wf. of Ichabod Spinnage.
" 17. Abijah Fairchild & wf. Sarah.
Oct. 1. Joseph Marsh & wf. Elizabeth.
" 25. Jane, wf. of Docr. Lewis Dunham.
1780.
Apr. 5. Joseph Byram & Esther his wf.
June 24. Wm. Satterly & Elizabeth his wf.
1781.
Jan. 1. Jesse Cutler & Elizabeth his wf.
1782.
Mar. 24. John Dickerson & Grace his wf.
May 3. Eph. Lindsley's wf. Martha.
" " Elizabeth, David Walker's wf.
" " Thomas Keen or Kein & wf.
" 5. Jacob Emery & Elizabeth his wf.
" 26. John Lindsly, Junr. & Sarah his wf.
June 2. Daniel Freeman, Jr. & Mary before.
" 23. Caleb Edy & Esther his wf., who was baptized.
July 22. Sarah, wf. of Sam'l Seward.
Sept. 15. George Marsh & Catharine his wf.
Oct. 10. Cornelius Loce & Mary his wf.
Oct. 20. Henry Clark & Mary his wf.
Nov. 3. Peter Hill & Charity his wf.
" " Ichabod Badgly & Sarah his wf.
(*To be continued.*)

(Continued from page 45.)

BAPTISMS.

—:o:—

1756.

April 4. Henry Primrose & wf., child Abigail.
" " Elijah Pierson & wf., ch. Sarah.
" " Demas Lindly & wf., ch. Zenas.
" 22. Philip Conduit & wf., ch. Hannah.
" 26. John Pitney & wf., ch. Comfort.
" " Christopher Woods & wf., ch. Sarah, born Jan. 15. 1756.
May 16. Doc. Sam'l Tuthil & wf., ch. Jane.
" " Philip Hathaway &, wf. ch., Shadrack.
June 27. David Gauden & wf., ch. Hopestill.
July 11. Stephen Freeman & wf., ch. John.
Aug. 1. John Fford & wf., ch. Mahlon.
" " Moses Prudden & wf., ch. Abigail.
" " Abel Lyon on wf.'s accompt., ch. John.
" 15. Dan'l Freeman & wf., ch. Elizabeth.
Sept.12. Gideon Riggs & wf., ch. Abraham, I think.
" 15. Gilbard Heady & wf., ch. Abraham.
" 19. Lorance Decker, ch. Josia, I think.
" " Wido. Rebecah Woods, ch. Phebe.
Oct. 3. David Beeman & wf., ch. Josiah.
" 10. John Cole & wf., ch. David.
Nov. 5. Sarah, wf. of John Hermon, Household—Abigail, Hannah, Lucretia Price & John.
" 21. Benjamin Woodruff & wf., ch. Joseph.
Dec. 5. John Lindly & wf., ch. Joanna.
" 8. Benjn. Freeman & wf., ch. Samuel.
" 15. Ebenezer Stiles & wf., ch. Rebecca.

1757.

Jan. 16. Robard Arnold & wf., ch. Ziba, born Nov. 12, 1756.
" 16. Benjn. Hathaway, Jr's wf., ch. Mary.
" 23. Jonathan Reeves & wf., ch. Rachel.
" 30. James Frost's wf., negro ch. Antony.
Feb. 6. Thomas Throop & wf., child Thomas, I think.
Mar. 21. Abraham Hathaway & wf., ch. Sarah.
" " John Burrel & wf., ch. Jedediah.
" " Shadrack Howard & wf., ch. Rebecca.

Apr. 24. Uriah Cutler & wf., ch. Jesse.
" " Peter Dickerson & wf., ch. Ester.
" " Demas Lindley & wf., ch. Daniel.
" 17. John Robond (?) & wf.,ch.Elizabeth.
" " Philip Hathaway & wf., ch. Bathia.
May 1. Deborah, wf. of Benjn. Bailey & ch. Phebe.
" " Benjn. Prudden & wf., ch. Eunice.
" " Stephen Hedges & wf., ch. Ame.
" " Phineas Fairchild & wf., ch. Deborah, born Feb. 22, 1757.
" " Phebe. Dan. Dickin's wf., ch. Mary
" 15. Timo. Mills & wf., ch. Timothy.
" " Zophor Gildersleeve & wf., ch. Elijah.
" " Junia Lindsley & wf., ch. Ruth.
June 6. Benjn. Coe & wf., ch. Rachel.
July 3. Thomas Tuttle & wf., ch. Jacob.
" " Henry Gardiner & wf., ch. Joseph.
" 10. Adoniram Prudden & wf.,ch. Sarah.
" 24. Sam'l Arnold & wf., ch. Samuel.
Aug. 7. Moses Prudden & wf., ch. Joanna.
" 21. John Marsh & wf., ch. Ephraim.
" " Dan'l Howard & wf., ch. Simeon.
" " John Lose, on wf.'s acompt., chn. Abigail & Hanna.
Oct. 3. Jabish Beers & wf., ch. Nathaniel.
" 16. Joseph Edmister & wf., ch. Joseph.
Nov. 6. Peter Norris & wf., ch. Ebenezer.
" 15. Charles Howell & wf., ch. Samuel.

1758.

Jan. 1. John Fford & wf., ch. Chilion.
" " Benjn. Pierson & wf., ch. Hannah.
" " Eleazar Hathaway's wf., ch. Zophar.
" 8. Tunis Spear of Rockaway, ch. Abraham.
" " Sam'l Shipman & wf., ch. Elizabeth.
" 15. Sollomon Munson & wf., ch. Joshua.
" " Elijah Pierson & wf., ch. Benjn.
" " Benjn. Prudden & wf., ch. Rachel.
" 22. Daniel Freeman & wf., ch. Phebe.
Feb. 5. Jonathan Wood & wf., Jerusha.
" 26. Sam'l Day & wf., ch. Jehial.
Mar. 12. Stephen Hodges & wf., ch. Nathan, I think.
" 19. Sarah Allen, wido., household—Amos, Elizbeth & Jonah.
Apr. 16. David Gauden & wf., ch. John.
" 23. Christopher Wood & wf. ch. Elizabeth, born Mar. 17, 1758.

(To be continued.)

(Continued from page 46.)

MARRIAGES.

———:o:———

1769.

Mar 30. David Moore & Bathiah Cutler.
Apr. 12. Isaac Southard & Rachel Goble.
"　" Asher Smith & Eunice Lum.
" 20. George Lefollet & Jemima Mint-
　　　horn, Mendham.
"　" Abner Wines & Kezia Pierson.
" 23. Joseph Benway & Ann Freeman.
May 22. Samuel Pierson & Rebeccah Garri-
　　　gas.
" 25. David Wheeler & Hannah Youngs.
June 1. Elias Hedges & Mary Ludlam.
"　7. Samuel Sutten & Easter Sutten.
"　15. Silas Flint & Mary Clark.
" 20. Aaron Lilly & Tamson French.
July 6. Devid Day & Deborah Halsey.
"　9. Daniel Lawrance & Charity Mills,
　　　Succasuney.
Aug. 31. Zenas Baldwin, of Sussex, & Dorcas
　　　Younglove.
Oct. 25. Isaac Prudden & Hannah Lum.
" 29. Matthew Rue & Lidia Adams,
　　　widow, both of Hunterdon.
Nov.13. Matthew Jennings & Ursula Coe.
" 15. Moses Gard & Sarah Lyon.
Dec. 6. David Raynor & Elizabeth Lindsley
" 10. John Ludlam & Sarah Headley.
" 14. Jacob Gard & Sarah Hathaway.
1770.
Jan. 10. John Prudden & Abigail Riggs.
" 24. Stephen Arnold & Phebe Guiering.
" Samuel Loree & Mary Reeve.
Mar. 8. Joseph Guierin, & Martha Fauger-
　　　son, of Mendham.
" 11. Jabish Rogers & Rachel Lee.
" 19. Samuel Carter & Susanna Frost.
July 16. Nathan Hall & Susanna Halbert.
Aug.29. Ursula Coe & Mary Burnet.
Sept.23. John Adams & Agnish Bloys wido,
　　　both of Woodbridge.
" I think, Ezek. Crane & Eunice Hay-
　　　ward.
Oct. 1. Jacob Arnold & Elizabeth Tuthill.
" 9. Nathanial Burt & Rebecah Throop.
" 11. Morris Sharphenstine & Catharine
　　　Miller.
" 8. Daniel Extell, of Mendham, & Ruth
　　　Tuttle.
Nov.14. Joseph Youngs & Izabel Berry.
" 27. Joseph Beers & Miriam Hathaway.

Dec. 27. Isaac Ayers & Mary Cooper.
"　" Stephen Cooper & Mary Swaine.
1771.
Jan. 9. Matthias Burnet & Phebe Brook-
　　　fied.
Mar. 5. John Sutten & Leah Balden.
" 12. Benjamin Woodruff & Phebe Pier-
　　　son.
May 1. Joseph Lefollet, widower, & Phebe
　　　Gobil.
" 9. James Gillispie & Jane Marsh.
" 13. William Stubs & Mary Headly.
" 15. William Hayward & Servia Hudson.
" 26. Robert Arnold & Mary Pierson.
June 4. John Day, of Newark Mountains,
　　　& Mary Ludlam, of ye town.
" 17. John Allison & Catarine Mitchel,
　　　both of Brookland Forge.
July 4. Joshua Lambart & Anne Johnson.
Aug.19. Aaron Lindsly & Abigail Halsey.
Sept. 3. Elijah Freeman & Hannah Smith.
Oct. 6. Benjamin Casterline & Ruth Mather
" 9. David Moureson & Elizabeth Hyler.
" 20. Job Hathaway & Lydia Johnson.
Nov. 7. Calvin Axtel & Mary Mills.
" 20. Herrick Benjamin & Joanna Wood-
　　　ruff.
Dec. 4. William Crane & Lydia Edmister,
　　　450 married.
" 12. Patrick McGill & Lucretia Harmon.
"　" Thomas Axtell & Mary Tuttle.
" 19. Jacob Hall & Damoras Moore.
" 23. Stephen Fairchild & Salome Tomp-
　　　kins.
"　" Silas Ayres & Mary Byram.
" 26. Epenetus Beach & Hannah Ayrs.
" 30. Usual Tompkins Susannah Benja-
　　　min.

　　　(The slippers worn by Miss Ben-
　　　jamin upon the occasion of her
　　　marriage are upon exhibition at
　　　Washington's Headquaters. Ed. of
　　　RECORD.)

1772.
Jan. 13. Gershom Hathaway & Sarah Free-
　　　man.
Jan. 30. Aaron Gobil & Charity Lindsley.
Feb. 26. Timothy Stiles & Anna Carter.
Apr. 9. David Jefferres (?) & Sarah Winings.
May 6. Abraham Gibbard & Joanna Free-
　　　man.
" 16. Joseph Casterling & Susannah
　　　Lyon.
　　　(To be continued.)

(Continued from page 47.)

BILL OF MORTALITY,

1776.

July 18. Silas, son of David Day, aet. 5, dysentery.

" — Norris, son of widow Stewart,† aet. 5, dysentery.

" 26. Jonathan, son of Nathan Reeve, aet. 5, dysentery.

" 28. Juba, servent of Nathan Reeve, aet. 2, dysentery.

" 29. David Anderson, aet. 24, dysentery.

" " Abraham Gilbert, aet. 28, dysentery.

Aug. 1. Eleanor, widow of Richard Easton,* aet. 78, old-age.

" " Phœbe, daughter of Nathan Reeve, aet. 4, dysentery.

" 7. Nathan, son of Nathan Reeve, aet. 2.

" " Joseph Hathaway, aet. 48, dysentery.

" 8. Joseph Condit,* aet. 48, fever.

" 11. Samuel, son of Nathan Reeve, aet 1, dysentery.

" 16. William Howard, aet. 27, dysentery.

" — Squire Lum, aet. 32, putrid-fever.

" — Ephraim Lyon, aet. 36, dysentery.

" 20. Isaac, son of Isaac Prudden, aet. 1,

" — Amos, son of Waitstill Munson, aet. 20, dysentery.

" 25. Phœbe, daughter of widow Howard, aet. 1, dysentery.

" 26. Bethuel, son of Samuel Baldwin, aet. 2, dysentery.

" — Child of Hezekiah Broadwell.

" 28. Zophar Gildersleve,* aet. 70, old-age.

" 29. Eunice, daughter of Jedidiah Gregory, aet. 1, dysentery.

Sept. 2. Jabez Lambert, aet. 14, consumption

" 11. Child of David Hoppen.

" 12. Child of David Hoppen.

" " Phillis, servant of Eleazer Hathaway, aet. 24, dysentery.

" " Servant child of Eleazer Hathaway, dysentery.

" 15. Child of Jesse Smith.

" " Julia, daughter of George Phillips.

" 18. Widow of Matthias Hoppen, aet. 68, fever.

" " Kezia Prudden, aet. 30, dysentery.

" 19. Child of Nathan Guering.

" 24. Peter Weizel, aet. 18, consumption.

" 26. Abigail, daughter of Moses Prudden, aet. 12, dysentery.

" 27. Deacon Joseph Prudden,* aet. 84.

" 29. Nancy, daughter of Moses Prudden, aet. 1, dysentery.

" " Ruth, daughter of Moses Prudden, aet. 10.

" 30. Child of Benjamin Clark.

Oct. 5. Sarah, daughter of Elijah Brown, aet. 13, dysentery.

" " Child of Stephen Fairchild,†

" 6. John Leconte, son of Joseph Lewis, aet. 1, teething.

" 12. Joshua Whitehead, jun., aet. 30, fever.

" 14. Hannah, widow of Elder Ezra Hallsey,* aet. 49, consumption.

" 16. Walter Irving, aet. 20, consumption.

" 19. Hannah Hathaway, aet. 17, dysentery.

" 21. Child of Jabez Condict.

" " Catharine, daughter of Moses Johnson, aet. 4, fever.

" 23. Elizabeth, daugher of Moses Pierson, aet. 10, fever.

" 26. Hannah, wife of Isaac Prudden,* aet. 33, dysentery.

" " Lydia, daughter of Nathan Turner, aet. 8, dysentery.

" 28. Child of David Fithian.

Nov. 4. Child of Constant Cooper.

" 5. Susanna, widow of Samuel Sweasy,* aet. 80, pleurisy.

" 6. Isaac Tuttle, aet. 55, pleurisy.

" 20. Rhoda, daughter of Moses Johnson, aet. 17, fever.

" 21. Ephraim Gard, aet. 40, dysentery.

" 29. Elizabeth, wife of Jeremiah Gard, sen., aet. 60, dysentery.

Dec. 1. Wife of Daniel Burnet, aet. 35, consumption.

" 2. Joseph Stiles, Esq., aet. 70, fever.

" 5. Child of Daniel Burnet.

" 16. Elizabeth, widow of Benj. Hathaway, Esq., aet. 67, remitting-fever.

" " Robert, son of Uzal Tompkins, aet. 1, consumption.

" " Child of Joseph Riggs.

" 17. Servant child of Peter Pruden, billious fever.

" 20. Rachel, wife of Benjamin Coe,* aet. 58, pleurisy.

" " Servant child of Jonathan Ford.

" " Servant man of Jonathan Ford, aet. 29, pleurisy.

(To be Continued.)

(Continued from page 48.)

TRUSTEES' BOOK.

—:o:—

The Trustees then appointed Doct. Tuthill and Mr. Lindsly a committee, to settle and collect the moneys Due for the use or Rent of the said House, and to hire out the said House for the future untill the further order of this Board ; Mr. Condict having declined serving any longer as Clerk of the Board, the Trustees unanimously choose Mr. Mills to be Clerk, and agreed that Mr. Condict deliver the money and obligations for money, with the Book to the said Clerk.

Nov. 20, 1781. The Trustees met at Jacob Arnold's, at the Request of the President, all present, and agreed to call for the money due on the Subscription for purchasing a parsonage, and if paid Before the first day of may next to be taken in State money (if offer'd) Allowing the Exchange of two for one, the Trustees appointed Mr. Tuthill, Mr. Ford & Mr. Mills to settle with Mr. Johnes, his Sallary, and charge for Ditching the parsonage meddow. And appointed Mr. Lindsly & Mr. Stiles to settle with Thos. Kinney on Acc't of a piece of Land the Trustees Bought of said Kinney. Trustees settled with Justice Lindsly for Repairing the Burrying yard fence and found Due to him thirty-three Shillings.

May 14, 1782. At a meeting of the Trustees at Mr. Johnes, present Mr. Conkling, Mr. Tuthill, Mr. Lindsly and Mr. Mills ; Agreed & appointed Mr. Tuthill & Mr. Lindsly a committe to call on Mr. Ferman, Q. M. & request him to remove the continental building on the parsonage land adjoining the house built by Mr. Huntington, Dec.

Agreed that Mr. Johnes should employ some of the silversmiths to make a vessel for the use of the communion table, & this Bord will pay for the Same (the workmanship only), and that Mr. Johnes employ some person to Ditch the parsonage meddow & this Bord pay for the Same.

May 25, 1782. at a meeting of the Trustees on Morristown green, present Mr. Condict, Mr. Tuthill, Mr. Lindsly, Mr. Stiles & Mr. Mills. Agreed & Bought the Continental Buildings on the parsonage Land adjoining the house Built by Mr. Huntington, Dec. for the use of the parish for the sum of £23. the trustees then agreed with the Q. Ms. Obale & Ferman by Leaving it to men for the Rent to be allowed for the house Built by Mr. Huntington while in publick use for the term of two years & nine Months, which expired in June 1781, for which Rent is to be allowed £9 per year. the trustees appointed Mr. Mills to call on Col. Obale & Mr. Ferman to Settle the purchase of Said Buildings & Rent of said house and Receive the Ballance if to be had.

April 25, 1783.—At a meeting of the Trustees at Morristown, all present but Mr. Condict. agreed and ordered the Clerk to Call on those persons Indebted to this Bord by note to pay at Least the Interest that is Due and that within three months or Depend on being prosecuted in Law.

The Trustees then appointed Mr. Conklin, Mr. Tuttle, Mr. Lindsly, Mr. Ford & Mr. Mills or any three of them to attend Vandue Next tuesday & to purchase (if they think proper) the Continental house on the parsonage Land for the use of the parish in behalf of the Trustees—and to See to the Settling of the Rent due to the Trustees for the use of the Land where Said house Stands.

May 23, 1783.—Trustees met at Morristown at the Request of the president, all present, Appointed Mr. Frederick King to employ some person to Ring the Bell & take care of the Clock.

The Trustees then appointed Mr. Tuttle & Mr. Mills or either of them to Settle with Mr. Johnes Respecting his Sallary from the year 1774, and to Draw a List of the Delinquents of the Rates and Subscriptions due for Sallary from that time and present a copy of Such deficiency to Each of the Parish collectors, and Desire them to Request the people thus behind to pay their deficiencies or give Notes for the Same. And that the Said Committee at a proper time lay before the Congregation the debt due for the repairs of the meeting house, Ringing the Bell &c., and fall on such meashures as the parish Shall approve for Discharging the same, and that the Said Committee take meashures to discharge the arrears. Either by applying the debts now due or by a new Subscription as shall appear most agreeable to the parish.

(To be continued.)

THE RECORD.

FIRST PRESBYTERIAN CHURCH, MORRISTOWN, N. J.

"This shall be Written for the Generation to Come."—Psalms 102 : 18.

VOL. 1.   AUGUST, 1880.   NO. 8.

(Printed with the approval of Session.)

THE RECORD

Will be printed and published monthly at Morristown, N. J. Terms, 50 cents per annum in advance; 75 cents after June.

Subscriptions will be received at the book-stores of Messrs. Runyon and Emmell, or through the mail, and may begin with the first number. ALL COMMUNICATIONS should be addressed to the

EDITOR OF THE RECORD,

Lock box 44.   Morristown, N. J.

Entered at the Post Office at Morristown, N. J., as second class matter.

——:o:——

(From New York Observer, January 29th, 1880.)

WASHINGTON'S COMMUNION

It is well known that Gen. Washington professed the Christian religion, and it is in evidence that he was a praying man, habitually kneeling in secret prayer, and sometimes with the Bible open before him while he was on his knees.

It is also in evidence that while the army was at Morristown, he requested of the pastor of the Presbyterian church, Dr. Johnes, the privilege of partaking of the Lord's Supper with the church at its regular communion. His request was cheerfully granted by Dr. Johnes, who said to the General: "We give the Lord's invitation to all his followers of whatever name."

A lady, an adopted daughter of Washington, and his wife's granddaughter, having lived in his family for twenty years, states in a letter to Mr. Sparks, that on communion Sundays the General was in the habit of leaving the church with her, before the communion, and the carriage was sent back for Mrs. Washington, who remained to commune.

Bishop White states in a letter to Rev. Mr. Parker that Washington habitually attended church during his Presidency, with Mrs. Washington, who was regularly a communicant. From which remark it is fairly inferred that Washington himself was not.

Perhaps other testimony may be adduced to throw more light on the subject. It seems probable that in early life the Father of his Country was a communicant, but that in later years he neglected his duty and privilege in this respect.

PHILO.

————

Sextons of the First Church.

There are probably few, if any, churches in the land in which the sextons have served longer or more faithfully than in our own church. The names of those who filled that office previous to the year 1784 are unknown. Under date of Nov. 23, 1784, mention is made in the Trustees' Book of Nathan Howell, but in such a way as to lead to the inference that he was already filling the position.

The list is as follows;

Nathan Howell, 1784 to June 21, 1790.

William Cherry, June 21, 1790, to Sept. 12. 1818.

Moses Cherry, son of Wm., Sept. 13, 1818 to Nov. 7. 1841.

Sevalon Mulford, Nov. 6, 1841 to July 29. 1865.

Francis L. Whitehead, Aug. 19, 1865 to ——

————

The "Bill of Mortality" begins in this number its mournful record of that terrible year, 1777. Gen. Washington's army encamped here in January of that year. Small-pox soon made its appearance with fatal effects. Sixty-eight were swept away by it in the parish alone, not counting those who died in the army. Good pastor Johnes attended in that one year over 200 funerals, more than half of which resulted from malignant diseases.

NEWARK, N. J., BOX-202,
June 28, 1880.

In the RECORD of July, 1880, is the following in relation to an article in the *Pres'n* of Oct. 3, 1846: "No one now in the office of the *Pres'n* is able to say who K. H., the author, is." He was the Rev. Richard Webster, then, and till his death, the pastor of the Pres'n church of Mauch Chunk, Pa., the finals of which, inverted, he used for his signature.   WM. P. VAIL.

ORANGE, N. J., July 3, 1880.
Rev'd. Rufus S. Green :

MY DEAR SIR : I am greatly obliged to you for the RECORD. I have been prompted by the last No. to send you some notes upon its historical glances,

Are there any memorials of Doct. Tuthill who is named as a Trustee of the Morristown church, or any in Morris to whom you can refer me for information concerning him ? I had no knowledge of such a man till I read the minutes of Trustees in your publication, You are doing a worthy thing in getting your early records in printed form. We ought to do it in Orange.
Very truly,   STEPHEN WICKES.

NOTES ON "GLANCES AT THE PAST,"

IN THE RECORD, VOL. 1, NO. 7.,

BY DR. WICKES.

The Tuttles, Kitchels and Lindsleys came from Eng., first to the N. Haven & Conn. colony and migrated thence to N. Jersey.

Joseph Tuttle was in Newark before 1738, removed to Hanover, d. 1789, a. 91. His will names Joseph, John, David and g. son Sam'l, son of Joseph (Conger's genealogies.)

Timothy Tuttle was of Hanover, 1755. Will names Dan'l, Thomas, Isaac, Stephen, Abraham, Mary, Joanna, Ibid, Timothy, Joseph & Stephen Tuttle, "all of Newark," gave rec't to Exec'rs Apr. 9, 1725, for legacy from their "honored father, Stephen Tuttle, of Woodbridge."

Robert Kitchel left Eng. in the first ship that ever anchored in New Haven bay. He & his son Samuel were two of the 41 associates from Milford who signed the "Fundamental agreement" in 1667, which document the 23 associates from Branford had signed the year previous. They each rec'd their home lots in the town of Newark.

Samuel (by his second wife, Grace Pierson,

sister of Abraham), had Abraham, who, in 1714, sold land in Newark, deed signed also by his wife Sarah. He was in Hanover in 1722. Was a deacon in the church there when he died, 1741, a. 62. Wife d. 1745, both buried in Whippany. (Conger, Stearns, *et aliis*.)

Francis Linle, (Lindly, Lindsly,) an associate in Newark, from Milford 1667, was a son of John of Guilford Conn, 1650. At Branford had Deborah in 1656, & Ruth, 1658, also sons John, Ebenezer, Benj., Jos., & Jonathan. (Conger.)

In 1699 gave lands to son John, 1703-4 to Benj., Joseph, Jonathan & Ebenezer. In the deeds he is "of Newark in the Prov. of East Jersey," and his sons therein described as of the same place. John in 1711-12 signed an agreement with John Baldwin, both "of Newark," Mar. 1726-7. John Lindsley "of Hanover in the County of Hunterdon," &c., "carpenter," conveyed to Sam'l & John Harrison "of Newark," lands therein.

Joseph migrated to Whippany, was bur'd there in 1753.

Jonathan was in Hanover in 1726.

Benj. & Ebenezer were of Orange and owned lands given by their father in 1704. Were bur'd here and their descendants are here.

The forge in Whippany was built "about 1710," (Pres. Tuttle.) As Francis had a child 1656, he must have been at least 69 when he gave lands in 1704 and 75 when the forge was started.

There was no other Francis than this one. As John removed to Hanover after 1712 and his brothers then or subsequently, he is probably the Lindsley named in the "Glances" of K. H.

Rev. Jno. Nutman was eldest son of James, Esq., from Edinburgh by 2nd wife Sarah, dau. of Rev'd John Prudden. James d. Mar. 8, 1739, a. 77 (Conger.)

Rev'd Jno. had a dau. Hannah, 2d wife of Jonathan Sergeant of Newark, who had Jonathan Dickinson Sergeant, the father of Hons. John, Thomas and Elihu Spencer Sergeant and Sarah, wife of Sam'l Miller, D.D. (Hatfield's Elizabeth p. 353.) Hatfield in his History furnishes notices of Rev'd Nath'l Hubbel and Rev.Jno. Cleverly.

In History of Long Island by N. S. Prime (Robt. Carter, 1845,) p. 104, s. 99. Will be found a very full record of Rev'd Azariah Horton 'prior to his migration to S. Hanover as 1st pastor when he served 25 years and d. 1777.

REPRESENTATIVES OF MORRIS COUNTY IN THE STATE LEGISLATURE.

The act setting off the County of Morris from Hunterdon was passed March 15, 1738-9, and the act setting off Sussex County from Morris June 8, 1753, but neither county was represented in the Colonial Legislature until the 22d and last, which met in 1772, when Jacob Ford and William Winds represented Morris County, and Thomas Van Horne, (and after his death Joseph Barton) and Nathaniel Pettit represented Sussex.

May 22d, 1756 in the minutes of the Assembly it appears that several petitions were presented to the House from the County of Morris signed by 190 hands setting forth "the Hardships they labour under by having no members allowed to Represent them in General Assembly; praying the Legislature to Grant them the. usual priviledges as the other counties Enjoy in being represented by two members in General Assembly for the future, which were read and ordered a second Reading."

By the First State Constitution adopted July 2, 1776, each county elected annually one member of the Legislative Council and three members of Assembly, the first election to be on the second Tuesday of August, and afterwards on the second Tuesday of October, and to convene the second Tuesday after election.

The members from Morris for each Legislature and the time of assembling are as follows:

1st Legislature, 1776, Aug. 27.
Council, Silas Condict.
Assembly, Jacob Drake,
Ellis Cook,
William Woodhull.

2d Legislature, 1777; Oct. 28.
Council, Silas Condict.
Assembly, Jacob Drake,
Ellis Cook,
William Woodhull.

3d Legislature, 1778, Oct. 27.
Council, Silas Condict.
Assembly, Jacob Drake,
Abraham Kitchel,
David Thompson.

4th Legislature, 1779, Oct. 26.
Council, Silas Condict.
Assembly, Abraham Kitchel.
Ellis Cook,
Alexander Carmichael.

5th Legislature, 1780, Oct. 24.
Council, Silas Condict.
Assembly, William Winds,
John Carle,
Eleazer Lindsley.

6th Legislature, 1781, Oct. 23.
Council, John Carle.
Assembly, Ellis Cook,
Aaron Kitchel,
John Starke.

7th Legislature, 1782, Oct. 22.
Council, John Carle.
Assembly, Ellis Cook,
Aaron Kitchel,
John Starke.

8th Legislature, 1783, Oct. 28.
Council, John Carle.
Assembly, Ellis Cook,
John Starke,
Jonathan Dickerson.

9th Legislature, 1784, Oct. 26.
Council, John Carle,
Assembly, Ellis Cook,
Aaron Kitchel,
Jacob Arnold.

10th Legislature 1785, Oct. 25.
Council, John Cleves Symmes.
Assembly, Ellis Cook,
John Starke,
Jacob Arnold.

11th Legislature, 1786, Oct. 24.
Council, Abraham Kitchel.
Assembly, Ellis Cook,
John Starke,
Aaron Kitchel.

12th Legislature, 1787, Oct. 23.
Council, Abraham Kitchel.
Assembly, Ellis Cook,
Aaron Kitchel,
John Starke.

13th Legislature, 1788, Oct. 28.
Council, Abraham Kitchel.
Assembly, Ellis Cook,
John Starke,
Aaron Kitchel.

14th Legislature. 1789, Oct. 27, at Perth Amboy.
Council, William Woodhull.
Assembly, Ellis Cook,
Aaron Kitchel,
Jacob Arnold.
(To be continued.)

(*Continued from page* 52)

HALF-WAY MEMBERS.

1783.

May 15. Zenas Condict & Hannah his wf.
" " Isaac Lyon & Rebekah his wf.
July 8. Aaron Howell, Junr., & Phebe his wf.
Aug.17. Theophilus Hathaway's wf. Phebe,
Sept.18. Phebe Stockbridge.
Nov.23. Joseph Halsey & Jerusha his wf.

1784.

Apr. 18. Mary wf. of Wm. Locy.
" 29. Abigail wf. of Abraham Munson.
June20. George Gwinnup & wf. Margaret.
Sept.19. Benj. Pierson & Abigail his wf.
" 26. David Reeve & Martha his wf.
Nov.18. Aaron Marsh & Nance his wf.

1785.

Jan. 20. Ben Woodruff & Patience his wf.
Apr. 3. Isaac Woolley & Hannah his wf.
" 28. Isaac Conckling & Comfort his wf.
May 1. Keziah Fairchild and her sister.
" " Jemima Fairchild.
" 22. David Tuttle & Phebe his wf.
Apr. 26. Paul Lee & Eunice his wf.
Nov. 4. Isaac Walker.
" 27. Dayton Talmadge & Charity his wf.
Dec. 8. Dan'l Pierson & Prudence his wf.
" 18. Moses Esty & wf. Anna.
" 29. Jacob Ball, bap. adult., & Mary his wf.
" 30. Hannah, Asa Beach's wf.

1786.

Jan. 19. Dan Phenix & Anna his wf.
" 29. Doc. Timo. Jones' wf. Abigail.
Mar. 30. Rob Arnold, Jun. & Mary his wf.
" " David & Bathia Pierson.
" " John Conckling & Elizabeth his wife.
" " Elizabeth, wf. of Jonathan Hayward.
Apr. 16. John Oliver.
July 2. Hannah, Cap. S. Howell's wf.
" 31. Martha, George Emmel's wf.
Sept. 3. Zebidiah Orsborn.
" 17. Gideon Riggs & Rachel his wf.
Nov.10. Phebe wf. of John Kirkpatrick.
" 19. Elizabeth wf. of Peter Fairchild.
Dec. 3. Phebe, wf. of William Wick.

1787.

Feb. 9. Nathaniel Bears & Ame his wf.
May 6. Abr.Tunis Schenck & Phebe his wf.
June17. James Vance & Amy his wf.
Nov.25. Isaac Lindsly & Phebe his wf.

1788.

Feb. 24. David Lindsly & Tapena his wf.
May 2. Benj. Freeman, Jun. & Elizabeth his wf., with her child.
July 6. Jno. Wilson & Mary his wf.
" " Jno. Sprout and Mary his wf.
Sept. 5. Caleb Tuttle & Mary his wf.
Oct. 19. Samuel Tuttle & Rebeka his wf.

1789.

Feb. 27. Stephen Burnet's wf.
June 2. Catharine, wf. of Jacob Reed.

1790.

Feb. 17. Asanath (?) wf. of Steph. Burnet.
(See above Feb. 27, '89.—ED.)
July 26. Joseph Godden & Eunice his wf.
Aug.23. Mary, wf. of Moses Sturge.
Sept.20. Larence Wilson & Jane his wf.
" " Thomas Johnson.
Oct. 4. John Alwood.
" 11. Abraham Core & bap., and Jane his wf.
" 17. Elizabeth, wf. of James Pitney,
" 25. Moses Johnson & Hulda his wf.

1791.

Jan. 3. Bethuel Hayward & Temperance his wf.
May 23. Will Hamilton & Nelle his wf.
July 2. Abraham Munson.
Sept.11. Abraham Conkling & Jemima his wf.
Oct. 6. Gabriel Ford & Francis Goldo his wf.

WHO CAN TELL.

The date of death or removal from town of the following persons :

NAME.	DATE OF JOINING CHURCH.
Jonathan Reeve,	Sept. 24, 1752.
Susanna, wf. of Joseph Jones,	June 27, 1753.
Stephen Freeman, Jr.,	Nov. 3, 1753.
Sarah,wf.of Abraham Ludlam,	Sept. 1, 1754.
Sarah, wf. of Samuel Munson,	" " "
Abigail. wf. of John Robards,	Apr. 11, 1756.
Stephen Mahurin,	July 3, 1757.
Timothy Riggs,	Sept. 4, "
Sarah, wf. of Timothy Peck,	" 3, "
Abigail, wf. of Isaac Pain,	Jan. 5, 1759.
Widow Rebecca Stockbridge,	" " "
Rachel, wf. of Uriah Cutler,	Sept. 6, 1761.
Widow Abigail Gilbard,	" " "
Sarah, wf. of Wm. Goodwin,	" " "
Stephen Munson,	Nov. 7, 1762.
Mary, wf. of Moses Prudden,	Sept. 2, 1764.
Ame, wf. of Joseph Lindsly,	" " "

(*Continued from page* 58.)

BAPTISMS.

——:o:——

1758.

June 18. Lorance Decker, child Job.

" 25. Benjn. Halsey & wf., ch. Ruth.

" " Isaac Tuttle & wf., ch. Isaac.

" " Philip Hathaway & wf., ch. Mary.

July 2. Thomas Coe & wf., ch. Stephen,

" 10. Seth Mahurin & wf. two youngest children, Bap. Rockaway.

Aug. 6. Joseph Pierson & wf., ch. Abraham.

" " Wido. Zervia Wines, ch. Loruhama.

" " Thomas Throop's wf., ch. Abigail.

" 13. Thomas Wilkerson on wf.'s accompt., ch. Mary.

" " Wm. Goodwin on wf.'s accompt., chn. Nance, Margere, Seth, John.

" 20. John Lindsly & wf., ch. John.

" " William Akeman & wf., ch. Jane.

" 27. Henry Primrose & wf., ch. James.

Sept. 17. Stephen Conkling & wf., ch. Mary.

" " Zophar Freeman & wf., ch. David.

" 24. Capn. Daniel Tuttle on wf.'s accompt., ch. Mary.

Oct. 8. William Brown & wf., ch. Uriah.

" 29. Matthias Burnet & wf., ch. Phebe.

" " Rob Arnold & wf., ch. Silvanus, born Sept. 21, 1758.

" " John Cole & wf., ch. Daniel.

Nov. 12. Matthew Fairchild & wf., ch. Rebecca.

Dec. 31. Joshua Ball & wf., ch. Phebe.

" " Thomas Tuttle & wf., ch. Caleb.

1759.

Jan. 5. Rebecca Stockbridge, ch. Phebe, her youngest.

" 21. John Mitchel & wf., ch. Benj., born Nov. 22, 1758.

Feb. 4. Abraham Hathaway & wf., ch. Jemima.

" 18. Abigail wf. of Constant Cooper, adult.

" " Phebe Wheler, adult.

" 25. Thomas Brandon & wf. Martha, two chn., William & Mary Ann.

" " Junia Lindsly, ch. Rachel.

Mar. 11. Tim. Mills & wf., ch. Phebe.

" 25. Moses Johnson & wf., chn. Mary & Eunice.

Apr. 15. Moses Prudden & wf., ch. Phebe.

" " James Frost, negro ch. Tubal.

Apr. 22. Benj. Coe & wf., ch. Jane.

" " Henry Gardiner & wf., ch. Ruth.

" " Sam'l Bayles, Junr. & wf., ch. Jemima.

" 29. Daniel Wick & wf., ch. William & servant ch. Hagar.

" " Phineas Fairchild & wf., ch. Sarah, Born Feb. 22, 1759.

May 8. Daniel Morris & wf., ch. Sarah.

" 12. Wid. Elizabeth Mott, ch. Ebenezer.

" 20. James Miller & wf., ch, Eleazar.

June 10. Joshua Geering, dult., & ch. Nance.

" " Seth Mahurin & wf., ch. Othiniel.

" " David Beeman & wf., ch. ——

" " Ephraim Burrel & wf., ch. ——

" 11. Jonathan Reeve & wf., ch. Jonathan.

" 24. Doc. Sam'l Tuthil & wf., ch. Sarah.

July 8. Petr. Dickerson & wf., ch. Nance.

" 15. Joshua Whitehead on wf.'s accompt., twins, Samuel & Isaac.

" 29. Deac. Matt. Lum & wf., ch. Sarah.

" " John Hunterdon & wf., ch. Symon.

Aug. 5. Abraham Campfield on wf.'s account, ch. Israel.

" " Willm. Bates & wf., ch. Martha.

Aug. 12. John Pierson & wf., ch. Mary.

" 19. Agnish ye wf. of Stepn. Lyon, chn. Joseph & David.

Sept. 2. John Fford, ch. John.

" 9. Jabesh Bears & wf., ch. John.

Oct. 1. John Robards & wf., ch. Silas.

" " Eleazer Hathaway & wf., ch. Theophilus.

" 7. Benjn. Bayles, Jun. & wf., ch. Robard.

" " Benj. Hathaway & wf., ch. Hannah.

" " Sam. Shipman & wf., ch. Phebe.

" " Moses Johnson & wf., ch. Rhoda.

" 14. The wid. of Charles Howell, ch. Mary, born July 28, 1759.

" " Shadrack Howard & wf., ch. Bethuel.

" " Adoniram Prudden & wf., ch. Elijah.

" 21. Capt. Dan'l Tuttle & wf., ch. Daniel.

" " John Burrell & wf., ch. Jemima.

" " Peter Norris & wf., ch. Mary.

" 28. Thomas Marigold on wf.'s accompt, ch. Samuel.

Nov. 4. Job Lorain on wf.'s accompt., chn. Sarah & Job.

(*To be Continued.*)

(*Continued from page 54.*)
MARRIAGES.
——:o:——
1772.

June 4. Icabod Johnson & Rhoda Headly.

" 25. Joseph Cathcart & Thankful Huntington.

Aug. 2. Joseph Lewis & Anne S. Johnes.

Sept. 8. Benjamin Suythard & Joanna Shaw.

" 20. Luke Devour, of Pepper Cotton & Elizabeth Masters,both of Harduston.

Oct. 4. John Cook & Jane Peer, both of Pequannock.

" 15. Daniel Baldwin & Margaret Wilson of Parsepaning.

" 22. John Lyon & Theodosia Fairchild.

" 25. Abraham Hudson & Abigail Hayward.

Nov. 4. John Wheler & Charity Stiles.

" 23. Asahel Shipman & Electa Riggs.

Dec. 3. John Perkhurst & Letitia Hathaway:

" 8. James Eddy & Miriam Wilkerson.

" " Moses Allen & Elisabeth Turner.

" 13. Jacob Johnson & Anne Veal.

" 21. Daniel Hall & Sarah Lace.

1773.

Jan. 18. Ralph Bridge & Catherine Rogers.

" 24. Silas Hathaway & Prudence Baldwin, of Rockaway, both.

" 25. Humphry Davenport & Elizabeth Erwin, of Pequanack, both.

Feb. 1. James Young, of Morris Co., and Elizabeth Lowraine, of Somersett.

" 17. Asher Fairchild & Martha Howell.

" 25. James Bullen & Phebe Primrose.

" " Caleb Howell & Rebecca Stiles.

Mar. 18. David Garrlgas & Abigail Loce.

" 21. James Cooper, of Roxbury & Mary Winnings, of this town.

" 23. Seth Gregory & Ruth Pierson,

April 22 Nathaniel Thompson & Hannah Pierson.

May 30: Benj. Freman, Junr., & Elizabeth Carter.

June 24. William Dote & Margeret Serren.

July 4. William Verguson & Jerusha Knapp.

Aug. 15. John Ward & Pamela Bridge.

" 16. William Ketchen & Eunice Robarts.

Sept. 5. Thomas Combs & Mary Johnson.

Sept. 8. Jonathan Fairchild & Sarah Howell.

Nov. 1. Dennis Comes, of Woodbridge, & Eunice Johnson.

" 21. Uriah Allen & Rachel Coe. •

" 22. Samuel Cob & Sarah Southard, both of Rockawny, false marriage—another husband.

Nov. 22. Josiah Ayrs, of Baskenridge & Clymene Conkling.

" 28. Daniel Smith & Joanna Gardiner.

Dec. 26. Samuel Morris & Joanna Woodruff.

1774.

Jan. 2. Job Allen & Mary Minton, of Rockaway, both.

" 26. Ephraim Castemore & Mary Whitehead.

" 27. Aaron Crane & Mary Hathaway.

" 30. John Pierson, of Rockaway, & Sarah Garragas.

" " Benj. Prudden & Eunice Baldwin.

Feb. 21. Abiel Wheeler & Sarah Dalrimple, Rockaway.

" 22. Ephraim Youngs & Phebe Cutler.

Mar. 7. Abraham Peer & Susanna Johnson, Rockaway.

" 9. Benj. Bridge & Elizabeth Hathaway.

" 13. Timothy Ward & Thankful Smith.

Apr. 19. Jesse Smith & Eunice Tingley.

May 16, Joshua Badger & Mary Hathaway, daughter of Philip.

" 20. William Bayles & Hannah Halsey.

June 15. Jonathan Ogden & Abigail Gardiner.

July 9. Samuel Merritt & Anna Garrigas.

" 10. Jabez Beach & Anne Ayrs.

" 20. Aaron Howell & Abigail Crane, widow.

" 25. Zerah Rolfe & Sibil Keen.

" 31. David Lee & Eunice Carter.

Aug. 1. Samuel Freeman & Sarah Crane.

" 28. Jacob Whitehead & Elizabeth Arnold.

Sept. 7. Abraham Day & Sarah Coe.

" 19. John Crane & Mary O'Harah.

Oct. 2. George King & Esther Dickenson.

" 17. Jeduthan Day & Phebe Wines.

" 25. Ezra Halsey & Sarah Johnson.

Nov. 2. Samuel Squire & Rhoda Kitchel.

" 29. Dan'l Prince Crane & Phebe Burnet.

531 married.

" 23. Col. Joseph Tuttle & Widow Isabel Drake.

(*To be continued.*)

(Continued from page 55.)

BILL OF MORTALITY,

1776.

Dec. 20. Captain Zenas Condict,* aet. 37, phrenzy.

" 21. George, servant of Peter Prudden, aet. 40, bilious fever.

" " Zervia, wife of Capt. Samuel Day,* act. 56, fever.

" 25. Isaac Brookfield,†* aet. 23, consumption.

" 30. James Gillespie, aet. 36, camp-fever.

" " Francis Casterline, aet. 68, black-jaundice.

" " Cæsar, servant of Ebenezer Condict, aet. 20, fever.

" 31. Rev. John Cleverly,* aet. 81, consumption.

1777.

Jan. 2. A child of Capt. Zenas Condict.

" 3. Ezekiel Day,* aet. 33, consumption.

" 4. Jerujah, wife of Henry Dow Trip, aet. 32, consumption.

" 5. Son of John Miller, aet. 19.

" 7. Benjamin, son of John Brookfield, Esq.,† aet. 15, fever.

" 11. Charity, widow of Benjamin Shipman,* aet. 81, old age.

" " Moses Prudden,* aet. 45, cholic.

" " Col. Jacob Ford, Jun., aet. 39, peripneumony. (Born Feb. 19, 1738. Ed.)

" " Martha, widow of Joshua Ball, aet. 55, small pox.

" " John Gwinup, aet. 28, fractured skull.

" 16. Peter, servant of Doct. Jabez Campfield,* aet. 76, old age.

" 19. Col. Jacob Ford, Sen.,* aet, 73, fever. (Born Apr. 13, 1704. Ed.)

" " Stephen Moore, aet. 39, consumption.

" 20. Cæsar, servant of Zachariah Fairchild, St. Vitus's dance.

" 21. Phœbe, wife of Benjamin Woodruff, aet. 36, consumption.

" 22. Esther, wife of Abiel Fairchild, aet. 35, consumption.

" 23. William Budd, aet. 45, inflammatory fever.

" 24. Gershom Hathaway, aet. 57, small-pox.

" " Nathaniel Lhomedieu; aet. 48, inflammatory fever.

Jan. 31. Widow of Nathaniel Lhomedieu, aet. 45, child-bed.

" " Ebenezer Winds, aet. 25, small-pox.

Feb. 1. David, son of James Losey, aet. 21, dysentery.

" 3. Sarah, wife of John Ward,† aet. 27, dysentery.

" " Frank, servant of Capt. Hallsey, fever.

" 3. Abraham, son of Uzal Tompkins,† aet. 2, fever.

" 4. Silas Hallsey,* aet. 73, fever.

" 6. Mary, widow of Thomas Bridge, aet. 70, fever.

" 7. Child of Mr. Kemper.

" " Mary, daughter of Matthias Burnet, aet. 3, dysentery.

" — Tom, servant of Deacon Burnet, aet. 70, pleurisy.

" 9. Richard Kinney, aet 60, fever.

" 11. Isaac Whitehead,* aet. 77, pleurisy.

" 16. Anna, daughter of Matthias Burnet, aet. 1, dysentery.

" 17. Jonathan Wilkison, aet. 38, putrid fever.

" " Joseph, son of Shubal Pitney, aet. 18, fever.

" " Elizabeth Whitehead, aet. 21, consumption.

" " Samuel, son of Eleazer Hathaway, aet. 13, small pox.

" 20. Eleazer Hathaway,* aet. 46, small pox.

" " Benoni, son of Eleazer Hathaway, aet. 5, small pox.

" " John, son of Eleazer Hathaway, aet. 1, small pox.

" " Servant Child of Eleazer Hathaway, aet. 2, small pox.

" " Child of Henry Dow Trip.

" " Joseph, son of Peter Norris, Jun., fits.

" " Sarah, wife of Constant Cooper, aet. 35, consumption.

" 21. Abraham Pierson,* aet. 70, pleurisy.

" 22. Mary, wife of Peter Metarr, aet. 42, small pox.

" 23. Robert, son of David Godden, aet, 6, dysentery.

" 24. Wife of Nicholas Comesau, aet. 50, small pox.

" 25. Phœbe, daughter of Waitstill Munson, aet. 19, small pox.

(To be continued.)

TRUSTEES' BOOK.

(Continued from page 56.)

Feb'y 9, 1784, at a meeting of the Trustees at Mr. Johnes's, present Mr. Condict, Mr. Conkling, Mr. Lindsly, Mr. Ford and Mr. Mills, agreed that the board cieling of the meeting house over head be Taken Down and a wall of Lime be put in its Stead and that the Side Cieling be painted. Also agreed that the Burying ground be put in fence with Boards, and appointed Mr. Lindsly & Mr. Mills a committee to doo the Same or Employ proper persons to do it. Also agreed to Draw Subscriptions to pay for the same,

Feb. 17, 1784.—Trustees met at the Minister's house, all present, agreed to Reconsider the matter of walling the meeting house overhead, and agreed to have the cieling overhead taken down and put up in a better manner and be painted. And ordered Mr. Fraderick King to pay to Samuel Huntington the Sum of Seven pounds and to Sara Winters the Sum of three pounds ten shillings of the parish money it being for Debts Due from Simon Huntington Dec. Mr. Mills Reported that he had Settled with Mr. Johnes Respecting his Sallary from a former Settlement in the year 1775 to the year 1780 Inclusive and found due to him for Said Six years Sallary £107,5,2 and that he had Delivered Lists of the Delinquents to the parish collectors according to order.

Trustees appointed Mr. Ford to provide and Set out 100 appletrees on the parsonage Land and this Bord will pay for the Same.

April 30, 1784.—Trustees met at the request of the president at Richard Johnsons, present Mr. Condict, Mr. Tuttle, Mr. Lindsly & Mr. Mills. Agreed and ordered Mr. Mills to prosecute in behalf of the Trustees those persons indebted on Subscriptions for purchasing a parsonage. Likewise those indebted to the parish by note.

Aug. 18, 1784.—Trustees met by the Request of the President at Mr. Johnes, present Mr. Condict, Mr. Conkling, Mr. Lindsly, Mr. Ford & Mr. Mills. Agreed to give Jonathan Ford an order on Capt. James Keen for the Sum of £3, 6, 8 of the parish money due to the Trustees from sd. Keen it being for 100 appletrees. The Trustees appointed Mr. Condict & Mr. Mills a committee to Settle with Mr. Fraderick King for the Repairs of the meeting house, Ringing the Bell, &c., and to pay the Ballance by giving order on those persons indebted to the parish by note or Subscription. Likewise to settle with Mr. Johnes Respecting his Sallary.

Nov. 23, 1784—At a meeting of the Trustees at the house of the minister, present Mr. Condict, Mr. Conkling, Mr. Tuthill, Mr. & Lindsly Mr. Mills. Agreed and appointed Nathan Howell, Frederick King & William Johnes to take care of the Steple, to guard it against the weather by Applying Sheet Lead, painted cloath, &c., as they Shall think best & this bord will pay for the same. the Trustees then at the Request of Mr. Nathan Howell agreed to Say what price he should have for Diging graves and Tolling the Bell for funerals, which was for Children under ten years old to be Seven Shillings & Six pence and for grown persons Eleven Shillings and three pence—the Bord then adjourned to 1st day of Dec. next to meet at this place at o'clock.

Dec. 1, 1784.—Trustees met pursuant to adjournment, all present but Mr. Ford. Agreed and appointed Deacon Allen to call on the Delinquents in Mr. Johnes' Sallary and urge them to pay of their arears or give notes for the Same, & that he shall make abatements at his Discretion and this Bord will pay him for his Services. Then agreed to purchase of Capt. Silas Howell the Land that Lies Common, Adjasant to his house for the purpose of Enlarging the publick parade and appointed Mr. Condict & Mr. Tuthill a Committee to Compleet the Buisness with Capt. Howell to take a Deed & pay him for the Same, the Sum of £25, 0, with the obligations in the hands of the Trustees the property of the parish. Then agreed to give of four years Interest on the obligations in the hands of the Trustees the property of the parish Such as have Layne through the Late War.

(To be continued.)

We are indebted to Hon. Edmund D. Halsey, Esq., for the valuable list begun on the third page of this number of the RECORD, of the Representatives of Morris County in the State Legislature. The list will be continued to the present time.

THE RECORD.

FIRST PRESBYTERIAN CHURCH, MORRISTOWN, N. J.

"This shall be Written for the Generation to Come."—Psalms 102 : 18.

| VOL. I. | SEPTEMBER, 1880. | NO. 9. |

(Printed with the approval of Session.)

THE RECORD

Will be printed and published monthly at Morristown, N. J. Terms, 50 cents per annum in advance; 75 cents after June.

Subscriptions will be received at the book-stores of Messrs. Runyon and Emmell, or through the mail, and may begin with the first number. ALL COMMUNICATIONS should be addressed to the

- EDITOR OF THE RECORD,
Lock box 44.   Morristown, N. J.
Entered at the Post Office at Morristown, N. J., as second class matter.

————:o:————

We again solicit the aid of our friends in correcting any mistakes or supplying any omissions in either of our lists, especially in the list of members which begins in the present number of the RECORD. Few can appreciate the amount of labor necessary to make this roll complete. First, the Sessional Books were read from the beginning of our church-history, and the names of members admitted to church-fellowship copied chronologically. Then for convenience of reference an alphabetical roll was needed. After this the Sessional Books were again read, and dismissions &c. noted. Then followed the great task of gathering some 3,000 names of persons deceased, not including those in "the Bill of Mortality." From these it was necessary to cull the names of the members of the church, that the dates of their death might be entered opposite their names in the membership-roll. Then followed the same work with the books of Evergreen Cemetery. It would be impossible to give one unfamiliar with this kind of work any adequate idea of the hundred sources of confusion which have furnished constant perplexity in the prosecution of this labor. We have done the best we could. It would be too much to

expect that no mistakes have been made. It has also been impossible to fill all the blanks. For the rest we must rely upon our friends. Bring out the old Bibles, the old diaries, the old family-trees, and give to THE RECORD in this good work of saving local history all the aid possible. If you have not time and patience to read them, hand them over to us. We will be responsible for their safe return.

Under Dr. Johnes's pastorate there were three lists of members.

1st. Of those whom he found in full communion when he came here in 1742, together with those who came afterwards from other churches.

This list is found on pages 12, 20 and 28.

2nd. Of the Half-Way Members, pages 28, 36, 44, 52 and 60,

Many of these half-way members became at a later date full members; and hence their names will appear again in the list which follows.

3rd. Of those who united with the church by the profession of their faith. This list begins on page 68 of the present issue.

WHO CAN TELL

The date of death or removal from town of the following persons :

	Joined the Church.
Sarah, w. of Abr. Ludlow,	Sept. 1, 1754.
Sarah, w. of Sam'l Munson,	" " "
Abigail, w. of John Robards,	Apr. 11, 1756.
Timothy Riggs,	Sept. 4, 1757.
Sarah, w. of Timo. Peck,	" 3, "
Abigail, w. of Isaac Pain,	Jan. 5, 1759.
Wid. Rebecca Stockbridge,	" " "
Rachel, w. of Uriah Cutler,	Sept. 6, 1761.
Wid. Abigail Gilbard,	" " "
Stephen Munson,	Nov. 7, 1762.
Mary, w. of Moses Prudden,	Sept. 2, 1764.
Jane, w. of Joseph Lindsley,	" " "

THE COLLEGE OF NEW JERSEY.

Or, as it is more popularly known, Princeton College, was chartered in 1746 by John Hamilton, acting governor of the colony. Rev. Jonathan Dickinson, pastor of the First Presbyterian Church of Elizabethtown, was its first President. At his death, Oct. 7, 1747, the students were removed from Elizabethtown to Newark, and placed under the care of Rev. Aaron Burr, who was chosen to succeed Mr. Dickinson as President. In 1757 the institution, then numbering about seventy students, was removed to Princeton.

Gov. Belcher made at this time a "generous donation of his library of books, with other valuable ornaments" to the College. Grateful for his liberality the trustees desired to name their first building, erected in 1757, in his honor. This honor was declined by the Governor; but the suggestion was added that it be called *Nassau Hall*, "to express the honor we retain in this remote part of the globe, to the immortal memory of the glorious King *William* the third, who was a branch of the illustrious House of Nassau; and who, under God, was the great deliverer of the British *nation* from those two monstrous furies, *Popery and Slavery*," &c. In accordance with this suggestion the Trustees resolved "that in all time to come," the building should be called Nassau Hall.

Princeton has received many munificent gifts. We doubt, however, if any have been more timely and helpful than the following which we copy from the last page of our earliest Records, and which shows the deep interest of the early inhabitants of this community in the cause of education.

SUBSCRIPTION FOR PRINCETON COLLEGE.

Morristown, Jan. 5th, 1769, the Trustees of the College of New-jersey having represented to the Presbyteries, that the interest of their capital was inadequate to the annual necessary expences of the College, The Presbyteries considering the necessity and importance of the object, are uniting their indeavours to increase said capital. And our Presbytery, viz., of New-york, the 18th of October agreed to open a subscription to exert ourselves on that head, which motion the members of our Ch. Session notwithstanding the publick expence now lying on them, do, both encourage it themselves, and recommend it to others—The subscription is as followeth—We whose names are under written do promise to pay or cause to be paid to the Treasurer of the College and to the use and benefit of the College the several sums affixed to our names Proc., &c.

	£	
Rev'd Tim. Johnes	9. 0. 0	
Jacob Ford, Esq'r	21.0.0	
Dea. Matthias Burnet	9. 0. 0	
Cap. Tim. Mills	6. 0. 0	
Elder Daniel Lindsley	3. 0. 0	
Abr. Ogden, Esq'r	3. 0. 0	
Elder Jno. Lindsley	3. 0. 0	
Joseph Wood	6. 0. 0	
Henry Gardiner	0.16.0	
Nathan Reeve	3. 0. 0	
John Ayres, Esq'r	9. 0. 0	
Thomas Kenney	3. 0. 0	
Will'm DeHart, Esq'r	3. 0. 0	
Thomas Morrell	4.10.0	
Jonas Phillips	4.10.0	
Isaac Pierson	3. 0. 0	
Jonathan Cheever	1. 0. 0	
Peter Condict	2.11.0	
Peter Prudden	2.11.0	
Moses Prudden	2.11.0	
Joseph Prudden	2.11.0	
Benjamin Pierson	9. 0. 0	
Samuel Tuthill, Esq'r	3. 0. 0	
Silas Condict	3. 0. 0	
Ezra Halsey, elder	12.0.0	
Samuel Robarts	3. 0. 0	
Augustine Bayles	3. 0. 0	
Wid. Phebe Wood	3. 0. 0	
Jonathan Stiles, Esq'r	1.15.0	
Cap. Benjamin Halsey	0.10.0	

140. 5. 0 Proc.

BENJAM'N LINDSLEY.

April 27, 1873. The Elders being met, Mr. Sergeant, the Treasurer of ye College receit for £140 Proc. was seen and acknowledged by the Elders and the overplush was allowed for incidental charges, testafied in behalf of ye Rest by   JACOB FFORD.

Sept. 29, 1787. Then presented to the Trustees of Nassau Hall for the education of poor and pious youth as followeth, viz:

Caleb Russell, Esq.	22 dol.	& 45 ninetieths
Joseph Lewis, Esq.	11 "	& 5 "
Silas Condict, Esq.	42 "	& 1 "
Icabod Cooper,	1 "	& 1 "
Dea. Gilbert Allen,	1 "	& 80 "
Phillip Lindsley,	3 "	& 66 "
Jonathan Dickerson, Esq.,	16 dol.	& 12 "
Col. Benont Hathaway,	3 "	& 30 "
John Mills,	9 "	& 2 "

£ 41. 3. 9

For which they received the thanks of the Board of Trustees.

Test, TIMO. JOHNES.

(*Continued from page* 50.)

REPRESENTATIVES OF MORRIS COUNTY IN THE STATE LEGISLATURE.

15th Legislature, 1790. Oct. 26, at Burlington.
Council, William Woodhull.
Assembly, Ellis Cook,
- Aaron Kitchel,
Jacob Arnold.
16th Legislature, 1791, Oct. 25.
Council, Ellis Cook.
Assembly, Silas Condict,
John Starke,
Hiram Smith.
17th Legislature, 1792, Oct. 23.
Council, Ellis Cook.
Assembly, Silas Condict, (speaker).
Hiram Smith
John Wurts.
18th Legislature, 1793, Oct. 22.
Council, Abraham Kitchel.
Assembly, Silas Condict, (speaker).
Aaron Kitchel,
David Welsh.
19th Legislature, 1794, Oct. 28.
Council, Abraham Kitchel.
Assembly, Silas Condict, (speaker).
Aaron Kitchel,
David Welsh.
20th Legislature, 1795, Oct. 27.
Council, Ellis Cook.
Assembly, John Starke,
David Thomson,
John Debow.
21st Legislature, 1796, Oct. 25.
Council, Abraham Kitchel.
Assembly, Silas Condict,
David Welsh,
John Cobb.
22d Legislature, 1797, Oct. 24.
Council, Abraham Kitchel.
Assembly, Silas Condict, (speaker).
David Welsh,
Aaron Kitchel.
23d Legislature, 1798, Oct. 23.
Council, Abraham Kitchel.
Assembly, Silas Condict,
William Corwin,
Cornelius Voorheese.
24th Legislature, 1799, Oct. 22.
Council, Abraham Kitchel.
Assembly, William Corwin,

24th Assembly Cornelius Voorheese,
William Campfield.
25th Legislature, 1800, Oct. 28.
Council, Abraham Kitchel.
Assembly, Cornelius Voorheese,
Silas Condict,
David Welsh,
26th Legislature, 1801, Oct. 27.
Council, David Welsh.
Assembly, Aaron Kitchel,
William Corwin.
27th Legislature, 1802, Oct. 26.
Council, David Welsh.
Assembly, Aaron Kitchel;
William Corwin,
Jonathan Ogden.
28th Legislature, 1803, Oct. 25.
Council, David Welsh.
Assembly, Aaron Kitchel,
William Corwin,
Jonathan Ogden.
29th Legislature, 1804, Oct. 23.
Council, David Welsh,
Assembly, Aaron Kitchel.
Jonathan Ogden,
Jesse Upson.
30th Legislature, 1805, Oct. 22.
Council, David Welsh.
Assembly, Jesse Upson,
Lewis Condict,
George Tucker.
31st Legislature, 1806, Oct. 28.
Council, David Welsh.
Assembly, Lewis Condict,
Jesse Upson,
Nicholas Neighbour.
32d Legislature, 1807, Oct. 27.
Council, Benjamin Ludlow.
Assembly, Lewis Condict,
Nicholas Neighbour,
Stephen Dod.
33d Legislature, 1808, Oct. 25.
Council, Benjamin Ludlow.
Assembly, Lewis Condict, (speaker).
Nicholas Neighbour,
Stephen Dod.
34th Legislature, 1809, Oct. 24.
Council, Bedjamin Ludlow.
Assembly, Aaron Kitchel,
Lewis Condict, (speaker).
Stephen Dod.
(To be continued.)

MEMBERS.

"THE NAMES AND·NUMBER OF THE PERSONS ADMITTED TO FULL COMMUNION BY
MY SELFE SINCE MY ORDÍNATION—WITH THE TIME OF THEIR ADMITION."

TIMO: JOHNES.

——:o:——

Names.	When Received.	When Dismissed or Died.
Benjamin Hathaway, Doc. .	June 26, 1743	April 21, 1762, aet. 63.
Samuel Bailey . . .	" " "	
John Perkis	" " "	
Mary Perkis (Ben.) . .	" " "	"Moved away."
Hannah Lindley (Da. of John Jr.)	" " "	
Elizabeth Johnes my Consort	" " "	Sept. 19, 1748, aet. 31.
Elizabeth Headley (Thomas) .	Dec. 28, "	
James Tompkins . . .	Feb. 24, 1744	"Moved away."
Sarah Fairchild (Mathew). .	Apr. 27, "	Jan. 6, 1750, aet. 32 y. 10 m.
Abraham Pierson . . .	Aug. 31, "	Feb. 21, 1777, aet. 70.
Peter Norris	" " "	"Moved away."
Eleanor Easton (Richard) .	" " "	Aug. 1, 1776, aet 78.
Jude, servant of Dea. Prudden .	" " "	
Deborah Fairchild (Zachariah)	" " "	Suspended May 27, 1765.
Zachariah Fairchild . .	Nov. 2, "	Suspended May 27, 1765.
Isaac Whitehead, Sr. . .	" " "	Feb. 11, 1777, aet. 77.
Mary Pierson (Abraham) .	" " "	Oct. 2, 1784, aet. 72.
Deborah Allerton (Thomas) .	" " "	"Moved away."
Thomas Alerton . . .	Jan. 11, 1745	Susp. June 29, 1752.
Sarah Freman (Stephen) . .	" " "	"Moved away."
Jacob Allerton . . .	May 10, "	" "
David Chitester . . .	July 5, "	" "
Abigail his sister . . .	" " "	" "
Rachel Stiles (John) . . .	" " "	" "
Rachel Samson (Samuel) .	Sept. 6, "	" "
David Gauden	Mrch 7, 1746	
Isaiah Wines (Winds) . .	" " "	Died Oct. 3, 1757.
Susanna Frost (John) . .	Oct. 24, "	
Phebe Baileys (Sam'l) . .	May 1, 1747	
Tabitha Frost (Daniel) . .	July 10, "	March 28, 1788, aet. 75.
Elisabeth Mott (Ebenezar) .	Sept. 25, "	"Moved."
Joseph Wood	Apr. 3, 1748	
Hannah Wood (Joseph) . .	" " "	Oct. 3, 1768, aet. 49.
Joseph Tichenor . . .	Sept. 2 1749	
Anne Holloway . . .	" " "	"Moved."
Samuel Hudson	May 25, 1750	"
—— Hudson (Samuel) . .	" " "	"
Thomas Wilkerson . . .	Feb. 17, 1751	"Moved." March 11, 1783, aet. 75.
Hannah Wilkerson (Thos.) .	Oct. 6, "	"
Daniel Lindley	July 7, 1752	Aug. 14, 1777, aet. 76 y. 6 m.
Grace Lindley (Daniel) . .	" " "	Sept. 12, 1777, " 68 y. 6 m.
Jonathan Reeve	Sept. 24, "	[aet. 70,
Zophar Gildersleeve . .	Oct. 15, "	Susp. Dec, 13, 1771, Died Aug. 28, 1776.
Mary Gildersleeve (Zophar) .	" " "	
Susannah Jones (Joseph) .	June 27, 1753	
Elizabeth Day (Samuel) . .	Aug. 29, "	Apr. 22, 1761, aet. 46.
Stephen Freeman, Junr. .	Nov. 3, "	

(To be continued.)

(Continued from page 61.)

BAPTISMS.
—:o:—

1759.
Nov. 11. Gideon Riggs & wf., ch. Rachel.
"   " John Lose, on wf.'s accmpt, ch.
Anne.
"   18. John Perkhurt & wf., ch. Daniel.
"   " Zophar Gildersleeve & wf., ch.
John.
"   25. Sam'l Lorain & wf., household—
Joanna, Moses & Samuel.
"   " James Losey, on wf.'s accompt,
household—Sarah, David, Phebe, Joanna.
Dec. 9. Stephen Freeman & wf., ch. Jehiel.
1760.
Jan. 3. Ebenezer Stiles & wf., ch. Hannah.
"   13. Benj. Pierson & wf., ch. Patience.
Born Nov. 24, 1758.
Feb. 10. Benj. Lindsly & wf., ch. Rachel.
"   21. John Hunterdon & wf., ch. Gilbard.
March 2. Benj. Halsey's ch. Sarah.
"   16. David Gauden & wf., ch. Providence.
"   23. Stephen Lyon, on wf.'s accompt,
ch. John.
April 13. Jonathan Wood, on wf.'s accompt,
ch. Joseph.
"   20. Stephen Hedges & wf., ch. Mary.
May 5. Benj. Prudden & wf., ch. Joseph.
"   11. Demas Lindsly & wf., ch. Joseph.
"   25. Rhoda Wheeler, adult. ⎱ Sisters.
"   " Sarah Wheeler,   " ⎰
"   " Daniel Howard & wf., ch. Jonathan.
"   " Essacar Huntington & wf., ch·
Lydia.
"   " James Keen & wf., ch. Sibbel.
June 8. Isaac Pain & wf., ch. John.
"   15. Philip Hathaway & wf., ch. Abigail.
"   22. Elizabeth Kenny, adult, and on
her accompt 2 children, John
and Jabish, which she had by
Thomas Kenny.
"   " Joseph Morris, on wf.'s accompt,
ch. Jonathan Ford.
"   " John Cole & wf., ch. Sarah.
"   29. Elizabeth, wf. of Wm. Loyd, ch.
William.
July ·13. Sam'l Bayles, Jun., and wf., ch.
Elias.

July 20. David Fairchild & wf., ch. Abijah.
Aug. 10. Dan'l Coe & wf., ch. Daniel.
"   " Bette Lyon, wid., ch. Jedidiah.
"   24. Joseph Person & ·wf., ch. Rachel.
"   " Isaac Tuttle, on wf.'s accompt, ch.
Daniel.
"   31. Juniah Lindsly & wf., ch. Junia.
Now of males Bap., 348; of
females, 354; total, 702; su-
periority of females, 6.
Sept. 5. Sarah, Philip Price's wf., adult.
"   " Philip Price & wf., Household,
Isaac, Philip, Samuel & Sarah.
Oct. 24. Samuel Arnold & wf., ch. Phebe.
Nov. 2. John Lindsly & wf., ch. David.
"   12. Humi, wf. of Dan. Camel, ch.
Daniel.
Dec. 14. Christopher Woods & wf., ch. Ra-
chel, born Sept. 15, 1760.
1761.
Jan. 4. Zophar Freeman & wf., ch. Phebe.
"   18. Silas Day & wf., ch. Rebecca.
"   25. James Miller & wf., ch. Ichabod.
"   " Eleazar Lindsly & wf., ch. Samuel.
"   " Thomas Coe & wf., ch. Betse.
"   " Thomas Throop & wf., ch. William.
"   " Constant Cooper, on his wf.'s ac-
compt, ch. David.
Feb. 5. Alexander Kermicle & wf., ch.
John.
"   15. Alexander Ralston & wf., ch.
James.
M'rch 1. Samuel Mills & wf., ch. Daniel.
"   " Elijah Person & wf., ch. Jane.
"   22. Sam. Lose or Lore & wf., ch. Eliz-
abeth.
"   " Job Lore, on his wf.'s accompt, ch.
Hannah.
"   29. Joseph Youngs, on his wf. Sarah's
accompt. ch. Joanna.
"   " David Fairchild & wf., ch. Rhoda.
"   " Wm. Akeman, on wf.'s accompt.
ch. Hannah.
Apr. 19. Benjamin Coe & wf., ch. Elizabeth.
"   " John Ford & wf,, ch. David.
"   " Daniel Morris & wf., ch. Phebe.
"   " Joseph Stiles, Junr. & wf., ch.
George.
May 3. Cap. Dan. Tuttle, on wf.'s accompt,
ch. William.
"   " Rob. Arnold & wf., ch. Betse.
"   " Benjamin Lindsly & wf., ch. Joseph.
Born April 1, 1761.
"   10. Philip Price & wf., ch. Edward.
(To be continued.)

(Continued from page 69.)

MARRIAGES.

—:o:—

1774.

Dec. 8. Jedidiah Orsborn & Abigail Stockbridge.

"   " Bezaleel Orsborn & Elizabeth Hill.

" 11. Daniel Freman & Mary Pollard.

" 28. Jonathan Pierson & Sarah Ferver.

1775.

Jan. 2. Abijah Cutler & Dinah Lee.

" 5. William Hamilton & Elizabeth
Rogers.

" 7. David Tredwell & Anne Loce.

" 12. Simeon Hayward Eunice Rogers.

" 24. George Mills & Mary Freeman.

" 26. Peter Ferver & Susanna Guierin.

Feb. 1. Nathan Guierin & Abigail Conger.

" 27. Philip Morris & Mary Flint, widow.

Mar. 2. Roberd Roff & Phebe Cooper.

" 26. Benjamin Coe & Margaret Beegle.

" " Josiah Tingley & Diademia Hazel.

" " John Lyon & Rachel Reeve.

" 30. David Pierson & Bathiah Hallock.

July24. Silas Gildersleeve & Sarah Woodruff.

Aug. 3. John Tuttle, Jun., & Mary Pitney.

" 10. Joseph Canliffe & Phebe Ayres.

Sept.3. Joseph Miller & Mary Johnson.

" " David Lawrence & Mary Burnet.

" " Samuel Broadwell & Mary Lindsley.

" 7. David Fithen (?) & Phebe Mills.

Oct.22 James Youngs & Ruth Halsey.

Nov 8. Samuel Minthorn & Margaret Crane.

" 14. Benjamin Fowler & Mary Cammel,
widow.

" 22. Jonathan Stiles, Jun., & Sarah Tuthill.

Dec. 31 John Harporee & Elizabeth Easton.

1776.

Jan. 10. Clement Wood & Sarah Canfield.

Feb. 21. Rev. Jos. Grover & Sarah Howell.

" 26. Nathan Arnold & Eliz Freman.

" 28. Joseph Hallsey & Jerusha Wood.

Mar. 20. John Beach & Sarah Chever.

Apr. 4. Richard Southerd & Phebe Prudden.

" 6. John Knowland & Mary Curtain.

May 2. Stephen Conkling & Abigail
Mitchel.

" 6. Daniel Tichenor & Anne Condict.

" 26. Hugh McConnel & Susanna Dil-
rimple.

May 30. Nehemiah Mills & Amy Hedges.

July 24. Amos Young & Sarah Mott, } Han-
"   " Joseph Kitchell and Jane } over.
Young.

" 28. John Tucker & Anne Treadwell.

Nov.28. John Crane & Catharine Davis.

1777.

Jan. 27. John Holden & Hannah }
Allibe. } Sol-
Feb. 6. Will. McCormick & } diers.
Dranna Gramer.

Mar. 27. Jacob Longhals & Martha } Soldier.
Rhoderick. }

Apr. 10. Codstant Cooper & Phebe Vander-
hoof.

" 11. Cap'n Jonas Simmons & Elizabeth
Kenny.

" 13. John Beach & Jane Akeman.

" 14. Abraham Day & Deborah Wines.

" 15. William Rogan, soldier, and Sarah
Greer.

May 4. Doc. Lewis Dunham & Jane Tuthill.

" 5. Benjamin Freeman & widow Esther
Marsh.

" 18. Matthew Rainer & Lotte Mass-
chalk.

" " David Walker & Elizabeth Ludlam.

" " Robert Day & Esther Wines, widow.

" 22. Keley Cutter & Hannah Marsh.

July 3. Ephraim Lindsley & Martha Gobell.

" " Nathaniel Coleman & Nancy Evans
Smart.

" 10. James Gardiner, soldier, and Nance
Burn.

Aug. 13. Ezra Brown & Nance Guiering.

" 23. John Pipes & Mary Morris.

Sept. 4. David Moor & Rachel Haden.

596 married to ye date.

Nov. 18. Sussex (?) Negro of Mr. Phenix &
Mary, negro of Mr. Doty by
their master's consent.

" 20. Vinson Guerin & Azuba Brown.

" 25. Nicholas Comesay & Miriam Smith.

Dec. 11. Silvanus Loree & Hannah Loree.

" 17. Zophar Hathaway & Elenor Carter.

1778.

Jan. 1. Samuel Frost & widow Sarah
Tuttle.

" 4. Peter Meter & widow Abigail
Hathaway.

" 4. Wm. Hambleton & Bette Hathaway.

(To be continued.)

(*Continued from page* 68.)

BILL OF MORTALITY.

1777.

Feb. 26. Waitstill Munson, aet. 47, small pox.

" " Samuel, son of Waitstill Munson, aet. 17, small pox.

" 27. Moses, son of Waitstill, Munson, aet. 4, small pox.

" " James Brookfield,* aet. 35, small pox.

" 28. Sarah, daughter of Joseph Youngs, aet. 4, putrid fever.

" " Ned, servant of Joseph Youngs, aet. 12, fever.

Mch. 1. Sarah, wife of John Scott, aet. 76, fever.

" " Widow Isabella Drake,* aet. 67, small pox.

" 2. Phœbe, wife of Jeduthun Day, aet. 27, fever.

" 3. Jonathan Carter, aet. 45, small pox.

" 4. Massey, wife of Jonathan Carter, aet. 41, small pox.

" 5. Child of Jonathan Carter, aet. —, small pox.

" " Jonathan Hinds, aet. 44, small pox.

" 10. Abel Tomkins, aet. 36, inflammatory fever.

" 20. Elizabeth, daughter of Dr. Timothy Johnes, aet. 4, putrid fever.

" 23. Shadrach Hildreth, aet. 19, putrid fever.

" 24. Dorcas, wife of Zebedee Brown, aet. 50, child-bed fever.

" " Ebenezer Howell, aet. 66, small pox.

" 25. Captain Samuel Day, aet. 63, small pox.

" " Child of Squire Lum, aet. 2, fever.

" 26. Abigail, widow of Silas Hallsey,* aet. 60, fever.

" " Child of Matthew Jennings, aet. —, small pox.

" 30. Wife of Benjamin Freeman, aet. 60, small pox.

Apr. 2. Child of Joseph Wood, aet. —.

" " Elizabeth, daughter of Peter Norris, Jun., aet. —, small pox.

" 3. Colonel Ebenezer Condict, aet. 41. small pox.

Apr. 5. Phœbe, wife of Nathan Turner, aet. 35, small pox.

" " Child of Nathan Turner, aet. —, small pox.

" 7. Jabez Beers, aet. 55, small pox.

" " Susanna, daughter of Hezekiah Stibbens, aet. 2, small pox.

" 8. Anne, wife of Caleb Fairchild, Esq.* aet. 86, fever.

" " Andrew Joline Whitehead, aet. 45, small pox.

" 9. Silas, son of Jeduthun Day, aet. —, small pox.

" 10. Lois, wife of Daniel Bishop,* aet. 36, small pox.

" 14. Ezra Fairchild, aet. 43, small pox.

" " Hannah, wife of Epenetus Beach, aet. 31, small pox.

" " Daniel Gard,†* aet. 70, sudden.

" " Mary, daughter of Epenetus Beach, aet. 1, small pox.

" 16. David Ogden, aet. 65, small pox.

" 29. John Ayres, Esq.* aet. 57, small pox.

" 20. William, son of Joseph Youngs, aet. 20, putrid fever.

" " Abigail Conkling, aet. 35, consumption.

" 21. Peter Prudden,* aet. 55, small pox.

" 23. Mehitable, Relict of Benjamin Campfield, aet. 62, putrid fever.

" 24. Child of David Gardner, aet. —, fits.

" " Abraham, son of Epenetus Beach, aet. —, small pox.

" 28. Ruth, wife of Seth Gregory, aet. 42, small pox.

" 30. Phœbe, wife of Ichabod Cooper,* aet. 32, small pox.

" " Sarah, daughter of Peter Ayres, aet. —, small pox.

" " Child of Capt. John Lindsley, aet. —, small pox.

" " Child of Demas Ford, aet. —, small pox.

May 3. Rebeckah Turner, aet. 20, small pox.

" " Caleb Fairchild, Esq.* aet. 84, small pox.

" 6. Rebeckah, daughter of Hur Osborn, aet. 15, small pox.

" 13. Lydia, widow of William Crane, aet. 23, small pox.

(*To be continued.*)

(Continued from page 64.)

TRUSTEES' BOOK.

——:o:——

March 23, 1785, Trustees met at the Request of the President at Capt. Howell's all present Deacon Allen Reported that he had called on the Delinquents in Mr. Johnes Sallary according to the Directions of the Trustees and had taken Notes to the amount of £140, 18, 6 and had received cash to the amount of £1, 6, 3 and that he had spent in doing said Business 9 1-2 days for which Service he charges 7 s. per day amounting to £3, 6, 5——the Trustees then proceeded to take a Deed of Capt. Silas Howell for a Small Lot of Land for the purpose of Enlarging the Publick parade on the Green and paid him the Consideration the Sum of £25, o by an order on James Keen for the Sum of £20, o, o, and an order on Benoni Hatheway for £5, o, o—and Likewise gave an order to sd. Silas Howell for £4, 7, o —due to him for Paying Timothy Humbervil for Ringing the Bell &c., the above sums to be paid out of the money belonging to the parish, due from said Capt. Keen & Col. Hatheway.

June 30, 1785.—Trustees met at the Request of of the President at Capt Howell's present Mr. Condit, Mr. Conkling, Mr. Lindsly and Mr. Mills.

Mr. Condit and Mr. Mills Reported that they had Settled with the Rev. Doct. Johnes respecting his Sallary as follows:

Settlement by Doct. Johnes & Committe of Trustees.

Agreeable to appointment of the Trustees Mr. Condit and Mr. Mills waited on Doctor Johnes and Delivered the notes obtained of the parishoners amounting to £141, 13, 3, having gone through the Rates and Subscriptions of the Doctor's Sallary for the Several years of 1775, 1776, 1777, 1778, 1779, 1780, 1781, 1782 & 1783 their appeared to be Due to the Doctor £19, 11, 1 agreeable to his offer to the Trustees the Doctor made an abatement of a half years Sallary, viz. £60 We then Revised the five first years of the said time and Canceled of the poor & Such as appeared too high in the Rate £24, o, 1 including the Notes of the widow Coe Solomon Brown Ashael Henmon and Stephen Person there then Remained of Said gratuity £16, 8, 10 which at the Request

of the Committe the Doctor agreed to Take out of the four Remaining years Viz. 1780, 1781, 1782 and 1783 by Canceling or abateing Such as he Should Judge most Needy or unable to pay, and finally to take the Rates and Subscriptions of the Said Several years and to Discharge the parish from any Further Demands for his Sallary for any time previous to the Sallary for the year 1784 as witness our hands this 26 day of March, 1785.

> TIMO. JOHNES
> SILAS CONDICT
> JOHN MILLS

Trustees agreed that Mr. Johnes Should Employ Some person to clear out the Ditches in the Parsonage medow and this Bord will pay for the same. The Trustees Likewise ordered Mr. Mills to pay the old paper money in his hands belonging to the parish to Mr. Frederick King for the purpose of Repairing the meeting house Ringing the Bell &c.

Jan. 10, 1787.—Trustees met at the Request of the President at the house of Daniel Hallsey. Present Mr. Condict, Mr. Conkling, Mr. Lindsly, Mr. Ford and Mr Mills— Trustees appointed Mr. Mills to give orders to Mr. Nathan Howell on James Smith contribution Treashurer Quarterly for his Salary for Ringing the bell &c., at the rate of Seven pounds per year—And that he should Likewise give to Jeduthan Day an order on Said Treasurer for the Sum of £0, 17, 6 for service done to the clock Some years ago— Trustees appointed Mr. Condict and Mr. Mills a Committe to Settle with Mr. Johnes Respecting his Salary and Present a list of the Delinqnents to Deacon Allen and Desire him to call on them to Discharge the Same and this Bord will pay him for his Services and if Deacon Allen refuse the Committe do Employ some other person——

Trustees Appointed Mr. Lindsly and Mr Ford a Committe to Repair the Meeting House to put the cieling in order and paint the Same——

Trustees Appointed Mr. Condict to Draw a Subscription for the purpose of raising a Revenue in Publick Securities for the Benefit of the parish. Agreed that Mr. Ford Should take of the Chestnut timber on the Parsonage wood Lot So far as the other Timber is Cut and Account to this Bord for the Same.

(To be continued.)

THE RECORD.

FIRST PRESBYTERIAN CHURCH, MORRISTOWN, N. J.

"THIS SHALL BE WRITTEN FOR THE GENERATION TO COME."—Psalms 102 : 18.

VOL. I.　　　　　OCTOBER, 1880.　　　　　NO. 10.

(Printed with the approval of Session.)

THE RECORD

Will be printed and published monthly at Morristown, N. J. Terms, 50 cents per annum in advance; 75 cents after June.

Subscriptions will be received at the book-stores of Messrs. Runyon and Emmell, or through the mail, and may begin with the first number. ALL COMMUNICATIONS should be addressed to the

EDITOR OF THE RECORD,

Lock box 44.　　　Morristown, N. J.

Entered at the Post Office at Morristown, N. J., as second class matter.

———:o:———

Below will be found a sermon of the Rev. Timothy Johnes, D.D.; the first, we believe, which has appeared in print. It is, as will be seen, a skeleton. His sermons were never written in full. To aid our readers we annex

A KEY TO CONTRACTIONS.

Wo—Who.
Wll—Will.
Wn—When.
Y'—This.
Wh—Out—Without.
Wy—Why.
Sll—Shall.
Wt—What.
Wld—Would.
Ym—Them.
Yr—Their—There.
Yt—That.
Yr—Your.
Yos—Thou.
Yee—Thee.
Ny—They.
Yee—Thee.
Ye—The.
Sld—Should.
Wh—With.
Yn—Than.
Ym—Selves—Themselves.

Doc—Doctrine.
Ev—Every.
W—Were.　Ws—Was.
F—For.
Sa—Said.
Yt—Fore—Therefore.
L—Lord.
X—Christ.　Xns—Christians.

SERMON BY REV. TIMO. JOHNES, D.D.

PREACHED AUG. 27, 1775:

"Joshua 7:18.—And he brought his household man by mail; and Achan ye son of Carmi, ye son Zabdi, ye son of Zerah of ye tribe of Judah, was taken.

Doc. yt secret sins make way for open and awful punishments.

1. Show wt is meant by secret sins.
2. Whence men seek secrecy for yr sins.
3. Ye great absurdity of so doing.
4. Prove ye doc.

1. Not only such sins as men especially conceal, but such as ny wld not commit if ny could not flatur ym selves ny sld conceal— ye hope and prospect of secrecy is ye great temptation to it, together with wicked propensities of ye heart such as secret neglect of duty in ye closet—of publick worship— or living in infidelity and not having God in all yr thoughts; and yet wld not be content wthout some form or appearance of religion —a man wld not live wthout Family Prayer, under a visi-profession if his conduct ws open before all—such, also, as theft and lying—as Anthanias such, also as family quarrels and contentions in ye house— such, also, as fornication and adultery— ye eye of ye adulterer waits for twilight, saying, no eye sll see me and ye morning is to ym as ye shadow of death—if one know ym ny are in ye terror of ye shadow of death—Job 24, 15, 17. So all soul idolatry could not be practiced if known,

it is an affront to subjection ye of it—
Ezekiel 12. So man has yos seen we
ye actions ye house of Israel do in ye
dark ev man in ye house of his imagery for
ny say. ye Lord seeth us not—so ny set up
Idols in yr heart—such, also, as flying from
duty—as Jonah.

2. When men seek secrecy f yr sins because ny are Atheists, and I don't believe yr
are any greater Atheists in ye world yn ys yt
habitually practice secret sins, if I had beheld
ye sun or moon etc., I sld have denied ye
God yt is above—Job 31, 26:28. And ny say
how doth God know—Psa. 73:11 and 139, 9:10
If I take ye wings of ye morning—
ye fear of man.

From ye odious nature of sin, it cannot
bear ye light—every one yt doeth evil—Jno.
3:20—especially some sins such as theft and
lying—all kinds of uncleanliness—indeed
such is ye vile nature of sin yt men must be
amazingly hard and impious yt do not in
some way cover its malignity and palliate it
—Adam's fig-leaf.

3. Ye great absurdity of secrecy in sin.
1. God created all—nothing can be hid—
sll ye thing framed say of him yt made it, he
hath no understanding—Isa. 29:16.

2. Upholds all.

3. Governs all—He rules by his power—
for ever, his eyes behold ye nations, let not
ye rebellious exalt ymselves—Psa. 66:7.

4. He has his scouts and witnesses alway
at hand—conscience, I mean—and if our
heart condemn, &c.

5. God knows our thoughts yt are more
secret yn actions—Psa. 139:2. Yos under-
standest my thoughts afar off.

6. God has discovered his knowledge of
ye most secret actions—Achan—David's
adultery—"yos didst it secretly, but, I wll
do it before all Israel and before ye sun"—
So Daniel calls him the revealer of secrets
—2:28.

7. He is to be the final Judge of all nations, ytfore must be acquainted wth all secrets—so he wll Judge the secrets of men by
Jesus Christ, and bring every secret thing
into judgement—Ecc. 12:14.

4. Prove ye doc. yt secret sins make way
for open and awful judgements—

1. Because secret sins pave ye way to
apostasy—sins do not rise to greatest
height at once, especially under a good

eduation or faithful ministry—like the
cloud Elijah saw.

2. God has threatened it and his word sll
not fall to ye ground—and be sure ye sin wll
find you out—Num. 32:23—an adequate punishment.

3. From ye nature of sin—ye designs of
Satan—sin is but ye fuel for a dreadful flame
like fire under ground yt anon bursts forth
wth terrible noise and destruction.

4. From example—strongest of evidence
—so Achan discovered to all Israel and destruction to himself—wy did he not fly the
lot? Joseph's br.: Gehazi secretly told a
lie ws openly struck with inveterate leprosy.
I have read of one Bassus, a murderer, wo
fancied ye chimney birds chattered out ye
sentence—"Bassus killed a man," so confessed—and ye know ye case of David's
adultry. Because yr is a day appointed to
discover and judge secret sins and villanies,
Luke 8, 17. Nothing but wt sll be made
known. Some yr fore sll rise to shame and
everlasting contempt. Psa. 90, 8, yos hast
set our iniquities before yee, our secret sins
in ye light of yr countenance.

Imp.—see how this sld caution us against
all sin and secret yt leads to others. God
beholds! and with detestation every secret
sin, puts his patience to great trial, endures
wth much longsuffering ye vessels of wrath,
registers all and one day will make you
see. I will set ym in order before yee. Psa.
50, 21, Yea, make all ye world see for he
wll make known the hidden council of ye
heart. How dreadful the case of open sinners yt declare yr sin as Sodom and seek
not a cover—drunkards, profane swearers,
Sabbath breakers, ungodly yt glory in yr
shame.

Wonderful patience of God yt bears wth
such a world of wickedness, secret and
open: wonder ye world stands, tis for X
sake: w' it not yt ye Lord had left us a rem-
nant we had been as Sodom. Isa. 1, 9.

How strong ye subject recommends virtue,
probity and sincerity, ye great guards
against secret and open sins; certainty of a
judgment day; some men's sins are open
before, others follow after.

Exhort Xns to live near to God and duty;
keep conscience clean and tender; sinners
to awaken to repentance; you think no
danger: always in danger out of X.

(*Continued from page* 67.)

REPRESENTATIVES OF MORRIS COUNTY IN THE STATE LEGISLATURE.

—:o:—

35th Legislature, 1810, Oct. 23.
Council, Benjamin Ludlow.
Assembly, Stephen Dod.
Jeptha B. Munn,
Nicholas Mandeville.

36th Legislature, 1811, Oct 22.
Council, Benjamin Ludlow.
Assembly, Stephen Dod.
Jeptha B. Munn,
Mahlon Dickerson.

37th Legislature, 1812, Oct 27.
Council, Benjamin Ludlow.
Assembly, Stephen Dod,
Jeptha B. Munn,
Mahlon Dickerson.

38th Legislature, 1813, Oct. 26.
Council, Benjamin Ludlow.
Assembly, Mahlon Dickerson,
Leonard Neighbour,
Nicholas Mandeville.

39th Legislature, 1814, Oct. 25.
Council, Benjamin Ludlow.
Assembly, Jeptha B. Munn.
David Thompson, Jr.
Nicholas Mandeville.

By act of Legislature approved Feb'y 10, 1815, (P. L. 11) Morris County was allowed four representatives in the Assembly instead of three.

40th Legislature, 1815, Oct. 24.
Council, Jesse Upson.
Assembly, David Thompson, Jr.
Nicholas Mandeville,
Benjamin Condit,
Ezekiel Kitchell.

41st Legislature, 1816, Oct 22.
Council, Jesse Upson.
Assembly, David Thompson, Jr.
Ezekiel Kitchell,
Samuel Halliday,
Benjamin Condit.

42d Legislature, 1817, Oct. 28.
Council, Jesse Upson.
Assembly, David Thompson, Jr.
Samuel Halliday,
John S. Darcy,
Benjamin McCurry.

43d Legislature, 1818, Oct. 27.
Council, Jesse Upson, (Vice President.)
Assembly, David Thompson, Jr., (Speaker.)
Samuel Halliday,
John S. Darcy,
William Brittin.

44th Legislature, 1819, Oct. 26.
Council, Jesse Upson, (Vice President.)
William Brittin,
Benjamin Condit,
David Thompson, Jr. (Speaker.)
Silas Cook.

45th Legislature, 1820, Oct. 24.
Council, Jesse Upson, (Vice President.)
Assembly, David Thompson, Jr., (Speaker.)
William Monro,
Silas Cook,
Benjamin Smith,

46th Legislature, 1821, Oct. 26,
Council, Jesse Upson, (Vice President.)
Assembly, David Thompson, Jr. (Speaker.)
William Brittin,
Benjamin McCurry,
William Monro.

47th Legislature, 1822, Oct. 22.
Council, Jesse Upson, (Vice President.)
Assembly, William Brittin,
David Thompson, Jr., (Speaker.)
Ebenezer F. Smith,
Benjamin McCurry.

48th Legislature, 1823, Oct. 28.
Council, Silas Cook.
Assembly, George K. Drake,
William Brittin,
William Monro,
Ebenezer F. Smith.

49th Legislature, 1824, Oct 26.
Council, Silas Cook.
Assembly, William Brittin,
Benjamin McCurry,
George K. Drake,
John Scott.

(*To be continued.*)

(Continued from page 68.)

MEMBERS.

[The third column on this page is the work of the RECORD. Information which will lead to the correction of any mistake, or the filling of any blank, will be thankfully received.—ED.]

—:o:—

Names.	When Received.	When Dismissed or Died.
Phebe Mills (Timothy)	July 2, 1754	May 4, 1808, aet. 86.
Sarah Ludlam (Abraham)	Sept. 1, "	
Sarah Munson (Samuel)	" " "	" Moved away."
Matthias Burnet	July 7, 1755	Oct. 18, 1783, aet. 60.
Stephen Conklin	" " "	Sept. 8, 1791, aet. 70.
Hannah Halsey (Ezra)	" " "	Oct. 26, 1776, aet. 33.
Rebecca Primrose (Henry)	" " "	Sept. 13, 1798, aet. 80.
Abigail Robards (John)	April 11, 1756	
Abigail Johnson (John)	July 4, "	June 4, 1793, aet. 85.
Stephen Mahurin	" 3, 1757	
Mary Burnet (Matthias)	" "	Dec. 24, 1782, aet. 59.
Timothy Riggs	Sept. 4, "	" Moved away."
Kezia Johnes, my consort	" " "	Nov. 2, 1794, aet. 79.
Sarah Peck (Timothy)	" 3, 1758	
Abigail Pain (Isaac)	Jan. 5, 1759	" Moved."
Rebeckah Stockbridge, wido.	" " "	
Hannah Lindley (Junia)	Aug. 19, "	~~Dec. 8, 1775, aet. 38.~~
Rachel Cutler (Uriah)	Sept. 6, 1761	
Abigail Gilbard wido.	" " "	
Sarah Goodwin (William)	" " "	" Moved away."
Elizabeth Reeve, wido.	Nov. 1, "	March 12, 1768, aet. 46.
Stephen Munson	Nov. 7, 1762	" Moved away."
Caleb Munson	" " "	Feb. 25, 1815, aet. 80.
Dorcas Eastoll	" " "	Sept. 23, 1784. aet. 58.
Gilbard Allen	Mch. 4, 1763	Jan. 6, 1816, aet. 80.
Elizabeth Allen (Gilbard)	" " "	Jan. 10, 1816, aet. 79.
These, the sweet fruites of yt wonderful effusion of God's adorable Grace, began on our Sacramental Day, July 1, 1764.		
Shadrack Howard	Sept. 2, 1764	Oct. 21, 1789, aet. 65.
Silas Condict	" " "	Sept. 6, 1801, aet. 63.
Joseph Prudden, Junr.	" " "	March, 20, 1816, aet. 87.
Moses Prudden	" " "	Jan. 11, 1777, aet. 45.
Mary Prudden (Moses)	" " "	
Joseph Lindsly	" " "	Oct. 8, 1822, aet. 87.
Anne Lindsly (Joseph)	" " "	
Nathaniel Peck	Nov. 1, "	March 28, 1782, aet. 40.
Mary Peck (Nathaniel)	" " "	Oct. 25, 1821, aet. 78.
Joseph Condict	" " "	Aug. 8, 1776, aet. 48.
Zophar Freman	" " "	Dec. 15, 1810, aet. 83.
Eleazar Hathaway	" " "	Feb, 20, 1777, aet. 46.
David Fairchild	" " "	Sept. 1, 1807, aet. 73.
Jabez Condict	" " "	Nov. 22, 1804, aet. 65 y., 9 m., 14 d.
Boys Prudden	" " "	" Moved."
Isaac Prudden	" " "	June 22, 1798, aet. 60.
John Prudden	" " "	" Moved."

(To be continued.)

(Continued from page 89.)

BAPTISMS.

——:o:——

1761.

June 7. Henery Gardiner & wf., ch. John.
" 14. Thomas Tuttle & wf., ch. Silvanus.
" 21. Absolam Bedell & wf., ch. David.
" " Jonathan Hathaway & wf., ch. Nathaniel.
" " Robard McCalve, on his wife's accompt, ch. Mary.
July 5. Abraham Campfield & wf., ch. Hannah.
" 12. Samuel Tuthill, Esq., & wf., ch. Theodorus.
" " Eleazar Hathaway & wf., ch. Betse.
" 26. Gilbard Ludlum & wf., Household —Ezekiel, Ziba & Stephen.
Aug. 2. Moses Prudden & wf., ch. Mary.
" 17. Gilbard Allen & wf. Elizabeth, adult, & ch. Abigail.
" " Timothy Mills & wf., ch. Sarah.
" " Joseph Cundit & wf., chn. Zenas and Rebecca.
" " Nathaniel Cundit & wf., ch. Benjamin.
" 30. Stephen Conkling & wf., ch. Isaac.
Sept. 6. Abraham Hathaway & wf., ch. Thomas.
Octl 11. John Mitchell & wf., ch. Luce, Born Sept. 4, 1761,
" 18. Tophat Byram, twins Rebecca & Elizabeth.
Sussex County. George McKenne, ch. Archibald
Laurance Decker, ch. Eunice.
Daniel McKenne, ch. Hannah.
Philip Bovee, ch. Philip,
John Loder, ch. John.
Nov. 1. Benj. Hathaway & wf., ch. Abigail,
" 22. Joshua Ball, on wf.'s accompt, ch. Jemima.
" " John Lose, Jun., on wf.'s accompt, ch. Stephen.
" 29. William Brown & wf., ch. Phebe.
Dec. 6. James McKey, ch. Robard.
" 20. Ebenezer Stiles & wf., ch. Daniel.
" " Shadrack Howard & wf., ch. Seruiah.
" 27. John Perkhurst & wf., ch. Ruth.
" " Joseph Cundict & wf., ch. Jemima.

1762.

Jan. 1. David Gauden & wf., ch. William.
" 17. Moses Johnson & wf., ch. Ruth.
" " Sary Nichols, adult.
" " Stephen Norris & wf., Household Shadrack, Born Mar. 28, 1756, Bethuel Born Oct. 26, 1758, Libeus & Thaddeus Born Feb. 23, 1760,
Feb. 7. James Keen & wf., ch. Elizabeth.
" 14. Matt'w Fairchild & wf., ch. Mehitabel.
" " Philip Hathaway & wf., ch. David.
March 7. Sarah Freeman, Wid., ch. Stephen.
" " Silas Day & wf., ch. Jonathan.
" " Humi Cammel, on her accompt, ch. Catharine.
" 28. Jabish Bears & wf., ch. Henry.
Apr. 5. Stephen Lyon, on wf. accompt, ch. Mary.
" 11. Doc. Goold on wf.'s accompt ch. Ame Bruister.
" " Peter Norris & wf., ch. Ziba.
May 2. Gilbard Ludlam, ch., Abigail.
" 16. Solloman Munson & wf., ch. Ezekiel.
" 23. Jeremiah Gard's Household—John, Phebe, Rebecca, Cornelius, Moses, Timothy, Daniel, Alexander.
" " Daniel Tichenor & wf., ch. Joseph.
" 30. Stephen Norris & wf., ch. Rhoda.
June 6. Zophar Gildersleeve & wf., ch. Mary.
" " Joshua Whitehead & wf., chn. Puah and Patience.
" 13. Sam'l Bayles & wf., ch. Augustin.
" " Moses Lindslv & wf., ch. Eunice.
" 27. Hannah & Mary Garrigas, adults.
" " John Cole & wf., ch. Masey.
" " Stephen Hedges & wf., ch. Ruth.
" " Josiah Beman & wf., ch. Abijah.
July 16. Will Goodwin's wf. had an adopted ch. Phebe Coles, ch. name Philip.
" " Gilbard Allen & wf., ch. Kezia.
" 25. Sam'l Shipman & wf., ch., Stephen.
" " Ephraim Howard, on wf.'s accompt, Household — Joseph, Ephraim, Caleb.
Aug. 1. Joseph Pierson & wf., ch. Abigail.
" 13. Thomas Throope & wf., ch. Isaac-Bacon-George.

(To be continued.)

(*Continued from page 70.*)

MARRIAGES.

——:o:——

1778.

Jan. 6. James Howell & Union Conkling.
" 8. Simeon Broadwell & Rachel Lindsly.
" 18. John Pumoroy & Elizabeth Beegle.
Feb. 11. David Mott & Widow Mary Manson.
" 13. John Bastedo & Nance Wade, of Mendum.
" 16. Phenix Ayrs, of Woodbridge, & Hannah Rolfe.
" 18. John Runyon & Mary Concling.
Mar. 12. Enoch Goble & Mary Cooper.
" 25. Samuel Wook & Rebekah Munson.
Apr. 22. John Milburn & Nancy Fielding.
" 23. David Leonard & Phebe Lum.
May 4. Ebenezer Stiles & Widow Abigail Goble.
" 7. Stephen Conklin, Jun., & Rachel Lindsley.
" 11. Edward Mills & Phebe Byram.
" 14. Enos free negro & Elizabeth also free.
" 19. Nathan Reeve & Joannah Day, Widow.
" 24. Matthew Lum & Hannah Leonard.
" 27. Daniel Riggs & Rhodah Condict.
June 1. Cuffe Negro & Cate Negro.
" 10. Abner Condict and Martha Leonard.
" 10. Luther Extell & Hannah Condict.
" 21. Ichabod Cooper & Hannah Lyon, Widow.
" 22. John Paine & Elizabeth Peterson.
July 5. James Bampfield & Elizabeth Clarkson.
" 8. Benjamin Woodruff & Patience Lum.
" " Isaac Prudden & Sarah Keen.
Aug. 1. Job Brown a Soldier & Ellzabeth Hopkins.
Sept. 20. Rubin Cooper of Virginia, Sergeant, & Elizabeth Cady.
" 24. John Van Cort & Mary Prudden.
Oct. 12. John Stevenson & Widow Rachel Gwinnup.
" 21. John Kenny & Phebe Arnold.
Nov. 1. Elis Bower of Mendam & Martha Butler.
" 2. Jeremiah Guard & Mary Ball.
" 4. Usual Crane & Sarah Pierson.

Dec. 2. Nathaniel Broadwell & Joanna Lindsley.
" " Joseph Tuttle & Esther Parkhurst.
" 3. George Thorborn Soldier & Nancy Kenny, late Nancy McGowen, Widow.
" 31. William Bowen & Lucrecia Loce.

1779.

Jan. 5. John Eddy & Mary Ward.
" 6. Timothy Stiles & Damaris Crane.
" 27. Stephen Whitaker & Ruth Conkling.
Feb. 8. Zenas Condict & Hannah Pierson.
March 15. Jeduthan Day & Anne Carns.
" 29. Benjamin Conger & Phebe Armstrong.
" 5. William Cheever & Catharine Freeman.
April 11. William Davis & Ruth Gardiner.
" 12. Nathan Tompkins & Phebe Morris.
" 20. David Tarbill & Phebe Riggs.
" 28. Thomas Johnson & Eunice Rayner.
May 9. James Ford & Elizabeth Odill.
June 3. Joseph Locy & Jerujah Kenny.
" 27. James Smith & Charity Pitney.
July 4. Samuel Allen & Hannah Beach.
" 5. Isaac Lyon & Rebekah Condict.
" 27. Daniel Jones & Abigail Pollard.
Aug. 1. Zebedee Brown & Widow Hannah Loring.
" 29. Jacob Doren & Mary Dun, Bedminster.
Sept. 16. Jonathan Whitaker & Mary Mitchell.
Oct. 8. Abijah Fairchild & Sarah Howell.
Nov. 1. Stephen Brown & Phebe Williams.
" 3. Joseph Marsh & Elizabeth Lum.
" " Gideon Riggs, Jun., & Rachel Minthorn.
" 11. Samuel Morrison & Mary Johnson.
" 15. George Marsh & Catharine Younges.
" 24. Timothy Gobil & Rebekah Morri
Dec. 1. Caleb Tuttle & Mary Fairchild.
" 8. Cap'n Joseph Williams & Mar Gard, Wid.
" 12. Frederick Hll molat. sol. Free he saith & Hannah Coran, S of Sam'l Hopping.

(*To be continued.*)

(Continued from page 71.)
BILL OF MORTALITY,

1777.

May 15. Jerusha, daughter of George Mills, aet. —, Small pox.

" 18. Rebeckah, wife of Hur Osborn, aet. 60, small pox.

" " Servant child of Silas Condict, Esq., aet. —, small pox.

" 20. John Brookfield,† aet. 25, small pox.

" 21. Deacon, Matthew Lum,* aet. 70, Fever.

" 22. Mary, wife of Matthew Ball, aet. 37, fever.

" " Mary, wife of Daniel Conger,† aet. 46, small pox.

" 24. Hannah, daughter of Lindsley Burnet, aet. 1, inflammation in the head.

" 25. Daniel Wick, aet. 65, small pox.

" " Jacob, son of Hezekiah Stibbens, aet. —, fits.

" " Child of Daniel Kemper, aet. —, small pox.

" 26. Augustine Steen, aet. 50, fever.

" 29. Servant woman of Doct. Johnes, aet. 35, consumption.

" 30. Benjamin, son of Dan Trowbridge,† aet. 12, dysentery.

June 8. Squire Price, aet. 89, small pox.

" " Servant girl of Abraham Talmage, aet. 10, small pox.

" " Abraham Ludlow, aet. 34, consumption.

" 16. Daniel Howard, aet. 53, pleurisy.

" 17. Child of Stephen Arnold, aet. —, hives.

" 21. Phœbe, daughter of Col. Jacob Ford, Jun., aet. 2, dysentery.

" —. Jacob Tuttle, aet. 23, drowned.

" 24. Bennui Freeman, aet. 33, epilepsy.

" 25. Sarah Stagg, aet. 45, consumption.

" 26. Martha, wife of Andrew Wade, aet. 34, small pox.

" " Servant Child of George Phillips, aet. —, ——

" 30. Timothy, son of Benjamin Lindsley, Esq., aet. 4, worms.

July 2. Elizabeth, daughter of Philip Tucker, aet. 11, small pox.

" 3. James, son of John Crane, aet. 1, dysentery.

July 7. Sarah, daughter of John Pool, aet. 1, small pox.

" 8. Child of Caleb Howell, aet. —, small pox.

" 10. Joseph Miller, aet. —, small pox.

" 11. Timothy Pierson, aet. 67, putrid fever.

" " Child of John Cobb, aet. —, ——

" 12. Phœbe, daughter of Thomas Miller, aet. 13, small pox.

" " Charity, daughter of David Muir, aet. 1, dysentery.

" 13. Anne, daughter of Thomas Miller, aet. 1, small pox.

" 16. Child of Elias Hedges, aet. —, ——

" 17. Child of John Harporee, aet. —,

" 18. Susanna, widow of Caleb Tichenor,* aet. 73, old age.

" " Sarah, wife of Jacob Garrigues, aet. 57, dysentery.

" 19. Susannah, widow of John Magee,†* aet. 63, dysentery.

" 20. Hur Osborn, aet. 67, dysentery.

" 21. A child of James Chadwick, aet. —, dysentery.

" 22. A child of David Garrigues, aet. —,

" " Peter, servant of Phillip Tucker, aet. 21, consumption.

" 23. Jarzel Turner,* aet. 39, fever.

" " A child of James Smith, aet. —,

" " Epenetus, son of Jabez Beach, aet. 1, small pox.

" 24. A child of Moses Wilkinson, aet. —,

" 28. A child of Doct. Samuel. Tuthill, aet. —, ——

" 29. A child of Joseph Gardner, aet. —, small pox.

" 31. Paul, son of Benjamin Pierson, Jun., aet. 8, dysentery.

" " Cato, servant of Silas Condict. Esq., aet. 35, nervous fever.

" " Hannah, widow of Col. Jacob Ford, Sen.,* aet. 76, dysentery. (Born Nov., 1701.)

" " A child of Nathan Arnold, aet. —, dysentery.

" " Indian child of Samuel Roberts, aet. —, dysentery.

(To be continued.)

(*Continued from page 72.*)

TRUSTEES' BOOK.

—:o:—

Sept. 20, 1787.—Trustees met at Mr. Johnes; present Mr. Condict, Mr. Conkling, Mr. Stiles, Mr. Lindsly, Mr. Ford & Mr. Mills, and Agreed to new Shingle the Ends & the South Side of the Ruff of the meeting house, and that Mr. Lindsly & Mr. Ford be a Committe to do the same, and other necessary Repairs to the house, they Likewise Drew a Subscription for the purpose of paying for the same, and that the Subscription formerly Drawn for Repairs of said house & Signed by a Number Should be Null & Void, and that those persons that have paid the Same or any part thereof, more than their part for fencing the Graveyard Shall have Credit towards the present Subscription—the Trustees appointed Deacon Allen to Carry the Subscription through the Congregation for Signers, and this Bord will pay him for the same.

March 25th, 1788.—Trustees met at the Request of the President at the house of Benjamin Freeman. Present Mr. Condict, Mr. Tuthill, Mr. Lindsly, Mr. Ford & Mr. Mills, Agreed to Sell the Chesut timber on the Parsonage wood-lot at Vendue next Friday, & Sold the Continental Building on the Parsonage Land near the meeting house to John Mills for £2,15s. The Trustees then Agreed unanimously to Resign their appointment as Trustees.

FINIS.

April 24th, 1788.—The Trustees having resigned their Office, the Congregation met this day agreeably to advertizements & elected 1st Silas Condict, 3rd John Mills, 2nd Jonathan Ford, 4th Benj. Lindsly, 5th Richard Johnson, 6th Joseph Lewis and 7th James Smith, to serve as Trustees.

April 27th, 1788.—The Persons elected on the 24th inst. as Trustees met at Mr. Lewis's viz., Silas Condict, Jonathan Ford, John Mills, Benj. Lindsly, Richard Johnson, Jos. Lewis & James Smith, and Severally took and Subscribed the Oath of Allegiance, and an Oath of Office as the Law directs before Alex'r Carmichael, Esq. The Trustees Elected Mr. Condict to serve as President, and Mr. Lewis to serve as Clerk of the Board. The Trustees then assumed the name of THE TRUSTEES OF THE FIRST PRESBYTERIAN CHURCH AT MORRISTOWN, & chose as their common Seal, one—the device & impression of which is a Sheaf of Wheat.

The Board appointed Mr. Lindsly & Mr. Smith, a Committee to take care of the house, where Jonath. Brown now lives, and to repair the same.

Ordered that the Ditches on the Parsonage Meadow be again cleared out at the expense of the Parish, that Mr. Lewis superintend the same.

The Board appointed Mr. Lindsly, Mr. Ford, Mr. Mills & Mr. Johnson, a Committee to superintend the Repairs of the Meeting House, & that they proceed to collect the money Subscribed for that purpose, provide materials, &c., as soon as convenient.

Voted that Mr. Mills, Mr. Johnson & Mr. Smith, be a committee to advertise & sell such Timber as is suitable for rails on that part of the parsonage Land where the wood has been cut off, and to pay Mr. Ford out of the money arising from the sales, for getting the rails now lying there.

Some persons having objected to the plan proposed for repairing the church, The Board agreed to call a meeting of the parish to consult & finally conclude in what manner the same should be repaired. Then adjourned.

1788, May 13th.—The Board met at Mr. Lewis's—all present. After some consultation had on the subject of repairs, some calculations made, some proposals rec'd, &c., the Board adjourned to meet at the meeting house, where the people of the parish were convened. The congregation voted that repairs be omitted, & that Justice Lindsly, Major Lindsly & Jos. Lewis, be a committee to make an estimate of the expense of a church to be built of Timber, & that Deacon Prudden & J——e Carmichael, be a committee to make an estimate of the expense of a Brick church, 65 feet long and forty-five feet broad, and that both estimates be laid before the congregation on Thursday, the 29th Inst.

By advice of the Elders & Trustees, the above meeting is put off till Thursday, the 5th of June next.

(*To be continued.*)

THE RECORD.

FIRST PRESBYTERIAN CHURCH, MORRISTOWN, N. J.

" This shall be Written for the Generation to Come."—Psalms 102 : 18.

VOL. I.   NOVEMBER, 1889.   NO. 11

(*Printed with the approval of Session.*)

THE RECORD

Will be printed and published monthly at Morristown, N. J. Terms, 50 cents per annum in advance; 75 cents after June.

Subscriptions will be received at the book-stores of Messrs. Runyon and Emmell, or through the mail, and may begin with the first number. ALL COMMUNICATIONS should be addressed to the
EDITOR OF THE RECORD,
Lock box 44.   Morristown, N. J.
Entered at the Post Office at Morristown, N. J., as second class matter.

—:o:—

" Alden's New Jersey Register and United States calendar, for the year of our lord, 1812.

The Thirty-Sixth, till the Fourth of July, of American Independence; with an Ephemeris and various Interesting Articles.

Second Edition, with corrections and additions, Newark, printed by William Tuttle, who, by agreement with rev. mr. Alden is the proprietor of this edition."

(A friend has sent to THE RECORD the above book, for which he will please receive our thanks. Below will be found so much of it as relates to Morris County. [EDITOR.]

COURTS, &C.

Master and Examiner, Stephen J. Ogden.
Surrogate, David Thompson, jun.
Clerk of County, Edward Condit.
Sheriff, David Mills.
Leg. Council, Benjamin Ludlow.
Assembly, Stephen Dodd,
              Jeptha B. Munn,
              Mahlon Dickerson.
Attornies and Counsellors at law ;
Gabriel H. Ford,   Charles Russell,
Sylvester D. Russell,   Stephen J. Ogden,
Hill Runyan,   Isaac Blackford.
    Isaac H. Williamson, assist. atty. gen.

Militia, Cavalry,	246
Artillery,	87
Infantry,	2741
Total in brigade,	3074

Lieut. colonel, Wm. Campfield.
Major,   Isaac Campfield.

MORRIS BRIGADE.

Brigadier-gen., John Darcy.
Lieut. colonels, 1st reg., Silas Axtell,
               2nd reg., John Smith.
               3rd "   Joseph Jackson.
               4th "   Lemuel Cobb.
Majors, 1st reg. 1st batt., Solomon Bayle.
               2nd "   Grover Youngs.
     2d reg. 1st   "   Benj. McCowny.
               2d "   Cadwallader Smith.
     3d reg. 1st   "   William Lee.
               2d "   Joseph Hurd.
     4th reg. 1st   "   Samuel Cobb.
               2d "   Daniel Farrand.
Judges of the common pleas, with time of their appointment :
23 Nov., 1808. William Woodhull, William Munro, Jesse Upson, Benj. Smith.
25 Nov., 1809. David Welsh.

JUSTICES OF THE PEACE.

2 Dec., 1807. Lot Dixon, David L. Bates.
23 Nov., 1808. William Woodhull, William Munro, Jesse Upson, Nicholas Mandeville, Richard Johnson, Nicholas Emmons, Benj. Condict, Dan Hurd, William Corwin, Benj. Lampson, Ezekiel Kitchell, Philip Schuyler, John Kelso, Henry Cooper, jun.
25 Nov., 1809. David Welsh, Nicholas Neighbour, Ebenezer Coe, William Spencer, Benj. Pierson.
1 Nov., 1810. David Pier, Daniel Hopping.
19 Nov., 1811. Thomas Vanwinkle, Benj. Smith, Isaac Lindsley, Benj. Beach, Preserve Riggs, Peter Smith, Thomas Parrot.

NOTARIES PUBLIC,
David Miller, Cornelius Voorheis.

POST OFFICERS AND MASTERS.
Chatham, Samuel Crane.
Chester, J. D. Gardiner,
Hanover, Cornelius Voorheis.
Mendham, Daniel Dodd.
Morristown, Henry King.
New Vernon, Jonathan Miller.
Rockaway, Joseph Jackson.

Suckasunna, James Hinchman.
Washington, David Miller.

NEWSPAPERS.
The Morris-Town Herald, pub. Tuesday
by Henry P. Russell.
Palladium of Liberty, pub. Thursday
by Jacob Mann.

MEDICAL SOCIETY OF NEW JERSEY.
Vice-President, Lewis Condict.

MINISTERS.
Presbyterian, Hanover, Aaron Condict.
Mendham, Amzi Armstrong.
Morris, Samuel Fisher.
Rockaway, Barnabas King.
Baptist, Morris, vacant.

MORRIS COUNTY PRESBYTERY.
Stephen Grover, Caldwell.
——— Phelps, Parsippany.
Without a pastoral charge,
Abel Jackson, res. Bloomfield.
Congregational.
Chester and Schooley's Mountain, Stephen
Overton.

MORRIS ACADEMY.
Trustees:
John Doughty, president,
Samuel Fisher, first director.
William Canfield, second do.
Sylvester D. Russell, third do.
Daniel Phœnix, treasurer.
Lewis Condict, secretary.

Instructers ;
Henry Mills, principal
James Whelpley, assistant.
Orland Whelpley, assistant.

A BOARDING SCHOOL
For young ladies is conducted by
Esther Scribner,
Elizabeth Scribner.
Ann Scribner.

CHATHAM ACADEMY.
Trustees:
Matthew LaRue Perrine, president.
William Spencer, Jeptha B. Munn,
Eliphalet Miller, Elijah Ward,
David Brown, Cornelius Meeker,
Enoch W. Jackson, preceptor.

MASONIC.
Cincinnati lodge, Hanover.

WASHINGTON TURNPIKE,
Directors:
David Welch, president.
John Doughty, treasurer.
Sylvester D. Russell, Wm. McCullough.
Nicholas Neighbour, Henry Dusenbery.
Jared Haines, John Bruteman.
The length of this turnpike from Morris
to Easton is 40 miles, 59 chains and 20 links.

MORRIS TURNPIKE.
Directors:
Gabriel H. Ford, president.
Elias B. Dayton, treasurer.
Jeremiah Ballard, secretary.
Aaron Ogden, Robinson Thomas,
Christopher Robert, Jonas Wade.
Isaac H. Williamson, John Gustin.

MORRIS LIBRARY COMPANY.
Officers:
William Campfield, president.
Mahlon Ford, vice-president.
Jabez Campfield, librarian.
Israel Canfield, treasurer.
Sylvester D. Russell, secretary.

MORRIS AQUEDUCT.
Officers:
Lewis Condict, president.
William Canfield, vice-president.
Daniel Pierson, director.
William Johnes, vice-director.
Charles Russell, treasurer.
William Beach, accountant.
Henry King, clerk.

SOUTH HANOVER LIBRARY.
Was instituted 1st Aug., 1803, and contains
180 volumes.
Trustees:
William Thompson President and treasurer.
Elias Thompson, Lewis Carter.
Elijah Ward, Jacob Bound,
Cyrus Bruen, librarian.

MEMBER OF CONGRESS.
Lewis Condict.

(*Continued from page 75.*)

REPRESENTATIVES OF MORRIS COUNTY IN THE STATE LEGISLATURE.

——:o:——

50th Legislature, 1825, Oct. 25.
Council, Silas Cook.
Assembly, George K.Drake,(Speaker.)
Ebenezer F. Smith,
Joseph Dickerson,
Ephraim Marsh.

51st Legislature, 1826, Oct 24.
Council, Silas Cook.
Assembly, George K.Drake,(Speaker.)
Ephraim Marsh,
Joseph Dickerson,
John D. Jackson.

52d Legislature, 1827, Oct. 23.
Council, Silas Cook, (Vice President.)
Assembly, Ephraim Marsh,
David Mills,
Stephen Thompson,
Walter Kirkpatrick.

53d Legislature, 1828, Oct. 28.
Council, Edward Condict.
Assembly, William Monro;
Joseph Jackson,
Charles Hillard,
John Hancock.

54th Legislature, 1829, Oct. 27.
Council, Edward Condict.
Assembly, William Monro,
John Hancock,
Joseph Jackson,
Charles Hillard.

55th Legislature, 1830, Oct. 26.
Council, Edward Condict.
Assembly, William Monro,
Joseph Jackson,
Charles Hillard,
John Hancock.

56th Legislature, 1831, Oct. 25.
Council, James Wood.
Assembly, Elijah Ward,
Thomas Muir,
Leonard Neighbour,
James Cook.

57th Legislature, 1832, Oct. 23.
Council, James Wood.
Assembly, William Brittin,
Samuel Beach,
Jacob W. Miller,
Joseph Smith.

58th Legislature, 1833, Oct. 22.
Council, Mahlon Dickerson.
Assembly, Joseph Dickerson, Jr.
Thomas Muir,
Henry Hillard,
Silas Lindsley.

59th Legislature, 1834, Oct 23.
Council, William Monro.
Assembly, Joseph Dickerson, Jr.
Henry Hillard,
Thomas Muir,
Silas Lindsley.

60th Legislature, 1835, Oct. 27.
Council, Jeptha B. Munn.
Assembly, Henry Hillard,
Isaac Quimby,
James Cook,
John D. Jackson.

61st Legislature, 1836, Oct. 25.
Council, Jeptha B. Munn, (Vice President.)
Assembly, John A. Bleeker,
William Dellicker,
Alexander Dickerson,
William Logan.

62d Legislature, 1837, Oct. 24.
Council, William Brittin.
Assembly, Lewis Condict, (Speaker.)
Silas Tuttle,
Robert C. Stephens,
Ezekiel B. Gaines.

63d Legislature, 1838, Oct. 23.
Council, William Brittin.
Assembly, Lewis Condict, (Speaker.)
Ezekiel B. Gaines,
Silas Tuttle,
Robert C. Stephens.

64th Legislature, 1839, Oct. 22.
Council, Jacob W. Miller.
Assembly, Abraham Brittin,
Ebenezer F. Smith,
Jacob Weise,
Paul B. De Bow.

65th Legislature, 1840, Oct. 27.
Council, James Wood.
Assembly, Abraham Brittin,
Ebenezer F. Smith,
Paul B. De Bow,
James W. Drake.

(*To be continued.*)

(Continued from page 76.)

MEMBERS.

[The third column on this page is the work of the RECORD. Information which will lead to the correction of any mistake, or the filling of any blank, will be thankfully received.—ED.]

—:o:—

Names.	When Received.	When Dismissed or Died.
Silas Halsey, Junr.	Nov. 1, 1764	" Moved."
Jedidiah Mills	" " "	Feb. 1, 1820, aet. 75 y., 8 m.
Sarah Mills (Jedidiah)	" " "	Aug. 15, 1784, aet. 35.
John Mills	" " "	Sept. 24, 1837, aet. 91.
Jonathan Tichenor	" " "	" Moved."
Nathan Reeve.	" " "	
Daniel Bishop	" " "	
Isaac Soverill	" " "	" Moved away.",
Ichabod Cermichael	" " "	
Crowel Wilkerson	" " "	
Peter Price	" " "	" Moved away."
Naptali Byram	" " "	
Mary Dikins, wido.	" " "	May 20, 1769, aet. 70.
Sarah Ayrs, (John)	" " "	" Moved away."
Lydia Hathaway (Jonathan)	" " "	
Phebe Gobil (Ezekiel)	" " "	
Abigail Peck	" " "	(Later Mrs. David Gardner.)
Elizabeth Keen (James)	" " "	
Hannah Roggers (John)	" " "	March 22, 1788, aet. 52.
Huldah Cundict (Ebenezer)	" " "	(Later Mrs. Geo. Philips.)
Abigail Cundict (Silas)	" " "	Jan. 14, 1823, aet. 80.
Agnish Bedle (Dan.)	" " "	" Moved."
Phebe Pierson (Benjamin)	" " "	July 6, 1799, aet. 63.
Hannah Cutler	" " "	" Moved away."
Susannah Allen	" " "	" "
Abigail Bates	" " "	" "
Rebecca Stockbridge	" " "	
Silas Hains	" 25, "	" Moved away."
Samuel Oliver	Dec. 1, "	Suspended July 1, 1782.
Sarah Oliver (Samuel)	" " "	July 18, 1786, aet 53.
Moses Munson	" " "	" Moved away."
Susan Easton (John)	" 16, "	
Job Lorain	Jan. 6, 1765	" Moved."
Jarzel Turner	" " "	July 23, 1777, aet. 39.
Zenas Condict	" " "	Dec. 20, 1776, aet. 37.
Joshua Winget	" " "	" Moved away."
Stephen Arnold	" " "	" "
Wick. Ludlam	" " "	" "
Garret Miller	" " "	" "
Patience Miller (Garret)	" " "	" "
Abigail Goble (Simeon)	" " "	
Elizabeth Miller (James)	" " "	
Phebe Miller (Zophar Freeman)	" " "	Sept. 28, 1789, aet. 54.
Mary Lindsley (Phil.)	" " "	" Moved."
Lois Burnet	" " "	
Sarah Lindsley	" " "	

(To be continued.)

(Continued from page 77.)

BAPTISMS.

——:o:——

1762.

Aug.22. Eleazer Lindsley & wf., ch. Anne.
" 29 Benjamin Woodruff.&°wf., ch. Benjamin.
Sept.12. Essaker Huntington's ch. Zervia.
" " Benj'n Halsey & wf., Negro ch. Pompe.
" 19. Nathaniel Condict, ch. Sarah.
" " Silas Condict, ch. Elizabeth.
" " Jonathan Wood's wf. on her own accompt., ch. Ruth.
" 26. John Lindsly & wf., ch. Sarah.
" " Jedediah Gregory & wf., ch. Ebenezer.
" ". Isaac Tuttle on wf.'s accompt, ch. Sarah.
" " Sarah,wf. of John Pitney, ch. Mary.
" " Thomas Kenny on wf.'s accompt., ch. Abraham.
" " Shuball Pitney's wf. on her own accompt., chn. James & Joseph.
Oct. 3. James Loce on wf.'s accompt, ch. Abigail.
" 24. Henry Primrose & wf., ch. Rebecca.
" 31. Junia Lindsly & wf., Rhoda.
" " James Millar & wf., ch. Enoch.
" " Jno. Burrel on wf.'s accompt, ch. Hannah.
Nov. 7. Lititia, Stephen Munson's wf., adult.
" " Susanna, Caleb Munson's wf., adult.
" " Stephen Munson & wf., Family, Hannah,Solloman, Sarah,Ruth.
" " Caleb Munson & wf., Family, Ruth & Joseph.
" " Dorcas, Zebide Brown & wf., Family chn. Experience, Hannah, Jabish.
" 14. Isaac Person & Rhoda his wf., adult, chil'n Jacob & Tapena.
" " Wilby Clark & wf., ch. John McKey.
" " Job Lorain on wf.'s accompt, ch. Elizabeth.
" 28. John Ayrs & wf., ch. Samuel Bayles.
" " Thomas Coe & wf., ch. Jerud.
" " Alexander Carmichael .& wf., ch. Elizabeth.
Dec. 8. Dan'l Howard & wf., ch. Shadrack.

Dec. 26. Joseph King's wf. on her accompt, ch. Prudence.

1763.

Jan. 16. Moses Lindsly & wf., ch. Daniel.
" 30. Doc. Barn. Budd on wf. accompt, ch. John Cozens.
" " Dan'l Morris, Jun. & wf., ch. Timothy.
" " Benj. Lindsly & wf., ch. Jonathan, born Dec. 26, 1762.
Feb. 6. David Fairchild & wf., ch. Phebe.
" 13. Jacob Ford & wf., ch. Timothy.
" 27. Cap. Tuttle on wf. accompt, daugh'r Cecil.
Mar. 5. Joseph Stites, Jun. & wf., ch. Benjamin, born Jan. 9, 1763.
" 12. Ebenezer Coe & wf., ch. Hannah.
" 27. Sam'l Arnold & wf., ch. Anne.
Apr. 28, Mattania Lyon & wf., ch. Hannah.
May 1. Joseph Lindsly & wf., ch'n Bathiah & Grace.
" 8. Nathaniel L'hommedou & wf., ch. Timothy.
" " Edward Byram & wf., ch. Sarah.
June 5. Henry Gardiner & wf., ch. Rachel.
" " Moses Prudden & wf., ch. Samuel.
" " Jonathan Hathaway & wf., ch. Sarah.
July 10. Ebenezer Condict & wf., ch. Abibail.
July 17. Deac. Matt'w Lum & wf., ch. Matthew.
" " Abraham Campfield & wf., ch. Isaac.
" " Zebedee Brown on wf.'s accompt, ch. Mary.
" 31. John Lose on wf.'s accompt, ch. Cornelus.
Aug. 7. Joseph Youngs & wf., ch. Catura.
" 14. Ebenezer Hathaway & wf., ch. Samuel.
" 21. Samuel Mills & wf., ch. Sarah.
Nov. 4. Constant Cooper on his wf.'s accompt, ch. Mehetabel.
Oct. 2. Stephen Lyon on his wf.'s accompt, ch. Ezekiel.
" 9. Benj. Pierson & wf., ch. David.
" " Zophar Freeman & wf., ch. Stephen.
" " Phineas Fairchild & wf.. chil'n Mary, born June 12, 1761 ; Timothy, born July 22, 1763.
No. of males, 442 ; females, 448.
Whole No. 890; superiority of females, 6.

(To be continued.)

(*Continued from page 78.*)
MARRIAGES.

——:o:——

1779.
Dec. 16. John Stevenson, of Philadelphia
& Anne Merrill, of Mor-Town.
" 22. Benj. Pierson, Jun. & Abigail
Condict.
" 23. Andrew Durham, of Baskenridge
& Jane Pierson.

1780.
Jan. 5. William Gregory, Corporal of Major Anderson Regiment & Je-
mima Burrell.
" 13. Isaac Headley, widower and Catharine Clark, widow.
" 24. Fulkerd Fulkerdson & Sarah
Schellenger, both of Roxbury.
" 31. John Carner, of 6 Pen. Reg. &
Margaret Packers.
" " Christopher Breackin & Mary
Briant.
March 6. Lawrence Brennan, Serj. 7 Mar'd
Reg. & Catharine Claney, of ye
1 Mor Brigade.
" 21. James Right & Jane Woodrough
of Cap. Harmon Stout 10 Pen.
Regiment.
" " David Irwin & Catharine Munson.
April 5. Griffith Davis & Sarah Conaway,
both in the army.
" 9. Michael Conner & Sarah Hamil-
ton.
" 18. Eliezer Miller & Hannah Mills.
May 3. Abraham Munson & Abigail Allen.
" 11. Allen McLane, a soldier & Mary
Robinson.
" 14. John McCarrall, a soldier of 10
Pen. Reg. & Kezia Clark.
" 20. ⎰ Thomas Brown, a soldier &
Elizabeth Nicholson.
" " ⎱ Patrick Rogers & Peggy
Brien, Camp folks.
" 21. Elijah Pollock, a soldier & Cathar-
ine Grear, Camp folks.
" 24. Matthew Dorham, a soldier &
Mary Davis, from the Camp.
June. 13. Silas Jennings & Loruhamah
Wines.
" 25. David Youngs & Catharine Bears.
July 23. Caleb Ball & Lois Gordon, Wid.
" 25. Samuel Sewerd & Elizabeth Keen.

July 28. William McMullen, soldier & Jemi-
ma Guirin.
Aug. 12. John Smith Waggoner & Margaret
Wilson, Camp woman.
" 15. ⎰ Joseph Morgan & Mary Cros-
man.
" " ⎱ John Dickerson & Grace
Lindsly.
Sept. 21. Jacob Whitehead & Mary Lyon—
Continental.
Oct. 1. Elemuel Bowers & Sarah Mills.
" 12. Jeremiah Rogers & Hannah Lam-
bert.
" 15. William Shippen, Master of Musick
& Lucretia Umberfield.
" 31. Paul Lee & Eunice Lindsly.
" " Israel Lee & Bethia Lindsly.
Nov. 14. David Reeve & Martha Bates.
" 21. Jonathan Johnson & Zipporah
Conger.
" 29. Bethuel Hayward & Temperance
Brown.
Dec. 4. James Pitney & Elizabeth Car-
michael.

1781.
Jan. 10. William Lawrence & Catharine
Slover.
" 29. Samuel Loree & Sarah Price.
Feb. 15. Henry Clark & Mary Smith.
Mar. 5. Jerud Day & Mary Gildersleeve.
Apr. 5. Timothy Mills & Abigail Ludlam.
" 18. Peter Hill, Jun. & Charity Badgley.
" " Ichabod Badgly & Sarah Hatha-
way.
July 11. Alexander Gard, son of Jeremiah,
& Hannah Keen, daughter of Cap.
Keen.
Sept. 5. Roberd Twiman & Sarah Odel.
Oct. 1. Major Joseph Lindsly & Mary Gar-
diner.
" 17. Joseph Shipman & Sarah Pool.
Nov. 15. Chatfield Tuttle & Deborah Car-
man.
" 25. James Cook & Phebe Condict.
Dec. 13. Col. Jacob Drake & Esther King.
" 30. James Griffith & Desire Easton.
To this Date Married 726.

1782.
Jan. 13. Armstrong Jones & Lea Sutten.
" 24. John Bolton, soldier 2d Jer. Reg.
Jonathan Holms Cap'n, & Cathar-
ine Devins.
(To be continued.)

(Continued from page 79.)
BILL OF MORTALITY.

1777.

Aug. 1. Mary, wife of Philip Tucker, aet. 36, small pox.
" 5. A child of Ephraim Howard.
" 6. Zachariah Fairchild,* aet. 77, dysentery.
" 7. A child of Amos Prudden, aet. —, dysentery.
" 8. A child of Ichabod Carmichael, aet. —, dysentery.
" " Elizabeth, daughter of Jonathan Ogden, aet. 2, dysentery.
" " Aron, son of Abraham Talmage,† aet. 4, dysentery.
" " Child of Zebedee Brown, aet. —, dysentery.
" " Simeon Goble,† aet. 51, consumption.
" 9. Child of Paul Farber.
" 10. Hannah, wife of Nathaniel Thompson, aet. 24, dysentery.
" 16. Elder, Daniel Lindsley,* aet. 77, dysentery.
" " Nathan Arnold, aet. 23, dysentery.
" 21. John Burwell, aet. 70, dysentery.
" " Cæsar, servant of Captain Keen, aet. 35, dysentery.
" 26 John Stevens, aet. 60, dysentery.
" —. Henry, son of Joseph Johnson, aet, 1, dysentery.
" 28. Child of Mr. Banker.
" 30. Cato, servant of Captain Keen, aet. 5, dysentery.
Sept. 5. Seth, son of David Godden, aet. 2, worms.
" 9. Child of Gilbert Ludlow.
" " Joel Loree, aet. 25, colic.
" 11. Hannah Duyckinck, aet. 17, consumption.
" 12. John Sutten, aet. 28, dysentery.
" " Child of Willits Simmons, aet. —, canker.
" 14. Grace, wibow of Elder, Daniel Lindsley,* aet. 68, dysentery.
" " Timothy Mills, Jun. aet. 30, consumption.
" 15. Elizabeth, daughter of John Day, aet. 3, dysentery.
" 20. David, son of John Day, aet. 1, fits.
" 21. Child of Ralph Bridge.
" 29. Philip Hathaway, aet. 46, fever.

" " Epenetus Beach, aet. 38, putrid fever.
Oct. 3. Ruth, wife of Nathan Reeve, aet. 30, consumption.
" 11. Ruth, daughter of Moses Johnson, aet. 16, putrid fever,
" " Daniel Parkhurst, aet. 18, consumption.
" 13. Rachael, wife of Joseph Williams, aet. 34, consumption.
" 16. Benjamin Tomkins, aet. 35; putrid-fever.
" 19. Child of Abner Winds.
Nov. 6. Child of Mr. Robertson.
" 13. Philip Tucker, aet. 41, consumption.
" 27. Abigail, widow of Joseph Edmister, aet. 50, consumption.
" 29. Abraham, son of Timothy Stiles, aet. —, convulsion-fits.
Dec. 14. Doct. Bern Budd, aet. 39, putrid fever.
" 16. Mary, wife of Jacob Freeman, aet. 23, child-bed.
" " A child of Jacob Freeman.
1778.
Jan. 5. Major Joseph Morris, aet. 46, gunshot wound.
" " Isaac, son of Nathaniel Armstrong, aet. 1, fever,
" 6. A child of Morsecholick, aet. —, fever.
" 6. Rachel, daughter of Ichabod Cooper, aet. 2, scald.
" 8. A child of Howell Osborn.
" 16. George Gordon, aet. 81, old-age.
Feb. 2. Hannah Burnet,* aet. 81, old-age.
Mar. 17. Huldah, daughter of John Arnold, aet. 2, consumption.
Apr. 12. Abigail, wife of Abraham Hudson, aet. 25, putrid-fever.
May 22. Kezia, wife of Capt. Joseph Beach, aet. 46, fever.
June 11. A child of Capt. John Lindsley.
" 26. A child of Enoch Conger.
July 17. Susanna, wife of Philip Castener,* aet. 51, fever.
Aug. 2. Sarah, wife of John Arnold, aet. 33, consumption.
" 9. Abijah Cutler, aet 31, consumption,
" 10. William, son of David Godden, aet. 16, dysentery.
Sept. 4. Benjamin, son of Uzal Coe, aet. 1, worms.
(To be continued.)

(Continued from page 80.)

TRUSTEES' BOOK.

June 5th, 1788.—The congregation met agreeably to the adjournment & notice,—& after some consultation & debate about Building a new, or repairing the old church, Voted that a new church be built—& the votes being taken there appeared to be a considerable majority for building it of Timber.

The Trustees then convened at Mr. Smith's—all present. Voted that Deacon Allen & Mr. Johnson carry a Subscription through the parish to get a sufficient sum for erecting a new meeting-house, 65 feet long, 50 feet wide & and 25 feet high, to be inclosed with shingles.

Voted that the Clerk draw orders on the receiver of collections (Jas. Smith) for thirty-five shillings in favor of the Sexton (Nathan Howell) for his services quarterly. Voted that no Book be purchased for the purpose of keeping accounts for the parish. Board adjourned.

At a meeting of the Trustees at Jos. Lewis's, the 23d Sept. 1788.—Present Mr. Mills, Mr. Lindsly, Mr. Johnson, Mr. Smith & Lewis. Voted that a fence (of post & 3 rails) be made on the parsonage from Mrs. Hambletons spring to the corner of the Rev. Doct. Johnes's lot, on the bank of the ditch.

That the timber for s'd fence be taken from the parsonage wood lot. That Mr. Lewis get the work done at the expense of the Trustees.

Board adjourned.

Oct. 14th, 1788.—The Board met at Mr. Smith's—all present. Voted that the president & Mr. Mills, be a committee to settle acc'ts with Rev. Doct. Johnes.

That Justice Lindsly & Mr. Ford be a committee to superintend the business of repairing the old meeting House (in a temporary way) so as to answer the purpose until a new House be built.

Board adjourned.

Dec. 3d, 1789.—The Board met at Mr. Lewis's.—Present the president, Mr. Lindsly, Mr. Ford, Mr. Johnson & Mr. Lewis. The minutes of some of the last meetings of the Board were read. Mr. Lewis who was appointed (the 23d of Sept. '88), to get a ditch

cleared, & fence made on the parsonage lot, reported that he had got the business done, & had p'd Geo. Kelly, 22.6 and William Johnes 21. for the ditching, & had paid to Will Johnes, 25.5 for the fencing. Ordered that the same be allowed.

Mr. President from the committee appointed (14th Oct. '88) to settle accts with the Rev. Doct. Johnes, reported that Mr. Mills and himself had proceeded in the settlement, but after having gone thro' the Doct. suggested some difficulties about it & to prevent it he was willing to accept the tax bills or duplicates and subscriptions (made for his salary) as they now stand and would take the whole risk of collecting it and the losses that may be sustained thereon in full for the present & all preceding years salary and discharge the parish therefrom, provided the Trustees will appoint some person or persons who shall at the expense of the parish go thro' the same & use their endeavors to obtain the cash or notes of the several subscribers or persons taxed & deliver the same to him. On motion whether the doctors proposal be agreed to, it passed in the affirmative—and thereupon Deacon Allen & Mr. Johnson were appointed to go to every person within the parish and indebted either on the subscriptions or duplicates (except Thomas Miller who for his service in making the assessments is to be discharged from the taxes laid on him) for the salary aforesaid—& after they shall have performed the business & delivered the money or notes by them collected to the Rev. Dr. Johnes or his order, they shall receive of the parish a reasonable compensation for their trouble.

Deacon Allen & Mr. Johnson who were appointed (in June, 1788) to carry subscriptions thro' the parish to get a sufficient sum subscribed for building a new meeting house —reported that they had presented the subscriptions to the greatest part of the people of this parish—they then laid the subscriptions before the Board. It appeared that there was a sufficient sum subscribed for inclosing a house of timber according to the estimate heretofore made, whereupon the Board agreed to lay the same before the parish at their first meeting, and that Mr. President wait on the Rev. Doct. Johnes, and request him to appoint a day of meeting for that purpose, and to preach a sermon on the occasion.

(To be continued.)

THE RECORD.

FIRST PRESBYTERIAN CHURCH, MORRISTOWN, N. J.

"THIS SHALL BE WRITTEN FOR THE GENERATION TO COME."—Psalms 102 : 18.

VOL. 1.   DECEMBER, 1880.   NO. 12

(Printed with the approval of Session.)

THE RECORD

Will be printed and published monthly at Morristown, N. J. Terms, 50 cents per annum in advance; 75 cents after June.

Subscriptions will be received at the book-stores of Messrs. Runyon and Emmell, or through the mail, and may begin with the first number. ALL COMMUNICATIONS should be addressed to the

EDITOR OF THE RECORD,

Lock box 44.   Morristown, N. J.

Entered at the Post Office at Morristown, N. J., as second class matter.

————:o:————

————:o:————

Vol. I. of THE RECORD is complete. The twelve numbers are a priceless contribution to local and genealogical history. With their successors they will prove invaluable to all who care for the history of our town and county.

————

NEW YORK, Nov. 17, 1880.

Rev. Rufus S. Green :

MY DEAR SIR : The eleven numbers of THE RECORD, received only two days ago, have afforded me a great deal of pleasure. Please find enclosed one dollar for another year. Fifty cents is entirely too cheap for so valuable a publication.

J. H. WALLACE, *Ed. Wallace's Monthly.*

We advise our readers carefully to preserve the files of THE RECORD, as they will grow in value as the years fly.—*Democratic Banner.*

The history of the "First Church" is so thoroughly interwoven and identified with the early history of Morris County that THE RECORD can but prove highly interesting to our citizens generally.—*Chronicle, Jan. 24th,* 1880.

Other old churches would do well to collect and preserve their histories in the same form, even if the publication were continued only for a single year—*N. Y. Observer, Jan. 29th,* 1880.

It contains much valuable information, and must be of great value as a reference in the future.—*Jerseyman, Jan. 23d,* 1880.

See also page 96. These are but samples of the kind words THE RECORD has received from many sources.

Notwithstanding some generous gifts, for which we desire again to express our thanks, THE RECORD has not paid expenses for the year. It has fallen behind about twenty dollars. Who will help make up this deficiency?

THE RECORD will be published monthly during 1881. Terms 50 cents in advance, 75 cents after June. Please send in your subscriptions at once.

Vol. I. complete can be had for seventy-five cents.

HALF-WAY COVENANT.

Editor of the Record:

Some of your readers, doubtless, desire information concerning the list of "Half-Way Members," found in THE RECORD, from time to time. Dr. Johnes' caption is as follows: "The Names and Number of Persons that have renewed their cov. or taken their Baptismal Vows upon themselves." (Record, p. 28.)

None but the children of church members were regarded, by the early churches of New England, as proper subjects of baptism. Baptized children were considered members of the church, and entitled, at a proper age, if irreproachable, to partake of the Lord's Supper. Certain civil privileges, also, were confined to church members.

The children of the second generation, however, it was found, were much addicted to unsanctified and worldly habits of life, such as unfitted them for full membership in the church. Others, by reason of the awe with which the sacrament of the Lord's Supper was regarded, refraining from the ordinance, until the later period of life. All such were denied the privilege of presenting their offspring to God in baptism. A large number of children were thus growing up unbaptized, and fears were seriously entertained that, in some places, the church would consequently become extinct.

To remedy this evil, it was proposed to recognize a qualified church membership in all baptized persons, even after coming to maturity, on their consenting to assume publicly the engagements made by their parents for them when baptized, and this without any profession of Christian experience, or converson, binding themselves simply to live a Christian life, but not to partake of the Lord's Supper; in consequence of this qualified membership they were to have their children duly baptized. This proposition, after considerable discussion and much opposition, was sanctioned, by the Synod of elders and messengers from all the churches of Massachusetts that met in 1662, at Boston, in the words following:

"Church members who were admitted in minority, understanding tne doctrine of faith, and publicly professing their assent thereto, not scandalous in life, and solemnly owning the covenant before the church, wherein they give up themselves and children to the Lord, and subject themselves to the government of Christ in the church—their children are to be baptized."

This obtained the name of "the half-way covenant," was introduced partially into the other New England Colonies, and found its way into other churches by emigrants from New England. It became a fruithful cause of contention and bitter alienation, and was the means of filling many of the churches with unconverted members, leading at length to great corruption of doctrine. It has long since been entirely abandoned.

E. F. HATFIELD.

(*Continued from page* 88.)

REPRESENTATIVES OF MORRIS COUNTY
IN THE STATE LEGISLATURE.

——:o:——

66th Legislature, 1841, Oct. 26.
Council, James Wood.
Assembly, James W. Drake,
Samuel B. Halsey,
William Stephens,
Thomas C. Willis.

67th Legislature, 1842, Oct. 25.
Council, Ezekiel B. Gaines.
Assembly, Sam'l B. Halsey, (speaker.)
William Stephens,
David T. Cooper,
James Clark.

68th Legislature, 1843, Oct. 24.
Council, John H. Stansborough.
Assembly, James Clark,
John M. Losey,
Samuel Willet,
George Vail.

69th Legislature, 1845, Jan. 14.
Senate, John B. Johnes.
Assembly, Timothy Kitchel,
Matthias Kitchel,
Henry Seward,
George H. Thompson.

70th Legislature, 1846, Jan. 13.
Senate, John B. Johnes.
Assembly, Henry Seward,
George H. Thompson,
Matthias Kitchel,
Calvin Howell.

71st Legislature, 1847, Jan. 12.
Senate, John B. Johnes.
Assembly, Calvin Howell,
Richard Lewis,
Charles McFarland.
Samuel Hilts.

72d Legislature, 1848, Jan. 11.
Senate, Ephraim Marsh.
Assembly, David T. Cooper,
Samuel VanNess,
Edward W. Whelpley.
Andrew J. Smith.

73d Legislature, 1849, Jan. 9.
Senate, Ephriam Marsh, (Pres.)
Assembly, David T. Cooper,
Samuel VanNess,
Ed. W. Whelpley, (Speaker)
Andrew J. Smith.

74th Legislature, 1850, Jan. 8.
Senate, Ephriam Marsh, (Pres.)
Assembly, John L. Kanouse,
Andrew B. Cobb,
Freeman Wood,
George H. Thompson.

75th Legislature, 1851, Jan. 14.
Senate, John A. Bleeker.
Assembly, Cornelius B. Doremus,
Horace Chamberlain,
Jonathan P. Bartley,
Josiah Meeker.

76th Legislature, 1852, Jan. 13.
Senate, John A. Bleeker.
Assembly, John D. Jackson,
Cornelius S. Dickerson,
Robert Albright,
Cornelius B. Doremus.

Hitherto the members of Assembly had
been elected on the general ticket; the last
legislature provided for election by districts.
(P. L. 464.) 1st District : Morris and Chatham ; 2d District : Hanover and Pequannoc;
3d District : Rockaway, Jefferson and Roxbury; 4th District : Randolph, Mendham,
Chester and Washington.

77th Legislature, 1853, Jan. 13.
Senate, John A. Bleeker.
Assembly, Robert Albright,   1st Dist.
John L. Kanouse,   2d "
John D. Jackson,   3d "
Cor. S. Dickerson,   4th "

78th Legislature, 1854, Jan. 10.
Senate, Alexander Robertson.
Assembly, Wm. P. Conkling,   1st Dist.
Andrew B. Cobb,   2d "
William Logan,   3d "
Aaron Pitney,   4th "

79th Legislature, 1855, Jan 9.
Senate, Alexander Robertson,
Assembly, Wm. P. Conkling,   1st Dist.
Edward Howell,   2d "
William Logan,   3d "
Aaron Pitney,   4th "

80th Legislature, 1856, Jan. 8.
Senate, Alexander Robertson.
Assembly, Wm. M. Muchmore, 1st Dist.
Edward Howell,   2d "
William A. Carr,   3d "
Daniel Budd,   4th "

[*To be continued.*]

(*Continued from page 84.*)

MEMBERS.
—:o:——

[The third column on this page is the work of the RECORD. Information which will lead to the correction of any mistake, or the filling of any blank, will be thankfully received.—ED.]

Names.	When Received.	When Dismissed or Died.
John Lindsly . . .	March 1, 1765.	Sept. 10, 1784, aet. 56.
Sarah Lindsly (John), later, wife of Benjamin Halsey .	" " "	March 29, 1803, aet. 67.
Benj., son of Doc. Hathaway .	" " "	
Jonathan Wood . .	" " "	Susp. July 5, 1782, d. Jan. 2, 1804, aet. 75
Deborah Raynor . .	" " "	
Phebe Clark, later, wife of Ichabod Carmichael . .	" " "	
Benjamin Lindsly . .	May 3, 1765.	Died Nov. 8, 1815, born Feb. 22, 1731
Samuel Mills . . .	" " "	June 17, 1805, aet. 85.
Eleazar Lindsly . .	" " "	
Caleb Halsey . .	" " "	"Moved away."
Ezekiel Day . .	" " "	Jan. 3, 1777, aet. 33.
John Pool . .	" " "	Dismissed Jan. 21, 1825.
John Cooper. . .	" " "	"Moved away."
Richard Johnson . .	" " "	Sept. 23, 1825, aet. 77.
Mary Perkhurst (John) .	" " "	"Moved."
Eliz. Easton . .	" " "	
Joanna Coe .	" " "	
Cloe Wines . .	" " "	
Susan. Gildersleeve .	" " "	"Moved."
Rachel Gildersleeve .	" " "	"
Charity Freeman . .	" " "	"
Ezra Halsey . . .	July 5, "	Oct. 23, 1775, aet. 48.
Johnathan Stiles . .	" " "	Oct. 6, 1806, aet. 85.
John Hathaway . .	" " "	"Moved."
Benjamin Coe, Jun. .	" " "	"
Onesimus Whitehead . .	" " " •	July 4, 1814, aet. 72 y. 10 m, and 21 d.
Rebecca Whitehead (Ones.)	" " "	Sept. 3, 1805, aet. 59.
Sarah Lindsly (Benj.) .	" " "	Dec. 16, 1811, born Aug. 12, 1738.
Jerusha Cade, later, wife of John Pool . . .	" " "	Dismissed Jan. 21, 1825.
Obadiah Robin, an Indian .	" " "	
Elizabeth Prudden (Boice) .	Oct. 31, "	
Samuel Roberts . .	Feb. 28, 1766	Jan. 31, 1802, aet. 86.
Abraham Campfield . .	" " "	July 29, 1789, aet. 57.
Dan. Tichenor . .	" " "	"Moved."
Phineas Fairchild . .	" " "	Nov. 12, 1801, aet. 71.
Ebenezer Coe . .	" " "	"Moved."
Isaac Ayers . .	" " "	June 7, 1794, aet. 51.
Silas Gildersleeve . .	" " "	
Nat. Condict . .	" " "	"Moved."
Abigail Condict (Nat.) .	" " "	"
Patience Pierson (Joseph) .	" " "	Dec. 9, 1813, aet. 89.
Rhoda Tuttle . .	" " "	"Moved away."
Ruth Tuttle . .	" " "	" "

(*To be continued.*)

(Continued from page 85.)

BAPTISMS.

1763.

Oct 30. Sam'l Tuthill,Esq. & wf., ch. Samuel
"   " Gilbard Ludlam & wf., ch. Hannah.
"   " Paul Fervor & wf., ch. Amos.
Nov. 6. Stephen Conkling & wf., ch. John.
"   " Robart McCalvin on his wf.'s accompt, ch. Elizabeth.
" 13. Increass Mather & wf., ch. Joseph.
Dec. 4. John Pierson & wf., ch. Sarah.

1764.

Jan. 1. John Michel & wf., ch. John, born Oct. 12, 1863.
Feb. 8. John Ford & wf., ch. Nathan, Bp. at their own home.
Mar. 4. Rob. Arnold & wf., ch. Sarah, born Dec. 24. 1763.
" 18. Benj'n Hathaway & wf., ch. Mabel.
Apr. 1. Cap'n Timothy Mills & wf., ch. Hannah.
"   8. Jabish Bears & wf., ch. Hannah.
"   " Gilbard Allen & wf., ch. Stephen.
May 6. Philip Lindsly & wf., ch. Isaac.
"   " Jedidiah Gregory & wf., ch. Naomi.
"   " Joshuah Guring & wf., ch. Abraham.
"   " David Gauden & wf., ch. Mary.
"   " Stephen Norris & wf., ch. Stephen, born Apr. 6, 1783.
"   " Wilby Clark, on wf.'s accompt, ch. Mehitable.
" 13. Ebenezer Cundict & wf., ch. Byram.
"   " Shadrach Howard & wf., ch. Silas Day.
" 27. Cap'n Benj. Halsey & wf., ch. Benjamin.
June 3. Ebenezer Stiles, on his own accompt, ch. Charity.
"   " Moses Johnson & wf., ch. Naomi.
" 14. Moses Tuttle on wf.'s accompt, ch. Simeon.
" 17. Elijah Pierson & wf., ch. George.
" 24. Job Lorain with his wf., ch. Sollomon.
July 1. Dan. Tichenor & wf., ch. Daniel.
"   " Dan. Carmichael & wf., ch. Phebe, born Sept. 3, 1763.
" 22. John Cole & wf., ch. Mary.
"   " Thomas Miller & wf., ch. Phebe.
" 29. Mary McMahon, ch. James.
"   " Nathan Price & wf., ch. Asee.
"   " Caleb Munson & wf., ch. Mary.

July 29. Nathan Turner & wf., ch. Benjamin.
Aug. 5. Peter Prudden & wf., ch. Peter.
"   " Boys Prudden & wf.,ch. Boys John.
"   " Sol'n Southard, on wf.'s accompt, ch. Phebe.
" 12. Moses Lindsly & wf., ch. Zenas.
" 26. Thomas Tuttle & wf., ch. Mehitabel
"   " Ebenezer Lindsly & wf., child'n Mary & Elizabeth.
" 31. Larence Cummin & wf., ch. Robard.
Sept. 9. Benj. Hathaway & wf., child'n Mary & Sarah.
"   " Augustus Bayles & wf., adopted ch. Rebecca Bayles.
" 23. Jarzel Turner & wf., Household— Joseph, Elizabeth, Rebecca, Catura, Stephen, Sarah.
Oct. 14. Wilky Ludlam, at between 12 & 13. on his own account.
"   " Joseph Lindsly & wf., ch. Susanna.
" 21. James Millar & wf., ch. Sarah.
"   " Tim. Johnes & wf., Negro child Cato; born Sept. 17, 1764.
" 27. Elizabeth Bridge, ch. Sarah.
"   " Susannah Tichenor, ch. Zuba.
"   " Anne Freeman, ch. Cornelius.
Nov. 1. Peter Price, adult.
"   " Hannah, wf. of John Roggers & her child'n Eunice, Elizabeth,Phebe & James.
"   4. Josiah Crane, adult.
"   " John Lindsley & wf., ch. Stephen.
"   " John Lose on wf.'s accompt, ch. Lucretia.
" 11. Thomas Coe & wf., ch. Darius.
"   " Joshua Whitehead & wf., ch. Phebe.
"   " Joseph Cundit & wf., ch. Timothy.
"   " Isaac Pierson & wf., ch. Asa.
" 24. Mattania Lyon & wf., Stephen Smith.
"   " Silas Hains, ch. Jemima.
"   " Sarah, Euben. Halbard's wf. on her own accompt, ch. Mary.
"   " Benj. Pool on wf.'s account, ch. Sibbel.
Dec. 1. Sam'l Oliver & wf., family—Phebe, John, Sarah.
"   " Moses Munson, family—Catharine, Jemima.
" 16. John Easton on wf.'s account, ch. Eunice.
"   " Peter Dickerson & wf., ch. Peter.
" 30. Nathaniel Peck & wf., ch. Phebe.

(To be continued.)

(Continued from page 88.)

MARRIAGES.

1782.

Feb. 1. David Lloyd, of Cap. Mead Company & 1st Jer. Reg., & Mercy Hayward.

" 5. Abraham Hudson & Sarah Oharrow.

Apr. 18. George Phillips & Widow Huldah Condict.

May 6. Jacob Casterlin & Eunice Squire.

June 3. Theophilus Hathaway & Phebe Carmichael.

July 7. George Kelle & Anne Ward, a widow.

" 21. Nehemiah Johnson & Sarah Bridge.

" " Amos Sackers, a soldier, & Elizabeth Godden.

Aug.27. Cornelius Mills & Catherine Looker.

" 29. Joshua Munson & Ruth Wood.

Sept 15. Benj. Holloway & Elizabeth Evolt.

" 30. John Garrigas & Elizabeth Shipman.

Oct. 3. Joseph Gardiner & Martha Lewis.

" 9. Hector & Juda.

Nov.14. Peter Prudden & Esther Prudden.

Dec. 10. William Marsh & Susanna Lindsly.

" 12. Job Loree & Elizabeth Hull.

1783.

Jan. 2. David Tuthill & Phebe Freeman.

" 7. Abner Fairchild & Theodosia Conger.

" 8. Isaac Walker & Ruth Tompkins.

" 13. Peter Davison & Phebe Roberds.

" 15. Tim. Fairchild & Mehitabel Tuttle.

Feb. 2. Nathaniel Carn & Hannah Dun.

Mar. 4. Thomas Fearels & Kezia Bayles.

" 6. Isaac Mills & Ruth Pain.

" 11. Jacob Ludlam & Margaret Pool.

" 16. Benj'n Prudden & Elizabeth Thompkins.

" 26. Daniel Burnet & Esther Jacks.

Apr. 3. Jacob Reed & Catharine Masters.

May 8. Joseph Lindsly & Sarah Lindsly.

" 11. Elijah Sneden & Sarah Gregory.

July 2. Pharis Doty & Phebe Freeman.

" 3. Joseph Munson & Joanna Johnson.

" " Abraham Godwin & Mary Munson.

Aug.17. Joseph Force & Elizabeth Bottinghouse.

" 21. Abraham Willis & Rebecca Ludlam.

" 24. John Hines & Elizabeth Prudden.

Sept.18. Timothy Morris & Malatia Gobil.

Oct. 2. Jacob Simson & Sarah Turner.

" 26. Jnula Riggs & Jemima Cooper.

Oct. 30. Jesse Saxon & Kezia Allen.

Nov. 5. Thomas Thompson & Anna Catreen Card.

" 6. John Freeman & Esther Larzelere.

" 12. Maj'r Leonard Bleeker & Joanna Abeel.

" 19. Lambert Merrell & Comfort Wheeler

" 20. Samuel Leonard & Abigail Pierson.

" 24. William Denine & Margaret Templeton.

Dec. 1. William Hulbard & Deborah Fairchild.

" 3. Joseph Prudden, Jun. & Providence Gordon.

" 16. Stephen Turner & Phebe Peck.

" 30. Isaac Garrigus & Phebe Locy.

Married to this date, 779.

1784.

Jan. 7. George Tucker Anne Arnold:

" " Daniel Phoenix & Anne Philips.

" 20. Ephraim Hayward & Phebe Dickerson.

Feb. 17. Jesse Locy & Martha Locy.

Mar. 3. Abijah Sherman & Mary Gregory.

" 4. Capt'n Alexander Thompson & Amelia DeHart.

" 31. Daton Talmage & Charity Stiles.

Apr. 15. Samuel Prudden & Sarah Oliver.

" 29. William Cross & Sarah Lasheleere.

May 9. Daniel Skelly & Catharine Headly.

June24. David Freeman & Rachel Pierson.

" " Stephen Headfield & Elizabeth Holloway.

July 24. John Christopher Smith & Elizabeth Ward.

" 25. Samuel Richards & Phebe Stockbridge.

Aug.24. Isaac Conkling & Comfort Pitney.

Sept. 1. Josiah Munson & Rachel Holloway.

Nov. 1. Lebbeus Norris & Elizabeth Hedglen.

" 8. George Cook & Phebe Totten.

" 11. Lodovicus Kent & Mary Tuthill.

" 18. Joseph Trobridge & Mary Locy.

" 22. Silvanus Tuttle & Mary Brown.

800 to this date.

" 30. Benj. Wilson & Mary Prudden.

Dec. 3. John Conkling & Elizabeth Mills.

" 15. Charles Smith & Cecelia Tuttle.

" 24. Matthew Lum & Hannah Ludlam.

" 26. Daniel Lewis & Elizabeth McCalvey.

" 29. David Hurd & Abigail Fairchild.

(To be continued.)

(*Continued from page 87.*)

BILL OF MORTALITY.

1778.

Sept.12. Anne, wife of Timothy Stiles,* aet. 27, consumption.

" 13. Elizabeth, wife of John Macferran,* aet. 77, old age.

" 29. Mehitabel, wife of James Smith,* aet. 27, consumption.

Oct. 7. Robert Day, aet. 28, putrid fever.

" 8. A child of William Hamilton.

Nov. 5. Widow Leonard, aet. 75, fever.

" 6. Isaac, son of Robert Arnold, Jun, aet. 5, worms.

" 8. Mary, daughter of David Gardner, aet. 5, consumption.

" 10. Mink, servant of Deacon Burnet, aet. 60, pleurisy.

" 22. John Macferren,* aet. 80, old age.

Dec.20. Joanna, daughter of George Mills, whooping-cough.

" 19. Stephen, son of Gilbert Deacon Allen, aet.15, consumption.

1779.

Jan. 17. William Hulbert, Sen., aet. 76, old age.

" 23. Elizabeth, daughter of Job Loree, aet. 16, nervous fever.

" 28. Tamer, widow of Capt. Solomon Munson,* aet. 77, old age.

" 29. Joshua Whitehead, aet. 70, consumption.

Feb. 17. Phœbe, wife of Zophar Freeman,* aet. 54, consumption.

Mar. 20. Servant of Benjamin Pierson, dysentery.

" 28. Wife of Elias Vancourt.

" 29. Jacob Allen,† aet. 77, old age.

Apr. 17. Betsey, wife of William Hamilton, aet. 17, child-bed.

May 1. Child of Christopher Woods.

" 2. Phœbe, wife of Christopher Woods, aet. 43, child-bed.

June 3. Elizabeth, daughter of Joseph Lewis, aet. 2, sudden.

July 22. Hannah, widow of Stephen Freeman,* aet. 85, old age.

Aug. 4. Ebenezer Norris, aet. 22, mortification in the hip and thigh.

Sept 10. A child of Samuel Broadwell.

" 15. Reuben Cherry, aet. 64, intermittent fever.

" 20. A child of David Gardiner, fits.

Sept.25. Son of George Mills.

Nov. 3. Rhoda, wife of Jedediah Gregory,* aet. 42, consumption.

" 4. A child of Marsh.

" 6. A child of James Bamfield.

Dec. 9. Anne, wife of Maj. Joseph Lindsley,* aet. 37, consumption.

1780.

Jan. 16. Polly, daughter of John Pool, Sen., aet. 18, consumption.

" 20. Jane, wife of David Youngs, aet. 26, consumption.

" 20. Esther, wife of John Brookfield, Esq.† aet. 60, consumption.

" " A child of Jonathan Carter.

Feb. 15. Charlotte, daughter of John Beach, aet. 1, hives.

Mar. 16. Sarah,wife of Doc. Timothy Johnes, aet. 28, asthma.

" 22. Hannah, wife of George Hall, aet. 28, dropsy of the breast.

" " A child of Daniel Freeman, Jun.

Apr. 12. Nancy, widow of Ezekiel Cheevers, aet. 55, consumption.

" 14. Jonathan Crane, aet. 61, consumption.

" 25. Jacob Johnson, aet. 30, consumption.

May 12. Capt. Peter Dickerson, aet. 54, inflammatory fever.

" 22. William Losey, aet. 85, old age.

June 10. Sarah, daughter of Peter Norris, Jun., fits.

" 28. Rachel, wife of John Lyon, aet. 23, consumption.

July 3. George King, aet. 34, consumption.

" 17. Michael Hoffman, aet. 19, fever.

Aug. 14. Joseph Lacey, aet. 60, consumption.

" 24. Eunice, wife of Benjamin Prudden, aet. 40, putrid fever.

Sept.15. Henry, son of William Cherry, fever.

" " David Lee, aet. 35, sudden.

Oct. 20. Henry Primrose,* aet. 70, asthma.

" 27. A child of Doct. Lewis Dunham.

Nov.18. Wife of Daniel Burnet, aet. 22, dysentery.

Dec. — Phœbe, wife of Asa Beach, aet. 18, consumption.

" — A child of Asa Beach.

" 21. Henry Wick,† aet. 72, pleurisy.

(To be continued.)

(*Continued from page 88.*)

TRUSTEES' BOOK.

——:o:——

Mr. Ford reported that the decay of some timber on the parsonage made it necessary to sell or use it to prevent any loss from further decay. Whereupon Mr. Ford & Mr. Johnson be a committee to dispose of the said trees or timber to the best advantage & to report their proceedings.

Mr. Lewis again suggested the necessity of having a book provided for entering the acc'ts of the Trustees. Voted that he provide a suitable book for that purpose.

December 11th, 1789.

At a meeting of the congregation of the first presbyterian church in Morris Town (at the request of the Trustees) on the 11th day of December, 1789, to instruct the Trustees respecting their proceedings in building a new meeting house or appoint a committee to direct the s'd building, & the congregation having met, the Rev. Doct. Johnes preached a sermon on the occasion and then the congregation proceeded to business. Presid't Condict opened the business of the day.

Voted that Deacon Allen serve as Moderator of this meeting. That Joseph Lewis serve as Clerk. A motion was made for appointing a committee to superintend the building a new meeting house, as there was now a sum subscribed sufficient to provide materials, raise & inclose the same. Elder Phillips, Elder Condict & others objected, & alleged the old house would do for a number of years with some repairs—after some desultory debates a vote was taken—whether we should repair the old, or build a new meeting house & there appeared a large majority for building a new house—after one year.

Deacon Prudden, Mr. Kinney and others proposed that a vote should again be taken, whether the house should be built of Brick or of Timber, & the votes being taken there appeared to be a large majority for building of Timber.

The congregation then proceeded to elect a committee to consist of three persons who should employ workmen, provide materials & superintend the said building—& it was agreed that if any of the Trustees were appointed to serve in the committee their place in the Board of Trustees should be considered as vacant—& the votes being taken by poll there appeared a majority in favor of Moses Estey, Joseph Lewis & Daniel Phoenix, Jun.

A motion was made for some general instructions to be given the committee respecting the size of the building, where it should stand, what it should be inclosed with, &c. The congregation declined giving any instructions at present but impowered the committee to appoint a meeting of the parish at some future time for that purpose —then adjourned.

(*To be continued.*)

———

TREASURY DEPARTMENT,
Room 30., Fourth Auditor's Office,
Washington, D. C., Feb. 19, 1880.

Rev'd Rufus S. Green :

Dear Sir: Less than an hour ago, I received by mail from the hands of Rev'd J. C. Rankin, of Baskingridge, a copy of Vol. I., No. 1 of the Record. After a careful perusal of the number received I passed it over to Hon. Edwin Salter, who occupies the desk nearest mine for his inspection, thinking he might perhaps like to join me in the remittance as a subscriber, which he voluntarily proposed and at once suggested the names of two or three others in the Treasury Department whom he thought would like to join us. I also had a friend, the grandson of the Rev. Timothy Johnes, whose name heads your "List of Pastors." We called upon them at once and found them as anxious to subscribe as we ourselves were, and have the pleasure herewith to furnish a list of 5 subscribers with remittance of 50 cents each—in all $2.50 with address of each, and request that we be furnished with copies beginning with No. 1, so that we may be able to preserve the full set for binding and better preservation.

If a similar enterprise were undertaken in every county in the United States, the Record would become invaluable and save immense labor and correspondence searching for such information as you propose to give in the Record. Every citizen of Morris county and every one whose ancestry dates back to the early days of New Jersey, ought and doubtless will subscribe and find it the best investment they have ever made of so small a sum of money.

Very respectfully your Ob't Serv't,

JOHN J. HAYDEN.

THE RECORD.

FIRST PRESBYTERIAN CHURCH, MORRISTOWN, N. J.

"This shall be Written for the Generation to Come."—Psalms 102 : 18.

VOL. II.	JANUARY, 1881.	NO. 1.

(Printed with the approval of Session.)

THE RECORD

Will be printed and published monthly at Morristown, N. J. Terms, 50 cents per annum in advance; 75 cents after June.

Subscriptions will be received at the book-stores of Messrs. Runyon and Emmell, or through the mail. All communications should be addressed to the

EDITOR OF THE RECORD,
Lock box 44.   Morristown, N. J.
Vol. I. complete, 75 cents.

Entered at the Post Office at Morristown, N. J., as second class matter.

———:o:———

Vol. II. of THE RECORD begins with this number. We hope to give our subscribers old and new historical matter of even more value than during the past year. We would esteem it a favor if our readers would call the attention of their friends to the merits of our little paper. May we also ask for the early renewal of subscriptions?

———:o:———

HARRISBURG, PENN., Oct. 7, 1880.

Dear Sir:

I am very desirous of ascertaining the names of the parents of Eleazer Lindsley, who was born, probably at Morristown, Dec. 7, 1737, was Lieutenant-Colonel of Col. Oliver Spencer's regiment in the continental service, and with all his family removed from Morris County in 1790. He with his wife Mary (Miller) became a half-member of your church, as I learn in the RECORD Jan. 25, 1761.

The information is desired for genealogical purposes alone. If in your power to throw any light on this point, or if you can refer me to any person likely to know the history of the Lindsley family, I would be greatly obliged.

Very respectfully,
EDWARD HERRICK.

FROM HARPER'S MONTHLY, FEBRUARY, 1859.

From Dr. Thacher's *Journal* and the *New Jersey Gazette*, we learn that "the distinguished gentleman, Don Juan de Miralles," visited the Short Hills on the 19th or 20th of April, 1780, and undoubtedly admired the magnificent prospect there spread out before him. It was then, and it is now, a paradisaical prospect, which, once seen, is not to be forgotten. When Baron Steuben, on the 24th of April, had arranged the grand review of his battalions to the delight of Washington, De la Luzerne and others, and that night, while the fire-works were flashing their beautiful eccentricities in the darkness, and the sounds of music and dancing were heard at O'Hara's, Don Juan de Miralles was tossing with death-fever. Four days afterward he died, and on the 29th of April his funeral took place in a style never imitated or equalled in Morristown since. Dr. Thacher exhausted all his expletive words in expressing his admiration of the scene, and doubtless would have used more if they had been at hand. Hear him:

"I accompanied Dr. Schuyler to headquarters to attend the funeral of M. de Miralles. The deceased was a gentleman of high rank in Spain, and had been about one year a resident with our Congress from the Spanish Court. The corpse was dressed in rich state and exposed to public view, as is customary in Europe. The coffin was most splendid and stately, lined throughout with fine cambric, and covered on the outside with rich black velvet, and ornamented in a superb manner. The top of the coffin was removed to display the pomp and grandeur with which the body was decorated. It was in a splendid full dress, consisting in a scarlet suit, embroidered with rich gold lace, a three-cornered gold-laced hat, a genteel-cued wig, white silk stockings, large diamond shoe and knee buckles, a profusion of diamond rings decorated the fingers, and from a superb gold watch set with diamonds several rich seals were suspended. His Excellency General Washington, with several other general officers, and members of Congress attended the funeral solemnities and walked as chief mourners. The other officers, of the army, and numerous respectable citizens, formed a splendid procession extending about one mile. The pall-bearers were six field-officers, and the coffin was borne on the shoulders of four officers of the artillery in full uniform. Minute guns were fired during the procession, which greatly increased the solemnity of the occasion. A Spanish priest performed the services at the grave in the Roman Catholic form. The coffin was inclosed in a box of plank, and in all the profusion of pomp and grandeur was deposited in the silent grave, in the common burrying ground near the church at Morristown. A guard is placed at the grave lest our soldiers should be tempted to dig for hidden treasure."

This pompous funeral, so pompously described, was quite in contrast with the funeral procession which the previous week entered the same burying ground. The numerous friends and neighbors of Jacob Johnson made a long procession, but his oldest son, Mahlon, who still survives, remembers that there was only one vehicle on wheels at that funeral. Dr. Johnes and the physician led the procession on horseback, and the only wagon present was used to convey the coffin to the graveyard. All the people, men, women and children, either rode on horseback or walked on foot. At the house the pastor drew heavenly consolation for the afflicted from the Word of God, and at the grave dismissed the people by thanking them for their kindness to the dead. And had Dr. Johnes officiated at the funeral of General Washington his services would have been just as simple and unostentatious. These two funerals make no uninteresting features in the social life of Morristown when Washington spent his last winter there.

(Continued from page 91.)

REPRESENTATIVES OF MORRIS COUNTY IN THE STATE LEGISLATURE.

81st Legislature, 1857, Jan. 13.
Senate,   Andrew B. Cobb.
Assembly, Benj. M. Felch,   1st Dist.
            Richard Speer,   2d   "
            William A. Carr,   3d   "
            Daniel Budd.   4th "

82d Legislature, 1858, Jan. 12.
Senate,   Andrew B. Cobb.
Assembly, Benj. M. Felch,   1st Dist.
            Richard Speer,   2d   "
            Lyman A. Chandler, 3d   "
            John Naughright.   4th "

83d Legislature, 1859, Jan. 11.
Senate,   Andrew B. Cobb.
Assembly, A. H. Stansburough, 1st Dist.
            James H. Ball,   2d   "
            Lyman A. Chandler, 3d   "
            John Naughright.   4th "

84th Legislature, 1860, Jan. 10.
Senate,   Daniel Budd.
Assembly, Eugene Ayers,   1st Dist.
            James H. Ball,   2d   "
            Nelson H. Drake.   3d   "
            Nathan Horton.   4th "

85th Legislature, 1861, Jan. 8.
Senate,   Daniel Budd.
Assembly, William W Beach, 1st Dist.
            John Hill,   2d   "
            Nelson H. Drake,   3d   "
            Nathan Horton.   4th "
In 1860 the representation of the county was reduced to three members, and the county was redistricted. (P. L. 532–548.)
1st District, Chatham, Morris, Mendham and Chester.
2d District, Hanover, Pequannock and Rockaway.
3d District, Randolph, Roxbury and Jefferson.

86th Legislature, 1862, Jan. 14.
Senate,   Daniel Budd.
Assembly, Jacob Vanatta,   1st Dist.
            John Hill,   2d   "
            Nelson H. Drake.   3d   "

87th Legislature, 1863, Jan. 13.
Senate,   Lyman A. Chandler.
Assembly, Jacob Vanatta,   1st Dist.
            William J. Wood,   2d   "
            Jesse Hoffman.   3d   "

88th Legislature, 1864, Jan. 12.
Senate,   Lyman A. Chandler.
Assembly, Henry C. Sanders. 1st Dist.
            John Bates,   2d   "
            Jesse Hoffman.   3d   "

89th Legislature, 1865, Jan. 10.
Senate,   Lyman A. Chandler.
Assembly, Alfred M. Treadwell,1st Dist.
     John Bates,   2d   "
     Jesse Hoffman.   3d   "
90th Legislature, 1866, Jan. 9.
Senate,   George T. Cobb.
Assembly, James C. Yawger, 'ist Dist.
     John Hill, Speaker, 2d   "
     Elias M. White.   3d   "
91st Legislature, 1867, Jan. 8.
Senate,   George T. Cobb.
Assembly, James C. Yawger,   1st Dist.
     Lewis Estler,   2d   "
     ' Elias M. White.   3d   "
In 1867 (P. L. 514) the county was redistricted as follows:
   1st Dist., Chatham. Hanover, Morris and Passaic.
   2d Dist., Pequannoc, Rockaway, Randolph and Jefferson.
   3d Dist., Roxbury, Washington, Chester and Mendham.
92d Legislature, 1868, Jan. 14.
   Senate,   George T. Cobb.
Assembly, Daniel Coghlan,   1st Dist.
     George Gage.   2d   "
     Jesse M. Sharp.   3d   "
In 1868, (P. L. 1043) county again redistricted :
   1st Dist., Passaic, Chatham. Hanover, Morris and Mendham.
   2d Dist., Jefferson, Rockaway and Boonton.
   3d Dist., Roxbury, Washington, Chester and Randolph.
93d Legislature, 1869, Jan. 12.
Senate,   George T. Cobb.
Assembly, Theo. W. Phoenix,   1st Dist.
     Columbus Beach,   2d   "
     Jesse M. Sharp.   3d   "
94th Legislature, 1870, Jan. 10.
Senate,   George T. Cobb.
Assembly, Theo. W. Phoenix, 1st Dist.
     Columbus Beach,   2d   "
     Jesse M Sharp.   3d   "
95th Legislature, 1871, Jan. 10.
Senate,   Columbus Beach.
Assembly, Nathaniel Niles,   1st Dist.
     Wm. B. Lefevre,   2d   "
     Aug. C. Canfield.   3d   "
In 1871, (P. L. 47) County again redistricted :
   1st Dist., Chatham. Hanover, Montville and Morris.
   2d Dist., Boonton, Pequannoc, Rockaway and Jefferson.
   3d Dist., Passaic, Mendham, Chester Washington. Roxbury and Randolph.

96th Legislature, 1872, Jan. 9.
Senate,   Aug. W. Cutler.
Assembly, N. Niles, (Speaker.) 1st Dist.
     Wm. B. Lefevre,   2d   "
     Aug. C. Canfield.   3d   "
97th Legislature, 1873, Jan. 14.
Senate,   Aug. W. Cutler.
Assembly, William H. Howell, 1st Dist.
     Jacob Z. Budd,   2d   "
     Aug. C. Canfield.   3d   "
98th Legislature, 1874, Jan. 13.
Senate,   Aug. W. Cutler.
Assembly, William H. Howell, 1st Dist.
     Jacob Z. Budd,   2d   "
     Elias M. Skellenger.3d   "
99th Legislature, 1875, Jan.. 12.
Senate,   John Hill.
Assembly, J. C. Youngblood, 1st Dist.
     Edmund D. Halsey, 2d   "
     Elias M. Skellenger.3d   "
100th Legislature, 1876, Jan. 10.
Senate,   John Hill.
Assembly, J. C. Youngblood, 1st Dist.
     Edmund D. Halsey, 2d   "
     Elias M. Skellenger. 3d   "
101st Legislature, 1877, Jan. 9.
Senate,   John Hill.
Assembly, A. C. VanDuyne,   1st Dist.
     C. O. Cooper.   2d   "
     C. P. Garrabrant.   3d   "
102d Legislature, 1878, Jan. 8.
Senate,   Aug. C. Canfield.
Assembly, Francis J. Doremus,1st Dist.
     C. O. Cooper,   2d }   "
     Joshua S. Salmon.   "
     C. P. Garrabrant. 3d   "
In 1878, (P. L. 542), the County was redistricted as follows:
   1st Dist.,Chatham, Passaic, Morris, Mendham and Chester.
   2d Dist., Boonton, Pequannoc, Rockaway, Montville and Hanover.
   3d Dist., Washington, Mount Olive, Roxbury, Randolph and Jefferson.
103d Legislature, 1879, Jan. 14.
Senate,   Aug. C. Canfield.
Assembly, Charles F. Axtell, 1st Dist.
     James H. Bruen, 2d   "
     H. W. Hunt.   3d   "
In 1879, (P. L. 36) the act redistricting the county passed in 1878 was repealed and the districts were left as before that act was passed :
104th Legislature, 1880, Jan. 12.
Senate,   Aug. C. Canfield.
Assembly, Charles F. Axtell,   1st Dist.
     James H. Bruen, 2d   "
     Holloway W. Hunt. 3d   "
105th Legislature, 1881, Jan. 12.
Senate,   James C. Youngblood.
Assembly, Wm. C. Johnson,   1st Dist.
     John F. Post,   2d   "
     Oscar Lindsley.   3d   "

(*Continued from page 92.*).

MEMBERS.

[The third column on this page is the work of the RECORD. Information which will lead to the correction of any mistake, or the filling of any blank, will be thankfully received.—ED.]

Names.	When Received.	When Dismissed or Died.
Jonathan Hathaway,	April 27, 1766	Died Aug. 26, 1814 or Feb. 17, 1821.
James Brookfield,	" " "	Feb. 27, 1777, aet. 35.
Mary Lindsly (Eliezer)	" " "	
Ruth Serren (James) of Middletown,	" " "	
Susannah Halbart,	" " "	
William Vergusen,	July 4, "	"Moved."
Jonas Philips,	Sept. 5, "	Dec. 26, 1813, born March 12, 1735.
John Allen,	July 2, 1767	"Moved."
Frederick King,	July 5, "	Nov. 11, 1796, aet. 58.
Mary Southard, (Solomon)	Aug. 25, 1768	
Sarah Loree (Sob)	Nov. 4, "	"Moved away."
Ichabod Cooper,	May 4, 1770	Nov. 29, 1809, aet. 68.
Abigail Prudden (John)	June 28, "	July 17, 1805, aet. 54.
Joseph Riggs,	Aug. 30, "	"Moved away."
Catharine Tichenor, (Dan.)	Nov. 2, "	Jan. 8, 1776, aet. 40.
Phebe Arnold (Stephen)	May 3, 1771	"Moved."
George Phillips,	Aug. 29, "	July 22, 1784, aet. 52.
Dehorah Phillips (George)	" " "	Jan. 25, 1782, aet. 47.
Phebe Phillips (Jonas),	" " "	Aug. 2, 1819, aet. 91.
Sarah Tuthill (Doc. Sam'l),	" " "	Nov. 12, 1811, aet. 80.
Rhoda Prudden (Peter)	" " "	Apr. 10, 1818, aet. 87,
Daniel Carmichael,	July 3, 1772	Aug. 24, 1804. aet. 64.
Miriam Wilkerson,	" " "	
Enos, Serv. of Elder Ezra Halsey,	" " "	"Moved."
Mehitabel Smith (James),	Sept. 4, "	Sept. 29, 1778, aet. 27.
Sarah Crane (Jonathan)	Nov. "	Feb. 3, 1787, aet. 63.
Hannah Norris (Peter)	July 1, 1773	
Phebe Condict (Zenas),	" " "	
Sarah Turner (Jarzel),	Sept. 2, "	Nov. 4, 1805, aet. 75.
Jonathan Raynor,	Oct. 10, "	
Tripena Raynor, (Jonathan)	" " "	
Phebe Budd (Doc. Bern),	Nov. 5, "	
Kezia Ball,	Dec. 31, "	Aug. 24, 1774, aet. 27.

"These yt. follow the ingatherings of yt. Divine harvest A. D., 1774; sweet drops of ye morning dew."

Stephen Conklin, Junr.,	May 1, 1774	Aug. 31, 1788, aet. 38.
Jonathan Stiles, Junr.,	July 1, "	
Jeduthan Day,	" " "	
Samuel Seward	" " "	"Moved."
Mabel Tuttle (Thomas),	Sept. 1, "	
Lydia Seward,	" " "	
William Hamilton,	" " "	"Moved."
Eunice Prudden,	" " "	
Deborah Carter,	" " "	"Moved."
Hannah Condict,	" " "	"
Hannah, wf. of Elen Hathaway.	" " "	

(*To be continued.*)

BAPTISMS.

(Continued from page 98.)

1765.

Jan. 4. Joshua Winget, adult.
" " Garret Miller & wf., household except oldest son, Mary Elizabeth, Garret, Absolam, Phebe, Sarah.
" 27 Joshua Ball on wf.'s account, ch. Joshua.
" " Alexander Kermichael & wf., ch. David.
" " Ebenezer Coe & wf., ch. Silas.
Feb. 10. Jacob Ford, Jun. & wf., ch. Gabriel.
" " Benj. Woodruff & wf., ch. Joseph.
" 24. David Fairchild & wf., ch. Samuel.
March 10. Daniel Cermichael & wf., ch. John born Jan. 23, 1763.
" 31. Joseph Stiles & wf., ch. Joseph.
Apr. 14. Sam'l Allwood & wf., ch. Mary.
" " Benj. Lindsly & wf., ch. Hannah.
" " Benj. Coe & wf., negro ch. Bathsheba, born March 23, 1765.
" 21. Paul Fervour & wf., ch. Paul.
" " Increase Mather & wf., ch. John.
" " Jno. Easton on wf.'s account, ch. Susanna.
" 28. James Keen & wf., ch. Hannah.
" " Cap. Dan. Tuttle on wf.'s account, ch. Catura.
May 12. Henry Gardiner & wf., ch. Henry.
" " Garret Miller & wf., ch. Samuel.
June 9. Jeptha Byram & wf., ch. Eleazar.
" " James Chadwick & wf., ch. Hannah.
" 30. Joseph Person & wf., ch. Hepsiba.
" " Jonathan Hathaway & wf., ch. Timothy.
July 5. Onesimus Whitehead, adult.
" " Jerusha Cade, adult.
" " Robin Indian, adult, name Obadiah.
" " John Hathaway, ch. Sarah.
" " Onesimus Whitehead & wf., ch. Ezekiel, born May 7, 1765.
" 7. Nat. Lhomedau & wf., ch. William.
" 21. John Ayrs & wf., ch. Elisha.
" " Abraham Campfield & wf., ch. Jacob.
Aug. 18. John Laporte on wf.'s account, ch. Cornelus.
Sept. 1. Dan. Freeman & wf., ch. John.
" 22. Moses Prudden & wf., ch. Abigail.
" 29. Stephen Conkling & wf., ch. Abraham.

Sept. 29 Eleazar Hathaway & wf., ch. Abigail.
Oct. 13. Eliphalet Clark on wf.'s account, ch. Eliphalet.
Nov. 17. Jonathan Wood & wf., ch. Jonathan Baldwin.
" " Joshua Guering & wf., ch. Penina.
" " Seth Crowell, Junr. & wf., ch. Hannah.
" 21. Sol. Munson, Junr. & wf., ch. Josiah.
Dec. 1. Job Lorain & wf., ch. Charity.
" " Philip Lindsly & wf., ch. Jacob.
" 12. Gil. Ludlam & wf., ch. Daniel.
" 22. Timo. Day & wf., Israel.
1766.
Jan. 19. Docr. Sam'l Tuthill & wf., ch. Mary.
" " Peter Norris on his acc., ch. Hannah.
Feb. 2. Wilby Clark & wf., ch. Sarah.
" 8. Jarzel Turner & wf., ch. Naomi.
" 23. Frederick King & wf., ch. Henry.
Mar. 10. Jabish Bears & wf., ch. Elizabeth.
" " Nathaniel Cundict & wf., ch. David.
" " Zenas Cundict & wf., ch. David.
" 23. Jabez Campfield & wf., ch. William.
" " Peter Prudden & wf., ch. Rhoda.
Apr. 6. Christopher Wood & wf., ch. Freeman, born Sept. 18, 1765.
" " Moses Johnson & wf., ch. Hannah.
" " John Mitchel & wf., ch. Sarah, born Jan. 4, 1766.
" 13. Robard Hinds & wf., ch. Mary.
" " Robard McKalvey on wf.'s account, ch. Rebeccah.
" 20. Ichabod Carmichael & wf., ch. Mary.
" " Stephen Norris & wf., ch. Rebecca, born March 15, 1766.
" " Robart Arnold & wf., ch. David, born March 18, 1766.
" " John Redman & wf., ch. Joseph.
May 18. Moses Munson & wf., ch. Eunice.
" " Sol. Southard on wf.'s account, ch. Rhoda.
" " Jedidiah Mills & wf., ch. Elizabeth.
June 15. Gilbard Allen & wf., ch. Elizabeth.
" " Samuel Mills & wf., ch. Phebe.
" " Zophar Gildersleeve on wf.'s account, ch. Patience.
" " Stephen Hedges & wf., ch. John.
" " James Chadwick on wf.'s account, ch. Rhoda.

(To be continued.)

(*Continued from page 94.*)

MARRIAGES.

1785.

Jan. 11. John Howell & Phebe Farrand.
" 12. David Lindsly & Tapena Pierson.
" 13. Docr. Timothy Johnes & Abigail Juline, daughter of Mr. John Blanchard.
" 23. John Prudden & Mary VanCort.
Feb. 13. Nathaniel Tingly & Sarah More.
" 14. Israel Lum & Patience Pierson.
" 9. William Johnes & Anne Brewster, ceremony by Rev. Mr. Roe.
" 24. John Oliver & Sarah Prudden.
Mar. 6. William Stevenson & Lucy Mitchel.
Apr. 7. Johnathan Lindsly & Jemima Stiles.
" " Henry Huffman & Lidia Parker.
May 26. Henry Willm. DeSaussure & Elizabeth Ford.
June 8. Benjn. Halsey, Esq. & Widow Sarah Lindsly.
Oct. 23. John Hayward & Widow Lydia Shipman, both of Rockaway.
" 25. Abraham Genung & Hannah Johnson.
" 27. John Parriot & Salomy Goble.
Dec. 14. Cornelius Loce & Anna Hill.

1786.

Jan. 19. Isaac Lindsly & Phebe Condict.
Feb. 16. Ezekiel Howell & Susannah Hill.
Mar. 26. Joseph Lindsly & Phebe Rogers.
Apr. 4. Cornelius Bald & Sarah Budd.
" 12. James Rogers & Massey Johnson.
" 13. Benjamin Marsh & Eunice Easton.
" 20. William Courtney & Mary Chamberlain.
" 23. John Sprout & Mary Cermichael.
" 25. Rev. Alexander Miller & Elizabeth Ayres.
May 9. Benjamin Lamson & Thankful Hathaway.
" 16. James Morrison & Sary Primrose.
June 16. John Devens & Eunice Wood, wid.
Aug. 3. James Cook & Ruth Pierson.
" 15. John Allerton & Rhoda Carter.
Sep. 24. Loaumi Casterling & Sharlotte Fairchild.
Oct. 31. Jacob Canfield & Eunice Munson.
Nov. 21. Amos Ward & Susanna Easton.
" " Bethuel Pierson & Anne Ogden.
Dec. 24. John Cummins & Mary Crane, widow.

1787.

Jan. 1. Samuel Hill & Susanna Lyon.
" 3. Anthony Squire & Sarah Mills.
" 8. Joseph Woodman & Anne Larkins.
Feb. 7. William Burnet & Hannah Lindsly.
" 13. Benjamin Hathaway & Phebe Baldwin.
" 22. Joseph Still & Martha Gardner.
Mar. 2. Jacob Conger & Phebe Johnson.
" 12. Francis Phillips & Mary Briant.
" 14. Peter Fairchild & Savia Squire.
" 25. Moses Johnson, Jun. & Hulda Kenny.
Apr. 10. John Sheppard & Sibbel Gardiner.
" 15. Nathaniel Heady & Phebe Carmen.
" 26. David Halsey & Phebe Fairchild.
May 24. John Dorcey & Phebe Johnes, my Grand-daughter.
July 5. Zena Mills & Phebe Headly.
" 18. Stephen Bunnel & Susanna Pierson.
" 22. William Maniken & Catharine Tarney.
" 29. John House & Joanna Prudden.
Oct. 18. Jacob Lindsly & Abigail Prudden.
Nov. 8. Alexander Kirkpatrick & Sarah Mitchel.

1788.

Jan. 3. Michael Mountz & Margaret Denmen.
" 13. Joseph Godden & Eunice Fairchild.
" 16. Steven Lindsly & Hannah Crowell.
" 27. Isaac Drake & Phebe Mills.
" 31. Zenas Lindsly & Rachel Ogden.
Feb. 7. Abraham Core & Jane Guierin.
" 23. Zebedee Jones, Esq. & Abigail Currey.
Mar. 3. Josiah Munson & Ruth Hathaway.
" 36. John Lyon & Jemima Smith.
Apr. 10. Ichabod Genung & Mary Pierson.
" 20. Jonathan Watkins & Susanna Larison.
May 14. Gabriel Pierson & Ruth Ward.
" 15. Daniel Stiles & Elizabeth Brookfield.
" 18. Coonrah Esler & Sarah Carns.
June 1. Will. Hardy, free negro, & Hannah, Jon. Dickerson's wench.
July 28. George Foster Tenney & Sarah Bayles.
Aug. 31. Silas Howell & Sarah Potter.
Sept. 29. Daniel Smith & Sarah Pierson.

(To be continued.)

(Continued from page 95.)

BILL OF MORTALITY.

1781.

Jan. — Andrew Wade, aet 44, consumption.

" 29. William, son of William Cherry, aet. 2, convulsion-fits.

" 31. Widow of Samuel Baldwin, aet. 64.

" " Caroline, wife of Michael Mounts, aet. 26, consumption.

Feb. 27. Wife of Charles Allen, aet. 90, old age.

" " Letitia, wife of Amariah Sutten, aet. 47.

" " Wife of Enos Limas, black woman.

Mar. 8. Ezekiel Gildersleves, aet. 28, consumption.

" 11. Huldah, daughter of John Mills, aet. 1, worms.

" 12. John Primrose, aet. 46, atrophy.

Apr. — A child of Ralph Bridge.

" — Sarah, daughter of Henry Dow Trip, aet. 10, tapeworm,

May 4. A child of Capt. Joseph Beach.

" 27. Mary, wife of Samuel Morrison, aet. 26, child-bed.

" — A child of Samuel Morrison.

June 24. Mary, wife of Joseph Williams, aet. 39, consumption.

July 10. A child of Capt. John Lindsley.

" 21. David, son of Daniel Smith, aet. 2, scald.

Aug. 11. Letitia, wife of Benjamin Bayles,* aet. 78, consumption.

Sept. 13. Charles Allen, aet. 106, old-age.

" 17. Joanna, wife of Jonathan Stiles, Esq., aet. 53, fever.

" " Abigail, daughter of Ezekiel Day, aet. 9, worms.

" 18. Phœbe, daughter of Joseph Tuttle, aet. 1.

" 21. Asher Fairchild, aet. 32, quinsey.

" 30. Child of George Phillips.

Oct. 1. Samuel, son of Nathan Reeve, aet. 2, intermittent fever.

" 8. Asa, son of Uzal Coe, aet. 6, worms.

" 9. A child of Hubert Duburk, aet. 6, consumption.

" 23. Wife of Evan Bevan, aet. 24, fever.

" " Elizabeth, wife of Capt. Jonas Simmons.

1782.

Jan. 13. Mrs. Robertson, of New York, aet. 40, consumption.

" 14. Child of Captain Jacob Arnold, small pox.

" 18. Samuel, son of William Cherry, consumption.

" 20. Ann Margaret, wife of Peter Hill,* aet. 52, putrid fever.

" 25. Deborah, wife of George Phillips,* aet. 47, small pox.

" 28. Jane, wife of Silas Goble,† aet. 30, consumption.

" 29. Betsey, daughter of George Phillips, aet. 20, small pox.

" 30. Mary, widow of Joseph Howard,* aet. 79, consumption.

Feb. 1. Elizabeth, widow of Henry Wick, Jun., aet. 36, consumption.

" 8. Jonathan, son of Simeon Broadwell, aet. 3, small pox.

" 15. Bethiah, daughter of Abijah Cutler, aet. 3, small pox.

" 22. Son of Nathaniel Armstrong, aet. 16, small pox.

" Capt. Agustine Bayles, aet. 46, ulcered leg.

Mar. 4. A child of Thomas Kane, aet. 8 scald.

" 11. A child of Amariah Casterline.

" 12. Shubal Trowbridge,† aet. 42, small pox.

" 15. Widow of Francis Casterline, aet. 65, fever.

" 20. A black man, aet. 28, man-slaughter.

" 25. Gershom, son of Capt. Daniel Gard,† small pox.

" 30. Nathaniel Peck,* aet. 39, fever.

Apr. 10. Mary, daughter of Aaron Pierson, aet. 1, quinsey.

" 11. Wife of George Badgley, aet. 53, small pox.

" 24. Mary, wife of Joseph Gardner, aet. 42, consumption.

" 27. Philip Price, aet. 70, small pox.

" 30. A child of David Gardner, fits.

May 1. Jonas Goble,† aet. 37, small pox.

" 6. John, a foreigner, aet. 50, sudden.

" 10. John W. Smith, Esq., aet. 42, gout.

" 16. Thomas Pierson, aet. 45, found dead.

" 20. Hannah, widow of Elijah Holloway, aet. 42, fever.

(To be continued.)

(Continued from page 96.)

TRUSTEES' BOOK.

Jan. 25, 1790.—At a meeting of the Parish on the 25th of Jan., 1790, for the purpose of giving Rev. Mr. Collins a call to serve the congregation as an assistant to Rev. Dr. Johnes in the Ministry.

Voted, That Deacon Allen serve as Moderator; That Joseph Lewis serve as Clerk.

Voted, Unanimously that the Rev. Mr. Collins be requested to serve the congregation as an Assistant to the Rev. Dr. Johnes in the Ministry, and that he shall receive beside the use of the House and Parsonage and fire Wood a Salary of one hundred and thirty pounds for the first year and one hundred and forty pounds for the second and one hundred and fifty pounds annually thereafter so long as he shall officiate in the said congregation.

Voted, That the said Salary be raised as the Law directs State Taxes to be raised excepting that three assistants or supervisors should be annually appointed by said parish whose duty it should be to make such abatements and alterations from the strict rules of Law as to them shall seem just and equitable in consideration of the distance of residence of some of the Parishioners from the place of worship, or for particular misfortune or embarrassment of circumstances. And voted that Silas Condict, Esq., Jonathan Stiles, Esq., and Jonathan Ford be appointed for the above purpose for the first year.

The Moderator presented a paper from the Rev. Dr. Johnes in the words following, viz:

"Whereas, God in his Providence has been pleased to disenable me in a great measure for performing the duties incumbent on a minister for so large a congregation as the one now in my charge, and it appearing necessary for the accommodation and benefit of the congregation that some other person should be employed in the Ministry as an assistant or otherwise, and Providence at present apparently having opened a door for such supply, and it being my desire that peace and harmony with which we have been so long been blessed should continue, and least it should appear burdensome to my people to support more than one Minister, I do freely relinquish the obligation now subsisting between my people and myself from the time that another minister shall be settled here and his salary commence. Notwithstanding this resignation I am content to assist in the sacred work of the ministry so far as God shall enable me, and it shall be acceptable to the people, and shall entirely submit to the discretion and generosity of my people to make me such compensation for the same as to them shall seem meet."

Voted, That an address containing the thanks of the Society be presented him in the words following, viz:

The congregation sensible of the long and faithful services which the Rev. Dr. Johnes has rendered this congregation by his care and prudence as a minister and the blessings they have been favoured with by means of his administration. Voted, That the thanks of the congregation be presented to the Dr. for such his services and for the friendly and benevolent manner in which he hath been pleased to relinquish the obligation subsisting between him and his people and for his kind offer of future assistance—and that Silas Condict, Esq., and Deacon Allen wait on him and inform him of this Vote. That the members of the congregation now present will endeavor that a generous compensation shall be annually contributed so long as his assistance and direction shall by a kind providence be continued.

Voted, That the same persons wait on Rev. Mr. Collins, inform him of the determination of the congregation and request his answer.

Voted, That the Trustees hire a house for Rev. Mr. Collins, and that the same be levied on the people in the same tax with the salary.

(To be continued.)

——:o:——

Erratum—Page 86, fourth line from bottom of page, omit "Miller" and read "Phebe Freeman (Zophar.")

The list of members in this number begins with Jonathan Hathaway. One Jonathan Hathaway died Aug. 26, 1814, aet. 76 years, 7 mos. and 7 days; another of the same name died Feb. 17, 1821, no age being given. *Who can tell which was the church member!*

THE RECORD.

FIRST PRESBYTERIAN CHURCH, MORRISTOWN, N. J.

"This shall be Written for the Generation to Come."—Psalms 102 : 18.

VOL. II. FEBRUARY, 1881. NO. 2.

(Printed with the approval of Session.)

THE RECORD

Will be printed and published monthly at Morristown, N. J. Terms, 50 cents per annum in advance; 75 cents after June.

Subscriptions will be received at the book-stores of Messrs. Runyon and Emmell, or through the mail. All communications should be addressed to the

EDITOR OF THE RECORD,
Lock box 44. Morristown, N. J.
Vol. I. complete, 75 cents.

Entered at the Post Office at Morristown, N. J., as second class matter.

——:o:——

With the present number of THE RECORD the list of Dr. Johnes' marriages—947 in all—is completed. It is now put beyond liability of destruction, and made forever accessible for genealogical and other purposes. For a few months we shall discontinue the list until the others have reached it in point of time.

HISTORICAL SERMON,

No. I.

BY THE

REV. DAVID IRVING, D.D.,
Pastor of the Church,
1855-1865.

PREACHED THANKSGIVING DAY, 1861.

Walk about Zion and go round about her: tell the towers thereof. Mark ye well her bulwarks, consider her palaces; that ye may tell it to the generations following.
—*Psalm xlviii.*: 12-13.

We appear here to-day at the call of our Governor as citizens. We come at the call of Jehovah as subjects and enter the church as Christians to give thanks for past blessings and present enjoyments. As members of a great confederacy we have much to awaken and perpetuate gratitude. As citizens of this State, in her laws, government and judiciary, we have much to establish confidence, and banish fears. As inhabitants of a place, rich in moral influence and a noble religious ancestry, we have much to foster gratitude and induce us to be conformed to divine precepts that we may shew forth the praise of our God. With hearts touched with the varied marks of divine beneficence the past year in continuing national and civil rights, and in causing the earth to yield her richest stores we turn to consider our own past as a church, that we may adore that superintending Providence, that has preserved and enlarged her, that has been with her in trials, and that has made her the nursery for heaven and for many churches in this and other communities. Let us like the grateful Hebrew walk about our Zion, go around about her and tell the towers thereof. Mark well her bulwarks, consider her palaces that we may tell it to the generation following.

Long before this region became instinct with a civilized and religious life it was the hunting ground of the Indians and the home of the wild beast. * When these wholly disappeared is as difficult to tell as when the white man first reared his cabin and where. Upward the tide of civilization rolled from Long Island, Elizabeth Town, Newark, until it reached this section in the early part of last century. Prior to this, Hanover, then called Whippany, and embracing the territory now included in the townships of Morris, Chatham and Hanover was settled. In 1685, says the author of the Historical Collections of New Jersey, but on the records of the church book of Hanover we have the following entry by Rev. Jacob Green, its third pastor settled 1746. "About the year 1710, a few friends removed from Newark and Elizabeth Town and settled on

———
*The Whippanongs from whom the river received its name, now called Whippany. All kinds of game were abundant in Morris County. Geese, wild duck, pigeons, etc., were particularly abundant along the streams; bears, wolves, panthers, wild cats, etc., were also numerous and destructive.

the West side of Passaic River in that which is now Morris County."

This region then called West Hanover, was surveyed in 1715 to a number of proprietors, and the land on which Morristown is built surveyed in the same year to Joseph Helby, Thomas Stephenson and John Keys. Keys having 2,000 acres and the others 1,250 each. The land now occupied by the park and church belonged to the claim of Keys; that of Helby ran from George W. Johnes' toward Speedwell and southwest to the residence of Mr. Lovell, whilst Stephens' included the farms now owned by Revere, Cooper, etc. These tracts of the first purchasers were not settled by them but were divided and subdivided by smaller purchasers until the thrifty farmer and the hardy mechanic were prosecuting their appropriate vocations on the designated and adjoining lands.

When, where and by whom the first house was reared in Morristown, tradition is silent. It was no doubt soon after the first survey, and was near to the stream of water which still flows in its accustomed channel. There the grist mill, the saw mill and the forge were erected; the two former of vast importance to the wants of a young colony; the latter, owing to the peculiar state of the iron trade in England at that time and the growing necessities of this country, called forth throughout a certain section of the country the resources and capital of many so that this region was known for a long time as the "Old Forges," the ore being brought on horseback from the mines and when converted into iron carried in the same way to market at Newark and Elizabeth Town. Gen. Washington in 1777 remonstrates against the exemption of men engaged in iron manufactories from military duty, except those establishments employed for the public. He says that there are in Morris County alone between 80 and 100 iron works, large and small.—Sparks V. 4, p. 397.

Whilst the improvement of their temporal condition was no doubt a leading motive of the early pioneers to this region, religion was not sacrificed but had a controlling voice in their movements. It was the religious element that led the New Englanders and the Scotch and Irish to this province, whose fundamental condition guaranteed the largest liberty of conscience to all settlers; it was here that many came to be freed from spiritual despotism which galled them at home and to certain localities some repaired to test their favorite scheme of a pure church and a godly government in which power was to be exercised only by those who were members of the church, and where everything in active antagonism with this principle was to be removed. On this basis Newark and a few other towns were founded. Those who came into this region from older settlements where religion was deemed vital to the best interests of the people brought with them the sacred love of liberty and of truth, and the highest regard for religious institutions which was operative here as elsewhere, in honoring the Sabbath and the sanctuary and in regulating social and domestic life.

Almost in immediate connection with the original survey of Morristown, one John Richards, of Whippany, school-master, in the year 1718, in consideration of the love and affection he had for his Christian friends and neighbors gave 3½ acres " for a meeting house, school house, burying-yard and training field," on part of which a church building was immediately reared and which forms to-day the burying-ground of Whippany. This place of worship was attended for many years by the inhabitants of Morristown, Madison, Parsippany, Hanover and Chatham. This was the first organized church in the county and constitutes what is now called the Hanover church, to whom the Rev. John M. Johnson, a son of this church, ministers. Its first pastor was the Rev. Nathaniel Hubbell, who supplied this congregation in connection with one at Westfield though residing in Hanover. The second pastor was the Rev. John Nutman, ordained and settled in 1730 by the Philadelphia Presbytery.

The first we hear of him is in the synod of Philadelphia in 1733, seeking relief from two grievances, and both occasioned by the acts of the people of West Hanover or Morristown. Soon after his installation a question was mooted by this section of the congregation about organizing a separate society which was strenuously opposed by the Eastern portion. To quiet matters a resort was had to the casting of lots, which resulted against the proposed division. This way of determining the case was opposed by this branch of the congregation so that they would not submit to the decision. (For their action in this matter, though they gained their point, yet the church when organized called them to account. The record is as follows : A public confession at the settlement of this church for a transgression relating to a lot cast with reference to the settling a house for public worship between Hanover and this town ; the persons that confessed are Joseph Coe, John Lindsley, Joseph Prudden, Matthew Lum, Uriah Cutler, Stephen Freeman, Peter Condit, Jacob Ford, Joseph Howard, Benj. Bailey, Philip Condit, &c.) The whole affair was carried up to Synod in 1733 who strongly disapproved of the casting of lots, and resolved that in their present circumstances of poverty and weakness it might be very advisable for the people of West Hanover, at least for some time, to join themselves with the congregations of East Hanover and Baskingridge as may be most convenient, until they as well as the said neighboring congregations be more able to subsist of themselves separately. Yet if reunion was impracticable " the Synod judge that the people of West Hanover be left to their liberty to erect themselves into a separate congregation." No doubt knowing the temper and state of feeling in this part of his field of labor this deliverance of Synod was in no way satisfactory to Mr. Nutman, for at the same session of the body he asked for a dismission from his Presbytery, if this action was enforced of forming a separate congregation, whereupon the Synod earnestly recommended the Presbytery of East New Jersey to travail with the people of West Hanover to effect a reconciliation, and if this was impossible then to dismiss Mr. Nutman upon his application. The next year the matter again came before the Synod in the reading of the minutes when the use of lots was condemned, and yet say they " we are afraid that much sin has been committed by many if not all that people in their profane disregard of said lot, and therefore excite them to reflect upon their past practices in reference thereunto in order to their repentance."

This implied censure in no way healed the breach. There had been too much said and

done, on both sides again to work in concert; so that, independent of the counsellings of Synod, this branch of the congregation made application to that body on the following year for the ordination of one who had recently come among them. The Synod referred the matter to the Presbytery of Philadelphia. In May, 1736, the people pressed the Presbytery to proceed in the ordination of Mr. Cleverly, when they directed the congregation to appoint a day and give them due notice that they might attend properly to the business. For some cause no day was designated. So that the Presbytery in August, 1737, met here but found opposition on the part of some of the people to his settlement ; in virtue of this state of things they urged him to seek another field of labor and wrote to the rector of Yale College to send a candidate, giving as a reason that " they knew no other way to supply them." This advice was not taken as he remained in Morristown till his death in December, in 1776. He never married. His small property became nearly exhausted toward the close of life and reduced him to hardships. (The church was most likely supplied by him till the settlement of Mr. Johnes.)

The Synod in 1738, finding the difficulties still existing and anxious to bring the case to a final issue, appointed a large committee which met on the 20th of July, at Hanover. The members present were Andrews, of Philadelphia, Gilbert Tennent, of New Brunswick, William Tennent, of Freehold, John Cross, of Baskingridge, Crowell, of Trenton, and Treat, of Abington. An opening sermon was preached by Gilbert Tennent from Ezek. xi : 19, " I will give them one heart." The Eastern part were still anxious for a union if it could be had on reasonable terms ; to this the Western portion were however averse and represented according to truth that they were much increased in number, being nearly one-half abler than they were, and the committee finding that they both were better able to support the Gospel, unanimously concluded that there should be two separate societies, and that no further attempts should be made to merge them into one, and in this decision all parties expressed their entire satisfaction.

(To be continued.)

(*Continued from page* 100.)

MEMBERS.

[The third column on this page is the work of the RECORD. Information which will lead to the correction of any mistake, or the filling of any blank, will be thankfully received.—ED.]

Names.	When Received.	When Dismissed or Died.
Catharine Beers (Jabish),	Sept. 1, 1774.	Oct. 19, 1801, aet. 77.
Phebe Cooper,	" " "	
Jerusha Wood (Jonathan),	" " "	April 23, 1803, aet. 75.
Philip Condict, Junr.,	" " "	
Silas Howell,	Nov. 4. "	Suspended.
Hannah Howell (Silas),	" " "	April 26, 1785, aet. 36.
David Hoppen,	" " "	"Moved."
Joseph Pierson, Junr.,	" " "	"
Ephraim Youngs,	" " "	Jan. 27, 1794, aet. 44.
James Youngs,	" " "	Sept. 20, 1783, aet. 28.
William Johnes,	" " "	Dec. 8, 1836, aet. 83.
Deborah Wright (Gabriel),	" " "	
Susan Guiering (Joshua),	" " "	Nov. 3, 1820, aet. 82.
Joanna Prudden,	" " "	
Sarah Lum,	" " "	July 10, 1809, aet. 64.
Mary Johnson,	" " "	"Moved."
Deborah Wines,	" " "	"
Sarah Keen,	" " "	
Eunice Raynor,	" " "	
Susanna Burwell,	" " "	"Moved."
Seth Crowell,	Dec. 27, "	
Joanna Crowell (Seth.)	" " "	
David Garrigas,	" " "	"Moved."
Ephraim Lindsley,	" " "	March 26, 1824, aet. 71.
Martha Munson (Moses),	" " "	"Moved."
Rachel Gwinnup (John)	" " "	
Deliverance Youngs,	" " "	"Moved."
Laban Ward,	March 2, 1775.	
Hannah Ward (Laban),	" " "	
Isaac Morris,	" " "	
Ezekiel Crane,	" " "	"Moved."
Daniel Beers,	" " "	April 21, 1790, aet. 37.
Azuba Beers (Daniel),	" " "	"Moved."
Widow Sarah Kent,	" " "	
Mary King (Frederick),	" " "	
Phebe Youngs (Ephraim),	" " "	June 3, 1786, aet. 34.
Phebe Riggs,	" " "	"Moved."
Bloom, serv. of Peter Prudden,		
Barnabus Evens,	May 4. "	April 2, 1802, aet. 72.
Jesse Smith,	" " "	"Moved."
Eunice Smith (Jesse),	" " "	"
Matthew Ball,	Aug. 31, "	
Hannah Lyon (Ephraim),	" " "	"Moved."
Mary Hedges (Elias),	July 4, 1776.	
Rachael Prudden, (da. of Benj.)	" " "	"Moved."
William Wick,	Nov. 3, "	" [4, 1802, aet. 70.
Sally Stiles, (Jonathan),	July 20, 1777.	(Later wf. of Wm. Woodbridge,) Feb.

(*To be continued.*)

BAPTISMS.

(*Continued from page* 101.)

1766.

June 22. Zenas Condict, ch. Ebenezer.
" 29. Cap. Dan. Tuttle on wf's accompt., ch. David.
" " David Gauden & wf., ch. Joseph.
" " Absolam Beegle on wf's accompt., ch. Daniel McFeran.
July 20, Jedidiah Gregory & wf., ch. Seth.
" 26. Philp Hathaway & wf., chn. Jonathan, Rhoda & Catharine.
Aug. 3. Joseph Youngs on wf's accompt., 2 negro chn. Robert & Ned.
" 8. Sam Alwood & wf., sick child bap. at ye house—Joseph.
" 10. Ben. Hathaway, Lieut. & wf., ch. Benjamin.
" 17. Cap. Ben. Halsey & wf., negro ch. Cato.
" 31. John Cole & wf., ch. Lydia.
" " Boys Prudden & wf., ch. Sarah.
Sept. 14. Will Halbard, ch. Jotham.
" " Ebenezar Cundict & wf., ch. Silas.
" " John Lose on wf's accompt, ch. John.
" 21. Lieu. John Lindsly & wf., ch. Silas.
" " Moses Lindsly & wf., ch. Phebe.
" 27. Cap. Timothy Mills & wf., ch. Zenas.
" " Sam'l Ward on wf's accompt., ch Elizabeth, bo n April 13, 1765.
" " Benj. Pool & wf., ch. Zuba.
Oct. 6. Croel Wilkerson on his own account., ch. Anne.
Nov. 5. Benoni Hathaway & wf., adult, name Ruth & ch. Mary.
" " Daniel Carmichael & wf., ch. bap. by Mr. Peppard as he saith, born Aug. 6, 1766—Ebenezar.
" 23. Elijah Pierson & wf., ch. Phebe.
1767.
Jan. 2. James Miller & wf., ch. Mary.
" " Ebenezar Stiles & wf., ch. Jemima.
" 11. Jacob Frazey & wf., ch. Henry.
" " Isaac Pierson & wf., ch. Cyrus.
" 18. Phineas Fairchild & wf., ch. Ester, born Nov. 20, 1766.
Feb. 1. John Mintonye & wf., ch. John.
" " Seth Crowel & wf., ch. Rhoda.
" 8. Stephen Beach on wf's accompt., ch. Peter.
" " Caleb Munson & wf., ch. Abigail.
" " James Brookfield & wf., ch. Elizabeth, born Dec. 4, 1766,

Mar. 8. John Hathaway & wf., ch. Phebe.
" 15. John Pierson on own account, ch. Catharine.
" " Dayid Ogden on wf's accompt., ch. Ester.
Apr. 5. Onesimus Whitehead & wf., ch. Silas, born Jan. 30, 1766.
" 26. Thomas Miller & wf., ch. Oliver.
" " David Fairchild & wf., ch. David.
" " Ebenezar Coe & wf., ch. Damoras.
May 10. Dan. Tichenor & wf., ch. Phebe.
" " Nathaniel Peck & wf., ch. Hannah.
" 24. Solomon Munson & wf., ch. Gabriel.
" " Benj. Pierson & wf., ch. Lydia.
June 7. Daniel Morris, Jun. & wf., ch. Stephen.
" " Zophar Gildersleeve & wf., ch. Zophar.
" 13. Nathan Price & wf., ch. John.
" " Joseph Condict & wf., ch. Usual.
" " Jonathan Hathaway & wf., ch. Thankful.
" 21. Abraham Canfidld & wf., ch. Abraham.
" 28. Job Lore & wf., ch Jemima.
July 2. John Allen, adult.
" 19. Moses Prudden & wf., ch. Ruth.
" 26. Peter Dickenson & wf., ch. Ruth.
Aug. 2. Eleazer Lindsly & wf., ch. Anne.
" " Eleazer Hathaway & wf., ch. Eleazer.
" 16. Moses Prudden & wf., ch. Elizabeth.
" " Jabish Cundict & wf., ch. Mary.
" " Daniel Bishop & wf., ch. Mary.
" 23. Ebenezar Stites & wf., ch. Ebenezar.
" 30. Samuel Allwood & wf., ch. Samuel.
" " Benjamin Coe & wf., ch. Titus.
Sep. 6. Solomon Brown & wf., ch. Solomon.
" " Ezek. Day & wf., ch. Phebe.
" " Abel Lyon on wf's accompt., ch. Joseph.
" 20. Philip Lindsly & wf., ch. Abraham.
" 27. John Redman & wf., ch. Joseph.
Oct. 4. Levi Lindsly & wf., ch. Levi.
" " Frederick King & wf., ch. Sarah.
" " Dan. Tuttle on wf's accompt., ch. Usual.
" 6. John Burrel on wf's accompt., ch. Theodocia.

(*To be continued.*)

(*Continued from page 102.*)

MARRIAGES.

1788.
Oct. 2. Jacob Marsh & Jane Tichenor.
Nov. 3. Samuel Ludlam & Sarah Serren.
" " Thaddeus Norris & Mary Bishop.
Dec. 3. George Pierson & Anne Marsh.
1789.
Feb. 4. David Coit, (N. York), & Sarah Ogden.
" " Joshua Stenback, (N. York), & Mary Wilkerson.
" 8. Jacob Brant & Comfort Johnson.
" \11. John Halsey & Jemima Bridge.
" " Abraham Conkling & Jemima Lindsley.
" 14. Henry King & Sharlotte Morrel.
April 2. Jacob Clayden & Mary Hambleton.
" 5. Samuel Crowell & Anne Squire.
June15. Matthias Williams, of Orange Dale, & Anne Fairchild.
July 8. Isaac Hathaway & Mary Kirkpatrick.
Sept.22. Stout Benjamin & Hannah Peck.
" 23. Moses Lindsly & Phebe Williams, widow, both of Rockaway.
Oct. 4. Daniel Dennis & Mary Wolfe.
" 8. John Dunning Wilkerson & Jemima Potter.
" " Daniel Mills & Susanna Pierson.
" 11. Reuben Brundyge & Hannah Shores.
" 15. Stephen Tunis & Mahittable Bishop
" 18. Timothy Pierson & Joanna Tuttle.
Nov.10. William Campfield, Docr., & Hannah Tuthill.
Dec. 8. David Wood & Mehitable Fairchild.
" 10. Jacob Turner & Naomi Turner.
" 24. David, servant of Mr. Faish, & Abigail, servant of Miss Kerney.
Dec.31. George Collis & Naomi Johnson. To this date 906 married.
1790.
Jan. 10. John Brian & Mary Howell.
Feb. — William & Bella, negro.
" 25. Eliazer Byram & Anne Prudden.
Mar. 4. Joseph Dickerson & Eunice Pierson.
" 7. Phineas Tuttle & Widow Mary Riggs.
" 10. Samuel Ford & Elizabeth Reeve.
" 18. John Seward & Deborah Conkling.

" 29. Silas Condict, Jun., & Charlotte Ford.
May 23. Jacob Timbrel & Sarah Stebbins.
June 9. William Denman & Elizabeth Aber.
" 17. Jeptha Wade & Sarah Allen.
July 22. Silas Lindsly & Jane Lindsly.
Aug. 8. Elijah Taylor & Jemima Pierson.
Oct. 14. John Johnson & Jane Squire.
Nov.22. William Broadwell & Sarah Hathaway.
" 30. Ezra Morris & Shearlotte Dalglace.
Dec. 25. Samuel Tucker & Patience Layton, Sussex.
1791.
Jan. 6. Benj. Halbard & —— Smith. Married to this date 924.
Mar.24. Thomas Guierin & Elizabeth Lindsly.
May 1. William Hambleton & Abigail Ludlam.
" 22. Joseph Fairchild & Phebe Bayly.
Aug. 3. James Linsly & Elizabeth Williams.
Sept.15. David Wheeler & Rhoda Ludlam.
" 20. Benj. Halbert & Elizabeth Lindsly, widow.
Oct. 10. Jonathan Thomson & Rhoda Pierson, widow.
Nov.10. Nathan Furman from New York, & Phebe Pierson.
" 27. Samuel Moore, Rockaway, & Zippora Johnson, widow.
1792.
Mar.16. Henry Carr & Elizabeth Hall.
Sept.16. James Coe & Naomi Speese.
Oct. 3. Elijah Holloway & Elizabeth Gamble.
" 4. Daniel Williams & Elizabeth Deniston.
" 16. Samuel Guirin & Fanny Brown.
Nov. 13. Theodorus Tuthill & Jane Hancock.
" " Silas White Howell & Hannah Arnold.
1793.
Jan. 1. John Loper & Jane Templeton.
Feb. 11. Job Hathaway & Esther Pierson.
June 6. George Dalglish & Hannah Ward.
Aug.26. Richard Bowen (?) and Hannah Sanders.
Nov. — Aaron Aber & Martha Easton.
1794.
May 3. Ebenezer Carter & Abigail Maccalvy.
" 10. Benger & Elizabeth Horton, widow.
(*To be Continued.*)

(*Continued from page* 108.)

BILL OF MORTALITY.

1782.

Aug.11. Josiah, son of Samuel Broadwell, aet. 4, Scald.

" 14. Ruth, daughter of widow Peck, aet. 14, nervous fever.

Sept.17. Ebenezer, son of James Wilkison, Fits.

" 18. Maria, daughter of John Kinney, aet. 2, hives.

Oct. 6. Sarah, widow of Philip Price, aet. 65.

Nov.15. Caleb Ball, aet. 54, Consumption.

" 24. A child of Moses Wilkison,

Dec. 7. Col, Abraham Brasher, aet. 60, apoplexy.

" 24. Mary, wife of deacon Matthias Burnet,* aet. 59, pleurisy.

1783.

Jan. 9. Jedidiah Gregory,*aet. 53, consumption.

Feb. 18. Rebeckah, wife of Zachariah Allen, aet. 35, decay.

" 19. Isaac, son of Robert Arnold, Jun., aet. 4, worms.

" 23. Elizabeth, wife of Moses Estey, aet. 23, consumption.

Mar. 5. Sarah, daughter of Daniel Gardner, Putrid fever.

" 11. Thomas Wilkison,* aet. 75, consumption.

" 20. Benjamin Bayles,* aet. 83, old age.

" 22. A child of Jedidah Mills.

" 29. William Bishop. aet. 23, consumption.

" " Robert Goble, Esq.,†* aet. 83, old age.

" 30. Speath's wife.

April 6. Phœbe Headley, aet. 20, consumption.

" 12. Jane, wife of Daniel Kemper, aet. 32, child-bed.

May 4. Phineas, son of Lindsley Burnet, aet. 11, fits.

" 13. Elisha, son of Eliphalet Clark, aet. 13, fall from a tree.

" 22. John Crane, aet. 35, fever.

" 28. A child of Timothy Mills.

" 30. Daniel Freeman, aet. 19, drowned,

June 1. A child of Nathaniel Sturges, fits.

July 4. A child of Aaron Furman.

" 6. A child of Jonathan Howard.

" 7. William, son of Thomas Mitchel, aet. 1, phrenzy.

July 19. Jeremiah Gard, aet. 66, inward ulcers.

" 22. Sarah, wife of Abraham Canfield,* aet. 50, hypocondriac affection.

Aug. 4. Benjamin Pierson,* aet. 82, dysentery.

" " Betty Howard, aet. 53, sudden.'

" 18. Rebeckah, wife of Samuel Wood,* aet. 24, consumption.

" 27. Aaron, son of Lindsly Burnet, aet. 9, fits.

" 31. A child of Demas Ford.

Sept. 8. Jonathan Pierson,* aet. 32, consumption.

" 17. Mary, wife of Demas Ford, aet. 28, child-bed fever.

" 20. James Youngs,* aet. 28, pleurisy.

Oct. 3. Walter, son of Peter Norris, Jun., aet. 1, whooping-cough.

" " A child of Gideon Riggs, Jun.

" 4. A child of John Pool, aet. 9.

" 12. Hannah, widow of Major Joseph Morris, aet. 43, consumption.

" 17. A child of Daniel Hallsey.

" 18. Widow D'Hart, mother of Col. D'Hart, aet. 60, fever.

" " Deacon Matthias Burnet,* aet. 60, colic.

" 28. A child of David Carter.

Nov. 4. A child of Abraham Talmage,† aet. 1, whooping-cough.

" 15. A child of Silas Ayers.

" 15. A child of Ichabod Clark.

" 23. Widow (Magdalene) Cook, aet 67, old age.

1784.

Jan. 16. Joanna, daughter of Samuel Wood, aet. 1, consumption.

Mar. 9. Naomi, widow of Jacob Allen,†* aet. 70, mortification in the blood.

" 24. Wife of James Losey, aet. 50, consumption.

‹ 26. A child of John Vancourt.

" 27. Andrew Burnet, aet. 22, inflammation in the head.

" 28. A child of Isaac Mills.

April 1. Phœbe, wife of David Fithian, aet. 25, fever.

Apr. 24. A child of Ziba Arnold.

May 5. Deacon Daniel Walling,†* aet. 73, sudden.

" 20. Aaron Furman, aet. 35, consumption.

(*To be continued.*)

(*Continued from page* 104.)

TRUSTEES' BOOK.

Feb. 1, 1790.—At a meeting of the Trustees at the house of Jos. Lewis present, The, president Mr. Lindsly, Mr. Ford, Mr. Mills and Mr. Johnson,

In consequence of the vote of the Parish meeting the 25th ult. the Trustees prepared an obligation for the Rev'd Mr. Collins' Salary and house rent in words following—viz.

Whereas on the 25th day of January 1790 at a parish meeting for that purpose appointed, it was unanimously voted that the Rev. Aaron Collins should be employed as a minister of the gospel of the first Presbyterian Church and Congregation in Morristown and that the said Mr. Collins should have besides the use of a house and parsonage and fire wood, as a salary the sum of one hundred and thirty pounds for the first year, and one hundred and forty pounds for the second year, and the sum of one hundred and fifty pounds annually thereafter so long as he shall continue to do the duties of a minister to the said Congregation, and it being also voted that the said salary together with the money for the hire of a house for the said minister, should be raised and levied upon the parishioners by the way of a tax as the law directs the State taxes to be raised excepting that three assistants or supervisors should be annually appointed by the Parish, whose duty it should be to make abatements and alterations from the strict rules of law as to them shall seem just and equitable in consideration of the distance of residence of some of the parishioners from the place of worship or for particular misfortune or embarrassment of circumstances. Therefore we the subscribers sensible of the general utility and vast importance to ourselves and posterity of supporting the gospel, and being desirous that unanimity may subsist and continue, and that the burden of such support may be borne as equitably as possible and hoping jointly to participate in the advantages and blessings of the Gospel ministry, do hereby bind ourselves to pay the sums that shall be so assessed and levied upon us annually to commence from the 1st day of March one

thousand seven hundred & ninety, unto the said Aaron Collins, or to such person or persons as shall by the said parish be appointed to collect or receive the same, and that during the time he shall continue to officiate, and do the duties of a minister to said congregation, and we continue to be members thereof, or until the mode of payment shall be revoked or altered by plurality of voices of the said Parishioners.

In witness whereof we have hereunto set our hands this first day of Feb. 1790.

The trustees also proposed a subscription for the Rev. Doct. T. Johnes' salary, in the words following, viz.

Whereas the Rev. Doct T. Johnes in consequence of his being by divine Providence disenabled at least in part of performing the duties of a minister of the Gospel to the people of his charge, and they by his consent and advice having agreed to employ another minister to assist and perform the duties of the Gospel ministry to the said people, and the said Doct. Johnes having generously relinquished the obligation his people were under to pay him his stipulated salary at the same time kindly offering to serve and assist by his counsel & administration, as far as God shall enable him in the sacred work of the ministry. We the subscribers being sensible not only of his past long and faithful services to our Fathers and to us, and the blessing we have thereby enjoyed, but also of the need we still stand in of his pious advice and instructions, do cheerfully agree and promise to pay to the said Doct. T. Johnes or order the sums severally affixed to our names and that from the time the other minister shall commence, annually, so long as the said Doct. Johnes shall continue to render such, his advice and assistance to the said congregation. or until we shall each for himself withdraw this our consent and choice of rewarding virtue.

Witness our hands this 1st day of Feb., 1790.

Voted, That Deacon Allen and Mr. Johnson be requested to go through the Society with the said obligation and subscription and endeavor to get them signed.

(*To be continued.*)

THE RECORD.

FIRST PRESBYTERIAN CHURCH, MORRISTOWN, N. J.

"This small be Written for the Generation to Come."—Psalms xos 1.18.

VOL. II.   MARCH, 1881.   NO. 3.

(Printed with the approval of Session.)

THE RECORD

Will be printed and published monthly at Morristown, N. J. Terms, 50 cents per annum in advance; 75 cents after June.

Subscriptions will be received at the book-stores of Messrs. Runyon and Emmell, or through the mail. All communications should be addressed to the

EDITOR OF THE RECORD,
Lock box 44.   Morristown, N. J.
Vol. I. complete, 75 cents.

Entered at the Post Office at Morristown, N. J., as second class matter.

———:o:———

Citizens Savings and Loan Association.
Cleveland, O., Feb. 5th, 1881.

Rev. R. S. Green:

My Dear Sir:—Would you be kind enough to insert in The Record, an inquiry as to the parentage of Andrew Wade, who married Martha Riggs at Morristown, Dec. 4th, 1765, and also the place where Andrew's parents resided before their removal to Morristown? I would like very much to correspond with any one who is interested in, and can throw any light upon, the Wade Family prior to Andrew's time,

Very truly yours,

J. H. Wade, Jr.

———

Having finished the list of Dr. Johnes' marriages, we give this month two pages, 117 and 118, of Baptisms.

ERRATA.

Page 107, 2nd column, 21st line from bottom, read 26th instead of 20th.

Page 102, 1788, May 18. Coonrad instead of Coonrah.

Page 102, 1788, July 28, Tennery instead of Tenney.

———

The order of Baptisms for 1768—May, June, July, May, June—is copied as found on the original record.

———

(Continued from page 107.)

HISTORICAL SERMON.

No. I.

BY THE

REV. DAVID IRVING, D.D.,

The way now being open for their organization, and being within the bounds of the Presbytery of New York, which was formed the same year by the union of the Presbyteries of Long Island and East Jersey, we have no doubt that in the fall of 1738, or the beginning of 1739, this church had a name and a place among the Presbyterian churches of the land. As Mr. Cleverly still sojourned in Mornstown*—a name about this time given to the township, the county being laid out in 1738 and named Morris after the Gov., Lewis Morris, and which included the region now covered by Sussex and Warren—he no doubt officiated occasionally or regularly until a pastor was chosen. For a period of four years, that is from the time the Synodical Committee authorized the organization of a church until Aug. 13, 1742, we can find no trace of the state of this Society in any of its ecclesiastical movements. At that time appeared the Rev. Timothy Johnes, a licentiate, who supplied the pulpit for six Sabbaths, and whose ministrations were so satisfactory that the congregation urged him to remain and become their pastor. To this he assented, brought his family, consisting of his wife and two children, and was ordained and installed by the New York Presbytery, Feb. 9, 1743.

Mr. Johnes was of Welsh descent and was born at Southampton, Long Island, May 24th, 1717, and graduated at Yale College in 1737. Mr. Webster in his history of the Presbyterian church, say "of the period between his leaving college going to Morristown we have no notice, except that, in that perilous time when some happy were found fighting against God, those who separated from the First Parish in New Haven worshipped in the house of Mr. Timothy Johnes." From this it would appear that he studied Theology at New Haven. He was no doubt licensed by the congregational body, and came to Morristown by means of the letter of Presbytery to the president of the college or by a subsequent request to the same. Tradition asserts that he labored for a short period on Long Island in some of the vacant churches. With Mr. Johnes this church assumes historic character, shape and life, as from the date of his settlement the church records begin, though for a time the entries of sessional business are meagre, yet they are sufficient to indicate the character of the church in its government and relations. Mr. Barnes in his manual of the church published in 1828, says "it is not known under what form of church government, whether congregational or Presbyterian, the congregation was first organized—as Ruling Elders are mentioned however as early as the year 1747, it is probable it was Presbyterian." But the history of the church as already detailed confirms its Presbyterian origin—the heading of the church records, and the first business transacted by Mr. Johnes prove it. These are as follows : "The affairs as determined by our session of the minister and elders.

1743. Was agreed that the minister's expenses in the service of the churches should be defrayed from church fund." The next entry gives the list of the elders—as constituting the session with the minister (1747,) viz.: Joseph Prudden, Matthew Lum, John Lindsly, Joseph Coe and Jacob Ford, and in 1745 at the first meeting of the synod of New York we find among its members the names of Timothy Johnes, minister, and Joseph Prudden, elder. Yet here we discover that whilst the session transacted all judicial business of which there is a full record, no allusion is made in their meetings to the reception of persons to full communion until 1791 when we have the following decision : "The question was then put

whether the elders shall act with the minister or either of them be a committee to examine all candidates for church membership which was unanimously agreed to "—from which it may be inferred that they were either examined by the pastor alone as in some Presbyterian churches—or that the examination was conducted before and by the members of the churches—according to the opinion of Mr. Barnes. I prefer the former opinion because there is no hint or trace that the congregation ever participated in this matter, and also from the heading of the list of those thus received, which is as follows, "The names and number of the persons admitted to full communion *by myself*, since my ordination with the time of their admission." This same practice prevailed in the First Church of Newark till 1790.

The strength of the church in numbers and wealth at its first organization cannot now be learned. Rev. Samuel L. Tuttle in his history of the Madison Presbyterian church, another off-shoot of Hanover, a few years later, says, "In or about 1740 a small and very feeble church was organized and established in Morristown." But it would seem from the action of the Committee of Synod as well as from the whole course of procedure of this section of the church, that they were able from the beginning to support the gospel. There were 99 in full communion when Mr. Johnes was installed pastor, by no means "a very feeble church," yet small in comparison with the power it has since attained; but by no means to be ranked in those days among the feeble churches in the land. As the records of the old Presbytery of New York are lost we cannot tell who were present to take part in the ordination and installation services of the first pastor of this flock, but it was at that time composed of the following ministers and churches, Dickinson of Elizabeth Town, Pierson of Woodbridge, Aaron Burr of Newark, Nutman of Hanover, Hubbel of Westfield, Horton of Connecticut Farms, Pemberton of New York City, Wilmot of Jamaica, Leonard of Goshen, Pomeroy of Newtown, and F. Horton missionary among the Indians on Long Island, covering territory now occupied by eight Presbyteries and three Synods. The church at Mendham, organized in 1735, received its first pastor a few months after the induction of Mr. Johnes. The only other church in this region was that of Baskingridge, organized in 1733, and at that time supplied by its second pastor. This was however in another county and belonged to another Presbytery. It thus appears that our church was the second in the county that had a settled minister though the third in age. Hanover the mother, born in 1718, and Mendham in 1735.

Among those who welcomed their young pastor to their hearts and homes, and whose descendants are still found on the roll of this church were Prudden, Pierson, Freeman, Condit, Cutler, Mills, Stiles, Johnson and one of the first received into communion with the church was Elizabeth Johnes, wife of the pastor. But the parish of to-day is vastly different from the one that became the home of Timothy Johnes. The village if it might be so named was centred mainly in Water street. In or near it were found the store, the mill, the blacksmith's shop and forge, though Morris street might boast of an occasional hut, and perhaps two or three might be found amidst the clearings of the Green. The forest trees were standing where we now are and what is now the Park could boast of the giant oak, the chestnut and other noble specimens of growth, with which its present shade trees are not to be named. The woods around were visited by the panther and the bear, while wolves in great numbers answered each other from the neighboring hills. The sheep and cattle were brought into pens for the night. Roads were scarcely known. The bridle path or Indian trail was all that conducted the occasional traveler to Mendham, who saw on his way thither a mill, a blacksmith's shop and two dwellings—in three separate clearings. There was scarcely a better path to Baskingridge. There were no postal routes, no newspapers and but few books to instruct and amuse.* Life was then a reality. In the

new settlement every one had to be busy in order to procure such comforts and necessaries as were required. Frugal habits and simple manners distinguished their every day life; and their domestic relations partook more of the patriarchal and less of the commercial, for worldly prosperity had not been sufficient to create that jealous distinction of rank with which we are so often charged as a community. Religion had a moulding influence upon the household, and which from dearth of news often formed the principal topic of converse between neighbors. The Sabbath was rigidly kept; the church was regularly frequented and the minister was highly revered and loved. Into a parish bearing largely the type of New England and with which the new pastor was well acquainted—both on Long Island and Connecticut—did he enter, which he further moulded by his influence, regulated by sound principles and which was blessed more than half of a century by his presence and instructions.

We can only conjecture as to the religious condition of the church at the commencement of his labors. The troubles and contest preceding the organization were in no way congenial to a healthy growth of piety, and after the church was established it was without a settled minister for years—a state of things by no means favorable to the graces of the flock and to their steady increase. Religion throughout the country was at low ebb. This deeply affected many of God's faithful servants and was a subject of lamentation in the church courts, but now better days had arrived. The ministrations of the Tennents and Whitfield were attended with the most remarkable results; a knowledge of which was wafted to the place, and perhaps Mr. Johnes brought with him the spirit of the awakening which might have been deepened at his induction into the pastorate by those who greatly sympathized in that wonderful movement. At the first communion he was privileged to admit to sealing ordinances, Benjamin Hathaway, Samuel Bailey, John Perkis, Mary Perkis, Hannah Lindly and Elizabeth Johnes—an earnest of what God had in store for this people.

*In 1743 the year that Mr. Johnes was installed, Franklin advertised that as the post between Philadelphia and New York had gone once a fortnight that it would from April 13 set out for New York on Thursdays at 3 o'clock in the afternoon till Christmas, and the southern post would be sent every fortnight during the summer. The first periodical published in New Jersey was at Woodbridge in 1758 called the *New American Magazine*.

(To be continued.)

(Continued from page 108.)

MEMBERS.

[The third column on this page is the work of the RECORD. Information which will lead to the correction of any mistake, or the filling of any blank, will be thankfully received.—ED.]

Names.	When Received.	When Dismissed or Died.
Jedidiah Gregory,	Oct. 1776.	Jan. 7, 1783, aet. 53.
Rhoda Gregory (Jedidiah,)	" "	Nov. 3, 1779, aet. 42.
Elizabeth Odell,	" "	
Elizabeth Lewis (Abraham),	Dec. 4, "	
Loruhamah Wines,	Jan. 1, 1778.	"Moved."
Jonathan Pierson,	Feb. 1, "	Sept. 8, 1783, aet. 32.
Sarah Pierson (Jonathan),	" " "	"Moved."
Eunice Ford (Jonathan,)	March 1, "	July 24, 1830, aet. 88 y. 4 m. and 20 d.
Eleanor or Anna Stiles (Timo.)	June 18, "	May 10, 1778, aet. 27.
Brister, negro,	July 3, "	
Silve, his wf., (bap. by Mr. Lewis),	" " "	
Ruth Youngs, (James),	May 2, 1779.	
Susanna Steward (Lewis),	July 4, "	"Moved."
Benjamin Halsey, Esq.,	Sept. 3, "	Feb. 19, 1788, aet. 66.
Jonathan Hallock,	" " "	"Moved."
Mary Hallock (Jonathan),	" " "	"
Anna Ogden, widow,	Nov. 5, "	
Ebenezer Stiles,	May 6, 1781.	Nov. 22, 1814, aet. 88.
Samuel Ludlum, Jr.,	Aug. 31, "	
Kezia, Bayles (Capt. Angus),	" " "	"Moved."
Sarah Wilkerson (James),	" " "	Died May — 1819.
Sarah Conner (Michael),	Sept. 18, "	"Moved."
	"MEMORABLE 1782."	
Joseph Thornton,	Jan. 4, 1782.	"Moved."
Jacob Symson,	" " "	"
Elizabeth Brown,	" " "	
Abner Wade,	" " "	"Moved."
Ruth Tompkins,	" " "	"
Providence Godden,	" " "	"
Jeremiah Stone,	" " "	
Benjamin Holloway,	" " "	Sept. 16, 1846, aet. 87.
Silas Ayers,	Feb. 28, "	"Excluded Oct. 3, 1797, died Dec. 29,
Abigail Byram,	" " "	"Moved." [1826, aet. 77.
David Dalglish,	" " "	
Henry Lane,	" " "	Nov. 18, 1815, aet. 82.
Elizabeth Evolt,	" " "	
Theophilus Hathaway,	" " "	1828 or 1830, aet. 75.
Sarah Bayles,	" " "	Apr. 22, 1789, aet. 80.
Moses Lindsly	May 3. "	May 7, 1793, aet. 59.
Irany Lindsly (Moses)	" " "	May 28, 1821, aet. 82.
John Garrigas,	" " "	"Moved."
Cornelius Looy, Jr.,	" " "	Jan. 17, 1846, aet. 84. [1, 1822, aet. 73.
Stephen Turner,	" " "	"Excluded" May 22, 1796, died Aug.
Elizabeth Arnold (Capt.)	" " "	May 9, 1803, aet. 50.
Mary Ayers (Silas),	" " "	Oct. 30, 1819, aet. 64.
Nancy Arnold,	" " "	"Moved."
Elizabeth Watcuk,	" " "	"

(To be continued.)

(Continued from page 109.)

BAPTISMS.

1767.

Oct. 25. Jacob Ford & wf., ch. Elizabeth.

" " David Woodruff & wf., son, I think ye name Asa.

" " Peter Norris & wf., ch. Nicolas.

Nov. 1. Moses Johnson & wf., ch. Seth.

" " John Allen & wf., ch. Aaron.

Dec. 6. Malcolm McCourry & wf., ch. Phebe, born Oct. 18, 1767.

" " Mattaniah Lyon & wf., ch. Harvey.

" 13. Henry Gardiner & wf., ch. Silas. 1768.

Jan. 24. Wilby Clark on wf.'s acc., ch. Anne.

Feb. 7. Ichabod Carmichael & wf., ch. Rebecca.

Mar. 9. Sam'l Stevens Johnes & wf., ch. bap. at his own house; Phebe, born Dec. 26, 1767.

" 27. Eliphalet Clark on wf.'s acc., ch. Elizabeth.

" " Sam'l Ward on wf.'s acc., ch. Silas, born Oct. 19, 1767.

" " Nathaniel Condict & wf., ch. Hiram.

Apr. 3. Joseph Lindsly & wf., ch. Squire.

" 10. Robert Arnold & wf., ch. Hannah, born Dec. 24th, 1767.

" " Jonas Phillips & wf., ch. George.

" " Thomas Tuttle & wf., ch. Timothy.

" 17. Philip Hathaway & wf., ch. Hannah.

May 1. Jedidiah Gregory & wf., ch. Lois.

" " Ebenezer Condict & wf., ch. Phebe.

" " Nathan Turner & wf., ch. Jacob.

" " Robert Hains & wf., ch. Noah.

June 11. David Ogden on wf.'s acc., ch. Sarah.

July 10. Doc. Sam. Tuthill & wf., ch. Hannah.

" " Peter Prudden & wf., ch. Joanna.

" " John Mitchel & wf., ch. Solomon, born April 15, 1768.

" " Jabish Bears & wf., ch. David.

" " Jonathan Wood on wf.'s acc., ch. Abraham.

July 24. Jonathan Ford on wf.'s acc., ch. Charlotte.

" " Sam'l Hains on wf.'s acc., ch. Stephen.

" " Jedidiah Mills & wf., ch. Abigail.

" " James Shadwick on wf.'s acc., ch. Bethanah.

May 15. John Lyon on his own acc., ch. Sarah.

" " Lieu Ben. Hathaway & wf., ch. Isaac.

" " Gilbard Ludlum & wf., ch. Samuel.

" " Alexander Carmichael & wf., ch. Huldah.

June 5. David Gauden & wf., ch. David.

" " Joshua Guering & wf., ch. Phebe.

" " Gilbard Allen & wf., ch. Phebe.

" " Joshua Whitehead & wf., ch. Jemima.

Aug. 4, 1768, bap. 1,168, majority of females, 10,

Aug. 7. John Metonge & wf., ch. Peter Bruer.

" " Jacob Frase & wf., ch. Elizabeth.

" 13. Paul Fervor & wf., ch. Anna.

" " Hezekiah Stebbins on wf.'s acc., ch. Sarah.

" 21. Widow Anne Pierson, relict of Moses, ch. Kezia.

" " Willm. Halbard & wf., ch. Joshua.

" " John Lose on wf.'s acc., ch. Mary.

" 28. Silas Howell & wf., ch. Hannah.

Sept. 11. James Wilkerson & Sarah his wf., ch. Willm. Burnet.

" " Cornelius Woodruff & wf., ch. John.

Oct. 9. Dan'l Howard & wf., ch. Abner.

" " John Rogers on wf.'s acc., ch. Hannah.

" 16. James Brookfield & wf., ch. Silas, born Sept. 16, 1768.

" 20. Benj. Lindsly & wf., ch. Jane., born Sept. 15, 1768.

" " James Miller & wf., ch. Samuel.

" 27. Daniel Carmichael & wf., ch. Daniel, born Sept. 14, 1768.

Nov. 13. Ephraim Burrel's wf. on her acc., ch. Phebe.

Dec. 14. John Pool & wf., ch. Ezra.

Dec. 25. Lieu. John Lindsly & wf., ch. Henry. " " Christopher Wood & wf., ch. John, born Oct. 4, 1768.

1769.

Jan. 1. Ezek. Day & wf., ch. Elizabeth.

" 15. Nathan Turner & wf., ch. Lydia.

" 22. Phineas Fairchild & wf., ch. Charlotte, born Oct. 10, 1768.

" " Zenas Condict & wf., ch. Abigail.

Feb. 19. David Woodruff & wf., ch. Demas.

" " David Fairchild & wf., ch. Silas.

" " Jerzel Turner & wf., ch. Daniel.

Mar. 5. Jabish Condit & wf., ch. Jonas.
" 19. Abraham Canfield & wf., ch. Abner.
" " John Pierson & wf., ch. Ruth.
" " John Hathaway & wf., ch. Gershom.
" 25. Moses Munson & wf., ch. John.
" " Seth Crowell, jun., & wf., ch. Mary.
Apr. 2. William Verguson & wf., ch. Elizabeth.
" " Nathaniel Armstrong and wf., ch. Nathaniel.
" 23. Nathaniel Peck & wf., ch. Ruth.
May 14. Benj. Pierson, jun. & wf., ch. Paul.
" 21. Robard McCalvey, twins on wf's acc., Sarah & Abigail.
" " Timo. Johnes & wf., negro child Juba, born March 30, 1769.
June 4. Sam Allwood & wf., ch. Jonas.
" 25. Moses Prudden & wf., ch. Elizabeth born May 17, 1769.
" " Daniel Tichenor & wf., ch. Jane, born May 4, 1769.
" " Jonathan Tichenor & wf., ch. Hannah.
" 29. Joshua Winget & wf., ch. Huldah.
July 16. Phil. Lindsly & wf., ch. Sarah, born June 15, 1769.
" 23. Stephen Conkling & wf., ch. Deborah, born April 17, 1769.
" " Joseph Condict & wf., ch. Jeduthan, born April 28, 1769.
" " Moses Lindsly & wf., ch. Elizabeth, born June 25, 1769.
July 30. Peter Hill & wf., ch. Abigail, born April 8, 1769.
Aug. 6. Eleazar Lindsly & wf., ch. Eleazar,
" " Stephen Norris & wf., ch. Phebe, born July 1, 1769.
" 13. Ichabod Carmichael & wf., ch. Anna, born June 30, 1769.
" 26. Dea. Matthias Burnet & wf., negro ch. Dol, born May, 1769.
Sept. 3. Elizabeth Easton, ch. Aaron Davis, born March 17, 1769.
" 24. Jonathan Hathaway & wf., ch. Phebe, born Aug. 18, 1769.
" " Onesimus Whitehead & wf., ch. Huldah, born July 30, 1769.
" " John Allen & wf., ch. Jehosheba, born Aug. 31, 1769.
Oct. 15. Malcom McCoury & wf., ch. Jane, born Sept. 8, 1769.
" 22. Eleazar Hathaway & wf., ch. Mary, born Sept. 12, 1769.

Oct. 29. Alexander Johnson, on wife's account, ch. Timothy, born Aug. 20, 1769.
Dec. 17. Joseph Lindsley & wf., ch. Jemima, born Nov. 15, 1769.
1770.
Jan. 14. Moses Johnson & wf., ch. Ebenezar, born Nov. 14, 1769.
" " Nathaniel Condict & wf., ch. Isaiah, born Nov. 26, 1769.
" 21. Junia Lindsly & wf., ch. Nehemiah, born Dec. 3, 1769.
" " Perkins Byram & wf., ch. Eliab, born Dec. 1, 1769.
Feb. 11. Peter Condict & wf., ch. Edward, born Nov. 15, 1769.
" 25. John Mills & wf., ch. Silas, born Jan. 23, 1770.
Mar. 4. Joshua Guerin & wf., ch. Thomas, born Jan. 11, 1770.
" 25. Isaac Pierson & wf., ch. Eunice, born Feb. 10, 1770.
" " James Keen & wf., ch. Eunice, born Feb. 25, 1770.
" " Silas Howell & wf., ch. Silas White, born Feb, 22., 1770.
April 1. Eliphalet Clark, on wife's account, ch. Elisha.
" " Peter Norris & wf., ch. Aaron.
" " Ezekiel Brown & wf., ch. Sarah.
" 8. John Lyon, on his own account, ch. Isaac, born Feb. 24, 1770.
" " Gilbard Allen & wf., ch. Silas, born Feb. 5, 1770.
" " Sam'l Ward, on wife's account, ch. Hannah, born Dec. 29, 1769.
" 22. Abraham Campfield & wife, ch. Phebe, born Jan. 5, 1770.
" " Thomas Miller & wf., ch. Moses, born Feb. 28, 1770.
" 26. Jonathan Ford, on wife's account, ch. John Odell, b. Mar. 13. 1770.
May 4. Lindsly Burnet & wf., ch. Joseph Lindsly, born Nov. 26, 1769.
" 6. Ichabod Cooper & wf., ch. Moses, born Feb. 15, 1770.
" " Richard Johnson & wf., ch. David, born Feb. 3, 1770.
" " Phebe, wf., of Jacob Palmer, on her acc., ch. Samuel, b. Nov. 20, 1769.
" " Phebe, wf. of Jacob Palmer, on her acc., ch. Samuel, born Nov. 20, 1769.
(To be continued.)

BILL OF MORTALITY.

(Continued from page 111.)

1784.

June 11. Anne, widow of Jacob Johnson, aet. 31, consumption.

" 12. Jacob Allen,† aet. 22, kick from a horse.

July 22. George Phillips,* aet. 52.

" 25. Elizabeth, wife of Moses Allen, aet. 29, billous fever.

Aug. 1. Phœbe, daughter of George Mills, aet. 1, quinsy.

" " Child of Joseph Prudden, Jun.

" 9. Rachael, wife of John Stevenson,* aet. 31, consumption.

" 11. Judith, daughter of Aaron Pierson, aet. 16, consumption.

" " John, son of Caleb Russell, aet. 2, remitting fever.

" 16. Sarah, wife of Capt. Jedidiah Mills,* aet. 35, remitting fever.

" 24. Daniel Brady, aet. 40, inflammatory fever.

" 28. Elizabeth, daughter of Benjamin Woodruff, aet. 3, sore throat.

Sept. 2. Sarah, wife of Joseph Lindsly, Jun., aet. 22, consumption.

" " Elizabeth Johnes, daughter of Jos. Lewis, Esq., teething and worms.

" " Daphne, servant of Rev. Timothy Johnes, aet. 55, inflammatory fever.

" 8. Rachel, wife of Josiah Munson, aet. 18, fever.

" " A child of Asa Beach.

" 11. Capt. John Lindsley,* aet. 56, consumption.

" 13. Prudence, daughter of John Prudden, aet. 14, fever.

" " Abraham Plum, aet. 14, dropsy.

" 19. A child of John Tuttle.

" 23. Dorcas Easton,* aet. 58, intermittent fever.

" " Philip, son of Abiel Fairchild, aet. 10, fever.

" " Sarah, daughter of John Harporee, aet. 3, intermittent fever.

" 29. A child of Moses Wilkinson.

" 30. Mary, wife of Philip Condict,* aet. 72, fever.

" " Experience, widow of Benjamin Conger,* aet. 73, old age.

Oct. 2. Mary, wife of Abraham Pierson,* aet. 72, remitting fever.

Oct. 2. Mary Pierson,† aet. 25, consumption.

" 8. Widow Seward, aet. 60.

" 10. Uzal Coe, aet, 37, putrid fever.

" " A child of Silas Casterline.

Nov. 25. Nathan, son of Nathan Reeve, aet. 2, worms.

" " A child of Hubert Duburk, aet. 2, consumption.

1785.

Jan. 7. Patience, widow of Benjamin Pierson,* aet. 77, old age.

" 9. An illegitimate child, casual.

" 15. Sarah, wife of Samuel Mills,* aet. 61, pleurisy.

" 23. Bethiah, wife of Benjamin Hallsey, Esq.,* aet. 62, consumption.

Feb. 8. Bethia, wife of Thomas Miller, aet. 45, consumption.

" 21. Jacob, son of Isaac Pruden, putrid fever.

Mar. 3. Phœbe, daughter of Peter Norris, Jun., aet. 1, measles.

" 4. A child of Samuel Pangborn.

Apr. 10. A child of Jedidiah Osborn.

" 15. Joanna, wife of Daniel Smith, aet. 33, consumption.

" 20. Daniel Frost, aet. 79, diabetes.

" 23. A child of John Tuttle.

" 27. Hannah, wife Capt. Silas Howell,* aet. 36, child-bed.

" " A child of Joseph Byram.

May 1. Daniel Conger, aet. 57, dropsy.

" 9. Joseph Pierson, aet. 72, fever.

" 17. Rebeckah, wife of Gideon Riggs, aet. 68, fever.

" 18. Sarah, daughter of David Muir.

" 19. Twins of Amos Prudden.

" 20. A child of Ziba Ludlow.

" 25. A child of Silas Gildersleve.

" 28. A child of William Meeker.

June 1. Sarah, daughter of David Brown,† aet. 1, plurisy.

" 5. Elder, Timothy Lindsley,* aet. 57, sudden.

" 13. A child of Silas Gildersleve.

" 14. James, son of Michael Conner, aet. 2, hives.

" 17. Comfort, widow of Joseph Stiles, Esq.,* aet 77, consumption.

" 21. Elizabeth Phœbe, wife of James Cook, aet. 22, child-bed.

July 21. Elizabeth, daughter of Deacon Allen, 19, consumption.

" 23. A child of John Lindsley.

(To be continued.)

(*Continued from page* 112.)

TRUSTEES' BOOK.

A request was made by Mr. Lewis to have a certain plot of ground appropriated for the purpose of making vaults for any families who would chose that method of burying their dead.

Voted, That Mr. Lindsley, Mr. Mills and Mr. Lewis be a committee to examine the ground and conveniences for it, and request the Sexton to dig no more graves within the space chosen by the committee for the said purpose, until he shall receive orders from this board, and that the committee report thereon.

Voted, That Mr. Lindsley and Mr. Mills be a committee to rent a house for the purpose of accommodating the Rev. Mr. Collins.

June 21, 1790.—

* 　　* 　　* 　　* 　　* 　　*

Mr. President proposed to have a Church Treasurer in the room of Mr. Smith who is absent—whereupon the Board appointed Mr. Mills to serve in that office. Mr. Mills was appointed to settle the accounts of the late Treasurer, and report to the Board. The Board appointed Mr. Cherry to serve as Sexton, and that he be paid five pounds per year by the Treasurer, and be allowed to demand and receive from five shillings to a dollar for digging a grave and tolling the bell at each funeral; and that the Sexton see that the meeting house is properly swept from time to time and be allowed three pounds five shillings to pay for that service with the reserve that Joseph Woodman be allowed to continue to do the business as heretofore.

Voted, That the Treasurer be directed to pay Nathan Howell the balance of his account for services as sexton to this day.

Sept. 6, 1790, at the house of Joseph Lewis. The weekly contributions falling short of the current expenses of ringing the Bell, sweeping the meeting house, &c. Voted that Mr. Lewis wait on the Rev. Doctor Johnes and request him to address the people upon this occasion and request their future attention to this part of their duty and to be more liberal in contributing, and the next succeeding Sabbath be appointed to make a collection for paying arrears which now amount to about 5 or 6 pounds.

Voted that Jesse Cuttler and Samuel Day be appointed to carry about the collection box in the gallery when contributions are to be made.

Voted, That the Assessor be requested to assess twenty-two pounds ten shillings (in addition to the Rev. Mr. Collins' salary) for the purpose of paying the rent of a house hired for the use of Mr. Collins.

* 　　* 　　* 　　* 　　* 　　*

Voted, That Messrs. Johnson and Lewis be a committee to superintend the repairs of the fence around the parsonage, make such part of it new as they may think necessary, and erect a fence around a plot of ground on the same sufficient for garden.

Oct. 8, 1790.—At a meeting of the congregation pursuant to advertisements for that purpose.

Resolved, That Deacon Allen serve as Moderator. That Joseph Lewis serve as Clerk.

James Smith having removed and Joseph Lewis having resigned his office as a Trustee, the congregation elected Jonathan Ogden and Jacob Arnold, Esq., to serve as Trustees.

Resolved, That the committee of Direction proceed to provide materials for the new meeting house as soon as convenient. That the house be built seventy feet long and fifty feet broad. That a committee of Council be appointed to give further instructions to the Committee of Directors from time to time as they may think proper.

That Judge Condict, Doct. Johnes, Jr., Doct. Jab. Campfield, Squire Carmichael, Squire Lindsly, Mr. Phillips, Mr. Jonathan Dickerson, Major Lindsly, Deacon Allen, Mr. Johnson, Mr. Mills and Mr. Halsey be a committee for that purpose. That the said committee have leave to add to or take from the length or breadth of the said new meeting house any number of feet not exceeding five. That the said Committee have leave to apply to the Legislature for the privilege of a Lottery to raise a sum of money equal to the expense of building the new meeting house. That the Board of Trustees have leave to purchase a stove for the Rev. Mr. Collins.

(*To be continued.*)

THE RECORD.

FIRST PRESBYTERIAN CHURCH, MORRISTOWN, N. J.

"This shall be written for the Generation to Come."—Psalms 102 : 18.

| VOL. II. | APRIL, 1881. | NO. 4. |

(Printed with the approval of Session.)

THE RECORD

Will be printed and published monthly at Morristown, N. J. Terms, 50 cents per annum in advance; 75 cents after June.

Subscriptions will be received at the book-stores of Messrs. Runyon and Emmell, or through the mail. All communications should be addressed to the·

EDITOR OF THE RECORD,

Lock box 44.   Morristown, N. J.

Vol. I. complete, 75 cents.

Entered at the Post Office at Morristown, N. J., as second class matter.

——:o:——

(Continued from page 115.)

HISTORICAL SERMON,

No. 1.

BY THE

REV. DAVID IRVING, D.D.,

The year previous to his coming to this place, the Presbyterian Church, then in its infancy in this land, had been rent in twain. It consisted at that time of 6 Presbyteries and one Synod, called the Synod of Philadelphia. Its ministry was gathered from different countries, whose early training and habits influenced their views, which, being diverse, interfered to some extent with the general harmony of the body. The points, which had elicited for years the warmest discussion, were strict adherence to Presbyterial order —the examination of candidates for the ministry, and their literary acquirements. Whilst there·had been continued friction on these topics the visit of Whitefield brought matters to a crisis. In the great awakening which attended his labors, frequent scenes of fanaticism and extravagance were witnessed, that awoke the displeasure of the more rigid in the Synod, who were not backward to pronounce the whole work a

delusion. Those who warmly favored the revival, were as earnest in its approval. This, with the other matters mentioned, led to a division of the Synod in 1741—the "Old Side," as it was called constituting the Synod of Philadelphia, and the "New Side" the Synod of New York. This church naturally came into connection with the New Side, with many of whose views by reason of association and education Mr. Johnes warmly sympathized.

We are now brought to his active labors in the congregation, in which we are to view him as a man of God, anxious to do good, to build up the waste places and bring his hearers to Christ. Of the style of his preaching but little judgment can be formed, as none of his sermons, as far as we know, were ever printed,* and but few of his MSS. remain, and scarcely any with us to-day are old enough to remember the style and character of his productions. We have, however, the record of these gathered from a former generation, and published in 1828, as follows : "As a preacher he is said to have been clear, plain, practical and persuasive. His discourses were rather an affectionate appeal to the heart, than profound and elaborate disquisition on abstruse points of theology. He aimed rather to win men to the practice of holiness, than to terrify and denounce them." And, says one yet amongst us, Dr. Lewis Condict, in a vigorous old age, and who was with him a great deal in his last days, "As a preacher he was popular, impressive and earnest, speaking from the heart with affectionate kindness—he seldom failed to reach the hearts of his hearers. His sermons were seldom written out, but consisted of brief notes, on which he enlarged extemporaneously. He dwelt

—————
*One of his sermons was printed in THE RECORD of October last.—ED.

on the practical duties of Christianity, with fervor and plainness, seldom, if ever, indulging in speculative theology or metaphysics. His favorite authors were Flavel, Baxter, Bunyan and Doddridge. His delivery was natural and unaffected, with animation and earnestness adapted to his subject and sufficient to show that he felt the full force of the truths he uttered.

As a pastor he was much with his people : visiting from house to house, and becoming acquainted with the circumstances of every family. In these interviews, he sought as in the pulpit to bring home the concerns of eternity to the hearts and consciences of each and by his kind words and genial manner he not only inculcated pure sentiments but was instrumental in training many in the ways of sobriety and godliness. He was particular in his attention to the children and youth, collecting them at stated periods in their respective neighborhoods and school houses, hearing recitations in the catechism, explaining its truths and occasionally bestowing upon those whose proficiency was most apparent, some little token of approbation. By his kind attentions he won their hearts and retained them through life. His admonitions became law and as they grew up, they treated him with respect, venerated his presence and loved him for his excellencies. Then the power of the clergy was great and was skilfully used by him. The child scarcely, if ever, heard their pastor disparaged and his instructions contemned and as a consequence, the seed that he scattered and his efforts to benefit were accompanied in due time with God's blessing, so that in his old age he found an entire congregation, whose hearts and minds had been moulded by his ministry, to be largely in unison with his own.

At certain seasons he held regular meetings for young men, giving written questions from the Bible to those who were willing to give written answers, which were publicly read and commented upon by him. The children when catechised always stood up as a mark of respect to the minister.

He was preeminently a lover of peace and a peacemaker. Quick to discern any coldness or contention between neighbors, he was not at ease until the difficulties were removed in harmony with the laws of affection and concord. He was dignified in deportment, yet easy of access ; still no one could trifle with him nor use unbecoming language in his presence. In church discipline he was strict as the many cases left on record abundantly testify, amounting in all to 170. This arose in part from the texture of society and from social usages which led the unwary astray.

He was a man of great system and order, having a time for every duty. His days and hours for study and preparation for the pulpit were understood by his people, as well as his days for visiting and receiving visits. His church records exhibit the name of every member from the commencement to the close of his ministry, as well as marriages, births, baptisms and generally the ages of the children. Says the aged member alluded to and to whom I am greatly indebted for important reminiscences of Dr. Johnes and who has had many opportunities of inquiring as to the time of marriage of parties, &c., "In but one instance have I found a disagreement as to the date of the marriage and that variance was but of a single day, and in that case the widow after much reflection admitted her own mistake and that the record of her minister was correct."

Whilst in all these things he was a model pastor, the same regularity is not apparent in his attendance upon church courts. As the records of the Presbytery are lost we cannot tell how punctual he was in attendance upon its meetings. But those of the Synods of New York and Philadelphia are preserved and we find him often absent. At the first meeting of the Synod of New York after the division, held in Elizabethtown, 1745 ; he was present, with Joseph Prudden, an elder from this church. In the following year a large number of absentees is recorded, among whom was Timothy Johnes, but with this insertion, "The Synod is informed that most of the absent members were upon their journey to New York to attend the Synod but were prevented through apprehensions of the small pox and other difficulties." In 1747 he is present with Joseph Prudden ; absent in the years '48, '49,' '51, '52, but present at Philadelphia in 1753 ; at Newark, 1754 and

'56; absent in 1758, when the two Synods of New York and Philadelphia after a separation of 17 years were happily reunited, after mutual concession had been made. In 1764 he is again present with his faithful elder Joseph Prudden and both are placed on the commission of Synod. In 1768 he is a member with Col. Jacob Ford as elder and is appointed one of a committee to visit Bedford, N. Y., and settle all the differences in the congregation. His last attendance upon the body was in 1779, when he opened the Synod with a sermon, having been moderator the preceding year.

I have not been able to learn the amount of salary promised to the young pastor on his acceptance of the call, or in what way it was to be paid. In those days many of the congregations furnished their ministers with a house and farm or else promised him, in the call, a sum of money to buy a plantation. Thus when Mr. Hubbel was settled at Hanover and Westfield, the congregation gave him as a settlement so many acres of parsonage land in fee simple, while all who chose bound themselves by a covenant to be assessed according to their property. The salaries were often paid in kinds, wheat, Indian corn, hemp and linen yarn being frequently specified in the call. Yea, every imaginable article from "a riddle to a Squire's publishment of a marriage" has been found on the count books of ministers as being received in payment of stipend. Tradition makes the cash part of Mr. Johnes' salary at first to be £20, a trifle over $50, His table was furnished principally from the parsonage land, which covered the triangular piece of ground bounded by Morris, South and Pine streets and stretching down to the Whippany river. The ploughing, planting of the ground and harvesting of the crops were performed mainly by the farmers of the parish, who also furnished and cut all the wood used, and at their visitations the parishioners carried large supplies for the table. when they were assured of a hearty welcome. "It was a rare occurrence" says one, "in those primitive days that a visitor carried away from the parsonage more good things than he or she brought, while in his social visits in the congregation, with his wife or alone, he scarcely ever returned home empty handed." The first allusion to salary on the church books is in April 1759, soon after the charter of the church was obtained* and is as follows: "We inquired into the overplus money of Mr. Johnes' rates including the year 1757, when it was found that of all past rates only £14, 13 was due to him, and after his demands were answered and the assessor collects from said rates, the remainder should be lodged in the trustees hands." These rates were assessed upon the property or income, and collected by a person or persons appointed by the congregation and this custom continued until the building of the present edifice, which was commenced upon the same plan of assessment. Though we find at times that notes for the rates and subscriptions were put into the Dr.'s hands which he took as an equivalent for salary, making such reduction for the poor as he deemed proper. As the congregation increased in members and wealth additions were made to his salary until it became £150. The dwelling now occupied by Eugene Ayers, in Morris street, was the parsonage, and was either given to Dr. Johnes or was purchased for a small sum which he afterwards enlarged, and to the lot, on which the house stood, other lands bought by him were added. His children were well educated and trained for usefulness, and at his death he left an estate, which at that day was deemed large and valuable.

*See charter in RECORD, Jan. 1880—ED.

(To be continued.)

Report of First Church to the Presbytery of Morris and Orange, for year ending April 1st, 1881 :

Added on Examination,	29	
" " Certificate,	22	
Present number of Members,	592	
Adults baptized.	8	
Infants "	8	
Sunday School Membership,	471	
Contributed to Home Missions,	$1,183	00
" " Foreign Missions,	1,581	00
" " Education,	411	00
" " Publication,	40	00
" " Church Erection,	127	00
" " Ministerial Relief,	171	00
" " Freedmen,	112	00
" " Sustentation,	24	00
" " Miscellaneous Objects,	1,053	00
Assessment for General Assembly,	51	75
Raised for Congregational purposes,	9,008	00

(*Continued from page* 116.)

MEMBERS.

[The third column on this page is the work of the RECORD. Information which will lead to the correction of any mistake, or the filling of any blank, will be thankfully received.—ED.]

Names.	When Received.	When Dismissed or Died.
Rebecca Pierson (Samuel)	May 3, 1782.	
Elizabeth Shipman	" " "	
Mary Lindsly (Major Joseph)	July 5, "	Apr. 14, 1828, aet. 79.
Mary Ayers (Isaac)	" " "	June 30, 1809, aet. 63.
Rebecca Hambleton (Benj.)	" " "	Dis. to So. Hanover, March 4, 1814.
Sarah Turner	" " "	"Moved."
Sarah Prudden	" " "	

" 320 added to the ch. by my min. to ys. date, with m yt ha come from other chs. 480."

Eunice Tompkins	Jan. 1. 1783.	"Moved."
Joseph Lewis, Esq., "My Son-in-law"	Feb. 27. "	[1748. Died July 30, 1814, born Dec. 23,
Mary Ward (Samuel)	May 2. "	"Moved."
Mary Tennery (Michael)	" " "	
Lydia Parker	" " "	"Moved."
Rebecca Wood (Samuel)	Aug. 1, "	Aug. 18, 1783, aet. 24.
Samuel Freeman	Sept. 5, "	Sept. 16, 1833, aet. 80 y. 7 m, and 25 d.
Sarah Freeman (Samuel)	" " "	Feb. 9, 1817, aet. 62.
Damaris Prudden (Amos)	" " "	
Hope Keen (Thomas)	" " "	
Ezra Halsey	Oct. 30, "	"Moved."
Damaris Stiles (Timothy)	" " "	
John Walker	" " "	"Moved."
Hannah Walker (John)	" " "	" [died July 2, 1821, aet. 63.
Sarah Wilkerson	Nov. 2, "	Dis. to Mt. Freedom, June 15, 1820,
Experience Pierson	Aug. 2, 1784	Feb. 15, 1793, aet. 48.
William Cherry	Nov. 5, "	Sept. 2, 1825, aet. 78.
Rachel Cherry (William)	" " "	March 27, 1827, aet. 70.
Elijah Holloway,	Jan. 1, 1785.	Feb. 24, 1826, aet. 61 y. 9m. and 9 d.
Philip Lindsley,	Mar. 4, "	"Moved."
David Gardiner,	" " "	
Abiel Fairchild,	Apr. 28, "	Dec. 15, 1789, aet. 50.
Mary Arnold (Ziba)	July 2, "	Apr. 30, 1791, aet. 38.
Benjamin Pierson,	" " "	Died Jan. 1, 1792, born Mar. 30, 1736.
Sarah Ross, (Isaac)	" 3, "	"Moved."
Catharine Crain (Moses),	Sept. 4. "	"
Margaret Faugerson (James),	" " "	
Phebe McGloclin (John)	Nov. 4. "	"Moved."
Silas Brookfield,	Dec. 30, "	Excom. Oct. 3, 1797.
Rachael Riggs,	" " "	Dis. as Mrs. Woods, Oct. 30, 1810,
Sarah Smith,	" " "	"Moved." [to Springfield.
Asa Beach,	" " "	"
Anna Humes (James)	" " "	
Thankful Tuttle (Nathaniel)	" " "	
Sarah Howell (Nathan),	April 5, 1786.	Aug. 7, 1813, aet. 81.
Zippora Johnson, widow,	" " "	
Joseph Prudden, Jr.,	June 30, "	
Jane Brown, widow,	" " "	

(*To be continued.*)

(*Continued from page* 118.)

BAPTISMS.

1770.

May 13. Sam'l Tuthill, Esq. & wf., ch. Jacob Ford, born April 6, 1770.

" " Job Loree & wf., ch. John, born March 28, 1770,

" " David Gardiner, on wf.'s accompt, ch. Lydia, born April 16, 1770. John Mitchel desired record of three children bap., as he saith, in New England, viz: Lydia, born Dec. 14, 1752. Thomas, born June 17, 1754. James, born March 29, 1756.

May 27. David Cermichael & wf., ch. Bathsheba, born April 16, 1770.

June 3. Jonas Phillips & wf., ch. Samuel, born April 9, 1770.

" " Silas Condict & wf., Negro, ch. John, born March 21, 1770.

July 1. Jabez Condict & wf., ch. Moses, born May 21, 1770.

" " John Redman & wf., ch. Joel, born May 11, 1770.

" 15. Jacob Fraze & wf., ch. Anne, born June 15, 1770.

" " Hezekiah Stebins on wf.'s accompt, ch. Lydia, born May 19, 1770.

" 19. Eldr. John Lindsley & wf., ch. Henry, born July 10, 1770.

Sept.16. Jedidiah Gregory & wf., ch.—born Aug. 12, 1770.

" 30. Henry Gardiner & wf., ch. Catharine, born Aug. 4, 1770.

Oct. 7. Joseph Pierson & wf., ch. Bethuel, born Sept. 2, 1770.

" " Ebenezar Coe & wf., ch. Stephen, born Sept. 1, 1770.

" 14. William Akeman on wf.'s accompt, ch. Rebeccah.

" 28. James Brookfield & wf., ch. James, born Sept. 21, 1770.

" " Isaac Prudden & wf., ch. Timothy, born Sept. 29, 1770.

Nov. 2. Joseph Benway on wf.'s accompt, two children, Prudence, born Nov. 11, 1766—Mary, born Feb. 6, 1770.

" 4. Jonathan Wood & wf., ch. Sarah, born Aug. 23, 1770.

" " James Miller & wf., ch. Kezia, born Aug. 10, 1770.

PREACHING TOUR IN SUSSEX 2 SABBATHS.

Nov.20. PAULEN KILL—Stephen Hagerty, ch. Sarah.

" " Richard Westbrook's wf., adult, Mary.

" " WARICK—William Decay & wf., ch. Enos.

" " John Wissner & wf., ch. Elizabeth.

" " HARDISTON—At Tim. Lindsley's, Alexander McCullock, renewed cov. & ch. bap.,name Alexander.

" 25. At Lawrence Decker's, Francis Headly & wf., ch. Susanna.

" 29. David Wheeler. adult.

" " David Wheeler & wf., ch. David Young, born March 12, 1770.

Dec. 9. James McBride on wf.'s accompt, ch. Walter Irwin, born Oct. 8, 1770.

" " John Rogers on wf.'s accompt, ch. David, born Oct. 25, 1770.

" " Caleb Munson & wf., ch. Jacob, born Oct. 8, 1770.

" 23. Cornelius Woodruff & wf., ch. Joab, born Nov. 11. 1770.

1771.

Jan. 4. Susanna Allen, ch. on own accompt, Jacob, born Nov. 11, 1770.

" " Margaret, Serv. of Sam'l Robarts, ch. on her own accompt, Cloe, born July 3, 1769.

Feb. 3. John Prudden & wf., ch. Prudence, born Dec. 16, 1770.

" 24. Jedidiah Mills & wf., ch. Mary, born Dec. 28, 1770.

Mar.17. Benj. Lindsly & wf., ch. Mary, born Feb. 6, 1771.

" " Nathaniel Armstrong & wf., ch. Silas, born Jan. 12, 1771.

Joshua Ball.

Joshua Ball's children desired to be registered. Kezia, born Sept. 12, 1747, Jacob, born Feb. 24, 1749. James, born Sept. 10, 1750, Rachael, born March 19, 1752. Mary, born Jan. 23, 1754, Hannah, born Oct. 7, 1756; all baptized by Mr. Green, Phebe, born Oct. 14, 1758; Jemima, born Oct. 14, 1761; Joshua, born Dec. 14, 1764; these bap. by Mr. Johnes. The following my present wife had by her former husband, John Tompkins, & baptized: Jonas, born Aug. 31, 1748; Martha, born May 23, 1752; Enos, born Mar. 26, 1754; John, born Jan. 4, 1771.

1771.
Mar. 24. Moses Lindsley & wf., ch. Irane, born Feb. 19, 1771.
" " Jonathan Tichenor & wf., ch. Caleb, born Feb. 12, 1771.
April 7. David Fairchild & wf., ch. Eunice, born Jan. 1, 1771.
" " Moses Prudden & wf., ch. Theodosia, born March 7, 1771.
" " Nathaniel Peck & wf., ch. Rachel, born Feb. 20, 1771.
" " Zenas Condict & wf., ch. Stephen, born Jan, 16, 1771.
" " Lindsly Burnet & wf., ch. Elizabeth, born Dec. 26, 1770.
" 11. Icabod Cermichael & wf., ch. Sarah, born Feb. 27, 1771.
" 14. John Mitchel & wf., ch. Hezekiah, born Aug. 14, 1770.
May 3. Phebe, wf. of Stephen Arnold, bap. at the same time,
" " Their son, Ezekiel, was bap., born Dec. 19, 1770.
" " Mercy, wf. of Joseph Pierson, Jr., bap. at the same time,
" " Their daughter, Rhoda, bap., born Dec. 3, 1768, and
" " Their daughter, Mary, born Feb. 4, 1771.
May 5. Rebecab, wf. of Sam'l Pierson, adult, born Sep. 2, 1741.
" " Sam'l & wf., ch. Joanna, born Feb. 18, 1770.
" " Moses Munson & wf., ch. Philip, born Mar. 12, 1771.
" " Joseph Riggs & wf., ch. Stephen, born Mar. 4, 1771.
" " John Hathaway & wf., ch. Ruth, born Mar. 22, 1771.
" 12. Solomon Southward on wf.'s accompt, ch. Mary.
" 19. Ebenezer Stiles & wf., ch. Moses, born Apr. 2, 1771.
" 26. Gilbard Ludlam & wf., ch. Henry, born Feb. 3, 1771.
June 23. Peter Dickenson & wf., ch. Joseph, born Dec. 8, 1770.
" " Joshua Winget & wf., ch. Sarah, born Mar. 10, 1771.
" " Onesimus Whitehead & wf., ch. Asa, born May 4, 1771.
" " Sam'l Ward on wf.'s accompt, ch. Charity, born Apr. 29, 1771.

June 23. James Loce on wf.'s accompt, ch. Jemima, born Apr. 10, 1771.
" 30. Daniel Tichenor & wf., ch. Elizabeth, born May 10, 1771.
" " Paul Farber & wf., ch. Hannah, born Nov. 17, 1770.
July 5. Phebe, wf. of Abr. Talmage, adult, born May 19, O. S., 1750.
" " Abraham Talmage & wf., ch, Aaron, born July 30, 1770.
" " Rachel, wf. of Jabez Rodgers, on her accompt, ch. Ruth, born Jan. 21, 1771.
" 15. Nathaniel L'homedau & wf., ch. born May 16, 1771.
" " Bois Jno. Prudden & wf., ch. Gabriel, born Apr. 3, 1771.
" " Rhoda, Dan'l Kenny's wf., on her accompt. Twins, John & Sarah, born Nov. 8, 1770.
" 21. Fane, daughter of Kezia Ball, by Francis Redman, Oct. 5, 1770.
" 28. Rob. McCalve on wf.'s accompt, ch. Rachel.
Aug. 4. William Walton's wf., Catherine, on her accompt, ch. Will Pitt, born Feb. 13, 1771.
" " John Poole & wf., ch. William, born May 22, 1771.
" 11. John Miller & wf., ch. John, born Feb. 18, 1769.
" " John Miller & wf., ch. Jean, born April 13, 1771.
" 18. David Gauden & wf., ch. Robard, born June 30, 1771.
" 25. William Gray & wf., ch. John, his son, by former wife, born May 27, 1764, & David, born of his present wife, & that on Oct. 3, 1769.
Sept. 1. Mattaniah Lyon & wf., ch. Jacob, born July 30, 1771.
" 3. Dr. Bern Budd, on wf.'s acct. ch, David, born July 28, 1771.
" " Martha. wf. of Shadrach Hathaway, family bap: on her acct. Jacob, born June 20, 1769; Ruth, born Aug. 31, 1767; Abraham, born Apr. 24, 1771.
" 14. Sam'l Alwood & wf., ch. Sarah, born Aug. 7, 1771.
" 22. Peter Condict & wf., ch. Byram, born Aug. 22, 1771.
(To be continued.)

(*Continued from page* 119.)

BILL OF MORTALITY.

1785.

July 26. Thomas, son of James Smith, aet. 7, poisoned by night-shade berries.

" 27. Ephraim Howard, aet. 46, drowned.

Aug. 16. Child of Peter Carr.

" " Child of Abraham Hudson.

" 18. A Child of Daniel Mackentire.

" " Phœbe, wife of John Blackman, aet. 30, fever.

" 20. A child of Moses Allen, aet. 2, dropsy.

" 22. Eleanor, widow of Richard Verguson,* aet. 71, consumption.

" 30. A child of Cornelius Losey.

Sept. 6. John, son of William Davis, aet. 2, fever.

" " A child of Jeduthun Day, whooping cough.

" 13. Peter Schuyler Rusco, aet. 26, fever.

" 16. Mary, wife of James Carter, aet. 68, consumption.

" 17. Wife of John Cummings, aet. 35, consumption.

" 20. Grand-child of Paul Farber.

" 25. John, son of Stephen Pierson, aet. 14, sudden.

Oct. 1. Child of widow Zipporah Johnson.

" 4. Grand-child of William Hulbert.

" 27. Mary Pierson, daughter of Abraham Munson, fever.

" " Elizabeth, daughter of Hezekiah Stibbens, aet. 3, fits.

Nov. 7. A child of Thomas Johnson.

" 11. A child of Daniel Gardner.

" 18. Kezia, wife of Michael Miller, aet. 36, consumption.

" 20. Anne Mackentire, aet. 17.

" 29. A child of Samuel Allwood.

Dec. 26. A child of Sylvanus Arnold.

" 30. Kezia, wife of John Tuttle, aet. 63, fever.

1786.

Jan. 1. Child of Ziba Arnold.

" " Stephen Cook, aet. 35, sudden.

" 20. George, son of Jonas Phillips, aet. 18, by the fall of a chimney.

" " Jack, servant of Israel Canfield, aet. 50, by the fall of a chimney.

" 23. Gideon Riggs, aet. 73, fever.

" 27. Samuel Wood, aet. 34, fever.

Feb. 16. Jemima, daughter of Deacon Allen, aet. 5, worms.

" 19. Sarah, daughter of Michael Miller, fever.

" 20. Mary, widow of Robert Goble, Esq.,†* aet. 85, old age.

" 25. Mary, daughter of deacon John Ball,† decay.

Mar. 1. Richard Walker, aet. 73, old age.

" 2. Isaac, son of Capt. Job Brookfield,† aet. 1. dysentery.

" 5. A child of Jedidiah Burwell.

" 21. Elizabeth, widow of Benjamin Hinds. aet. 80, palsy.

" 30. Phœbe, daughter of Deacon Allen, aet. 18, consumption.

May 9. Aseneth, wife of Stephen Burnet, consumption.

" 22. Phœbe, daughter of Joshua Whitehead, aged 19, consumption.

" " Phœbe, wife of deacon John Ball,†* aet. 41, consumption.

" 24. Elisha Johnson,† aet. 51, pleurisy.

June 3. Phœbe, wife of Ephraim Youngs,* aet. 34, nervous fever.

" 16. Rachel, widow of Stephen Arnold, aet. 98, old age.

July 18. Sarah, wife of Samuel Oliver,* aet. 53, rupture.

" 20. Widow of Aaron Furman, aet. 30, consumption.

Aug. 27. James Searing, aet. 47, tetanus.

" 30. Phœbe, widow of William Losey, aet. 70, old age.

Sept. 21. Mary, widow of Francis Casterline, aet. 62, fever.

" 23. A child of John Pool the third.

" 28. Child of Wm. Hulbert.

Oct. 15. Esther, wife of Caleb Edy, aet. 30, jaundice.

" 27. Sarah, wife of Dan Trowbridge,† aet. 42, asthma.

Nov. 4. A child of Price Thompson.

" " Zenas, son of Jesse Muir, aet. 24, remitting fever.

" 18. Mary, wife of John Vancourt, aet. 26, consumption.

" 22. Elizabeth, wife of Peter Fairchild, aet. 33, fever.

Dec. 19. Sharod Fairchild, aet. 22, consumption.

(*To be continued.*)

(Continued from page 128.)

TRUSTEES' BOOK.

November 24th, 1790.

The Trustees met at Mr. Lewis', present: the President, Mr. Lindsley, Mr. Ford, Mr. Johnson & Jonathan Ogden attended in consequence of his being appointed instead of Joseph Lewis, who had resigned his seat in the board, & Mr. Ogden being duly sworn, and subscribed the oath as the law directs, took his seat in the board.

Voted that the subscriptions signed for the purpose of building a New Meeting House, dated 15th day of Sept., 1788, be delivered to Joseph Lewis, Moses Esty & Daniel Phœnix, Jr., appointed a Committee of Directors to superintend the said Building—and that the several sums therein subscribed be, & the same are hereby made payable to them.

Voted that Mr. Ogden be & he is hereby appointed Clerk—voted that the Clerk call on such persons as are indebted to the board on note or otherwise, for the interest due on sd. Notes or Obligations, & that he receive the Interest now due, or renew the Obligations, or prosecute for the whole debt as the Clerk shall judge most proper. Voted the President do purchase a stove for the use of the Reverend Mr. Collins, agreeably to the vote of the Parish.

Voted Mr. Johnson be appointed with Mr. Lindsley, in the stead of Mr. Lewis, to take care of the house where Jonathan Brown now lives. Voted that Mr. Lindsley, Mr. Ford & Mr. Johnson be a committee to view the lands proposed by Jonathan Dickerson to be exchanged for a part of the parsonage wood-lot, and report the terms of Mr. Dickerson, & their opinion thereon.

At a meeting of the Trustees on the 11th day of April, 1791, Mr. Condict, Lindsley, Johnson, Mills & Ogden being present. Agreed to continue on the present base of Mr. Duykink to Mr. King for the House the Rev. Mr. Collins now lives in.

17th October, 1791.

The Congregation being met, Mr. Jonathan Ogden & Mr. George Tucker was appointed to collect the present arrear of the last Church Tax, including the Rev. Mr. Collins' salary.

At a meeting of the Trustees on the 6th day of Feb., 1792, the President, Messrs. Lindsley, Mills, Johnson & Ogden being present. The Rev. Mr. Collins wished to know if he could have one & a half acres of the parsonage land adjoining Esquire Carmicals garden, for the purpose of a building spot and garden. Ordered that Mr. Mills pay William Cherry twenty-one shillings & nine pence, for repairs done to the Clock by Christian Bachman.

Resolved a decision on the Rev. Mr. Collins application be postponed. Thomas Miller's account for assessing the Ministers' Tax, presented by John Mills for settlement, postponed to the next meeting of the Trustees, Mr. Mills to give said Miller notice to attend. Resolved all the moneys now due to the Parish on Bonds, Notes or other ways be immediately collected by the Clerk.

At a meeting of the Parish on the 22nd Feb., 1792. Voted that in the room & stead of a Dwelling House an addition be made to the Rev. Mr. Collins' Salary equal to the interest a House proper for a Minister would cost; to be estimated by a committee consisting of Benj. Lindsley, Deacon Alling, Joseph Lindsley, John Britton, Silas Condict, Cornelius Locy & Jonas Phillips. The Trustees wished the Parish to determine on the propriety of selling the Parish land to the Rev. Mr. Collins for building on. And the proprietors of the Academy for a building spot on which to place an Academy.

Voted the Trustees shall act in the business above mentioned as they think proper.

At a meeting of the Trustees on the 22nd, Feb., 1792. The President, Messrs. Lindsley, Ford, Mills, Johnson, Arnold & Ogden being present. A Committee being appointed to inquire of Silas Howel the terms on which he would relinquish his reserve on a piece of land purchased of him by the Trustees, lying directly between the dwelling house of Caleb Russell and the dwelling house of Elisha Ayres, Esq. Report—Silas Howel will quit claim to said land on condition his Note of hand in the hands of the Trustees, & his subscription for the new Meeting House be canceled. The Trustees agreed to accept the same.

(To be continued.)

THE RECORD.

FIRST PRESBYTERIAN CHURCH, MORRISTOWN, N. J.

"THIS SHALL BE WRITTEN FOR THE GENERATION TO COME."—Psalms 102 : 18.

| VOL. II. | MAY, 1881. | NO. 5. |

(Printed with the approval of Session.)

THE RECORD

Will be printed and published monthly at Morristown, N. J. Terms, 50 cents per annum in advance; 75 cents after June.

Subscriptions will be received at the book-stores of Messrs. Runyon and Emmell, or through the mail. All communications should be addressed to the

EDITOR OF THE RECORD,

Lock box 44.   Morristown, N. J.

Vol. I. complete, 75 cents.

Entered at the Post Office at Morristown, N. J., as second class matter.

—:o:—

(Continued from page 123.)

HISTORICAL SERMON—No I.

By REV. DAVID IRVING, D.D.

As to the benevolence of the church in matters pertaining to the well being and furtherance of Christ's Kingdom, but little can be gathered. At the time of Mr. Johnes' installation David Brainard was preaching to the Stockbridge Indians, and in 1744 he came to the Forks of the Delaware, and in 1745 he visited the Indians at Crosswicks, near Freehold of this State. He was in that day the missionary of the church, and of the monies collected in 1745 in connection with his mission, I find in his life the sum of £1, 5 credited to Morristown. This was the first Foreign Mission collection ever made by this congregation.

The only other record is of sums contributed to Princeton College. This institution commenced its operations in Elizabethtown in 1746, under Jonathan Dickinson—removed to Newark in 1747, and was under the control of Aaron Burr, and was then removed to Princeton in 1757. In 1769, Dr. Rodgers was appointed by Synod to visit the churches in Morris county, but in January of the same year the session of this church determined, notwithstanding, the public expense now lying on them to exert themselves in behalf of the college, and collected the sum of £140—of which Dr. Johnes gave £9, and Jacob Ford £21. In 1787, the sum of £41 3s. 9d. was sent for the education of poor and pious youth in the college.

The first church edifice was no doubt reared some time before the coming of Mr. Johnes. We judge that this was so from the fact that prior to his induction there were no less than nine public confessions. It was a wooden building nearly square and stood a few rods east from this structure on land given by Benjamin Hathaway and Jonathan Lindsly for a parsonage and burial ground. On this land the house already mentioned and occupied for many years by Dr. Johnes was reared and the land enlarged by purchase by order of trustees in 1762. It was stated by some of those who seceded from Hanover that when the frame was raised, a small platform of boards, with a chair and small table served for a pulpit and the congregation were seated on the sills and on other timbers. The congregation slowly increased—at the First Communion six were added and in the next 21 years 67 were admitted to full communion on profession and more by certificate—from which we infer that the growth of the country was not rapid—among this number was Kezia Ludlow second wife of the pastor. At this time the taste and ability of the congregation were somewhat improved. The barn-like church did not suit them with its shingled sides and its plain exterior. After considerable discussion, the trustees granted permission on January 24, 1764, to the congregation to erect a steeple, and also agreed that Col. Ford should have the care, management and oversight of its erection which he accepted—a tower with a spire was raised to an elevation of about 125 feet, at the west end of the building and a bell hung

—the same bell which still summons the people to the house of God.. The traditional history of this bell is that it was presented to the church at Morristown by the King of Great Britain. It has on it the impress of the British Crown and the name of the makers, "Lister & Pack of London,—fecit." The vane of this steeple decorated the spire of the. old Academy of New Vernon.

In the year 1771, (Sept. 7) "the trustees, Henry Primrose, Benjamin Bayles, Benjamin Cox, Samuel Roberts, Joseph Stiles, Samuel Tuthill and Stephen Conkling, in consideration of £5 and also for and in consideration that the Justices and Freeholders of Morris county, and successors do constantly and continually keep full and in passable repair that part of the hereafter mentioned Lott of land commonly called the Gully (a portion of the present 'Green') containing one acre strict measure for the sole use and purpose of a Court House, Gaol," etc. This deed specifies "that if the Court House aforesaid shall be removed to any other place then this indenture and everything herein contained to be void and title to the aforesaid lot of land to revert to said Henry Primrose," etc. When the present Court House was built, the land reverted to the church. But the whole now embraced in the park was sold by the trustees in 1816 to certain parties for $1,600, and in virtue of this sale, the land occupied by the Court House became according to the deed a part of the "Green."

By the revivals of 1764 and 1774, the church was greatly enlarged, so that room could scarcely be had for the congregation in the old square building—on the latter year the trustees agreed that the Society might enlarge the meeting house at their discretion—whereupon the timbers running lengthwise were sawn asunder in the centre and the western half moved about 25 feet and the space built up to conform with the old parts—a spacious gallery was raised on the front and each end—the pulpit high and cup like in the centre of the north side, the main entrance door on the S. side in front of the pulpit. Two other entrances, one at each end were provided, and thus in this building the first pastor of Morristown began and ended his labors.

Such was the church and the minister, but ere we can complete the whole, we must glance at the congregation. The Sabbath was the great day of the week—the sermon the principal event and chief topic of converse. There were two services on the Sabbath, with an hour intermission. In winter there were no means of warming the old church, yet from all parts of the parish, embracing a much larger circumference than at present, they came—many on foot, especially the boys and the men—and the rest on horseback. Sometimes in carts with a sheaf of straw laid across for a seat. Before the Revolution there were very few wagons or carriages—all are warmly clad especially in cloth of domestic manufacture, prepared for the rigors of winter—the females having generally foot stoves. They enter the building and a division made nowhere else in all their social and religious customs at once takes place. The men are seated promiscuously on the W. side of the broad aisle, which serves for a partition, the wives and the little ones on the opposite side—the same distinction holding good in the gallery, and kept up until this house was reared. Access was to the galleries by two stairways, and this part of the building was reserved for the youth and the unmarried. A few overseers of grave character were distributed through the galleries to preserve order, and which seems to have been necessary in those days. As there were no pews claimed as private property the front seats were generally filled by the old. The services begin—the prayer is offered—the Psalm or Hymn read. Watts' was alone used in those days and continued until supplanted by the "Church Psalmody." When the pastor sits down, up rises the Psalm setter as was his title in those days, and standing at the foot of the pulpit commences the tune—when the first line is sung, the second line is read which was also sung, and thus reading and singing alternately till the end of the Psalm. It was nothing very unusual to have considerable variety both in the music and the sentiment of the line, some forgetting the words and some the tune adapted to the metre of the line.

This part of worship was in due time remedied through the labors and perseverance of the pastor, who as a lover of good sacred music, was instrumental in organizing singing schools in the parish. He encouraged the young to attend and was often present himself, advising with the teacher in the proper selection of music suitable for the sanctuary. By degrees a great reform was effected. Psalm books were procured. The rising generation could read, which was not true of all their fathers, and in time the lining was discontinued to the joy of the younger, but to the grief and displeasure of some of the older members of the congregation. We have heard that one good man was so incensed at this innovation that he would not come to Communion for years. Improvement in singing led to the formation of a choir, and during the latter part of the ministry of Dr. Johnes, the superiority of the Morristown choir was universally admitted.

For many years this was the only house of worship in Morristown—then the Baptist church was organized. Benedict in his history of the Baptists says, "As early as 1717, (this is a mistake) one David Goble with his family of the Baptist persuasion removed to this place from Charleston, S. C., and some ministers of the same order began to preach at their house; a small company after many years of patient effort were collected as a branch of old Piscataway, which in 1752 was formed into a distinct church." The first building was erected on the lands of the said Goble, about two miles from town and just beyond the brick school house on the road to Baskingridge. In 1770 their first building in the village was erected.

There are many matters of a private and public character with which the name of Dr. Johnes is connected, but I must pass by all and allude to one of historic value, relating to a religious act in the life of Washington. At the commencement of the year 1777, Washington reached Morristown and took winter quarters at the Arnold tavern—scarcely had he arrived before he encountered a new enemy—the small pox. It attacked soldier and citizen so that we find from the Bill of Mortality 68 deaths in this congregation alone from this terrible disease, and during the year from various causes 205 deaths in the parish, exclusive of soldiers. Never in the history of the town has death chained so many to his chariot

wheels as in that year of suffering and sadness. Every public building was seized for the soldiery—the church was a hospital, and often in the morning were the dead found lying in pews. Dr. Johnes, son of the pastor was intrusted with the care of the sick. This state of things compelled the congregation to meet in the open air for divine service. As the time of Communion drew near, which was then observed semi-annually, Washington accosted Mr. Johnes with the inquiry "if membership with the Presbyterian church was required as a term of admission to the ordinance." To which he replied "that all who loved the Lord Jesus were welcome." This pleased and satisfied the General, and on the coming Sabbath in the cold air, he was present with the congregation assembled in the orchard in the rear of the parsonage, and in the natural basin, still found there, he sat down at the table of the Lord, and in the remembrance of redeeming love obtained no doubt relief from the scenes that appalled and the cares that oppressed him. The common opinion is that the Lord's Supper was administered in the church. This is so stated in Spark's life of Washington and by other writers, but the true version is as already given. The church was occupied by invalid troops till the close of the year 1777, if not till some time in 1778, as the records of the trustees show. This was the only time after his entrance upon his public career that Washington is certainly known to have partaken of the Lord's Supper.

We have seen Mr. Johnes in different parts of his ministry, let us look at him at the grave. It is towards the last of October, 1775; the foliage is changed and falling; in the spring, he had stood there in the same spot and deposited the remains, in the open tomb, of a beloved grandchild. Now it is over all that is mortal of a Godly elder that he is deeply moved. The coffin is lowered—he lifts his voice in prayer—of the weeping and afflicted mourners, one is absent, a wayward youth, at that time captain of a company, and seemingly hardened in guilt. For that son earnest petitions are arising to a covenant God, that he would answer the cryings and intense desires of the departed for that erring boy, the prayers that were registered in the court of heaven for him—that son draws near, he has visited his home and found it desolate—a neighbor has told him of the death of his father, and of the funeral services—he hastens to the grave and unseen by the pastor he listens to the allusion to the prayers that are on high. These words reach his soul and by the Spirit they are instrumental in leading him to Jesus, when he consecrates himself to his service and for his glory.

Thus did God own his labors, in the performance of his official duties at the grave of a friend—let us follow him a few years later to the couch of the invalid—to one who has seen service in the army. He is approaching his end. The ambassador of Christ tells him of deliverance and beseeches him to be reconciled to God. The message thus brought finds a lodgment in his soul, it drives him to the cross, when a change great and marked is apparent to his Quaker wife. This with his death so affects her that she too is touched, and in due time she embraces Christ as her only hope, and publicly professes her faith in Christ in the old church. The faithfulness of the aged pastor impresses itself upon the mind of the orphaned boy, which never lost his power over him. That boy grew to man's estate and for 54 years was a member of this church —and his children's children are, members of it to-day—while numbers of his descendants in various parts of the country are connected with the Presbyterian church. In 1783, Mr. Johnes received the degree of D. D. from Yale College, no mean honor in those days. Soon after this he began to feel the infirmities of age, but kept on laboring actively till the year 1791, when Aaron C. Collins was installed as Collegiate pastor, which lasted only for a short time and was in no way fruitful of good.

About this time Dr. Johnes fractured his thigh bone by a fall, which confined him for months to his bed, and made him a cripple for the remainder of his life. After more than a year's confinement he was able to attend public worship. Aided by one or two of his elders he reached the desk where seated on a high cushioned chair he would occasionally address the people. In this condition he preached in 1793, his half century sermon to a crowded assembly, who came from all quarters to hear it. His text

was, "I have fought a good fight, I have finished my course," etc., 2 Tim. 4; 6—8. Of that review of his ministerial labors and their results no trace is found. In the delivery of that discourse he manifested unusual animation, and in the closing prayer he seemed to breathe out his whole soul in fervent petition for the peace, prosperity and salvation of his people. The service closed by singing the 71st Psalm—"God of my childhood and my youth," etc. In reading the 1st verse says an eye-witness, "his voice began to falter and became tremulous. He proceeded with much emotion, whilst the tears trickled over his venerable cheeks, and before he could utter the last line his voice seemed to die away amidst the sobs and tears of the whole assembly."

Seldom did he address his people after this. In the following winter, as he was riding to church on Sabbath morning his sleigh was upset a short distance from his house which broke his other thigh bone. He was carried to his home and never left it till he was removed by the hands of others to the graveyard, where he had so often stood, his body to repose in silence to the resurrection morn. He died Sept. 15, 1794, in the 78th year of his age, and 52d of his pastorate and 54th of his ministry, and his sepulchre is with us unto this day.

His tombstone bears the following inscription "as a Christian few ever discovered more piety—as a minister few labored longer, more zealously, or more successfully than did this minister of Jesus Christ."

He received into communion with the church over 500, baptized 2,827 persons and married 948 couples.

As a people have we not reason to-day to thank God for this church, and as a church have we not reason to bless its great head for such a pastor—so well suited to lead his people to Christ—to preach the great doctrines of redeeming love, and to exemplify in his life so much of what he recommended to others—reason to be thankful for his moulding influence—his strong Christian character by which he guided the young and the old in the ways of truth and righteousness;—and whilst we thus seek to revere the memory of the departed and tell to those who knew them not their virtues and achievements, we desire in the acts to honor not the mere instrument but God the agent, To him be all the glory.

(Continued from page 124.)

MEMBERS.

[The third column on this page is the work of the RECORD. Information which will lead to the correction of any mistake, or the filling of any blank, will be thankfully received.—ED.]

Names.	When Received.	When Dismissed or Died.
Elizabeth Alwood,	June 30, 1786.	Oct. 25, 1820, aet. 81.
Sarah Serren,	" " "	[Country."
Aaron Riggs,	" 29, 1787.	Dis. June 12. 1811 to " Western
Sarah Allen, widow,	Aug. 23, "	Nov. 28, 1789, aet. 92.
Daniel Burnet,	" 30, "	
Esther Burnet (Daniel),	" " "	
Elizabeth Eddy (Thomas)	Nov. 2, "	
Joshua Lambert,	" " "	Feb. 14, 1803, aet. 73.
Abigail Munson (Abr.),	" 25, "	Dis. Feb. 11, 1810 to N. Y. State.
Moses Wilkerson,	July 4, 1788.	" Moved."
Hannah Wilkerson, (Moses)	" " "	"
Ame Bears (Nathaniel)	" 6, "	
John Burnet,	Sept. 15, "	"
Samuel Day,	" 28, "	Aug. 12, 1796, aet. 44.
Ezekiel Ludlam,	Nov. 9, "	Dec. 1, 1800, aet. 44.
Joseph Woodman,	Feb. 27, 1789.	April 4, 1809, aet. 100.
Ann Woodman (Joseph),	" " "	
Jesse Cutler,	July 5, "	Sept. 4, 1827, aet. 70 y. 6 m. 14 d.
Mary Broadwell (William)	Aug. 9, "	June 19, 1790, aet. 25.
Charity Goble (Aaron)	Sept. 6, "	June 4, 1795, aet. 44.
Martha Johnson (Richard),	" " "	Nov. 7, 1825, aet. 75.
Nathaniel Bruen,	" " "	" Moved."
Kezia Pierson,	" " "	"
Armstrong Johnes,	Oct. 23, "	April 28, 1790, aet. 34.
Leah Johnes, (Armstrong,)	" " "	Jan. 30, 1809, aet. 62.
Phineas Chitester,	" " "	Excom. Sept. 24, 1808.
James Chitester,	" " "	Excom. July 15, 1807.
Phebe Wick (William.)	" " "	
John Alwood,	" " "	" Moved."
Cap. Joseph Halsey,	Nov. 1, "	May 18, 1811, aet. 56.
Rachael Redman,	Jan. 3, 1790.	" Moved."
Moses Johnson, Jr.,	" " "	"
Martha Ward,	" " "	
Phebe Plummer,	" " "	
Jerusha Halsey, (Cap. Joseph,)	" 12, "	
Elizabeth Cutler (Jesse)	" " "	March 4, 1849, aet. 90.
John Arnold,	" " "	Dec. 14, 1830, aet. 87.
Hannah Johnson,	" " "	
John Lindsley,	April 30, "	Excom.
Sarah Lindsly (John),	" " "	Jan. 11, 1821, aet. 60.
David Lindsly,	" " "	
Tahpenes Lindsly (David),	" " "	
William Meeker,	" " "	" Moved."
Samuel Tuthill, Jr.,	" " "	July 27, 1834, aet. 71.
James Stiles,	" " "	Dis. April 26, 1813 to Basking Ridge
Phebe Schenck (Abr.),	" " "	Dec. 21, 1835, aet. 73.
Eunice Johnson,	" " "	" Moved."
Ruth Johnson,	" " "	"

(To be continued.)

(*Continued from page* 126.)

BAPTISMS.

1771.

Sep. 22. Mary Chever, bap. adult, on a sick and expectedly dying bed, died Oct. 2, 1771.

" 29. Phineas Fairchild & wf., ch. Jestus, born July 20, 1771.

Oct. 3. Thomas Cheever, bap. adult, and expectedly on dying bed.

" 6. Thomas Lashley & wf., ch. Sarah, born Oct. 15, 1770.

" " Seth Crowell & wf., ch. Silas, born Sept. 4, 1771.

" 13. David Ogden on wf's accompt, ch. Huldah Tapping, born Aug. 22, 1771.

" 29. John Mills & wf., ch. bap. at ye own house, Ruth, born Oct. 3, 1771.

Nov. 17. Joseph Condict & wf., ch. Cyrus, born Oct. 21, 1771.

" 24 Eleazar Hathaway & wf., ch. Benoni, born Sept. 29, 1771.

Dec. 22. Joseph Lindsley & wf., ch. Anna, born Nov. 23, 1771.

" 29. Sam'l Hains on wf's accompt, twins, Elizabeth & Ruth, born Nov. 9, 1771.

" " Abraham Talmage & wf., ch. Nathan, born Nov. 14, 1771.

1772.

Jan. 6. Nathan Reeve, 2 children, Elizabeth, born Mar. 27, 1770, & Jonathan, born June 29, 1771.

Feb. 2. Philip Lindsley & wf., ch. Israel, born Dec. 18, 1771.

" 9. Benj. Woodruff & wf., ch. Daniel, born Aug. 26, 1770.

" 16. Jonathan Hathaway & wf., ch. Abigail, born Jan. 15, 1772.

" 21. John Bridge & wf., children Jemima, born Nov. 15, 1767; Ketchel, born Sept. 21, 1769.

" 23. David Youngs & wf., ch. William, born Dec. 13, 1771.

" " John Allen & wf., ch. Phebe, born Dec. 14, 1771.

Mar. 1. Silas Howell & wf., ch. Charles, born Jan. 21, 1772.

" 8. Alexander Cermichael & wf., ch. Ann, born Jan. 27, 1772.

" " Lydia, wife of John King, ch. William Turner, born Jan. 14, 1772.

Mar. 8. Benj. Pierson & wf., negro, ch. Cezar, born Oct., 1771.

" 15. Stephen Arnold & wf., ch. Elizabeth, born Feb. 14, 1772.

Apr. 1. Sam'l Pierson & wf., ch. Timothy, born Feb. 24, 1772.

April. 1378. Majority of males—3.

Apr. 12. Jacob Ford, Jr. & wf., ch. Jacob, born Mar. 15, 1772.

Apr. 26. Thomas Millar & wf., ch. Bethiah, born Jan. 23, 1772.

" " Eleazar Lindsley & wf., ch. Jemima, born Jan. 28, 1772.

" " Silas Stiles & wf., ch. William, born Feb. 18, 1772.

" " Nathaniel Condict & wf., ch. Phebe, born Feb. 28, 1772.

" " Daniel Cermichael & wf., ch. Rebeccah, born Jan. 4, 1772.

May 3. James Smith & wf., ch. Hannah, born Feb. 8. 1772.

" " Jabez Condict & wf., ch. Ira, born Mar. 6, 1772.

" 10. Job Lorain & wf., ch. Martha, born Mar. 1, 1772.

" " Lindsley Burnet & wf., ch. Phineas, born Mar. 18, 1772.

" 17. Peter Prudden & wf., ch. Phebe, born Mar. 20, 1772.

" " David Wheeler & wf., ch. Sarah, born Mar. 1, 1772.

" 31. Abraham Canfield & wf., ch. Anne, born Jan. 20, 1772.

June 7. Ben. Hathaway, Lieut. & wf., ch. Jacob, born Mar. 28, 1772.

" 14. James Gillespie & wf., ch. William, born Feb. 26, 1772.

" 28. John Loce on wf's accompt. 2 children, Abner, born June 28, 1770. Silas, born Mar. 24, 1772.

July 3. Sam'l Robart's servant, ch. Pompe.

" 5. Gilbard Allen & wf., ch. Sarah, born —1772.

" " Jonathan Ford on wf's accompt. ch. Julia, born May 15, 1772.

" 12. Wid. of David Case, ch. Elizabeth, better than a year old.

" " Edward Byram's wf., in his absence, ch. Ebenezar Olden, born June 13, 1772.

Aug. 2. Doc. Bern Budd & wf., ch. William, born —— 1772.

(*To be continued.*)

(Continued from page 127.)

BILL OF MORTALITY.

1787.

Jan. 20. A child of Samuel Logan.
" " Peter Hill,* aet. 66, asthma.
Feb. 5. Sarah, widow of Jonathan Crane,* aet. 63, consumption.
" 28. Teresa, daughter of Capt. James Rodgers, surfeit.
Mar. 16. Widow Biglow, aet. 65, decay.
" 18 Widow of Solomon Bates, aet. 97, old age.
" 28. A child of Timothy Humpherville, still-born.
Apr. 14. A child of Mr. Moles.
" 22. Philip Castenor, aet. 66, hurt and fever.
May 12. Abraham Allen, son of Jedidiah Osborn, aet. 9, drowned.
" 28. Widow of James Searing, aet. 43, consumption.
June 2. A child of Benjamin Marsh, still-born.
" 9. A child of Vincent Guering.
" 26. John Bloomfield, aet. 10, found dead.
July 7. Mary, wife of Henry Wick,† aet. 69, palsey.
Aug. 14. A child of John Freeman.
" 19. Samuel, son of Chatfield Tuttle.
" 20. A child of Phinehas Ayres.
" 26. A child of John Arnold.
Oct. 10. A child of Moses Wilkison.
Nov. 4. Joseph Benway, aet. 57, erysipelas.
" 7. Capt. Daniel Gard,† aet. 50. apoplexy.
" 14. Seth, son of Moses Johnson, aet. 20, consumption.
" 26. Wife of Benjamin Hulbert.
Dec. Mary, widow of deacon Daniel Walling,† aet. 77, old age.
" 11. A child of Caleb Howard.

1788.

Jan. 3. Elizabeth, daughter of Joseph Beers, aet. 1, fever.
" 12. Phœbe, daughter of deacon John Ball,† fits.
" 28. Wife of James Carven, aet. 40, found dead.
" 29. Widow Hyler, aet. 70, decay.
" 31. Mary, widow of John Armstrong, 84, old-age.
Feb. 8. Ebenezer, son of Jedidiah Gregory aet. 25, consumption.

Feb. 11. Ebenezer Cooper, aet. 70, old-age.
" 20. Benjamin Hallsey, Esq.,* aet. 66, Insanity.
" 25. Elizabeth, wife of John Jacob Fæsch, Esq., aet. 36, phrenzy.
" 29. Hiram, son of Jacob Casterline, aet. 2, fever.
Mar. 12. Child of Timothy Goble,†
" 22. Hannah, wife of John Rodgers,* aet. 52, remitting-fever.
" 25. Alexander Johnson, aet. 66, consumption.
" 28. Tabitha, widow of Daniel Frost,* aet. 75, old-age.
" A child of David Brown,† fits.
" 30. Esther, wife of David Fithian, aet. 21, child-bed.
Apr. 2. Isaac Searing, aet. 82, old-age.
" 26. Cornelia, daughter of Daniel Phœnix, jun., aet. 2, scald.
May 9. Hannah, daughter of Jacob Ball, aet. 2, sudden.
" Sarah, wife of John Crowell, aet. 37, inflammatory-fever.
" 21. Daniel, son of Doct. Ebenezer Blachly,† aet. 19, bleeding at the lungs.
" 30. Rhoda, wife of Daniel Sturges, aet. 22, consumption.
June 16. Lewis, son of Lindsley Burnet, aet. 5, fits.
" 15. Daughter of Jonas Goble,† aet. 10.
" 30. Moses Willis, aet. 40, found dead.
Aug. 6. Joseph, son of Joseph Lewis, relax.
" 26. Mary, widow of Timothy Pierson, aet. 76, fever.
" 31. Stephen Conkling, jun.,* aet. 38, fever.
Sep. 5. A child of Samuel Mills, jun., still-born.
" 28. Phœbe, wife of Zophar Freeman,* aet. 54, fever.
Nov. 5. Daniel Freeman, aet. 71, arthrax.
Dec. 9. Samuel, son of Ephraim Lyon, aet. 15, fever.
" 27. Rebeckah, wife of Eliphalet Clark,* aet. 63, fever.

1789.

Jan. 17. Benjamin Freeman, aet. 77, peripneumony.
" 25. Esther, wife of Benjamin Freeman, aet. 70, fever.

(To be continued.)

(Continued from page 128.)

TRUSTEES' BOOK.

At a meeting of the congregation of the First Presbyterian Church, at Morris Town, the 15th day of March, A.D., 1792.

Voted that Jonathan Dickerson serve as Moderator; that Joseph Lewis serve as Clerk.

A letter was presented by Silas Condit, Esq., signed by Jacob Arnold, dated Feb. 25, 1792. On motion whether the said letter shall be read, it passed in the affirmative, and is in the words following: "Gent'n., I know not who to direct to, but if I understand the Subscription, the Subscriber is at liberty at the end of every year to declare of from Mr. Collins, if so the second year ends next March; I declare of from paying any further Sallery to Mr. Collins as a preacher than two years, and further: if his subsistance as a preacher depends on the trustees to the congregation, I declare off and mean to apply to the Presbytery to silence or discharge said Collins from Morris Congregation as a preacher. This notification I give in behalf of myself and the Congregation. I remain Gent'n. Your humble Serv't, Jacob Arnold.

Silas Condit, Esq., president of Morris Congregation & to the Deacons & Elders of said church."

On motion whether Mr. Arnold was authorized by the Congregation to give the aforesaid notice, and sign said letter in their behalf, it passed in the negative. On motion whether the Congregation approves of the contents of said letter, it passed in the negative. On motion, it is resolved, that this Congregation highly disapprove of the conduct of the said Jacob Arnold, as it directly tends to disunite and disturb the peace of this congregation and that his assuming to act in behalf of this Congregation in a matter of so great importance and that so essentially affects their interests and happiness, without their knowledge or consent & contrary to their desire, is altogether unjustifiable, and that he the said Jacob Arnold be discharged from the office of Trustee to the congregation.

At a meeting of the Trustees at the House of Mr. Mills on the 12th day of May, 1792. Present: the President, Mr. Mills, Mr. Lindsley, Mr. Johnson & Mr. Ogden attended t the close of the business.

Voted Mr. Mills & Mr. Ogden be appointed to collect Mr. Collins' rate for the present tax.

Voted that Mr. Johnson's acc't in the books of the Trustees be discharged by way of the land sold to the proprietors of the Academy.

At a meeting of the Trustees at the house of Caleb Russel, Esq., 5th day of September, 1792. The President, Mr. Lindsley, Mr. Ford, Mr. Mills, Mr. Johnson and Mr. Ogden being met, a deed being made out for one hundred feet of land in front and one hundred and thirty feet deep on the hill opposite the Conners land agreeable to a vote of the parish requesting the trustees to act discretionary on this affair, the 22d Feb. 1792—the sd. deed was then signed conveying twenty-nine hundredths of an acre of land to the proprietors of the intended Academy for the sum of thirty pounds Jersey money. Caleb Russell, Esq., gave his obligation for sd. sum. A committee consisting of Mr. Condict, Mr. Johnson and Mr. Ogden, was appointed to examine the acct. of the managers of the new Meeting House.

At a meeting of the Parish on 24th Jan.1793, Dea. Gilbert Alling chosen Moderator, and Isaac Canfield chosen Clerk, Silas Condict, Esq., one of the committee appointed to examine the acct. of the managers of the new meeting house—reported a settlement of sd. accounts.

Resolved, That in order to discharge the debts contracted, on acct. of Building sd. Church and to proceed in further furnishing the same that the sum of twelve hundred pounds be raised this year by subscription.

Resolved, sd. subscription be payable the 1st of April next. Resolved, that Israel Canfield draw the subscription, and that Deacon Alling and George Tucker call on the people of the parish to subscribe on or before the first of March next.

The parish proceeded & chose Joseph Marsh in place of John Mills who declines as manager. Doctor William Canfield, manager in place of Joseph Lewis who declines. Benja. Linds, Esquire, declines serving as manager, whereupon Israel Canfield was chosen manager in his stead. The congregation having been advertised agreeable to law in order to chose a Trustee, Benjamin Pierson was duly elected to that office.

(To be continued.)

THE RECORD.

FIRST PRESBYTERIAN CHURCH, MORRISTOWN, N. J.

"This shall be Written for the Generation to Come."—Psalms 102 : 18.

VOL. II.　　　　　JUNE, 1881.　　　　　NO. 6.

(Printed with the approval of Session.)

THE RECORD

Will be printed and published monthly at Morristown, N. J. Terms, 50 cents per annum in advance; 75 cents after June.

Subscriptions will be received at the book-stores of Messrs. Runyon and Emmell, or through the mail. All communications should be addressed to the

EDITOR OF THE RECORD,
Lock box 44.　　　　Morristown, N. J.

Vol. I. complete, 75 cents.

Entered at the Post Office at Morristown, N. J., as second class matter.

——:o:——

(Continued from page 132.)

HISTORICAL SERMON—No. 2.

By REV. DAVID IRVING, D.D.

Preached Thanksgiving Day, 1862.

In our preceding discourse we traced the history of this church till the death of Dr. Johnes, its first pastor in the year 1794, but prior to this there were two important movements which exerted a great influence upon the after prosperity of this Zion ; the one, the visit of Rev. James Richards, resulting in his settlement ; the other, the building of the edifice in which we now worship. We have glanced at the exterior and interior of the old building when enlarged and improved in 1774 to meet the growing necessities of the congregation, but as the population of the township increased that structure became too small, and in an attempt to repair it in 1788, those who had been agitating the subject of a new building objected to the plan proposed. Finding the opposition influential, the trustees agreed to call a parish meeting which convened in the church May 13, 1788; there the congregation voted that repairs be omitted and that Justice Lindsly, Major Lindsly and Jos. Lewis be a committee to make an estimate of the expense of a church to be built of timber, and that Deacon Prudden and Justice Carmichael be a committee to make an estimate of the expense of a brick church 65 feet long and 45 feet broad, and that both estimates be laid before the congregation on June 5th On that day the congregation assembled, and after consultation and debate the votes were taken, when it was decided by a "considerable majority" that the house should be built of timber. A committee was appointed "to carry a subscription through the parish, to get a sufficient sum for erecting a new meeting house 65 feet long, 50 feet wide and 25 feet high to, be enclosed with shingles." This committee were successful and reported to the Board of Trustees on the following year, that "there was a sufficient sum subscribed for enclosing a house of timber according to the estimate heretofore made." This was laid before the parish meeting Dec. 11, 1789, when Elder Philip Condict and others opposed the whole movement, alledging that the old house would do for a number of years with some repairs, but to this the majority would not listen, and it was again voted that a new house should be built after one year. Deacon Prudden and those who sympathized with him were still anxious for a brick structure, but were a second time defeated by a large majority.

This subject occupied much of the thoughts of the people in their social interviews, both as to the size, shape and location of the building. Before the expiration of the year the parish are assembled to talk over the new enterprise, when the following resolutions are passed :

"That the Committee of Directors proceed to provide materials for the new meeting house as soon as convenient.

"That the house be built 70 feet long and 50 feet broad, with the privilege of adding to or taking from any number of feet not exceeding five.

"That a committee of council be appointed to give further instructions to the Committee of Directors from time to time as they may think proper, &c.

—"That the said committees have leave to apply to the Legislature for the privilege of a lottery to raise a sum of money equal to the expense of building the new meeting house."

If this application was ever made it was refused, as we hear no more about it.*

The meeting was held Oct. 8. 1790, and in a memorandum book of one of the committee for the purchasing of materials, we have the following entry: "Timber to be all white oak, cut in old moon of Dec., Jan'y or Feb'y, and delivered on the green by the —— day of —— next, Nov. 1790." Then follows the prices of the posts, girts, plates, beams, rafters, &c.

After various plans had been canvassed the committee decided upon the one adopted—to have the building 75 feet long, 55 wide, the steeple 20 feet square, 9 of which were taken from the main building, leaving ing an audience room of 66 feet in length. The work was commenced in the spring of 1791. The head carpenter was Major Joseph Lindsly, assisted by Gilbert Allen, both Elders in the church and men of great moral worth and highly beloved by the congregation. The frame was raised on Sept. 20, 1791, and on several successive days. Some 200 men assisted in the work, from which we may form some conception of the amount of timber embraced in this noble edifice, which says one, "for strength, solidity and symmetry of proportion was not excelled by any wooden building of that day in New Jersey."

The first site selected for the building was in the grave yard not far from the old church; this fact is gathered from an ac-

count book of that date which has been very much mutilated but in which is the following entry:
"William Cherry,   Cr.
By one days work done in the grave yard towards the foundation where the house was first ordered to be built, 5, 0"

It was changed chiefly through the agency of Dr. Jabez Canfield, but why, I can find no satisfactory reason? The location has never given satisfaction and several attempts have been made to move the church but without success, and it will no doubt stand where it is until superceded by a new house of worship.

It is very difficult to arrive at any definite conclusion respecting the cost of the building from the different (and seemingly conflicting) statements on the parish records. In Jan'y, 1792, it is "resolved, that in order to discharge the debts contracted on account of building said church and to proceed further finishing the same that the sum of £1,200 or $3,000 be raised this year by subscription." More than two years after this, a committee of 24 is appointed to go on and finish the building and all that is paid beyond the sums subscribed and received shall be assessed on the pews when sold. On January 1, 1796, another committee is chosen to make an equitable assessment on the parishioners for the purpose of raising £4,000. This subscription list we have seen containing 394 names, and the total sum assessed amounting to £4,496, 8, ranging from £5 to £100; but several demurred to the amount affixed to their names which had to be lowered and several refused, and in twenty cases I find that the assessment on the property was too low and they were taxed higher. The sums thus corrected fell £527 below the £4,000 needed, so that this method failed and the one finally adopted was, after reserving certain seats, appraising the remainder so as to yield $10,000; at that time the estimated expense of the building on which 5 per cent. was to be paid to meet the minister's salary. On Nov. 26, 1795, the congregation worshipped in this house for the first time, though it was not until several months afterwards that the whole was completed. The pulpit was not finished and furnished until some time in 1796, when this fell as in later times to the ladies who collected from their own sex the sum of $125 "for the purpose," as their subscription paper ran—"of dressing the pulpit, getting curtains for the large windows of the meeting house, a new funeral pall, and a gown for the minister." In the following year the walls were whitewashed and "the inside of the church ordered to be a light blue." Gradually the whole was finished at a cost considerably over $10,000. We have heard the sum stated at $12,000.

This for the times was a great undertaking. Commenced soon after the close of the protracted war with Great Britain when taxes were heavy and must be paid ; when the country was burdened with debt ; paper money the only currency ; nearly every farm mortgaged and when creditors ran from their debtors, afraid of the Continental money, when a silver dollar was scarcely seen, and gold was if anything rarer—yet steadily was the work prosecuted in the midst of the most trying discouragements while the willingness of the people to be taxed nearly $10,000 for the purpose of defraying the expenditure, shows a noble spirit ; and the readiness with which so many came forward—over 360 persons in all to contribute to the undertaking, reveals the fact that more were willing to share and bear the burdens of the sanctuary than at present. The communicants at that time numbered but little more than half of the subscribers as scarcely 40 pews were reserved for sacramental days, and only the name of one person now living is on that long list, telling us of death's doings in 64 years, and showing us how one generation goeth and another cometh.

The house commenced in 1791 ; consecrated in 1795, completed in 1797 ; still stands as firmly and compactly as when first erected. Twice has it been struck with lightning, oft has its lofty spire creaked in the wintry blast, against it have the storms of Heaven beat, but all have been in vain to injure and destroy. It still points in all its massive grandeur to Heaven, and though the work of a former it may well be the pride of the present generation, and should be cherished by us as a spot hallowed by the sweetest memories and as the grand achievement of a noble ancestry.

Twice has it been renovated to corres-

pond with the demands of the age ; the first time in 1841, when the floor was raised and the ceiling lowered, the high backed and square pews reduced in size, and other corresponding improvements at a cost of some $3,000 ; the second time in 1859, when a thorough alteration was made in both the interior and exterior at an expense of some $6,000. The church can boast of three pulpits ; the first small in size and high in position, remained till 1819. When the church was thoroughly painted and cleaned at a cost of $817, then the old pulpit was removed and given to the church at Newfoundland, and another more modern in style was built which cost nearly $300, and which was enlarged by two new panels in 1841. The present pulpit was erected last year at much less expense than the former and is in every way to be preferred.

The first pastor of the new church was Rev. James Richards ; the old edifice which stood 60 years and was taken down in 1797, could boast of but one pastor—this of many ; both were built in troublous times, and in the midst of much that was oppressing ; both were erected by men of a former generation ; both have been blessed to the good of hundreds of souls, who are now in glory and have been of incalculable benefit to this region of country. Our fathers may have wept when they saw their old shepherd removed and the house in which he had so long led them to the green pastures and the still waters of the gospel ; some may have wept when they thought of the glory of the former in 1764 and 1774, the years of the right hand of the Most High, but in this we can truly say that "the glory of this latter house is greater than the former."

The building of the new church was the development of a new life and the introduction of a new order of things. The Revolutionary war gave new views to the country, higher conceptions of its future, which brought the different States into one grand union, and under one and the same constitution. This had a great influence upon the different Christian organizations of the land, making all in time independent of the civil power and sweeping away every vestige of colonial law that interfered with the religious rights of the people. Under the influence of this, hopeful progress and expansion came to our ecclesiastical body, which in 1786 determined to form a constitution adapted to the state of the Presbyterian church in America, to form four Synods and a General Assembly composed of delegates from the several Presbyteries, so that whilst delegates from different States were in session at Philadelphia framing a constitution, ours was formed and being discussed in the lower judicatories, and was adopted and went into operation near the same time as that of the United States.[*] With something of this expansive feeling was our own church building contemplated; at first in 1787 the old house 30x50 was good enough, then a new structure 65x45 was needed in 1788 which was enlarged to 65x50 in 1789, which grew to 70x50 in 1790, and when the frame was raised in 1791 assumed its present proportions 75x55.

As Dr. Johnes had come from Long Island to mould and consolidate this church in its infancy; so from the same place came Richards in its transition and formative state with all the energies and vigor of youth around it to direct its interest, control the energies of its members, guide their impulses and lead their heaven born tendencies to God and truth, Like Johnes he was also of Welsh descent, and was born at New Canaan, Ct., Oct. 29, 1767. In his early years he suffered much from bodily weakness, but gave at that same time great evidence of fine intellectual powers. Reared in a Christian home, strong religious impressions were made in the buddings of youth upon his heart, which were never afterwards effaced. In his 19th year he became thoroughly awakened to his condition as a sinner and soon afterwards publicly consecrated himself to God, and united with the Congregational church in Stanford. The reigning desire of his heart was now to live for God in the work of the ministry and who opened up a way for his young servant to enter upon a preparatory course of study, which though interrupted by serious sickness was assiduously prosecuted until his licensure in 1793 when he com-

menced the active duties of the ministry; first laboring at Ballston, N. Y., and then supplying two small congregations on Long Island.

Soon after the dismissal of Mr. Collins, a parish meeting was called for the especial purpose of consultation, prayer and inquiry as to the best mode of supplying the pulpit, which resulted in the appointment of a discreet and influential member of the church to take such measures as his judgment would approve to obtain a suitable pastor for the church. In the discharge of their trust he was led to consult several ministers and was finally led to Dr. Buel, the early and constant friend of Dr. Johnes and his college companion, who directed him to young Richards then laboring in the adjoining parish, who listened on the Sabbath to his pulpit ministrations and with which the commissioner was so well satisfied that he invited him to visit Morristown, which he did, bringing with him the highest testimonials from Dr. Buel who was well known to the congregation, and who wrote: "the man who on a thorough acquaintance with James Richards does not love him, cannot himself be deserving the love of any man." He not only preached to the people with great satisfaction but also to the aged pastor in his own dwelling that he might judge of his fitness, and to both with such acceptance, that on the 21st of July, 1794, a call was made and put in to his hands the same day, in which he was to receive $440 salary in quarterly payments, the use of the parsonage and fire wood. This was in due time accepted by him, and on the 1st of May, 1795,[*] he was ordained and installed pastor of the church by the Presbytery of New York. Dr. McWhorter, of Newark, preached the ordination sermon from Acts 20:24. Dr. Rogers, of New York, presided; Mr. Austin, of Elizabeth gave the charge to the people.

(To be continued.)

---

[*]And here we may remark on the authority of Chief Justice Tilghman that in determining the structure of our national government the framers of the United States constitution borrowed very much of the form of our republic from that form of church government found in the constitution of the Presbyterian church of Scotland.

[*]The two following facts are of interest in connection with this date: George O'Hara advertised that his stage would commence running from Morristown to Powles Hook (Jersey City), on first Monday of April, 1795, twice a week for 9 shillings, and one penny a pound for all baggage above 7 lbs., way passengers 4 d a mile. Morristown post office was the only one in the county in 1795. In it letters were advertised for persons at Bedminister, Mendham, Baskingridge, Bottle Hill (Madison), New Market, Flanders, Hanover, Bound Brook, Franklin, Mt. Hope, Pompton, Ramapaugh.

(*Continued from page* 138.)

MEMBERS.

[The third column on this page is the work of the RECORD. Information which will lead to the correction of any mistake, or the filling of any blank, will be thankfully received.—ED.]

Names.	When Received.	When Dismissed or Died.
Jonathan Johnson, . .	July 2, 1790.	" Moved."
Phebe Johnson, (Jonathan,) .	" " "	"
Sarah Meeker, (William,) . .	" " "	"
Ephraim Muir, . .	" " "	Died in 1821.
Abraham T. Schenck, . .	Nov. 5, "	Feb. 12, 1830, aet. 63 y. 6 m. and 19 d.
Bathsheba Carmichael (Dan.,)	" " "	Aug. 30, 1803, aet. 62.
Rhoda Pierson, (wid. of Isaac,) .	" " "	
Ame Byram, (16 yrs. old,) .	" " "	Dis. Nov. 26 to 3rd Ch., Newark.
Elizabeth Burnet, (Lindsley,) .	June 26, 1791.	
Phebe Burnet, (Matthias), .	" " "	Dec. 10, 1828, aet. 78.
Burnet, (Ralph), .	July 4, "	
Jacob Pierson, . . .	Nov. 6, "	Excom. Dec. 16, 1816,
Jacob Ball, . . .	" " "	Nov. 26, 1808, aet. 60.
Mary Ball, (Jacob), . .	" " "	May 14, 1833, aet. 81.
Phebe Lindsley, (Isaac), . .	" " "	

[This completes the list of those who united with the church upon profession of their faith, during the pastorate of Rev. Dr. Johnes, 424 in all. Add to these 179, who " were in full communion when the ch. was first collected and founded, together with the number of those that came since from other churches," (RECORD, p. 12), and we have the total number of 603 communicants under Dr. Johnes' pastorate of half a century. Besides these, is a list of 589 " half-way " members, found on pages 28, 36, 44, 52, and 60, of THE RECORD.—ED.]

REV. AARON C. COLLINS, COLLEAGUE OF REV. DR. JOHNES.

Bethuel Hayward, . .	Jan. 3, 1791.	
Temperance Hayward, (Bethuel),	" " "	
William Hamilton, . .	May 23, "	
Hamilton, (William) .	" " "	
Abraham Munson, . . .	July 2, "	
Abraham Conkling, . .	Sept. 11, "	
Jemima Conkling, (Abraham), .	" " "	
Gabriel Ford, . . .	Oct. 6, "	
Frances Gold Ford, (Gabriel), .	" " "	
Charlotte Ford Condict, (Silas, Jr.), Dec.	"	Died March 6, 1850, born Dec. 8, 1776.
Jeptha Wade, . . .	Jan. 2, 1792.	
Wade, (Jeptha), .	" " "	
Matthias Crane, from 1st ch., N. Y.,	" " "	Dis. Jan. 7, 1825, to Union Town, Pa.
Jane Crane, (Matthias), .	" " "	
Henry Vail, . . .	June 1, "	Nov. 12, 1832, aet. 79.
Phebe Vail, (Henry), . .	" " "	March 28, 1814, aet. 56.
Damaris Hall, (Jacob), . .	" " "	
Pruda Marsh, (Joseph), .	" 3, "	Died Feb., 1821.
Enoch Miller, . . .	" " "	
Sally Miller, . . .	" " "	
Sarah Clark, (Enoch), : .	" " "	
Joseph Marsh, . .	Sept. 2, "	Excom. Oct. 3, 1797.
Abigail Mills, (Timothy), .	" " "	
Anna Losey, (Cornelius), .	" " "	

(*To be continued.*)

(Continued from page 134.)

BAPTISMS.

1772.

Aug.23. Elder John Lindsley & wf., ch. Phebe, born July 7, 1772.

"　" Nathaniel Morris on wf's account, ch. Elizabeth, born July 28, 1772.

"　" Usual Coe & wf., ch. Matthias, born July 30, 1771.

" 30. Henry Gardiner & wf., ch. Esther, born July 20, 1772.

"　" Matthias Burnet, Jr., & wf., ch.——

Sept. 4. Sarah, wf. of William Charlot, adult.

"　" Wm. Charlot & wf., ch. Stephen, born Feb. 16, 1772.

" 6. James Miller on wf's acct., ch. Elizabeth, born Aug. 20, 1772.

Oct. 4. Joshua Guering & wf., ch. Aram, born July 2, 1772.

" 11. John Redman & wf., ch. Rachael, born Sept. 10, 1772.

" 15. Abijah Cheever, adult.

"　" Abijah Cheever & wf., ch. Abijah, born Aug. 10, 1772.

" 25. Geo. Phillips & wf., ch. Ruth, born Sept. 28, 1772.

"　" Isaac Pierson & wf., ch. Phebe, born Sept. 3, 1772.

"　" Ezekial Day & wf., ch. Abigail, born Sept. 1, 1772.

"　" John Prudden's wf., husband absent, ch. Anne, born Sept. 15, '72.

Nov.15. Jonas Phillips & wf., ch. Mary, born Sept. 18, 1772.

"　" Jedidiah Gregory & wf., ch. Mabel, born Oct. 6, 1772.

"　" Peter Norris & wf., ch. David, born Sept. 18, 1772.

"　" Jno. Jacks on wf's acct., children, Wm., born May 8, 1770, Lidia, born Oct. 23, 1772.

" 20. Abraham Ludlam bap. and with his wf. had ye family bap. John, born Mch. 15, 1762, Sarah, born Aug. 21, 1763, Abigail, born Dec. 4, 1766.

Dec. 6. Moses Johnson & wf., ch. Catharine, born Sept. 12, 1772.

"　" Wm. Charlot & wf., ch. Aaron, born Oct. 20, 1772.

Dec. 6. Benoni Hathaway & wf., ch. Silas, born Oct. 26, 1772.

" 13. Ichabod Carmichael & wf., ch. Phebe, born Oct. 24, 1772.

"　" Hezekiah Stebbins on wf's acct., ch. Hannah, born Oct. 11, 1772.

1773.

Jan. 10. David Phillips on wf's acct., ch. Jonathan, born Oct. 24, 1772.

" 17. Doc. Goold, ch., at wf's, request & grandmother presenting, was bap. name, Wm. Budd.

" 24. Zenas Condict & wf., ch. Sarah, born Nov. 2, 1772.

"　" Caleb Munson & wf., ch. Silas, born Dec. 23, 1772.

"　" Silas Ayers & wf., child Abigail, born Nov. 28, 1772.

"　" Zebedee Brown on wf's account, ch. John Thompson, born Nov. 24, 1772.

" 31. Moses Prudden & wf., ch. Moses, born Dec. 17, 1772.

Feb. 14. Moses Lindsley & wf., ch. Sarah, born Jan. 10, 1773.

"　" Richard Johnson & wf., ch. Hannah, born Jan. 8, 1773.

" 28. David Day on wf's acct., ch. Silas, born Oct. 9, 1770.

"　" Ichabod Cooper on wf's acct., ch. Samuel, born Jan. 15, 1773.

Mch.21. James Brookfield & wf., ch. John, born Feb. 13, 1773.

"　" James McBride on wf's account, ch. Mountrose Irwin, born Jan. 9, 1773.

"　" Jonathan Tichenor & wf., ch. David, born Feb. 6, 1773.

"　" Joseph Pierson, Jun. & wf., ch. Ezekiel, born Jan. 17, 1773.

Apr. 1. Peter Condict & wf., ch. Lewis, born Mch. 3, 1773.

"　" Joseph Bears & wf., children Silas, born Apr. 23, 1771, Hannah, born Feb. 8, 1773.

" 11. Dr. Timothy Johnes & wf., ch. Elizabeth, born Jan. 13, 1773.

"　" Thomas Tuttle & wf., ch. Ebenezar, born Feb. 22, 1773.

"　" Sam'l Allwood & wf., ch. Joseph, born Feb. 16, 1773.

"　" Widow of Solomon Southard, ch. Benjamin, born Feb. 14, 1773.

(To be continued.)

BILL OF MORTALITY.

(Continued from page 135.)

1789.

Jan. 30. Child of Ziba Ludlow.

Mar. 2. Mary, daughter of David Freeman, worms, aet. 1.

" 22. Esther, wife of Joseph Tuttle,* consumption, aet. 36.

April 3. Lucinda Lee, daughter of Ephraim Youngs, meazles, aet. 1.

" 22. Sarah, widow of Solomon Boyles,* old age, aet. 80.

" 23. Elizabeth, wife of Thomas Kinney, Esq.,dropsy of the breast, aet.53.

" 24. A child of Luther Axtell.

May 30. Samuel, son of Daniel Coleman.

June 7. Ephraim, son of John Sutten, dropsy, aet. 17.

" 9. Mary, widow of Michal Tennery,* fever, aet. 41.

July 6. A child of Reuben Woods, still-born,

" 24. Esther, wife of William Johnes, consumption, aet. 21.

" 29. Abraham Canfield,* tabes, aet. 57.

Aug. 5. Phinehas Ayres, drowned, aet. 38.

" " John Lyon, drowned, aet. 40.

" 13. A child of Abraham Hudson.

" 15. Daughter of John Powers, fever, aet. 20.

" 15. Joseph Youngs, obstruction in the bladder, aet. 57.

" 18. Herrick Benjamin, old age, aet. 70.

Sept. 3. Child of John Morris.

Oct. 4. Richard, son of Zenas Mills, consumption.

" 12. Sarah, daughter of Richard Johnson, fever, aet. 3.

" 21. Shadrach Howard,* fever, aet. 65.

Nov. 1. Child of Benjamin Thomson.

" 16. Child of Vincent Guering.

" 19. Jonathan Elmer, son of Jonathan Dickerson, lingering decay, aet. 8.

" " Child of Thomas Johnson.

" 24. William, son of Joseph Marsh, colic, aet. 1.

" 28. Widow Sarah Allen,* old age, aet.92.

" 30. Hannah, widow of Jonathan Lindsley, old age, aet. 77.

Dec. 1. Widow Stillwell, old age, aet. 87.

" 15. Abiel Fairchild,* consumption, aet. 50.

1790.

Jan. 13. Ruben Cooper, fever, aet. 32.

Jan. 24. Hannah, widow of John Burwell, carbuncle, aet. 65.

Feb. 7. David Godden,* dropsy, aet. 66.

" 18. Joanna, daughter of Abraham Gilbert, phrenzy, aet..15.

Mar. 6. Robert M'Calvey, inflamed brain, aet. 66.

" 17. Cyrus, son of David Freeman, fever and ague, aet. 3.

Apr. — John Crowell,* hasty consumption, aet. 45.

" 3. Child of Joseph Shipman.

" 21. Daniel Beers,* drowned, aet. 37.

" 28. Armstrong Johnes,* consumption, aet. 34.

May 2. Sam'l Pierson, consumption, aet. 42.

" 10. Hubert Duburk, dropsy, aet. 52.

" 11. Stephen Smith Lyon,sudden, aet.26.

" 21. Deborah, wife of David Day, consumption, aet. 43.

" 22. George Riddles,consumption,aet.38.

June 4. Rachel, daughter of widow Conkling, worms, aet 5.

" 5. Matthew Fairchild, nervous fever, aet. 69.

" 12. Thomas Guering, fever, aet. 77.

" 19. Mary, wife of William Broadwell,* consumption, aet. 25.

July 1. Sophia Burk, consumption, aet. 23.

" 6. Margaret, wife of Michael Mounts, consumption, aet. 25.

" 24. A child of Isaac Mills, still-born.

Aug. 9. A child of James Stiles, fits.

" 24. Isaac Pierson, dropsey of the breast, aet. 53.

Sept. 9. Daughter of Peter Carr, consumption, aet. 13.

" " Servant child of Benjamin Freeman, fits.

" 16. Hannah, daughter of Jacob Casterline, fits.

" 21. An illegitimate child, found dead.

" 25. Elizabeth, daughter of John M'Collom, consumption, aet. 2.

Oct. 7. A child of Solomon Brown.

" 14. Huldah, daughter of Benjamin Pierson, consumption, aet. 3.

Dec. 25. Hannah, wife of Timothy Peck,* dropsey, aet. 79.

" 31. A child of Daniel Nixon, aet. 3.

1791.

Jan. 8. A child of Nathan Reeve.

" 25. Mary, daughter of Simeon Broadwell, sudden, aet. 1.

(To be continued.)

(Continued from page 136.)

TRUSTEES' BOOK.

At a meeting of the Trustees at the house of George O'Hara, the 28th Jan'y, 1793, the President, Mr. Lindsley, Mr. Mills, Mr. Ogden, and Benjamin Pierson attended in consequence of his being elected—who, being duly sworn and subscribed the oath as the Law directs took his seat in the board.

Joseph Munson applied for a piece adjoining the lands of Sam'l Morrison and James Pitney. Voted, Mr. Munson shall have the Refusal of a building spot at sixty pounds per acre. Mr. Munson, satisfied with the conditions, a committee consisting of Mr. Condit and Mr. Mills be appointed to survey sd. land and make out a Deed.

At a parish meeting held at the meeting house, 2nd Sept., 1793.

Resolved that the confession made by the Rev'd. Aaron C. Collins before the association, be read.

Whereas, the Rev. Mr. Collins has requested to be discharged from this Church and congregation as their pastor, and at the same time submitted to them to fix the period when his salary should terminate, and the church and Congregation having maturely considered the same, Resolved that they agree to his proposition for a separation from him as their pastor. Resolved, that the Trustees take charge of the parsonage & that they settle with Mr. Collins with respect to that part thereof which contains the nursery of mulbery trees agreeable to justice at their discretion. Resolved, that Silas Condit, Jacob Arnold, Caleb Russell, Gilbert Alling, Joseph Prudden, Benj. Lindsley, Jonas Phillips, Jonathan Stiles, Joseph Lewis, Matthias Crain, Dr. Wm. Campfield & Timothy Johnes, Jr., be a committee to ascertain and settle with Mr. Collins the arrears of salary that may be due to him.

Resolved, that the Deacons & Elders of this church be a committee for supplying the pulpit—that the said committee be authorized to employ any person duly qualified to preach the Gospel whether as Supplies or Candidates for any time not more than three months, & in order that such service be duly rewarded, the said Committee are directed to prepare and present a subscription to the parishioners of this Congregation for the purpose of raising the sum of one hundred pounds or there abouts to be appropriated for the payment of such supplies or Candidates, including the service already performed by the Rev. Mr. Baldwin, & if the sum so raised should not be all expended as above directed previous to the settlement of another minister in this Congregation—that such remaining sum shall be disposed of as the Congregation shall hereafter direct, & the sd. Committee are directed to keep an accurate account of their receipts and disbursements & lay the same before the Congregation whenever thereunto required, and, whereas it becomes us as professing Christians always to take notes of & wisely improve the dispensations of Divine Providence & as it is abundantly evident that God is now frowning on us as a Congregation, not only in permitting our pastor to conduct unbecoming his character and profession, but also in suspending those divine influences which are absolutely necessary to the being & continuance of Christian Love and Unity, the lamentable consequences of which obviously appear in the recent divisions & animosities that take place among us, with this view of our situation and in the same measure sensible of our guilt and vileness, our lukewarmness, sloth & want of Zeal in the cause of Religion, and of the justice of God in his dealings with us, and of our entire dependence on him for every degree of grace, wisdom and prudence; we think it proper and do agree to set apart the   day of this   as a day of humiliation, fasting and prayer to Almighty God that he would pour out his Spirit upon us and grant us that penitent & forgiving temper of mind that may dispose us to peace and union and that he would direct us in the path of duty in our future endeavours for the settlement of the ministry and perpetuating the Ordinances of the Gospel among us.

(*To be continued.*)

The part of the second historical sermon by Rev. Dr. Irving, published in this number of THE RECORD, will be especially interesting in its account of the building of the present edifice in which the First church worship. The frame was raised Sept. 20, 1791.

THE RECORD.

FIRST PRESBYTERIAN CHURCH, MORRISTOWN, N. J.

"This shall be Written for the Generation to Come."—Psalms 102 : 18.

VOL. II.   JULY, 1881.   NO. 7.

(*Printed with the approval of Session.*)

THE RECORD

Will be printed and published monthly at Morristown, N. J. Terms, 50 cents per annum in advance; 75 cents after June.

Subscriptions will be received at the book-stores of Messrs. Runyon and Emmell, or through the mail. All communications should be addressed to the

EDITOR OF THE RECORD,

. Lock box 44.   Morristown, N. J.
Vol. I, complete, 75 cents.

Entered at the Post Office at Morristown, N. J., as second class matter.

——:o:——

(*Continued from page* 140.)

HISTORICAL SERMON—No. 2.

By REV. DAVID IRVING, D.D.

Between the period of his call and his induction into the pastoral office, the aged and faithful shepherd was gathered to his fathers—his last hours cheered with the thought of his flock again united under one whom Providence had sent to heal the breaches occasioned by the misconduct of Mr. Collins. "The unanimity and cordiality in the settlement of Mr. Richards was as the balm of Gilead to his wounded spirit." Mr. Richards was paid for his services as a supply till September 12th, when his salary commenced, and from that time to this, this has been the close of the fiscal year of the parish.

This congregation was at that time the largest and most influential in the whole of this region. It had outgrown in strength the mother and the younger members of the same family; so that it was a post of great responsibility to the young licentiate, and owing to its peculiar state, one requiring great tact, prudence and discretion, but he proved himself equal to the task and more than met the expectations of the flock.

In alluding to the state of things, at his settlement in a letter to Dr. Condict in 1840, he says : "your fathers differ greatly in opinion and for a time were strongly opposed to each other in feeling, but they judged it best not to divide but to make sacrifices and endeavor to harmonize ; their endeavors were successful ; they were harmonized ; peace and brotherly love became the order of the day and with some slight exceptions have marked the course of things in the congregation for almost half a century." Whilst thus seeking to unite the people to each other, he was instant in season and out of season in striving to make them better acquainted with the Lord Jesus. He was abundant in labors. "I had," says he, "the sick and afflicted to visit, the dead to bury, the wandering to look after, the captious and uneasy to soothe, besides schools to catechise, and lectures to preach and prayer meetings to attend ; altogether creating a vast amount of labor, independent of regular family visitations and preparing for the pulpit." Besides these he had social calls to make and receive, and duties at times outside of his congregation to occupy his attention and time, but in his movements among his people and especially among the more spiritual and devoted, he sought to derive instruction and subjects for his pulpit ministrations. The doctrinal, practical and experimental were thus blended both to his own and the profit of those who listened to his preaching. Immediate fruits among the impenitent were not so perceptible as among the members of the church. Harmony with each other was more speedily seen than harmony between the wicked and God. Only three were added to the communion of the church during the first two years of his ministry, but in the two following years God poured his spirit upon his labors and 75 were added.

This revival commenced in the spring of 1797, and took the congregation by surprise; few were looking for it and when it came the members generally were unprepared for such manifestations of divine favor. As the result of this awakening about 100 united in this and the succeeding year; of the fruits of that revival but two remain, Phebe Burnet, widow of John Burnet, and Lewis Mills, the one received on March 5th, 1797, and the other May 1st, 1797. Once and again did God manifest his revival power during his pastorate, comforting and strengthening saints and bringing many aliens into the family of heaven. Whilst thus blessed at home, and highly revered by his people, his influence over the surrounding congregations was great, as well as extending over the church at large. In the year 1801 he received the degree of Master of Arts from Princeton College, and in 1805, at the age of 37, was chosen Moderator of the General Assembly of the Presbyterian Church. We can find no trace of anything published by him whilst here, but in 1816 he preached in this church a discourse entitled "This world is not our rest," which was afterwards printed. He was ever ready to assist others by ministerial labor and sought in this way to extend the Kingdom of the Messiah. One plan pursued by him and some of his brethren was to meet together in private or in school houses, in places lying between their churches and hold union meetings in some afternoon of the week, which were occasions of interest to the people and a means of mutual profit; another plan adopted in his day and for years afterwards was with some other minister to make preaching tours among the mountains or sparsely settled regions, now occupied by the Presbyteries of Passaic, Rockaway and Newton, and there proclaim Christ and him crucified to many destitute families or feeble struggling churches. In one of these excursions he met Dr. Griffin and spent the night with him in pleasant and profitable conversation. Part of this conference is detailed by Dr. Stearns, in which matters experimental and doctrinal are discussed, and doubts proposed and dissipated. On the atonement, Griffin unburdened his heart and spoke of his difficulty in apprehending Christ as a proper substitute, whereupon

Richards disclosed to him a distressing conflict which he had formerly upon that point and which was quieted by a transporting view of Heb. 7: 26. "For such an high priest became us who is holy, harmless, undefiled, separate from sinners and made higher than the Heavens." At this the agitation of Griffin's mind became relieved and he fell asleep, "when I awoke," he adds, "that same glorious High Priest was before me, just as he is expressed in Heb. 7: 26." The influence upon the character of such men by these conversations and the influence of labors such as they put forth beyond the limits of their own charges for the spiritual well being of others, eternity only can disclose. Their flocks were willing to be unsupplied an occasional Sabbath that their pastors might break the bread of life to those deprived of the stated means of grace, and they did not suffer in consequence. "They that water shall themselves be watered." Revivals here and there have been traced to these self denying but pleasant labors.

The old church building was vacated in Nov. 1795, and was soon afterwards taken down and sold in lots. And as truth must be spoken a large part of it was converted into a distillery and cider mill, and which, in Water street, did their work of mischief in those times of ignorance for many years. That church in which the sainted Johnes so long preached, where Drs. Buel, of Long Island, and Rogers of New York, and Mc-Whorter of Newark, proclaimed the words of life; where the voice of Green, and Darby, and Elmer, and Caldwell, and others was occasionally heard warning men of sin and pleading with them to be reconciled to God those walls that echoed back the praises of those, now at rest, and everything about i hallowed with the most joyous remen brances; where sweet communion with th unseen was enjoyed, and solemn vows mad that building converted to such an use mu have been trying to those who had be blessed in the privileges there possess and who were attached to it by t sweetest and holiest memories.

The new edifice was first occupied on N 26, 1795, the sermon preached by Mr. R ards, but from what text I have not b able to discover. On the 18th of Feb. 1 the seats of the new church were sold the old plan of rating and collecting was discontinued; several of the pews on the first floor were large square pews, and were appraised considerably higher than the single pews, (four of them at £120 each), the number of the pews in the main audience room was 101; in the gallery 57. The number of the pews since the alteration is 126 in the former and 57 in the latter besides the reserved seats for the choir. The principal seats in the body of the church ranged in value from $70 to $87, on which 5 per cent. was assessed to meet the current expenses of the congregation; 8 pews were reserved for the poor and some for the deaf. The number purchasing or renting pews or parts of pews was 158, who paid the sum of $533.35. The expenses of 1797 were for "salary $440, sweeping the church $15, sexton $15, cake for wood cutters $19, printing $2, cyder $5.62." The salary continued the same till 1804, when it was increased to $565, with certain privileges, the current expenses for that year were $605.

Among matters of note and that peculiarly belong to the annals of the church we may mention the spinning and wood frolicks, as they were called. The spinning visit was collecting together the various amounts of linen, thread, yarn, and cloth, proportioned to the "gude" wife's ability or generosity. The thread was woven into cloth for the use and comfort of the pastor and his family, and as it was not always of the same texture and size, it sometimes puzzled the weaver to make the cloth and finish it alike. The wood frolick brought together the greater part of the congregation, the ladies preparing supper at the parsonage, which was heartily enjoyed by those who were busy during the day in bringing together the years supply of fuel for their minister, which averaged about 40 cords. We find the amounts expended by the parish for these frolicks in 1797, to be for cake and cider, $25.62; 1798, bread and beef, $18.94; in 1799, 1 cwt. of flour and 200 lbs. of beef, $10.83. Besides these remunerative tokens, his own heart was oft refreshed and his family benefitted, by numerous acts of kindness performed by his people.

During his ministry here, politics largely agitated the public mind, and as in later

times sectional animosity was bitter if not unscrupulous. As an instance of this in our own State we find that Thomas Paine, a strong partisan of Jefferson, wished to ride in the public stage from Trenton to New York, but the proprietors of both stages were Federalists and refused with strong oaths to give a seat to an infidel. If not carried to such an extreme in this region, parties were as decided, zealous, and prejudiced as in any other part of the State, and were as jealous of pulpit interference as at the present day; hence its utterances were watched and faithfully scanned on fast days or occasions on which allusion was in any way made to public men or matters of State. On one of the fast days held during the administration of John Adams, a sermon suited to the times was preached by Mr. R., with which but little if any fault was found by the congregation. A few years later, Mr. R. preached again on a similar occasion, during Mr. Jefferson's administration, which gave great offence to one of the political parties as seemingly reflecting upon their men and measures. Sectional feeling was at once aroused and could only be allayed by some of the leaders waiting upon Mr. R., acquainting him with the facts and if need be require a retraction. The committee called upon the preacher; to their statements and grievances he politely listened, when he replied that they had approved of all that he had said. This they denied, he then told them that owing to a pressure of other matters upon him, he was unable to prepare a sermon, he therefore found that upon a perusal of the discourse preached a few years previous, that it was well suited to the present times; with it then no fault was found, but commendation was bestowed upon it, he had therefore repeated it as it was written and this was the only thing which they could blame. They saw the MS. and knew that it was the old sermon. Perceiving that they were caught, the committee soon retired and the matter was at once hushed. Here as elsewhere Mr. Richards showed that discretion and tact for which he was famed, a prudence that characterized all his movements among this people and that made him a wise counsellor, a strong leader, a faithful pastor and a true friend, so that he was regarded a model minister, throughout this region and the church at large.

Except some slight friction in his pastorate, like the one alluded to, Mr. R. lived in the affections of his people, they treated him with respect and esteemed him highly for his work's sake. His charge was laborious but pleasant, of the relation in after years, he thus speaks: "Never was a minister more happy with his people than I with mine during the 15 years I spent among you. I can truly say that if there be a spot on earth to which my mind turns with more than ordinary affection it is that where I was ordained to the work of the gospel ministry." Of one thing he felt that he had ground to complain, and that was of an inadequate support. His salary as we have seen was $440 per annum, with certain perquisites. Immediately on his marriage he purchased a lot of the church in South street, consisting of half an acre for $300, on which he erected the house now occupied by Mr. George King, afterwards he purchased 1 1-2 acres for $200 and enlarged the grounds attached to it. Some of the congregation lent him money, which he paid when convenient. His salary was increased in 1804 to $565 per annum. But this was inadequate to meet the growing necessities of his family. For a time he kept boarders, which added largely to his cares and against which some of his warm friends demurred. To relieve him of this burden and pay him a salary more in proportion to the ability of the congregation and his just claims a parish meeting was called in 1808. To this measure some were opposed, as they could not see why the minister could not live on his salary, which was more than many received; others were in favor of the movement, but thought it was ill-timed. These two combined carried their motion for delay over those who were anxious for immediate action. The matter was postponed till the next parish meeting; they met, talked and separated without coming to any result. Again they met and did the same. This was a severe trial to the pastor and preyed upon his mind. But rising above the trials and the mortification attached to it, he devoted himself with greater energy to his work, believing that God would make all things plain. Thus laboring, an application was made to him to become the successor of Dr. Griffin, as pastor of the First Church of Newark. This call, after a painful conflict, he accepted. When it was too late the congregation increased his salary to $1,000, yet hoping that it might with other considerations brought before him, so influence his action as to make it favorable to his remaining. Two formal memorials were addressed to him, one sent from a meeting of 71 ladies, which did honor to both pastor and people, but all were unavailing, he had gone too far to draw back, yet he was heard to say that had he known in time the strength and tenderness of affection of his people, he would never have accepted the call. At the spring meeting of the Presbytery, 1809, his pastoral relation with this congregation was dissolved, when he immediately entered upon his new field of labor. Mr. Richard's ministry here continued nearly 14 years. During that time there were admitted to the communion of the church on examination, 214; and on certificate, 29; baptisms, 444. Of these and now living members of this church, are only Phebe Burnet, Lewis Mills, Catharine, widow of David Mills, Silas Johnson, Rhoda, widow of Simeon Cory, Rebecca Beers, wife of Wm. Enslee, and Phebe Mills, widow of D.C. Dusenberry. The elders who were in office at the time of his installation were Gilbert Allen, Joseph Lindsley, Philip Condict, Jonas Phillips, Caleb Munson, Philip Lindsly, Ezra Halsey, Isaac Prudden, Samuel Freeman, Jesse Cutler, Matthias Crane, Joseph Pruden. These were reduced in 1805 to seven, when the bench of elders was increased by the ordination of Henry Vail, David Lindsly, Zophar Freeman, James Stephenson, Sept. 11, 1805. These have all gone, reunited no doubt to their beloved pastors, Johnes and Richards, in the realms of purity. Of the number of communicants at his installation we cannot learn from the manner in which the books were kept, three months after his departure, a new roll was made and there were 298 in full communion.

Mr. Richards was dismissed by Presbytery April 26, 1809; moved to Newark May 17th. Soon after this Mr. Fisher was invited to preach as a candidate, having a short time before been introduced to the people by Mr. Richards, which he did with such acceptance that on the 29th of May, an unanimous call was presented to him by the congregation which he accepted and was installed pastor Aug. 9th, 1809.

(To be continued.)

(Continued from page 141.)

MEMBERS.

[The third column on this page is the work of the RECORD. Information which will lead to the correction of any mistake, or the filling of any blank, will be thankfully received.—ED.]

PASTORATE OF REV. JAMES RICHARDS.

Names.	When Received.	When Dismissed or Died.
Hannah Kinney (Abraham),	Feb'y 1795.	
Phebe Kinney (John),	" "	
Katey Emmick, (widow,)	July 3, "	
Esther Scott (John),	"	
Anna Phœnix (Daniel),	July 1, 1796.	
Anna Beach (Jabez),	" " "	Dismissed Apr. 19, 1815 to N. Y. City.
Martha Lindsly (Ephraim),	" " "	
Phebe Hathaway (Abrm.),	" " "	
Polly Condict (Edward),	" " "	
Joanna Munson (Joseph),	" 24, "	
Eunice Marsh (Benj.),	Nov. 6, "	March 27,1823, aet. 60 y. 1 m. and 5 d.
Rhoda Lindsly (Dan'l),	" " "	
Sarah Losey (John),	" " "	
Esther Munson (Jacob),	" " "	Died 1820.
Abigail Lee (Wm).,	" " "	Dismissed May 28, 1840.
Jane Wilson (Lawrence),	" " "	
Phebe Hathaway (Theophilus),	" " "	
Polly Lyon,	" " "	
Sally DeCamp,	" " "	
Abigail Charlot,	" " "	
Abigail Ayers,	" " "	Feb. 18, 1812, aet. 39 y. 2 m. 22 d.
Polly Ayers,	" " "	
Patty Shipman,	" " "	
Edward Condict,	" " "	Died Dec. 1, 1855, born Nov. 15, 1769.
Stephen Jones Wheeler,	" " "	Dismissed Apr. 3, 1826, to Hanover.
Jonas Alwood,	" " "	Dis. Jan. 26, 1841 to 2d P. ch. Mor-
Stephen Wood,	" " "	[ristown,died Dec. 25,1841,aet. 71.
Ruth Pierson, (Gabriel),	" " "	Dis. Jan. 26,1841, 2d P.ch.,Morristown.
Gabriel Pierson,	Dec. 1, "	" " " "
David Pierson,	Jan. 1, 1797.	Died Mar. 22, 1824, born Aug. 29,1763.
Abigail Pierson (David),	" " "	Died Apr. 4, 1842, born Jan. 13, 1769.
Jeduthan Condict,	" " "	April 8, 1833, aet. 64.
Hannah Condict (Jed),	" " "	Sept. 6, 1837, aet. 63.
Theodocia Condict (Uzal).	" " "	
Anna Byram (Eleazar),	" " "	Later Mrs. Henry Vail,
Esther Prudden (Peter),	" " "	Dec. 10, 1827, aet. 65.
Rachel Bond (Nath'l),	" " "	
Hannah Lum (Matthew),	" " "	
Betsey Ward,	" " "	Dis. Apr. 26, 1813, to Hanover,
Sally Ball,	" " "	Dis. Jan. 26, 1841, 2d P. ch., Morris-
Abigail Condict Whitehead,(Abner),	" " "	[ristown, died Mar. 27,1848, aet. 67.
Rachel Roff,	" " "	
Nancy Bowen,	" " "	Disciplined Dec. 19, 1803.
Betsey McClure,	" " "	
Rachel Arnold,	" " "	
Polly Trowbridge,	" " "	
Nancy Douglass,	" " "	Dis. June 15, 1820 to Mt. Freedom.

(To be continued.)

(Continued from page 142.)

BAPTISMS.

1773.

Apr. 11. Nathaniel Armstrong & wf., ch. Phebe, born Feb. 9, 1773.

" 25. Nathaniel Peck & wf., ch. Mary, born March 11, 1773.

" 29. Cornelius Woodruff & wf., ch.

May 2. Christopher Wood & wf., ch. Phebe, born Sept. 3. 1772.

" " Phineas Fairchild & wf., ch. Sarah, born Feb. 26, 1773.

" 9. Gilbard Ludlam & wf., ch. Elizabeth, born Nov. 26, 1772.

" " Daniel Bishop & wf., ch. Ruth, born March 29, 1773.

" 23. Usual Coe & wf., ch. Phebe, born April 8, 1773.

" 30. James Wilkerson & wf., ch. Mary, born March 28, 1772.

" " Isaac Prudden & wf., ch. Daniel, born April 19, 1773.

" " Moses Munson & wf., ch. Solomon, born April 18, 1773.

June 13. Daniel Tichenor & wf., ch. Jacob, born April 8, 1773.

" " John Hathaway & wf., ch. Henry, born May 8, 1773.

June 27. John Winnup & wf., ch. Jabez, born April 22, 1773.

" " Howell Orsborn & wf., ch. Rhoda, born Nov. 8, 1772.

July 1. Peter Norris & wf., chn. by Bevens, Moses, born Dec. 6, 1760, and Evan, born Dec. 22, 1763.

" 18. Joseph Lewis & wf., ch. Stevens Johnes, born May 27, 1773.

" " David Moor & wf., chn. Rachel, born April 29, 1771 ; Phebe, born Aug. 10, 1772.

" " Timo. Loce on wf's acct., chn. Anne, born March 25, 1768 ; Stephen, born July 9, 1769.; Silas Sayre, born April 25, 1773.

" " Calvin Extel & wf., ch. Timothy, born Sept. 11, 1772.

" 25. Capn. Peter Dickerson & wf., ch. William, born June 18, 1773.

" " Andrew Whitehead & wf., ch. Elizabeth, born June 2, 1773.

" " Jedidiah Mills & wf., ch. John, born June 24, 1773.

Aug. 8. John Jacks on wf's acct., ch. John Reed, born June 2, 1773.

" 15. David Day's wife in absence of her husband, ch. David, born July 7, 1773.

" " John Pool & wf., ch. Silas, born July 6, 1773.

" " Wm. Gray on wf's acct., ch. Elizabeth, born Dec. 7, 1772.

" 22. David Woodruff & wf., ch. David, born June 29, 1773.

Sep. 5. John Mills & wf., ch. David, born Aug. 6, 1773.

" " Nathan Turner & wf., chn. Silas, born April 26, 1771; Phebe, born July 17, 1773.

" " John Rogers on wf's acct., ch. Jabish, born July 13, 1773.

" 12. Eliphalet Lyon & wf., ch. James, born Aug. 4, 1773.

" 19. Benj. Lindsley & wf., ch. Timothy, born Aug. 13, 1773.

" 26. Philip Hathaway & wf., ch. Philip, born Aug. 26, 1773.

" " Lindsley Burnet & wf., ch. Aaron, born Aug. 15, 1773.

Oct. 3. Eleazar Hathaway & wf., ch. Stephen, born Aug. 23, 1773.

" 10. Jonathan Raynor & wf., ch. Parnela, born Aug. 1, 1773.

" " Silas Condict & wf., a negro child, Cezar, born Aug. 18, 1773.

" 17. Onesimus Whitehead & wf., ch. Isaac, born Aug. 29, 1773.

" 30. Abner Wines' ch. on Timo. Person's & wf's acct., grand parents, Elizabeth, born Jan. 18. 1770.

" " Capn. James Keen & wf., ch. Jane, born Sept. 28, 1773.

Nov. 5. Jane Burnet, ch. Mehitabel, born Aug. 22, 1773.

" 21. Boyce Jno. Prudden & wf., ch. Silas, born Oct. 10, 1773.

" " Stephen Arnold & wf., ch. Naomi, born Oct. 13, 1773.

" 18. James Gillespie & wf., ch. John Marsh, born Oct. 8, 1773.

" 28. James Smith & wf., ch. Sarah, born Oct. 12, 1773.

" " Daniel Carmichael & wf., ch. Abigail, born Oct. 14. 1773.

Dec. 14. Jacob Arnold on wf's acct., ch. Hannah, born July 29, 1772.

(To be continued.)

(*Continued from page* 148.)

BILL OF MORTALITY,

1791.

Jan. 30. William, son of Doct. Ebenezer Blachly,† bleeding at the lungs, aet. 23.

Feb. 1. Mary, wife of Elijah Brown, old-age, aet. 61.

" 23. A child of Samuel Leonard, still-born.

Mar. 6. Mahlon, son of Zenas Mills, whooping-cough.

" 17. Elizabeth, widow of Rev. John Walton,†* consumption, aet. 49.

Apr. 4. Mariah, daughter of James Pitney, small-pox, aet 3.

" 5. A child of William Davis, whooping-cough, aet. 2.

" 18. Silas, son of Zophar Freeman, Jun., Whooping-cough, aet. 1,

" 23. Nancy, daughter of Samuel Prudden, small-pox, aet. 7.

" " Anthony, son of William Ford, small-pox, aet. 8.

" 24. Baldwin, son of David Wood, small-pox.

" " Benjamin Sylvester, small-pox, aet. 16.

" 30. Mary, wife of Ziba Arnold,* consumption, aet. 38.

May 14. A child of Vincent Guering.

" 16. William, son of Timothy Humpherville, sudden, aet. 8.

" 22. Elias, son of Peter Prudden, whooping-cough.

" 26. A child of Stephen Ludlow, still-born.

June 26. Deacon Jonas Goble,†* decay, aet. 84.

July 7. Silas Stiles, son of James Pitney, dysentery.

" 14. A child of David P. Tuttle.

" 17. James, son of James Louhhead,† bleeding, aet. 10.

Aug. 16. William, son of John Bryan, worms and fits.

Sept. 5. Thomas M'Speldon, consumption, aet. 34.

" 6. A child of Elijah Taylor, still-born.

" 9. Stephen Conkling,* fever, aet. 70.

" 12. Isaac Conkling, remitting-fever, aet. 30.

Sept. 24. Harvah, son of Mattaniah Lyon, consumption, aet. 23.

Oct. 3. Sarah, daughter of Stephen Norris, nervous-fever, aet. 20.

" 20. Thomas Doughty, Esq., old-age, aet. 73.

1792.

Jan. 3. Benjamin Pierson,* consumption, aet. 55.

" 5. John Pool, pleurisy, aet. 69.

" 14. Keziah, daughter of Abraham Manson, fever.

" 16. Elizabeth, wife of Henry Howell, consumption, aet. 45.

" 18. Wife of Simeon Hathaway, fever, aet. 24.

" 20. Abraham Pierson, pleurisy, aet. 57.

" 22. Child of Ichabod Badgley.

" 27. Lydia, widow of David Trowbridge,†* old-age, aet. 76.

" 28. Elizabeth, wife of Daniel Stiles, consumption, aet. 25.

Feb. 5. James, son of William Meeker, burn, aet. 3.

" 15. Wife of Abraham Lyon, fever, aet. 40.

" 23. David Muir, colic, aet. 52.

" " Child of John T. Howell, still-born.

Apr. 12. Elizabeth, daughter of Theophilus Hathaway, scarlet-fever, aet. 9.

" 13. Servant child of Frederick King, Quinsey, aet. 1.

May 25. Sarah, widow of Samuel Stevens Johnes, consumption, aet. 46.

June 20. Rebeckah, wife of Timothy Humpherville, consumption, aet. 59.

July 10. Child of Matthias Ward.

Sept. 3. Daniel Stiles, bilious-colic, aet. 30.

" 10. Servant woman of Joseph Morgan, consumption, aet. 30.

" 19. Child of Anthony Cazatt.

" 21. Hannah, wife of Zebedee Brown, old-age, aet. 77.

" 24. Timothy Goble,† accidental, aet. 34.

Dec. 15. Phœbe, daughter of Ichabod Cooper, hives, aet. 3.

" 16. Benjamin, son of Thomas Mitchell, putrid-fever, aet. 3.

1793.

Jan. 1. Child of Daniel Guering.

" 19. Child of James Chidester, sudden.

Feb. 5. Sarah, widow of Joseph Hathaway, consumption, aet. 58,

(*To be continued.*)

(Continued from page 144.)

TRUSTEES' BOOK.

At a meeting of the Trustees at Mr. Crain's on the 10th of Sept., 1793—present, the President, Mr. Lindsley, Mr. Mills, Mr. Pierson. Mr. Ogden.

Mr. Condict informed the Board Mr. Collins offered his right to the Mulberry nursery, provided the Congregation would pay up his salary to the time affixed by the committee immediately. This gratuity Mr. Collins considers 'as' some acknowledgment of the many inconveniences and great difficulties he has been the means of involving this society in. The trustees having taken into consideration said offer, agree to postpone the determination to a subsequent meeting.

At a meeting of the Trustees at Mr. Mill's house, 23d Sept., 1793. Mr. Condict, Mr. Lindsley, Mr. Mills, Mr. Pierson and Mr. Ogden being present. Rev. Mr. Collins made a present to the Trustees for the use of the congregation his right to the Mulberry Nursery.

Voted Mr. Mills & Mr. Ogden be a committee to settle with the Rev. Mr. Collins his accounts with the congregation.

Voted the Trustees shall discharge Mr. Collins, obligation in favour of Phineas Fairchild and such other debts agt. Mr. Collins, not to exceed the sum due from the congregation to Mr. Collins, and that the committee procure and advance to Mr. Collins near the amount probably due him after the above payments are made, and that the Trustees obligate as a body to pay the moneys which may be advanced. Voted Mr. Mills and Mr. Lindsley be a committee to take care of the parsonage and sell the mulberry trees.

At a meeting of the Trustees at Mr. Mills' house the 7th of Nov., 1793. The President, Mr. Lindsley, Mr. Mills and Mr. Ogden being met.

Voted that Mr. Lindsley and Mr. Pierson be a committee to sell the old wood lying down on the parsonage lot.

Voted that the stove be sold which was purchased for Mr. Collins.

At a meeting of the congregation 25th of Dec., 1793. Deacon Alling, Moderator and Israel Canfield, Clk.; Eliza Holloway, John Oliver and Silas Alling be appointed choristers.

At a meeting of the Trustees at the house of George O'Hara, Jan. 28th, 1794. Present, Mr. Condict. Mr. Lindsley, Mr. Mills, Mr. Ogden. Benj. Pierson appeared and was sworn agreeable to law. Joseph Munson applied for a piece of land adjoining the lands of James Pitney and Sam'l Morrison. Voted Mr. Munson should have the refusal of a building spot at sixty pounds per acre.

At a meeting of the Trustees 3d of March, 1794, at Mr. Mills' house, the Pres. Mr. Lindsley, Mr. Mills, Mr. Pierson and Mr. Ogden being present. Mr. Mills was appointed to collect the arrears of taxes due on Mr. Collins' salary and take up Mr. Collins' bond in favor of Phineas Fairchild—that Mr. Mills will inform delinquents they must be sued immediately in case of non-payment as the congregation is in needy circumstances. Mr. Lindsley & Mr. Pierson, a committee appointed for that purpose, report they have agreed with Jonathan Dickerson for two shillings and six pence per cord for old tops of trees lying on the parsonage lot. Voted the committee appointed to take care of the Mulberry Nursery shall advertise in Elizabethtown & Newark papers, to sell trees at ten shillings per hundred, the leaves remaining on the trees unsold to be sold also at public vendue trees not to be sold after the first of May.

At a meeting of the Trustees at the Court House, 22d of April, 1794, Mr. Lindsley, Mr. Mills, Mr. Ogden & Mr. Pierson present. Voted the parsonage lot in town be hired out by vendue until the 1st of Nov. next, that Mr. Mills & Mr. Ogden be a committee to superintend this business.

(To be continued.)

The roll of membership begins this month with the pastorate of Rev. James Richards. The Historical Sermon of Rev. Dr. Irving covers the whole period of his ministry in this church. He was pastor here about fourteen years, and was obliged to leave on account of insufficiency of salary. His predecessor, the Rev. Mr. Collins, the colleague of Rev. Dr. Johnes, will be found in the Trustees' Book to have had trouble of another sort.

THE RECORD.

FIRST PRESBYTERIAN CHURCH, MORRISTOWN, N. J.

"This shall be written for the Generation to Come."—Psalms 102 : 18.

VOL. II.	AUGUST, 1881.	NO. 8.

(Printed with the approval of Session.)

THE RECORD

Will be printed and published monthly at Morristown, N. J. Terms, 50 cents per annum in advance; 75 cents after June.

Subscriptions will be received at the book-stores of Messrs. Runyon and Emmell, or through the mail. All communications should be addressed to the

EDITOR OF THE RECORD,

Lock box 44.   Morristown, N. J.

Vol. I. complete, 75 cents.

Entered at the Post Office at Morristown, N. J., as second class matter.

——:o:——

(Continued from page 148.)

HISTORICAL SERMON—No. 2.

By REV. DAVID IRVING, D.D.

Jonathan Fisher who held a commission of Lieutenant in the Revolutionary army, was taken sick in the performance of his duties and died of camp fever in this town in March, 1777, and three months before the birth of Samuel Fisher, the successor of Mr. Richards. His remains are entombed in the grave yard. He was a man of ardent piety and his last moments were spent in prayer for his family and his country. Of his four sons three became ministers of the gospel. Mr. Fisher was born in Sunderland, Mass., June 30, 1777, received his collegiate education at Williams College, graduated in 1799, and was appointed tutor, which office he filled for some time. (His first public performance was delivering an eulogy on George Washington, Jan. 8th, 1800. A few days after his predecessor, Mr. R., delivered a sermon and eulogy on the same in this church.) Mr. Fisher was ordained to the ministry Nov. 1, 1805, and was settled over the Congregational Church of Wilton, Connecticut, when he was called to this church as already stated and installed pastor by the Presbytery of New York, which was divided in Nov. of the same year into two Presbyteries, the one retaining the old name and the other known as the Presbytery of Jersey; the first meeting of this new Presbytery was held in this church, April 24, 1816.

The salary promised to Mr. Fisher in the call was $1,000. The pew rents according to the old assessment yielded only $566. A vote was passed by the parish that the trustees should assess the deficiency in proportion to the original appraisal, which was rescinded at the next meeting. The fund owned by the church at this time was nearly $6,000, besides real estate in town lots and wood land which were occasionally sold to meet current expenses, until all disappeared, so that the church owns now no property to trouble and restrain our liberality, and thanks to an overruling Providence and the short sighted policy of our fathers, we have nothing but the parsonage house and lot and the grave yard to keep in repair. As the funds dwindled away the assessment had to be increased to meet the deficiencies until it is now more than treble the amount imposed at the first sale of the pews, yet not as high as upon pews in other churches of the same size throughout our country.

Mr. Fisher was a man of fervent piety, untiring industry, and of strong practical sense. There was a directness in his efforts that did not always win the active co-operation of those who differed from him. His aim was to do good to the souls of men and bring them under the control of the noblest principles. In the first year of his pastorate seven were received into the church on profession and eleven by certificate ; in 1813, twenty-four were admitted to sealing ordinances on confession and nine by letter. In October, 1812, he reported to Presbytery a membership of 325, and in 1813, 346. Dur-

ing the y... ...e ...o...a census of
the villa... a... ...hi... a... found the
number... m...e...to...e...6, ...emales 511,
black... 3... ...l...r... ...tan... ut of
the village, males 1,018, females 1,020, blacks
68—total, 2,106, in all 3,217. Number of
baptized persons in village 152, in the country 378—total of 530. Church members in
the village 102, in the parish out of the village 206—total 308.

Political excitement was very high during
the latter part of his ministry ; he was a decided federalist, while the larger part of his
congregation belonged to the opposite
party, who watched for an unwise word in
sermons and in prayers. Umbrage was
taken to two discourses preached in 1812,
as censuring those in authority, introducing
political discussion into the pulpit, and
stirring up strife without profit. To show
the groundlessness of the charge, he printed the sermons, together with an address,
in which he vindicates his course and nobly
defends himself against certain unrighteous
assaults. Says he, "when called to bear
testimony against vice, in any shape or form
whatever—no frowns, no flatteries, no promises nor threatenings shall ever deter me.
Earth and hell combined shall never silence
my voice till it is silenced in death." He
then meets the accusation that he was an
enemy to his country, and that he was
haughty and imperious, and of feeling above
the congregation. Both were unjust as he
feelingly and ably declared, but it is only
another evidence of what party spirit and
prejudice will seize upon in times of great
political excitement to injure one who occupies a prominent position in his honest
differences from them. There is nothing in
them of a partizan character, though he
does not spare the infidel, the vicious, the
Sabbath breaker, the profane swearer, the
gambler, the intemperate, the duelist, the
murderer who are in the National Council, who walk with impugnity the floor
of Congress and who are seated on the
bench of justice ; whilst thus condemned
by one part of his congregation for any allusion to national topics, he was upheld by the
mass of his people in all his ministerial duties, and over such his influence and preaching were not in vain. His congregation was
very large, covering a large territory and

embracing 500 fam...e... a... though all did
not attend the sanc...ry, ... i... case of marriages and deaths these families wished to
be considered as ...e... his pastoral charge.
These, together with twenty-seven families
of other denominations, he visited during his
pastorate. He was a laborious minister and
was active in everything that promoted
the well-being of his people and the
prosperity of the town, but all was in vain
to allay the opposition against him, and
finding that this crippled his usefulness,
he sought in the early part of 1814 a
dissolution of his pastoral relation. At a
parish meeting held on Feb. 15, the following question was put to the house : "Does
this congregation wish their minister to
join with them requesting Presbytery to
dismiss him from his present charge ?" It
was decided in the negative by 19 majority.
He applied however to Presbytery for a dissolution of the relation and was dismissed
by that body on April 27, 1814. The last
person received into the communion of the
church was an aged woman, who had 37
years before attended his father in his last
illness.

From his private records we have the following items : value of presents received
during his pastorate from his people, $917.37;
marriages 86, marriage fees, $276.10 ; deaths
from Sept. 5, 1809 to May 1, 1814, 279.
There were added to the church in the same
time 65 on profession and 32 by certificate.
In 1812, Stephen Young, Jacob Pierson,
Lewis Mills, Peter A. Johnson and Frances
Johnes, were ordained and added to the
bench of Elders, and here I may record it as
a singular fact that only one of the ninety-
seven admitted to the church under Mr.
Fisher's ministry is at present connected
with it.

The congregation was supplied by
Messrs. Chandler, How, Gildersleeve, Clark,
Condit, McDowell from the beginning of
May till the coming of the latter in Octo-
ber, the society having on Sept. 29, 1814,
made out a call to Mr. McDowell.

Wm. A. McDowell, was born at Lamington, N. J., in May 1789 ; received part of his
classical education at Elizabethtown, where
he was taught by Mr. Henry Mills, a son of
this church and afterwards professor in the
Theological Seminary, Auburn ; graduated

in Princeton College in 1809, and became a tutor in the same the following year; studying Theology under the direction of the President of the college, Dr. Samuel Stanhope Smith. Owing to failure of health he had for a season to abandon his studies but resumed them in 1812, when he entered the Theological Seminary of Princeton and was a member of its first class. On the following year he was licensed by the Presbytery of New Brunswick, and ordained and installed pastor of the church of Bound Brook by the same, on Dec. 22, 1815. This relation was dissolved on the ensuing October and on the 13th of December, he was inducted into the pastoral office here by the Presbytery of Jersey. His ministry was from the first characterized by great acceptableness and usefulness. He was a faithful pastor, entering largely into the sufferings of his people and was full of tenderness and sympathy. His sermons were simple, rich in Evangelical instruction and delivered with fervor and unction. He was diligent in family visitation and in dealing with the consciences of his people. God soon set the seal of his approval upon his labors, and ere the first year of his pastorate closed 42 united with the church on confession. The first indication of God's converting presence was in his weekly Bible class from which a large number were savingly brought to a knowledge of Jesus. On the following year a still larger number swelled the communion roll, and his heart was often cheered by seeing one and another coming out from the world and allying themselves with the cause of Christ. A blessing to his people they in turn did not forget him, but remembered his wants and cheered his heart and home by memorials of their regard. Among such evidences we have the following resolutions passed at a parish meeting Sept. 1816: Resolved, that the Trustees be instructed to inquire whether the salary of our minister for the last year has been sufficient for his support and make report to some future meeting. On the report of the Trustees they were empowered by the meeting to present to the pastor in addition to his salary for the past year the sum of $250—and here I would say that among all the charges brought against this people, a lack of gen-

erous support to the pastor has never reached my ear.

At the meeting to which I have already referred it was also voted that the sexton's salary should be increased to $60 per annum, and that he should be denied the privilege of pasturing cattle of any kind in the graveyard. On Jan'y 1, 1816, the society through its Trustees sold to certain parties chiefly belonging to the congregation for the sum of $1,500 all of that part of the parish land called Morristown Green to remain as a common forever, subject to certain restrictions and exceptions; two of which were as far as we are concerned the building of a lecture room, and a church; as the former has been located, the latter is a right which belongs to us and which we may be called upon to excise at some future period.

Permission was also given to the Trustees and others who would assist them to build a lecture room, which was completed in 1819 under the management and supervision of Mr. John Mills, who took much interest in the work, and who expended in its completion more than was subscribed; the balance was afterwards paid him. About the same time the church was thoroughly cleaned and painted at an expense of $817. The Trustees were also requested to employ a chorister at such salary as can be agreed on, not to exceed $50.

In 1816, a Sabbath school in connection with this church was established. Before this a few active friends met on Sabbath to instruct the colored people, which may be considered as the first movement in this section of planting that institution which God has so much honored and blessed to both teacher and scholar. This school was first under the superintendance of one or two devoted ladies assisted by an efficient corps of teachers, among whom I find the names of Mills, Condit, Johnson, Johnes, Schenck, etc., all ladies. Several of whom are with us unto this day and some have fallen asleep.

Whilst 1820 and '21 were years of comparative drought, God again remembered his heritage and appeared in a most glorious manner. Yea in a way that he had never done before. The whole congregation was moved in the spring of 1822; the church became crowded to overflowing and benches were brought in to accommodate the people. At one communion nearly 100 were added to the church, from the aged sire to the youth of fourteen ; thirty were baptized, the scene was overwhelming, few refrained from tears. A Scotch clergyman who was present, said afterwards to the pastor, "Ah my brother, I stood it very, very well, until I saw your youthful hand come down on the bald head of that old man and then I could refrain no longer but burst into tears." As the fruits of this revival there were received in 1822-3 over 160. Whilst abundant in labors, serious inroads began at length to be made upon the pastor's health. At the age of twelve he had suffered severely from small pox, and from that time never was robust and vigorous ; but in the fall of 1822 he was threatened with a pulmonary complaint, so that he was obliged to go South and spend the winter at Charleston. He returned in the spring much improved, but soon his strength failed. At this juncture a call came to him from the Presbyterian church of Charleston, S.C., and being benefitted by his former sojourn there he felt it a duty to ask for a dissolution of the pastoral relation which was reluctantly granted and a very feeling and touching address was presented to him by the congregation. On the 8th of October, 1823, he ceased to be pastor, but his love for his charge did not here end. This was a place dear to his heart, and in his last sickness he came back to place himself under the care of Dr. Johnes, his former physician, and in whom he had special confidence ; but he had only been here a few days when he breathed his last on the 17th of September, 1851.

Under his ministry the church was more highly blessed than under any of its pastors, if we regard the additions that were made to its strength. During his pastorate of nearly nine years, 271 were admitted on profession of their faith and 46 by letter, 317 in all. There were no elders ordained during his ministry, but of those afterwards set apart to that office were five, who joined the church under his ministry.

Besides the improvement and changes in the edifice already referred to, we may mention the introduction of stoves and lamps in 1822. The former innovation was very much resisted by a few as leading to effeminacy. Their fathers and mothers had faithfully attended the sanctuary without any such comforts, being satisfied with the smell of fire from the foot stoves. One good man affirmed that they had always trusted Providence for keeping warm and should do so still ; opposition was slight however and stoves and lamps were soon fixtures in the church, at an expense of $254. Previous to this when the church was lighted, which was but seldom, it was done by candles taken by different members of the congregation. Opposition to stoves was on a par with the repugnance of many to insuring the church, which was deemed a wanton disregard of God's Providence and an act that boded no good. These wood stoves continued till 1835, when they were found insufficient for warming the building ; coal stoves were then substituted and were used until the furnaces were introduced. The lamps remained until 1842, when others were purchased sufficient to give a fine light over the whole church. These were rendered useless by the introduction of gas.

We have now grouped together the leading characteristics and acts of the first four pastors of this church—Johnes, Richards, Fisher and McDowell. We have seen the blessings that attended their labors and their influence upon this community, during their pastorate of nearly 80 years, but they have finished their earthly course ; first Johnes went up, then Richards, then McDowell and lastly Fisher. Before them and after them came one and another whom they knew here and who constitute their joy and crown of rejoicing ; of the 424 added to the church by Johnes, all have died. Few, very few remain of the ingatherings of Richards and Fisher, and the member that tarry with us of those brought to Christ under McDowell, is rapidly diminishing. A few years more and the last will be gathered of the 974, that professed their faith in Christ under their united pastorate. Still their influence upon this church and community will never die. May we who remain be not slothful but followers of them who through faith and patience inherit the promises.

We are now brought with one exception to consider a living ministry and your patience, with the time already expended require that on these I should dwell briefly and a further reason is that some of you are better acquainted with them than I am.

(To be continued.)

(*Continued from page* 149.)

MEMBERS.

[The third column on this page is the work of the RECORD. Information which will lead to the correction of any mistake, or the filling of any blank, will be thankfully received.—ED.]

Names.	*When Received.*	*When Dismissed or Died.*
Huldah Byram,	Jan. 1, 1797.	Died Oct. 18, 1860, born Nov. 19, 1779.
Ezekiel Condict,	" " "	
Abner Pierson,	" " , "	
Lot Hamilton,	" " "	
Polly Peck,	" " "	
Ruth Smith (widow),	" " "	Apr. 22, 1818, aet. 86.
Timothy Tuthill,	Mar. 5, "	Jan. 26, 1841 to 2nd P. ch. Morristown.
Joanna Tuthill, (Tim.),	" " "	" .. " " " . "
Abraham Ball,	" " "	
Lydia Hathaway,	" " "	
Chloe Pierson, (Timothy),	" " "	Jan. 29, 1816, aet. 40.
Eunice Casterline, (Jacob),	" " "	
Uzal Condict,	" " "	
Timothy Prudden,	" " "	Feb. 2nd, 1802, aet. 32.
Phebe Wood,	" " "	Oct. 29, 1820, aet. 77.
Sarah Peck,	" " "	
Phebe Freeman.	" " "	(Married Abram Ball.)
Rheuma Smith.	" " "	
Polly Ayers,	" " "	
Stephen Charlot,	" " "	
Rachel Charlot. (Stephen),	" " "	
Mary Johnson,	" " "	
David Easton,	May 13, "	
Isaac Headly,	" " "	
Lydia Baldwin, (Silas),	" " "	
Eunice Fairchild,	" " "	
Mary Bollin,	" " "	
Phebe Alwood, (John),	" " "	Jan. 27th, 1850, aet. 71.
Phebe Codnor, (Robt. N.,)	May 13, "	
Daniel Prudden,	" " "	May 22, 1817 to Ohio.
John Burnet,	" " "	Died June 6, 1857, born Mar. 7, 1778.
Joseph Prudden,	" " "	
Elizabeth Pierson,	Sept. 24, "	
Mary Armstrong,	" " i "	
Martha Aber, (Aaron),	" " "	
Jonathan Johnson,	" " "	
Eleazer Byram,	" " "	
Daniel Lindly,	" " "	May 17, 1815, aet. 52.
Benjamin Coe,	" " "	
Lewis Mills,	" " "	Jan. 26, 1841 to 2nd P. ch. Morristown.
Moses Prudden,	Jan. 9, 1798.	Diciplined, April 19, 1815.
Hannah Sutton,	" " "	
Polly Prudden, (Timo.)	Mar. 4, "	
Lydia Peck,	May 4. "	
Theodosia Halsey, (Henry),	" " "	(Rec'd from church at So. Hanover.)
John Smith, (from Colwell)	July 1, "	Apr. 23, 1855, aet. 92.
Polly Philips,	" " "	
Mary McCarl, (David),	Sept. " "	

(*To be continued.*)

(*Continued from page 150.*)

BAPTISMS.

1774.

Jan. 2. Isaac Ayres & wf., ch. Sam'l, born Oct. 29, 1773.

" 9. John Allen & wf., ch. Abigail, born Nov. 13, 1773.

" 16. Silas Howell & wf., ch. David, born Dec. 10, 1773.

" 23. Jonathan Hathaway & wf., ch. Jonathan, born Dec. 21, 1773.

Feb. 6. Seth Crowel, Jr., & wf., ch. Moses, born Jan. 1, 1774.

" " Jabez Condict & wf., ch. Ezekiel, born Dec. 20, 1773.

" " Timo. Mills, Jr. & wf., ch. Jacob, born Aug. 29, 1773.

" 20. Job. Loree & wf., ch. Josiah, born Dec. 30, 1773.

" " Matthias Burnet & wf., ch. Mary, born Dec. 22, 1773.

" 27. Abraham Talmage & wf., ch. Anne, born Jan. 13, 1774.

Mar. 13. David Fairchild & wf., ch., bap. by Mr. Horton, Mabel.

Apr. 29. John Mitchel & wf., ch. Joseph, born Jan. 22, 1774.

May 22. Abraham Canfield & wf., ch. David Sealy, born Feb. 24, 1774.

" " John Milborn & wf., ch. Abigail, born March 10th, 1774.

" " Johnathan Ford on wf's acct., ch. Charles, born April 9th, 1774.

" " Thomas Miller & wf., ch. Joseph, born April 5th, 1774.

" " John Pierson on wf's acct., ch. Esther, born Jan. 21st, 1774.

" 29. Gilbard Allen & wf., ch., baptized by Mr. Kennedy, Hannah, born March 31st, 1774.

June 5. Alexander Carmichael & wf., ch. Keturah, born March 28th, 1774.

" " Aaron Pierson & wf., children, Judith, born Sept. 22d, 1768; Ebenezer Howell, born Feb. 10th, 1771; Charlotte, born Feb. 20th, 1774.

" " James Hume & wf., ch. Adam, born March 31st, 1774.

" 19. Silas Ayres & wf., ch. Ebenezer, born May 11th, 1774.

" " Jacob Frase & wf., ch. Phebe, born May 7th, 1774.

June 26. Eleazer Lindsley & wf., ch. Micajah, born May 23rd, 1774.

July 9. David Youngs & wf., ch. Elizabeth, born May 18th, 1774.

" " Sam'l Pierson & wf., ch. Silas, born May 30th, 1774.

" 17. Elias Hedges & wf., family, Elias, born Feb. 14th, 1770; Ludlam, born Oct. 4th, 1771; David, born Nov. 24th, 1773.

Aug. 14. David Dalglish & wf., ch. Anna, born Dec. 14th, 1771.

" " David Gardiner on wf's acct., ch. Mary, born July 9th, 1774.

" 21. Cap. John Lindsley & wf., ch. Elizabeth, born July 10th, 1774.

" " Jedidiah Gregory & wf., ch. Eunice, born July 8th, 1774.

" 28. Henry Gardiner & wf., ch. Abigail born July 8th, 1774.

" " Abraham Gibbard & wf., ch. Phebe, born July 18th, 1773.

Sept. 1. Deborah Carter, adult.

" " Phebe Cooper, "

" " William Hamilton, adult.

" 18. Robert Youngs, Jun. on wf's acct., ch. Hannah, born June 2nd, 1773.

" " Jacob Arnold on wf's acct., ch. Samuel, born Aug. 8th, 1774.

" " Isaac Morris and wf., children, Jacob, born Jan. 17th, 1769; Benjamin, born Feb. 20th, 1774.

" " Ichabod Carmichael & wf., ch. Stephen, born July 24th, 1774.

" " John Prudden & wf., ch. Phebe, born Aug. 15th, 1774.

Oct. 16. David Phillips on wf's acct., ch. Catharine, born June 19th, 1774.

" 23. Isaac Pierson & wf., ch. Jacob, born Aug. 28th, 1774.

" " James Eddy on wf's acct., ch. Hannah, born Sept. 20th, 1774.

" " John Redman & wf., ch. Barnabas, born Sept. 25th, 1774.

" 30. Josiah Broadwell & wf., ch. Josiah, born Sept. 14th, 1774.

Nov. 4. David Hoppen, family, Jeremiah, born Aug. 9th, 1764; Stephen, " Feb. 25th, 1766; Ezekiel, " Feb. 6th, 1768; Ananias, " Apr. 6th, 1770; Moses, born Oct. 6th, 1773.

(*To be continued.*)

(Continued from page 151.)

BILL OF MORTALITY.

1793.

Feb. 15. Experience Pierson,* consumption, aet. 48.

Mar. 12. Rolfe, son of widow Hannah Ayres, Colic, aet. 12.

" 18. Samuel Minton, consumption, aet. 37.

Apr. 2. Nathan, son of Joseph Guering, scarlet-fever, aet. 6.

" 3. Thomas Kinney, Esq., gout in his breast, aet. 62.

May 7. Moses Lindsley,* consumption, aet. 59.

" 10. Cyrus Maxson, son of Stout Benjamin, scarlet-fever, aet. 3.

" 12. Sarah, servant of Alex. Carmichael, Esq, consumption, aet 14.

" 17. Cornelia, daughter of Abraham T. Schenck, scarlet fever, aet. 5.

June. 4. Abigail, widow of John Johnson,* sudden, aet. 85.

" 11. Joanna, daughter of Abraham T. Schenck, scarlet fever, aet. 2.

" 15. Doctor Abraham Howell, consumption, aet. 22.

" 16. Child of James Stiles, sudden.

July 1. Hannah, daughter of Capt. Ezra Brown, consumption, aet. 15.

" 12. Daniel, son of Nathaniel Mathers, putrid fever, aet. 11.

" 17. Hannah, widow of Phinehas Ayres, consumption, aet. 45.

" 22. Abigail, widow of Thomas Troup, dropsy, aet. 60.

" 27. Child of Thomas Jenkins, fits.

" 31. Marcia, daughter of Silas Condict, Jun., scarlet fever.

Aug. 4. Child of Vincent Guering.

" 22. Abby, daughter of Jacob Conger, consumption, aet. 6.

" 29. Sarah, widow of Daniel Freeman, dysentery, aet. 71.

Sept.10. Sarah Tuthill, daughter of Rodolphus Kent, scarlet fever, aet. 6.

" " An illegitimate child.

" 13. Stephen Pierson, decay, aet. 57.

" 15. David Douglas,* consumption, aet. 48.

Oct. 1. William, son of Stephen Charlotte, decay, aet. 2.

" " Cato, servant of Peter Prudden, billious fever, aet. 19.

Oct. 16. Charles, son of Joshua Munson, fever, aet. 4.

Nov. 2. Child of Jonathan Dickerson, fits.

" 3. Eleazer, son of James Miller, consumption, aet. 35.

" 16. Nathaniel Peck, son of Stephen Turner, scald, aet. 7.

" 28. Margaret, wife of Thomas Cody, dropsy, aet. 22.

Dec. 9. Robert Arnold, lingering decay, aet. 73.

" 31. Servant child of Doct. Abraham Canfield, aet. 1.

1794.

Jan. 3. A child of Anthony Cazatt.

" 9. Silas Armstrong, a hurt and fever, aet. 23.

" 27. Ephraim Youngs,* drowned, aet. 44.

Feb. 4. Mattaniah Lyon,* decay, aet. 60.

" 10. Cyrus, son of Samuel Mills, Jun., third day ague.

" 15. Joseph, son of James Swift, dropsy, aet. 13.

" 17. Hannah Pierson, consumption, aet. 65.

Mar. 3. Jane, widow of John Hodges, old age, aet. 90.

Apr. 12. A child of Caleb Russell, Esq.

" 25. George Badgley, colic, 68.

" " A Child of Isaac Noe,† aet. 2.

May 11. A child of Zebulon Sutten,† aet. 2.

" 24. Mary, wife of John Bryan, consumption, aet. 27.

June 1. Richard Crooks, drowned, aet. 32.

" " A child of James Stiles, fits.

" 7. Isaac Ayres,* consumption, aet. 51.

" 13. Eliza Ann, daughter of Daniel Pierson, dysentery, aet. 1.

July 5. Widow of Thomas Coe, fever, aet. 69.

" " Jane, servant of Alexander Carmichael, Esq., consumption, aet. 8.

" 9. Benjamin, son of Benjamin Pierson, dysentery.

" 29. Peggy, daughter of Jep. a black man, dysentery, aet. 6.

Aug. 12. A child of Henry Badgley, dysentery.

" 19. Silas, son of James Ford, dysentery, aet. 4.

" 22. Jane, widow of Samuel Rolfe, old age, aet. 83.

(To be continued.)

(Continued from page 152.)
TRUSTEES' BOOK.

At a meeting of the congregation of the first presbyterian Church of Morris-Town for the purpose of determining whether they should give Mr. James Richards a call to become the pasture of this parrish, or to invite him to preach here a longer time upon tryal, and also for the purpose of entering into some resolution respecting the compleating the new meeting house, and for other purposes held July 21st, 1794.

After singing a psalm and prayer by Deacon Alling, the congregation appointed as moderator Deacon Alling; Tobias Bodinot & Mahlon Dickerson, Clerk.

It being moved a pole should be taken in voting for Mr. Richards, a pole was accordingly taken by which it was agreed that a call should be preferred to him to become the pasture of this parish, one hundred and forty-two votes being taken for the call and two for inviting him to preach here a longer time upon tryal. Voted that presbytery be requested to write to the congregation of Sagg harbour on Long Island to solicit them to relinquish a part of the time which Mr. Richards is engaged to them, in order that he may return the sooner to this place.

Voted that the sum of four hundred and forty dollars a year be paid to Mr. Richards in regular quarterly payments, that he have the use of the Parsonage, belonging to this Parish (except a small part planted with a nursery of mulberry trees before Col. De-Hart's door) and to be found fire wood so soon as he shall keep house, while he shall continue to do the duty of a preacher of this congregation.

Voted that Mr. Richards be supported in this congregation by a tax to be raised by an obligation for that purpose in the words following, viz:

Whereas on the 21st day of July, 1794, at a Parish meeting of the first presbyterian Church and congregation in Morris-Town duly noticed for that purpose, it was voted that a call be prefered to Mr. James Richards to take on him the pastoral charge of the said Church and congregation, and that as a compensation during the time, that he continue to do the duties of his office as a minister or pasture to the said congregation he shall be paid at the rate of four hundred and forty dollars per annum in quarterly payments, with the use of the parsonage lands near the meeting house, excepting the small lot that contains the nursery of mulberry trees, and it being also voted that the said sallary should be raised and levied by the parishioners by way of tax as the law directs the state taxes to be raised, excepting that four assistants or supervisors annually chosen to assist the assessor whose duty it shall be to make such abatements on the tax of individuals as to them shall seem just and equitable in consideration of their being in debt or any particular misfortune or embarrassment of circumstances.

Therefore we the subscribers sensible of the general utility and importance to ourselves and posterity of supporting the Gospel and being desirous that unanimity may subsist, and that the burden of such support may be borne as equitable as possible and hoping jointly to participate in the blessings and advantages of the gospel ministry, do hereby bind ourselves to pay the sums that shall be assessed and levied upon us annually to the said Mr. James Richards or to such person or persons as shall be appointed to collect the same, to commence from the time Mr. Richards shall return to supply the said congregation, and to be paid quarter yearly during the time he shall continue to do the duties of a minister to them, and we continue members of the said congregation, or until this mode of payment shall be revoked or altered by a majority of the said parishioners, provided that any subscribers may within three months after the expiration of any year erase his name by applying to the Clerk of the Trustees, whose duty it shall be to keep this obligation. In witness whereof we have hereunto subscribed our names this 22d day of July, 1794.

(To be continued.)

NOTE FROM A MS. OF THE REV. JOSEPH F. TUTTLE, D.D.—Rev. Baker Johnson some years ago conversed with a Mr. Shipman (father of lawyer S. of Belvidere) whose father aided in building the first house in Morristown, somewhere on the stream. It was in 1727 as Mr. J. thinks Mr. S. stated. This was the same year that Hackett put up the first house in Hackettstown.

THE RECORD.

FIRST PRESBYTERIAN CHURCH, MORRISTOWN, N. J.

"This shall be Written for the Generation to Come."—Psalms 102 : 18.

VOL. II.   SEPTEMBER, 1881.   NO. 9.

(Printed with the approval of Session.)

THE RECORD

Will be printed and published monthly at Morristown, N. J. Terms, 50 cents per annum in advance; 75 cents after June.

Subscriptions will be received at the book-stores of Messrs. Runyon and Emmell, or through the mail. All communications should be addressed to the

EDITOR OF THE RECORD,

Lock box 44.   Morristown, N. J.

Vol. I, complete, 75 cents.

Entered at the Post Office at Morristown, N. J., as second class matter.

——:o:——

(*Continued from page 156.*)

HISTORICAL SERMON—No. 2.

By REV. DAVID IRVING, D.D.

Hitherto there has been a short period between the removal of one pastor and the calling of another, but from the time of Mr. McDowell's dismissal to the settlement of his successor was a period of 14 months. Mr. Barnes, receiving a call Nov. 29, 1824, was ordained and installed Feb. 8, 1825, by the Presbytery of Elizabethtown, then but recently organized, being a part of the old Presbytery of Jersey. In the interval Rev. W. J. Hamilton's services had been sought by the congregation, who were anxious to "hire" him for two years, which he declined and soon after he became the successor of Dr. Richards, of Newark. Then the Rev. Darius O. Griswold was called which call he accepted and afterwards declined. But the church was not wholly vacant it being supplied by Prof. Bush for several months and who was the means of introducing the Rev. Albert Barnes to the congregation. This was Mr. B.'s first charge, and to his Master's work here he consecrated all his powers. His sermons were close, pungent, discriminating and pointed, making no compromises with sin and fearlessly uttered. There was a practicalness about many of them that met the inquiries of the timid and doubting whose cases he would gather up in their interviews with him, con over in his study, and from the pulpit, the minister's throne, would he utter truths suited to their individual wants. He would also lay bare the hypocrisy and sins of many, who individually felt that he was the man of whom the preacher was speaking. One of the self-convicted ones came to him with the inquiry who had been speaking to him about her, and then indignantly repelling the charge by saying, "she would not have cared if they had told the truth."

The greatest commotion was excited in the early part of his ministry by his decided and unflinching course on Temperance. That great work was beginning to occupy the thoughts of many. Here he found drinking customs in vogue, and distilleries dotted all over the parish. Few places needed reforming more, said Dr. Fisher in a Fast Day sermon preached in 1812, "In the guilt of this loathsome vice intemperance, this congregation is deeply involved for such is its awful prevalence in some of our borders that if the destroying angel were to pass over, for the purpose of separating the infected from the sound we have reason to fear that very few would escape," and then in a foot note says this is peculiarly applicable to a distant limb of the congregation. Mr. Barnes found with the limits of his pastoral charge 19 places where ardent spirits were made and 20 where they were sold. To arrest the evils that are ever associated with this vice and remove if possible the curse from the community he early called the attention of his people to the subject by a series of sermons in which he appealed to their reason, conscience and religion, and sought to lead them to an abandonment of social drinking usages, and of the places where intoxicating drinks were manufactured and sold. Some engaged in the traffic were first indignant at his interference and radical measures, and after listening to his discourse, determined never again to be present to listen to another, but at the time for the delivery of the next sermon they were in their places anxious to hear what he would say, and at last so convinced were they of the injury that they were doing to the morals of the place and the happiness of families that soon 17 of the distilleries were closed, and not long after his departure the fires of the other two went out. One has, however, lately been commenced in a neighborhood that suffered formerly very much from intemperance, but it is not under my pastoral charge, still I hope that it will soon be converted into something more meet for man's wants and those of the community.

Here also was commenced that system of early rising and literary labor, resulting in good to the church and pecuniary benefit to the author, and that has been kept up with but little intermission ever since. Sabbath Schools demanded not only a new kind of literature, but of comments upon the Word of God. To meet the want with reference to the latter Mr. Barnes commenced the preparation of a commentary on the Gospels which at once became popular, and which has been followed by several others upon different portions of the Word of God. These studies were a great aid to his pulpit ministrations, and were regarded by him as a side work, occupying his time from 4 till 9 A. M. These publications are all of a popular cast.

Here also was preached and published the sermon called "The Way of Salvation," which was greatly instrumental in his being called to the First Church of Philadelphia, and which from its statements in regard to certain doctrines led to discussion, opposition, censure, trial and a temporary suspension of his ministerial duties.

When Mr. Barnes came to Morristown there was only one other church in this region the Baptist, organized in 1752, but which had frequently to struggle for an existence, not having attained to the strength

that it now possesses. In 1826 the Methodist church was organized which soon advanced with great rapidity and has made its impress upon a large portion of this community. Its first edifice was built in 1827, and the present structure in 1841. (In the great revival of 1827-8 over 200 joined the society on probation.) According to last report it has 310 members, 40 probationers and a property worth $16,000. Besides this two other churches of this connection have sprung up at Green Village and New Vernon with a joint membership of 80 and 33 probationers.

In Jan. 1, 1827 the Episcopalians were organized into a church which took the name of St. Peter's. This edifice was consecrated in 1828, and its first Rector was the Rev. Benjamin Holmes. It was recently enlarged and improved under its present Rector and contains at present a membership of 112. An offshoot from this afterwards took place owing to certain theological tendencies on the part of its minister, which was organized into the Church of the Redeemer and contains a membership of 41.

During Mr. Barnes' ministry this building was crowded every pew being taken and from the great revival which occurred while he was here and to which on a former occasion I have fully alluded, the church was greatly strengthened. It was more powerful and extensive than any that has ever occurred in the history of this place, and then as in the revival under McDowell this church reached a membership that it has never possessed since and never will again, owing to the number of churches covering the territory then occupied solely by it.

Mr. Barnes' power while here lay in the pulpit and not in social and pastoral visiting, and in this he differed from the former pastors. His pulpit ability, ministerial faithfulness and success directed the attention of other churches to him, so that a committee from the First Church of Philadelphia, came to hear him; the sermon to which I have alluded, was circulated in that congregation and as a result a call was in due time extended to him. When that call came before the Presbytery of Philadelphia it was resisted by some on the ground of his sermon containing doctrinal errors, this was overruled and the commissioners allowed to prosecute the call. Mr. Barnes' removal was opposed strongly by the whole congregation before the Presbytery, but believing it to be his duty to resign his charge, the congregation gave way, and at a second meeting of the Presbytery June 8, 1830, Mr. Barnes' was dismissed to the Presbytery of Philadelphia. The occurrences before that body, the Synod of Philadelphia and the General Assembly in connection with the sermon "the Way of Salvation" are matters of history and do not belong to the history of this church. The sermon as here delivered, was designed says the author to bring together the leading doctrines of the Bible respecting God's way of saving men, "And is an outline of the way of salvation by the gospel." By a singular oversight the great doctrine of justification of faith is not alluded to in this "way," while there are to say the least unguarded expressions respecting other doctrines that were sufficient to provoke controversy and awaken suspicions on the part of a strong portion of the church who clung to old measures and a distinctive and well understood phraseology.

No man has left his impress upon this congregation more than Mr. Barnes, he came here in his youthful vigor, and God largely owned his labors, and few ministers have had a more attached people, who loved him for his excellencies, revered him for his piety and have followed his after life with undeviating interest. 296 were admitted to the church, of these 228 were on profession and 68 by certificate. On Oct. 1, 1826 Timothy Tucker, William Enslee, Geo. K. Drake, Frederic King, Jonathan Thompson and Jonathan Oliver were ordained elders, then the session consisted of 14.

There was after Mr. Barnes' removal, a long interval before another pastor was settled; one and another had been listened to as candidates, but no pastor was obtained till Dec. 26, 1831, when the Rev. Mr. Hoover was called. He commenced his labors Jan. 20, and was installed pastor Feb. 8, 1832. In the performance of his duties he had the sympathy of his people and God did not leave himself without a witness among them. Several were added to the communion during the first year of his ministry and in the Spring of the ensuing year a greater interest in divine things was manifested on

Morris Plains, Christians there were revived, prayer was more earnest, and on the labors of the pastor in that district God poured out his Spirit. Several were awakened and brought to Jesus. The school house was crowded and many could not gain admittance. When the work was seemingly arrested a day of fasting and prayer was appointed which gave a new stimulus to the interest and those who were halting and doubting soon gave decided evidence of conversion. The opposition of the infidel gave way and he acknowledged Jesus to be his hope and Saviour, and the youth fled for refuge to the same deliverer and rejoiced in the tokens of redeeming love. Some of these have done a good work in that neighborhood. Other sections that had scarcely been moved were visited with God's gracious smiles the latter part of the following Winter and Spring. Before this the church was in a cold state. Worldly conformity was seen, and earnest, living piety was lacking. This the pastor and a few others saw and lamented, it was brought before the session and the church, when special meetings for prayers and special visitation were determined on. The parish was districted and 34 directors were appointed, who went two and two. This was blessed to some and soon signs of awakening were seen, and a succession of religious services were commenced in the month of February, in which he was assisted by neighboring pastors and which continued for some time. In Reed and Matthesoa's visit to the American churches we have the following minute with reference to this place. "In the morning, says Mr. R., I worshipped at the Presbyterian church. The avenues and green were animated by the little groups hastening to the house of God. Some 60 light wagons stood about the green and church fence which had already delivered their charge. The people were all before the time. The exercises were well and piously conducted. Mr. Hoover read his sermon, but he read it with tears. It was on the duty of parents to their children and made a good impression. It was adapted to this end, for it was excellent in composition and, in feeling. The people did not show much interest in the singing nor all the interest in the prayer which I expected, but on the whole it was perhaps the best time of both pastor and people, for they were still surrounded by the effects and influence of a revival which had lasted most of the winter." As the fruits of this gracious refreshing 52 were added during the year 1834. Of this work Mr. H., says, "the very air seemed laden with awful influence. It seemed to me as if some mighty presence hung down from heaven penetrating all, oppressing all, and I was often afraid to move or speak lest I should say or do something wrong." This church was at the time the largest in the State of New Jersey according to its report to the General Assembly.

On June 26, 1833, Mr. Hoover assisted in the organization of a church at New Vernon, drawn mainly from this society, 30 were dismissed that year from this church and several during the next two years. That enterprise received material aid in the erection of their building, from this church. On March 1, 1836, the pastor sent to a parish meeting a letter giving reasons why he wished a dissolution of the pastoral relation. These were such as to induce the congregation to accede to his proposal, but from their regard for him they continued his salary some time longer. On Sept. 9, 1832, Stephen A. Prudden, Jonathan D. Marvin, John B. Johnes, John R. Freeman, Jonathan Pierson, Sylvester Whitehead and John W. Cortelyou were added to the bench of elders. On April 7, 1836, John B. Johnes and Jonathan Thompson resigned their seats in the Session. The funds of the church were reduced at this time to $2,000, besides certain real estate, the principal having been used, with the interest to meet as the occasion demanded the deficiency upon the pews. At the meeting in which this statement was made, it was also unanimously decided to make the salary $1,200 for reasons forcibly presented in a written report to the parish.

A call was presented to the Rev. James W. Adams, of Syracuse which he declined, and on Dec. 19, 1836, the same was extended to Rev. O. L. Kirtland which he accepted and entered on his labors Jan. 13, 1837, and was installed by the Presbytery of Elizabethtown, March 23, 1837. This year a corrected list of members was made and the number found to be in actual communion at that time and reported to the next Assembly was 453. The year 1837 was one of vital moment to the Presbyterian church. The acts of the assembly were to be approved or condemned according to the standpoint taken in regard to them, as at that meeting "the plan of union" was repealed and certain Synods exscinded. This led in the following year to a division of the church at large into two bodies, both claiming the same name and rights. On that year the representatives of our Presbytery adhered to the Old School. The Synod of New Jersey met that fall in this church and did the same, though the Presbyteries of Newark and Montrose cast in their lot with the New School. The decision of Presbytery and Synod caused this church to remain in connection with the Old School though there was naturally much sympathy with those who became identified with the measures and acts of the other portion in which were Richards, Fisher and Barnes the former leaders of this pulpit.

During the latter part of Mr. Kirtland's pastorate another division took place that had a more immediate bearing upon the interests of the town and church. Owing to causes to which I need not here allude, a portion of the congregation felt it to be their duty to withdraw and erect a second church, and the present tasteful edifice in South street is an evidence of the spirit by which they were swayed. Party feeling ran high and much was said and done that was neither for the glory of God nor the honor of religion. Amidst the excitement attending upon such a measure two things are at present matters of rejoicing, the one that the house was built and the church organized, the other that the bitterness of feeling has been removed and something truer and nobler is reigning. The present pastors are strangers to all that then occurred; and whilst I can speak of the unanimity and cordiality that has ever existed on our part, I can also testify to the good feeling on the part of my flock towards those who thus felt it a duty to go out and build.

(To be continued.)

(*Continued from page* 157.)

MEMBERS.

[The third column on this page is the work of the RECORD. Information which will lead to the correction of any mistake, or the filling of any blank, will be thankfully received.—ED.]

Names.	When Received.	When Dismissed or Died.
Mehetabel Condict (Ebenezer,) .	1799.	
Nathaniel Littell, .	"	(Rec'd from New Providence.)
—— Littell, (Nathaniel), .	"	" "
Ebenezer Fairchild, . .	May 4, 1800.	(Rec'd from Mendham.)
Phebe Fairchild (Ebenezer), .	" " "	" . "
Theodocia Ford, (wid. of Jacob, Jr.,		[13, 1741.
dau.of Rev.Timothy Johnes,D.D.) " " "		Died Aug. 31, 1824, born Sept.
Simeon Cory, . . .	Oct. 30, "	June 25, 1847, aet. 73.
Elizabeth Holbert, . .	June 1801.	
Isaac Hinds, . . .	Oct. 30, "	Dis. March 4, 1814 to Rockaway.
Martha Hinds (Isaac), .	" " "	" " " died
		[Feb. 13, 1835, aet. 69.
Abraham Hedges, . .	Mar. 7, 1802.	Died Sept. 27, 1830, born July 7,
		[1768, at Bridgehampton, L. I.
Phebe Hedges (Abraham) .	" " "	Died Mar. 18,1830, born Dec.11,1768.
Susanna W. Riggs, . .	July 11, "	Dis. Dec. 26, 1810, Md. Wm. F.
Rachel Dady, (widow), .	Sept. 6, "	[Lazzalere.
Kezia Sexton (Jesse), . .	" " "	Aug. 3, 1832, aet. 71.
Hannah Lindsley, (Stephen)	" " "	March 11, 1809, aet. 44.
Phebe Mills, (Samuel) . .	" " "	June 2. 1837, aet. 76.
Zophar Freeman, Jr., .	" " "	Dis. Aug. 26, 1825 to Chatham.
Briant Swain, . . .	Nov. 27, "	
Mary Freeman (Zophar, Jr.)	" " "	Dis. Aug. 26, 1825 to Chatham.
Mahlon Johnson, . . .	Feb. 25, 1803.	Dec. 20, 1857, aet. 82 y. 1 m. and 15 d.
Sally Johnson (Mahlon), .	Mar. 14, "	(Rec'd from Parsippany.)
Sarah Tuthill (Ebenezer), .	Apr. 29, "	" Chester.
Eunice Johnson, . .	July 3, "	
Sarah O'Conner, . .	" " "	
Elizabeth Enslee, . .	" " "	
Phebe Turner (Stephen), .	" " "	Nov. 6, 1848, aet. 84.
Sally Ferris, . . .	" " "	Dis. Jan. 26, 1841 to 2d P. ch. Mor-
Sarah Stiles, (Silas), . .	Sept. 4, "	[ristown.
Eunice Canfield (Jacob), .	" " "	March 3, 1810, aet. 44.
Mary Day (John), . . .	" " "	April 7, 1818, aet. 68, [York.
Nancy Guerin, (Jonas,) .	" " "	Dis. Nov. 2, 1813 to Western New
Sara Enslee, . . .	" " "	Aug. 26, 1825 to Westfield, died
		[Oct. 20, 1849, aet. 79.
Samuel Arnold (son of John), .	" " "	Died Jan. 18, 1832.
Elizabeth Taylor (Isaac), .	" " "	
Zilpah Jackson, . . .	" " "	Dis. March 4, 1814 to 1st ch. Newark
Elizabeth Cutler (Joseph), .	" " "	Died Jan. 27, 1846, born Dec. 9, 1782.
Matsy Condict (Lewis) .	" " "	
Mary Garrigus, . . .	" " "	
Anna Enslee, . . .	" " "	July 17, 1806, aet. 37.
Abigail Talmadge (Abraham), .	" " "	

(*To be continued.*)

(Continued from page 158.)

BAPTISMS.

1774.

Nov. 4. Deborah, the wife of Gabriel Wright on her acct., had her family baptised, Jonathan, born Nov. 13, 1766; Sarah, born Jan 15th, 1770: David, born March 31, 1772; Anna, born April 5, 1774.

" 6. Nathaniel L'homedau & wf., ch. Mary, born Sept. 11, 1774.

" " Moses Johnson & wf., ch. Timothy, born Sept. 7, 1774.

" " James Miller & wf., ch. Jane, born Sept. 3, 1774.

" " Calvin Extell & wf., ch. Anne, born Sept. 29, 1774.

" 27. Philip Lindsley & wf., ch. Mary, born Oct. 16, 1774.

Dec. 18. Joseph Riggs & wf., ch. Cyrus, born Oct. 15, 1774.

" 27. David Garrigus & wf., ch. Sarah, born April 21, 1774.

1775.

Jan. 10. Ezek. Crane, adult.

" " Ezek. Crane & wf., ch. Shadrack born May 24, 1773.

" " Samuel Baldwin & wf., family, Phebe, born Sept. 25, 1768; Silas, born March 3, 1771; Bethuel, born Aug. 18, 1774.

" 15. Zenas Condict & wf., ch. Samuel, born Nov. 6, 1774.

" " Daniel Smith & wf., ch. David, born Oct. 17, 1774.

Feb. 5. Peter Norris & wf., ch. Abraham, born Nov. 20, 1774.

" 19. Moses Lindsley & wf., ch. Matthew, born Jan. 10, 1775.

Mar. 2. Laban Ward & wf., family, Ebenezer, born July 31, 1756; Joshua, " Dec. 27, 1758; Elizabeth, " Sept. 21, 1763; Matthias Hoppen, born April 30, 1766.

" " Ephraim Youngs & wf., ch. ———— born Nov. 28, 1774.

" " Bloom, servant of Peter Prudden, adult.

" " Peter Prudden & wf., with yr. servant Bloom, her child Cato, born Dec. 18, 1774.

" 12. Lindsley Burnet & wf., ch. Phebe, born Nov. 21, 1774.

Mar. 12. Ezekiel Day & wf., ch. John, born Jan. 15, 1775.

" 19. Richard Johnson & wf., ch. Eunice, born Jan. 23, 1775.

" 26. Joshua Winget & wf., ch. Anne, born Jan. 24, 1775.

Apr. 2. Joseph Lewis & wf., ch. John Le-Conte, born March 5, 1775.

" 6. Nathan Reeve, two chn. bap. at his own house, Phebe, born Sept. 6, 1772; Nathan, born Dec. 16, 1773.

" " Nathan Reeve, at the same time 2 negro chn. James, born June 25, 1772; Zuba, born Aug. 22, 1774.

" 18. John Hunt on wf. Mary's acct., ch. Mary, born April 11, 1775.

" 23. Usual Coe & wf., ch. Asa, born Jan. 25, 1775.

" " Benj. Pierson, Senr. & wf., negro ch. Lucas, born March 25, 1775.

" " Isaac Prudden & wf., ch. Isaac, born April 4, 1775.

May 4. Jonathan Ogden & wf., ch. Elizabeth, born Jan. 3, 1775.

" " Samuel Freman & wf., Mary, born Sept. 10, 1774.

" " Jesse Smith & wf., ch. bap., adult Eunice & yr. ch. Nathaniel, born Jan. 26, 1775.

" " Barnabus Evens, adult.

" 7. Moses Munson & wf., ch. Martha, born March, 1775.

" 14. James Keen & wf., ch. Mary, born April 17, 1775.

" 28. Abraham Gilbard, ch. Joanna, born April 25, 1775.

" " John Hathaway & wf., ch. Calvin, born May 1, 1775.

" " Joseph Bears & wf., ch. Simeon Hathaway, born May 2, 1775.

" " Hezekiah Stebbins on wf's acct., ch. Susanna, born Jan. 17, 1775.

" 4. Col. Jacob Ford, Jun. & wf., ch. Phebe, born May 3, 1775.

" " Jonathan Tichenor & wf., ch. Sarah, born April 26, 1775.

Jun. 11. Jonathan Rainer & wf., ch. Cyrenius, born May 18, 1775.

" 18. Howel Orsborn & wf., ch. Jonathan, born April 25, 1775.

" " Ebenezer Coe & wf., ch. Phebe, born May 8, 1775.

(To be continued.)

(Continued from page 159.)

BILL OF MORTALITY,

1794.

Aug. 23. Rebeckah, widow of Matthew Fairchild, dysentery, aet. 73.

" " Hannah, daughter of Maj. Lemuel Minton,† dysentery.

" 26. Josiah, son of Simeon Broadwell, Esq., dysentery; aet. 2.

" 30. Isaac Garrigues, fever, aet. 31.

Sept. 2. William Morgan, decay, aet. 40.

" 9. William, son of William Meeker, fever, aet. 10.

" 17. Rev. Timothy Johnes, D. D.* dysentery, aet. 78.

" 21. Daniel, son of Ezekiel Howell,† dysentery, aet. 4.

" 24. Rachel, wife of Henry Gardner, consumption, aet. 64.

" 28. Jesse, son of John Enslee, decay.

Oct. 9. Thomas Lee, son of widow Youngs, scarlet fever, aet. 1.

" " Jacob, son of Aaron Goble,† dysentery, aet. 9.

" 14. Doct. Jonathan Cheever, consumption, aet. 50.

" 18. Sarah, daughter of Edward Carey, dysentery, aet. 21.

" 21. Amzi, son of Jeduthun Day, fever, aet. 7.

Nov. 2. Kezia, Widow of the Rev. Doct, Johnes,* decay, aet. 79.

" 4. A child of Jonathan Dickerson.

Dec. 1. Samuel Loree, sudden, aet. 36.

" 9. Widow Squire,†* old age, aet. 81.

" 23. Julia, wife of Silas Dickerson, dropsy, aet. 22.

" 26. Sarah, wife of Joseph Shipman, burn, aet. 37.

" 30. Robert Clark, dropsy, aet. 57.

1795.

Jan. 2. Reuben Gildersleve, decay, aet. 66.

" 11. A child of John Casterline,

" 12. Mehitable, wife of Thomas Tuttle,* consumption, aet. 62.

" 21. A child of Aaron Whitehead, fits.

Feb. 5. Uriah Cutler,* fever, aet. 86.

" 6. Elizabeth, daughter of Abraham Willis, inflammatory fever, aet. 11

" 24. David, son of Capt. Silas Howell, consumption, aet. 21.

" 26. Elijah Pierson, dropsy, aet. 66.

" 27. A child of Moses Crane,

Mar. 5. Christopher Lindenor, fever, 89.

" 11. Major Lemuel Minton,† fever, aet. 38.

" 22. Anna, widow of David Ogden,* fever, aet. 77.

" 25. Jeduthun, son of Silas Allen, white swelling.

Apr. 26. Sally, wife of Daniel Guerin, consumption, aet. 26.

" 29. Servant child of Silas Condict, Jun., rickets, aet. 1.

May 8. Henry, son of William Kirk, fever, aet. 5.

" 10. Anna, wife of Samuel Crowel,†* putrid fever, aet. 27.

" 13. A child of John Green.

" 26. Thomas Jones, pleurisy, aet. 36.

" " Lydia, widow of John Howard, palsy, aet. 70.

" 24. Sally, daughter of George Noble, died in liquor, aet. 7.

June 4. Charity, wife of Aaron Goble,* consumption, aet. 44.

" 11. John Brookfield, Esq.,†* apoplexy, aet. 80.

" 14. Charity, daughter of John Enslee, decay, aet. 1.

July 14. Jane, widow of Thomas Guering, old age, aet. 85.

" " Nathan, son of Whitehead Guering, scarlet fever, aet. 1.

" 18. Elizabeth, wife of Samuel Roberts,* asthma, aet. 71.

" 29. Child of James Chidester, aet. 2.

Aug. 6. Samuel, son of Isaac Prudden, dysentery, aet. 4.

" " Jeduthun, son of John Crowell, dysentery, aet. 16.

" 6. Servant girl of Elijah Pierson, consumption.

" 22. Phœbe, wife of Edward Mills, dysentery, aet. 37.

" 31. Child of Joseph Ludlow.

Sept. 4. Sarah, daughter of Silas Lindsley, worms, aet. 1.

" 7. Charles, son of Zenas Lindsley, dysentery.

" " Servant child of Silas Condict, Jun., hives, aet. 3.

" 19. Abigail, daughter of Isaac Garrigues, consumption, aet. 1.

" 21. Hannah, daughter of Ichabod Cooper, dysentery, aet. 3.

(To be continued.)

(Continued from page 100.)

TRUSTEES' BOOK.

Voted that Deacon Joseph Pruden and Mr. Jonas Philops be a committee to wait upon Mr. Richards this evening, and inform him of the resolutions of this society respecting him.

Voted that the Elders & Trustees sign the call in behalf of the Congregation to be given to Mr. Richards.

Voted that Messrs. Joseph Lewis, Jonas Stiles, Jonas Philops & Lindley Burnet be directed to circulate the obligation for raising the sallery of Mr. Richards & also the subscription for raising money to finish the new meeting house.

Voted that the obligation dated the 28th of March, 1794, for the support of the ministry be null and void.

Voted that the managers of the new meeting house be directed to procede to the plastering, glazing and puting in seats this season—& that Silas Condit, Esq., Mr. Benja. Lindsley, Mr. Jos. Lewis, Dr. Johnes, Mr. Richard Johnson, Mr. George Tucker, Major Kinney, Mr. Jonathan Ogden & Caleb Russell, Esq., be a committee to confer with the managers respecting the same.

Oct. 21, 1794. At Mr. Crain's house. Present, the President, Mr. Lindley, Mr. Mills, Mr. Johnson, Mr. Ogden & Mr. Pierson.

Voted that Mr. Mills be directed to call on the delinquents of Mr. Collin's sallery or tax & request them to confess Judgment, in case of refusal to prosecute for the same.

Nov. 19, 1794. Parish meeting. Allex'r Carmichal, Esqr., was chosen Moderator & Jonathan Ogden, Clerk.

Voted Mr. Thomas Miller be appointed to make the tax for Mr. Richard's sallery the present year.

Voted that Jonathan Stiles, Esqr., Lindsley Burnet, Jonas Philops & Allex'r. Carmical, Esqr., be appointed supervisors agreeably to the obligation for raising & levying Mr. Richard's sallery.

Voted Mr. Richard Johnson be appointed to circulate thoughroughly through the Congregation the obligation & receive seven shilling per day for his services from the Trustees.

Voted Messrs. Joseph Lewis, Jonathan

Stiles, Jonas Philops, Esqr., Ezra Halsey & Lindley Burnet be appointed collectors of Mr. Richard's sallery.

Voted that Mr. Lewis, Mr. Lindsley, Mr. Mills be appointed to attend the vendue for furnishing materials for the new meeting house, vendue this day two weeks at the Court House, 2 o'clock P. M.

Jan. 5, 1795. Voted that a vendue to sell the Mulberry Nursery be held on the premacies on the first day of April next. (The following were purchasers: Geo. O'Hara, Seley Campfield, Johnathan Ford, Dr. Jabez Campfield, William Jones, Silas Condit, Esqr., Henry Howell, Ebenezer Stiles, Aaron Pierson, John Veal, Benj. Lindley, Benj. Pierson, Jos. Lewis, Esqr., John Mills, Nathaniel Bull, Gilbert Alling, Joseph Beers, Isaac Wolley, Jos. Johnson. The amount realized was $37.99.)

April 1, 1795. Ordered that William Cherry be directed to take charge of the parsonage lot & to inform those who owns swine that gits into sd. lot to keep them out or ring and yoke them, in case of noncomplyance that he kill them after 'notis if they again trespass, & that he proceed according to law, that he pound horses or cattle in case they treepass contrary to law.

April 8, 1795. Parish meeting. Deacon Alling, Moderator; Israel Canfield, Clerk.

Voted that Benjamin Holloway be appointed to call on the parishoners with the subscription for the new meeting house, and inform the people that unless a sum sufficient be previously signed, the parrish propose at the next parish meeting to direct the managers to finish the house & sell the seats to reimburse themselves, & that the parrish meet for that purpose on Wednesday, two weeks from this 8th day of April, 1795.

(To be continued.)

THE RECORD.

. FIRST PRESBYTERIAN CHURCH, MORRISTOWN, N. J.

"This shall be Written for the Generation to Come."—Psalms 102 : 18.

| VOL. II. | OCTOBER, 1881. | NO. 10 |

(Printed with the approval of Session.)

THE RECORD

. Will be printed and published monthly at Morristown, N. J. Terms, 50 cents per annum in advance; 75 cents after June.

Subscriptions will be received at the book-stores of Messrs. Runyon and Emmell, or through the mail. All communications should be addressed to the

EDITOR OF THE RECORD,

Lock box 44.   Morristown, N. J.

Vol. I. complete, 75 cents.

Entered at the Post Office at Morristown, N. J., as second.class matter.

——:o:——

(Continued from page 164.)

HISTORICAL SERMON—No. 2.

By REV. DAVID IRVING, D.D.

We are brethren possessing the same name, the same faith and belonging to the same great family, and as such should labor for the same end in harmony and in love. It has been to me a matter of regret that the church did not divide before. Besides, Morris township was larger in population in 1810 than in 1830, the church was much larger in regard to attendance and in membership in 1820 than in 1840, and everything demanded that a new enterprise should be started. Had the spirit that reared this building been manifested in church extension in later times, Presbyterianism would be much more influential in the community than it now is, but self more than God's glory kept together a large hive, so that when God saw that they would not swarm he permitted another spirit to enter and thus drive them apart. For the result we thank God. Mr. K. went out with the colony, when those that remained called the Rev. A. H. Dumont, D. D., which call he accepted and was installed January 17, 1841. His ministry was exercised under trying circumstances. There was much excitement in the community, the congregation was greatly reduced, pew rents were inadequate to meet the expenditures, and a few had liberally to meet the deficiencies, but it was done, a large salary was given, the church building thoroughly repaired, and other large sums contributed that at least showed a willing mind and a desire to perpetuate the old prestige of the church. In one of the old papers of the town we have the following respecting Mr. D.'s ministry : "The lover of oratory could have no greater treat nor the intellectual man a richer repast than in listening to those productions so replete with admirable reasoning and beautiful imagery. It is true he was no visitor but his deficiency in this respect was by no means owing to any want of colloquial talent or natural aversion to the delights of social intercourse, but he seemed to prefer the retirement of his study and the uninterupted enjoyment of his peculiar pursuits to everything else." During his ministry of four and a half years 53 were added on examination and 58 by letter. On Sept. 21, 1843, Ezra Mills was ordained elder. In Mr. D. sent in his resignation, and in due time he was loosed from his pastoral charge. On Sept. 1, 1845, a call was made and presented to Rev. Jonathan B. Condict—it was not accepted. On the ensuing November a call was given to Alex'r R. Thompson, licentiate, which he accepted and was ordained, and installed by the Presbytery of Elizabeth Town, Jan. 14, 1848, the Rev. Dr Broadhead, of Brooklyn, preached the sermon. On May 3d of the same year Ira C. Whitehead was ordained Ruling Elder. Measures were taken this year for the erection of a parsonage house, which was finished in 1847, and has been occupied since by the successive pastors. [Owing to certain difficulties arising respecting church Psalmody Mr. Thompson felt constrained in the month of June to tender his resignation, and to his request the congregation reluctantly assented, and his pastoral connection with this church was dissolved by Presbytery July 28, 1847 ; 31 were added to the communion roll, 10 by examination and 21 by certificate.

The Rev. James Richards, of Penn Yan, was the next pastor, being inducted into that office by Presbytery Dec. 28, 1847. This installation was fruitful in pleasant associations. Dr. Magie acquainted with his father, the former pastor of this church, delivered a solemn charge to the pastor in which he alluded to the bright constellation of ministers that constituted the Presbytery when he entered it in his youth and then said: "Among all, I say it with the earnestness of thorough conviction, there is not one to whom my mind reverts with a deeper and more filial reverence than to James Richards. He was so wise, so judicious, so prudent. His counsel in those days was as if a man inquired at the oracle of God. Everywhere, in the pulpit, the lecture room, the parlor and the market place, he was the same upright, dignified, consistent Christian minister. You will oft be reminded of your honored sire as you go in and out among this people. The aged pilgrim here will live to speak of his preaching, his prayers, and his counsel, and they will thank God for one who bears his name and fills his place. May his mantle fall on you and your heart be imbued with a double portion of his spirit." How this was realized, his walk, conversation and deportment you well know. The rumors that arose and the painful recollections that followed, together with the tedious trial of Presbytery are all fresh in your minds and need not be enlarged upon ; as a preacher he was popular, earnest and vehement ; in social intercourse he was affable and winning. The last sermon he preached was instrumental in the conversion of a young man who was a few months ago called from our midst, just after he had finished his theological course and had commenced preaching the gospel of the Son of God. He resigned his pastoral charge in July, 1851, having, during his ministry, received

in to fellowship of the church 13 on examination and 40 by certificate.

On Dec. 16, 1851, the Rev. John H. Townley was installed pastor by Presbytery, the Rev. Dr. Murray preaching the sermon. Mr. Townley had for several years been pastor of the church at Hackettstown, where he was beloved and where God had blessed his ministrations. He came here at a trying time, yet by his holy walk and conversation, his devotedness to his master's service, his untiring zeal and his faithful exhibition of the truth, he commended himself to many hearts, winning their esteem, confidence and affection. God blessed his labors. He brought with him the seeds of that disease that closed his ministry on earth and that cut him off in the strength of his days, but to the last he sought to preach the unsearchable riches of Christ, and he only yielded when he was unable to declare the message of God, and on the 5th of Feb. 1855, he was gathered to his fathers, the second pastor that died sustaining this relation to this church.

Mr. Townley was born at Westfield, Essex County, N. J., on March, 1818, was a graduate of the College of N. Jersey and of the Theological Seminary, Princeton, after which he accepted a call to the Presbyterian Church of Hackettstown and then to the First Church of Morristown. His funeral services took place on Feb. 8, 1855. Dr. Murray preached the sermon on the text, "God so loved the world," &c., a text selected by the deceased that the gospel might again be preached to his people over his remains. Of him the Session have recorded "that as a pastor his qualities of mind and heart, and his excellencies of life and character have made him a rich blessing to this church and congregation." During his three years pastorate 85 were received into communion with the church, 35 on examination and 50 by certificate.

On Nov. 5, 1855, the present pastor was inducted into the pastoral office, the Rev Chas. K. Imbrie, of Jersey City, preached the sermon. During these official relation the word preached has not been in vain There has been an actual gain to the church of about 80. In this period 176 have been added, the larger portion on confession of their faith. The church edifice has been thoroughly renovated, which, with the payment of an old debt, has amounted to $7,000 Four active elders have been added to the other excellent body of men that constituted the session, Messrs. Stevenson, Olyphant, Davis and Little. The benevolence of the church has largely expanded so there is not a church in the state in proportion to its ability that has contributed more for the spread of the gospel than this during the last four years.

A few brief reflections and I have done.

(1) When the First Church edifice was reared there were no buildings around the park, no streets except Water street, leading to it; the park was a forest and the roads to Baskingridge and Mendham were principally the Indian trail. Hanover was the only church organized in the county—now there are 11 in the township. Then the Province had no newspaper, no printing press and scarcely a decent road. There was no regular mail in the state—a weekly mail between Philadelphia and New York in Summer and bimonthly in Winter, and these were only Provincial towns. The Jerseys could boast of no newspaper, and no printing press—now they are counted by thousands in our country.

(2) When the church was organised there were only two in the whole county, embracing at the time the counties of Sussex and Warren and Morris, containing a population of some 4,000 inhabitants. Now, in Morris county alone we have 48 churches, 24 Presbyterian, 13 Methodist, 5 Episcopal, 2 Reformed Dutch, 1 Congregational, and 1 Lutheran—then the membership did not exceed 300. Now there are 6,000 communicants, then there were only 40 churches in the State, now there are about 850 evangelical churches with a membership of about 100,000.

(3) When the first pastor was called to the pastorate in 1742, there were 54 Presbyterians ministers in the United States, now there are 6,254.

(4) When a minister was wanted to supply the pulpit, this congregation knew not where to look. The Presbytery therefore wrote to the Rector of Yale College if he knew of a minister to send him thither—we had then no college in the Province and no Theological Seminary, but were dependent on Foreign ministers or those educated in New England. Now we have hundreds of candidates. More than a 100 colleges and nearly 40 Theological Seminaries in the land under Presbyterian influence. Then there was no associated effort for the spread of the gospel or assisting the feeble. In our branch of the church alone over $3,000,000 were expended last year for the support of the gospel at home and abroad.

If these indicate progress throughout our land there are also healthful indications of spirituality in our own branch; there is more piety in the churches and fewer cases requiring discipline, now than a hundred years ago. There were 170 public confessions for various gross sins during Dr. Johnes' minister. The number was also great under Dr. Richards. There are, again, more professors in proportion to the population now than formerly, In the 520 families alluded to by Dr. Fisher there were only 308 professing christians; now we have over 1,300 members in the town churches, besides those that belong to the churches in New Vernon and Green Village.

Another cheering sign is that of those who unite with the church, more are from the young than formerly. Then again there is more active benevolence and less bitter party political spirit, than in the days of Richards and Fisher, and also less intemperance.

Then, as a church we have had no sympathy with the ultraisms of the day, either on the right hand or on the left, in politics, religion or moral reforms. This church has pursued a steady onward course from the beginning. Fanaticism has never crept into the pulpit or the pew; it received a healthful direction in its infancy, and from that it has never swerved. May the same noble conservatism mark its after history—what that future is we cannot now tell. Soon our pilgrimage will end and our relation to this church cease. Let us live nobly for heaven, cherish the previleges bequeathed to us by our fathers—adhere to their principles as they were based upon God's word, and never forsake the faith that bears the impress of heaven, but bequeath it unsullied to our children, that, thus standing between the past and the future, we may look back to the one with gratitude, and forward to the other with budding hope and joyous anticipation.

(*Continued from page* 166.)

BAPTISMS.

Jun. 23. Paul Ferver & wf., ch. Elizabeth,
born March 16, 1775.

" " James Wilkerson on wf's acc., ch.
John, born Aug. 29, 1774.

" 29. Abel Tompkins & wf., household,
Phebe, born Feb. 6, 1766 ; Mary,
born Aug. 23, 1768 ; Anne, born
Sept. 23, 1770; Jacob, born
Aug. 17, 1772.

" " Uriah Allen on wf's acc., ch.
Aaron, born Feb. 24, 1774.

July 6. Daniel Tichenor & wf., ch. Timothy,
born Jan. 16, 1775.

" . 9. Sarah Chever, adult.

" " Demas Ford & wf., ch. Anne, born
May 20, 1775.

" 20. Abraham Day & wf., ch. Isaac, born
May 29, 1775.

" 23. Benoni Hathaway & wf., ch. David,
born June 25, 1775.

" " Moses Prudden & wf., ch. Nance,
born June 23, 1775.

" 30. Doc. Bern Budd & wf., ch. Mary,
born May 13, 1775.

" " John Crowell & wf., chn, William,
born Dec. 21, 1772; Luther, born
Feb. 3, 1774.

Aug. 3. Eunice, wf. of John Primrose, on her
acc., family—Jacob, born Jan. 1,
1764 ; James, born Sept. 3, 1766;
Sarah, born Oct. 21, 1769 ;
Henry, born Dec. 3, 1772 ;
Abigail, born June 29, 1774.

" " Hannah, wf. of Ephraim Lyon, on
her account, family—Rebecca,
born Sept 3, 1764 ; Isaac, born
Nov. 20, 1766 ; Ezekiel, born
Feb. 17, 1769; Samuel, born
Nov. 23, 1773; Mary, born
March 12, 1775.

" 13. John Gwinnup & wf., ch. Sarah,
born June 29, 1775.

" " Icabod Cooper & wf., ch. Rachel,
born July 8, 1775.

" " John Pool & wf., ch. John, born
June 27, 1775.

" 20. Job Loree & wf., ch. Mary, born
July 8, 1775.

" " Elias Hedges & wf., ch. Sarah, born
July 9, 1775.

Aug. 20. Joseph Pierson, junr. & wf., ch,
Hephzibah, born July 12, 1775.

" " Roberd Youngs on wf's acc., ch.
Joseph, born July 3, 1775.

" 27. Wido. of David Wheler, ch. Stevens Johnes, born July 15,
1775.

" " Nathaniel Peek & wf., ch. Tirzah,
born July 21, 1775.

" 31. Joseph Cook & wf., family—Elizabeth, born Aug. 21, 1769;
Mary, born Feb. 7, 1772 ; Abraham, born Aug. 11, 1774.

" " Matthew Ball & wf., family, Mary
Hathaway, born Feb. 1, 1762 ;
Abigail Hathaway, born Feb. 3,
1764 ; Jonathan Hathaway, born
May 6, 1766 ; Jonas Ball, born
Dec. 2, '71; Sarah Ball, born
May 8, '74.

Sept. 7. George Phillips & wf., ch. Jonas,
born July 2, '75 ; also his negro
chn., Cato, born Dec. 5, 1768 ;
Surreen, born April 24, '70 ; &
Silve, born Jan. 3, '73.

" 17. David Godden & wf., ch. Seth, born
Aug. 1, '75.

" " Eleazar Hathaway & wf., ch. John,
born Aug. 16, '75.

" " Onesimus Whitehead & wf., ch.
Elizabeth, born July 8, '75.

" 24. James Smith & wf., ch. Mehetabel,
born Aug. 13, '75.

" " Daniel Bishop & wf., ch. Elizabeth,
born Feb. 22, '75.

Oct. 1. Lieut. Benj. Hathaway & wf., ch.
Joseph, born July 20, '75.

" " Dan Carmichael & wf., twins, Silas
& Nathaniel, born July 26, '75.

" 15. Silas Howell & wf., ch. Phebe, born
Sept. 10, '75.

" " John Mills & wf., ch. Ezra, born
Sept. 12, '75.

" 22. Benj. Lindsley & wf., ch. Elizabeth,
born Sept. 5, '75.

" 29. Stephen Arnold & wf., ch. Phebe,
born Sept. 24, '75.

Nov. 5. Jabez Condict & wf., ch. Martha,
born Sept. 20, '75.

Dec. 10. James Brookfield & wf., ch. Mary,
born Oct. 27, '75.

" 17. David Day, on wf's acc., ch. Elizabeth, born Nov. 12, '75.

1776.

Jan. 14. Timo. Mills & wf., ch. Timothy, born Nov. 7, '75.

" 21. Samuel Freman & wf.. ch. Phibe, born Nov. 27, '75.

" 28. Matthias Burnet & wf., ch. Anna, born Dec. 12,"75.

Feb. 11. Nathan Guiering & Abigail, adult, & yr. son Levi, born Nov. 6, '75.

" 18. Seth Crowell & wf., ch. Esther, born Dec. 31, '75.

" " Zippora Conger, adult.

Mar. 3. Samuel Allwood & wf., ch. Henry, born Oct. 11, '75.

" 24. Jabez Beach & wf., ch. Epenetus, born Nov. 15, '75.

Apr. 14. Robert Rolfe, adult, & with his wf., ch. Mary, born Jan. 5, '76.

" " David Hopper & wf., ch. Phebe, born Dec. 3, '75.

" 21. Jedidiah Mills & wf., ch. Ruth, born March 8, '76.

" " Capt. Benj. Halsey & wf., negro ch. Sharper, born Dec. 25, '75.

" " Doc. Timo. Johnes & wf., sick ch. bap. at ye house, name Oliver, born April 15, '75.

May 5. Moses Wick's wf. Mary on her acc.,ch. Anne born Feb. 15,1776.

" " Ezra Fairchild & wf., ch. Ebenezer, born Jan. 18, 1776.

" 12. Lindsley Burnet & wf., ch. Hannah born March 20, 1776.

" " James Hume & wf., ch. John, born Jan. 9, 1776.

" 26. Daniel Phenix & wf., Elizabeth Platt, yr ch. Elizabeth, born April 23, 1776.

" " Silas Condict & wf., negro ch. Zenas,, born April 7, 1776.

June 2. Abel Tompkins & wf., ch. John, born April 11, 1776.

" " Jonathan Hallick & wf., chn. Mary, born Nov. 10, 1770, and Martha, born May 2, 1775.

" " Dan. Wick on wf's acc., negro chn. Harry, born ——, 1769; Tabitha, born March, 1764, and Antony, born March, 1776.

" 16. Abraham Talmage & wf., ch. David, born May 7, 1776.

" " Ichabod Carmichael & wf., ch. Ichabod, born May 11, 1776.

June 16. Shadrach Hathaway, on wf's acc., ch. Jane, born May 1, 1776.

" 23. Gilberd Allen & wf., ch. Anne,born April 29, 1776.

" " Elizabeth, wf. of Thomas Pierson on her acc., family—Susannah, born Aug. 8, 1763; Abigail, born Feb. 14, 1766 ; Esther, born March 16, 1771 ; Jemima, born June 21, 1773; Kezia, born Dec. 23, 1775.

" " James Eddy on wf's acc., ch. John, born April 20, 1776.

" 30. James Bullen on wf's acc., ch. John Paimrose, born July 28, 1774.

July 7. David Garrigas & wf., ch. Jeptha, born June 7, 1776.

" 21. John Milborn & wf., ch. Lidia, born Jan. 5, 1776.

" 26. Nathan Reeve, ch. Samnel, born July 7, 1775.

" 27. James McMullon & Jane, ch. Jane, born July 11, 1775.

" 28. Abrm. Hathaway on wf's acc., chn. John, born April 14, 1779; and Abner, born Oct. 11, 1775.

" " Alexander Cermichael & wf., ch. Richard Mongomory, born June 22, 1776.

" " Wm. Pierson & wf., ch. Anne, born June 8, 1776.

" " Mary, wido. of Will Crane, ch. Mary, born Sept. 20, 1764.

Aug. 4. Moses Lindsley & wf., ch. William, born June 30, 1776.

" " Jonathan Ford on wf's acc., ch. Catharine, born June 18, 1776.

" " John Allen & wf., ch. Silas, born June 26, 1776.

" 8. Joshua Guiering & wf., ch. Parne, born May 27, 1776.

" 11. Barzillai Orsborn on wf's acc., ch. Barzillai, born Aug. 27, 1775.

" 18. Jesse Smith & wf., ch. Sarah, born June 14, 1776.

" 25. David Youngs & wf., ch. Bathiah, born July 10, 1776.

Sept. 1. George Phillips & wf., negro ch. Gillis.

" 15. David Moor & wf., ch. Loammi born April 12, '76.

Oct. 6. Jacob Arnold, on wf's acc., ch. Sarah, born Aug. 7, '76.

Oct. 6. Isaac Morris & wf., ch. John, born Aug. 31, '76.

" " Joseph Bears & wf., ch. Cloe, born Sept. 12, '76.

" " Jacob Frazy & wf., ch. Hannah, born Aug. 18, '76.

" 13. David Woodruff & wf., ch. Aaron.

" " Thomas Miller & wf., ch. Anne, born June 5, '76.

" 27. Christopher Wood & wf., ch. Terresse, born Nov. 26, '75.

" " Nathaniel Condict & wf., ch. Rhoda, born Aug. 25, '76.

Nov. 3. Jeduthan Day & wf., ch. Silas, born July 29, '76.

" " Daniel Smith & wf., ch. Joseph Gardiner, born Sept. 17. '76.

" 17. John Primrose, on wf's acc., ch. Phebe, born Oct. 10, '76.

" 24. Capt. James Keen & wf., ch. Dorcas, born Sept. 30, '76; also a negro ch. Pompey, now about 5 years old.

1777.

Feb. 16. Isaac Ayrs & wf., ch. Mary, born Oct. 19, '76.

" " Silas Ayrs & wf., ch. Sarah, born Nov. 28, '76.

Apr. 16. John Mills & wf., ch. Phebe, born March 22, '77.

May 4. Joseph Lewis & wf. ch. Elizabeth, born Feb. 12, '77.

" 25. Lewis Stewerd & wf., ch. Lewis, born Dec. 3, '76.

June 1. Col. Eleazar Lindsley & wf., ch. Sarah, born June 8, '76.

July 3. Nathan Guiering & wf., ch. David Conger, born Dec. 24, '76.

" " Nathaniel Armstrong & wf., ch. Isaac, born Feb. 23, '77.

" 6. Walter Buchaman & Ally Camel, his wf., ch. Walter, born June 4, '77.

" 7. John Harparee & wf., ch. Dorcas, born Dec. 22, '76.

" 10. Joseph Riggs & wf., ch. Daniel, born Dec. 22, '76.

" " Andrew Wade, ch. Gideon, born Aug. 11, '76.

" 20. Jonathan Stiles & wf., ch. Jacob, born May 22, '77.

" " Jonathan Ogden & wf., ch. Samuel, born May 3, '77.

July 20. Stephen Simson. on his acc., ch. Elizabeth, born May 25, '77.

" 27. Samuel Freman & wf., ch. Elizabeth. born May——'77.

Aug. 10. George Phillips & wf., ch. Deborah, born June 29, '77.

" 18. Daniel Kemper & wf., ch. Sophia Cornelia, born Aug. 14, '77.

" 28. Ezra Halsey & wf., ch. Ezra, born July 15, 1776.

Sept. 21. John Beach & wf., ch. Jonathan, born Oct. 12, 1776.

" " Ezekiel Crane & wf., ch. Abigail, born July 20, 1777.

" 29. Henry Ross & wf., ch. Phebe, born Jan. 19, 1777.

Oct. 19. Howell Orsborn & wf., ch. Sarah, born April 28, 1777.

" " Silas Gildersleeve & wf., ch. Phebe, born Oct. 22, 1776.

" " Samuel Pierson & wf., ch Stephen, born March 10, 1777.

" 26. Job Loree & wf., ch. Jane, born July 28, 1777.

" " Samuel Ward on wf's acc., ch. Phebe, born Sept. 24, 1777.

" 30. Nathaniel Thompson, chn. Samuel, born Jan. 26, 1774; Jeremiah Pierson, born May 18, 1775.

" " John McLaulin on wf's acc., chn. Hugh, born Oct. 20, 1774; Rachel, born Dec. 18, 1776.

Nov. 2. Onesimus Whitehead & wf., ch. Hannah, born Aug. 29, 1777.

" " David Douglass & wf., ch. Israel, born Sept. 14, 1777.

" " Jonathan Hallock, ch. Matthew, born Feb. 23, 1777.

" 12. Doc. Timo. Johnes & wf., ch. Maria, born Oct. 29, 1777.

" 16. Abr. Hathaway on wf's acc., ch. Esther, born Oct. 17, 1777.

" " Aaron Crane's widow., ch. Damaris, born Aug. 9, 1776.

Dec. 4. Abrm. Lewis on wf's acc., ch. Elizabeth Dodridge, born April 23, 1771.

" " Samuel Alwood & wf., ch. Elizabeth, born Oct. 7, 1777.

" 14. Benj. Archer & Charity his wf., ch. Philip Pain, born Aug. 15, 1777.

" 21. Leah, wido. of Jno. Sutton, household—John, born July 14, 1770;

Ephraim, born March 17, 1772 ;
Hannah, born Nov. 14, 1773;
Mary, born Oct. 7, 1775.

1778.
Jan. 8. Usual Coe & wf., ch. Benjamin,
born April 8, 1777.
" " Deac. Matthias Burnet & wf., negro ch. Cesar, born May, 1776.
" 11. Capt. Silas Howell & wf., ch. Harriot, born Nov. 23, '77.
" 15. Wido. of Moses Prudden, ch. Daniel,
born Aug. 5, '77.
" 18. Joseph Pierson, Junr., & wf., ch,
Joseph, born Nov. 24, '77.
" 25. Jabez Condict & wf., ch. Phebe,
born Sept. 16, '77.
Feb. 1. Robert Towt (Todd, ed.) & Sarah,
his wf., ch. Cornelia Hardecker,
born Dec. 26, '77.
" " Jonathan Pierson & wf., ch. Elizabeth, born Nov. 16, '77.
" 8. Robert Rolph & wf., ch. Rachel,
born Nov. 16, '77.
Mar. 1. Benj. Lindsley, Esq., & wf., ch.
Latta, born Jan. 18, '78.
" 30. Daniel Phenix & wf., Elizabeth
Platt, ch. Alexander, born Feb.
28, '78.
Apr. 5. Abijah Cutler & wf., ch. Joseph
born Oct. 16, '75.
" 22. Nathaniel Peck & wf., ch. Lydia,
born March 4, '78.
" 26. James Humes & wf., ch. James, born
Feb. 21, '78.
" " Jesse Smith & wf., ch. Jacob, born
March 12, '78.
" " John Arnold & wf, ch. Cloe, born
April 24. '74.
May 3. Lindsly Burnet & wf., twins, Mat-
thias & Mary, born March 8, '78.
" " Matthias Burnet, Junr., & wf., ch.
John, born March 7, '78.
" " Stephen Arnold & wf., ch. Jacob,
born Jan. 14, '78.
" " Jedidiah Orsborn, on wf's acc., ch.
Abraham Allen, born Nov. 4,
1777.
" 17. David Fairchild & wf., ch. Silas,
born Oct. 3, '77.
June 4. Moses Munson & wf., ch. Mary, born
June 30, '77.
" 7. Richard Johnson & wf., ch. Silas,
born April 21, '78.

June 14. Elias Hedges & wf., ch. Ruth, born
May 3, '78.
" " David Douglace & wf., ch., adopted,
Samuel Ludlam, (son of Wick
Ludlam) born Aug. 27, '75.
" 18. Anner or Elenor, wf. of Timo. Stiles,
adult, with her chn., Mary, born
April 4, '73 ; Hannah, born Oct.
30, '74,
" 28. James Smith, on wf's acc., ch.
Thomas, born May 30, '74.
" " Shadrach Hathaway's wido., ch.
Shadrach, born Jan. 13, '77.
July 27. Col. Henry & Cornelia Remson, ch.
Cataline, born June 27, '78.
Aug. 2. Capt James Keen & wf., ch, Joseph
Ayres, born July 1, '78.
" " David Garrigas & wf., ch. David,
born June 30, '78.
" " Mary, wf. of Daniel Freman, Junr.,
adult, born Feb. 17, '75, and her
household, James, born March
13, '75 ; Hannah, born March 2,
1778.
" 13. Joseph Lewis & wf., ch. Jacob, born
Sunday morn., Aug. 9, '78.
Sept. 6. Demas Ford & wf., ch. Lewis, born
Aug. 4, '78.
" " Ichabod Carmichael & wf., ch. Alex-
ander, born July 30, '78.
" " Jonathan Rainor & wf., ch. Eunice,
born July 14, 1778.
" " Ephraim Youngs & wf., ch. Bathiah,
born Aug. 8, 1778
" " Dinah, wido. of Abijah Cutler, ch.
Bathiah, born Aug. 8, 1778.
" 13. Naphtali Byram & wf., family—
Abigail, born March 3, 1771 ;
Anne, born Nov. 17, 1774 ;
Ebenezer, born April 9, 1778.
" " John Day on wf's acc., ch. Sidney,
born Aug. 6, 1778.
Oct. 4. Amos Prudden & Damaris his wf.,
twins Sarah & Mary, born July
9, 1778.
" " Councillor Silas Condict & wf., ne-
gro ch. Cato, born July 18, 1778.
" 18. Jacob Fraze & wf., ch. Jacob, born
Aug. 6, 1778.
" " David & Martha Burnet, ch. Mary
Dickerson, born Sept. 5, 1778.
" " Daniel Smith & wf., ch. Daniel, born
Aug. 31, 1778.

Nov. 15. Asahel Hinman & wf., ch. Samuel, born Sept. 2, 1778.

" " Esther, wido. of Rob. Day, ch. Roberd, born Aug. 13, 1778.

" 22. James Youngs & wf., ch. Samuel, born Oct. 22, 1778.

1779.

Jan. 3. Col. Benoni Hathaway & wf., ch. Jabez, born Nov. 20, 1778.

" 24. John Prudden & wf., ch. Anne, born Oct. 6, 1778.

" " John Pool & wf., ch. Elizabeth, born Nov. 30, 1778.

" 31. David Day & wf., ch. Sarah, born Dec. 29, 1778.

" " Nathaniel Armstrong & wf., ch. Rhoda, born Dec. 13, 1778.

" " Nathan Guerin & wf., ch. Roberd, born Dec. 9. 1778.

Feb. 21. Daniel Carmichael & wf., ch. Ruth, born Dec. 27, 1778.

" " Joseph Beers & wf., ch. Phebe, born Jan. 12, 1779.

" 28. John Beach & wf., ch. Charlotte, born Jan. 2, 1779.

" " John Primrose on wf's acc., ch. Anne, born Nov. 30, 1778.

Mar. 4. Thomas Miller & wf., twins Jonathan & David, born Dec. 25, 1778.

" 21. David Ogden on wf's acc., ch. David, born Nov. 4, 1778.

" " Moses Wick on wf's acc., ch. Jane, born Oct. 10, 1778.

" " John Allen & wf., ch. Hannah, born Feb. 5, 1779.

Apr. 11. Deac. Allen & wf., ch. Timothy, born Dec. 26, 1778.

" " Alexander Carmichael & wf., ch. Charles, born Feb. 27, 1779.

" " Jonathan Ford on wf's acc., ch. Apollos, born Feb. 28, 1779.

" " Daniel Tichehor & wf., ch. Jerud, born Feb. 28, 1779.

" " Silas Ayrs & wf., ch. Mary King, born March 2, 1779.

" " Thomas Pierson & wf., servant ch. John, born March 1, 1779.

" " Matthew Rainer & wf., ch. Cornelius, born Nov. 23, 1778.

" " John Harporee & wf., ch. Elizabeth, born Feb. 4, 1779.

" 25. Luther Extel & wf., son, March, 1779.

May 2. Jonathan Wilkerson on wf's acc., ch. Matthias.

" Ichabod Cooper & wf., ch. Ephraim, born May 4, 1779.

June 27. George Phillips & wf., ch. Phebe, born May 15, '79.

" " Benj. Prudden & wf., ch. John Stevens, born May 8, '79.

" " Jonathan Hallock & wf., ch. Jonathan, born May 7, '79.

July 4. Ebenezer Stiles & wf., chn. bap. by Simon Gobill, names, Abner Gobill, born June 27, '65; Luther Gobill, born May 24, '70; Calvin Gobill, born March 6, 1773.

" 18. Isaac Pierson & wf., ch. John, born May 16, '79.

" 22. John Mills & wf., ch. Hulda, born June 25, '79.

Aug. 1. Jonathan Ogden & wf., ch. Oliver, Wayne, born July 5. '79.

" 8. Isaac Ayrs & wf., ch. Anne, born July 8, '79.

" 29. Levi Lindsly & wf., ch. Benjamin, born July 13, '79.

" " Eunice, late Prudden, now Rowley, ch. Hannah, born Feb. 7, '79.

Oct. 13. John Stevenson on wf's acc., ch. John, born Aug. 1, '79.

" 17. Jer. Bird, on wf. Eliz. acc., ch. Freman, born Jan. 18, '79,

" " Isaac Morris & wf., ch. Robert, born Sept. 2, '79.

" " John Lyon & wf., ch. Mary, born April 18, '78.

" " Abner Condict & wf., ch. Rhoda, born July 22, '79.

" 24. Daniel Kemper & Jane, his wf., ch. Daniel Darby, born Aug. 30. '79.

" 27. Daniel Phenix & wf., ch. Sidney, born Oct. 7, '79.

" 31. James Bampfield & wf., twins, Rebeka & Jemima, born Sept. 5, 1779.

" " Jonathan Hathaway & wf., ch. Lydia, born Sept. 25. '79.

" " Joseph Tuttle, on wf's acc., ch. Phebe, born———'79.

" " Joseph Riggs & wf., ch. Rebekah, born Sept. 6, '79.

" " Usual Coe & wf., ch. Benjamin, born Sept. 5, 1779.

(To be continued.)

THE RECORD.

FIRST PRESBYTERIAN CHURCH, MORRISTOWN, N. J.

"This shall be Written for the Generation to Come."—Psalms 102 : 18.

VOL. II.　　　　NOVEMBER, 1881.　　　　NO. 11

(Printed with the approval of Session.)

THE RECORD

Will be printed and published monthly at Morristown, N. J. Terms, 50 cents per annum in advance; 75 cents after June.

Subscriptions will be received at the book-stores of Messrs. Runyon and Emmell, or through the mail. All communications should be addressed to the

EDITOR OF THE RECORD,

Lock box 44.　　　　Morristown, N. J.

Vol. I. complete, 75 cents.

Entered at the Post Office at Morristown, N. J., as second class matter.

——:o:——

(Continued from page 176.)

BAPTISMS.

Oct. 31. Boys Pruden & wf., ch, Bethuel, born Aug. 10, 1779.

" " Sussex Negro on wf's acc., with her Mrs. Doughty, ch. Sarah, born Sept. 7, 1779.

Nov. 3. Jedidiah Gregory, motherless infant, Jedidiah, born Nov. 1, '79.

" 5. David Muire on wf's acc., ch. Araunah, born March 28, '78.

" 25. Lewis Nichol & wf., ch. Lewis, born Oct. 24, '79.

" " Timothy Stiles & wf., ch. Phebe, born Sept. 28, '79.

Dec. 9. Samuel Allwood & wf., ch. Phebe, born Oct. 25, '79.

" 26. Jabish Condict & wf., ch. Abigail, born Oct. 10, '79.

1780.

Jan. 23. David Youngs, ch. David, born Jan. 9, '80.

" 30. Jonathan Pierson & wf., ch. Kezia, born Oct. 2, '79.

" " Stephen Arnold & wf., ch. Thomas, born Nov. 29, '79.

Feb. 6. Onesimus Whitehead & wf., ch. Abner, born Oct. 22, '79.

Feb. 6. Naphtali Byram & wf., ch. Huldah, born Nov. 19, '79.

" " Samuel Pierson & wf., ch. Isaac, born Dec. 23, '79.

" 13. Abrm. Hathaway on wf's acc., ch. Ruth, born Dec. 24, '79.

" " John Kenny, junr. on wf's acc., ch. Harriot, born Nov. 14, '79.

" " Abraham Talmage & wf., ch. Hannah, born Dec. 4, '79.

" 20. Capt. Silas Howell & wf., ch. Mary, born Nov. 22, '79.

" " Robert Rolfe & wf., ch. Henry, born Oct. 18, '79.

Mar. 19. Jonathan Stiles, junr. & wf., ch. Elizabeth, born Jan. 26, '80.

" " Capt. Jacob Arnold on wf's acc., ch. Gitty, born Nov. 29, '79.

April 2. Ichabod Carmichael & wf., ch. Elizabeth, born Jan. 30, '80.

" 9. Ezekiel Crane & wf., ch. Silas, born Jan. 30, '80.

" " Jabish Beach & wf., ch. Elizabeth, born Jan. 9, '80.

" " Elias Hedges & wf., ch. Anne, born Jan. 29, '80.

" 12. Caleb Munson & wf., ch. Caleb, born Jan. 4, '80.

" " Moses Munson & wf., ch. Tamar, born Jan. 16, '80.

" 23. Joseph Lewis & wf., ch. Timothy, born March 10, '80.

" " Reuben Wood & wf., ch. Zenas, born Sept. 26, '79.

" 30. David Dalglish & wf., ch. Timothy, born March 13, '80.

" " Daniel Smith & wf., ch. David, born Feb. 19, '80.

May 7. Col. Jno. & Catharine Nelson, ch. Gertrude, born April 25, '80.

" 9. Walter Buchanan & wf., ch. Elizabeth, born April 11, '80.

May 14. Matthias Burnet & wf., ch. Esther, born March 5, '80.

" 14. William Carn a soldier, & wf., ch. Graa, born Jan. 7, '80.

" 21. James Humes & wf., ch. William, born March 10, '80.

" " Joseph Pierson, Junr., & wf., ch. Phebe, born April 6, '80.

" " James Youngs & wf., ch. Hannah, born April 13, '80.

" 25. Jedidiah Orsborn, on wf's acc., ch. Isaac, born Sept. 21, '79.

" 28. Benj. Archer & wf., ch. William, born March 21, '79.

June. 4. Nathan Reeve & wf., ch. Samuel, born Oct. 26, '79.

" 18. John Lyon & wf., ch. Rachel, born Feb. 10, '80.

" 25. Nathaniel Peck & wf., ch. Sarah born May 6, '80.

" " Andrew Wade & wf., ch. Rachel, born Feb. 10, '80.

" " Nathaniel Broadwell & wf., ch. John, born Aug. 23, '79.

" " Joshua Guerin & wf., ch. Susanna. born March 25, '80.

July 2. John Hathaway & wf., ch. Jemima, born March 12, '80.

" " Sam Day, on wf's acc., ch. Phebe, born Oct. 22, '79.

" " Abraham Day & wf., ch. William Windes, born March 10, '80.

" " Lindsly Burnet & wf., ch. William, born March 9, '80.

" 9. Samuel Freman & wf., ch. Stephen, born May 2, '80.

" " Calvin Extel & wf., ch. Philip Lindsley. born Dec. 3, '79.

" 21. Col. Henry & Cornelia Remson, ch. Cornelius, born June 18, '80.

Aug. 6. Wido. of Philip Hathaway, ch. Phillip, born May 22, '77.

" 13. Nathaniel Armstrong & wf., ch. Samuel born Aug. 21, 1779.

" " Stephen Conkling, Junr., & wf., ch. Sarah, born Sept. 14, '79.

" 17. Moses Lindsly & wf., ch. Rhoda. born July 7, '80.

" " Nathan Guierin & wf., ch. Jabesh, born July 23, '80.

" 20. Daniel Bears & wf., ch. Triphena, born July 17, '80.

" 27. John Day, on wf's acc. ch. Abraham, born July 24, '80.

Sept. 10. Richard Johnson, Esqr., & wf., ch. Paul, born Aug. 6, '80.

" " Ichabod Spinnage & wf., ch. John Pierson, born Dec. 25, '79.

" 17. Abijah Fairchild & wf., ch. William, born July 24, '80.

" " David Tarbill, on wf's acc., ch. Martha, born May 14, '80.

Oct. 1. Joseph Marsh & wf., ch. Martha, born July 23, '80.

" 8. James Eddy, on wf's acc., ch. Phebe, born Aug. 13, '80.

" 25. Docr. Lewis Dunham, on wf's acc., chn. Mary & John.

" 26. James Ford, on wf's acc., nephew, adopted Samuel Moor, born March——'73.

" " Peter Parcel, on wf's acc., ch. Sarah, born Nov. 26, '79.

Dec. 21. Corporal John Smith & wf., from camp, recommended by yr. Capt., ch. Ann, born Jan. 12, '80.

" " Edward Blake, soldier, recommended by his Capt., & wf., ch. Edward, born Oct. 29, '80.

1781.

Jan. 14. Robert Towt & wf., ch. Margaret, born Oct. 4, '80.

" " Ichabod Cooper & wf., ch. Daniel, born Nov. 20, '80.

" 28. Isaac Prudden & wf., ch. Isaac, born Oct. 16, '80.

" " Matthew Rainer & wf., ch. Hannah, born Dec. 20, '80.

Feb. 7. Daniel & Elizabeth Phenix, ch. Rebekah, born Jan. 17, '81.

" " Doc. Tuthill & wf., negro, ch. Pero, born Jan. 18, '79.

Mar. 18. Alexander Carmichael & wf., ch. Mary, born Dec. 29, '80.

" " David Garrigas & wf., ch. Stephen, born Dec. 1, '80.

" " John Pool & wf., ch. Phebe, born Jan. 28, '81.

Apr. 1. Enos Limus, negro ch. Adam, born Feb. 6, '81.

" 8. John Beach & wf., ch. Harriot, born Jan. 9, '81.

" 15. Joseph Byram & wf., chn. John Reed, born Jan. 14, '79; and Ebenezar Alden, born Feb. 3, '81.

" 29. David Fairchild & wf., ch. Lewis, born Feb. 12, '81.

Apr.29. David Porter, on wf's acc., ch,
John, born March 14, '81.

May 3. John Allen & wf., ch. Rachel, born
March 12, 81.

" 13. Elder Jno, Lindsley & wf., ch. Azariah, born March 28, '81.

" " Jonathan Ford, on wf's acc., ch.
Catharine, born March 25, '81.

" " Joseph Bears & wf., ch. Jabez, born
March 25, '81.

" 20. Aaron Pierson & wf., ch. Mary,
born, March 26, '81.

" 27. Luther Extel & wf., ch. Phillip,
born Feb. 10, '81.

" 3. Deac. Gilbard Allen & wf, ch. Jemima, born March 18, '81.

June10. Isaac Pierson & wf., ch. Abraham,
born March 6, '81.

" " Ephraim Youngs & wf., ch. Abijah,
born May 2, '81.

" 12. Stephen Arnold & wf., ch. Sarah,
born April 5. '81.

" 24. Wm. Satterly & wf., ch. David, born
May 3, '81.

July 1. Silas Ayrs & wf., ch. Hannah, born
May 12, '81.

" 8. Jacob Frazy & wf., ch. Isaac, born
Feb. 21, '81.

" 22. Jeduthan Day & wf., ch, Phebe,
born Dec. 22, '80.

Aug.15. Charity, wido. of Jno. Wheeler, chn.
Susanna, born Dec. 8, '76; and
Elizabeth, born March 18, '79.

Sept. 2. Wido. Bette Dobbin, ch. Elizabeth.

Aug.31. Samuel Ludlam, Jun'r, bap. and
joined ye. ch. in full, adult.

Sept17. Elizabeth, Rich Watcuk's wf.,
adult, and 2 chn. Maty Kent,
born Oct. 15, '69; and Elias,
born Aug. 22, '76.

" " Sarah, wf. of Michael Conner, adult
& ch. Elizabeth,born Feb. 1, '81.

" 23. Jesse Cutler & wf., ch, Abijah,born
Aug. 13, '81.

" " Ichabod Carmichael & wf., ch.
Hannah, born Aug. 5, '81.

Oct. 7. Wido. of Nathaniel Condict, ch.
Abigail.

" 14. Ichabod Spinnage & wf., ch. Isaac
Watts, born Aug. 21, '81.

" " Silas Gildersleeve & wf., ch. John,
born Aug. 16, '81.

" " John Mills & wf., ch. Jonas, born
Sept. 13, '81.

Oct. 21. John Harparee & wf., ch. Sarah,
born Sept. 29, '81.

" " Robert Rolle & wf., ch. Samuel,
born Sept. 3, '81.

Nov. 1. Joseph Pruden & wf., ch. Joanna,
born Sept. 25, '81.

" " David Day on wf's acc., ch. Joseph,
born April 28, '81.

" " Loruhama, ye wido. of Silas Jennings, ch. Phebe, born Sept. 6,
'81.

" 19. Nicholas Carter & wf., family—Silas, born July 9, '65; Elenor,
born May 18, '67; Sarah, born
Aug. 1, '69; Elizabeth, born
Jan. 5, '73; Rhoda, born April
13, '77; and Nicholas, born
Dec. 25, '80.

" 21. Abraham Talmage & wf., ch. Joseph, born Oct. 27, '81.

" " Joseph Tuttle on wf's acc., ch. William, born Aug. 19, '81.

" 22. Of 2,016 bap. a majority of males 6.

" 29. Capt. Jacob Arnold on wf's acc.,
ch. Jacob, born Sept. 21, '81.

Dec. 2. Jabez Beach & wf., ch. Phebe, born
Oct. 14, '81.

" 13. Jonathan Ogden & wf., ch. Stephen,
born Nov. 13, '81.

" " John Prudden & wf., ch. John,born
Nov. 11, '80.

" 23. Jonathan Hallock & wf., ch. Elizabeth, born Nov. 2, '81.

" 27. Samuel & Mary Teressa Flemin, ch.
Sam'l Dunham, born Nov. 3, '81.

1782.

Jan. 3. Anthony & Mary Bleecker, ch.
Elizabeth DeHart, born Aug.
2, '81.

" " David Ogden on wf's acc., ch. John
born Oct. 30, '81.

" 4. Jeremiah Stone, adult, & chn.
Lewis, born Dec. 28, '77; &
Silas, born Feb. 8, '81.

" 19. Dan. & Jane Kempel, ch. Ann Gertrude Miller, born Aug. 4, '81.

Feb. 3. Abner Condict & wf., ch. Rebekah,
born Dec. 7, '81.

" 28. Naptali Byram & wf., ch. Susanna,
born Jan. 22, '82.

" " Henry Lane, adult.

Mar.24. John Dickerson & wf., ch. Joseph
Lindsley, born Oct. 7, '81.

April 7. Jonathan Johnson, on wf's acc., ch.
　　William, born Oct. 22, '81.
　" " Abner Wade & wf. ch. Abigail More-
　　house, born March 3, '82.
　" 14. Timothy Stiles, & wf., ch. Sarah,
　　born Feb. 6, '82.
　" 21. Usual Coe & wf., ch. Rachel, born
　　Nov. 16, '81.
　" " Matthias Burnet, Junr., & wf., ch.
　　Anne, born Jan. 16, '82.
　" 25. Jon. Stiles, Junr., & wf., ch. Gitty,
　　born March 20, '82.
　" 28. Capt. Silas Howell & wf., ch. Sarah,
　　born March 1, '82.
　" " Capt. Dan. Tuttle & wf., ch. John
　　Alexander, born Dec. 24, '81.
　" " Jonathan Raynor & wf., ch. Pru-
　　dence, born Feb. 3, '82.
May 3. Ephraim Lindsly & wf., family,
　　Sarah, born June 20, '78 ; Hyram,
　　born Feb. 27, '80 ; David, born
　　March 10, '82.
　" " David Walker's wf., Elizabeth, adult,
　　& on her acc., ch. Richard, born
　　Aug. 7, '75.
　" 5. Jedidiah Mills & wf., ch. Sarah, born
　　March 27, '82.
　" " Abijah Fairchild & wf., ch. Cathar-
　　ine, born March 6, '82.
　" " Samuel Allwood & wf., ch. Stephen,
　　born Jan. 5, '82.
　" 7 Abrm. Hathaway, on wf's acc., ch.
　　Peter Dickerson, born Mar. 17,
　　1782.
　" " Larence Dowling, on wf's acc., ch.
　　Elizabeth, born Jan. 3, '81.
　" " Jacob Emery, adult, & wf., chn.
　　Jonathan, born July 29, '79 ; &
　　Joanna, born March 12, '82.
　" 19. David Muir, on wf's acc., ch. Josiah,
　　born July 6, '80.
　" 22. Ruben Wood & wf., ch. Stephen,
　　born Dec. 19, '81.
　" 26. John Lindsly, Junr., & wf., ch. Anne,
　　born Oct. 30, '81.
　" " Nathan Reeve & wf., ch. Nathan,
　　born Jan. 3, '82.
　" 29. Jno. Kenny on wf's acc., ch. Maria,
　　born Dec. 13, '81.
June 2. Daniel Freman, Junr., & wf., ch.
　　Phebe, born Dec. 31, '81.
　" 9. Abr. Day & wf., ch. Abraham, born
　　March 23, '82.

June 16. Elias Hedges on wf's acc., ch. David,
　　born April 10, '82.
　" 23. Isaac Ayers & wf., ch. Stephen
　　Cooper, born May 16, '82.
　" " Caleb Edy & wf., adult Esther, their
　　ch. also Timothy, born March
　　4, '81.
　" 30. James Wilkerson on wf's acc., ch.
　　Ebenezer, born April 25, '82.
July 5. Widow Deborah Brookfield, ch.
　　Sarah, born April 3, '82.
　" " Ben. Hamilton's wf., Rebekah,
　　adult, & on her acc., ch. Lot,
　　born April 29, '81.
　" 7. Major Joseph Lindsly & wf., ch.
　　Phebe, born Feb. 11, '82.
　" 16. Joseph Pierson, Junr., ch. Abigail
　　born April 13, '82.
　" 21. Samuel Seward & wf., ch. Sarah,
　　born Sept. 22, '82.
　" 28. Caleb Russel & wf., chn. Henry
　　Pierson, born March 25, '80. &
　　John, born June 7, '82.
　" " Jabez Condit & wf., ch. Zenas, born
　　May 20, '82.
　" " Daniel & Elizabeth Phoenix, ch.
　　Jinnett, born July 15, '82.
Aug. 1. Capt. John Stevenson on wf's acc.,
　　ch. Elizabeth, born June 9, '82.
　" 4. Nath'l Broadwell & wf., ch. Sarah,
　　born Nov. 17, '81.
　" 11. Richard Johnson & wf., ch. Peter,
　　born June 27, '82.
　" 18. James Humes & wf., ch. Samuel,
　　born March 16, '82.
　" " Nathan Guierin & wf., ch. Mary,
　　born July 18, '82.
　" 25. Isaac Prudden & wf., ch. James,
　　born July 29, '82.
Sept. 2. David Burnet & wf., ch. Ann, born
　　July 18, '82.
　" 12. Doc. Lewis Dunham on wf's acc.,
　　ch. George Tuthill, born March
　　22, '82 ; also a negro ch. Harry,
　　born May, '76.
　" 15. George Marsh & wf., ch. Sarah,
　　born July 3, '82.
　" 22. James Youngs & wf., ch. Sarah,
　　born Aug. 2, '82.
　" " John Day, on wf's acc., ch. William,
　　born Aug. 18, '82.
　" 29. Silvanus Arnold, on wf's acc., ch.
　　Anne.

Oct 6. Samuel Pierson & wf., ch. Mary,
born Sept. 9, '82.

" 10. Cornelius Loce & wf., family;
Phebe, born May 14, '68 ; Aaron,
born April 12, '70 ; Mary, born
Nov. 2, '72 ; Daniel, born Nov.
30, '75 ; Charity, born Aug. 18,
'78 ; and James, born Nov. 3,
'81.

" " John Loce, on wf's acc., chn. Leti-
cia, born March 3, '74, David
and Sarah, born March 13, '77 ;
and granddaughter Naomi, born
April 21, '73.

" " Hezekiah Stebbins, on wf's acc., ch.
Elizabeth, born Feb. 22, '80.

" 13. Onesimus Whitehead & wf., ch,
Ruth, born Aug. 22, '82.

" 19. James Ford, on wf's acc., ch. Sarah,
born Sept. 12, '82.

" " Demas Ford, on wf's acc.; ch. Sarah,
born Oct. 25, '81.

" 20. Henry Clark & wf., ch. John, born
Dec. 6, . '81.

" " Jed. Orsborn, on wf's acc., ch. Mary,
born Sept. 3, '82.

{
" 23.
Shon-
gum.
{

Deac. Jno. Hunterdon & wf., ch.
John, born Nov. 2, '79.
Daniel Clark & wf., Han., chn. Icabod, born July 13, '75 ; Hannah,
born Jan. 16, '78 ; Phebe, born
March 22, '81.
John Dean, on wf's acc., chn. Matthias, born Oct. 2, '72 ; Aaron,
born Oct. 22, '74 ; William, born
Feb. 7, '76 ; Mary, born June 9,
'78 ; Daniel, born Dec. 23, '81.

Nov. 3. Peter Hill & wf., ch. Rachel, born
June 4, '82.

" " Samuel Day & wf., ch. Susanna,
born Feb. 6, '82.

" " Ichabod Badgly & wf., ch. Lydia,
born Jan. 23, '82.

" 10. Jonathan Pierson & wf., ch. Sarah,
born Dec. 1, '81.

" 24. David Hoppen & wf., chn. David,
born Feb. 25, '78 ; & Matthias,
born Jan. 31, '82.

" 27. Col. Henry Remsen & wf., ch. William, born Sept. 25, '82.

Dec. 15. Matthew Rainer & wf., ch. David,
born Nov. 4, '82.

" " Joseph Marsh & wf., ch. Elizabeth,
born Oct. 7, '82.

1783.

Jan. 1. Eunice Tompkins, adult.

Jan. 5. Col. Benoni Hathaway & wf., ch
Ruth, born Nov. 15, '82.

" " Ichabod Cooper & wf., ch. David,
born Dec. 5, '82.

" 7. Joseph Riggs & wf., ch. Hannah,
born Sept. 3, '82.

" 26. Stephen Conkling, junr., & wf., ch.
Elizabeth, born Sept. 15, '82.

" " Armstrong Jones on wf's acc., ch.
John Sutton, born Nov. 11,'82.

Mar. 16. Wil. Saturly & wf., ch. Elizabeth,
born Jan. 15, '83.

" 11. Lydia Parker on her acc., chn.
Moses Johnston, born Aug. 20,
1771 : David Johnson, born
Oct. 30, '73 ; Jacob Johnson,
born April 22, '76 ; Morris
Johnson, born May 15, '79.

" 26. David Garrigas & wf., ch. Hannah, born Jan. 26, '83.

" " David Dalglish & wf., ch. David
born Dec. 28, '81.

" 30. John Pool & wf., ch. Luther, born
Feb. 1, '83,

April 6. David Tarbill & wf., ch. David,
born Jan. 25, '83.

" " Sarah, wf. of Michal Conner on her
acc., ch. James, born Jan. 16,'83.

" 12. Daniel Kemper & wf., ch. Thomas
Wair, born April 11, '83.

" 27. Daniel Smith & wf., ch. William,
born Feb. 2, '83.

May 2. Capt. Jacob Arnold on wf's acc., ch.
Abrm. Brasher, born March 29,
'83.

" " Gilbert Thornton on wf's acc., chn.
Mary, born Jan. 30, '77 ; Phineas, born July 1, '79 ; Ann,
born Nov. 17, '81.

" " Michael Tennery on wf's acc., chn.
Jno. Merry, born Sept. 13, '69 ;
Mary, born Sept. 1, '71 ; Michael,
born Sept. 3, '75 ; Joseph, born
June 26, '79.

" 11. Moses Crane & wf., ch, Phebe, born
Feb. 28, '83.

" " Joseph Byram & wf., ch. Rulatte,
born Feb. 28, '83.

" " Aaron Riggs on wf's acc., ch. Susanna Wood, born March 2, '83.

" " Caleb Edy & wf., ch. David, born
Feb. 1, '83.

" 18. Nathaniel Armstrong & wf., ch.
Hannah, born March 10, '83.

June 1. Richard Watcuk, on wf's acc., ch.
Francis, born April 29, '83.
" " David Day on wf's acc., ch. Anna,
born Jan. 28, '83.
May 15. Zenas Condict & wf., chn. Joseph,
born Nov. 25, '79; Angelina,
born Oct. 15, '81.
" " Isaac Lyon on wf's acc., chn. Mattaniah, born Dec. 12, '80; Cyrus, born March 29, '83.
July 8. Aaron Jowell, Junr., adult, with
Phebe his wf., who had been
christened before, ch. Catharine, born March 22, 83.
" 13. Samuel Seward & wf., ch. Ruth,
born May 9, '83.
Aug. 1. Sam. Wood on wf. Rebekah's acc.,
family, Jerusha, born June 27,
'78; Phebe, born Aug. 21, '80;
Jehannah, born Feb. 1, '83.
" 17. Theophilus Hathaway & wf., ch.
Elizabeth, born March 24, '83.
" " Abr. Wade & wf., ch. Noah Beach,
born June 23, '83.
" 31. Lindsly Burnet & wf., ch. Lewis,
born June 15, 83.
" " Silas Ayrs & wf., ch. Huldah, born
July 17, '83.
Sept. 5. Jonathan Ford, on wf's acc., ch.
Henry, born Aug. 4, '83.
" " Thomas Keen, on wf's acc., chn.
Roberd, born May—'78, David,
born April 10, '80.
" 7. Jeduthan Day & wf., ch. Silas, born
July 23, '83.
" " Benj. Hambleton & wf., ch. Phebe,
born July 20, '83.
" 18. Luther Extel & wf., twins, Luther &
Lucretia, born July 20, '83.
" " Phebe Stockbridge, ch. Eliab, born
Dec. 19, '75.
" 21. Icabod Carmichael & wf., ch. John,
born June 25, '83.
Oct. 5. Benj. Holloway & wf., ch. David,
born Aug. 17, '83.
" 12. Robert Rolfe & wf., ch. Sears, born
Aug. 18, '83.
" " Mrs. Doughty had two servant chn.
bap., Sussanna Sussex, born
Oct. 9, '81; & David Sussex,
born Sept. 14, '83.
" 20. Christopher Banker, on wf's acc.,
ch. Will. Stevens Smith, born
Jan. 31, '83.

Oct. 26. Joseph Lindsly & wf., ch. Joseph,
born Aug. 13, '83.
" " John Lindsly & wf., ch. Mary, born
Aug. 30, '83.
" 31. John Walker & wf., chn. Anne, born
Sept. 7, '80; Oliver, born July
11, '82.
Nov. 16. John Garrigas & wf., ch. Mary, born
Aug. 27, '83.
" 23. Capt. Ezek. Crane & wf., ch. Ann,
born July 14, '83.
" " Joseph Halsey & wf., ch. Elizabeth,
born Sept. 12, '83.
" 27. Joseph Tuttle, on wf's acc., ch.——
born Oct. 27, '83.
" " Jonathan Stiles, Esq., & wf., negro,
ch. Phillis, born Oct. 16, '81.
Dec. 11. Boys Prudden & wf., ch. Rhoda,
born May 17, '82.
1784.
Jan. 18. James Wilkerson on wf's acc., ch.
Elizabeth, born Nov. 13, '83.
" 24. John Mills & wf., ch. Elizabeth,
born Dec. 21, '83.
" 29. Ruben Wood on wf's acc., ch.
Phebe, born Sept. 11, '83.
" " Jesse Smith & wf., ch. Phebe, born
Oct. 20, '83.
Feb. 1. Joseph Lewis & wf., ch. Elizabeth
Johnes, born Dec. 25, '83.
" " Naptali Byram & wf., ch. Silas
Condict, born Nov. 24, '83.
" 8. Capt. Jabez Beach & wf., ch. Cy-
rus, born Dec. 7, '83.
" " Stephen Arnold & wf., ch. Susanna
Reve, born Sept. 15, '83.
" 15. Timo? Stiles & wf., ch. Jonathan
Tuttle, born Dec. 24, '83.
" 22. Job Loree & wf., ch. Experience,
born Dec. 31, '83.
Mar. 14. Sarah, wido. of Jonathan Pierson,
ch. Jonathan, Jan. 25, '84.
April 5. Jacob Emery & wf., ch. Experience,
born Jan. 29, '84.
" 18. David Raynor & wf., ch. Naomi,
born Feb. 3, '84.
" " Wil. Locy on wf's acc., ch. Barnabas, born Nov. 20, '83.
" " Matthias Burnet & wf., ch. Mary,
born Jan. 22, '84.
" 25. Ichabod Badgly & wf., ch. Charity,
born Nov. 24, '83.
" 29. Abraham Munson on wf's acc.,
chn. Stephen, born March 14,
'81; Elizabeth, born Dec. 15, '82.

May 2. Nathaniel Broadwell & wf., ch. Ira, born March 20, '84.

" 9. Dea. John Prudden & w.., ch. Gideon, born Feb. 24, '84.

" 16. Elias Hedges on wf's acc., ch. Mary, born March 14, '84.

" " Isaac Prudden & wf., ch. Jacob, born April 9, '84.

" " Zenas Condict & wf., ch. Paul Pierson, born Feb. 29, '84.

" " Peter Hill & wf., ch. Daniel, born Sept. 11, '83.

" 30. Samuel Morrison & wf., ch. Catharine Maria, born March 4, '84.

" " Richard Johnson & wf., ch. Elizabeth, born April 1, '84.

" " Jonathan Hallock & wf., ch. William, born April 25, '84.

June 10. Abrm. Hathaway, on wf's acc., ch. Augustine Bayles, born May 2, '84.

" " George "Gwinnup & wf., ch. John, March 17, '84.

" 24. John Stevenson, on wf's acc., ch. John, born May 1, '84.

" 27. Alex. Cermichael & wf., ch. Sophia, born May 6, '84.

" " Abijah Fairchild & wf., ch Gabriel, born May 21, '84.

" " Caleb Russell & wf., ch. Charles, born May 9, '84.

July 2. Mat. Rayner & wf., ch. Hannah, born April 12, '84.

" " Silvanus Arnold, on wf's acc., ch. Joanna, born May 17, '84.

" 25. Armstrong Jones & wf., ch. Catherine, born June 14, '84.

Aug. 15. Joseph Beers & wf., ch. Samuel, born July 1, '84.

" " John Walker & wf., ch. John Wood, born June 11, '84.

" 29. Nathan Guerin & wf., ch. Isaac Whitehead, born July 19, '84.

" " John Day, on wf's acc., ch. Barnabas, born April 21, '84.

" " Sam. Wines, on wf's acc., ch. Ebenezar, born April 21, '84.

Sept 19. Benj. Pierson, Jun'r & wf., chn. Ebenezar Condict, born Dec. 26, '83; Mary Armstrong, born Dec. 30, '83.

" " Jos. Pierson, Jun'r, ch. Amos, born July 2, '84.

Sept. 26. Ephraim Lindsly & wf., ch. Ruth born June 27, '84.

" " David Reeve & wf., chn. Abraham, born Sept. 9, '81; Daniel, born May 10, '84.

Oct. 3. Abner Condict & wf., ch. Silas Haines, born July 29, '84.

" 10. Henry Clark & wf., ch. Massa, born Oct. 17, '83.

" 24. Wido. of Usual Coe, ch. Mary Lindsly, born Aug. 17, '84.

" 27. James Ford, on wf's acc., ch. William Bdell, born Oct. 6, '84.

" 31. Abr. Talmage & wt., ch. David, born Sept. 17, '84.

Nov. 7. William Cherry & wf., chn. Ruben, born Nov. 4, '68; Euphemia, born Sept. 28, '83.

" 18. Thomas Kein's wf., ch. Bartholemew, born Oct. 8, '83.

" " Aaron Marsh & wf., family, Samuel, born May. 7, '68; Israel, born Feb. 11, '71; Anne, born March 8, '80; David, born Dec. 18, '82.

" 28. Amos Prudden & wf., ch. Jabesh. born Oct. 8, '84.

" " Peter Hill & wf., ch. Elizabeth, born Sept. 3, '84.

" 30. Nathan Reeve & wf., ch. Ezekiel, born Aug. 16, '84.

Dec. 12. George Marsh & wf., ch. William Youngs, born Sept. 1, '84.

1785.

Jan. 9. Joseph Riggs & wf., ch. Eunice, born Oct. 9 '84.

" " Cornelius Locy & wf., ch. Benjamin, born Sept. 1, '84.

" " Stephen Conkling & wf., ch. Rachel, born Oct. 30, '84.

" 16. Abraham Day & wf., ch. Elizabeth, born July 31, '84.

" 20. Silas Ayers & wf., ch. Huldah, born Sept. 1, '84.

" " Benj. Woodruff & wf., family, James, born Jan. 30, '72; Charles, born Jan. 18, '74; Phineas Lyman, born May 10, '76; Hannah, born May 17, '79; Benjamin, born July 31, '83.

Feb. 6. Abr. Munson on wf's acc., ch. Mary Pierson.

" 13. David Burnet & wf., ch. Foster, born Dec. 16, '84.

Feb. 20. Caleb Edy & wf., ch. Elizabeth, born Dec. 9, '84.

Bap'd, 2273 ; majority of males, 19.

" 27. Samuel Day & wf., ch. Samuel, born Nov. 5, '84.

" " Samuel Freman & wf., ch. Luis, born Dec. 8, '84,

Mar. 4. David Gardiner & wf., ch. Timo. Peck, born Dec. 26, '84.

Apr. 3. Isaac Woolley & wf., ch. Williams, born Dec. 13, '84.

" 17. John Pool & wf., ch. Jerusha, born Feb. 3, '85.

" " George Tucker & wf., ch. William, born Jan 25, '85.

" 25. Jesse Cutler & wf., ch. David, born March 10, '85.

" " James Farguson & wf., ch. Daniel, born March 15, '85.

" " Samuel Pierson & wf., ch. Samuel, born March 22, '85.

" 28. Abiel Fairchild, family, Jemima, born June 25, '69; Kezia, born April 29, '67; Rebekah, born Sept. 28, '71; Noah, born Nov. 22, '73; Hannah, born Jan. 8, 1780.

" " John Ensly, on wf's acc., ch. Jno. Scudder, born Feb. 11, '85.

" " Isaac Conkling & wf., ch. Sarah, born Nov. 25, '84.

May 1. Theophilus Hathaway & wf., ch Benoni, born March 21, '85.

" 19. John Kenny, Junr., on wf's acc., ch. Elizabeth, born March 1, '85.

" 22. David Tuttle & wf., ch. Isaac, born Jan. 18, '84.

June 5. Eld. Jos. Lindsly & wf., ch. Ira, born April 21, '85.

" " Capt. Silas Howell, ch. Charles, born April 12, '85.

" 26. Ephraim Youngs & wf., ch. Phebe, born May 13, '85.

" " Aaron Allen & wf., ch. Phebe, born April 11, '85.

" " Stephen Arnold & wf., ch. Hannah, born March 26, '85.

" " Samuel & Mary Ann Wilkerson, ch. Baxter, born Jan. 6, '85.

" 2. Ziba Arnold, on wf's acc., fam., Elizabeth, born July 30, '71 ; Sam., born April 20, '75; Mary, born April 11, '78; Rachel, born Dec. 16, '80.

" 3. Isaac Ayrs & wf., ch. Enos, born May 17, '85.

July 10. Michael Conner, on wf's acc., ch. James, born June 16, '85.

" 31. Isaac Ross, on wf's acc., ch. Elizabeth; born———, '83.

Aug. 3. Silas Condict, Esqr., & wf., grand ch. Elizabeth Phebe, born Dec. 9, '82 ; at same time, negro, ch. Chloe, born Jan. 28, '82.

Aug. 7. Zip. wido. of Jonathan Johnson, ch. Jonathan, born June———, '85.

Sept. 9. David Dalglish & wf., ch. John, born Aug. 22, '83.

" 18. David Garrigas & wf., ch. Silas, born Aug. 18, '85.

" 25. Icabod Cooper & wf., ch. Lewis, born Aug. 16, '85.

Oct. 9. Capt. Joseph Halsey & wf., ch. Maria, born Sept. 2, '85.

" 26. Paul Lee & wf., family, Anna, born Aug. 23, '81 ; Daniel, May 31, '83 ; Phebe, born Sept. 28, '85.

Nov. 4. Joanna Prudden, ch. Ruth, born Nov. 17, '84.

" " Isaac Walker, adult, & wf., ch. James, born Dec. 14, '84.

" 6. Joseph Lewis & wf., ch. Anna, born Oct. 4, '85.

" 10. Michael Miller on wf's acc., chn. Michael, born Aug. 25, '82; Sarah, born Aug. 28, '85.

" " Rodolphus Kent & wf., ch. Catharine, born Oct. 9, '85.

" " Samuel Tuthill & wf., negro ch. Violet, born March 15.

" 20. Icabod Badgly & wf., ch. Timothy, born Oct. 11, '85.

" 27. Benj. Holloway & wf., ch. Moses, born Oct. 12. '85.

" " Dayton Talmage & wf., ch. Esther Case, born Aug. 29, '85.

Dec. 8. Daniel Pierson & wf., ch. Clarissa, born Sept. 19, '85.

" 14. Peter Hill & wf., ch. Aaron, born Oct. 18, '85.

" 18. Moses Esty & wf., ch. David, born Oct. 21. '85.

" 25. Capt. Jabez Beach & wf., ch. Sarah, born Oct. 26, '85.

" " William Cherry & wf., ch. Phebe, born Nov. 23, '85.

" 30. The names and ages of Jacob and Mary Ball, and babtized, Phebe, born Sept. 11, '70; Abraham, born Sept. 22, '74 ; Sarah, born July 5, '77 ; Isaac, born Aug. 17, '83.

" " Asa Beach. adult, born Aug. 6, '61.

" " Asa & Hannah Beach, family, John Kenny, born Jan. 23, '79 ; Henry, born March 17, '82.

(To be continued.)

THE RECORD.

FIRST PRESBYTERIAN CHURCH, MORRISTOWN, N. J.

"This shall be Written for the Generation to Come."—Psalms 102 : 18.

VOL. II.	DECEMBER, 1881.	NO. 12

(Printed with the approval of Session.)

THE RECORD

Will be printed and published monthly at Morristown, N. J. Terms, 50 cents per annum in advance; 75 cents after June.

Subscriptions will be received at the book-stores of Messrs. Runyon and Emmell, or through the mail. All communications should be addressed to the

EDITOR OF THE RECORD,

Lock box 44.   Morristown, N. J.

Vol. I. complete, 75 cents.

Entered at the Post Office at Morristown, N. J., as second class matter.

• ——:o:——

VALE !

The Presbytery of Morris and Orange met in the First Church Chapel Tuesday, Oct. 11, 1881, and voted to dissolve the pastoral relation then existing between the Rev. Rufus Smith Green and the First Presbyterian Church of Morristown, N. J., the dissolution to take effect after the following Sunday. Mr. G. resigns his charge to assume the pastorate of the La Fayette St. Church of Buffalo, N. Y., whither he removes Oct. 19th, 1881. To meet engagements with the subscribers to *The Record* he continues its publication to the end of the year, issuing the last two numbers in advance. He sincerely regrets that he can not carry forward the work now fairly under way. He hopes that some one may be found to continue it.

For the kindly interest of his readers he desires to express his hearty thanks.

That their names may be found upon The Record of the Book of Life is his earnest prayer.

THE SIXTEENTH PASTORATE

Of the First Church, that of Rev. R. S. Green, began June 17, 1877, and closed Oct. 19, 1881. During this time there have been added to the church on examination, 57 ; by certificate from other churches, 77 ; total, 134. 18 adults and 35 children have been baptized, 22 marriages have been solemnized, 103 funerals have been attended.

The contributions of the church for the same time have been :

For Foreign Missions,		$6,205
" Home Missions,		4,500
" Education,		4,149
" Church Erection,		1,010
" Ministerial Relief,		564
" Freedmen,		457
" Sustentation,		303
" Publication,		157
" Miscellaneous Objects,		5,225
Total,		$22,570
Congregational Expenses about		$31,000
Total,		$53,570

OMITTED

Inadvertently from the List of Members of the Church the name of Martha Emmell, (George.) Mrs. Emmell was born Nov. 12, 1760, united with the Church Sept. 1st, 1786, and died Feb. 23d, 1845.

THE RECORD

Has been published from its commencement at the office of the *True Democratic Banner* of this city. To the Messrs. Vogt, editors, our thanks are due for uniform courtesy.

The records of the church members, baptisms, marriages and deaths are now completed through the pastorate of the Rev. Timothy Johnes, D.D. The Trustees Book has also reached the same date.

BAPTISMS.

178

Jan. 1. John Lindsly & wf., ch. John, born Nov. 20, '85.

" " John Garrigas & wf., twins Thankful & Anna, born Oct. 19, '85.

" 19. Daniel Phoenix & wf., ch. Cornelia, born Nov. 8, '85.

" 29. Doc. Timo. Johnes & wf., John Blanchard, born Dec. 1, '85.

Feb. 19. Isaac Prudden & wf., ch. Hannah, born Jan. 1, '86.

" 26. Robert Rolph & wf., ch. Robert, born Nov. 27, '85.

" " Isaac Pierson & wf., Mary, ch. Eliza Miller, born Dec. 26,'85.

" " David Tuttle & wf., ch. Sarah, born Dec. 19, '85.

Mar. 19. Jacob Emery & wf., ch. Nathan, born Feb. 8, '86.

" " Jonathan Hallock & wf., ch. Joanna, born Feb. 25, '86.

" 26. Benj. Woodruff & wf., ch. Obadiah Lum, born Nov. 1, '85.

" " David Pierson & wf., family— David, born July 24, '76; Silas, born Aug. 20, '78; Elias, born Jan. 14, '81; John, born May 27, '83; Phebe, born April 12, '85.

" 30. Robert Arnold, Jun. & wf., family— Hannah, born Nov. 21, '71; Abraham, born Oct. 15, '76; Elizabeth, born May 2, '82; Nathan, born Sept. 9, '84.

" " John Conkling & wf., ch. Deborah, born April 21. '85.

" " Jonathan Hayward on wf's acc., family—Daniel, born Jan. 28, '80; Nathan, May 3, '84.

April 6. Luther Exell & wf., ch. Mary, born Feb. 7, '86.

" " David Tarbill & wf., ch. Rebekah, born Feb. 23, '86.

" " John Oliver & wf., ch. Abagail, born Jan. 4, '86.

" 9. Daniel Freeman, Junr. & wf., ch. Carolina, born Feb. 6, '86.

" 16. Jonathan Dickerson & wf., ch. John, born March 10, '86.

" 23. John Mills & wf., ch. Henry, born March 12, '86,

Apr. 30. Samuel Seward & wf., ch. Ann-julina, born March 6, '86.

" " Asa Beach & wf., ch. Sarah, born March 7, '86.

" 5. Boys Prudden & wf., ch. Luce, born March 6, '86.

May 7. Jacob Ball & wf., ch. Hannah, born March 17, '86.

" 14. Isaac Woolley & wf., ch. David, born March 25, '86.

June 4. Nap. Byram & wf., ch. Sarah, born April 18, '86.

" " Zenas Condict & wf., ch. Phebe, born March 26, '86.

" " Joseph Marsh & wf., ch. Sarah, born April 4, '86.

" 18. Samuel Freman & wf., ch. John Ross, born April 6. '86.

" " Jonathan Dickerson & wf., family desired to be recorded as followeth: Mahlon, born April 17, '70; Silas, born Oct. 3, '71; Mary, born Sept. 8, '78; Jonathan Elmer, born Sept. 8, '81; Aaron, born Sept. 10, '83; baptized by different ministers; John, born March 10, '86; the cast bap. by myself, (see April 16, '86, above; Ed.)

" " Henry Clark & wf., ch. Jane, born Jan. 12, '86.

" 30. Sarah Serren, adult.

" " Joseph Prudden & wf., ch. Elizabeth, born Jan. 10, '86.

July 2. Capt. Silas Howell & wf., ch. Susannah, born May 6, '86.

" " Nathaniel Broadwell & wf., ch. Lindsly, born May 14, '86.

" " David Day & wf., ch. Benjamin, born Nov. 23, '86 (?)

" 9. Abijah Fairchild & wf., ch. John Flavel, born May 18, '86.

" 30. John Hayward's wf., on her acc., ch. Jonathan, born July 1, '86.

" " Richard Johnson & wf., ch. Sarah, born June 18, '86.

" " Nathaniel Armstrong & wf., ch. John, born June 21, '86. Bap. to this date, 2392.

Aug. 20. Elizabeth Arnold's grand-ch. Catharine, born Jan. 13, '83.

Sept. 1. George Emmel on wf's acc., chh. Susanna, born Oct. 12, '83; Elizabeth, born Feb. 29, '86,

Sept. 3. Jedidiah Osborh & wf., ch. Jacob, born July 16, '86.

" 17. Gideon Riggs & wf., chn. Sarah, born Dec. 3, '80; Ashbel, born March 9, '86.

" " Abr. Talmage & wf., ch. John, born June 23, '86.

" " Silvanus Arnold on wf's acc., ch. Lewis, born Feb. 16, '86.

" 24. Caleb Russell & wf., ch. Robert Morris, born July 30, '86.

Oct. 8. Dea. Jos. Prudden & wf., ch. Jane, born Aug. 17, '86.

" " Jno. Prudden & wf., ch. Aaron Riggs, born July 29, '86.

" " Nathan Guierin & wf., ch. Phebe, born Aug. 30, '86.

" 22. Benj. Pierson & wf., ch. Elijah, born Aug. 31, '86.

" 27. Nap. Tuttle & wf., her niece Mary Post, born Oct. 25, '86.

" 29. David Reeve & wf., ch. David Hallock, born Aug. 28, '86.

" " John Harporee & wf., ch. Hannah, born Sept. 2, '86.

Nov.10. John Kirkpatrick on wf's acc., ch. Hannah, born Sept. 30.

" 15. Elizabeth wf. of Peter Fairchild,ch. Hannah, born Oct. 26, '86.

" 30. Abner Condict & wf., ch. Anna, born Sept. 26, '86.

Dec. 3. Wil. Wick & wf., ch. Daniel, born Sept. 10, '86.

" 17. George Tucker & wf., ch. John, born Oct. 14, '86.

" 17. Stephen Conkling & wf., ch. Stephen, born Oct. 27, '86.

1787.

Jan. 15. George Gwinop & wf., ch. Samuel, born Jan. 31, '86.

" " Armstrong Jones & wf., ch. Elizabeth, born Sept. 3, '86.

Feb. 2. Stephen Turner & wf., ch. Nathaniel Peck, born Nov. 11, '86.

" 4. Abr. Day & wf., ch. Isaac, born Nov. 12, '86.

" " Joseph Bears & wf., ch. Elizabeth, born Dec. 27, '86.

" " Nathaniel Bears & wf., ch. Jacob, born Oct. 7, '86.

" " Abr. Hathaway & wf., ch. Abraham, born Sept. 26, '86.

Mar. 4. Jesse Cutler & wf., ch. Jonathan, born Jan. 7, '87.

April 1. Matthias Burnet & wf., ch. Rachel, born Jan 17, '87.

" " Silas Ayrs & wf., ch. Silas Condict, born Feb. 12, '87.

" 5. Ruben Wood & wf., ch. Israel, born Oct. 16, '86.

" " Capt. Jacob Arnold, on wf's acc., ch. Jacob, born Sept. 16, '86.

" 8. Nathan Reeve & wf., ch. William, born Dec. 3, '86.

" 10. Joseph Tuttle, on wf's acc., twins, Elizabeth and Jacob, born Aug. 26, '86..

May 6. Maj. Joseph Lindsly & wf., ch. Matthew, born Jan. 27, '87.

" " Moses Crane & wf., ch. Elizabeth, born Feb. 6, '87.

" " James Ford & wf., ch. John, born March 23, '87.

" " Abr. Tunis Schenck & wf., ch. Peter, born Jan. 16, '87.

" 27. Michael VanCourt, on wf's acc., ch. Elizabeth, born April 3, '87.

June 10. Rob. Arnold, Junr., ch. Phebe, born May 7, '87.

" " John Paul & wf., ch. Susanna, born March 1, '87.

" " Icabod Badgly & wf., ch. Demas, born March 27, '87.

" 17. James Vance & wf., family, Martha, born Jan. 1, '81; Alexander, born Sept. 9, '82; Rebekah, born March 15, '85.

" 25. Joseph Pierson & wf., ch. Timothy, born Dec. 24, '86.

" " Benj. Holloway & wf., ch. Hannah, born Apr. 4, '87.

" " John Conkling & wf., ch. Sarah Roberts, born May 18, '87.

July 1. Joseph Byram & wf., ch. Esther, born May 7, '87.

" 15. Isaac Conkling & wf., ch. Jonathan Dimon, born July 7, '87.

" 22. Doc. Timo. Johnes & wf., ch. Elizabeth Sophia, born June 14, '87.

" " David Ogden, on wf's acc., ch. Phebe, born April 7, '87.

" " Jonathan Rainer & wf., ch. Jonathan, born April 11, '87.

" 29. Capt. Silas Howell & wf., ch. Stephen, born May 28, '87.

Aug. 5. Jno. Lindsly, on wf's acc., ch. Ephraim, born June 23, '87.

Aug. 19. Moses Estey & wf., ch. Elizabeth, born July 8, '87.

" " Ziba Arnold, on wf's acc., twins, Robert & Jonathan Reeve, born July 2, '87.

" 26. Peter Hill & wi., ch. Sarah, born July 25, '87.

" 31. Daniel Burnet's wf., ch. Samuel Jacks, born Dec. 11, '76.

Sept. 2. John Oliver, ch. Catharine, or Gette born July 5, '87.

" 30. David Tuttle & wf., ch. Kezia, born Aug. 19, '87 ; Mr. Miller.

Oct. 28. David Pierson & wf., ch. Charles, born Sept. 1, '87.

" " Capt. Jed. Mills, ch. Sarah, born Sept. 22, '87.

Nov. 2. Capt. Jabez Beach & wf., ch. Ira, born Sept. 16, '87.

" 11. Jeduthan Day & wf., ch. Amzi, born Sept. 29, '87.

" " Icabod Cooper & wf., ch. Silas, born Oct. 4, '87.

" 25. Lambert Merrel, on wf's acc., ch. Anna, born Oct. 16, '87.

" " Abr. Munson, on wf's acc., ch. Gil. Allen, born Sept. 3, '87.

" " Isaac Lindsly & wf., ch. Philip, born Dec. 21, 86.

Dec. 2. Robert Rolfe & wf., ch. Enoch, born Nov. 16, '87.
Bap. to this date, 2465.

" 25. Capt. Joseph Halsey & wf., ch. Juliana, born Nov. 18, '87.

" " Cornelius Locy, ch. Elizabeth, born Sept. 20, '87.

" " Ephraim Lindsly & wf., ch——

" 30. Samuel Pierson & wf., ch. Ebenezer, born Oct. 3, '87.

" " James Vance & wf., ch. James, born Nov. 3, 87.

1788.
Feb. 10. Isaac Prudden & wf., ch. Josiah, born Dec. 27, '87.

" 24. Abner Wade & wf., chn. Dorothy Wells, born Feb. 13, '85 ; Susanna, born Oct. 21, '97.

" 25. David Lindsly & wf., ch. Mahlon, born Jan. 3, '88.

" 29. Daniel Phenix & wf., ch. Jonas Phillips, born Jan. 14, '88.

Mar. 30. Isaac Walker & wf., ch. Sarah, born Dec. 11, '87.

April 6. William Cherry & wf., ch. Moses, born Dec. 31, '87.

" 10. Jonathan Stiles, Junr., on wf's acc., ch. Chilion Ford, born Dec. 17, '87.

" " Daniel Tuthill & wf., negro ch. Timon, born Mar. 19, '88.

" 13. Abr. T. Schenck & wf., ch. Cornelia, born Feb. 24, '88.

May 2. Benj. Freeman & wf., ch. Charles, born Dec. 20, '87.

" 4. Nathaniel Bears & wf., ch. Elizabeth, born Feb. 25, '88.

" " John Garrigas & wf., ch. Lidia, born Jan. 4, '88.

" 18. Sam. Seward & wf., ch. Elizabeth Ayrs, born April 4, '88.

" 25. Joseph Riggs & wf., ch. Joseph Cook, Mar. 28, '88.

June 1. Richard Johnson & wf., ch. James, born Mar. 30, '88.

" " John Hayward, on wf's acc., ch. Deborah, born April 2, '88.

" " Naphtali, Byram & wf., ch. Anna, born April 21, '88.

" 8. Lnther Extel & wf., ch. Hannah, born April 13, '88.

" 22. Isaac Woolley & wf., ch. John, born April 29, '88.

" 26. Josh. Lambert, grandch. Jabez Lambert, born Oct. 3, 81.

" 29. John Day, on wf's acc., ch. Sarah, born May 8, '88.

July 4. Moses Wilkerson & wf., family, Hannah, his wf., adult; Phebe, born April 6, '74, Mary, born Mar. 15, '80; Elizabeth, born Dec. 17, '81.

" " George Emmel, on wf's acc., ch. Phebe, born April 30, '88.

" 6. John Sprout & Mary, his wf., ch. Margaret, born Jan. 31, '88.

" " John Wilson & wf., ch. Henry, born April 16, '88.

" 13. Joseph Lewis & wf., ch. Joseph, born July 8, '88.

" 20. Benj. Pierson, jun'r., & wf., ch. Huldah, born June 11, '88.

Aug. 3. Jonathan Dickersou & wf., ch. Philemon, born June 26, '88.

" " Timothy Stiles & wf., ch. Elizabeth, born June 14, '88.

" " Samuel Freeman & wf., ch. Sarah, born June 9, '88.

Aug. 17. George Gwinnup & wf., ch. Pamelia, born April 21, '88.

" 31. Caleb Russell & wf., Eliza Pierson, born July 19, '88.

Sept. 5. Caleb Tuttle & wf., family, Ann, born Sept. 20, '80; Sarah, born Jan. 26, '82 ; Phebe, born June 6, '83 ; Jacob, born May 10, '85.

" 10. David Day, on wf's acc., ch. Ezra Halsey, born April 29, '88.

" 17. Joseph Marsh & wf., ch. William, born July 11, '88.

" 21. Jonathan Hallock & wf., ch. Abigail, born Aug. 16, '88.

" " Zenas Condict & wf., ch. Hannah, born Aug. 17, '88.

" 28. Jonathan Ogden & wf., ch. Elias, born Aug. 19, '88.

" " Ephraim Youngs & wf., ch. Lucinda Lee, born July 3, '88.

" " Gideon Riggs & wf., ch. Calvin, born June 1, '88.

" " Samuel Day & wf., ch. Ira, born July 21, '88.

Oct. 5. Aaron Riggs & wf., ch. Mary, born Aug. 14, '88.

" " Mary, servant of Mr. Doty, on her mistress' acc., as well as on her own, chn. Maria, born June 17, '85 ; Cretia, born Jan 12, '88.

" " Wm. Jones & wf., negro ch. Amos, born July 1, '88.

" 12. Capt. Silas Howell & wf., ch. Lewis, born Aug. 17, '88.

" " Henry Wil. Desausure's wf., ch. Henry Alexander, born Sept. 15, '88.

" 19. Samuel Hill & wf., ch. Jonathan, born Dec, 17, '88.

Nov. 2. Isaac Lindsly & wf., ch. Ebenezer, born Sept. 15, '88.

" " Stephen Conkling's wido., ch. Benoni, born July 22, '88.

" 16. Abr. Talmage & wf., ch. Mehitabel, born Sept. 17, '88.

" " Joseph Beers & wf., ch. Elizabeth, born Sept. 24, '88.

Dec. 21. George Tucker & wf., ch. George Phillips, born Oct. 29, '88.

1789.

Jan. 4. Silvanus Arnold, on wf's acc., ch. Stephen Harrison, born Oct. 4, '88.

Feb. 27. Stephen Burnet & wf., ch. Sam. Landson, born Oct. 30, '88.

Mar. 1. Wm. Wick & wf., ch. Ann, born Jan. 13, '89.

May 4. Maj. Jos. Lindsly & wf., ch. Mary, born Feb. 20, '89.

" " John Oliver & wf., ch. Jonathan, born Jan. 25, '89.

" " Caleb Tuttle & wf., ch. Stephen, born Dec. 31, (?) '89.

June 14. Jesse Cutler & wf., ch. Lewis, born March 14, '89.

" " Capt. Jed. Mills & wf., ch. Hannah Hedden, born April 7, '89.

" " Matthias Burnet & wf., ch. Matthias Lindsly, boan April 26, '89.

" " Silas Ayres & wf., ch. John, born, March 27, '89.

" 19. Capt. Ja. Arnold, on wf's acc., ch. Charles, born Sept. 29, '88.

" 21. Nathaniel Broadwell & wf., ch. Mary, born March 14, '89.

" 28. Jacob Read, on wf's acc., chn. Thomas, born March 27, '84 ; Penina, born March 30, '88.

" " Michel VanCourt, on wf's acc., ch. Elias, born March 7, '89.

July 4. Doc. Timo. John es & wf., ch. Francis Childs, born March 19, '89.

" " Daniel Pierson & wf., ch. John, Alfred, born May 3, '89.

" " Moses Estey & wf., ch. Charles, born May 12, '89.

" 26. Abr. Hathaway on wf's acc., ch. Elizabeth, born Feb. 6, '89.

" " Joseph Godden & wf., ch. Lewis, born Oct. 30, '88.

" " John Pool & wf., ch. Rebekah, born June 8, '89.

Aug. 9. Mary, wf. of Wm. Broadwell, chn. Ebenezar, born Jan. 3, '84 ; William, born June 20, '86 ; Baxter, born Jan. 5, '88.

" 23. Mary, wf. of Moses Sturge, on wf's acc., ch. Walter, born Jan. 24, '89,

" " Daniel Smith on wf's acc., ch. Joanna, born July 3, '89.

" 30. David Reeve & wf., ch. Bathia, born May 9, '89.

Sept. 6. Samuel Hill & wf., ch. Henry, born June 10, '87.

" " Stephen Turner & wf., ch. Joseph, born ―― 22, '89.

Sept. 6. Benj. Holloway & wf., ch. William, born July 26, '89.

———Larance Wilson & wf., ch. James, born July 10, '89.

" 20. Thomas Johnson & wf., family, Zenas, born July 26, '82; Ruth, born April 11, '84; William, born Jan. 7, '87; Daniel, born Jan. 3, '89.

" 22. David Ogden on wf's acc., ch. George, born Jan. 18, '89.

" 27. Jno. Ensley on wf's acc., ch. Phebe, born Aug. 11, '89.

Oct. 4. John Alwood, adult.

" 11. Joseph Lewis & wf., ch. William Johnes, born Aug. 22, '89.

" " Abr. Coe & wf,, ch. Lewis, born Mar. 30, '89.

" 17. James Pitney on wf's acc., family— Charity, born March 31, '82; Catherine, born Feb. 5, '84; Joseph Stiles, born June 18, '86; Maria, born Aug. 5, '85.

" 25. Moses Johnson bap. adult, & Hulda, his wf., renewed covenant ch. Joseph, born July 2, '88.

Nov.— David Larence & wf., ch. Sarah, born March 17, '88.

" 8. Ichabod Cooper & wf., ch. Phebe, born Sept. 1, '89.

" 29. Joseph Byram & wf., ch. Elizabeth, born Oct. 12, '89.

Dec. 6. Jacob Ball & wf., ch. Mary, born Oct. 5, '89.

" 20. Dea. Jos. Prudden & wf., ch. Joseph, born Oct. 6, '89.

1790.

Jan. 10. James Ford & wf., ch. Silas, born Nov, 27, '89.

" 17. Robert Arnold & wf., ch. Mary Pierson, born Nov. 15, '89.

" " Bethuel Hayward & wf., family— Darius, born March 17, '83; Isaac, born Aug. 15, '85; Rebecka, born May 23, '88.

" 31. Isaac Prudden & wf., ch. David, born Dec. 1, '89.

Bap. to this date 2,580.

Mar. 12. Capt. Joseph Halsey & wf., ch. Joseph, born Jan. 31, '90.

" " Capt. Jabez Beach & wf., ch. Fanna, born Nov. 24, '89.

" " Wm. Cherry & wf., ch. Elizabeth, born Oct. 15, '89.

Mar. 12. John. Arnold, chn. Samuel, born Oct. 6, '82, Sarah, born Oct. 5, '85: Abigail, born Jan. 30, '89.

" " Hannah Johnson, a young woman.

" 20. Abner Condict & wf., ch. Mary, born Dec. 21, '89.

" 28. Icabod Badgley & wf., ch. Joanna, born Oct. 30, '89.

Apr. 4. Dan. Phoenix & wf., ch. Lewis, born Feb. 22, '90.

" 30. Enuice Johnson, a young woman.

" " Ruth Johnson, a young woman.

" " James Stiles, a young man.

" " Abr. Schenck & wf., ch. David, born Feb. 26, '90.

" " David Tuttle & wf., ch. Phebe, born March 1, '90.

May 2. Caleb Russell & wf., ch. Israel, born March 10, '90.

" " Isaac Woolley & wf., ch. Mary, born Feb. 21, '90.

" " Nathaniel Beers & wf., ch. Rebekah, born Feb. 12, '90.

" " Jonathan Raynor & wf., ch. Triphena, born Jan. 2, '90.

" " Benj. Pierson & wf., ch. Silas, born Jan. 17, '90.

" " Joseph Pierson & wf., ch. Esther, born Oct. 5, '89.

" 23. Wm. Hamilton & wf., family, Elizabeth, born April 19, '79; Silas, born Feb. 14, '81; William, born Feb, 20, '83; Sarah, born April 15, '88.

June 6. Isaac Lyon & wf., ch. Rhoda, born Nov. 20, '89.

" 13. John Howel, on wf's acc., ch. Rachel.

" 20. Richard Johnson, ch. John, born April 29, '90.

" 23. Isaac Canfield on wf's acc., ch. James, Caldwell, born Jan. — '90.

" 26. John Garrigas & wf., ch. Charity, born Jan. 30, '90.

" " Jacob Reed, on wf's acc., ch. Mary, born May 20, '90.

July 2. Jonathan Johnson & wf., chn. Mary born March 4, '75; David Parkhurst, born July 24, '77; Jonathan, born July 5, '79; Elizabeth born Nov. 10.

July 2. Will. Meeker & wf., bap., and chn.
William, born Dec. 8, '84 ; Sam.,
born Nov. 12, '86 , James, born
Dec. 6, '88 ; Henry, born Jan,
8, '90.

" " Ephraim Muir, a young man.

" " Abr. Munson & wf., ch.—— ·

" 3. Phineas Chitester, family, Phebe,
born Feb. 21, '81 ; Melinda,
born Oct. 27, '83 ; Stephen,
born Oct. 7, '85 ; Ruhamah,
born Jan, 22, '87 ; Ame, born
Mar. 2, '89.

" 31. Jonathan Hayward on wf's acc., ch.
Martha, born April 20, '90.

" " George Foster Tennery on wf's
acc., ch. John Bayles, born
June 7, '80.

Aug. 15. Dea. Allen's adopted ch. John
Frase.

" " Elijah Sneden & wf., ch. Mary,born
April 28, '90.

" 22. Aaron Cook Collins, ch. Salle Ann,
born May 1, '90.

Sept. 7. Caleb Howell on wf's acc., chn.
Charles, born Sept. 24, '78 ;
William, born Jan. 21, '79 ;
Ebenezer, born March 20, '81 ;
Daniel, born March 28, '83 ;
Deborah, born March 6, '85 ;
Anna, born July 21, '87 ;
Elizabeth, born Aug. 21, '89.

" 12. John Conkling & wf., ch. John,
born Sept. 5, '89.

" " Abraham Conkling & wf., ch. Anna,
born July 25, '90.

" " Joseph Marsh & wf., ch. Henry,
born Aug. 7, '90.

" " Samuel Ludlam & wf., ch. Timothy,
born July 11, '90.

Oct. 24. John Kenny on wf's acc., ch. Jacob
Arnold, born Sept. 14, '90.

" " Moses Sturge on wf's acc., ch.
Anne, born Sept. 21, '90.

" " Sam. Day & wf., ch. Mahlon, born
Aug. 17, '90.

" 31. Toomas Johnson & wf., ch. Phebe,
born Sept. 3, '90.

Nov. 5. George Emmell on wf's acc., ch.
Mary, born Sept. 18, '90.

" " Isaac Pierson & wf., ch. Maltby
Gelstone, born Sept. 8, '90.

" " Capt. Silas Howell & wf., ch. Anne
Lewis, born Oct. 6, '90.

Dec. 19. Gideon Riggs, ch. Henry, born
Sept. 25, '90.

1791.

Jan. 2. Isaac Lindsly & wf., ch. Fanny,
born Sept. 2, '90.

" " Robert Rolfe & wf., ch. Elias, born
Oct. 12, '90.

" " Aaron Riggs & wf., ch. Rachel, born
Oct. 11, '90.

" 23. Stephen Arnold & wf., ch. Stephen
born Sept. 23, '89.

" " Abraham Talmadge & wf., ch.
Eunice, born Dec. 2, '90.

" " Zenas Condict & wf., ch, Elias, born
Oct. 3, '90.

" " Wm. Wick & wf., ch. Wm., born
Dec. 10, '90.
Bap. to this date 2,777.

" 30. Gabriel Pierson & wf., chn. Matthias, born May 1, '89 ; Enos,
born Nov. 9, '90.

Feb. 7. Joseph Lindsly & wf., ch. Rachel,
born Nov. 24, '90.

" 28. Ziba Arnold on wf's acc., twins
Joanna & Gitty, born Nov. 13,
'90.

Mar. 4. Wm. Hambleton & wf., ch. Jane,
born Oct. 9, '90.

" 10. Caleb Tuttil & wf., ch. Mehytable,
born Oct. 10, '90.

April 4. Silas Stiles on wf's acc., ch. Silas
Stiles, born Dec. 17, '90.

" 17. David Burnet & wf., ch. Aaron Lee,
born March 14, '91.

May 15. Dan. Pierson & wf., ch. William
Horase, born Feb. 12, '91.

" " Phineas Chistester & wf., ch. ——

" " George Tucker & wf., ch. Samuel,
born Dec.' 25, '90.

" 29. Isaac Ayrs & wf., ch. Isaac, born
April 11, '91.

" " William Meeker & wf., ch.——

June 15. Rodolphus Kent, on wf's acc., chn.
Sarah Tuthill, born April 4, '88,
John Vaness, born Oct. 7, '89.

" 26. Silas Ayrs & wf., ch. Elias, born
May 17, '91.

" " Matthias Burnet, on wf's acc., ch.
Job Brookfield. born April 27,
'91.

July 1. Doc. Timo. Johnes, Jun'r & wf., ch.
Joanna Nitel, born May 16, '91.

" 3. Sil. Arnold, on wf's acc., ch. Isaac,
born April 5, '91.

July 4. Ralph Burnet, on wf's acc., chn.
Susanna, born April 18, '80;
Phebe, born April 25, '84;
Sarah, born May 15, '86,
" 5. Aaron Hoell, of N. York, & wf., ch.
Mary, born Dec. 15, '90.
" 10. Ephraim Youngs & wf., ch. James
Pershal, born Oct. 12, 90.
" " John Wilson & wf., ch. Ezra. born
March 8, '91.
" " David Pierson & wf., ch. Lewis,
born Jan. 7, 91.
Aug. 7. Cornelus Loce on his acc., ch.
Lewis, born Feb. 14, '91.
" " John Dav on wf's acc., ch. Mary,
born April 15, '91.
" 14. Sussex Johnes on wf. & Mrs.' acc.,
(Mr. Doughty), chn. Peter,born
June,'89 ; Jane, born May 3,'91.
" 21. Jno. Oliver & wf., ch. Phebe, born
May 2, '91.
Sept. 30. Moses Johnson & wf., ch. Ben.,
born July 22, '91—Collins.
" " Benj. Woodruff & wf., ch. John,
born Oct. 19, '88—Collins.
Oct. 6. Gabriel Ford & wf., ch. Anna Elizabeth, born July 21, '91.
" 9. Moses Estey & wf., ch. William,
born July 9, '91.
" " Lorance Wilson & wf., ch. Mary,
born July 17, '91.
" " Benj. Woodruff & wf., ch. Timothy,
born March 10, '91.
" 20. Isaac Prudden & wf., ch. Samuel,
born Sept. 12, '91.
" " Benj. Holloway & wf., ch. Elijah,
born Sept. 19, '91.
" " George Tenery on wf's acc., ch.
Mary, born Sept. 5, '91.
" 6. Samuel Freman & wf., ch. Hulda,
born Aug. 28, '91.
1792.
Jan. 10. Rodolphus Kent on wf's acc., ch,
David Ford, born Dec. 10, '91,
July 3. Capt. Arnold on wf's acc., ch. bap.
at Aaron Pierson's, name Eliza
Maria,,born March 2, '92.
Sept. 23. Daniel Phoenix & wf., ch. Julia
Anna, born July 25, '92.
1793.
Apr. 10. James Pitney on wf's acc., ch.
Charles Alex, born Sept. 21,'92.
Aug. 5. Daniel Pierson & wf., ch. Elizabeth
Ann, born March 19, '93.
Also negro chn. Pegg, born Feb. 6,
'93 ; Rose, born March 24, '90.
Aug. 1. James Vance & wf., ch. Mary, born
Aug. 1, '93—by Mr. Acley. (?)
Oct. 29. Thomas Johnson, ch. Rhoda, born
Dec. 5, '92.
Total baptisms (by Rev. Timothy
Johnes) 2,827.

(Continued from page 188.)

TRUSTEES' BOOK.

April 22, 1795. Silas Condict, Moses Estey, Benj. Lindsly, Isaac Canfield, Wm. Canfield, John Mills, Jonas Philops, Richard
Johnson, Jonathan Dickerson, Jonathan
Ogden, Jonathan Stiles, Joseph Lewis, Daniel Phœnix, Ezra Halsey, Alex. Carmichael,
Benj. Holloway, Gilbert Alling, Joseph Pruden, Joseph Halsey, David Lindley, John
Lindley, Caleb Russell, Abraham T.
Schenck, and Samuel Oliver appointed undertakers or managers to finish with the
advice and consent of the Com. of Council
the new meeting house.

Oct. 29, 1795. Voted that the money collected last Sabbath be applyed to the support of Missionarys on the frontiers.
Agreed that no public provisions be made
for those employ'd in giting wood for Mr.
Richards.

Jan. 1. 1796. Voted that Mr. Johnson,
Mr. Ogden and Ezekiel Whitehead be requested to set with the singers, and lead the
Tenor & Bass. Committee also appointed
to raise money by "an equitable assessment
on the parishioners for the purpose of paying for the new meeting house."

Feb. 18, 1796. Com. reported they could
not raise the money. As worship had already begun in the new building (on the
26th of Nov., 1795), it was resolved that
the seats be sold for the purpose of re-
imbursing the undertakers or managers for
moneys advanced or promised.

Among the regulations of this sale we
find that seat No. 1 on the East side was to
be reserved for the minister's family, and on
the West side for strangers, and No. 31 and
32 for those hard of hearing and for the
poor.

That the undertakers affix such a price to
the remaining seats as will in the whole
amount to £4,000, the estimated expense of
said house.

That five per cent. of the valuation be
assessed upon the pews to pay the minister's salary.

Feb. 25. 1796. Parish meeting voted to
make eight seats free, and fixed the assessments on the others at sums ranging from
£29 to £120. The front seats brought the
higher price.

March 5, 1796. Parish meeting authorized the Trustees to have the old meeting
house taken down at parish expense.

MEMBERS

Received in the Pastorate of Rev'd James Richards, D. D.

Names.	When Received.			Remarks.
Hannah Bailey, wid. of Wm.,	1 Jan.,	1804,	Conf.	
Timothy Axtell, . .	"	"	"	
Stephen Tunis, .	"	"	"	
Timothy Johnes Lewis, .	"	"	"	Died 19 Jan., 1814.
Susan Day, (w. Silas), .	4 May,	"	Cert.	
Sarah Shipman, (w. Sam'l,)	6 "	"	Conf. B.	Died Aug. 1, 1824.
Elizabeth Ludlum,(w. Jonas).	6 "	"	" B.	Died Jan. 14, 1810.
Betsey Bonnell, . .	8 July,	"	"	Died Aug. 21, 1821.
Enos Ayers, . . .	"	"	"	Dis. April 28, 1815.
Jane Douglas (widow,) .	"	"	"	
John McCord, . .	2 Sept.,	"	"	Dis. Nov. 15, 1832.
Mary McCord, (w. John),. .	"	"	"	Dis. Dec. 14, 1826.
Stephen Cooper Ayers, .	"	"	"	
Jabez Mills, . . .	"	"	"	Dis. Jan. 26, 1841. died at Dover,N.J.
Susan Byram, . .	"	"	"	
Hannah Prudden, (d. Isaac and				[P. Howell.
Sarah Keene,) .	"	"	"	Dis. Nov. 1, 1811, later Mrs. Elias
Patience Woodruff, (w. Benj.)	"	"	"	
Lydia Guerin, . .	4 Nov.,	"	"	Later Mrs. Moses Prudden.
Jacob Smith, . .	1 Mar.,	1805,	Cert.	Died April 30, 1811. [13, 1855.
Catharine Smith, (w. Jacob),	"	"	"	Later Mrs. David Mills, died Sept.
David Talmadge, .	3 May,	"	"	
Catharine Talmage,(w.David,)	"	"	"	
Jane Tuthill, (w. Theodorus),	1 Sept.,	"	Conf.	
Lois Emer, (w. Levi,) .	5 Nov.,	"	"	
Sylva, (servant Benj. Pierson,)	2 Feb.,	1806,	"	
Samuel Whepley, Rev.	1 July.	"	Certf.	Dis. Mar. 29, 1813. died July 15,1817.
				Princ. Morris Academy,
Silas Johnson, (son of Richard)	3 "	"	Conf.	Died Nov. 17, 1861.
Richard Horton, . .	27 "	"	"	
Samuel DeGrove, .	7 Sept.	"	"	
Hannah Brookfield, (w. John)	31 Oct.,	"	"	Died Jan. 28, 1810.
Jared D. Filer, .	2 Jan.,	1807,	"	
Rebecca Willis,(w. Abraham,)	3 "	1808,	"	
Richard Blackman. .	"	"	Cert.	
Mary Blackman,(w. Richard,)	"	"	"	
John Campfield, .	1 May,	"	"	Died Sept. 25, 1845.
Mary Munson, (widow), .	"	"	Conf.	
Mary Campfield, (w. John),	"	"	"	
Lydia Halsey, (w. Henry),	"	"	"	Died Jan. 29, 1871.
Mary Lain, (w. Samuel,) .	"	"	"	Dis. May 22, 1817.
Elizabeth Arnold, .	"	"	"	
Anna Byram, . .	"	"	"	
Sarah Lewis, (w. Isaac),	"	"	"	Dis. Nov. 11, 1826.
Rhoda Cory, (w. Simeon,)	"	"	"	Died Sept. 30, 1865.
Amy Byram, (w. Napthali,) .	3 July,	"	"	Died May 23, 1823.
Phebe Swain, (w. Bryant),	"	"	"	Died Nov. 16, 1835.
Hannah Miller, (w. Sam'l,) .	"	"	"	
Comfort Ayers,(w.Stephen C.)	"	"	"	
Mary Armstrong,(w.William),	"	"	"	

Name				Notes
Abigail Smith,	3 July,	1808,	Cont.	
Eliza Hoppock,	"	"	"	
Elizabeth Frost,	"	"	"	Dis. Apr. 19, 1810.
William Addison,	"	"	"	
Catharine Addison,(w. William,)	"	"	"	
Mathew G. Lindsley,	"	"	"	Dis. Jan. 6, 1841, died July 23, 1855, aged 68-5-24.
Matthias Pierson	"	"	"	
Philemon Depoe,	"	"	"	Dis, June 22, 1814.
Stephen Young.	"	"	"	Dis. Jan. 6, 1841, died Feb. 10, 1867 aged 93.
Samuel Miller,	18 Aug.,	"	Cert.	Dis. Aug. 27, 1813.
Jane Miller, (w. Sam'l,)	"	"	"	" " "
Eliza Woodruff,(da. Rev.Benj.)	"	"	"	Died June 10, 1835.
Mary VanArsdale,	"	"	"	
Desire Ross, (w. Dan'l),	"	"	"	
Peter A. Johnson,	4 Sept.,	"	Conf.	For many years a ruling Elder, died Feb. 12, 1854. aged 72.
Moses Sayre,	"	"	"	Dis. Nov. 2, 1825.
Ira Lindsley,	"	"	"	
Josiah Prudden,	"	"	"	Died Dec. 4, 1809.
Loammi Moore.	"	"	"	Died June 25. 1841, crushed by a falling house.
Mary Hoppock,	"	"	"	
Hannah Jane Wick,	"	"	"	
Rebecca Beers,	"	"	"	Dis. Mar. 1, 1842.
Huldah Beers,	"	"	"	Dis. Jan. 6, 1841.
Joanna Dickerson,	"	"	"	
Eliza Russell,(w.Sylvester D.)	"	"	"	Died May 25, 1843.
Hannah Benjamin (w. Stout,)	"	"	"	Died April 11, 1839.
Elizabeth Godden,	"	"	"	
Ichabod Miller,	"	"	"	Died Sept. 26, 1816.
Enos Pierson,	"	"	"	Died Feb. 28, 1816.
Lewis Cutler,	4 Aug.,	"	"	
Abagail Vail,	6 Nov.,	"	"	
Sarah Lewis,	"	"	"	
Charlotte Tuttle,	"	"	"	Dis. Jan. 6, 1841.
John Ayers,	"	"	"	
Joel Jones,	"	"	"	
Francis Jones,	"	"	"	
Hannah Wooley, (widow),	"	"	"	
Mariah Halsey.	"	"	"	Later Mrs. Charles Burnet, dis. May 3, 1816, and again dis. June 8, 1841.
Sarah Ann Ford,	"	"	"	Died Feb. 2, 1830.
Harvey Goble,	"	"	"	
Tunis Hoppock,	"	"	"	
Jonathan Oliver	"	"	"	
Susannah Conger,	"	"	"	
Moses Fairchild,	"	"	"	Died June 26. 1829.
Wealthy Fairchild,(w.Moses),	"	"	Cert.	
Isaac Lewis,	"	"	"	

Clarissa Pierson,	1 Jan., 1809, Conf.	Dis. April 22, 1814, died in 1863, at Cincinnati, Ohio.
Elizabeth Lum,	" "	Died March 29, 1813.
Abigail Harris,	" " "	
Mary Post, (w. Joseph,)	" " "	
Elizabeth Freeman, (w. Benj.,)	" " "	Dis. Jan. 3, 1813.
Nathan Hedges,	" " "	Dis. Aug. 27, 1825.
Hannah Ruttan,	" " "	
Mary Wooley,	" " "	
Susan Wade,	" " "	Dis. Oct. 24, 1809.
Phebe Vail,	" " "	Died Oct. 5, 1847.
Caroline Richards,(w.Rev.James,)	" " "	Dis. March 29, 1813.
Charlotte B. Arden,(w. Thos.)	" " Cert.	
Abigail Mills, (w. David),	5 Mar., " Conf.	Died Aug. 13, 1816.
Phebe Mills,	" " "	Dis. Dec. 4. 1838, as Mrs. Daniel. C. Dusinberre,died Mar. 3, 1870
Phebe Pierson	" " "	Dis. Apr. 15, 1823,
Silas C. Ayers,	" " "	
Albert Ogden Pierson,	" " "	Died Oct. 14, 1862.
Betsey Campbell,	" " Cert.	
Timothy Drake,	7 May, " Conf.	
Mary Pierson,	24 June, " "	
John Ray,	" " "	Dis. Oct. 30, 1810.
Sarah Ray, (w. John),	" " "	" "

Dr. Richards was dismissed April 26, 1809. His successor, Rev. Samuel Fisher, D. D., was settled in July or August, 1809. It will be noticed that there are recorded above, the admission of four persons, apparently uniting with the church after Dr. Richards was dismissed. They were admitted in the time between the two pastorates of Dr. Richards and Dr. Fisher; but are recorded here so as to preserve the continuity of the registry. When the RECORD again introduces the admissions to the church it will begin with those admitted in Dr. Fisher's time.

BAPTISMS.

THE RECORD for December. 1831, completed the list of Baptisms, as found in the Register of Rev. Dr. Timothy Johnes, which comes down to 29 October, 1793 For two years previous to this latter dat· the Rev. Aaron C. Collins was colleague pastor with Dr. Johnes, and the second Register, apparently begun by Mr. Collins, continues some names for the years 1792 and 1793, which were not recorded by Dr. Johnes. In resuming the publication, therefore, we go back to the date, at which the two Registers begin to diverge and include, thereafter, all the names appearing in both.

Mr. Collins was dismissed 2d Sept. 1793, and Dr. Johnes died 17 Sept., 1794. These facts, probably, account for the lack of a record of Baptisms in 1794.

The Rev. Dr. James Richards was install-

ed 1 May, 1795, and the Baptisms after this last date belong to his Pastorate.

1791.

Nov. Joseph Byram & wife, child Joseph, born Sept. 30, 1791.

Dec. Benjamin Pierson & wife, child Mahlon, born Oct. 21, 1791.

Abraham Schenk & wife, child Joanna, born Oct 27, 1791.

Boas Prudden & wf., child Huldah, born June 15, 1789.

1792. JOHNES.

Jan. 10. Rodolphus Kent on wf.'s acc., child David Ford, born Dec. 10, 1791.

19. Silas Condict, Junr. & wf. ch. Ebenezer, born July 22, 1791.

29. Bethuel Howard & wf, ch. Shadrack, born Oct. 27, 1791.

Feb'y 5. Nath'l Broadwell & wf., ch. Julia, born Dec. 16, 1791.

12. Calib Russell & wf., ch. William, born Dec. 1, 1791.

19 James Stiles & wf., ch. ———, born

26. Isaac Wolly & wf., ch. Harriet, born Jan. 17, 1792.

Jesse Cutler & wf., ch. ———, born

Mar. 2. ——— Godden & wf.,ch. Elizabeth, born Feb. 7, 1791.

Jeptha Wade & wf., ch. ———, born ———.

April 1. Joseph Beers & wf., ch. Abegail, born February 29, 1792.

Abrah. Hathaway & wf., ch. ———, (son), born Sept. 23, 1791.

8. Nathanael Beers & wf., ch. Nathanael, born Jan. 31, 1792.

22. Aaron C. Collins & wf., ch. Love Lee, (da.), born Feb. 19, 1792.

Jonathan Ogden & wf., ch. Charles, born Mar. 10, 1792.

Abram Conkling & wf., ch. Maria, born Jan. 14, 1792.

May 13. Mrs. Howard, wid. of Jona. Howard, ch. Anna, born Feb'y 20, 1792.

June 5. Kennery Veal.

Damaras, wf. of Jacob Hall.

John Garrigus & wf., ch. John, born Feb. 7, 1792.

John Hall & wf., ch. Kata, aged 15 years on Feb. 14, 1792.

John Hall & wf., ch. Ruth, aged 13 years on Aug. 5, 1792.

John Hall & wf., ch. Josiah, aged 10 years on Feb. 15, 1792.

John Hall & wf., ch. Caleb, aged 7 years on Aug. 18, 1792.

John Hall & wf., ch. Nancy, aged 4 years on Feb. 19, 1792.

John Hall & wf., ch. Elizabeth, aged 1 year on Oct. 5, 1792.

10. Abnor Condict & wf., ch. Philip, born Mar. 4, 1792.

July 3. Capt. Arnold on wf.'s acc., baptised at Aaron Pierson's, name Eliza Maria, born March 2, 1792, (Johnes.)

15. Ichabod Cooper & wf., ch. Huldah, born Jan. 6, 1792.

July 15. Joseph Halsey & wf., ch. Benjamin Foster, born June 10, 1792.

Aug. 24. Timothy Mills & wf., ch. Nancy, aged 10 on Dec. 31, 1792.

Timothy Mills & wf., ch. Sally, aged 8 on Aug. 7, 1792.

Timothy Mills & wf., ch. Pheby, aged 5 on May 10, 1792.

Timothy Mills & wf., ch. Abigail, aged 3 on Mar. 8, 1792.

Timothy Mills & wf., ch., Betsey. aged 1 on Nov. 9, 1792.

Sept. 2. Richard Johnson & wf., ch. Phebe, born July 17, 1792.

Catharine Reed, wf. of Jacob Reed, ch. Richard, born April 29, 1792.

" 23. Daniel Phœnix & wf., ch. Julia Anna, born July 25, 1792.

Ephraim Youngs & wf., ch. Thomas Lee, born September 28, 1792.

1793.

Jan. 6. George Emmell & wf., ch. George Alexander, born Dec. 2, 1792.

Mar. 17. William Wick & wf., ch. Lemuel Justus, born Jan. 22, 1793.

Silas Condict, Junr. & wf.,ch. Martia, born Dec. 27, 1792.

Jacob Ball & wf., ch. Electa, born Jan. 3, 1793.

William Hambleton & wf., ch. Benjamin, born Dec. 27, 1792.

Robert Rolfe & wf., ch. Charles, born Oct. 18, 1792.

William Meeker & wf., ch. Phebe, born Oct. 31, 1792.

Jeduthan Day & wf., ch. Anna, born Jan. 12, 1792.

April 10. James Pitney on wf's acc., ch. Charles Alex, born Sept. 21, 1792.

Aug. 5. Daniel Pierson & wf., ch. Elizabeth Ann, born March 19, 1793.

Also negro children, Pegg, born Feb. 6, 1793, and Rose, born March, 24, 1790.

James Vance & wf., ch. Mary, born Aug. 1, 1793. (By Mr. Acley?)

Oct. 29. Thomas Johnson, ch. Rhoda, born Dec. 5, 1792.

Total Baptisms (by Rev. Timothy Johnes) 2,827.

BAPTISMS.

BAPTISMS IN PASTORATE OF REV. JAMES RICHARDS.

1795.

May 9. Benjamin Holloway, ch. Jacob.

" 31. John Kinney, on wf's acc., children Mariah and George.

June 7. Elijah Holloway, ch. Gilbert.

July 3. Timothy Stiles, on wf's acc., ch. Timothy.

Jacob Hall, on wf's acc., ch. Isaac, born Dec. 1793.

" 5. John Oliver, on wf's acc., ch. Anne.

Jeduthan Day, ch. Elizabeth.

Aug. 23. George Emmell, on wf's acc., ch. Martha, born June 2, 1793.

Sept. 4. Bethuel Howard, ch. Solomon Brown, born April 23, 1794.

Phineas Chidester, ch. Sarah.

George Tucker, ch. Jacob.

Oct. 29. Daniel Phenix, on wf's acc., ch. John Doughty.

1796.

Jan. 10. Elijah Holloway, ch. Richard.

" 29. Mark Walton, on wf's acc., ch. Clarissa. born Aug. 9, 1793.

" 31. Isaac Pruden, ch. Keen, born Dec. 2, 1795.

Feb. 28. James Chidester, ch. Stephen Ogden, born Dec. 5, 1795.

" 29. Joseph Marsh, on wf's acc., ch. Peggy.

Mar. 10. Silvanus Arnold, on wf's acc., ch. Lydia, born Oct. 9, 1795.

" 12. Silas Ayres, on wf's acc., ch. David.

April 3. Benjamin Pierson, on wf's acc., ch. Julian.

" 16. Abraham Schenck, ch. John, born March 1, 1796.

June 5. William Jones, ch. Charles Alexander, born March 30, 1796.

" 12. Matthias Crane, ch. Hannah Johnson, born 1796.

July 1. Ephraim Lindsly, ch. Abby.

Jabez Beach, on wf's acc., ch. Hannah.

17. Robert Rolfe, on wf's acc., ch. Phebe, born March 11th, 1795.

Bethuel Hayward, ch. Silas, born May 31, 1796.

24. Jacob Piersons, ch. Phebe, born May 4, 1796.

Aug. 14. Abraham Hathaway, on wf's acc., ch. Jesse.

Sept. 12. Joseph Munson, on wf's acc., ch.

Samuel, together with these which follow : Jabez, Rebekah, Anna, Ira, Abraham, Godwin, children of the above Joseph Munson, and baptised an infant.

Sept. 25. Bethuel Howard, ch. Silas, born 1796.

Nov. 2. James Richards, ch. Anna, bap. by Rev. Aaron Condict, born Sept. 21, 1796.

6. Nathaniel Beers, ch. David, born 1796.

Benjamin Holloway, ch. Polly, born 1796.

Dec. 1. Gabriel Pierson, ch. Sarah.

8. Mark Walton, on wf's acc., ch. James Youngs, born 1796.

Mark Walton, on wf's acc., ch. Ruth Halsey, born 1796.

18. Jacob Munson, on wf's acc., ch. Lewis.

Jacob Munson, on wf's acc., ch. Marian.

21. Reuben Wood, on wf's acc., ch. Martha, born 1795.

1797.

Feb. 5. Abner Condict, on wf's acc., ch. Abner, born 1796.

Nathaniel Bond, on wf's acc., ch. John.

April Joseph Halsey, ch. Schuyler.

May 12. Edward Condict, ch. Eliza, born Sept. 17, 1795.

28. Uzal Condict, ch. Moses, born Nov. 1792.

Uzal Condict, ch. Betsy, born Aug. 1794.

Uzal Condict, ch. Jemima, born May 1, 1797.

July 9. Jeduthan Condict, ch. Sally Condict, born Dec. 22, 1794.

J. Condict, ch. Electa Condict, born May 14, 1797.

16. John Oliver, on wf's acc., ch. Samuel Oliver, born May, 1797.

Amos Ward, on wf's acc., ch. Nancy Ward, born May 28, 1797.

Dan'l Lindsley, on wf's acc., ch. Elias, born May 26, 1797.

26. Jacob Reed, on wf's acc., ch. William Reed, born May 25, 1797.

July 26. Benj. March, on wf's acc., children.

Aug. 6. Stephen Charlot, ch. Joannah Charlot, born May 29, 1794.

Stephen Charlot, ch. Aaron Charlot, born Dec. 5, 1796.

McFarland, on acc. Stephen Charlot and his wife, ch. Joppha Matilda, born March 11, 1795.

13. Theophilus Hathaway, ch. Samuel, born June 21, 1797.

Sept. 17. Aaron Riggs, ch. Phebe, born June 25, 1797.

22. William Jones, ch. Joseph Lewis, born 1797.

Jacob Hall, on wf's acc., ch. Joseph, born April 1796.

George Emmell, on wf's acc., cn. Sophia, born July 27, 1797.

Jacob Caterline, on wf's acc., ch. Polly Caterline.

Jacob Caterline, on wf's acc., ch. Charles Caterline.

Jacob Caterline, on wf's acc., ch. Francis Caterline.

24. Susser Blackman, on acc. his wf. Mary, ch. Anne.

Oct. 6. Isaac Pruden, ch. Peter, born Sept. 2d, 1797.

Widow Mary Armstrong, ch. Silas Armstrong, born April 21, 1792.

Amos Pruden, ch. Sally Pruden, born Dec. 15, 1791.

Amos Pruden, ch. Amos Pruden, Feb. 16, 1794.

Nov. 5. Eleazer Byram, ch. Phebe, born Jan. 26, 1791.

Eleazer Byram, ch. Harriet, born Dec. 23, 1792.

Eleazer Byram, ch. Clarissa, born Aug. 19, 1795.

David Easton, ch. Phebe, born July 13, 1794.

David Easton, ch. Susan, born April 23, 1796.

David Pierson, Jr., ch. Stephen Harris, born Sept. 29, 1797.

Timothy Tuthill, children, on acc., Tim. Tuthill.

14. Mat. Lum, on wfs. acc., ch. David, born Oct. 11, 1785.

Mat. Lum, on wfs. acc., ch. Henry, born Aug. 8, 1787.

Mat. Lum, on wf's acc., ch. Sally, born Dec. 12, 1789.

Nov. 14. Mat. Lum, on wf's acc., ch. born Nov. 1, 1795.

Dec. 21. Baptised in January or February last:

Albert, son of David Pierson, born Jan. 10, 1791.

Benjamin Thompson, son of David Pierson, born Sept. 21, 1793.

Jonathan, son of David Pierson, born Oct 2, 1795.

1798.

Jan. 7. Job Pierson, ch. Mehitable, born Dec. 1797.

14. Nathaniel Bond, on wf's acc., ch. ——, born Dec. 1797.

21. John Howard, on wf's acc., ch. Abner Pierson, born Dec. 1797.

Feb. 4. Jacob Caterline, on wf's acc., ch. Jacob, born 1797.

Benj. Marsh, on wf's acc., ch. Elisha, born Dec. 6, 1797.

Mar. 10. Timothy Pruden, ch. Daniel Owen, born Sept. 23, 1792.

Timothy Pruden, ch. Ira Pruden, born Nov. 27, 1794.

Timothy Pruden, ch. Sally, born May 6, 1797.

April 1. Silas Condict, Jr., on wf's acc., ch. Julia.

15. Abraham Conklin, on wf's acc., ch. Richard.

James Chidester, ch. Joanna Chidester, born Feb. 19, 1798.

29. Eleazer Byram, ch. Peter Pruden, born Feb. 26, 1798.

May 4. Aaron Aber, on wf's acc., ch. Hannah, born July 27, 1794.

Aaron Abor, on wf's acc., ch. Timothy Jones, born April 14, 1797.

Lawrence Wilson, on wf's acc., ch. Ester.

Lawrence Wilson, on wf's acc., ch. Henry Runyon.

Daniel Pierson, ch. Alexander, born April 20, 1798. Baptised by Doctor Rodgers.

June 3. Benj. Pierson, on wf's acc., ch. Jane, born Feb, 27, 1798.

Jeduthan Day, ch. Christian DeWint, born April 28, 1798.

June 10. Matthias Crane, ch. Josiah Ferris.

17. Jeptha Wade, ch. Silas Allen, born Sept. 4, 1797.

June 17. George Tucker, ch. Charles Tucker, born May, 1798.

29. Jacob Hall, on wf.'s acct., ch. Timothy Hall, born April, 1798.

Silas Baldin, on wf.'s acct., ch. Phebe.

Silas Baldwin, on wf.'s acct., ch.

Silas Baldwin, on wf.'s acct., ch.

July 1. Benj. Holloway, ch. Lott, born 1798.

John Kinney, on wf.'s acct., ch. Marian, born 1798.

15. Edward Condict, ch. John, born 1798.

Aug. 5. Bethuel Howard, ch. Sarah, born 1798.

12. Jesse Cutler, ch. Phebe, born July, 1798.

30. Moses Pruden, ch. Mary Pruden, born March 21, 1793.

Moses Pruden,ch. Matilda Pruden, born May 2, 1797.

Oct. 4. —— Garrigus, ch. Isaac, Aug. 28, 1798.

Silas Piersons, on wf.'s acct., ch. Phebe Piersons, born 1798.

1799.

Jan. 4. Lawrence Wilson, on wf.'s acct., ch. Joseph Wilson, born 1798.

12. Silas Ayers, on wf.'s acct., ch. Lewis Ayres, born 1798.

Feb. 24. David Easton, ch. Betsey Easton, born ——

March 1. Jabez Beach, on wf.'s acct., ch. Mary Ann Beach, born Nov. 22, 1798.

April 4. Timothy Prudden, ch. Ezra Prudden, born January 8, 1799.

John P. Bollin, on wf.'s acct., ch., Sally Ann, born 1799.

May 3. Wm. Jones, ch. Elizabeth Caroline, born Mar. 23, 1799.

Abm. Schenck, ch. Eliza Schenck, born Jan. 4, 1799.

5. Nath'l Little, ch. David Colwell.

June 30. Usual Condict, James Harvey Condict, born 1799.

Joseph Marsh, on wf.'s acct., ch. Jane Marsh, born May 1799.

July 14. James Stiles. ch. Polly Cooper.

James Stiles, ch. Aaron Abor.

July 11. Matthias Crane, ch. John Crane, born 1799.

28. Wm. Stiles, on wf.'s acct., ch. Eliza Stiles, born Feb. 1799.

Aug. 1. Henry Halsey, on wf.'s acct., ch. ——, born March, 1799.

30. Silas Condict, Jr., on wf.'s acct., ch. Sidney Condict, born July 1, 1799.

Mahitabel, the wife of Ebenezer Condict.

Ebenezer Condict, on wf.'s acct., ch. Ann Mariah, born Feb. 12, 1799.

Ebenezer Condict, on wf.'s acct., ch. Wickliff, born Jan. 2, 1796.

Ebenezer Condict, on wf.'s acct., ch. Hannah, born Dec. 27, 1797.

Wm. Lee, on wf.'s acct., ch. Isaac Byram, born Mar. 14, 1792.

Wm. Lee, on wf.'s acct., Henry Perin, born Sept. 20, 1795.

Wm. Lee, on wf.'s acct.,ch. Lucinda Young, July 30, 1797.

Wm. Lee, on wf.'s acct., Susanna Washbourn, born Oct. 4, 1793.

Wm. Lee, on wf.'s acct., ch. Joseph Cutler, born Apr. 29, 1799.

Sept. 22. Dan'l Pruden, ch. Huldy, born 1799.

Stephen Charlott, ch. Luther Charlott, born 1799.

Nov. 1. Abm. Kinney, on wf.'s acct., ch. Wm. Augustus Burnett, born Sept., 1799.

Moses Prudden, on his own acct., ch. Charles Morris, born Sept. 13, 1799.

Wm. Bedell, on wf.'s acct., ch. Juli, born Sept. 8, 1799.

Ebenezer Byram, ch. Sukky Ann, born Sept. 13, 1799.

Dec. 22. John Day, ch. Elizabeth Day, born Nov., 1799.

1800.

Jan. 28. Silas Pierson, on wf's acc., ch. Cornelia Dixon, born Nov. 29, 1799.

May 11. Ebenezer Condict, on wf's acc., ch. Phebe Condict, born 1800.

June 1. John Burnett, ch. Brookfield Burnett, born 1800.

8. Benj. Holloway, ch. Julian Holloway, born 1800.

June 8. Elijah Holloway. ch. Anna Holloway, born 1800.

19. George Emmell, on wf's acc., ch.
Silas Brookfield, born 1800.

July 6. Joseph Halsey, ch. Alfred, born
May 17, 1800.

Aug. 24. George Tuker, ch. Lewis, born
June 24, 1800.

Jacob Caterline, on wf's acc., ch.
Betsy, born 1800.

Oct. 12. John Oliver, on wf's acc., ch.
Primrose, born 1800.

Dec. 29. Loammi Moore, on wf's acc., ch.
Sally Ann, born Oct. 1800.

1801.
April 5. Silas Pierson, on wf's acc., ch.
Jane Pierson, born Feb. 1801.

12. John Smith, on wf's acc., ch. Mahitabel Smith, born 1801.

19. Daniel Lindsly, ch. William Lindsly, born Feb. 1801.

Daniel Prudden, ch. Archibald
Prudden.

May 1. Joseph Goddin, on wf's acc., ch.
Amzi Goddin.

Joseph Goddin, on wf's acc., ch.
Ezra Fairchild.

Dan'l Phenix, on wf's acc., ch. Sarah Amelia, born Aug. 29, 1800.

Wm. Johnes, ch. Aaron Pierson
Jones, born March 23, 1801.

Benj. Marsh, on wf's acc., ch.
Charles Marsh, born Nov. 30,
1800.

Timothy Prudden, ch. Timothy
Prudden, born 1801.

17. Bethuel Howard, ch. Betsy Howard, born Jan. 21, 1801.

31. James Stephenson, ch. Martha
Washington, born Apr. 10, 1801.

June 3. Nath'l Beers, ch. Caty Ann Beers,
born 1800.

Jacob Piersons, ch. Polly Piersons,
born Feb. 25, 1799.

Jacob Piersons, ch. Jonathan Piersons, ch. April 13, 1801.

21. Wm. Lee, on wf's acc., ch. William
Lee, born April 21, 1801.

Sept. 4. Usual Condict, ch. Mary Condict,
born July 22, 1801.

Wm. Stiles, on wf.'s acct., ch,
James Smith, born Oct. 29, 1800.

Wm. Bedell, on wf.'s acct., ch.
Harriott Bedell, born July 23,

Sept. 4. Simeon Corey, ch. James Corey,
born 1801.

12. Rev. James Richards, ch. James
Henry, Bap. by Rev. Asa Hillyer, born Sept. 6, 1801.

30. Jesse Cutler, ch. James Richards,
born Sept., 1801.

Nov. 15. Ezekial Condict, ch. Minerva
Condict, born Sept. 30, 1801.

Dec. 13. Amos Ward, on wf.'s acct., ch.
Lewis Ward, born Oct., 1801.

H. P. Bollin, on wf.'s acct., ch.
Henry Primrose, born 1801.

1802.
Jan. 3. Lawrence Wilson, on wf.'s acct.,
ch. Eliza Wilson, born 1801.

Mar. 7. Abm. Conklin, on wf.'s acct., ch.
Zeba Conklin, born 1802.

21. John Burnett, ch. Samuel Crane
Burnett, born Feb., 1802.

31. Isaac Hinds, ch. Hannah Hinds,
born Nov. 13, 1789.

Isaac Hinds, ch. Mary Hinds, born
Aug. 15, 1791.

Isaac Hinds, ch. Elizabeth Hinds,
born May 22, 1793.

Isaac Hinds, ch. Sarah Hinds, born
Jan. 24, 1795.

Isaac Hinds, ch. Jerusha Hinds,
born July 21, 1797.

Isaac Hinds, ch. Hetty Hinds
born Sept. 5, 1799.

Isaac Hinds, ch. Ezra Hinds, born
Sept. 21, 1801.

April 25. Matt Crane, ch. Alletta Mary
Crane, born 1802.

May 2. —— Enslee, (widow), on acct., ch.
Ester, born May 11, 1793.

Wm. Enslee, on wf.'s acct., ch.
Phebe Enslee, born Feb. 21,
1802.

9. Abm. Hedges, ch. Julia Ford, born
Oct. 10. 1797.

Abm. Hedges, ch. Unice, born
Feb. 2. 1800.

July 11. Loammi Moore, on wf.'s acct., ch.
Napthali Byram, born June 23,
1802.

John Garrigus, ch. Samuel Garrigus, born Jan. 26, 1802.

Sept. 3. Abm. Hedges, ch. Sarah Hedges,
born July 7, 1802.

Sept. 26. Jonathan Condict, ch, Cyrus Condict, born Aug. 22, 1802.

BAPTISMS.

BAPTISMS IN PASTORATE OF REV. JAMES RICHARDS.

1802.

Sept. 26. Stephen Pierson, ch. Samuel Pierson, born Aug. 13, 1802.

Eleazer Byram, ch. Lewis Byram, Aug. 6, 1802.

Nov. 20. Silas Condict, on wf's acc., ch. Marcia Condict, born Aug. 28, 1802.

25. George Tucker, ch. Henry Tucker, born Oct. 3, 1802.

Ebenezer Condict, on wf's acc., ch. Sarah Condict, born Oct. 11, 1802.

28. Joseph Halsey, ch. Seymour Halsey, born Oct. 8, 1802.

Dec. 2. Zophar Freeman, ch. Peter Freeman, born Jan. 30, 1792.

Zophar Freeman, ch. Lewis Freeman, born April 13, 1794.

Zophar Freeman, ch. Joanna Freeman, born Oct. 7, 1797.

Zophar Freeman, ch. Phebe Freeman, born Dec. 3, 1799.

Zophar Freeman, ch. Elias Freeman, born Sept. 7, 1802.

Stephen Lindsly, on wf's acc., ch. Anna Lindsly, born Aug. 20, 1798.

Stephen Lindsly, on wf's acc., ch. Moses Lindsly, born Aug. 28, 1790.

Stephen Lindsly, on wf's acc., ch. Seth Lindsly, born Aug. 28, 1792.

Stephen Lindsly, on wf's acc., ch. Phebe Lindsly, born March 26. 1795.

Stephen Lindsly, on wf's acc., ch, David Lindsly, born March 9, 1801.

Sam'l Mills, on wf's acc., ch. Mary Mills, born April 27, 1790.

Sam'l Mills, on wf's acc., ch. Sarah Mills, born Oct. 27, 1791.

Sam'l Mills, on wf's acc., ch. Anna Mills, born Feb. 18, 1798.

Jeptha Wade, on wf's acc., ch. Keziah, born Aug. 6, 1800.

1803.

Jan. 16. David Pierson, ch. Mary Ann Pierson, born Nov. 6, 1802.

Mar. 4. Dan'l Phenix, on wf's acc., ch. Dan'l Alexander, born Nov. 14, 1803. by Mr. Aaron Condict.

21. James Richards, ch. Henry Smith Richards, born Dec. 6, 1803, by Mr. Aaron Condict.

27. Nath'l Beers, ch. Hannah Beers, born 1802.

April 24. John Day, on wf's acc., ch. Lavina Day, born 1802.

29. Abm. T. Schenck, ch. Margaret Schenck, born Feb. 7, 1803.

Simeon Corey, ch. Phebe Corey, born March, 1803.

May 1. Wm. Lee, on wf.'s acct., ch. Cyrus Lee, born Feb., 1803.

Baptized about this time Elizabeth, daughter of Ezekiel Condict, born Oct. 26, 1802.

2. Wm. Jones. ch. Wm. Jones, born 1803.

June 12. Bethuel Howard, ch. Bethuel Howard, born 1803.

July 1. Dan'l Lindsly, ch. Francis Lindsly, born May 3, 1803.

Aug. 7. Benjamin Piersons, on wf.'s acct., ch. Caroline Piersons, born 1803.

Jacob Caterline, on wf.'s acct., ch. Charles Stephens, born 1803.

14. Isaac Hinds, ch. Stephen Hinds, born 1803.

Sept. 4. Wm. Enslee, on wf.'s acct., ch. Mary Owen Enslee, born July 29, 1803.

20. Jonas Guering, on wf.'s acct., ch. Joseph Guering, born May 17, 1802.

Nov. 4. Widow Archibald Ferris, ch. Phebe Ferris, born 180-.

John Burnet, ch. Sarah Burnet, born July, 1803.

Joseph Cutler, on wf.'s acct., ch. Silas Condict Cutler, born Jan. 13, 1802.

Joseph Cutler, on wf.'s acct., ch. Abagail Sophia Cutler, born June, 1803.

Jacob Canfield, on wf.'s acct., ch. Lindsly Canfield, born 1800.

Jacob Canfield, on wf.'s acct. ch. Hannah Little Canfield, born 1803.

Dec. 21. Bryant Swain, ch. Jacob Smith Swain, born Apr. 20, 1793.

Bryant Swain, ch. Matthias Swain, born Dec. 24, 1794.

Bryant Swain, ch. David Arnold, born June 12, 1797.

Bryant Swain, ch. Richard, born Apr. 19, 1799.

Bryant Swain, ch. Mahlon, born Jan. 3, 1803.

Jonas Alwood, ch. Elizabeth, born Sept., 1800.

30. Usual Condict, ch. Eleanor Condict, born Oct. 2, 1803.

1804.

Jan. 19. Stephen Turner, on wf.'s acct., ch. Ruth Turner, born Jan. 3, 1794.

Stephen Turner, on wf.'s acct., ch. Ira Turner, born July 8th, 1796.

Stephen Turner, on wf.'s acct., ch. Jarzel Turner, born Mar. 24, 1800.

Apr. 1. Mahlon Johnson, ch. Baker Johnson, born Oct. 23, 1803.

May 4. Joseph Godden, on wf.'s acct., ch. Robert Godden, born Oct. 19, 1803.

May 4. John Smith, ch. Jacob Socrates, born Feb. 22, 1804.

29. Wm. Jones, ch. Harriot Jones, born March 24. 1804.

June 24. Isaac Conkling, on wf's acc ch. Joseph Lindsley, born 1804.

July 6. Wm. Bedell, on wf's acc., ch. John Sutton, born Feb. 14, 1804.

Wm. Stiles, on wf's acc., ch. John Primrose. born Aug. 28, 1803.

Sam'l Shipman, on wf's acc., ch. Mary Stephens, born Dec. 1799.

Geo. Emmell, on wf's acc., ch. Cornelia Ann, born May 18, 1804.

Timothy Decamp, on wf s acc., ch. Eliza Decamp, born Oct. 4, 1803.

James Stephenson, on wf's acc., ch. Richard Wilson, born April 19, 1804.

July 8. Abm. Ball, ch. Jacob Ball, born —

George Templeton, on wf's acc., ch. Albert Bonaparte, born 1804.

July 19. Timothy Axtel, ch. Jehiel Freeman, born Sept. 23, 1795.

Timothy Axtel, ch. John, born May 23, 1797.

Timothy Axtel, ch. Charles, born Nov. 30, 1798.

Timothy Axtel, ch. Sarah, born Sept. 1, 1800.

Timothy Axtel, ch. Stephen, born March, 12, 1803.

Aug. 19. Silas Condict, on wf's acc., ch. Henry Ford, born 1804.

26. Ezekiel Condict, ch. Bethsheba, born 1804.

31. David Pierson, ch. Charles born July 21, 1804.

Jonas Ludlow, on wf's acc., ch. David W., born Dec. 25, 1795.

Jonas Ludlow, on wf's acc., ch. Charles, born Aug. 15, 1797.

Jonas Ludlow, on wf's acc., ch. Eliza Russell, born July 11, 1799.

Sept. 2. Jonas Guering, on wf's acc., ch. Affy Guering, born April 23, 1804.

Mark Walton, on wf's acc., ch. Charles, born 1804.

Oct. 7. Loammi Moore, on wf's acc., ch. Susan Mariah, born July 22, 1804.

21. John Dayton, on wf's acc., ch. Julian Kitchell Day, born 1804.

Nov. 4. Wm. Enslee, on wf's acc., ch. Elizabeth Scudder, born 1804.

1805.

BY REV. MR. FINLEY.

Feb. 24. Amos Ward, on wf's acc., ch. Susann Wood, born 1804.

Mar. 1. Simeon Corey, ch. Anna, born Dec. 5, 1804.

George Tucker, ch. Mary Anna, born Nov. 12, 1804.

Moses Prudden, ch. Phebe, born Oct. 5, 1804.

17. John Keyes, ch. Mary Ogden, born Feb. 7, 1805.

Ebenezer Condict, on wf.'s acct., ch. Mehitabel, born Feb. 10, 1805.

Apr. 15. Elijah Holloway, ch. Henry Holloway, born Feb. 2, 1805.

May 3. Zophar Freeman, ch. Mary Freeman, born March 3, 1805.

June 16. Malon Johnson, ch. Alfred Johnson, born Apr. 5, 1805.

30. Wm. Lee, on wf.'s acct., ch. Anner Lee, born May 19, 1805.

July 5. Stephen Pierson, ch. Anor Pierson, born Apr. 1, 1805.

Aug. 30. Dan'l Phenix, on wf.'s acct., ch. Henrietta Phœnix, born May 1805.

Timothy DeCamp, on wf.'s acct., ch. Lewis Allen DeCamp, born May, 1805.

Sept. 12. Silas Day, on wf.'s acct., ch. Amzi Day, born July, 1805.

Widow Jane Tuthill, ch. Margaret Elizabeth, born Dec. 25, 1799.

Nov. 3. Loamni Moore, on wf.'s acct., ch. Phebe Bethiah, born Aug. 27, 1805.

5. Levi Emes, on wf.'s acct., ch. Silas Gregory, born July 11, 1795.

Levi Emes, ch. John Odel, born Dec. 9, 1796.

Levi Emes, ch. Rhoda Ann, born Mar. 16, 1799.

Levi Emes, ch. Louisa Elizabeth, born Feb. 3, 1801.

8. Silas Piersons, on wf.'s acct., ch. Sally Margaret, born Aug. 22, 1805.

Briant Swain, ch. Chilion, born 1805.

Dec. 1. Jeduthan Condict, ch. Uzal Condict, born 1805.

1806.

Jan. 4. Lewis Condict, on wf.'s acct., ch. Silas Condict, born 1805.

5. Wm. Bedell, on wf.'s acct., ch. Henry Bedell, born 1805.

Feb. 23. David Talmage, ch. Phebe Vanness, born Dec. 24, 1805.

Mar. 26. John McCord, ch. Margaret, born Aug. 29, 1794.

John McCord, ch. Joseph, born May 30, 1797.

John McCord, ch. James, born Mar. 19, 1800.

John McCord, ch. Samuel, born July 18, 1803.

John McCord, ch. William, born Dec. 31, 1805.

May 11. Silas Condict, ch. Silas Byram, born Dec. 1805.

June 8. David Pierson, Sr., ch. Ira, born April 26, 1806.

Abner Whitchead, on wt's acc., ch. Jabez Condict, born Mar. 26, 1806.

July 5. Rev. James Richards, ch. Edward Conres, by Mr. Perrine, born Mar. 26, 1806.

Edward Condict, ch. (a son), by Mr. Perrine, born 1806.

27. Baptised Richard Horton, aged 22 years, on a sick bed.

Sept 7. Baptised Samuel DeGrove, aged 21 years.

Oct. 5. Mahlon Johnson, ch. Susannah, born Aug. 26, 1806.

19. Wm. Enslee, on wf's acc., ch. Rachel, born 1806.

31. Timothy DeCamp, on wf's acc., ch. James Hughes, born Aug. 28, 1806.

Nov. 13. Stephen Tunis, ch. Dan'l Bishop, born Feb. 20, 1794.

Stephen Tunis, ch. Jane, born April 17, 1796.

Stephen Tunis, ch. Mary, born Oct. 1, 1798.

Stephen Tunis, ch. Matilda, born Sept. 2, 1800.

Stephen Tunis, ch. Penina, born April 1, 1804.

Simeon Corey, ch. Axtel Corey, born 1806.

1807.

Feb. 28. Abm. Hedges, ch. James Henry, born Oct. 12, 1806.

Apr. 19. George Templeton, on wf's acc., ch. Mary Caroline, born Sept. 24, 1805.

May 13. Sam'l Halliday, ch. (a son), born 1807.

24. Stephen Pierson ch. Stephen, born Mar 17, 1807.

30. Loammi Moore, on wf's acc., ch. Phebe Bethiah, born April 13, 1807.

June 14. Wm. Lee, on wf's acc., ch. Phebe, born April 24, 1807.

July 3. Wm. Jones, ch. William, born Sept. 30, 1806.

Moses Prudden, ch. Hyram Lindsly, born April 16, 1807.

July 3. Zophar Freeman, ch. Elizabeth,
born ——, ———.
Breese. ch. Louisa, born
Aug 25, 1803.

July 3 —— Breese, ch. Sylvester W., born
Aug. 11, 1805.

Oct. 11. Wm. Bedell, on wf.'s acct., ch.
Phebe, born July 30th, 1807.

Dec. 20. Abner Whitehead, ch. (a son),born
1807,

27. George Templeton, on wf.'s acct.,
ch. George William, born 1807.

1808.

Jan. 1. Jabez Mills, ch. Caroline Conkling, born Sept. 24, 1807.

3. Rebecca Willis, wife of Abm.
Willis.

31. David Talmage. ch. James Richards, born Dec. 10, 1807.

Mar. 4. Rev. Sam'l Whelpley, ch. Mel-
ancton.

Rev. Sam'l Whelpley, ch. Sam'l
Waldo.

Rev. Sam'l Whelpley, ch. Alger-
non Sidney.

Rev. Sam'l Whelpley, ch. Albert
Ogden.

Rev. Sam'l Whelpley, ch. William
Oscar.

Rev. Sam'l Whelpley, ch. Par-
menio.

Mar. 27. Richard Blackman. ch. Mariah,
born Nov. 13, 1806.

Apr. 30. Mahlon Johnson, ch. Elizabeth
Ann, born Feb. 16, 1808.

May 1. Wm. Enslee, on wf.'s acct., ch.
Henry Roff, born Mar. 18, 1808.

Sam'l Roff, on wf.'s acct., ch. Mari-
anna, born June 1806.

Mary Campfield, wife of John
Campfield.

Mary Lain, wife of Sam'l Lain.

Lydia Halsey, wife of Henry Halsey.

19. Fanny Ann Miller, on account of
her grandmother Elizabeth Miller, born April 3, 1800.

29. John McCord, ch. Elizabeth, born
1808,

July 3. Hannah Miller, wife of Sam'l
Miller.

Comfort Ayres, wife of Stephen C.
Ayres.

July 3. Elizabeth Frost.
Eliza Hoppock.
Philemon Depoe.

17. Rev. John Reyes, ch. Wm. Mulford, born May 4, 1808.

Aug. 2. Benj. Holloway, on wf.'s acct., ch.
John, born July, 1807.

14. Sam'l Miller. ch. Jane Williams,
born May 8, 1808.

Aug. 25. Sam'l Lain, on wf.'s acct., ch.
Richard, born Sept, 15, 1798.

Sam'l Lain, on wf.'s acct., ch.
Sarah, born July 10, 1800.

Samuel Lain, on wf.'s acct., ch. Jacob, born April 14, 1802.

Sam'l Lain, on wf.'s acct., ch. Mar-
ianna, born April 12, 1804.

Sam'l Lain, on wf.'s acct., ch.
Samuel, born Jan. 26, 1808.

Sam'l Lain, on wf.'s acct., ch.
James; born Feb. 12, 1806.

Sept. 4. Joanna Dickerson, an adult.
Mary Hoppoc, an adult.

8. Silas Johnson, ch. Sarah Louisa,
born Sept. 8, 1808.

Peter A. Johnson, ch. Julia Ann,
born Oct. 16, 1807.

Sylvester D. Russell, on wf.'s acct.,
ch. Anna Lucretia.

Sylvester D. Russell, on wf.'s acct.
ch. Francis Antoinette.

Sylvester D. Russell, on wf.'s acct.,
ch. Robert Morris.

18. David Piersons, ch. Lewis, born
Aug. 14, 1808.

Oct. 9. Loammi Moore, ch. Henry Southard, born 1808.

Nov. 4. Dan'l Lindsley, ch. Cornelia Ann,
born Aug. 18, 1808.

Jacob Campfield, on wf.'s acct.
ch. Ira Day.

Jacob Campfield, on wf.'s acct.,
ch. Phebe Piersons, born 1808.

Dec. 25. Sam'l Holliday, ch. ——, born 1808,

1809.

Jan. 1. Susan Wade, an adult.
Hannah Rutan, an adult.
Phebe Vail, an adult.

11. Stephen Youngs. ch. Ephraim,
born July 28, 1799.

Stephen Youngs, ch. Benjamin
Franklin, born July 14, 1801.

BAPTISMS.

BAPTISMS IN PASTORATE OF REV. JAMES RICHARDS.

1809.

Jan. 11. Stephen Youngs. ch. Eliza Seers, born Apr. 27, 1803.

Stephen Youngs. ch, Phebe Cutler, born Apr. 16, 1805.

Stephen Youngs, ch. Juliann, born Feb. 11, 1808.

Wm. Addison, ch. Sally Ann, born Dec. 17, 1804.

Wm. Addison, ch. John Montgomery, born Mar. 15, 1808.

26. John Day, on wf's acc., ch. Mary Byram, born 1808.

Mar. 3. Stephen C. Ayers, ch. Elizabeth Lyon, born 1808.

24. Moses Seers. ch. Keziah, born April 27, 1799.

Moses Seers, ch. Moses, born Mar. 1, 1801.

Moses Seers, ch. Oliver, born Dec. 21, 1803.

Moses Seers, ch. Joseph, born Sept. 4, 1805.

Moses Seers. ch. Benjamin, born Dec. 18, 1807.

April 30. Stephen Piersons, ch. Phebe,

May 5. Samuel Roff, on wf's acc., ch. Charles, born Dec. 4, 1808.

Dan'l. Phœnix, on wf's acc., ch, Elizabeth Waldron. born June 22, 1807.

Stout Benjamin, ch. Nathaniel Tenk, born 1795.

Stout Benjamin. ch. Mary, born June, 1797.

Stout Benjamin, ch. Timothy, born Sept 1799.

Stout Benjamin, ch. Lewis Condict, born Feb. 1807.

David Mills, on wf's acc., ch. Huldah Maria, born April 25, 1800.

David Mills, on wf's acc., ch. Sarah Eliza, born Dec. 17, 1801.

David Mills, on wf's acc., ch. Cornelia, born Oct. 26, 1803.

David Mills, on wf's acc., ch. Phebe Ann, born June 5, 1805.

May 7. Hannah Rutan, ch, Manning, about 5 years of age.

Wm. Lee, on wf's acc., ch. Mary, born Mar. 5, 1809.

May 7. Timothy Drake, adult, about 20 years of age.

14. Wm. Bedell, on wf's acc., child Mary, born Mar. 13, 1809.

Elijah Holloway, ch. Cephas, about 1½ years old.

Abraham Ball, 3 children baptised.

Whole number of baptisms by Mr. Richards. 444.

MARRIAGES.

BY REV. JAMES RICHARDS, D.D,

1795.

June 18. Jacob Piersons to Jane Burnett.

20. Henry Blackman to Belinda Camfield.

21. John Arnold to Hannah Eddy.

28. John Hill to Rebekah Goble.

Aug. 17. Mons'r. Le Breton to Harriet Butler at Rahway.

28. Aaron Freeman to Betsy Butler.

Sept. 6. Joseph Lord to Euphemia Hyler.

Oct. 28. John Brookfield to Hannah Allen.

29. Joseph Garner to Sarah Bonnel.

Nov. 10. Silas Pruden to Rebekah Carmicle.

19. Ara Broadwell to Phebe Munson.

24. Andrew Charles to Sally.

26. Barnet Doty to Elizabeth Sutton.

Dec. 20. Joseph Scot to Betsy Bishop.

28. Moses Force to Sarah Wood.

1796.

Feb. 12. John McCloud to Patience Decker.

May 26. Ezra Post to Abigail Minthom, both of Morristown.

June 9. Silas Guering to Sally Bowers, both of Morristown.

Aug. 20. Zebedee Wood, of Mendham, to Sally Lindsly, of Morristown.

Oct. 2. Sealy Camfield to Polly Dickerson, both of Morristown.

31. John Harris, of Newborough, to Phebe Post, of Morristown.

Nov. 12. David Y. Wheeler to Caty Baker, both of Hanover.

16. Jonas Smith, of Roxbury, to Nancy Losier, of Morristown.

23. John Hinchman to Deborah Luker, both of Morristown.

24. James Corce, of Mendham, to the widow Ruth Goble. of Morris.

Dec. 7. Ebenezer Howard, of Hanover, to Phebe Willis, of Morristown.

8. Sylvester Halsey and Abigail Cook, both of Hanover.

Dec. 28. John Mills and Sally Prudden, both of Morristown.

1797.

Feb. 16. Philip Easton to Sally Alwood, both of Morristown.

Mar. 1. Jonathan Miller, of Baskingridge, to Polly Hedges, of Westfield.

23. Jacob Hathaway to Betsy Lyon, both of Morristown.

Apr. 11. Charles Leyton, of Baskingridge, to Nancy Allen, of Morristown, Josiah Lorin, of Mendham, to Phebe Bower, of Long Island.

May 28. Wm. Shelley, of Hanover, to Jemima Pruden, of Morristown.

July 26. John Primrose Bollin to Polly Lion, both of Morristown.

Aug. 6. David Halsey to Anna Whitehead, both of Hanover.

Oct. 4. Silas Mills to Irene Lindsley, both of Morristown.

Nov. 3. Ebenezer Byram Ayres to Abigail Byram, both of Morristown.

18. Mahlon Johnson to Sally Baker, both of Hanover.

Dec. 3. Timothy Garner, of New York, to Betsy Pierson, of Morristown.

7. Joseph Coleman to Ruth Mills, both of Morristown.

25. Sam'l Lain to Mary Decker, both of Hanover.

1798.

Jan 4. Joshua Guering, of Somerset Co., to Mary Arnold, of Morristown.

18. Abner Hathaway to Hannah Kirkpatrick, both of Morristown.

Feb. 22. Cyrus Condict to Phebe Piersons, both of Mendham.

27. Patrick Brown, township of Hardwick, in Sussex Co., to Betsy Freeman, of Morris township.

Mar. 1. Henry Primrose to Jane Baley, both of Barnardstown, Somerset Co.

15. Ebenezer Hathaway, of Hanover, to Chloe Arnold, of Morristown.

17. Wm. Bedells to Hannah Sutton, both of Morristown.

31. Frazier Stephens, of Morristown, to Mary Shipman, of Hanover.

Apr. 2. Jacob Ricky, of Barnardstown, Somerset Co., to Parnell Geering, of Morristown.

Apr. 28. Wm. Stiles to Mary Bollin, both of Morristown.

May 1. Dan'l Prudden to Phebe Prudden, both of Morristown.

12. John Bryan, of Albany, to Huldah Carmicle, of Morristown.

16. Rev. Robert Finley, of Baskingridge, to Easter Colwell, of Newark.

June 5. John F. Ellis to Maria Wilrocks, both of New York.

June 23. Josephus Guard, of Hanover, to Sally Goble, of Morristown.

28. Moses Johnson, of Hanover, to Elizabeth Pierson, of Morristown.

July 29. John Steward, Moreland township, Philadelphia Co., Penn., to Anna Douglas, of Morristown.

Oct. 25. Dan'l Prudden to Elizabeth Freeman, both of Morristown.

Dec. 12. Thomas Day, of Barnetstown, Somerset Co., to Phebe Ward, of Morristown.

20. Jonas Alwood to Rachel Arnold, both of Morristown.

26. Charles Ford to Rachel Burris, both of Hanover.

30. Jonas Meeker, of Wantage, Sussex Co., to Elizabeth Miller, of Morristown.

1799.

Jan. 10. Ezekiel Crane to Hannah Stebbens, both of Morristown.

12. John Day to Polly Ayres, both of Morristown. John Blackman to Sarah Blackwoman.

Feb. 12. Thomas Miller to Margaret Gordon, both of Morristown.

Mar. 30. Loammi Moore to Huldah Byram, both of Morristown. John Burnet to Phebe Freeman, both of Morristown.

May 15. Robert Codner to Phebe Chidester, both of Morristown.

June 15. Wm. Loveridge, of Mendham, to Widow Caty Youngs, of Morristown.

July 14. Ezekiel Right to Phebe Potter, both of Essex.

16. Bethuel Prudden to Sally DeCamp, both of Morristown.

Aug. 4. Nathaniel Little to Elizabeth Youngs, both of Pequanock.

Oct. 12. Caleb Ward, of Newark, Essex Co., to Nancy Hathaway, of Morristown.

30. Robert James Gillaspie to Abigal Charlotte, both of Morristown

Nov. 24. William Dickerson to Keziah Sturges, both of Morristown.

Dec. 15. James Baker, Hanover, Morris Co., to Elizabeth Price, of Morristown.

17. Wm. Goble to Hannah Price, both of Morristown.

Wm. Goble to Hannah Tompkins, both of Morristown.*

25. John Seers, of Bedminster, Somerset Co., to Margaret Taylor, of Morristown.

1800.

Feb. 12. Abraham Ball to Phebe Clerk, both of Hanover township, Morris Co.

Mar. 2. John Veal to Lecta Goble, both of Morristown.

22. Ebenezer Byram to Polly Little, both of Morristown.

Mar. 29. Albert Ogden to Margarett Wood, both of Morristown.

April 13. Joseph Cutler to Elizabeth Cook both of Morristown.

19. Pompey Blackman to ――――

20. Benjamin Halsey to Jerusha Wood, both of Morristown.

May 3. David Carmicle to Jane Silcoat, both of Morristown.

4. David Miller, town of Hanover, Morris Co, to Eliza Wheeler, of Morristown.

10. Archibald Ferris to Sally Mills, of Morristown, by Rev. Rob. Finley.*

11. Jonathan Tomkins to Nancy Lindsley, both of Morristown.

29. James Leiddle, of Sussex Co., to Hannah Camfield, of Morristown, by Rev. Mr. Sloan.*

July 6. Amos Rogers to Jane Loree, both of Mendham, Morris Co.

Sept. 4. Stephen Freeman to Betsy Harperee, both of Morristown.

8. John French to Rebecca Ensley, both of Morristown, by Rev Mr. Armstrong.*

Oct. 11. Joseph Deming, of Mendham, to Polly Trobridge, of Morristown.

Nov. 3. John Arnold, near this town, to Phebe Larey, of N. Y. State, by Rev. Amsay Armstrong.*

8. Sylvester Russell to Elizabeth Stiles, both of Morristown.

Dec. 9. Abraham Richards, of N. Y. City, to Sarah Arnold, of Morristown, by Rev. Asa Hillyer.*

1801.

Jan. 3. Dan'l Potter to Betsy Drew, both of Springfield, Essex Co.

Isaac Pierson to Hannah Ayers, both of Whatnung, by Rev. John J. Carle.*

Mar. 22. William Douglas to Charity Ward, both of Morristown.

April 20. William Robinson, of New York City, to Eliza Faesch, of Morristown.

May 21. Sam'l Williams, of Calwell township, Essex Co., to Huldah Whitehead, Morris Co.

June 3. Stephen Piersons, Hanover Township, Morris Co., to Phebe Beer, of Morristown.

6. John Ryly to Saloma Coe, both of Upper Bethel Township, Northhamton Co., Penn.

July 4. Stephen Veal to Bethia Youngs, both of Hanover, Morris Co.

11. Alexander Muckle Wrath to Rhoda Condict, both of Mendham Township.

Aug. 15. James Prudden to Sally Halsey, by Rev. Mr. Benedict.*

Sept. 20. Charles H. Morrel to Anna B. Lewis, both of Morristown.

Oct. 11. Micah Hawkins, of Brookhaven, Suffolk Co., N. Y., to Lettey Lindsley, of Morristown.

Nov. 14. Stephen Freeman, of Morristown, to Ester Burnett, of Hanover, Morris Co.

25. Isaac McCombs to Catherine Bagley, both of New York City.

30. Elias Piersons to Hannah Armstrong, both of Morristown.

Dec. 8. Moses Phillips, of Goshen, Wallkill township, Orange Co., N. Y., to Harriot Kinney, of Morristown.

Dec. 26. Samuel Cooper to Hannah Freeman, by Rev. Sam'l. Whelpley,
all of M.*
John Brown to Phebe Piersons,
both of Morristown.

1802.

Jan. 27. James Ely, of Calwell township,
Essex Co., to Phebe Carmicle,
of Morristown.

Feb. 13. John Howell, to Polly DePoe,
both of Morristown.

16. Thomas Whitnack, of M., to Sarah
Breeze, of B. Ridge, by Rev.
Mr. Finley.*

Feb. 20. James Wood to Elizabeth Meeker,
both of Morristown.

22. Jacob Lawrence, of Roxbury
Township, to Jane Geering, of
Morristown.

Mar. 5. Elias Squire, of Springfield Township, Essex Co., to Charlotte
Robinson, of Morristown.

29. Israel Munson, of Sussex Co.. to
Nancy Conger, of Morristown.

April 1. David Johnson to Phebe Badgly,
both of Morristown.

3. Benj. Humphreyville to Hannah
Dalrymple, by Rev. Mr. Black-
well.*

May 8. Jacob Allen to Polly Minton, both
of Morristown.

16. John Thomas Bently, of New York,
to Phebe Sturges, of Morristown.

June 5. Isaac Howel, of Jefferson, Cayuga
Co., N. Y., to Rhoda Piersons,
of Morristown.
Hiram Lindsley to Phebe Wood,
both of Morristown.

July 18. Benjamin Leek to Dinah Brown,
both of Mendham Township.

Aug. 12. David Cooper to Susanna Hinds,
both of Morristown.

29. Jedediah Gregory to Elizabeth
Marsh, both of Morristown.

Sept. 8. John Broadwell to Phebe Lindsly,
both of Morristown.

25. Hyram Quimby to Polly Baldin,
both of Orangedale, Essex Co.

Nov. 21. James G. Conway to Elizabeth
Easton, both of Morristown.

25. Azael Broadwell, of New York, to
Ruth Hathaway, of Morris-
town.

Nov. 29. Jared Russell to Gertrude Arnold,
both of Morristown.

Dec. 4. James Munroe to Elizabeth Munson, both of Morristown.
Timothy DeCamp to Jane Hughes,
both of Morristown.

18. George Templeton to Sarah Ball,
both of Hanover Township.

1803.

Feb. 10. David Lindsly to Charity Guard,
both of Morristown.

26. Foster Day, of Hanover township,
to Susanna Smith, of Roxbury
Township.

Mar. 14. Jarzel Allen to Polly (Mary) Piersons, both of Morristown.

19. Henry Berry to Nancy Ayres, both
of Pequannoc Township.
Isaac Gaston to Annie Hedges,
both of Morristown.

20. David Townly, of New York City,
to Mary Marsb, of Morristown.

21. John Brown to Sarah Hall, both
of Barnardstown, Somerset Co.

24. Dan'l Cockran to Susanna Hedges,
both of Morristown.

Mar. 26. Jonathan Hathaway, of Hanover
township, to Sarah Prudden, of
Morristown.

April 3. Joseph Smith, of Pequannoc township, to Polly Caterline, of Hanover Township.

10. Jonathan Lindsly to Hannah Rodgers, both of Morristown.

21. Jonathan Miller to Ruth Lindsly,
both of Morristown.

30. Drake Ludley to Sarah Morris,
both of Morristown.

May 5. Grover Youngs to Mary Burnett,
both of Hanover.

7. Sam'l Holiday, of Newburg,
Orange Co., N. Y., to Anna Byram, of Morristown.

14. Elias Howel, of Hanover Township, to Rebeca Tucker, Township of Newark, Essex Co.

June 2. Timothy Johnson to Sally Johnson, both of Littletown, by Rev.
Mr. Perine.*

12. David Kitchell, of Hanover township, to Rebekah Norris, of
Morristown.

MARRIAGES.

BY REV. JAMES RICHARDS, D.D.

1803

July 2. Thomas B. Whitman, of Hanover township, to Anna Garrigus, of Hanover township.

4. Sylvanus Jessup, of New York, City, to Margaret Stanbury, of Morristown.

5. Isaac Prudden to Nancy Miller, both of Morristown.

6. Barnabus Winds to Phebe Howard, both of Hanover township.

23. David Osborne to Lydia Peck, both of Hanover township.

Aug. 27. Ezekiel Lyon to Nancy Stillwell, both of Hanover township.

Sept. 3. Ezekiel Day, of Morristown, to Elizabeth Mooney, of Baskingridge, by Rev. R. Finley.*

15. Sam'l Camp, of Springfield, N. J., to Mary Burnett, of Hanover township.

24. Jacob Allen, of Coldwell township, Essex Co., to Hannah Whitehead, of Mendham township, Morris Co.

Andrew Meeker to Peggy Shipman.*

Andrew Meeker to Margaret Parker, both of Hanover township.

Nov. 2. Silas Day, of Morristown, to Susan Breese of Baskingridge, by Rev. R. Finley.*

17. Josiah Muir to Mary Tucker, both of Morristown.

Dec. 2. Phillip Wicker, of New York City, to Catharine Bell, of Hanover township.

11. Mons. Carney to Susanna Doughty, both of Morris County.

19. Israel Canfield to Rachel Wetmore, both of Morristown.

1804.

Jan. 7. Benj. Hathaway, of Morris Plains, to Mahalah Bitenger, of Mendham, by Rev. R. Finley.*

12. Sylvanus Piersons, of Mendham township, to Betsy Inkle, of Hanover township.

14. Frederick Alsover to Jerusha Halsey, both of Hanover township.

Jan. 15. Jason Hix to Rachel Lafever both of Mendham township,

17. Sam'l Wright to Phebe Casterline, both of Byram township, Sussex Co.

Joseph Harriman, of Pequannock township, to Abigail Clark, of Hanover township.

Feb. 10. Silas Carmichael to Nancy Lum. (†see below.*)

13. Edward Kimble to Caty Canfield, both of Morristown.

14. Joseph Talmage to Catharine Beers, both of Mendham township.

16. †Silas Carmichael, of Hanover township, to Nancy Lum, of Morristown.

22. Luther Spelman to Anna Vail, both of Hanover township.

Mar. 4. Kitchel Bridge to Susan Day,both of Morristown, by Rev. S. Whelpley.*

10. Charles Carmichael to Temperance Blachley, both of Morristown.

24. Joseph Hinds to Hannah Youngs, both of Morristown.

Apr. 12. John Prudden, of Morristown, to Lucinda Halsey, of Hanover.

May 3. Sam'l Roffe. of Morristown, to Sarah Mills, of Mendham.

June 16. George Dixon to Elizabeth Bryant, both of Morristown.

John P. Losey to Sarah Woods, both of Hanover township.

July 7. Harry Halsey, blackman of John Halsey, to Rose Ford, blackwoman of Mahlon Ford, both of Morristown.

25. Sylvanus Lorin, of Minyink township, Orange Co., N. Y., to Phebe Tuttle, a widow, of Mendham township, Morris Co., N. J.

Aug. 25. John Henry Wonderly to Mary Sweeny, both of New York.

Sept. 5. Robert McCleanen, of Hanover township, to Lydia Shores, of Mendham township.

6. Abijah Youngs to Harriet Cook both of Hanover township.

29. John Harrison to Betsy Day, both of Morristown.

Sept. 29. Paris, servant of Richard Kimble, to Abigail, servant to Joseph Lewis, both of Morristown,

Sept. 29. York, servant of Jonathan Ogden, to Mercy, servant of Richard Kimball, both of Morristown.

Cato, servant man of Richard Kimble, to Zilpah, servant woman of Lewis Condict, both of Morristown.

Oct. 20. Abraham Johnson to Jane Price, both of Hanover township.

Dec. 13. Wm. F. Larzelere to Susannah Woods Riggs, both of Morristown.

15. James Cooper to Elizabeth Shipman, both of Morristown.

23. Jacob, servant man of Gen'l Doughty, to Jane, servant woman of Elizabeth DeHart, both of Morristown.

30. Joseph Guard, of Hanover township to Phebe Norris, of Morristown.

1805.

Jan. 2. Elisha Piersons to Sarah Norris, both of Morristown.

13. Samuel McCurdy, of Mendham township to Alice Steward, of Morristown.

Feb. 21. Joseph Garner to Caroline M. Freeman, both of Morristown.

Abner Whitehead to Abigail Condict, both of Morristown.

Mar. 17. Dennis Dalrymple to Sarah Marsh, both of Morristown.

22. Henry Lindsley to Abigail Mills, both of Morristown.

April 6. Brister, servantman of Abigail Condict, to Dinah, servant woman of Samuel Ford.

7. Obadiah Hedden, of Newark township, Essex Co., to Sarah Miller, of Morristown.

13. Martin Cameron to Frances Gray, both of Hanover township.

17. Silas Broadwell to Sally Byram, both of Morristown, by Rev. Mr. Perine.*

20. Jacob Chamberlain to Mary Conklin Halsey, both of Morristown.

June 8. Cuff, servantman of Matthias Meeker, to Sayre, servantwoman of Daniel Phenix.

27. Samuel Beach, of Pequannock, to Jane Hoff, of Pequannoc, Morris Co.

July 22. William Hyar to Nancy Bowen, both of Morristown.

24. Gideon Humphreys, of New York city, to Mary Bradley, of the same place.

28, Moses Cherry, aged 17, to Nancy Badgley, aged 17, both of Morristown,* married at Springfield, N. J., by Rev. Mr. Williams.

Aug. 9. John Piersons to Hannah Freeman, both of Morristown.

Sept. 18. Ebenezer Pierson, of Morristown, to Phebe Day, of the same place.

Dec. 8. Clement Cary, of Mendham township, to Phebe Jennings, of Roxbury.

1806.

Jan. 1. David Kitchel, of Hanover township, Puah Whitehead, of Mendham township.

9. Lewis Lorin to Phebe Fithin, both of Mendham township.

17. David Mann, of Newark township, Essex Co., to Phebe Youngs, of Morristown.

25. Jeremiah Mott, of Elizabeth township, Essex Co., to Mary Hand, of Morristown.

29. Wm. Lawrence, of Warwick, Orange Co., N.Y., to Rhoda Lindsley, of Morris township, N. J.

Feb. 22. Peter Blackman to Phillis Blackwoman, servants of Isaac Canfield, of Morris township.

Apr. 8. William Osborne, of New York City, to Hannah Ayres, of Morristown.

May 1. Ezra Brown, of Randolph township, Bethiah Piersons, of Morristown.

31. Halsey Guerin, of Morristown, to Ann Stephens, of Mendham township.

Thomas Gold, of Colwell township. Essex Co., to Eliza Ayres, of Bernardstown, S. Co.

June 14. Peter A. Johnson to Elizabeth Mills, both of Morristown.

28. Stephen Prudden to Nancy Guerin, both of Morristown.

July 10. ——, blackman of Joseph Prudden, to Hannah, blackwoman of Jabez Canfield, both of Morristown.

19. Stephen C. Bonnell, of Chatham township, to Sarah Simpson, of Springfield township, Essex Co.

20. Nathan Arnold to Huldah Mills, both of Morristown.

Aug. 9. Samuel Day to Jane Beach, both of Morristown.

14. Archippus Parish, of Bergen township, Bergen Co., to Phebe Miller, of Morristown.

16. Timothy Douglas, of Morristown, to Ann Peer, of Pequannock township.

24. Thomas Foster, of Hanover township, to Jerusha Hayden, of Morristown.

Sept. 11. Joseph Byly to Jane Doty, both of Morristown.

16. David Douglas, of Savannah, Ga., to Elizabeth Piersons, of Newark township, Essex Co., N. J.

Sept. 18. Silas Johnson, of Morristown, to Sarah Stansbury, of Scotch Plains.*

20. Jabez Mills, of Morristown, to Hannah Coe, of Succasunna. by Rev. L. Fordham.*

Nov. 4. Charles Russell to Ann Barkins, of Morristown.

15. Jacob Mitchel, of Pompton township, to Mary Goble, of Morristown.

23. Peter Bockoven to —— Riggs, both of Morristown.

Dec. 13. Samuel Kilpatrick, of Morristown, to Mary Hazel, of Chester township.

22d. Moses Allen to Sarah Lindsley, both of Morristown.

30. Ezekiel Reeve, of Morristown, to Mary Youngs, of Hanover.

1807.

Jan. 3. David Fairchild, of Morristown, to Nancy Loper, of Hanover township.

*Feb. 5. Ephraim Fairchild to Gitty Oliver, both of Morristown.

Jan. 29. Lewis Freeman, of Morristown, to Electa Voorhees, of Hanover, by Rev. John McDowell, at Elizabethtown, N. J.

Feb. 6. Joseph Blackman, servant of Oliver Woodward, to Judah Blackwoman, servant of Elizabeth Kinney.

19. John Lindsly, Jr., to Martha Tomkins, both of Morristown.

Mar. or Apr. Hiram Prudden, of Morristown, to Eliza Ball, of Newark, by Rev. Mr. Williams.*

Apr. 5. George Murray, of Newark township, Essex Co., to Abigail Piersons, of M'town.

May 2. Isaac Johnson to Unice Vail, both of Hanover township.

6. Thos. B. Van Horne, of Scotch Plains, to Sophia Carmichael, of Morristown, by Rev. Wm. Van Horne.†

16. Rociter Lum to Rebecca Condict, both of Morristown.

20. Wm. O. Ford, of Hanover township, to Sarah Martin, of Chatham township.

Sam'l DeHart to Betsy Cherry, both of Morristown, by Rev. Sam'l Whelpley.*

30. Stephén Mills, of Morristown, to Experience Loree, of Mendham township.

June 20. Aaron Boylan, of Bernard, Somerset Co., to Phebe Breeze, of Morristown.

July 17. Thomas Martin to Sally Little, both of Morristown.

19. Jared Kitchell, of Hanover township, to Sarah Freeman, of Morristown.*

Aug. 6. Lewis Prudden to Mary Baird, both of Morristown.

Aug. 6. Abraham Stage to Jane Mitchel, both of Pompton, Morris Co.

Oct. 10. Robert M. Bedell to Keziah Goble, both of Morristown.

Jesse Johnson, of Frankfort, Sussex Co., to Elizabeth Loree, of Mendham township.

Dec. 10. John Armstrong to Rhoda Norris, both of Morristown.

17. Charles Freeman to Harriet Beach, both of Morristown.

26. Jacob Arnold to Sarah Nixon, both of Morristown.

1808.

Jan. 16. Ashbel Tuttle to Harriet Halsey, both of Morristown.

Feb. 7. John R. Freeman, of Morristown, to Rachel Pierson of Chatham.

17. Hiram Lindsly to Abigail Oliver, both of Morristown.

Joseph Wheeler, of ————to Nancy Douglas, of Hanover township.

Apr. 14. Elias Howell to Hannah Prudden, both of Hanover township.*

May 3. Col. Joseph Jackson to Mrs. Electa Dickerson, by Rev. J. Richards, at Stanhope, N. J.*

12. James Stevens, of Mendham township. to Sarah Tompkins, of Morristown.

July 31. Jabez West to Rachel Whitehead, both of Morristown, by Rev. M. L. R. Perine, at Bottle Hill.*

Sept. 6. Hezekiah Hurlbut to Elizabeth Martin, both of Morristown.*

17. Wm. Reeve, of Morristown, to Hannah Bryant, of Morris Plains, N. J.*

1809.

Jan. 19. Lewis Mills, of Morristown, to Mary A. Pierson, of Chatham, N. J., by J. Richards.

21. Timothy J. Lewis, of Morristown, to A. L. Perine, Long Hill, N.J., by Rev. Mr. Finley.

Wm. Tucker to Phebe Canfield, of Hanover, N. J., by J. Richards.

Mar. 8. James Willis to Elizabeth Dickerson, of Morris Plains, N. J., by J. Richards.

Apr. 3. Wm. Dalrymple to Susannah Crilly, all of Morristown, by J. Richards.

BILL OF MORTALITY

Continued from page 167 of " The Record" September, 1881.

1795.

Sept. 26. Jacob, son of Zenas Lindsley, dysentery, aet. 7.

27. George, son of Zenas Lindsley, dysentery, aet. 3.

Oct. 1. Lewis, son of David Pierson, Sr., dysentery, aet 5.

4. Electa, daughter of Stephen Ludlow, fever.

15. Israel Penier, nervous fever, aet. 53.

William Henry, dysentery, aet. 22.

Charlotte, daughter of David M. Carle, fever, aet. 1.

20. Rachel, daughter of George Mills, dysentery, aet. 1.

21. Samuel Ludlow, old age, aet. 77.

Nov. 2. Hiram Howard, fever, aet. 40.

4. Phebe, daughter of John Enslee, dysentery, aet. 6.

6. Child of Joseph Byram.

7. Seth, daughter of Elijah Sneden, hives, aet. 3.

19. Child of John Casterline.

Dec. 22. Elizabeth, widow of Robert Arnold, fever, aet. 70.

26. Child of Vincent Guering.

1796.

Jan. 3. Esther, daughter of Abraham Hathaway, drowned, aet. 18.

3. Servant girl of Geo. O. Hara, fever, aet. 10.

15. Aaron, son of Elisha Rolfe, consumption, aet. 25.

Feb. 2. Maria, daughter of Maj. John Kinney, hives, aet. 3.

3. Eliphalet Clark, old age, aet. 86.

Mar. 11. Daniel Owen, sudden, aet. 50.

Apr. 2. Sylvanus Arnold, consumption, aet. 38.

5. Frederick King, Esq., wound and fever, aet. 58.

12. Abigail, daughter of Edward and Mary Condict, diarrhœa, aet. 2.

May 15. Child of Widow Arnold.

June 6. Hannah Tunis, daughter of George Mitchel, consumption, aet. 3.

27. Child of Maj. Clement Wood.

July 28. Mary, daughter of David Conger, fits.

31. Child of Silas Ayres.

Aug. 12. Samuel Day, dysentery, aet. 44.

Sept. 9. Silas, son of David Pierson, Sen., inflammatory fever, aet. 18.

15. John, son of William Templeton, consumption, aet. 21.

18. Child of David P. Tuttle.

Mary, wife of Doct. Ebenezer Blachley, an enlarged liver, aet. 57.

Oct. 1. Servant child of Gabriel H. Ford, Esq.

Nov. 22. Henry Gardner, dropsy, aet. 72.

23. Mary, wife of Jeremiah Pierson, consumption, aet. 22.

BILL OF MORTALITY.

1796.

Nov. 25. Daniel, son of Henry Gardner, phrenzy, aet. 41.

Dec. 1. Child of Calvin Sayre, decay.

13. James Carven, decay, aet. 49.

21. Mary Ann, daughter of Barnabaş Tuttle, inflammation in the head, aet. 1.

29. Sarah, widow of Uriah Cutler, old age, aet. 76.

1797.

Jan. 6. Eliab Clark, consumption, aet 21.

28. Child of Abraham Conkling, fits.

29. Nancy, daughter of Capt. James Rodgers, consumption, aet. 3.

Feb. 7. Hannah, widow of Amos Stark, colic, aet. 70.

James O. Hara, consumption, aet. 36.

18. Lydia, wife of Abraham Ludlow, child-bed, aet. 33.

27. Lemuel Pierson, old age, aet. 80.

Mar. 16. Fanny Phœnix, consumption, aet. 41.

Apr. 7. Child of Jedidiah Osborn, fever, aet. 3.

9. Martha, daughter of Abraham Ludlow, fits.

May 14. Josiah, son of Elijah Taylor, small pox.

June 19. Jacob Riggs, dysentery, aet. 34.

July 9. Child of Joseph Ludlow, fits.

23. Henry, son of Capt. James Rodgers, thrush, aet. 1.

Aug. 1. Naomi, wife of Moses Johnson, consumption, aet. 65.

4. Child of John Casterline.

Sept. 12. Jarzel, son of Jacob Turner, dysentery, aet. 6.

23. Daniel, son of Ephraim Hulbert, dysentery, aet. 14.

28. Phœbe, daughter of David Freeman, accidental, aet. 2.

Oct. 1. Rachel, servant child of Ebenezer Stiles, rickets.

5. Benjamin, son of David Day, dysentery, aet. 12.

8. Hannah, daughter of Samuel Shipman, dysentery, aet. 3.

27. Rhoda, widow of John Sturges, fever, aet. 57.

Timothy Peck, old age, aet. 88.

Nov. 2. Lois, widow of Alexander Johnson,* cancer, aet. 68.

16. Thomas Stillwell, old age, aet. 84.

17. Abraham Munson, phrenzy, aet. 43.

Dec. 3. Wife of John Pernell, consumption, aet. 46.

4. A child of Patrick Cammel, fits.

8. Daniel, son of Widow Zipporah Moore, hives, aet. 3.

9. A child of Jube Ford, worms, aet. 2.

13. Samuel, son of David Fairchild, Jr. fever, aet. 3.

14. Wife of Benjamin Dooly,†* consumption, aet. 36.

17. Child of Vincent Guering.

1798.

Jan. 13. John, son of Isaac Miller, fits.

18. George, son of George Mitchel, hives, aet. 1.

21. Abraham Ludlow, killed in a well, aet. 43.

Feb. 4. Rebeckah, wife of William Woodruff, sudden, aet. 47.

8. Electa, daughter of Wm. Denman,†* consumption, aet. 17.

Abraham Ogden, Esq., apoplexy, aet. 55.

Mar. 9. William Hulbert, Jr., consumption, aet. 34.

11. Robert Brown, apoplexy, aet. 56.

28. John Enslee, pleurisy, aet. 57.

Apr. 12. Kezia, daughter of Moses Sayre, sudden.

17. Rachel, wife of Zenas Lindsley, dropsy, aet. 31 y. 3 mo. 13 d.

May 13. Jacob Garrigues, fever, aet. 82.

17. A child of John Hill.†

22. Pompey, servant of Benj. Pierson, convulsions, aet. 48.

June 19. Rachel, wife of Francis McCarty, consumption, aet. 40.

6. Mary, wife of Frazy Stevens, child-bed, aet. 19.

21. Jacob, son of Bethuel Pierson, fits,

22. Elder Isaac Pruden,* fever, aet. 60.

July 6. Aaron, son of Simeon Broadwell, Esq., fall from a tree, aet. 10.

9. A child of Elijah Holloway.

22. Archibald Parrit, son of Thomas Cobb, inflammatory fever, aet. 4.

Aug. 6. Sarah, wife of John Mitchel, fever, aet. 66.

18. Sarah, wid. of Capt. Peter Dickerson, fever, aet. 69.

Aug. 22. Elias Hedges, dropsy of the brain, aet. 52.

30. Daniel, son of Samuel Crowel,†dysentery, aet. 1.

Sept. 13. Rebeckah; widow of Henry Primrose,* fever, aet. 80.

17. Lucretia, wife of William Bowen, child-bed. aet. 35.

22. Elisha Ayres, Esq., consumption, aet, 33.

25. A child of Samuel Ludlow, decay, aet. 1.

29. Gideon Arhart. yellow fever, aet. 23.

Oct. 1. John Marsh, yellow fever, aet. 44. 8 m. 15 d.

21. Mary; wife of Enoch Goble, consumption, aet. 52.

Nov. 12. David P. Tuttle, drowned, aet. 43.

15. Peter Prudden, son of Elezer Byram, mortification.

19. John Dennis, son of Widow Ayres, consumption, aet. 7 mos.

24. Jonathan,son of Simeon Broadwell, Esq., inflammatory fever, aet 15.

27. A child of John Mabée.†

Dec. 2. Abner Canfield, consumption, aet. 29.

1799.

Jan. 1. A child of Ichabod Clark.

6. George, son of Samuel Mills, Jr., quinsy, aet. 3.

29. George Kelly, burn, aet. 60.

30. Henry, son Doct. Wm. Leddle,† sudden, aet. 22.

Feb. 20. Lemuel, son of Nathan Willson,† scald, aet. 3.

A child of Abraham Lyon.

Mar. 1. Rebeckah, wife of Silas Prudden, consumption, aet. 27.

7. Daniel Carmichael, Jr., pleurisy, aet. 30.

9. Elisha Rolfe, Jr., consumption, aet. 23.

17. Sarah, wife of Maj. Clement Wood, consumption, aet. 40.

20. Servant child of Doct. Johnes, epileptic fits, aet. 1.

21. Wife of Abraham Lyon, consumption, aet. 39.

24. Jack, servant of Joseph Johnson, old age, aet. 75.

26. William, son of Capt. Benj. Holloway, accidental, aet. 9.

Apr. 2. Ruth, daughter of Timothy Tucker, hives, aet. 3.

3. John Woodruff,†accidental, aet. 24.

17. Samuel Ward,† decay, aet. 75.

Isaac Wooley, accidental, aet. 39.

19. Abigail, widow of Wm. Johnes,† old age, aet. 87.

May 3. Mary, daughter of Jonathan Hathaway, Jr †

10. Sarah, widow of Shadrack Howard, fever, aet. 72.

11. A child of John Hill.†

16. Catharine, daughter of Benjamin Hulbert,Jr.,nervous fever,aet. 4.

29. John Jacob Faesch, Esq., dropsy. born in Canton of Basil, came to America in 1764.

June 9. Servant child of Doct. Campfield, rickets.

10. Elizabeth, widow of John Marsh, old age, aet. 76.

20. Mary Simpson,consumption, aet.45.

July 6. Phebe, widow of Benj. Pierson,* rupture, aet. 63.

Aug. 22. A child of Michael Pierce.†

25. Stephen,son of Nathaniel Tingley,† worms, aet. 2.

Sept. 1. A child of Byram Ayres, thrush.

8. David Hallsey, yellow fever, aet. 43.

10. Patrick Dadey, consumption, aet. 51.

22. Amos Prudden,* yellow fever, aet. 54.

Nov. 6. Sally, daughter of Capt. James Rogers, thrush, aet. 1.

18. John Mitchel, old age, aet. 70.

Dec. 27. Jacob F. Tuthill, son of Sam'l. Tuthill, Esq., dysentery, aet. 29.

28. Jack, servant of Gabriel H. Ford, Esq., found dead, aet. 70.

1800.

Jan. 13. Widow of Christopher Lindsnor, old age, aet. 94.

14. Timothy Humphreville, sudden, aet. 54.

28. Lydia, daughter of Dan. Trowbridge,† consumption, aet. 26.

Feb. 20. Catharine, wife of David Fairchild, Sen., consumption, aet.65.

Mar. 5. Jube, servant of Jonathan Ford, consumption, aet. 40.

8. Child of James Stiles, fits.

26. Belinda, servant of Doctor Campfield, consumption, aet. 29.

Mar. 28. Cornelia Dixon, daughter of Silas Pierson, sudden.

30. Benjamin, servant of Jonathan Ford, consumption, aet. 2.

April 4. Sylvester, son of Charles Ford, hives.

11. John O'Neil, sudden, aet. 65.

16. Servant child of Silas Condict, Esq. epilepsy.

18. Ruth, wife of Col. Benoni Hathaway, decay, aet. 57.

20. A child of Cuff, a blackman.

May 23. Aaron Howell,†* old age, aet. 93.

28. Rachel, wid. of Ephraim Goble,†* sudden, aet. 58.

June 5. John Scott, old age, aet. 87.

18. Wife of Joseph Holdren, dysentery, aet. 23.

July 9. Jemimah, wife of Jonathan Lindsley, decay, aet. 34.

18. Widow Chloe Adams, consumption, aet. 42.

27. Richard Montgomery Carmichael, yellow fever, aet. 24.

28. Jude, servant of Seth Gregory, decay, aet. 45.

Phœbe, daughter of Silas Pierson, dysentery, aet. 2.

31. William Wickham, son of Capt. Wm. Tuttle, born Jan. 4, 1789, dysentery, aet. 11.

Aug. 7. Deborah, daughter of John Brookfield,† dysentery.

15. Theodocia, wife of Henry Hallsey, consumption, aet. 34.

28. Mary, daughter of Jeduthan Gardner, dysentery, aet. 8.

Sept. 12. Nathaniel Tingley,†* leprosy, aet. 67.

22. Ann, servant of Doct. Tuthill, consumption, aet. 45.

Oct. 2. Belinda, servant of General Doughty, scrofula, aet. 26.

20. Elizabeth, daughter of Samuel Alwood, dysentery, aet. 22.

John Merrick, consumption, aet. 65.

19. Col. Chileon Ford, cholera, aet. 42 y. 9 mos. 23 d.

Nov. 24. John, son of Nathaniel Tingley,† sciatic, aet. 14.

25. James Wilkison, rheumatism, aet. 65.

28. John Beers, drowned, aet. 41.

Dec. 1. Ezekiel Ludlow,* fever, aet. 44.

1801.

Jan. 8. A child of Silas Guering.

30. Moses Force, consumption, aet. 27.

Feb. 1. Sarah, wife of Gabriel Meeker, consumption, aet. 60.

4. Henry White, old age, aet. 98.

12. A child of Matthias Crane, sudden.

Mar. 2. John Wallis, son of George Mitchel, decay.

7. Michael Conner, inflammatory fever, aet. 49.

11. Zenas Lindsley, pleurisy, aet. 36.

14. Joline, daughter of Samuel Leonard, inflammatory fever.

18. John, son of Augustine Trowbridge, fever, aet. 2.

30. Jasper Langsley, pleurisy, aet. 42.

31. Reuben Woods, pleurisy, aet. 57.

April 19. Wife of Elisha Bedell, dropsy, aet. 54.

26. Shuah, daughter of Matthew Lum, Sen., whooping cough.

30. Archibald Ferris, born Sept. 10, 1780, peripneumony, aet. 21.

May 4. Eliza, daughter of Benjamin Pierson, fever.

5. Mary, wife of Thomas Osborn,†* apoplexy, aet. 43.

8. Miranda, daughter of Jacob and Catharine Smith, whooping cough, aet. 2 y. 8 mos. 26 d.

10. Caty, daughter of William A. Fabricius, worms, aet. 3.

13. Matthew Rayner, consumption, aet. 49.

23. John Ferris, son of Amos Ward, fits, aet. 1.

26. Servant child of Matthias Crane, consumption, aet. 1.

June 6. A child of Bryant Swain.

16. Col. William D'Hart, consumption, aet. 54, born Dec. 7, 1746.

20. Servant boy of Doctor Abraham Canfield, consumption, aet. 14.

July 1. Aaron Kitchel, son of Joseph Lindsley, Jun., drowned, aet. 4.

3. A child of John Edwards.

July 12. Servant child of Silas Condict, Jun., rickets, aet. 1.

30. Lewis, son of Samuel Mills, Jun., a hurt and fever, aet. 1.

Aug. 4. Rhoda, daughter of Moses Sayre, whooping cough, aet. 7.

Sept. 16. Silas Condict, Esq.,* born March 7, 1738, cholera, aet. 64.

22. Charity, widow of Capt. Daniel Gard, consumption, aet. 52.

26. John T. Howell, consumption, aet, 46.

Oct. 1. Abraham Brasher, son of Col. Arnold, yellow fever, aet. 18.

9. Albert, son of Rev. Samuel Whelpley, dysentery, aet. 2 y. 9 mos.

12. Edward, son of Rev. Samuel Whelpley, dysentery, aet. 8 mo. 3 d.

James, son of Rev. James Richards, born Sept. 6, 1801, whooping cough.

19. Catharine, widow of Jabez Beers,* consumption, aet. 77.

21. Sucky Ann, daughter of Elezer Byram, whooping cough, aet. 2.

25. Abigail Troup, consumption, aet. 44.

Nov. 6. David Pierson, Sen., colic, aet. 47.

9. Martha, wife of Joseph Still, consumption, aet. 34.

11. Gilbert Ludlow, fever, aet. 74.

12. Phinehas Fairchild,* gravel, aet. 71.

25. A child of Joseph Post.

30. Jacob, son of Henry Vail, putrid fever, aet. 21. 3 months and 16 days.

Dec. 2. David, son of Joseph Parker, phrenzy, aet. 21.

3. A child of Elijah Holloway, whooping cough, aet. 2.

2. Phœbe, wife of Jonathan Winings Harris,* consumption, aet. 38.

12. Enoch Conger, decay, aet. 59.

23. Elder Philip Condict,* old age, aet. 92, 8 mos.

1802.

Jan. 10. Timothy, son of Ebenezer Johnson, whooping cough.

29. Zophar Hathaway, phrenzy, aet.45.

31. Samuel Robarts,* sudden, aet. 86.

Feb. 1. Aaron Goble,† decay, aet. 51.

2. Timothy Pruden,*apoplexy, aet. 32.

5. A child of Joseph Dickerson.

4. Sarah, wife of Jonathan Stiles, Esq.* consumption, aet. 70.

10. A child of Timothy Pierson.

20. John Vail,† meazles, aet. 47.

Mar. 3. Mary Shute, meazles, aet. 35.

Mar. 8. A child of Bethuel Howard. meazles, aet. 9.

Eunice, widow of John Scott,* formerly wife of Stephen Moore, fever, aet. 60.

9. Samuel Cooper, meazles, aet. 22.

19. Cato, servant of Benjamin Pierson, meazles, aet. 8.

25. Sarah, daughter of Capt. Solomon Munson, consumption, aet. 48.

April 2. Barnabas Evans,* fever, aet. 72.

10. Joseph Tuttle, palsy, aet. 49.

May 5. Sarah, daughter of Davis Vail, hives, aet. 6 months and 7 days; removed from Baptist yard.

12. Phœbe,. wife of Kitchel Bridge, consumption, aet. 22.

17. Elizabeth, widow of Creed Ludlow, fever, aet. 47.

24. Jedocia, daughter of David Brown,†* consumption, aet. 24.

June 1. Susanna, widow of George Kelly, found dead, aet. 60.

July 25. Ezra, son of Isaac Hinds, meazles.

Aug. 5. Elizabeth, wife of John Hill,† childbed, aet, 35.

6. Charles, son of Samuel Ayres, dysentery.

7. William Bayles, dysentery, aet. 59.

Zophar, son of George Mills, dropsy in the head, aet. 13.

Sept. 9. Joseph, son of Nathan Minton,† scarlet fever, aet. 10.

Isaac, son of Nathan Minton,† dysentery, aet. 4.

10. Lydia, wife of Jonathan Hathaway,* dropsy, aet. 66.

12. Dick, servant of Jonathan Ford, dropsy, aet, 60.

Oct. 4. Mary, daughter of Jacob Canfield, sore throat, aet. 1.

7. A child of Jonathan Smith, hives, aet. 2.

10. A child of Jacob Goble,† quinsy.

24. Cyrus, son of Jeduthun Condict, decay.

Dec. 7. John Edwards, rupture, aet. 45.

Jane Ann, daughter of George Pierson, fits.

9. Phillis, servant of Jonas Phillips, old age, aet. 75.

17. Harriot, widow of Col. Chileon Ford, nervous fever, aet, 31.

18. Philip Post, consumption, aet. 57.

1802.

Dec. 24. Elias. s. of Daniel Lindley, phrenzy, aet. 6.

1803.

Jan. 2. Aaron Pierson, aet. 57 yrs., 3 mos., 18 days.

11. Antoinette Regnaudot, w. T. L. Mesle, child-bed fever, aet. 26.

21. Julia, d. Daniel Tunis, sudden.

21. Charles, s. Stephen Hayden, decay.

22. Gideon Howell†, asthma, aet. 75.

23. Aaron Pierson, colic, aet. 56.

23. Jane, d. Silas White Howell, dropsy in the head, aet. 5.

24. Moses Johnson, phrenzy, aet. 72.

28. Timothy, s. Eliakim Smith, scrofula, aet. 1.

28. Sarah, serv. Joseph Lewis, Esq., child-bed, aet. 26.

31. Sam'l Cooke 2d, s. Capt. David Ford, scarlet fever, aet. 2 y., 6 m., 5 d.

Feb. 1. Sally, d. Daniel Guering,† whooping cough, aet. 1.

8. Capt. Solomon Munson, palsy, aet. 78.

14. Joshua Lambert,* old age, aet. 73.

17. Stephen, s. Deacon John Ball†, scarlet fever, aet. 1.

Phœbe, w. Hiram Lindsley, consumption, aet. 22 y. 6 m.

20. Sarah Amelia, d. Major Daniel and Anna Phœnix, scarlet fever, aet. 2 y., 6 m., 10 d.

Mar. 4. Capt. Timothy Mills,* fever,aet. 85.

17. Child of David Johnson.

20. Wm. Gay, s. Gabriel H. Ford,Esq., scarlet fever, aet. 4.

25. Phœbe, d. Jeduthun Day, consumption, aet. 22.

30. Sarah, wid. Benjamin Halsey,Esq., formerly w. Capt. John Lindsley, fever, aet. 67.

31. Nathan Howell,* fèver, aet. 74.

31. Child of Benj. Pierson.

April 8. Parnel, d. Abraham Beach, peripneumony, aet. 15.

22. Margaret, serv. Maj. Mahlon Ford, sudden, aet. 8.

23. Jerusha, w. Jonathan Wood,* fever, aet. 75.

May 6. Child of David P. Tuttle, aet. 6.

May 9. Elizabeth, w. Col. Jacob Arnold,* consumption, aet. 50.

19. Harriot, d. David Pierson, Jun., scarlet fever, aet. 3.

26. Nathaniel Armstrong, Jun., consumption, aet. 34 y., 3 m., 20 d.

June 4. Henry Allen, decay, aet. 71.

30. Jane, wid. Daniel Wick, old age, aet. 85.

July 2. Servant child of Matthias Meeker, aet. 1.

Aug. 3. Levisa, d. Whitehead Guering, putrid fever, aet. 7.

12. Matilda Dove, convulsions, aet. 15.

20. Delia, d. Capt. James Rodgers, diarrhea.

24. Lydia, d. Stout Benjamin, swelling of the spleen, aet. 1.

24. Mary, wid. William Hulbert, dropsy, aet. 78.

30. Bathsheba, w. Daniel Carmichael,* decay, aet. 62.

31. Jeremiah Kirk, fever, aet. 16.

Sept. 23. John Lawson, suicide, aet. 50.

28. Abraham, s. Bethuel Pierson, scarlet fever, aet. 14.

28. Catharine, d. Tho. L. Ogden, Esq., quinsy, aet. 2.

Oct. 23. Sarah, wid. Gideon Howell;†* palsy, aet. 71.

27. Rachel, d. Henry Minton,† fever.

30. Hannah, w. John Losey, inflammatory fever, aet. 70.

Nov. 13. Joanna, d. Isaac Miller, Jun., fits.

Benjamin Hulbert,† consumption, aet. 70.

20. Henry, s. David Fairchild, Jun., fever.

Dec. 1. Child of Jonathan Winings, convulsions.

7. Philip Losey, pleurisy, aet. 53.

19. Rachel, w. Wm. Martin, child-bed. removed from Baptist yard, aet. 37.

20. Charlotte Johnes, aet. 81 y., 7 m., 17 d.

25. Eliza, w. Doctor Wm. Hampton,†* consumption, aet. 22.

27. William S., s. Wm. Johnes, decay.

1804.

Jan. 2. Jonathan Wood, decay,* aet. 75.

18. Dorothy, w. Jonathan Stiles, Esq., a hurt and fever, aet. 68.

1804.

Feb. 20. Kezia, d. James Miller, consumption, aet. 34.

Mar. 5. Massey, w. Wm. Bowen, polypus, aet. 48.

7. A child of Jedediah Gregory. Joseph Winget,*† old age, aet. 83.

25. Lewis, s. Edward Condict, convulsions, aet. 1.

28. A child of Stephen Pierson, still born.

April 18. John, s. Abraham Shipman, pleurisy, aet, 30.

19. Child of James Stiles, fits. Stephen Beach,*† decay, aet. 81.

May 3. Lydia, d. Timothy Tucker, consumption, aet. 3.

9. Anne Vashti, d. Bethuel Pierson, pleurisy, aet. 5.

13. Charles Morris, s. Moses Prudden, decay, aet. 5,

13. Jacob, s. Elias Parshals,† hives, aet. 2.

24. Widow of Robert M'Calvey, old age, aet. 80.

June 5. Keziah, w. Joseph Gard,†consumption, aet. 48.

10. Nathaniel Sturges, s. John T. Bentley, fever, aet. 1.

12. Margaret, w. Sylvanus Johnson, consumption, aet. 38.

July 6. Mary, d. Jacob Ball, consumption, aet. 14.

9. John Day, Esq., consumption, aet. 43.

Aug. 2. Elijah Brown, sciatica, aet. 78.

4. Sarah, wid. Isaac Whitehead, old age, aet. 104.

8. Jonathan Benjamin, decay, aet. 58.

10. David Seely, s. David Wood, putrid fever.

24. Phœbe, wid. Nathanael Tingley,†* intermittent fever, aet. 66.

24. Daniel Carmichael*, consumption, aet. 64.

Sept. 16. Charlotte, d. Wm. Martin, scald, removed from Baptist yard, aet. 4.

25. Phœbe, wid. Col. Ebenezer H. Pierson, consumption, aet. 35.

Oct. 1. Col. Reuben Ferris,†* a fall from a young horse, aet. 72.

5. Joseph Fairchild,† fever, aet. 80.

11. Jacob Minton, Esq.,†* consumption, aet. 79.

Nov. 22. Jacob Reed, fever, aet. 54.

22. Jabez Condict,* dropsy of the brain, aet. 65 y., 9 m., 12 d.

23. Jemima, wid. Israel Penier, decay, aet. 46.

Dec. 1. Susanna, d. of George Emmel, consumption, aet. 21.

6. Eliakim Smith, consumption, aet. 30.

26. Cæsar, a free blackman, old age, aet. 85.

26. Sarah, d. James Losey, cancer, aet. 50.

1805.

Jan. 9. Thomas Lee,* decay, aet. 76.

24. Monsieur Delisle Dupres, sudden, aet. 38.

Charity, wid. Daniel Owen,†* consumption, aet. 76.

25. James, s. John Brookfield,† inflammatory fever, aet 1.

28. An illegitimate child, decay.

Feb. 9. James, s. Thomas Cobb, inflammatory fever.

March 4. William Woodruff, sudden, aet. 56.

29. Cæsar, serv. Doct. Samuel Tuthill, old age, aet. 70.

April 8. Child of David Cooper, still born.

9. Child of Ezekiel Day, sudden.

14. John Morris, sore leg, aet. 52.

19. Doctor Ebenezer Blachly,† dropsy, aet. 69.

27. Mehitabel Cobb, d. John Smith, scarlet fever, aet. 4 y., 6 m., 3d.

May 11. Zeruiah, w. Peter Fairchild,† inflammatory fever, aet. 39.

24. Jacob, s. Stephen Ogden, consumption, aet. 19.

June 8. John Drewer, epilepsy, aet. 50.

8. Caleb Russell, Esq., born 4th June, 1749, palsy, aet. 56.

10. Ruth, w. James Cory, dropsy, aet. 60.

17. Samuel Mills,* fever, aet. 85.

24. Phillis, serv. Gabriel H. Ford,Esq., dropsy, aet. 80.

July 7. Sarah, serv. Maj. Daniel Phœnix, colic, aet. 26.

11. Child of William Dickerson, still born.

17. Abigail, w. John Prudden,* consumption, aet. 54.

18. Rhoda, d. Jacob Garrigues, dropsy, aet. 9.

1805.

July 26. Silas Howard, consumption, aet. 41.

Aug. 3. James, s. Rev. James C. Richards, born 3d March, 1805, dysentery.

13. John Carvin, fever, aet. 15.

16. Theodorus Tuthill, consumption, aet. 44.

21. Child of Cuff, a blackman, decay.

24. Child of James Cooper, still born.

28. Servant child of Capt. Israel Canfield.

29. Israel, s. Jacob Turner, thrush.

29. Davis Youngs, s. Stephen Vail, hives, removed from Baptist yard, aet. 1 y., 6 m., 24 d.

Sept. 2. Henry Wick, s. Capt. Wm. Tuttle, born 29th Oct., 1804, diarrhœa.

3. Rebeckah, w. Onesimus Whitehead,* dysentery, aet. 59.

15. Abraham, s. Abraham Clark,† convulsions, aet. 2.

16. Jane, wid. Elijah Pierson, decay, aet. 72.

21. Alexander Hamilton, s. Nathaniel Bull, decay, aet. 1.

27. Daniel B. Fletcher, yellow fever, aet. 29.

Oct. 2. Silas S., s. Doct. Lewis & Martha Condict, born June 25, 1803, Whooping cough, aet. 2.

3. Child of David Conger, fits.

5. William Robarts, fever, aet. 85.

9. Cæsar Dumaine Gachet, sudden, aet. 25.

9. Charles, s. Stout Benjamin, decay.

27. Nancy, w. Capt. Ezra Brown, dysentery, aet. 47.

28. Louise Dovillard Vanschalkwic, w. Vincent Boisaubin Beauplan, child-bed, aet. 33.

Nov. 1. Pamelia, d. of Gideon R. Drake, aet. 1.

4. Sarah, wid. of Jarzel Turner,* pleurisy, aet. 75.

28. Nancy, d. of Thomas Watson, hives, aet. 5.

Dec. 10. Charity, w. of Stephen Ogden, consumption, aet. 46.

12. Mary, d. of John Brookfield,† thrush.

15. Thomas Johnson, colic, aet. 53.

19. Deborah, wid. of William Hulbert, Jun., consumption, aet. 41.

21. Stephen Munson, pleurisy in the head, aet. 25.

Dec. 23. Servant child of General John Doughty.

24. Lois, w. of Levi Emes, rose cancer, aet. 37.

27. Susanna, serv. of John Doughty, Esq., child-bed, aet. 24.

30. Samuel Morrison,* sudden, aet. 52.

1806.

Jan. 9. Alfred, s. of Capt. James Rodgers, teething.

14. Child of Cuff, a black man, decay, aet. 1.

15. Elizabeth Jones, consumption, aet. 19.

16. Mary, wid. of Jacob Minton, Esq.†* fever, aet. 77.

16. Elijah Sneden, decay, aet. 52.

25. Sarah, w. of Jabez Campfield, Esq., dropsy of the breast, aet. 65.

30. George, s. of George Schroeppel, drowned, aet. 11.

31. An illegitimate child, found dead.

Feb. 15. Joseph Ludlow, consumption, aet. 53.

Mar. 2. Rachel, wid. of Enoch Goble,† debility, aet. 39.

3. Child of William Thomas, sudden, aet. 3.

6. Eliza, d. of David Freeman, inflammation in the head, aet. 4.

10. John Hinds,†* diabetis, aet. 74.

17. Samuel, s. of Nathanael Tingley,† pleurisy, aet. 17.

18. Cæsar, serv. of Jonas Phillips, old age, aet. 75.

19. David Byram, s. of Sam'l. and Sarah Holliday, fever, aet. 7 m. 17 d.

27. Eunice Darling, dropsy of the brain, aet. 18.

April 2. Widow of William Roberts, old age, aet. 90.

3. Servant child of wid. Mary Pierson, teething.

4. Jabez Ogden, consumption, aet. 13.

4. Lafford, serv. of George Tucker, Esq., pleurisy, aet. 21.

11. Pompey, serv. of Col. Ebenezer H. Pierson, dropsy, aet. 75.

14. Phebe Cook, aet. 19 y. 6 d.

28. Child of David Pierson, Sen., fits.

30. Joshua Munson, s. of Benj. Beach, Esq., pleurisy, aet. 20.

1806.

May 10. Phebe Bethiah, d. of Loammi Moore, quinsy.

William Boyd,† old age, aet. 80.

June 2. Child of James Stiles, fits.

13. William Wheeler, nervous fever, aet. 35.

15. Phebe, w. of Doct. Wm. Leddle,†* polypus, aet. 61.

22. Jacob Ford, s. of Joseph and Annie Lewis, Esq., consumption, aet. 29.

27. Rebeckah, w. of Abraham Hyer, consumption, aet. 30.

28. Silas, s. of Daniel Guering, quinsy.

July 2. Abigail, wid. of Joseph Fairchild,†* old age, aet. 77.

3. Violet, serv. of wid. Condict, sudden, aet. 62.

12. George, s. of James Patten, accident, aet. 1.

12. Rachel, d. of Jacob Garrigues, dropsy, aet. 13.

17. Anne Enslee,* consumption, aet. 37.

27. Rebeckah, d. of Wm. Hulbert, dropsy, aet. 12.

Reuben Tharp,†* consumption, aet. 60.

Aug. 3. Thomas, serv. of Timothy Fairchild, dropsy of the breast, aet. 61.

6. Mary, d. of Jonathan Winings, dysentery, aet. 1.

12. Rhoda, w. of Capt. Job Brookfield,†* dyspepsy, aet. 50.

15. Richard Horton, consumption, aet. 22.

Sept. 20. Isaac Tomkins,† apoplexy, aet. 53.

24. Child of Elias Howell, sprew.

29. Sarah, w. of Timothy Johnson, consumption, aet. 23.

29. Mary, w. of Samuel Oliver,* dropsy, aet. 69.

Oct. 6. Jonathan Stiles,Esq.,old age,aet.85.

8. Christiana Hoffman,wid. of Samuel Morrison, consumption, aet. 53.

17. A child of Jonathan Hathaway, Jun.,† whooping cough.

26. Phœbe, d. of widow Ferris, born Sept. 27, 1801, inflammation in the head, aet. 5.

George O'Hara, consumption, aet. 53.

Nov. 2. James Thompson, apoplexy, aet.60.

12. Nicholas Comissau, old age, aet. 90.

20. Servant child of Daniel Pierson.

Dec. 2. Edward William, s. of Timothy J. Lewis, convulsions.

4. Lydia, w. of William Tarney, consumption, aet. 52.

4. Child of Nathan Arnold.

10. Child of John P. Clark, fits.

23. Keziah, wid. of John Morris, fever, aet. 52.

24. Joshua Gordon, sudden, aet. 40.

24. Joseph Prudden, Jun., sudden, aet. 37.

25. Servant child of widow Dewint, whooping cough, aet. 2.

1807.

Jan. 2. Sally, w. of Drake Ludlow,pleurisy, aet. 23.

3. Joanna, d. of Deacon Joseph and Esther Prudden, consumption, aet. 25.

10. Colonel Silas Dickerson, born Oct. 3, 1771, killed by a nailing machine at Stanhope, N. J., aet. 35.

11. David Hathaway, inflammatory fever, aet. 31.

Jan. 13. Child of Stephen Hayden, decay.

14. Child of Lewis Hughs, convulsions.

15. Eliza, d. of Timothy Allen, dropsy, of the brain, aet. 2.

30. Isaac, s. of widow Mary Ayers, killed by the fall of a log, aet. 16.

31. Isaac Miller, killed by a waggon, aet. 50.

Feb. 2. Child of Peter Fairchild.

16. Elizabeth, wid. of David Hathaway, insanity, aet, 27.

17. Servant child of Joseph Lewis, Esq., dropsy, aet. 2.

21. Jonathan Bigelow, inflammation in the head, aet. 52.

Mar. 27. Keziah Gard, consumption. aet. 45.

April 2. Child of Widow Gordon.

3. Mary, wid. of Elias Hedges, consumption, aet. 54.

16. Phebe Cook, consumption, aet. 19.

18. Mary Harden, fever, aet. 31.

18. Sylvanus Johnson, consumption, aet. 61.

May 31. Iane, wid. of William Brown, old age, aet. 84.

1807.

June 7. Priscilla Price,† consumption, aet.
        20.

    10. Child of Thomas Mann, convulsions.

    21. Child of Captain David Congar.

    22. John Johnson, consumption. aet. 39.

    28. Child of Abraham Hedges.

    29. Phebe, w. of Stephen Hayden, insanity, aet. 26.

July 3. Servant child of widow Condict, convulsions, aet. 2.

    9. Child of Mary Hardin, fits.

    20. Catharine, d. of widow Johnes, consumption, aet. 23.

    24. Nanny, serv. of Capt. I. Canfield, dropsy, aet. 66.

Aug. 2. Servant child of Sylvester D. Russell, Esq., decay, aet. 6.

Aug. 9. Rhoda, w. of William Stilwell, pleurisy, aet. 51.

    9. Nathan Reeve, decay, aet. 62.

    12. Mary Clifton, consumption, aet. 23.

    23. Leah, w. of Timothy Druer, influenza, aet. 48.

Sept. 1. David Fairchild,* consumption, aet. 73.

    15. Julianna, d. of Joseph Halsey, Esq., consumption, aet. 19.

    17. Anna, w. of George Tucker & d. of Sam'l Arnold, consumption, aet. 44y. 7m. 17d.

    19. Child of Abraham Johnson, scald, aet. 1.

    19. Sophia, w. of Timothy J. Lewis, fever, aet. 21.

Oct. 8. William Templeton, Jun., killed by the fall of a bridge, aet. 28.

    10. Child of John Brookfield.

    11. John Frost, fever, aet. 32.

    12. Child of William Dickerson, convulsions.

    14. Chloe, servant of widow Condict, bleeding at the lungs, aet. 28.

    20. George Tucker,* consumption, aet. 45y. 8m. 9d.

    26. Flora, servant of Jonathan Ford, aet. 37.

    29. William Denniston, sudden, aet. 71.

    30. Rebekah, w. of Elias P. Howell, consumption, aet. 40.

Nov. 3. Child of John Craft, hives, aet. 1.

Dec. 12. John McCarter, Esq.; jaundice, aet. 54y. 5m. 4d.

    23. Child of Jack Condict, consumption, aet. 6.

1808.

Jan. 20. Child of William Atwood.

    21. Stephen Ogden, consumption, aet. 58.

    25. Alexander Carmichael, Esq., dropsy of the breast, aet. 74.

Feb. 17. Charles Ogden, consumption, aet. 30.

    19. Jemima, d. of Peter Prudden, consumption, aet. 19.

Mar. 4. Widow Phebe Leonard, decay, aet. 60.

    11. Child of Joseph Wares, convulsions.

    11. Cato, serv. of William Johnes, aet. 51.

    18. Child of Abraham Hyer.

    24. Frank, serv. of Capt. Benj. Holloway, pleurisy, aet. 24.

    25. Servant child of Daniel Pierson.

    29. Elizabeth, wid. of Lemuel Pierson,* consumption, aet. 81.

    31. Gabriel Meeker, decay, aet. 61.

April 3. Aaron Deacon, consumption, aet. 54.

    4. Joshua Guerin, old age, aet. 70y. 7m.

    8. Mary, w. of Moses Sturges, consumption, aet. 41.

    17. Child of James Monroe, fever, aet. 1.

    24. Child of William Marsh.

May 2. Jack Condict, dropsy, aet. 38.

    4. Phebe, wid. of Capt. Timothy Mills,* old age, aet. 86.

    9. Thankful, wid. of Ralph Tucker, aet, 75y. 5m. 3d.

    10. John, s. of Edward Condict, Esq., fall from a horse, aet. 10.

June 1. Hannah, wid. of Junia Lindsley, old age, aet. 80.

    5. Matthew Lum, s. of Silas Carmichael, hives, aet. 1.

    8. William B. Delaplaine, gout, aet. 50.

    10. Davis Youngs, second s. of Stephen Vail, hives, removed from Baptist yard, aet. 2y. 8m. 10d.

    18. Child of Robert N. Codner.

    23. Sally Crane, w. of Dennis Dalrymple, fever, aet. 22.

1808.

July 18. Rachel, wid. of Daniel Howard, sudden, aet. 81.

Aug. 4. Child of John Till, aet. 2.

25. Alexander, s. of John Campfield, convulsions, aet. 5.

Sept. 19. Simeon, s. of Silas Broadwell, fever, aet. 3.

25. Child of Thomas Watson.

" Child of William Dickerson.

Oct. 13. Mary, w. of John H. Wonderly, childbed, aet. 33.

14. Robert Morris, s. of S. D. Russell, Esq.

Nov. 10. Thomas Robbins, decay, aet. 52.

23. Servant child of widow Dewint, aet. 1.

29. Jacob Ball,* accidental, aet. 60.

Dec. 7. Amy, w. of Abraham Hudson, Jun., consumption, aet. 29.

7. Child of Peter Bockoven.

29. Servant girl of Charles T. Day, sudden, aet. 8.

1809.

Jan. 3. Servant woman of Major Isaac Canfield, aet. 24.

3. Child of Henry Lindsley, fever, aet. 1.

4. Child of Abraham Hedges.

12. Grandchild of Joshua Wilson.

21. Child of Silas Condict, infantile weakness.

24. Servant child of Doct. Wm. Campfield, hives.

28. Charles Russell, s. of Nathaniel Bull, fever, aet. 1.

30. Leah, wid. of Armstrong Johnes,* consumption, aet. 62.

Feb. 7. Aphia, wid. of Abraham Pierson, fever, aet. 68.

9. Sophia, d. of Maj. David & Abigail Mills, consumption, aet. 1y. 5m.

11. Grandchild of Cato Hallsey.

28. Elizabeth, wid. of Timothy Humphreville, apoplexy, aet. 55.

28. Joseph Marsh, apoplexy, aet. 53.

Mar. 1. Amzi, s. of Silas Day, fever, aet. 3.

7. Child of Enoch Miller.

20. Sophia, w. of Jacob Tingler, consumption, aet. 44.

24. David M'Carl, decay, aet. 50.

25. Child of John Crane, sudden.

29. Elizabeth, wid. of Benjamin Halbert,* old age, aet. 80.

April 4. Child of Jabez Mills.

4. Joseph Woodman,* old age, aet. 100.

11. Hannah, w. of Stephen Lindsley,* consumption, aet. 44.

15. Nancy, w. of Jacob Losey, childbed, aet. 37.

TRUSTEES' BOOK.

[Continued from page 192, vol. II., Dec., 1881. As heretofore * * * will indicate where portions of the original are not transcribed; and a [ ] will inclose all words or marks not found in the original. The spelling and the use of capitals will also conform strictly to the original minutes. And it may be well to remember that those who inscribed these minutes lived before the days of our bondage to an arbitrary system of spelling; a system which is öften as absurd as it is etymologically false, a great barrier in the education of every child and a disgrace to the English language. In punctuation some liberty will be taken, since the original pointing is mainly limited to the period and the dash; a paucity which would needlessly obscure the meaning for a reader whose eyes are accustomed only to a modern page.]

PARISH MEETING, March 5, 1796. Proposed and agreed that the former persons who were appointed as choristers be a committee to elect the leading singers to fill the reserved seats for the singers. The chief of the seats were this day struck off. Agreed that the trustees may rent any of the seats on which no `bid is or shall be made by the first day of April next, on condition that the same be occupied only for the purpose of decent public worship, and that the rent be not less than the proportion of the sallery attached to such seat at the time and the Interest of the money at which the seat was apprised, unless the person hiring the same hath previously contributed and paid towards the expense of building the house, and in that case the interest of the same so paid shall be abated from the Interest of the apprisal; and that the Trustees reserve the right of selling at the expiration of any year when opportunity may offer for that purpose; and enter in the sd. book the number of the seat, to whom entered, at what rate, and the sallery arising thereon; and that the year of renting and sallery generally to begin on September the 12th, * * * Agreed that the seats No. 1, 2, 3, 6, 7, 28, 29, &c., to 53 inclusive be reserved on sacramental days for the communicants.

PARISH MEETING, March 23, 1796. Agreed that after the 1st of April the Trustees may dispose of any of the seats which are not at that time sold at the apprisal.

Voted that Amos Pruden be appointed to carry around the subscription for the Minister's sallery, and to collect the same and pay it to the Treasurer.

Voted that John Mills and Jonathan Ogden be appointed to collect and receive the moneys due on Mr. Collin's sallery.

Voted that the undertakers continue to superintend the finishing of the meeting house, and that they may do it by contract if necessary.

Voted that Mr. Crain be appointed an agent for the purpose of Superintending the fences of the parrish ground and burying Ground, and keep them in repair, and keep an account of the Said superintendance to be Settled with him by the Trustees.

Voted that Nathan Howell, Ephraim Lindsley and Usual Condict be appointed to collect in the galleries in the parts where they sit.

PARISH MEETING, 8 Ap'l, 1796. Deacon Alling, moderator; William Campfield, clerk.

Voted that so much of a former vote be resinded as respects the power given the Trustees to rent out the seats unsold at the sallery apprised on them and the Interest of the apprisal; and that the Trustees have the power of renting out the Seats unsold to the best advantage and not under the sum of the Sallery apprised on them, with a reserve that they may be sold at any time when a purchaser applies; and if any person applies to rent a Seat, who has transferd his property in the books of the parrish, he shall pay the Interest of that transfer: that Israel Canfield, Joseph Halsey and William Campfield be managers to dispose of the overplus on the Seats sold, to finishing of the House; the pulpit first to be finished:—that the former vote respecting the old meeting house be resinded, and

that the Trustees dispose of the same to the best advantage.

Voted that after one month from this time, the ballance due on the sale of the Seats be held good for the present undertakers, after paying the former undertakers the ballance due them.

Voted that the whole of the year sallery be paid Mr. Richards of the year when he was absent some time.

TRUSTEE MEETING, 25 June, 1796. At Mr. Mill's house. Present all the Trustees.

Voted that the report of the Committee appointed to Settle with Mr. Collins, stating the sum of one hundred and twenty-four pounds due to him on the first day of September, Seventeen hundred and ninety-three, with the interest thereon, be accepted.

Ordered that the Trustees pay the above sum to the discharge of Phineas Fairchild's bond ag't Mr. Collins.

PARISH MEETING, 4 July, 1796. Richard Johnson, Moderator; Jonat'n Ogden, clk.—

Voted the second sale of seats of delinquents be postponed to the 15 day of Aug't. next.

Voted the reserv'd seat near the pulpit be apprised and sold by the Trustees.

* Voted that the parrish Treasurer affix one person at each of the meeting house doors, and pay them not to exceed 6d each Sabath during three months, for the purpose of keeping dogs out of the Meeting house.

Voted that the proprietors of the pews No. 2, 3, 4 and 5 be allowed to raise the flowers equal with No. 1, at their own expence.

Voted that Mr. Philops be requested to put in windows in the corner pews No. 4 and 5, agreeable to a vote of a former Parish meeting.

PARRISH MEETING, 29 Aug't, 1796. Alexander Carmichael, Moderator; William Campfield, Clerk.

Voted that the sale of the Seats of delinquent purchasers be postponed to September 12 next, and that the seat of every person, or part thereof, that is not settled on that day be exposed to public sale on that day at 3 o'clock afternoon, agreeable to the articles of Sale.

MEETING OF THE TRUSTEES, at Mr. Mills house, 20 Sept., 1796. Present all the Trustees. Mr. Condict, from the Committee appointed for that purpose—Reported that George Emmil and Silas Brookfield are willing to purchase the lotts inclosed in front of their respective lands the same width as Alex'r Carmichael dore yard—that Mr. Jones is not willing to Submit the setling the line of his land and parsonage to Arbitration, but will releas to the Trustees what is south of the road and west of the shop, provided they will releas to him the lands on the north side of the road.

Voted that Mr. Emmil & Brookfield have the lands afforesaid at one hundred and forty pounds pr. Acre ; and that Mr. Condict and Mr. Mills be appointed to agree with Messers. Emmil and Brookfield, survey sd. Lands, and prepare deeds, &c.

Voted that the parrish Treasurer inform the delinquents of Mr. Richards salery, by letter or otherwise, that, on neglect or refusal of spedy payment, the sd. Sallery delinquents shall be immediately prosecuted by reason of Mr. Richards· necesituous circumstances.

Voted that Mr. Johnson, Mr. Mills and Mr. Ogden be a committee of Accounts— there being a number of old Acc'ts unsetled by delays of the accountants therefore.

Resolved that all such Acct's shall not draw Interest untill a settlement of the same.

TRUSTEE MEETING, 18th October, 1796, at Esquire Lindsleys ; present, the President, Mr. Lindsley, Mr. Johnson and Mr. Pierson.

Voted that Mr. Mills and Mr. Pierson be appointed to call on the executors of the late Rev'd Doct'r Jones for a settlement respecting a certificate or money said to have ben given to the sd. Dr. Johnes for the parsonage fence destroyed by the army in the late war ; and if a settlement is not obtained to the Satisfaction of the sd. Committee, that they shall proceed to take the testimony of Jonat'n Stiles, Esquire, agreeably to law for perfectuating Testimony, &c.

The President presented a, Deed for a small lott of Land to George Emmell which

was signed and Sealed by the members present, and ordered that the Clerk deliver it and secure the money.

PARRISH MEETING, 4 Nov.. 1796. Deacon Alling, Moderator ; William Campfield, clerk.

Voted that the reconsideration of the vote at a former parrish meeting respecting Raising the flowers of the pews No. 2, 3, 4 and 5, which were to be taken up this day, be postponed unto friday of next weak.

PARRISH MEETING, 8 Nov., 1796. Jonathan Mills, Moderator; Mahlon Dickerson, Clk.

Voted that it be recommended to the proprietors of the pews No. 2. 3, 4 and 5 to lower the floors of their sd. pews as low as they were when originally sold by the parrish, from which they have lately raised them."

MEETING OF THE TRUSTEES, at Mr. Fords, the 8th day of Nov., 1796. Present, Mr. Lindsley, Mr. Ford, Mr. Mills, Mr. Johnson, Mr. Ogden and Mr. Pierson.

Voted that Mr. Johnson read a Notis to the Congregation the next Sabath in the words following, viz.: that the members of this Congregation, who have receits for Sallery pd. to Mr. Richards, will pleas to deliver the same to the parrish Treasurer, in the course of the present weak ; by request of the Trustees.

Voted that Mr. Johnson call on the Treasurer and Mr. Richards for a state of the arrears of Sallery due Mr. Richards, and report the same to the Trustees at their next meeting.

PARRISH MEETING, 10th day of Jan'y, 1797. Alexander Carmichael, moderator ; and Joseph Lewis, clerk. Resolved that the vote passed the 4th day of July last, requesting the Parrish treasurer. to addopt measures to keep the dogs out of the meeting house, be continued until the further order of the parrish."

MEETING OF THE TRUSTEES, 19 Jan'y, 1797, at Mr. Condict,s House. Present all the Trustees.

" Voted that the Committee appointed to call on Mr. Jones be instructed to inform him (provided Mr. Johnes refuses to pay the order drawn by the Trustees in favor of B. Lindsley,) that the committee will be under the necesaty of prosecuteing for the same, and that sd. committee offer to leave the demand of the Trustees, respecting the land said to be in the inclosure of Wm. Jones and belonging to the parrish, also the rails burnt by the Army and paid for to Rev'd Doctor Jones, to Arbitration.

" Voted that Matthias Crain, Usual Conlict and Zenus Lindsley be appointed to collect in the Gallery.

[PARRISH MEETING, 25 May, 1797. Deacon Alling chosen Moderator, and Matthias Crain, Clerk.

Voted that the large windows each side of the pulpit be fixed so that they may be raised when they are wanted, and that a committee of three be appointed to fix the above windows, and all the other windows in the house to be raised also at their discretion, and that Alexander Carmichael, George Tucker and Deacon Alling be the committee to superintend said business. .

Voted that the same committee attend to stoping the leaks about the house and repairing the upper part of the steeple.

Voted that Col. Hathaway be appointed to superintend whitewashing the meeting house.

Voted that Alexander Carmichael, Dr. Wm. Campfield, and Moses Estey be appointed to proceed to paint the inside of the meeting house, and that it be a light sky blue.

Voted that the contributions for sweeping the meeting House and ringing the bell be discontinued, and that the parrish Treasurer for the minister's salery be directed to pay the above expenses, quarter yearly, out of the funds collected from the rents of the seats and pews, and that he settle with the late Treasurer and receive what money remains in his hands.

[TRUSTEES.] 19 June, 1797. At the meeting House. Present, the President, Mr. Mills, Mr. Ogden and Mr. Pierson.

Voted that the president do assign to Capt. Joseph Halsey obligations belonging

to the Congregation in the hands of Dr. William Campfield, to the amount of his demand against the parrish, on account of finishing the meeting House."

Voted that [1] Hyer be prosecuted in behalf of the Congregation on account of his injureing the ball on the steeple by shooting a ball through it, and that John Mills and Jonathan Ogden be a committee to prosecute sd. Hyer to effect.

9 Dec., 1797. At a meeting of the Trustees at Mr. John Mills' house, this 9th day of December, 1797, present, the President, Mr. Lindsley.[2]

[TRUSTEES,] Dec. 23, 1797, Trustees met at George O'Haras, all present; and in consequence of agreements made prior to this meeting, they executed a Deed to Daniel Phœnix for a small lott of Land in front of his lot now occupied by Wm. Tuttle; also a deed to Benja. Lindsley for a small lott near the Grave yard, and sd. Lindsley executed a Deed to the Trustees for a part of the grave yard. The President rec'd the consideration money from Mr. Phœnix, viz.: ten dollars and fifty cents— 10 dls. 50 cts.

[TRUSTEES, Feb. 8, 1798.] The trustees met at George O'Haras house this 8th day of feb'y, 1798. All present except the President.

Voted that Mr. Mills publish the lotts for sale in the Morris paper that were lately surveyed of the parsonage for building lotts.

Voted that Mr. Tucker make a box suitable to keep the pall in, and that the saxton be requested to keep sd. pall in the meeting house.

Voted that Dr. Wm. Campfield and Alexander Carmichael be appointed to settle the several accts. respecting painting, whitewashing, and sundry other accounts relating to finishing the meeting house.

Voted that the Treasurer Credit Mr. Russell one dollar for printing letters Circulated in the Congregation.

Voted that the Trustees proceede and sell the seats of Delinquents, agreeable to a resolution of the parrish the 18th day of feb'y, 1796.

Voted that Esq'r Lewis be appointed to

[1]A blank was left for the first name and never filled in.
[2]A blank of half a dozen lines follows,

collect the arrears of Mr. Richards' Sallery, encluding that due on the last year rented scats ; and that Mr. Johnson be appointed to attend on the part of the Trustees in case of prosecutions.

[PARISH, Feb. 13, 1798.] Parish meeting held at the meeting house the 13th day of feb'y, 1798. Deacon Alling, moderator.

"Voted that the seats or pews now unsold and not Rented shall be Rented at vendue on tuesday of next weak, 3 o'clock P. M., until the 12 day of September next ; and that on the first Monday in September annually, the seats or pews that are then unsold be Rented at vendue for the sucseeding year, with reserve that if any person shall offer to buy any of sd. seats, the persons that rented them shall give them up and pay the rent for the time they posses them, unless they will buy them themselves; and this mode to continue untill the Congregation shall other wise direct.

[TRUSTEES,] 15th may, 1798. Trustees met at the house of George Oharra ; present Mr. Condict, Mr. Lindsly, Mr. Ford, Mr. Mills, Mr. Johnson and Mr. Ogden. The trustees present Signed a Deed to Israel Canfield for a lot of Land in front of Elisha Ayers house and adjoining Jon'n Ogden, for 375 Dollars. Also Jonathan Ogden took a Deed of Trustees for a Lot of Land, dated Jan'y last ; said lot joind his house lot and George Oharra's lot. Said Ogden gave his note for Seventy Dollars.

[TRUSTEES,] 24th may, 1798. Meeting Trustees at Mr. Oharras ; all present except Mr. Mills. Executed a Deed to Loammi More for Lot No. 1, containing 64 hundredths of an acre, amounting to 192 Dollars ; also appointed Mr. Mills, Mr. Johnson and Mr. Ogden a Committee to Settle accompts with Mr. Condict and others ; and to meet at the house of Capt. Canfield on tuesday.

[TRUSTEES, 18 June, 1798.] Meeting of the Trustees at Mr. O'Haras house 18 June, 1798 ; present Mr. Ford, Mr. Mills, Mr. Johnson, Mr. Ogden and Mr. Pierson. Voted that Mr. Ogden obtaine advice from Aaron Ogden, Esq'r, on the business of Samuel Tuttle, Esq'r, Ag't Silas Howell and Peter McKee Ag't Silas Howell, executions and sherriff sale of lands sold by the trustees to Israel Canfield and Jonathan Ogden.

PARRISH MEETING, 5th Sep'r, 1798. Gilbert Allen, Moderator ; and Matthias Crane, Clerk. Silas Condict gave notice to the meeting that he resigned his office as Trustee in the Congregation.

Voted that the Trustees advertize for the Election of a Trustee, agreeable to Law, at the next parish meeting.

Voted that the Seats and pews that are unsold be rented by the Trustees at their discretion for the ensuing year ending the 12th of September, 1799, provided that if any person appears to purchase, the person renting Shall give up the Seat and pay rent for no longer time than he possesses the Seat.

TRUSTEE MEETING, 12 Sep'r, 1798, at the house of George Oharra ; present, Jon'n Ford, Jno. Mills, Rich'd Johnson, Jon'n Ogden and Benj'n Person. Voted that John Mills Settle accounts with Jonathan Stiles with him, or if they cant agree, then to appoint men to Settle the same. Silas Condict, late president of the Trustees, attended and delivered to Jon'n Ford, President pro tem., the bonds, Deeds and other papers, with the Seal belonging to the Corporation.

PARISH MEETING, 19th Oct., 1798. Deacon Allin, Moderater ; Joseph Lewis, Clerk. Benjamin Lindsly resigned his office as Trustee to the Congregation. The Congregation then proceeded to choose George Tucker and Daniel Lindsly Trustees in the room of Silas Condict and Benjamin Lindsly.

[TRUSTEES, 21 Dec., 1798.] At a meeting of the Trustees at Mr. Ford's house this 21st of Dec'r, '98 ; present, Mr. Ford president pro tem., Mr. Mills, Mr. Johnson, Mr. Ogden, Mr. Pierson, also Mr. George Tucker and Mr. Daniel Lindley who were lately elected trustees and quallified agreably to law before Joseph Lewis, Esq., the 19th day of Dec'r instant.

Voted that the burying yard fence be repaired, and that Mr. George Tucker be appointed to cut and draw the logs, for bords and posts for sd. fence, from the parsonage.

Voted that the chesnut timber not wanted for the above fence, nor any other parrish purpose, be sold at public vendue, meaning such trees as are decaying and injureing the young groth ; that Mr. Johnson and Mr. Tucker superintend the above vendue.

Voted that the meeting house be inclosed with a decent pale fence of chesnut timber, together with a raleing on the oute side; and that Mr. Tucker be appointed to cut and draw the timber for the same.

Voted that Jonathan Ogden settle with and pay Wm. Cherry his account for repairs done to the clock when in the old Meeting house.

Voted that Mr. Mills and Mr. Johnson be a committee to settle the accounts of the parrish with Joseph Lewis, Esquire; and that they make report to the trustees at their next meeting.

MEETING OF THE TRUSTEES, the 13th day of Ap'l, 1799, at the house of George O-Hara; all present.

Voted that Mr. Mills and Mr. Tucker be a committee to settle the Meeting house acc'ts with the managers of the new meeting house.

Voted that the burying yard be fenced with a frame fence ; the boards be put up and down, or picket fassion. [3]

Voted that the Clerk draw an order on William Tuttle, in favour of Mr. Richards, for twelve pounds, ten shillings, being his half the interest on lands belonging to the parsonage and sold by the trustees.

Voted that Mr. Ford, Mr. Mills and Mr. Lindley be a committee to superintend the laying out the burying yard with Mr. Condict, and stake oute the same.

[TRUSTEES, April 20, 1799.] The Board met at Esquire Tuttles [?], the 20 Ap'l, 1799, all present. Mr. Ogden, appointed to settle and pay Wm. Cherry his acct. for repairing the Clock when in the old meeting, reported that he has paid Wm. Cherry thirty shillings and 4d for the above repairs, including four shillings sd. Cherry paid Moses Force for mending the clock of a late date, and produced his receipt.

Voted that Mr. Ford, Mr. Johnson and Mr. Tucker be a committee to attend the fenceing of the burying yard and git it done

[3] In a duplicate report of this meeting the word *fashion* is spelled "facion."

by the great or Job, or by the day, at their discretion.

Voted that Mr. Mills, Mr. Johnson and Mr. Pierson be a committee to Call on Coll. Hathaway for security for the money he owes the congregation.

Voted that Mr. Ford be directed to pay Joseph Marsh for mending a sash in the meeting house, broken in by the wind.

Voted that Mr. Lindley git the candlesticks and bason belonging to the Congregation cleaned, and charge the Trustees.

[PARISH MEETING, May 3, 1799.] At a Parrish Meeting held the 3d day of May, 1799; Major John Kenney, moderator, and Capt. Joseph Halsey, cl'k.

Voted that the Trustees be directed to credit, on the bonds of Jonathan Ogden and Israel Canfield, the amount of the Sherriffs sales on the lands purchased by sd. Ogden and Canfield of the Trustees, on the south side of the green.

Voted that the Trustees shall not call for the old tax due to Mr. Collins, nor 'refuse the money if any should be offered.

Voted that Usual Condict and Jaduthan Condict be request to take charge of, and prevent as much may be, disorderly and ill-behaved boys siting on the stares, from playing and making disturbance in time of public servis.

PARRISH MEETING, 3d September, 1799. Deacon Allin chosen moderator, and Matthias Crane, Cl'k.

Voted that that the Trustees be directed to continue same mode of renting the seats and pews that remained unsold, that was adopted the last year, until the further order of the Congregation.

Voted that the Trustees be requested to apply to the proprietors of the Steple school house, or such of them as may be conveniently found, and request them to move oute of the burying yard sd. house ; that in case sd. proprietors neglect or refuse to take measures for this purpose, so as to have sd. house mooved, as affore said, by the fifteenth Instant, in that case the Trustees are directed to dispose of sd. house at Public vendue, the product to remain in the hands of the Trustees without Interest, to be applyed to the benefit of the Town whenever they choose to apply it to the use of building another school house ; and, if the Town see proper to remove the sd. house, the Trustees are directed to point out the ground on which sd. house may stand.

[TRUSTEES, Sept. 17, 1799.] Meeting of the Trustees at the house of George O'Hara, 17 September, 1799, all present.

Voted that the c,l,k advertise the Steple School house to be sold at the public vendue on the first day of October next, at four o'clock P. M.; if not taken oute of the burying yard before that day ; that Mr. Mills and Mr. Ogden be a committee to attend the vendue and give six months credit.

Mr. Lindley, who was appointed, reported that he had mended the parsonage fence with Coll. Hathaway to assist him, 'who charged two shillings and Mr. Lindley two shillings.

[TRUSTEES ——.] Trustees paid Mr. Tucker eleven shillings and 3 d. on order of Mr. Crain on David Freeman.

[TRUSTEES ——.] The Trustees present, viz: Mr. Mills, Mr. Johnson, Mr. Ogden, Mr. Tucker and Mr. Lindley; and appointed Mr. Mills to collect the money due to Trustees from Israel Canfield. Mr. Lindley appointed to call on Mr. Timo. Tuttle and Mr. Wm. Tuttle and request them to attend a meeting of the Trustees at Mr. Tucker's house on friday next, 4 o'clock P. M.

[Trustees ——.] The Trustees met at Mr. Ford's House ; all present, except Mr. Lindley. Voted that Mr. Ford furnish Iron hooks and put them in to the burying yard fence, to hitch horses, and place them Six feet distance, from near Cherrie's house to the Huntington sellar. Gave Mr. Tucker to colJect Jos. Johnson's note of fifteen shillings and 1d. Voted that Mr. Richards have the old wood left at Dr. Condicts house, at a price that Mr. Mills shall agree on with Mr. Richards.

Voted that Jonathan Ogden pay Wm. Cherry his account for repareing a shath in the New Meeting house.

[TRUSTEES, Dec. 23, 1799.] Meeting of the Trustees at Mr. Lindley's house, 23 day Dec'r, 1799, all present. Voted that the Saxton be directed to cleane the steps of the meeting house from snow, so that the steps before the oute side doors are free from snow on sunday mornings; and that Cherry be paid by the Trustees for sd. servis.

[TRUSTEES, 30 Dec., 1799.] Meeting of the Trustees at Mr. Mill's house, 30 Dec., 1799 ; all present, except Mr. Pierson.

Voted that Mesers. Mills and Ogden be a committee to sell the saddles, had of Benja. Holloway, at their discretion ; and that the above named committee be directed to enquire where the lime is, said to belong to the congregation, and make report at the next meeting of Trustees.

[TRUSTEES, 6 Jan., 1800.] Meeting of the Trustees at the house of Jonathan Ogden, the 6th day Jan'y, 1800 ; present, all except Mr. Ford. Voted that Mr. Mills and Mr. Johnson be a committee to Settle with Mr. Lewis as parrish Treasurer.

Voted that Mr. Tucker have a Note of hand agt. Joseph Young, dec't, dated 14 day of March, '87, for 20s. proc., to be charged if he recovers it, and to prosecute in case of refusal to pay.

[TRUSTEES, 13 Jan., 1800.] The Trustees met at Mr. Johnson's house this 13 day of Jan'y, 1800 ; all present except Mr. Ford. Voted that Mr. Mills, Mr. Johnson and Mr. Pierson be a committee to settle the accounts with the Trustees and Israel Canfield, and all other accounts that appear to them nessasary in connection with said Canfield's acct., in point of settlement with him.

Voted that Jno. Ogden call on Coll. Hathaway respecting his obligation to the Trustees, and report at the next meeting of the Trustees, which will be at Mr. Ford's house on Monday next at Early candle light.

PARRISH MEETING, 28 day Jan'y, 1800. Deacon Alling, moderator ; and Mr. Jos. Halsey, clerk.

Voted that the Trustees, with the Treasurer, be directed to pay to Mr. Richards, instead of his firewood for one year, eightyseven dollars and fifty cents, or such other sum as shall be sufficient to purchase thirtynine cords of good fire wood, delivered at his house, one-half to be hickory ; and the year to begin the 12 day of September next

Sold at public vendue this day, after parish meeting, two women's saddles; one to Ebenezer Stiles for ten dollars and ten cents; the other to Benja. Pierson for ten dollars and four cents, payable in three months with interest from this day.

[TRUSTEES, 18, Feb., 1800.] Meeting Trustees at Mr. Crain's house, the 18th day Feb'y, 1800, Mr. Mills, Mr. Ogden, Mr. Tucker and Mr. Lindley, present. Voted that Matthias Craine have one-third of pew No. 13, at thirty-four pounds, thirteen shillings and 4d.

[TRUSTEES, 31 March, 1800.] Meeting of Trustees at Mr. Mill's house, 31 day March, 1800, all present.

Elijah Snethen applyed for a building lot in the hollow, near the Academy, adjoining Dr. Tuttle, The Trustees agreed to take 100£ York money; to which Mr. Snethen agreed, and also to maintain the fence around said premises as others have agreed with the Trustees. Voted that Mr. Mills and Mr. Johnson be a committee to attend to the unfinished business respecting the sold Seats. Voted that Mr. Tucker and Mr. Pierson be a committee to collect from Gabriel Ford, Esqr., the sum due for a lather [ladder?] belonging to the Parrish, at their Discretion. Voted that Mr. Mills and Mr. Ogden convers with Mr. Woodmen, and obtain his consent to give up the swaping of the meeting house; and in that case to give Wm. Cherry the work to doe. Voted that Mr. Ford be, and he is, unanimously appointed President of this body of Trustees.

TRUSTEES, 8 May, 1800.] Meeting of Trustees at George O. Hara's house, this 8th day of May, 1800. Mr. Ford Mr. Mills, Mr. Ogden, Mr. Pierson and Mr. Lindley met and executed a Deed to Elijah Snethen, for a lot of Land, to build on, adjoining Dr. Tuthill, for the consideration of one hundred pounds York money; sd. Snethen gave a Mortgage for security.

[TRUSTEES, 2 Jan., 1801.] Meeting of the Trustees at the Court house, 2d day Jany, 1801; present all the Trustees. Voted that the Clerk collect the money due from Ebenzer Stiles to the Parrish and pay the same to George Tucker.

Voted that John Rogers be allowed two pounds, nineteen shillings and sixpence for shaveing shingles for New Meeting house and raising, including Interest on sd. account.

[TRUSTEES, 12 Jan., 1801.] Meeting Trustees at Mr. Mill's house, 12th day Jany, 1801; Mr. Pierson absent.

Voted the Clerk be directed to write to Loami More or his security, requesting the Immediate payment of his Interest.

Voted that the President git the Morgages belonging to the Parrish acknowledged and recorded.

[TRUSTEES, 9 June, 1801.] Meeting Trustees at Mr. Crain's house, 9th day of June, 1801; present, the President, Mr, Mills, Mr. Johnson, Mr. Ogden, Mr. Pierson, Mr. Lindley.

Voted that the burying yard fence be whitewashed; and that Wm. Cherry be paid twenty-eight shillings for whitewashing, and the Trustees find him lime and allum.

[TRUSTEES, 4 Sept., 1801.] Meeting of the Trustees, 4th day Septr., 1801; all present. Voted that Mr. Mills take care of the burying yard fence and mend the same if needed.

Voted that Wm. Cherry, the sexton, be allowed two dollars for cleaning the meeting house of goos dung and the meeting house steps of human dung and goos dung sundry times.

Voted that Mr. Mills and Mr. Lindley be a committee to enquire into the business of dirtying the meeting house with goos dung, &c.; and prosecute, if sd. committee think proper.

Voted that Mr. Ogden be directed to pay the above two dollars on account of cleaning the meeting house as above directed.

[PARISH, 26 Oct., 1801.] Parrish meeting, at the Meeting house, 26 Octr., 1801. Doctor Tim'o Johnes, Moderator; Silas Condict, clk. Voted that the trustees pay Mr. Richards, instead of his firewood for one year, the sum of eighty dollars; the year to end the 12 day of Septr., 1802.

TRUSTEES, 9-17 Nov., 1801.] Meeting Trustees, at Mr. Johnson's in Morris Town, 9th day Novr., 1801; all present. Adjourned til to-morrow, two of the clock P. M. Met agreable to adjournment; the president and Mr. Tucker absent. Adjourned to meet on the 17 Insant, at this place, at two of the clock P. M. The Trustees all met except Mr. Tucker.

Mr. Mills, one of the committee appointed for that purpose, reported that Mr. Crain declined takeing the pew heretofore agreed on with Mr. Crane.

Voted that Mr. Mills, Mr. Ogden and Mr. Lindley be a committee to sell a building lot, near the meeting house, at public vendue. Voted that the aforesaid committee be directed to sell, at public vendue, part of the wood on the parsonage, in small lotts at their discretion.

[TRUSTEES, 17 Dec., 1801.] Meeting of Trustees, 17 Dec'r, 1801, at Mr. Mills house ; all present, except Mr. Pierson.

The committee appointed for that purpose reported that they had sold the lot of Land North of the meeting house, which contains forty-eight hundredths of an acre, to Mr. Pierson, for four hundred and eleven dollrs.; and that they had sold the timber on thirty-three half acre lots, which amounted to three hundred and forty-five dollars and 93 cents, as follows : [Here follow the designations of the thirty-three lots, with the name of purchaser and amount paid, ranging from $5.61 to $15.90 each.]

Voted that Mr. Mills and Mr. Ogden be a committee to make a statement of the accounts and obligations belonging to the congregation.

[Parish, 10 March, 1802.] At a Parrish meeting, 10 march, 1802. Deacon Alling, Moderator ; and Jos. Lewis, Esqr., Clerk.

The meeting considering the necessity of raising money to pay the arrears due to sundry persons for building the church, and to raise enough to compleat it, Voted that the Trustees be authorised to sell the seats by vendue, at such price as they can obtain, not less than one-half the original price and subject to the payment of the original Sallery; that the first Vendue be held on the 24th instant. On motion of Mr. Carmichael, Voted that Alexander Carmichael, Joseph Lewis and Dan'l Phoenix be a committee to examine the trustees Accounts, and report a state of the Debts, funds and property of the Congregation.

[TRUSTEES, 2 April, 1802.]   2 April, 1802.

Trustees met at Benjamin Lindsleys, all present but Mr. Johnson and Mr. Person, and executed a deed to Benj'n Lindsley for a small Lot of Land near the meeting house, Containing 16 hundredths of an acre, for 325 dollars ; and took a bond and Mortgage for the same.

[PARISH, 3 Sept., 1802.] At a Parish Meeting, held this 3rd of Sept'r, 1802, David Lindsly was appointed Moderator and Joseph Halsey, Clerk.

Voted that the Trustees pay to Mr. Richards eighty dollars in lieu of firewood for the ensuing year, to commence the twelfth instant.

Voted that the committee appointed to examine the state of the funds of the Parish and make report to the parish be dismissed from their appointment.

Voted that the Trustees make a report annually to the parish, at a parish meeting in September, of the property, debts and funds belonging to the parish.

Voted that the Venitian blinds which are put to one of the windows of the meeting House be taken away.

Voted that the pew belonging to Doctor Wm. Campfield, which has been raised, be put down to its former situation ; and that the President of the Trustees wait on Doct'r Campfield and request him to put it in its former situation.

[TRUSTEES, 17 Nov. 1802.] Mr. Mills and Mr. Lindley of the committee appointed the 17 Nov'r 1801, to sell wood on the parsonage land, report that in addition to what was sold the 25 Nov'r, 1801, they have sold on the 17 Nov'r, 1802, twenty small lots to the amount of 173 Dls. 20 cnts.

[TRUSTEES, 29 Dec. 1802.] Meeting Trustees at Mr. Johnson's house, 29 Day Dec'r, 1802 ; all present. Voted that Mr. Mills on the part of the Trustees settle Joseph Marsh's Account with him, and make report at the next meeting of the Trustees.

Voted that Mr. Mills attend to settleing Gen'l Doughties account with the parrish, and make report at the next meeting of the Trustees,

Voted that the President call on Isaac Pierson and secure the payment of his Note to the Trustees in such way as he shall deem proper.

[TRUSTEES, 29 Oct. 1802.] Meeting Trustees 29 Oct'r 1803, [1] at Mr. Johnson's house; present Mr. Ford, Mr. Mills, Mr. Johnson, Mr. Tucker and Mr. Lindley. Voted that the parsonage land lying between the meeting house and Israel Canfields cyder works, from the grave yard fence to the public road that leads from the Court house to Mr. Rineharts tavern, be sold at public vendue, Voted that John Mills and Dan'l Lindley be a committee to advertise and sell the same.

[TRUSTEES, 19 Nov. 1802.] 19 Nov'r 1803, [1] at a meeting of the Trustees at Mr. Johnsons house, all present except Mr. Pierson; Mr. Mills and Mr. Lindley reported that they had sold the parsonage land between the meeting house and Israel Canfields cyder works, containing sixty four hundreths of an acre, to James Stephenson for one hundred and forty four dollars, and presented the deed for signing.

[TRUSTEES, 5 Jan, 1803.] At a meeting of the Trustees at Mr. Johnson's house the 5 day of Jan'y, 1803, Mr. Mills, Mr. Johnson, Mr. Ogden, Mr. Pierson and Mr. Lindley present. Mr. Mills, of the committee appointed to settle with Gen'l Doughty, reported that his account against the parrish for scaffeling [scaffolding ?] poles was setled at three pounds, four shillings and 3d. Voted that the treasurer be directed to prosecute all delinquents in arrears with the parrish on account of Sallery after two years become due; that the Clerk furnish the Treasurer with a coppy of the forgoeing resolution.

[TRUSTEES, 24 March, 1803.] At a meeting of the Trustees at Mr. Johnson's house this 24 day of March, 1803; all present. Voted that widow Day have the refusal of a lot of parrish ground adjoining the Accademy lot, for one hundred pounds until monday next. Recompence Stanbury applyed for a lot of parrish land; the Trustees agreed with him, for seventy pounds, for a lot adjoining one he now owns and occupies. Mr. Mills and Mr. Lindley appointed, and they are hereby instructed, to collect the money for which wood was sold

[1] The position and dates of these two entries are as given above. It seems probable that the Clerk put "1803" inadvertently for 1802, when he inscribed the minutes after the entry of Dec. 29, having omitted them in their proper order.

at vendue, agreably to the articles of said vendue, and prosedute if nessasary. Mr. Johnson and Mr. Tucker appointed to take care of and see that no wood, or other property, belonging to the parrish, be taken of the parrish land after the 1st day of April next; and that if wood heretofore sold at vendue and not taken of agreably to articles of vendue by the 1st day of April, said committee are hereby directed to sell said wood immediately at vendue for the benefit of the Congregation.

[TRUSTEES, 1 April, 1803.] At a meeting of the Trustees at Mr. Johnson's house, 1st April, 1803; all present & executed a Deed to Recompence Stanbury for the lot he applyed for the 24 last month, for seventy pounds; also a deed to Nancy Day for a lot adjoining the Accademy and Elija Snethen, for one hundred pounds. Voted that Mr. Johnson be directed to write to Richard Meeker requireing payment for arrears of Sallery due on a seat he owns 'in the church; also a Note of hand in the possession of the Trustees against him. Voted that Mr. Mills be directed to furnish Mrs. Day her deed and receive her bond and morgage; also to make oute R. Stanberries deed and receive his bond and morgage.

Voted that Mr. Mills and Mr. Johnson be a committee to Settle with the Treasurer, and lay before the trustees a list of those Names supposed bad debts; and make report if practicable at the next meeting of the Trustees. Voted that the book of transfers and register be kept by Mr. Johnson; that he be requested to make all entries nessasary and proper to be made in said book. Mr. Mills is appointed to keep the book of Accounts; to make all charges and entries proper to be made in said book.

[TRUSTEES, 25 June 1803.] At a meeting of the Trustees at Mr. Johnson's house, the 25 June, 1803; all present but the President.

Mr. Johnson and Mr. Lindley are appointed to repair the fence between the parrish and Wm. Johnes, and all other fence partition between the parrish and others. Voted that the Saxton be, and he is here by, directed to demand and to receive for the use of the takel belonging to the Congregation, fifty cents per day, meaning each and every day until returned, or for any part of said takel ; that the Saxton report in writeing to Mr. Johnson the several accounts due, or that may become due, by virtue of this order. Voted that Mr. Daniel Pierson pay one dollar and fifty cents for the use of said takel, which Mr. Pierson agreed to. Mr. Johnson is hereby directed to call on and collect from those persons charged as above & not paid to the Saxton. Voted that Mr. Mills collect all or any money due to the Congregation, not secured by morgage, and put it oute at his discretion for the use of the parrish, to be had if wanted by the 1st of october next. Voted that Mr. Johnson be directed to receive the principal only of the Note of hand ag't Wm. Meeker and the Sallery due on his seat in the Church, in full satisfaction of any demand against said Meeker. Voted that Mr. Mills and Mr. Johnson repair the stepel and clock.

[TRUSTEES, 27 Aug., 1803.] Meeting of the Trustees at Rich'd Johnson's House, 27 Augt., 1803; all present. Voted that John Mills, Rich'd Johnson and Daniel Lindley or any two of them, be a committee to prevent,, by legal means, the turn pike company or any person or persons breaking ground on the green belonging to the parish for the purpose of makeing a turn pike road.

Voted that the President be directed to receive a Mortgage from James Stephenson for the one now in his keeping against Ebenezar C. Pierson in favor of the Trustees for

[PARISH, 2 Sept., 1803.] At A parrish meeting held in the Church the 2d Day of September, 1803 ; Gilbert Alling, Moderator, and Joseph Halsey, Clerk. Voted that the Minister be paid ninety dollars in lieu of his fire wood for one year next ensuing. A statement of the parrish funds was laid before the Congregation.

[TRUSTEES, 13 Sept., 1803.] At a meeting of the Trustees at Richard Johnson's house, 13 September, 1803 ; the President. Mr. Mills, Mr. Johnson, Mr. Ogden, Mr. Tucker, and Mr. Lindley, Present.

Voted that Mr. Mills and Mr. Johnson be a committee to call on John and Abraham Kinney's, or on Abraham's Agent, for the moneys due to the parrish from them ; that on neglect or refusal on the part of the said Kinnes, or either of them, of the payment of the said arrears, said committee are hereby directed to procede and collect the money by prosecution and by the sale of there pew ; & that the committee report there procedings at the next meeting of the Trustees.

[PARISH, 1 Dec, 1803.] At a meeting of the Congregation on the 1st day of December, 1803 ; Deacon Alling, moderator, and Joseph Lewis, Clerk, the moderator gave notice that the business in part was to agree about raising, or increasing, Mr. Richard's Sallery, and after some conversation, Resolved, that there be an addition to Mr. Richards present sallery of one hundred and twenty five dollars annually, from the 12th day of September last ; and that the parrish Treasurer be directed to pay to him in advance all the surplus sallery money on hand ; and if there be any yet uncollected, ' that was due the 12th day of September last, that he pay the whole to him as soon as collected : That the Trustees be directed to sue all delinquents whose sallery may remain unpaid for three months after the sallery for one year shall become due.

That the Trustees be requested to paint the church as early next spring as they can with convenience, & that they repaire the clock and put one or more faces to it ; also that the Trustees be authorised & requested to provide two branch candle sticks to each window below, & two for the desk in front of the pulpit, & one for each pillar ; and that they provide as many candels for each eavening meeting as may be nessasary.

[TRUSTEES, 21 Jan. 1804.] At a meeting of the Trustees at Esquire Johnson's house, 21 Jan'y, 1804, Mr. Ford the President, Mr. Mills, Mr. Johnson, Mr. Ogden, and Mr. Lindley present.

Voted that six years interest be allowed on Jonathan Browns account.

[TRUSTEES, 23 April, 1804.] At a meeting of the Trustees at Esq'r Johnson's house, the 23 April, 1804, all present.

Esq'r Johnson reported that he had received thirty dollars & sixty three cents in full of Wm. Meekers Note of hand to the Trustees. Voted that Mr. Mills collect the small debts due to the parrish before the first of October next. Voted that Messers Mills & Ogden be a committee to settle the accounts of the Trustees with Individuals.

[TRUSTEES, 31 Aug., 1804.] Meeting of the Trustees at the house of Rich'd Johnson, Esq'r., this 31st of August, 1804 ; Mr. Ford the President only absent.

Voted that Esq'r Johnson employ some proper person to repaire the clock. Voted that Mr. Mills be appointed to purchase the whitelead and oils to paint the meeting house. Voted that Mrs. Woolley have the refusal of two lots of ground situate between the Stanbury house and Lewis Mills's house, for one hundred and forty pounds, York money.

[PARISH, 19 Sept, 1804.] At a Parrish meeting held at the meeting house the 19 September, 1804, Deacon Alling was appointed Moderator and Henry Mills, c,l,k.

On motion, voted that the Minister be supplyed with wood in the same manner as last year. Resolved that Mr. Jaduthan Condict and Mr. Usual Condict be authorised and directed to prevent all disorderly behaviour in the galleries and on the stairs, during public worship ; and more particularly to prevent young people from disturbing the congregation by moveing down stairs before the blessing is pronounced.

Also resolved that Mr. Richards be requested to publish the foregoing resolution on the next Sabath.

Resolved that Richard Johnson, Esquire, Dr. Lewis Condict, and Joseph Lewis, Esquire, be a committee to superintend the singing in the church ; who are authorised to appoint Chorristers, point out proper tunes to be suug, and generally to do all things necessary for the promotion of harmony in the singing and with the singers.

[TRUSTEES, 8 oct. 1804.] At a meeting of the Trustees, at the house of Richard Johnson, Esquire, this 8th day of October, 1804, all present. Voted that Mr. Mills and Mr.

Johnson be a committee to sell at public vendue those seats and pews which are delinquent in the payment of sallery, for the purpose of paying the same, agreeable to a resolution of the parrish, of the 18th of february, 1796, viz. * * * * [Nos 2, and half of 13 in the gallery, with 14 and half of 53 on lower floor, the names of their owners being mentioned.] Voted that Mr. Mills, Mr. Johnson, and Mr. Tucker be a committee to superintend painting the meeting house, and put one face to the clock ; also to errect two or more hors blocks near the church.

Voted that Mr. Pierson be directed to collect from Ga. H. Ford, Esq'r, money to the amount of a lather [ladder ?] he borrowed belonging to the Congregation.

Voted that Mess'rs Mills and Johnson be directed to call on Dr. Canfield for the books and papers belonging to the Congregation.

[REPORT OF A COMMITTEE.] Mr. Mills and Mr. Johnson, the committee appointed to sell forfited seats, reported that they had given public notice, on the preceeding sabeth, of a parrish meeting for the purpose of seling a number of forfited seats, and that they had put up advertisements in 6 diferent places, describeing the particular seats to be sold & who were the owners ; &, according thereto, on the 2 day of Nov. 1804, they had sold at public vendue the seats & pews hereafter named, viz : * * * * * * [Here follows a description of same pews mentioned under last entry, with the prices and names of purchasers. In the gallery No. 2 sold to John Smith for $7.50 ; half of 13 to Joseph Beers, for $9 : on main floor, 14 sold to George Tucker, in behalf of "Jonas Philops," for $8 ; and half of 53, to David Hedges for $12.]

[MEMORANDUM, 27 DEC., 1804.] EXPENSE OF PAINTING MEETING HOUSE, 1804.

40 Gls. of oil, at 10,	£20. 0. 0
28¾ Do. of Do. 10-6,	15. 1.10
13l. of whitelead, 1456 @ ¼,	84.18. 8
N. York price,	120. 0. 6
Expense of giting to Morristown,	3.15. 9
	————
	£123.16.9
2¼ Gls. of oil of J. Dixon at 13,	1. 9.3

5 brushes, 16,	16. 0
1 qt. Sps. turpentine 2-6 lamback 3,	5. 6
Jonatn. Ford,s acct.	11. 0
Jesse Cutler acct.,	1. 4 .0
Benja. Halloways,	10. 0
Benoni Hathaway,	1. 4. 0
David Hathaway,	11. 1. 10
Wm. Woolley,	19. 8. 5
James Cooper,	14.15. 9
Stephen Ayers,	15. 0
John Mills acct. about	4.12. 0
Richard Johnson,	15. 0. 0
	70. 3.6
Work at the Steple,	12. 0.0
	£207. 9.0

27 Dec., 1804, the committee for painting the meeting house Report that they had painted the oute side of the house twice over; & had painted some of the inside, & had expended in doeing the same about four hundred and 90 dollars, & in Ironing the frame of the steeple about thirty dollars.

painting the house,	490 dollars.
Ironing the Steeple,	30
	$520

[Trustees, 29 April, 1805.] Meeting of the Trustees at Esquire Johnson's house, 29 Apl., 1805 ; all present except Mr. Johnson.

On application of Wm. Cherry, the Saxton, Voted that he receive from the treasurer for his services for ringing the bell and sweeping the meeting house, thirty-five dollars pr. annum, after this date.

Voted that Snethens Mortgage be exchanged for one from Stephen Pierson, provided that Mr. Mills shall be satisfied that no encumbrance has been done or made by said Snethen respecting sd. premises. Voted that Mr. Ford attend to clearing oute the old ditches on the parsonage lands and pay for the same.

[PARISH, 12 Sept. 1805.] At a Parrish meeting held at the meeting house, 12 Sept. 1805 ; Alexander Carmichall, Moderator, & Jo's Halsey, Clerk. Voted that Jaduthan Condit, Jaduthan Day, Moses Pruden & Elija Holloway be, and they are hereby, appointed to take charge of the galleries & of the stairs, in order to prevent disturbance & disorderly behaviour on the Sabeth.

[PARISH, 4 Sept. 1806.] At a Parrish meeting held at the Church on the 4 September, 1806 ; Gilbert Allen, Moderator, and John McCarter, Clerk. Voted that the parrish pay to the Minister Ninety dollars in lieu of his fire wood for the ensueing year, commenceing the 12 Instant. A statement of the parrish funds were réd to the parrish.

[TRUSTEES, 15 Feb., 1806.] At a meeting of the Trustees, at Grover Coes, 15 Sept'r, 1806 ; Present Mr. Mills, Mr. Johnson, Mr. Ogden, Mr. Tucker, Mr. Lindley.

Voted that the trustees sell two acres of the low lands belonging to the parrish, adjoining lands of Mr. Richards ; & that Mr. Mills, Mr. Johnson and Mr. Lindley be a committee to advetise & sell the same at Public vendue.

[TRUSTEES, 26 Feb., 1807.] At a meeting of the Trustees at the house of George Tucker on 26 day of feb'y, 1807 ; present Jonathan Ford, John Mills, Jonathan Ogden, George Tucker, Benj'a Pierson, Richard Johnson, & Dan'l Lindley.

Voted that the Trustees pay Henry Lindley twenty nine shillings & sixpence, & Deacon Jos. Pruden the money due him on the meeting house books with interest from the year 98. Said Lindleys demand is also on the meeting house books ; and that John

Mills collect the money due from John Lindley on sd. books.

Voted that   *   be prosecuted for the arrears of sallery due the parish on his Seat.

Voted that Mr. Mills, the parrish treasurer, be directed to collect arrears due to the Parrish, by prosecution or otherwise immediately.

[TRUSTEES, 12 March, 1807.] At a meeting of Trustees on 12th March, 1807, at Grover Coes, all present except Mr. Johnson and Mr. Tucker. Voted that the delinquents of Sallery, who are more than a year & a half in arrears on their pews & Seats, be prosecuted for the same by the treasurer, agreably to a resolution of the parrish of the 18 of february, 1796. [Then follows a list of five "delinquents," three of whom are described as " Dect.'' or deceased, and three of the pews were in the gallery.]

[TRUSTEES, 29 May, 1807,] Meeting of Trustees, all present except Mr. Tucker ; met at Mr. Coes, 29 May, 1807.

Voted that Mr. Mills be directed to prosecute delinquents of Sallery, and pay the costs of such prosecution provided the defendant pay the demand before Judg't entered.

Voted that Mr. Mills and Mr. Pierson be a committee for the purpose of waiting on the board of chosen freeholders, & to inform the board that the trustees request them to relinquish the rent due from Moses Estey for the privalege & use of the land on which his store is placed, adjoining the Court House , & to present them' with a writeing in the following words or to that effect, viz.; Morris town, 29 May, 1807. To the board of chosen freeholders for the County of Morris, we, the Trustees of the first Presbyterian Church at Morris town, would again solicit your attention to a matter we think of Sufficient importance. The board will remember that some time in the year 1805 we addressed you with a few lines, in which we remonstrated against the erecting of a building at the West end of the Court House, which was then goeing on. For two reasons we requested that Said building might be stoped. 1st that we consider it was a trespasing on the property of the congregation ; and 2d that erect-

ing a building on that ground for private use would effectually destroy the title of the County to the whole Court house lot. It seems that our application and remonstrance has been totally disregarded, and Said building has been sometime occupyed for private use. Altho you have hereby destroyed the Title of the County to the Court house lot, we have no objections to the County's useing Said lot for the purposes Specified in their deed from the Trustees, which was for the Court house only, provided they pay to this board the whole of the ground rent paid and to be paid by Moses Estey.

Sighned by order of the board,

Sighned, Jon'n. Ford,

President.

Mr. Mills committee for seling forfeited seats in the church, reported that he had sold at public vendue, on 29 March, 1807, at a parish meeting duely published & and advertised for that purpose—seats as follows, viz :

Half No. 28 in the gallery, formerly the property of Ebenezar Condict, which was sold to Elias Jagger for five dollars, who gave his note to the trustees for the whole $1.56 salery due, which said Mills, Treasurer, credited in Salery book and charged to the Trustees.

Also No. 49 in Gallery, formerly the property of Zopher Hathaway, Dect., Sold to Mahlon Ford for eight dollars and fifty cents, who paid the whole money to Sd. Mills, and Mills has credited in Salery book $5.31 for Salery due, and to the Trustees the surplus $3.19.

Also No. 17 in the Gallery, formerly the property of John Morris Dect., Sold to Drake Ludlow for five dollars and one cent, who paid to Mr. Richards $4.19, and to John Mills 68 cents for Salery & 14 cents surplus which is credited to the trustees.

Also pew No. 9 formerly the property of Jonathan Dickerson, Dect., Sold to George Tucker for twenty-seven dollars and fifty seven cents, amount of Sallery due, who paid the same to John Mills, Sallery Treasurer.

Also one fourth part of a pew No. 24, formerly the property of Matthew Lum, Junr., Sold to Vincent Gerin for eight dollars and fifty cents ; $2.26 due for Sallery was paid to John Mills, Sall'y Treasurer, and $6.24, the surplus, said Gerin retained in his hands, by order of Jacob Arnold, Att,y for Said Lum, said Gerin to credit Lum towards money due him from said Lum.

[TRUSTEES, 13 Nov., 1807.] At a meeting of the Trustees at Grover Coes, the 13 Nov'r 1807; present the President, Mr. Mills, Mr. Johnson, Mr. Ogden, Mr. Pierson, Mr. Lindley.

Voted that Messers. Johnson and Ogden be a committee to settle the treasurer, acc't with the Parrish, and acc'ts generally with the trustees.

Voted that John C. Willing be paid by Mill his acc't ag't the parrish in the parrish meeting house books, the principle only.

Voted that Mr. Mills take an obligation with security of Mr. Stevenson, for the Interest now due to the parrish from him.

[PARISH, 24 March, 1808.] At a parrish meeting held at the Presbeterian Church on 24 march, 1808; Jno. Kinney, moderator, Timo. I. Lewis, Clerk.

Voted that one of the Seats reserved for deaf people, No. 31. be rented from this time to 12 of Sept'r next.

Voted that the Trustees procure an estimate of the expense of painting inside of the Church, lettering of the Seats, repairing of the clock, and ascertaining whether the Clock can carry three hands and the expense of them. Resolved that the business of the meeting be adj'd to the Second wednesday in April next, at three in the afternoon.

[PARISH, 13 april, 1808.] At a meeting of the Parrish held at the Church in morris town, on 13 ap'r, 1808, by adjournment, Edward Condict, Esq'r., moderator; Henry King, Clerk.

On motion of Dr. Condict, Resolved that the appointment of two of the Trustees shall be vacated Annually, from and after the yearly parrish meeting to be holden in Sept'r next; and, that it may be ascertained in what order their respective appointments shall become vacant, be it further resolved that the said Trustees be, and they are hereby, requested to divide themselves into three classes, the two first classes consisting of two members each and the third of three members; the term

of the first class to Expire at the time before mentioned; of the second class, one year thereafter; and of the third, one year after the expiration of the second.

And be it resolved that, at the Annual meeting of the Parrish before mentioned, the Congregation shall procede to fill the vacancies which shall happen in pursuance of the above resolution; and that occasional vacancies by Death or resignation shall be filled as heretofore.

Richard Johnson & Jonathan Ford resigned their offices as Trustees, whereupon Richard Johnson was reappointed; Silas Condict, in place of Jonathan Ford resigned, and Jacob Smith, in place of George Tucker, Dec't., were also appointed Trustees.

Resolved that the Trustees be authorised to pay Mr. Richards the ballance due him oute of any money in their hands, or compromise by paying him the Interest on Said ballance.

Resolved that a Subscription be set on foot by the Trustees to purchase a new Clock with three faces, & lay the same before the next annual parrish meeting.

[TRUSTEES, 18 April, 1808.] A meeting of the Trustees at the house of G. Coe; present John Mills, Jon'n Ogden, Benj'n Pierson & Daniel Lindsly; when Richard Johnson, Silas Condict & Jacob Smith attended and took the oaths required by Law as Trustees. The Trustees then proceeded to the choice of a president, and appointed John Mills their president for the time being.

TRUSTEES, 2 June, [1808.] At a meeting of the Trustees at Grove Coes, Mr. Person absent. Mr. Mills and Mr. Johnson appointed a Committee to meet the Committee of the Board of Chosen Freeholders for the County, respecting the building erected by Moses Estey on the Courthouse lot.

[TRUSTEES, 31 Aug., 1808.] At a meeting of Trustees, at the house of Grover Coe, Mr. Person absent. Mr. Mills and Mr. Johnson, a committee appointed to meet a committee from the board of chosen Freeholders of the County of Morris, respecting the building erected by Moses Estey, Esq'r, Reported that they had met with Said Committee, who disagreed to the proposal made by the Trustees,

Mr. Mills, from the Committe for Selling forfited Seats in the Meeting house, Reported that they had Sold at publick vendue, at a parish meeting which was duly Advertised & publick notice given. which vendue began on the 24th day of march, 1808, and a part of the Sales adjourned to the 13th Apriel: the Seats Sold were as follow : ⅜ No. 77, below. of Jehabod Coopers, Sold to David Cooper for $14.20. ⅜ of No. 58, below, of Jabez Condicts, Sold to Abner Whitehead for $15.00. ⅜ of No. 50, in Gal'y, of Jabez Condicts, Sold to Jacob Tingler for $7.00. ⅜ of No. 40, in Gal'y, of John Coplins, Sold to Thomas Gering for $6.85. ¼ of No. 69, below, of Philip Eastens, Sold to George Emmel for $11.00. ¼ of No. 62, below, of Timothy Fairchilds, Sold to Jacob Smith for $30.05. ¼ No. 45, in Gal'y, of Silas Hathaway, Sold to Isaac Lewis for $1.50. ¼ No. 57, in Gal'y, of Jeptha Wades, Sold to Moses Sayr for $1.30.

How the amount of the above Sales were Setled may be Seen in the Sallery book and the Trustees book of Accounts.

[PARISH, 15 Sept. 1808.] 15th Sept'r., 1808. A parish Meeting was this day held, agreeable to publick notice from the pulpit last Sabbath, when Deacon Gilbert Allen was chosen Moderator, and Lewis Condict, Clerk.

John Mills, one of the Trustees, presented a Subscription, circulated by order of the last parish meeting, the object of which was to purchase a new Town Clock. Ordered to lie on the table, & that the Trustees circulate it at their discretion in future.

Voted that Mr. Richards be paid Ninety dollars instead of firewood for this year.

John Mills, in behalf of the Trustees, reported a Statement in writing of the funds of the Congregation, to which is Subjoined a Statement of the Ministers Sallary, the amount of the assessments on the Seats in the meeting house, & a deficiency of the Same to defray the annual Sallary. Mooved & seconded that the annuities on pews and Seats be encreased, for the ensuing year, at the rate of _____ Resolved that the further Consideration of the matter be posponed to the next parish meeting, to be held at this place three weeks from this day.

[PARISH, 6 Oct., 1808.] 6th Oct'r., 1808.

At a parish held this day, ageeeable to publick notice & adjournment, Deacon Gilbert Allen was chosen Moderator. & Peter A. Johnson, Clerk.

A motion that was made at last parish meeting wether the annuities on the pews & Seats be raised or not, was carried in the negative.

Moovd & voted that a Subscription be opened, and circulated by Joseph Lewis, for raising money to make up a deficiency which now appears on our Ministers Sallery, and report at next parish meeting.

Moovd & Seconded whether Mr. Richards Sallary Shall be raised or not ; &, if raised, how much, and in what way. Resolved that this motion lie over untill next parish meeting.

Adjourned to this day two weeks.

[PARISH, 20 Oct. 1808.] 20 Octr., 1808. At a parish meeting held this day by adjournment & publick notice ; Henry Vail, Moderator, and Silas Condit, Clerk : when the Trustees Sold at vendue one half of Seat No. 30, below in the meetinghouse, formerly the property of Ezra Halsey, to Peter A Johnson for 35 dollars ; and Seat No. 46, formerly Benoni Hathaways, to Edward Mills for 56 dollars ; the meeting then adjourned to thursday the 10th day of November next at 2 oclock, P. M.

[PARISH, 10 Nov. 1808.] 10 Novr. 1808. At a parish meeting held this day, Simeon Broadwell, Moderator, & Peter A. Johnson, Clerk. Voted that three Seats each Side of the meetinghouse, in the corner where the negroes now Set, be converted in two pews, and be done in 2 weeks from this day, and the Trustees to fix a Sallary to the same. The Trustees Sold at vendue one half Seat No. 91, that was Moses Shipmans, to Joseph Johnson for seven dollars. The meeting then adjourned to 24th this month. [There is no record of a meeting on the 24th Nov. 1808; that of 12 April, 1809, follows immediately below the entry just given.]

[PARISH, 12 April, 1809.] 12th April, 1809. At a parish meeting held this day, at the meetinghouse ; Edward Condit, Moderator, Nathl Bull, Clerk.

On motion, Shall Mr. Richards Sallary be raised to a Sum Sufficient to Support himself & family ? was carried unanimously.

On motion that there should be an addition to Mr. Richards's Sallary Annually the Sum of three hundred & thirty five dollars, from the 12th of September last: which was carried unanimously, Except 2 votes; and a Committee apointed to wate on Mr. Richards immediately and inform him of the above proceedings, viz. Jonas Philips, Jon'n Ford, Henry Vail & Jno. Mills.

Voted that the Trustees, instead of raising the Sallery on the Seats & pews in the meetinghouse, do Circulate a Supscription through the parish, for raising the addition made to Mr. Richardss Sallary, provided he continue with us.

[PARISH, 24 April 1809.] 24th April 1809, at a parish meeting, held at the request of Mr. Richards & in pursuance of publick notice, the Revd. Matthew L. Perine was

chosen Moderator, & Timothy Lewis, Clerk; when the following resolutions were passed unanimously.

Resolved that a Committee of three persons be appointed as Commissioners to represent this Congregation at the Ensuing meeting of presbytery, at Elizabethtown; & that they be instructed not to oppose Mr. Richards's Removal; & that they lay before Presbytery the proceeding of the last parish meeting, at which time Mr. Richards intention to leave us was not known; & that the Committee be instructed to make and lay before Presbytery, Such extracts from the proceedings of this parish as they may deem necessary.

Voted that John Mills, Henry Vail and Lewis Condict be the Committee for that purpose.

PROSPECTUS OF SUPPLEMENT FOR 1884.

Beginning with the next number, for Jan. 1884, the *Supplement* will be enlarged from four to eight pages each month. It is proposed thus to print all the salient facts of record from the books of the Church, in a form suitable for binding in a separate volume. The January number will begin the publication of extracts from Dr. Johnes' Session Book, which dates back to 1742. Lists of baptisms, communicants, marriages and burials will appear in the order of the pastorates under which they occurred, as during the past year; but *Supplements* containing these lists will be paged to be bound with Vols. I and II of THE RECORD. Extracts from the Session and Trustees' books will be paged continuously for the separate volume; and, should the proposal meet with sufficient encouragement, an alphabetical list of all the names which appear on the Registers of baptisms, communicants, marriages and burials, will be prepared, and arranged in family groups, to close the volume. For this new volume, a reprint will be made of the more interesting portions of the Trustees' Book, which have already appeared in THE RECORD. This reprint will *not* be issued as a regular part of the publication, but as an extra; and it will be supplied *gratuitously* to subscribers.

CORRECTIONS.

A few errors have been discovered in previous numbers of THE RECORD, for the correction of which the present offers a favorable opportunity.

LIST OF RULING ELDERS.

Pages 34 and 35.

John Lindsley met with Session 29 June, 1752 Is there not an error in the date of his death as there given?

Abner Beach, the sixth name on this list and also on that of Mr. Barnes, should probably be erased. The only reason now apparent for calling him an Elder is the fact that in the minute recording his suspension, (the only place where he is mentioned,) he is styled "a member of our Body." But, as Dr. Johnes elsewhere uses the word Body to designate the Church membership, it seems insufficient evidence for the conclusion that he here includes Abner Beach in the Session by this term.

Joseph Prudden, Jr. is first mentioned as an Elder in 1783, not 1785. Isaac Prudden Samuel Freeman, Jesse Cutler, and Matthias Crane do not appear till 1795; Barnes' Manual says they were "first in office between 1792 and 1795."

David Lindsley appears for last time at meeting of Session, 23 May, 1733, not 11 Dec., 1832; and was dismissed May, 1833, to New Vernon, where he died 15 Nov., 1858.

James Stevenson should be recorded as appearing last at Session meeting 28 Oct., 1807; he is not mentioned even among the absentees after 3 May, 1809.

Stephen Young was dismissed to the 2d Church 26 Jan., 1841, and Lewis Mills at the same time, but the latter returned 24 Feb., 1848.

The name of Francis Johnes should be inserted after that of Peter A. Johnson, as he was elected an Elder at the same time with the four whose names precede, 14 May, 1812; although not ordained with them, "being on a journey at the time," according to the record, but ordained 4 Mar., 1814, and present at one meeting of Session, that of 22 April, 1814. The fact that he met once with the Session gives his name a right to a place in the list along with the name of George K. Drake, since the latter never attended even one Session meeting.

Jonathan Oliver met last with Session 11 Dec., 1832, not 23 May, 1833.

Jonathan Thompson and John B. Johnes, M. D., resigned 7 April, not 30 March, 1836.

John W. Cortelyou met last with Session 22 May, instead of 20 Feb., 1834.

MEMBERS.

Rebecca, Matt. (not Zach.) Fairchild s wife, page 20.

Hannah Lindley, page 68, wife of Junia, received 19 Aug., 1759, is recorded as having died 8 Dec., 1779, but this death was that of Hannah, wife of Joseph Lindsley.

Zophar Freeman, received 1 Nov., 1764, was an Elder and dismissed to Chatham, 26 Aug., 1825.

Benoni Hathaway and Damaris, his wife; should be added to the roll under date of 9 Nov., 1766; Damaris died 24 Feb., 1829.

Martha Emmell, wife of George, should be added to roll under date of 1 Sept., 1786, she died 23 Feb., 1845.

Nathanael Beers should be added, 6 May 1787; died 1825.

The following 8 names, which appear on rolls prepared by Mr. Fisher and Mr. Barnes, have not been identified with any hitherto published.

Prucia (Meeker), widow of Wm. Woodruff, wrongly given as Jerusha in Mr. Barnes' Manual, received on certificate, 1798,

Jane Meeker, wife of Matthias, received ———; d. 1 Mar., 1815.

Sarah Post, wife of Wm., received on conf. 3 June, 1792.

Phebe Burnet, wife of John, received on cert. 5 March, 1795; died 1861.

Rachel Enslee, wife of Wm., conf. 1 Jan., 1797; d. 4 Aug., 1843, aet. 46.

Mary Williams, wife of Matthias, conf. 24 Sept., 1797.

Elizabeth Fairchild, wife of Joseph, conf. 3 July, 1808; dismissed Jan., 1848.

Mary Day, wife of David, conf. 4 Sept., 1808.

Page 149. Phebe Kinney, died Feb., 1820.
" Anna Phœnix, died 12 March, 1854.
" Martha Lindsly, dismissed.
" Rhoda Lindsly, died April, 1857, aet. 92.
" Abigail Charlot, married Robert Gillespie, 11 May, 1801.
" Polly Ayres, appears on Mr. Fisher's roll as Polly King, wife of John Day.
" Patty Shipman, dismissed into Sussex, 1809.
" Ruth Pierson, on Mr. McDowell's roll is marked "died 16 Sept., 1814."
" Anna Byram, died 1818.
" Sally Ball, married George Templeton, 18 Dec., 1802, died 1839.
" Abigail Condit Whitehead, dismissed May, 1816.
" Nancy Bowen, married Wm. Hyer, 22 July, 1805, and dismissed to Meth. Church.
" Nancy Douglass, married Joseph Wheeler, 17 Feb., 1808.

Page 157. Huldah Byram, married Loammi Moore, dismissed to East Bloomfield, 1 Mar., 1842.
" Abner Pierson, dismissed to Baskingridge.
" Abraham Ball, dismissed to 2d Ch., 26 Jan., 1841.
" Eunice Casterline, dismissed to Chatham.
" Sarah Peck, dismissed to 2d Ch., 26 Jan., 1841.
" Phebe Freeman, married John Burnet, d. 1861.

Page 157. Eunice Fairchild, dismissed Oct., 1815.
" Phebe Condnor, was Phebe Chitester before marriage.
" Hannah Sutton, married Wm. Bedell, and died 12 Sept., 1812.
" John Smith, dis. to 2d Ch., 26 Jan., 1841.
" Polly Phillips, died 2 July, 1811.

Page 165. Abraham Hedges, dis. to Bottle Hill, 1 Sept., 1825.
" Phebe Hedges, dis. to Bottle Hill, 1 Sept., 1825.
" Sally Johnson, died 17 April, 1837.
" Eunice Johnson, mar. Silas Mills, joined Bap. Ch.
" Add name of Mehitable Tunis, wf. of Stephen, rec'd 20 June, 1803.
" Phebe Turner, dis. to 2d Ch., 26 Jan., 1841.
" Sally Ferris, wid, of Archibald; d. 13 April, 1841.
" Matsy Condit, died 22 Oct., 1820.

Page 193. Susan Byram, dis. to Carmine St. Ch., N. Y. City, 17 Aug. 1839.
" Lydia Guerin, dis. to 2d Ch., 30 Oct., 1841.
" Jared D. Filer, "from ye Cong. of Pleasant Valley," "ordained;' later Prof. in Princeton Col.
" Rebecca Willis, dis. to 2d Ch., Newark, 2 June, 1830.
" John Campfield. dis. to Hanover, 4 Mar., 1839.
" Mary Munson, died 1820.
" Mary Campfield, died Feb., 1833

HALFWAY MEMBERS.

1747, Nov. 8, Capt. Benj. Hathaway's son and son's wife.
1752, July 7, Junia Lindsley.
1764, July 1, Dan'l Carmichael and Bathsheba his wf.
1771, July 21, Rachael, wf. of Jabish Rodgers; see Baptisms of July 5.
1775, Jan. 10, Ezek. Crane, Bap. and Eunice his wf. renewed cov.
1786, Sept. 1, not July 31, Martha, George Emmel's wf.
1791, Oct. 6, Gabriel Ford and Frances Gwaldo, his wf.

BAPTISMS.

1745, Dec. 8, Bathiah, wf. of Nat. Wheler.
1748, July 31, Stephen Mahurin, ch. Samuel, not Sarah.
1749, Aug. 6, Joseph Moore, not Mears.
1754, April 1, Shadrack Howard, not Halward.
1754, Dec. 30, Joseph Pierson, not Josiah.
1757, April 17, John Robard (or Roberts) not Robond.
1758, Mar. 12, Stephen Hedges, not Hodges.
1763, Mar. 5, Joseph Stiles, not Stites, Jun. and wf., ch. John, not Benjamin.
1763, Mar. 5, add. Christopher Wood and wf., ch. Benjamin, born 9 Jan., 1763.
1763, July 29, Caleb Munson, not Manson.
1766, Mar. 10, Nathaniel Condict and wf., ch. Sarah, not David.
1767, Aug. 16, Moses Pierson, not Prudden.
1767, Aug. 23, Ebenezar Stiles, not Stites.
1770, May 27, Daniel, not David, Carmichael.
1771, Jan. 4, ch. Jacob born 19 March, not Nov. 11, 1770.
1771, May 5, Samuel *Pierson.*
1773, June 27, John Gwinnup not Winnup.
1776, July 28, Lydia, not Mary, wid. of.
1778, Aug. 2, Mary, wf. of, &c. born Feb. 17, 1757, not 1775.
1781, Nov. 19, to children of Nicholas Carter add Phebe, born 17 Feb., 1775.
1782, Jan. 4, add 3 adults, Jacob Simson, Elizabeth Brown and Ruth Tompkins.
1782, April 21, add Lindsly Burnet and wf., ch. Benajah, born 2 Jan., 1782.
1783, Aug. 1, add Caleb Munson and wf's grandch. Phebe Goodwin, born 26 Nov., 1782.
1784, May 9, Dea. Joseph, not John, Prudden' ch. *Stephen Ayrs, born* 5 April, 1784.
1784, add, May 13, David Hoppen and wf., ch. Gideon, born 24 Feb., 1784.
1786, June 18, add Silas Gildersleeve and wf., ch. Sarah, born 5 May, 1786.
1787, June 10, John Pool not Paul.

MARRIAGES.

1747, Sept. 17, Preserve Primrose.
1748, May 25, Catharine Muir, instead of Catheront Mace.
1760, Jan. 31, Phebe Armstrong, not Ann Strong.
1769, Aug. 29, Usual, not Ursula, Coe.

THE RECORD.

FIRST PRESBYTERIAN CHURCH, MORRISTOWN, N. J.

" This shall be Written for the Generation to Come."—Psalms 102 : 18.

| VOLUME III. | JANUARY, 1883. | NUMBER 1. |

[Printed with the Approval of the Session.]

Entered at the Post Office at Morristown, N. J. as second class matter.

PROSPECTUS.

The publication of the RECORD was suspended in December, 1881. The issue for that month closed the second volume ; this month's number begins the third volume. The former, indefatigable editor, the Rev. R. S. Green, through whose almost unaided efforts the paper had, theretofore, been prepared, removed from Morristown to Buffalo in October, 1881. But, though transferred to a very extended field of labor, involving new efforts, and therefore demanding his almost undivided time, his interest in the publication did not cease, and he continued his care over it until the close of the year. It would not have been possible for his successor, coming here as he did, an entire stranger, to have taken up the work and continued it. It has been in his mind, however, and means have been taken, by which it is expected that the paper will now be regularly issued. It was thought proper, for many reasons, that the first number of the new series should appear in January, 1883.

It will be perceived that the RECORD assumes somewhat a different form. This difference consists in the number of pages, being twelve, instead of eight—which, if proper support be afforded, will be continued hereafter—in the character of the paper upon which it is printed, and in the method of presenting the records of the church. The number issued in December, 1881, completed the records of the members, baptisms, marriages and deaths in the pastorate of the Rev. Dr. Timothy Johnes. The extracts from the Book of the Trustees also reached the same date in that number. Hereafter, the separate records will be begun and carried through succeeding issues, until completed for the several pastorates, instead of presenting parts of the different records in the same number. The paging of all matter taken, hereafter, from the records, including the Book of the Trustees, will follow that of the second volume, but the other part of this series will begin with a new paging. This plan is adopted so that the records may appear consecutively, instead of being scattered through the different issues, and may be bound together, when sufficient is furnished for binding in one volume.

The Rev. Mr. Collins was associated with Dr. Johnes, and was dismissed during the life time of his senior ; so that there will not any records appear as distinctively belonging to his ministry.

This number begins the record of members received into the church during the time of Dr. James Richards, beginning with January, 1804. All the other records in Dr. Richards's time will be taken up and finished seriatim, before those of another pastorate are begun.

It is hoped to continue, from time to time, as material may be obtained, another feature of this number. Short, biographical notices will be given of prominent individuals, who appear in the annals of the church, or, who were so connected with it that they may be claimed as members of the Congregation. These notices must necessarily be short. The one given this month is that of a man of Revolutionary fame, whose name and that of his wife, one of the mothers in Israel, are household treasures in many families. His name appears quite early in the Book of the Trustees and he seemed to have taken a very lively interest in the affairs of the church and congregation.

It was also deemed eminently proper, at this time, to give a biographical sketch of the Rev. Mr. Green, the former editor of the

RECORD. His great exertions in preparing its pages for publication, his unwearied efforts in sustaining it, his interest abiding in it, even after he left Morristown, as well as his untiring service for the church as its pastor, present great claims for gratitude upon those who read the RECORD, and upon the members of the congregation.

The object in the publication of the paper is to give those, who are interested in the subject, information about the church, its pastors, its officers and members, and, generally, to present such a monthly paper as will interest and instruct. It is not expected, it is not even hoped, that it can be made more than self-sustaining. Whatever editorial, or other labor, is performed in its preparation is a free will offering to the church.

The price of subscription will be increased from fifty cents to one dollar, *in advance.*

Perhaps some apology is required for this increase. It is found in two or three facts. The RECORD has not been self-sustaining, but has been a source of expense to the church. The present number will, it is hoped, show such improvement in paper and type, and such an amount of new matter as will warrant the increase.

The request is renewed for information, for old pamphlets, papers, sermons and lectures, books, family histories and genealogies, old family records obtained from Bibles or otherwise.

Any corrections of errors will be most thankfully received. The record of marriages in the pastorate of the Rev. Dr. McDowell, from 1814 to 1825, is deficient. The records of the church do not, of course, contain the marriages of members of the congregation, solemnized by clergymen who were not pastors of the church. Information in these particulars is respectfully solicited.

THE RECORD will essentially be a church paper, in the main devoted to the interests of the First Presbyterian Church at Morristown. It will, however, by no means, be confined, exclusively, to those interests, but will seek to extend its influence and sphere, embracing in its aims, all proper objects of interest connected with the county and town. Communications, therefore, relative to the early history of Morristown, of the county, the early settlers, and their descend-

ants, will be gladly received. These must necessarily be brief.

This number will be sent to all the former subscribers, and it is earnestly requested that they will not only renew their subscriptions but also induce others to subscribe.

Subscriptions for the RECORD may be made at the book stores of Messrs. Runyon and Emmell, or to Messrs. James R. Voorhees and William D. Johnson, or through the mail, by letter, addressed to

"THE EDITOR OF THE RECORD.

CONGRATULATIONS.

BY REV. WILLIAM DURANT.

The season is propitious. THE RECORD awakes from a long nap—not as long as Rip VanWinkle's—to greet its readers with a Happy New Year.

But where is the suggestion of those garments all tattered and torn? We mistake. It is not Rip VanWinkle, but the Sleeping Beauty who comes to us, by fairy enchantment, decked in the latest fashion. Sleep has given her growth and new attractions.

Happy we who may receive her visits with the changing moons, and scan her treasures old and new. Her bright look shows a quick glance to catch flashes of present interest. And there is depth, too, a far-offness, about her glance. Its gleam of the present is the shimmer that lies on the surface of a deep well of memory. What stories she can tell us of the past! Though so youthful her appearance, she romped with our grandmothers and made lint for the hospital and blankets for the camps, that winter Washington was here, when his bare-foot soldiers shivered in the snows on Mount Kemble or lay dying by scores in the old First Church. Yes, she was a girl of comely parts, albeit of temper to enjoy a tiff with her good mother of Hanover, when our city was a frontier settlement, full only of log cabins and primitive hardships in the struggle against wild nature.

For a maiden still, and one who has seen so many summers, marvelous is her cheery, youthful look. Ponce de Leon made the mistake of his life when he sought his enchanted fountain in Florida instead of where Morristown was to be. It is not on the Green, for the aqueduct folks now hold the title.

From lips still ruddy with youth, is it not delicious to hear the gossip of olden time! And our maiden knows it all, for she was present at all the baptisms, danced at all the weddings, thrilled with heavenly joy when our ancestors confessed the Son of Man before the high pulpit, and stood with tears in her eyes when one after another they were laid in the graves behind. Their names are still on her tongue's end, and it is with loving recollection that she tells off the long lists, like the one she brings this month.

But her gossip is not all of names. What she will tell of events and progress, of the unwritten history that has given character to families, to State or Nation, there is no need of predicting. We have only to welcome her at our fireside and listen while she speaks.

Happy we who may hear these lips again! And thrice happy he who has pushed through the tangled briars and scaled the castle walls and unravelled the labyrinth of halls and found the enchanted chamber and awakened the Memory Maiden. Yes, it is the hearty sentiment of all who listen to this voice that has been long silent: A Happy New Year to Mr. John Whitehead, the new editor of THE RECORD.

REV. RUFUS SMITH GREEN.

Mr. Green was the sixteenth pastor of the church. He was born April 1, 1848, at Sidney Plains, Delaware Co., N. Y., and was prepared for college at the Gilbertsville Academy, in Otsego county of that State. When only fifteen years of age he entered the sophomore class in Hamilton College, Clinton, N. Y., where he graduated in 1867. He would have graduated earlier, but, like many other men who have made their mark, he was not provided largely with this world's goods. Soon after entering College he accepted a position as classical teacher in the Academy at Norwich, N. Y. Securing, in this manner, the means to continue, he re-entered college and pursued his studies with great success, taking, at various times, prizes in English composition, mathematics and the classics. At the time of his graduation he took the

second position in his class and was honored with the salutatory.

After leaving college, Mr. Green, for a year, taught in the seminary at Cooperstown, N. Y., and the next year became the principal of the academy at Penn Yan, N. Y.

Being desirous of learning German, as it can only be learned, and also of improving himself by foreign travel, he spent the third year, after his graduation, at the university in Berlin, Prussia, and in visiting places of interest in Europe. In this manner he became so well acquainted with German, as to be able to read the works of the profoundest German theologians, printed in that language. He could also speak that language fluently, and while settled at Morristown, preached in their own vernacular to a small congregation of German Protestants, who occasionally gathered for worship.

Mr. Green's ardent desire for many years had led him to regard the preaching of the gospel as the dearest object of his life. At last he found himself in a position where he could hope to carry out his cherished intention. In 1870 he entered the Theological Seminary at Auburn, as a student of divinity, and there finished a full three years course, graduating in 1873. In September of that year he accepted a call from the Presbyterian church at Westfield, N. Y., where he remained until June 1877,when he was installed pastor of the First Presbyterian church at Morristown. In October, 1881, he became pastor of the Lafayette Street Presbyterian Church at Buffalo, N. Y., where he is now engaged in an extended field of labor and where he fills a large space in that wide awake city. His congregation is one of the largest, most active in every good word and work, and alertly follows the lead of its pastor.

Mr. Green, while at Morristown, gained the respect and won the love of his people. Faithful in the discharge of his duties, untiring in his devotion to his church and its work, instant in season and out of season, he served the church and his parishioners with a zeal and a fidelity which could only emanate from one whose highest and best pleasure was to benefit mankind and do his Master's will.

His mind is logical, analytical, and he delighted in presenting to his congregation thoughts matured by reflection and adorned by scholarly studies. His perceptions of the nice shades between right and wrong are alert ; and his judgment, if exercised after due time was given to his subject, rarely failed in the proper presentation of truth. He delights in literary pursuits, particularly those which are of a statistical character, and, while never suffering his taste in that direction to interfere with the full discharge of duty, he often devoted his mind and pen to subjects not exactly germane to his profession.

While pastor of the church here he wrote the article on Morristown, which appeared in the history of Morris County, recently published. It was well and conscientiously done. He must have expended much time in the investigation of his subject, and great labor in reducing his materials to the excellent shape in which they appeared. Mr. Green married, July 23, 1873, Miss Lucy Anna, daughter of the Rev. Samuel N. Robinson, and has three children.

The heartiest wishes of his former parishioners in this city will ever attend Mr. Green in any field of labor in which he may be placed.

SILAS CONDICT.

Among the names of the men of Morristown, of Revolutionary times, none appears oftener or with greater honor than that of Silas Condict. Born in Morris County, within the limits of the present township of Morris, early connecting himself with the Church, he was ever foremost in promoting the interests of both the church of his adoption and the county and State of his birth. His name very early appeared on the pages of the book of Trustees and the frequency of its occurrence, and the circumstances surrounding its record there fully prove that he was an honored and trusted member of that body. In any emergency, when wisdom was required, and promptness of action demanded, he seems ever to have been called to the front, to aid by his counsel and to give the congregation the benefit of his alert endeavor. When the country, in its times of direst peril, needed patriots willing to devote themselves to its assistance, he never swerved from a

patriot's true duty, but with high resolve and firm devotion, gave to that country the best of his intelligence, and would have sacrificed life, if necessary, for its salvation. And when peace came he sat in the councils of State and Nation and aided by his voice and wise judgment in directing the unsettled affairs of the new commonwealth and of the new Republic to a firm and substantial basis.

The frequency with which his name has been repeated, since his time, on the records of the church, given by those who cherished his memory, fully attest the estimation in which he was held by those who knew him best. The name, Silas, does not seem to have been borne by any of his ancestors. The inference, therefore, is proper, that to the veneration for him is due the fact that so many have perpetuated his name by giving it to their children. This has not been confined to the Condict family simply, but has found its way into the collateral branches bearing other patronymics.

It is well that some notice of such a man, so identified with church and State, especially with this church, should appear on the pages of the RECORD. It is much to be regretted that it must necessarily be very meagre.

Silas Condict was born at Morristown, March 7, 1738, and was the fifth child of Peter Condict, the third of his name, who died in 1768. The family was of Welsh extraction and its genealogy can be traced back to the first settlement of the country and, beyond that, into Wales. The first of the family in America was named John. There is a family record in the possession of Frederick G. Burnham, Esquire, one of whose ancestors was a brother of Silas Condict, which gives many items of interest relative to the original family.

In 1760, April 10, Mr. Condict married Phebe Day, twin sister of Ezekiel Day, and daughter of Captain Samuel Day and Elizabeth, his wife. Mrs. Condict was born July 10, 1743, and consequently was not quite seventeen years old when she married. She died July 16th, 1762, soon after her marriage, leaving one child, born just before its mother's death. This child was named Elizabeth Phebe, and subsequently married, November 25, 1781, James

Cook and died June 21, 1785. Mrs. Cook, like her mother, died in early life and left one child, a daughter, born December, 1782, called Elizabeth, who was taken by her grand-father, Silas Condict and his second wife, and reared by them in their Christian home. This grand-daughter afterwards married Gen. Joseph Cutler and died January 27, 1846, having had four children, Silas Condict, James Richards, Abigail and Augustus W. Cutler. Silas Condict Cutler became a physician and died several years ago; Abigail married the Rev'd James B. Hyndshaw, and is now dead; James became a clergyman and died in early manhood unmarried; Augustus W. is the only one surviving. He is living on a part of the farm formerly belonging to his great-grand-father Silas Condict. He has represented, several times, the Congressional District in which he resides, and is now practising his profession, that of the law, at Morristown.

Silas Condict married a second wife, Abigail Byram, March 16, 1763. Abigail Byram was the daughter of Ebenezer Byram and Abigail Alden, who was the great-great grand-daughter of John Alden, of Mayflower memory,

"Fair-haired, azure-eyed, with delicate Saxon complexion,
Having the dew of his youth and the beauty thereof, as the captives
Whom Gregory saw, and exclaimed, "Not Angles but Angels."
Youngest of all was he of the men who came in the Mayflower."

Three sisters, Huldah, Abigail and Anna Byram married three brothers, Ebenezer, Silas and Peter Condict, and from these three families have descended many of the name and many collateral branches which have given to Morris County and the State illustrious names. The late Lewis Condict, for many years a member of Congress from New Jersey, came from one of them. Frederick G. Burnham, Esq., is a lineal descendant from Ebenezer Condict and Huldah Byram. Abigail Byram, Silas Condict's second wife, died January 14, 1822, at the ripe old age of eighty years. By her Mr. Condict had no children. The name of Mrs. Abigail Condict, who was familiarly known as "Aunt Abby," is cherished to this day by many of

the old inhabitants of Morristown as one of the best of women. Childless herself, her motherly heart went out with all its tenderness to the orphan, and many motherless children were nourished and nurtured with loving care and Christian grace by this mother in Israel. She was the step-mother of the baby child of her husband's first wife, but that child showed her appreciation of her second mother's love by a filial affection, and when her daughter had children of her own, she gave her grand-father's name to her first-born and the name of the only grand-mother she ever knew, to her only daughter. Silas Condict preceded his wife in death, dying in 1801, September 6, aged 63 years.

He was elected Trustee of the church, October 19, 1772. The choice seems to have been made by the Elders. This is the entry of the fact which appears in the Book of the Trustees. "*October 19, 1772, the Elders met at Mr. Jones and made choyce of Silas Condict for a Trustee in the Roome of Samuel Roberts.*" At the next meeting he was chosen Clerk of the Trustees, and placed on two important committees. So that, at the outset of his connection with the Board, he was charged with weighty duties and put in places of responsibility. Early, his fellow Trustees discovered his fitness for the performance of these duties, and while he continued to be connected with the Board, which was for several years and even after he was called to a more extended sphere of action, he was always regarded as the man most fitted to be intrusted with any business which required sagacity and sound judgment. For several years he acted as President of the Trustees, and a reading of the minutes fully shows the opinion of the Board to have been that when peculiar tact and wise action were required, Silas Condict was the man selected. October 18, 1773, it was "*agreed*" "*that Silas Condict "again" request the Inhabitants who Subscribed on the old subscription for the purchasing a parsonage to discharge the same or "confess a judgment to the Trustees for the same."* August 22, 1774, he was directed to "*goe to Perth Amboy and get the charter recorded,*" and at the same meeting, he was requested to "*draw a copy of said Charter and keep for common perusal to save the original.*" March 22,

1776, "*agreed that Silas Condite take the further trouble to call on such of the Inhabitants as have hitherto neglected to discharge their subscription for a Parsonage.*" April 27, 1778, he was elected President of the Board, and, at the same meeting, was appointed one of a Committee to settle with the Rev. Dr. Johnes. This seems to have been a very important settlement, as the time over which it extended, ran from 1769 to 1775; but Mr. Condict reported July 13, 1778, that he "*had settled accounts with Mr. Johnes Respecting his salary from a former Settlement in the year 1769 untill the year 1775 inclusive and made an even Ballance.*" Mr. Condict appears, not only to have filled the position of President of the Board, but also to have been its Secretary and Treasurer. In April, 1781, he declined serving any longer as Clerk, and Mr. John Mills was selected to fill his place, so that he held that position for nine years, but continued to fill the Presidency until at least the year 1788, and for some time after that date. In that year a new organization of the Board was made. March 25th, 1788, the members of the old Board unanimously resigned their appointment as Trustees. April 24, 1788, the congregation met according to advertisement, and elected " 1*st, Silas Condict ; 2d, Jonathan Ford ; 3d, John Mills ; 4th, Benj. Lindsley ; 5th, Richard Johnson ; 6th, Joseph Lewis ; 7th, James Smith, to serve as Trustees.*" Mr. Condict was again chosen President of the new Board, and seems to have held this position for several years after the new organization.

While performing these duties in the church, Mr. Condict was not unmindful of those calls upon him, leading him to assume positions in more public and more extended spheres. He was a member of the State Council of New Jersey from its organization in 1776 to 1780. In 1781 he became a member of the continental Congress, and continued such member until 1784. From 1791 to 1800, excepting the two years, 1792 and 1799, was again a member of the New Jersey Legislature and was Speaker of the house for four sessions, 1792, 1793, 1794 and 1797.

In whatever position he was placed he secured that loving respect, that great confidence, which could only be rendered to one who had the rare combination in his nature of the greatest integrity, of true justice, of kindness of heart, of an intuitive perception of right and wrong, and of an inherent judgment of human nature.

He was of a loving nature and his heart went out to the young. His brothers died early in life, leaving children. The orphans were transferred to his Christian home, and under the godly tuition of his wife, educated and nurtured with loving care to become honored and respected members of society.

His home was open to the needy to be fed, and his large heart delighted in finding under his roof and around his table, those whom he could delight and honor with his hospitality.

During the Revolution and while the army was encamped on the hills around the then sparsely settled village, he gathered in his house officers and men and dispensed with a liberal hand such good gifts as he had to bestow. While thus mindful of the duties of neighbour and friend, of the bountiful host and of the almsgiver, he did not forget his then distressed country. He was untiring in her service and heartily devoted to her cause. He and his only surviving brother Ebenezer, spared no effort to secure the independence of the colonies and cheerfully gave their time and their substance to accomplish that end.

A part of the house, which he then occupied, is still standing near Sussex avenue on the road which formerly ran from that avenue, toward the farm formerly owned by Boyd Headley, and which left Sussex avenue, near the former residence of Mr. Samuel Eddy. The house has been designated by some of the older residents of Morristown, the "Hyndshaw Place," for the reason that his great-grand-daughter, Abigail, daughter of General Jos. Cutler and the wife of the Rev. J. B. Hyndshaw, formerly owned the old house and some of the surrounding land, receiving it as her portion of her mother's estate.

Mr. Condict had large possessions, his farm containing many hundred acres. Its bounds cannot now well be defined, but the land now owned and occupied by the Hon. A. W. Cutler is a portion of the old homestead. Our church is largely indebted to this excellent man. His wisdom guarded it from many dangers; his cheerful counsel inspirited its members and officers, when evil menaced its existence; when immediate action was required his alertness led others with prompt energy; when emergencies arose which required sagacity to meet, his tact never failed; when it became necessary to direct, his voice of command was heard and always succeeded in leading towards the right; when entreaty was needed, his was the kindly heart which persuaded, and when great endeavor was required for the church's best interests, his was the beneficence which led the way and prompted others, by an excellent example, to provide the means for the church's wants. His piety led him to seek in the Church of God for that worship which alone could satisfy such natures as his. His patriotism was manifested at a time when dangers crowded around the patriot. His name has come down to us unsullied, without a blot. Time may take away from his memory but cannot destroy the good he has accomplished. That good will remain so long as the church lasts, for it is the work of one who loved God, feared evil and trusted in his Savior.

THANKS!

To Mr. Jotham H. Condit, of Orange, who has given, from his very extensive notes on the genealogy of the Condit family, much information which has been used in the preparation of the biographical notice of Silas Condit, appearing in this month's RECORD.

Mr. Condit has been, for many years, gathering these genealogical notes. He has sought for information in all directions, and has obtained a mass of knowledge on the subject of his family which is perhaps unequalled in its extent and variety. He is still seeking to extend these notes and will gladly receive any additional information relative to the pedigree of the family, of which he is a worthy member. If the readiness with which he afforded aid to the RECORD, when it was needed, be any criterion of his good will, it can be very confidently asserted that any proper inquiries made to him, on a subject which he undoubtedly has very near his heart, will receive a hearty response.

Thanks! too, to our excellent fellow townsman, F.G. Burnham,Esq., for his kindness manifested in substantially aiding by information on the subject of the life and memory of Silas Condict.

WANTED.

Information is needed as to the precise date of the installation of the Rev. Samuel Fisher, D. D. It was in July or August, 1809. The actual dates of the installations of all the other Pastors are known, but, for some reason, that of Dr. Fisher does not appear.

If possible, sketches of the lives and characteristics of other Pastors of the church will be given hereafter. Any information respecting them, of any kind, is earnestly requested and will be appreciated.

The Rev. Dr. McDowell was dismissed in 1823, and was succeeded by the Rev. Albert Barnes, who was ordained and installed Feb. 3, 1825, and remained in charge until June, 1830. The Rev. Charles Hoover came next to Mr. Barnes and he was Pastor until March 1836 The Rev. A. Henry Dumont was settled over the church in January, 1841, and was dismissed July 1845. His successor was the Rev. A. R. Thompson, who came January, 1846, and remained only until July of the next year. Then came the Rev. Jas. R. Richards. D. D., who was installed December, 1847, and dismissed April, 1851. The lamented Townley, who died in February, 1855, while Pastor, came December, 1851. The Rev. David Irving, D. D., still living, was' with us nearly ten years, from 1855, in November, until May, 1865. The Rev. Mr. Langmuir, whose recent death saddened so many hearts, came in July, 1866, and remained until Sept. 1868. The Rev. John Abbott French was Pastor for a little more than nine years, from December, 1868, until January, 1877. Then came the Rev. Mr. Green, of whom, a short notice, too short for the subject, appears this month. These dates are repeated so as to enable those, who are able and willing, to recall, if possible, some facts, relative to the various Pastors with whose names they are connected. It is very desirable to put those facts in some enduring form, that they may be accessible, for future reference.

CHURCH DIRECTORY.

PASTOR: REV. WILLIAM DURANT.

RULING ELDERS:

Joel Davis,	Enoch T. Caskey,
Theodore Little,	Joseph H. VanDoren,
Henry M. Dalrymple,	Aaron D. Whitehead,
Lebbeus B. Ward,	James R. Voorhees,
William W. Stone,	William D. Johnson.

Theodore Little, . . *Stated Clerk.*

Joseph H. VanDoren, . . *Clerk pro. tem.*

DEACONS:

Victor Fleury, Henry M. Olmsted.

TRUSTEES:

Aurelius B. Hull, . . . *President.*

Henry C. Pitney, Edward Pierson,
Committee on Buildings and Grounds.

William E. Church, Joseph H. VanDoren.
Committee on Seats, Music, &c.

Thomas C. Bushnell, Stephen Pierson, M. D.,
Committee on Finance.

Joseph H. VanDoren, . *Clerk of the Board of Trustees.*

The President is, *ex-officio*, a Member of each Committee.

A. B. Hull, ... *Treasurer.*
James R. Voorhees, . . . *Parish Clerk.*
Francis L. Whitehead, . . . *Sexton.*

THE RECORD.

FIRST PRESBYTERIAN CHURCH, MORRISTOWN, N. J.

" This shall be Written for the Generation to Come."—Psalms 102 : 18.

VOLUME III.   FEBRUARY, 1883.   NUMBER 2.

[Printed with the Approval of the Session.]

THE RECORD

Will be published monthly at Morristown, N. I Terms $1.00 per annum, *in advance*: Subscriptions may be made at the bookstores of Messrs. Runyon and Emmell, or to Messrs. James R. Voorhees and William D. Johnson, or by letter addressed to the EDITOR OF THE RECORD, Morristown, N. J.

Entered at the Post Office at Morristown, N. J., as second class matter.

In the RECORD for January an error occurs in the statement of the death of Mrs. Catharine Smith, afterwards Mrs. David Mills. Mrs. Mills died in 1865 and not in 1855. A great favor will be conferred upon the editor if any person discovering mistakes will report them. Proper corrections will always be made.

A very strange omission occurred in the mention of the names of the pastors of the church, made in the last number of THE RECORD It was an inadvertence very much regretted No notice was made of the Rev'd Orlando L. Kirtland. It was simply an oversight, entirely accidental. Mr. Kirtland was installed March 23, 1837, and dismissed August 26, 1841, becoming then the first pastor of the South Street Presbyterian church of this city. The request made for facts and information relative to our former pastors is renewed, especially with reference to Mr. Kirtland. This saintly minister of God cannot be forgotten.

The first and second volumes of the RECORD may be had upon application to either Mr. James R. Voorhees, Mr. Wm. D. Johnson or to Francis L. Whitehead, the sexton of the church.

Price 75 cents, each volume,

REV. JOHN ABBOTT FRENCH.

Of the seventeen pastors, who have ministered to the First Presbyterian Church, five only survive. One of these bears the name at the head of this article. He is still in the full flush of manhood. He came to us in his youth, when he had the hope of a life of usefulness before him, and left us before the bloom of that youth had left him. We had the freshness of his young life and the energy of his opening manhood. The few years, which he gave us, were filled with the evidences of his desire to serve his Master and to benefit his kind. None of the present generation who have listened to his efforts, will forget him and none speak of him but to praise.

John Abbott French was born at Boscawen, N. H., in 1840. He was prepared early for college in the high school at Nashua, N. H., and in 1858, he entered Williams college, where he graduated, in 1862. After graduation he entered the Union Theological Seminary of N. Y., where he remained a short time and finished his theological course with the Rev. Charles Robinson, D. D., now of the Memorial Church in N. Y. He was ordained in 1867, and, shortly after ordination, took charge of the Congregational Church, at Flushing, L. I. While preaching at Flushing he received a call from the First Presbyterian Church of Morristown, N. J., which was accepted and on December 21, 1868 he was installed pastor. He remained in charge of our church until January 31, 1877, when he was transferred to the Fourth Presbyterian Church at Chicago, succeeding Professor Swing, at the close of the Swing and Patton controversy. His health failing, he resigned in January, 1880. Improving his health by rest and travel, he became so far restored that in October, 1881, he resumed the charge of the Congregational Church at Flushing, where he now is.

The relations between Mr. French and his people here in Morristown were peculiarly pleasant and his memory will long be cherished.

Mr. French possesses great cordiality and sprightliness of manner. He has a keen sense of the ludicrous and much native wit. His ability to clothe his utterances, while addressing an audience, when the severe rules, which checked him in presenting religious truth, could be cast aside, was almost marvellous. The irrepressible smile, often he merry laugh, were sure to follow his addresses when he gave full expression to his humor and wit. His wit was never exercised at the expense of others. It was keen but it never wounded, and never descended. The smile, the laugh which it excited, were never the boisterous merriment induced by broad humor, and his wit was such, that if he chose, he could make it appreciable by all. It was simply a delight to see him and hear him in the Sunday school, or at some meeting, where children formed the larger part of his audience.

This characteristic of Mr. French was born with him; it was as natural to him as the breath he drew. He never abused it, but always knew when to use it, and when to restrain it. Delightful as it was, to his hearers, he lost it when he was in the pulpit. There he was the minister of God, delivering the message of his Master to his people. He did not lose the sprightliness of manner and matter, which marked his efforts elsewhere; that would have been a simple impossibility. But he threw around his pulpit utterances a dignity, which told his hearers, that he, at least, fully felt the importance of his position. His sermons were rarely, if ever, threatening; his gentle nature did not delight in holding up to his hearers the terrors of the law, but he chose rather to dwell upon the love and mercy of the Savior. His efforts were persuasive, full of similes and comparisons, in which he peculiarly delighted, and which he invested with a directness of purpose, a fitness of adaptation, and a propriety in their application to the subject in hand, which charmed and never failed to arrest attention.

His command of language was great, and his selection of words, with a view to their nice adjustment for the proper expression of his ideas, seemed intuitive. It is barely probable that his power, in that direction, was the consequence of study; but he so seized the subtle differences in the meaning of words that it appeared as if his was an inherent ability.

He was particularly successful in those subjects, in which fancy and imagination could be made subservient to his purpose. His was the fancy which delighted in tracing similes between natural scenes and those higher thoughts which lead man from nature to nature's God. His was the imagination which, with metaphor and figure, charged home upon the conscience of the sinner, taught him his duty to repent and believe, showed the mercy of God, the love of the Savior, and enforced all those inducements, which can be brought to bear upon sinful man, to change the evil of his ways and become reconciled with an offended Deity. His eyes were always open to the scenes which surrounded him, and the quick play of his fancy readily seized upon any event, and passing it through the crucible of his brain, made it subservient for the enforcement of a truth. The play of the moonlight, following the foot of the rambler upon the shore of the ocean; the eddying stream; the little inlet, into which the creeping waves came with ripple and shimmer, to gladden and brighten; the same wave, caught in its retreat, as the tide went down, by the obstructing sand, and changed from crystal, sparkling health into noisome decay; the rays of the sunlight on the mountain side, now caught and obscured by the passing cloud, and now coming forth in all their glory; the unshapely mass of unsightly ore, drawn from the dark mine, submitted to the force of art and transmuted into the shining metal—how he wove all these and a thousand others, like them, taken from nature, with a subtle grace and a master hand into his sermons, bringing home to heart and conscience truth and precept, with a power and a charm which logic and argument, could not so well have enforced.

Mr. French was always true to himself, he never brought crudities nor inequalities to the pulpit; his sermons were the result of study and patient labor, but they were not scholastic, simply derived from books. The scholar appeared in them, but they were such as could only proceed from a man who had a loving heart and a gentle nature. He was enthusiastic, but it was enthusiasm tempered with wisdom. He was fearless in his delivery of truth ; but it was a fearlessness founded upon love, a love which went out for all, and desired by a display of truth, though it might sound harsh, to accomplish the best for those who heard.

It would, indeed, have been most difficult for such a mind and such characteristics as were possessed by Mr. French, not to have left their impress upon our church and congregation. They did impress us and their influence is with us now and will long linger with us.

He gained the respect of all, he won the love of all. His flock were happy under his ministry, happy in their young pastor and he was happy in his people, in his ministrations to them and happy in the many manifestations of love he received from them. His presence was a delight to all. The eyes of the scholars in the Sunday school flashed with joy as his slender form appeared among them, and his bright. laughing glance beamed upon them. They expected something pleasant from their pastor and he never failed them.

Our church has been peculiarly blessed in its pastors, but none of them all will be remembered with greater affection than John Abbott French.

The first number of the *Palladium of Liberty* was published at Morristown, Thursday, March 30, 1808. Jacob Mann was its first editor and publisher, Mr. Mann's address to the public, which occupies the first two columns of the first page, closes thus, " I therefore pledge myself to the patrons of this paper, that its columns shall never be *poluted* with sentiments derogatory to national unanimity—at variance with truth or injurious to private reputation ; but as far as my judgment will direct me, I shall endeavor to strengthen the just maxim, that *a free press* is THE PALLADIUM OF LIBERTY."

The paper was printed *"on the Green."* All of the four pages, except one single column, were devoted to news, to original poetry and communications. One column alone was all that was required for advertisements. There was soon, however, a change in this feature, as nearly a whole page in subsequent issues was devoted to that kind of literature. The paper began its publication at a most stirring period in the history of the world. Thomas Jefferson was President of the United States, James Madison, Secretary of State, and James Monroe, Minister at the British Court. Bonaparte, or, Buonaparte, as he was invariably called in the newspapers of the day, both in Europe and in this country ; was in the full tide of victory. The celebrated " *Orders of Council*" had been made in the preceding November. There were serious fears of a rupture between England and the United States. In the first number news from Europe, happening there from January 28th to February 6th, were published, making an interval of nearly two months, during which no information was received from the old country. The paper is remarkable, certainly, for one feature. It is wanting entirely in any news of events happening either in town or county ; not a single item of gossip, no mention of wedding dresses nor wedding gifts. An examination of its columns, when it appeared at the time of the installation of the Rev. Dr. Fisher, gave no information whatever of that event.

It contains some advertisements, which show the difficulties and delays connected with a trip then to New York, compared with the ease and swiftness with which the journey can be made to-day. May 30, 1808, John Halsey advertises that " having furnished himself with a pair of good horses, and a careful driver, he intends to run a stage from Morris-Town to Elizabeth-Town-Point, which will start from his house in Morris-Town on Mondays. Wednesdays and Fridays at 6 o'clock in the morning of each day, so as to arrive at the Point for the first boat and return on each succeeding day." Fare one Dollar. "The driver will leave New York with the first boat on the returning days." "The *Four Horse Stage* will run to Powles-Hook as usual, that is, on Tuesdays and Fridays in each week, so that passengers can be accommodated in either Stage."

Mr. Martin, "lately from New York,."

May 23, 1808, "informs the Ladies and Gentlemen of Morris-Town and its vicinity, that he will open his FRENCH SCHOOLS on Thursday, the 26th inst., from *five to eight in the morning* for young men, and from nine to twelve for young ladies."

April 14, 1808, the death of John Newton is thus noticed:

"On the evening of the 21st December last, in the 83d year of his age, the Rev. JOHN NEWTON, Rector of St. Mary, Woolnorth, Lombard street, London. He was 29 years Rector of that Parish, and had formerly been a long time Curate of Olney, Bucks.

He was the intimate friend of the celebrated Cowper, as may be seen in Mr. Newton's preface to Cowper's poems; and while living together at Olney, these two composed the well-known Olney Hymns, which are certainly among the best extant.

Mr. Newton is well known by his numerous works, among which are his 'Omicron Letters.' These were the first he published and were universally admired. He had a peculiarly happy talent at letter writing, and his epistolary style has justly been considered a model. His works have undergone several editions in England and Scotland and have also been published in America."

Immediately following this notice of Mr. Newton's death, is an announcement by the editor, that he had issued proposals for printing the works of Mr. Newton in nine volumes, Duodecimo, at the low price of seven dollars a complete set. Each volume was to contain 340 pages, and was to be issued every two months "*or thereabouts.*" This edition was actually published, and no doubt is in the possession of some of the families of the congregation. Will not some one, possessing a copy, place it in the Library?

The intense patriotism of Mr. Mann is apparent in almost every line, certainly upon every page of his paper. It is quite interesting to notice the manner in which events, then crowding fast upon each other, and which have since become recognized as decisive upon subsequent history, were received. Mr. Mann was a close observer, and, in his intense love of country, he did not fail to give full expression to his views

as in his opinion those events might affect the interests of the Republic.

Much interesting matter will be found in the *Palladium*, and reference may hereafter be made to it to show change and progress, and how our ancestors thought and lived,

---

PULPIT ECHOES. NO. I.

A wise man, like Socrates; a powerful executive, like Cæsar; an enthusiastic philanthropist, like Howard, continues to exert a certain sway over all the generations that remember the thoughts and deeds of such a heroic leader. But the influence of Jesus Christ in the world to-day is as real and active and direct as the mysterious influence of the sun upon vegetation. Yes, that is but a faint figure. It is more than an influence; it is a personality. The work of the Holy Spirit is the work of Jesus Christ. We are influenced not merely by a memory, or an example, or an inscrutable force; but by the living, present Jesus, our Savior, the Son of God.

Take the inspired idea of Redemption as a guide in reading the history of the world. As surely as the law of gravity draws the water of the mountain springs towards the sea, so all the events of time have trended to the broad estuary of christian civilization where we are now resting. Before the advent, patriarch and law giver, priest and prophet, the flood and the dispersion, the rise and fall of kingdoms, the culture of Egypt and Greece, the power of Babylon and Rome, famine and plenty, the regular course of the heavenly bodies, and the wonderful Star of the East—all events are seen now to have been the preparation of the world for the advent of its Redeemer.

Upon no other principles can subsequent history be explained. What but Redemption reveals an intelligible purpose in the conversion of the Roman Empire and its overthrow?—that thus both the civilized states around the Mediteranean, and the barbarous hordes of pagan Europe, might learn the story of the Cross.

What but a Redemptive aim can account for the occurrences of the 16th century?—the revival of learning, the invention of printing, the opening of a new world, the Reformation; all factors in the establishment of vigorous christian nations.

The present century will be most memorable for two things : the marvellous achievments of physical science, and the enthusiasm of missions. Why were the secrets of steam, electricity and chemistry—which now, though still in the infancy of their development, have so stimulated industry and commerce as to bring the ends of the earth nearer together than Rome and Jerusalem were in the days of the apostles— why were these potent secrets kept hidden from man until the Reformation had crystalized into enduring forms and begun to exhibit an unprecedented missionary zeal ? Why, unless the Son of God is ruling in all things so that the good news of Redemption shall 'go forth to every creature in all the world.

In the light of the gospel of Redemption, past and present display one, grand, beneficent purpose for the future of mankind. If the pessimists, whether professed infidels like Shopenhauer and Hartmann or professed Christians like the Plymouth Brethren, would read the signs of the times, as Jesus bade us do, their creed for humanity would not be, " The goal of Christian civilization is barbarism ; Christ is surrendering the world to Satan ;" but, instead, they would be praising the Redeemer,who makes each new dispensation of his grace wider and more effective than the last. If the materialists could be induced to read the indelible marks of design on the face of the heavens, on the rocks of the earth, in the historic life of man, they would discard a creed which makes Eden a frog-pond, and whose gospel has been aptly called by Carlyle, " the gospel of dirt." If the Christian, who does not believe in foreign missions, were more desirous of learning his Lord's will in the signs of the times, he would perceive that the secrets of steam, electricity and chemistry, with all the material benefits they bring, were not disclosed for our selfish indulgence, but, on the contrary, are the wards of the providential key with which the doors of heathen souls are being opened. By thus opening doors our Lord himself beckons for our prayers and our self-denying gifts, to send the message of Redemption within.

The Redemptive aim of Providence is individual as well as general. It must be so.

A machine cannot be manufactured, an army cannot be marshalled, without designing and constructing each smallest part, without drilling each common soldier, for special adjustment to the plan that covers the whole. Whosoever will may receive the new life, may share the glory of the redeemed. Do all the Christian influences which have surrounded each one of us, from the cradle to the present moment, go for nothing ? In whose ears has not the word of life sounded ? With whom has the Holy Spirit not striven long ? Look back over the way you have come and see if the trend of the whole has not been to show you the vanity of this world and the value of your soul, to reveal your need of pardon and the hope of it in Christ Jesus, to exhibit your own weakness and sin and the power and holiness to be had through faith in the Redeemer.

There are times, indeed, in the lives of sincere Christians, when providence is dark and bitter and hard. But redemption and suffering are not incompatible ; suffering is the heroic drill for perfection ; our Redeemer himself was made perfect through suffering. A child does not appreciate the love which prompted its mother to govern it by painful discipline. But the child, grown to be a man, whose character has thus been built up in noblest principles, looks into the placid eyes, or stands over the grave of that mother,with a heart full of tender gratitude for the love that did not shrink from keenest pain to herself in giving him the painful discipline which has made him noble and godly. An infinitely greater love, even that of our crucified Redeemer, sends trial and chastisement, affliction and tribulation, into the earthly lives of his disciples for their eternal good. Now we see through a glass darkly, and often murmur that our Lord deals so severely with us ; but when we shall see him face to face, the wisdom and the love in all his providence will shine out clear and bright ; and we shall praise Him because all things have worked for our redemption.

CHRIST'S INCARNATION.
Christ took our nature on him, not that he
'Bove all things lov'd it for the puritie ;
No, but he drest him with our humane trim
Because our flesh stood most in need of him.

THE RECTOR'S ASSISTANT

is welcome. It is an excellent church paper, a credit to its editor and his parish. Its reference, in the last issue, to the Rev. Mr. Green's sermon, on church worship, is peculiarly graceful, and has the true Christian, brotherly spirit. With this spirit ever animating the various denominations, there could be no contentions, no strife, but one, and that who should serve the Master in the best manner.

The Presbyterians in Fredonia are a wide-awake people. The *Fredonia Presbyterian* is a bright, spicy publication of ten pages, full of Presbyterian news and published monthly. Its proprietors promise to issue one thousand copies monthly, and do not require payment as a condition for sending the paper, but leave its support to voluntary contributions. It states some facts which deserve notice. The salaries of all the ministers in the United States amount to six million of dollars. Dogs cost seventy millions; lawyers, thirty-five millions; over *six hundred millions* are expended annually for tobacco and *twice that sum* for liquors.

We will always be glad to receive the *Fredonia Presbyterian.*

Our good friend and former pastor, Rev'd R. S. Green, of course, would not be satisfied, in his new field of labor, if he did not fill up his time with useful work. So he edits and issues his excellent church organ "*Our Church at Work.*" An exceedingly appropriate name, for the paper shows conclusively that the Lafayette Street Presbyterian church at Buffalo, is a most industrious organization, fully alive, alert and abounding in every good word and work, from pastor down.

The paper is an eight-page issue, well printed, and like all that Mr. Green does, is well edited, and shows a lively interest in all matters pertaining to church labor. *Our Church at Work* will always receive a hearty welcome in Morristown.

So many congratulations crowd upon the RECORD, at its reappearance, that their very wealth embarrasses. They come from the great West, from the North, from our own State and now Morristown has added its word of greeting. Is this the result of conspiracy, or does the RECORD, really, deserve it all?

The West always gives words of hearty cheer; the north never flatters; staid New Jersey, severely just, should speak the truth. What shall be said then to the greeting of the *Banner*, so warm in its congratulations; so strong in its commendations, both of paper and editor? All are received with thanks and will act as incentives to future effort.

Will kind friends, who make such generous donations, please accept hearty thanks. It would afford great pleasure to mention names, but the liberal giver is always modest.

One sends fifty dollars; he is of our kith and kin. Another, not worshipping with us, bearing another denominational name, but always alive to every good word and work and ever alert in Christian benevolence, unsolicited, donates a smaller amount.

But the kind words accompanying the gift and the kinder sympathy prompting it, add a hundred fold to the pecuniary value.

A pleasant word comes from Cleveland, Ohio. So pleasant that it is repeated.

"The receipt of THE RECORD was a very pleasant surprise and I wish you every success for its publication."

The words are few, but they are more than encouraging.

Another good word comes from nearer home, from Cranford, N. J. "I assure you," says our correspondent, "I was pleased to receive the RECORD again. I hope you will have as much and greater success than the Rev. Mr. Green, who so nobly commenced."

CHRIST'S ACTION.

Christ never did so great a work, but there
His humane nature did in part appeare;
Or ne're so meane a peece, but men might see
Therein some beames of his divinitie;
So that, in all he did, there did combine
His humane nature and his part divine.

THE FIRST PRESBYTERIAN CHURCH

Of South Orange, will dedicate their new house of worship on Friday evening, Feb'y 2, 1883.

The following correspondence speaks for itself:

"SOUTH ORANGE, N. J., Jan. 25, 1883.

To the Pastor and Congregation of Morristown First Church :

The Session of the First Presbyterian Church of South Orange, cordially invite you to attend the dedication of their new house of worship on Friday evening, February 2d, 1883, at half-past seven o'clock. By order of the session.

JAS. W. CONROW,
EDW'D D. SHEPARD,
Committee.

To Messrs. Conrow and Shepard, Committee :

The old First Church of Morristown rejoices in the prosperity which your service of *dedication* bespeaks, and desires to unite in your prayers that the Spirit of God may fill your new house of worship with his wisdom and power for the saving and sanctifying of souls through many generations.

W. DURANT, Pastor."

The teachers in the Sunday schools of the various churches in Morristown deserve a library. Books of reference, encyclopedias, commentaries, church histories and other books, useful for Sunday school teaching, could be easily procured and in sufficient numbers, at comparatively trifling expense. Two or three hundred volumes would be all that is necessary. Each church, of course, could have its independent library. If the First Presbyterian church should adopt this plan, the books might be placed in the study in the chapel.

But a suggestion comes from a friend of Sunday schools worthy of attention, not only by reason of its source, but also because of the excellence of the suggestion.

Combine all the strength of our churches and provide a library exclusively for the use of the Sunday school teachers of the city and make it free to all. In this way the necessary number of volumes could be readily procured. Doubtless the directors of the Library and Lyceum would devote a place to them in their building and provide means for access to them. If each congregation have a separate library, some room, in connection with the church, must be provided for the books and some person to take charge of them. If the combination suggested be formed and a general library procured and placed under the charge of the librarian at the Lyceum, access could be had to the books at all times, a pleasant place would be at the service of the teachers and means provided for full examination and reference and for taking extracts and notes.

If thought necessary to procure distinctive denominational books, so much the better. Each sect would have its own commentaries and the others could ascertain the opinions held by their fellow Christians of different name. More than one advantage could be derived from the plan proposed of a general library. Want of space forbids a further discussion of the plan. Let the subject be brought to the attention of superintendents and teachers and the friends of Sunday schools.

A newspaper was published in Morristown prior to the *Palladium of Liberty*, called the *Genius of Liberty*. Some files, perhaps the whole of it, may be in the possession of some one who would be willing to donate it to the Library, or, at least, place it at the disposal of the editor of THE RECORD, for a short time. A favor will be conferred if this can be done. It is hoped that, by an examination of its colums, in connection with those of the *Palladium of Liberty*, some defective registries of deaths and marriages may be restored. Some of these, about the time of the publication of these two papers, are missing.

There were not many newspapers published, in this country at the close of the last century; but there were a number sufficeut to show that they had become a necessity and that the cammunity was a reading one. The citizens of Morris County, in Revolutionary times, were overwhelmingly Whig in their political sentiments. They had no organ, so far as is known, through which to express their views. For news, they depended, generally, on papers published in the city of New York. The principal one, printed there, was called *Rivington's Gazette*, which was published before and during the Revolution. It was intensely loyal to King and Parliament. Some of its utterances, indeed its general tone, gave great offence to the Whigs of Morris County, during the exciting period, just before the breaking out of the war between the Colonies and the mother country. The paper and its editor were denounced in the severest terms, the paper burnt with great indignity, an effigy of the proprietor tarred and feathered, and other measures taken to show the disgust felt at the sentiments uttered by the publisher.

These facts give occasion for some statements about newspapers, which are taken from the *Portland "New Northwest."*

The first daily newspaper printed in the world, was published and edited by a woman named Elizabeth Mallet, in London, in 1702. In her address to the public she announced as her reason for publishing a newspaper, that she desired "to spare the public half the impertinences which the ordinary papers contain." It was to her credit that like most enterprizes undertaken by women, her paper was reformatory in its character.

The first paper published in America was in Massachusetts. It was called the Massachusetts *Gazette and News Letter.* After the death of the editor his widow edited it for two or three years in the most spirited manner. It was the only paper that did not suspend publication when Boston was besieged by the British. The widow's name was Margaret Craper.

In 1732, Rhode Island issued its first newspaper. It was owned and edited by Anna Franklin. She and her two daughters did the printing and their servants worked the printing press. History tells us that for her quickness and correctness she was appointed printer to the Colony, supplying pamphlets, &c., to the colonial officers. She also printed an edition of the colonial laws of 340 pages.

In 1776, Sarah Goddard printed a paper in Newport, R. I., ably conducting it; afterwards associating with her John Carter. The firm was announced as Sarah Goddard & Co., she taking the partnership precedence as was proper and right.

In 1782 Clementine Reid published a paper

in Virginia, favoring the colonial cause and greatly offending the Royalists, and two years after, another paper was started in the interests of the Crown by Mrs. H. Boyle, who borrowed the name of Mrs. Reid's paper, which was the Virginia *Gazette*; but Mrs. Boyle's paper was short lived. Both of the papers were published in the town of Williamsburg. The colonial paper was the first newspaper in which the Declaration of Independence was printed.

In 1773, Elizabeth Timothy published and edited a paper in Charleston, S. C. After the Revolution, Anne Timothy became its editor, and was appointed State printer, which position she held seventeen years. Mary Crouch published a paper in Charleston about the same time, in special opposition to the Stamp act. She afterwards removed her paper to Salem, Mass., and continued its publication there for years after.

———

Louis Richards, Esq., of Reading, Penna., has gathered much information and many facts about the genealogy of the Richards family in America. Through his kindness much of this information has been placed at the disposal of the RECORD.

It will be used for a sketch of the Rev. Dr. James Richards, former pastor of the church, which will appear in the March number.

In the meantime a great favor will be conferred if any one will furnish facts, anecdotes or other information about Dr. Richards. It is desirable to place correctly upon record these sketches of the men, who have ministered to the church.

———

Information received from Hon. A. W. Cutler settles a matter about which there was no certain knowledge at the time the article in the last number of the RECORD, relative to SILAS CONDICT, was written. The house now occupied by Mr. Cutler was built by his great grand father, Mr. Condict, and in it he actually lived. The building was erected by Mr Cutler's father, Gen. Cutler, for Mr. Condict.

The house has been altered and improved by its present occupant, but the main building still remains.

Solidity in houses as well as in character marked the times of our ancestors.

THE RECORD.

FIRST PRESBYTERIAN CHURCH, MORRISTOWN, N. J.

"This shall be written for the Generation to Come."—Psalms 102 , 18.

| VOLUME III. | MARCH, 1883. | NUMBER 3. |

[Printed with the Approval of the Session.]

THE RECORD

Will be published monthly at Morristown, N. J. Terms $1.00 per annum, *in advance*:

Subscriptions may be made at the bookstores of Messrs. Runyon and Emmell, or to Messrs. James R. Voorhees and William D. Johnson, or by letter addressed to the EDITOR OF THE RECORD, Morristown, N. J.

Entered at the Post Office at Morristown, N. J., as second class matter.

The Sunday School of the church reports as follows for 1882 :

Officers :

William D. Johnson,	Superintendent.
Mahlon Pitney,	Assistant Supt.
P. B. Pierson,	Sec'y and Treas.
O. F. Lozier,	Librarian.
William Leek,	Henry Potts,
Assistant Librarians.	

Miss Emma Campbell, Miss Lottie Campbell, Superintendents of Primary Department, Miss Laura Pierson, Assistant Supt.

Number of Officers,	9
" " Teachers,	47
" " Scholars in primary department,	85
" " Scholars in main school,	263
Total,	404

Average Attendance in 1882.

Officers,	7
Teachers,	38
Scholars,	205
	250
Average attendance,	250
Largest attendance,	278
Smallest attendance,	128
Number of Books in the Library,	502
Contributions by the Children's Missionary Society,	$566 59

A history of the Sunday School would be interesting. Mrs. Condict, wife of Dr. Lewis Condict, it is said, was its first Superintendent. She was the daughter of the Rev. Nathan Woodhull, of Long Island, a very successful and noted preacher.

Will not some kind friend furnish the material for an article on that history or, what is better, write the article ? The RECORD will gladly publish it.

A new order of service was introduced at the first Sunday evening worship, in February. This was the result of unanimous action on the part of the session. The service was certainly a success. It has been continued to this time and for the present will be retained in the evening worship of the church. The order of service and the church calendar for February and March, 1883, appear in this issue of the RECORD.

The rebound, at the outset of the Puritan Revolution in England, from what many deemed to be prelatical formalism, was so great as to carry the reformers to the opposite extreme. An excess of reform is sometimes a greater evil than the mischief intended to be remedied. Zeal is not always controlled by wisdom. The severe simplicity of worship introduced into Scotland by the Covenanters, and into England by the Puritans and brought to this country by the Pilgrim Fathers, served its purpose. It was a necessity when first introduced, but the time for that necessity has passed. The Covenanter, the Puritan, the Pilgrim Fathers were grand men ; they worked out a great revolution, grander in its results than they dreamed ; but they would be sadly out of place now. Their influence lingers with us yet, but it is tempered by a warmer heart, a kindlier spirit, than could possibly have existed in their time.

They accomplished the purpose for which God intended them. We are of a different mould, and live in a different atmosphere and must work on a loftier plane, for the same great end, it is true, but with more various means. They broke the sod, levelled the primeval forest, met the stern realities of the first years of a radical reform. We are plucking the fruit from trees of their planting; we are reaping the harvest of their sowing; we are rejoicing in the peaceful years which follow their rugged, stormy times. They could not avoid harshness, sternness. It was an absolute necessity for them to repress the softer promptings of human nature, and that repression extending, as it did, to the whole of their life, went, of course, into their worship. They believed as implicitly in the necessity for all this as they did in their existence. We are the better for it and they must ever be foremost in our love and in our admiration, as the men who laid the foundations of religious reform which has given us so many blessings.

But Presbyterianism, while always rejoicing in, and clinging tenaciously to, a simple order of service, is neither puritanical, nor is it bound by the harsh severe rules which, some centuries since, seemed right to the Scotch Covenanters, and *was* right then. There can be no good reason why Presbyterians should not enjoy a liturgy or liturgical exercises.

There is, however, no intention to offer an excuse for the apparent innovation. Whatever is right in any church is right in the Presbyterian. Let but the heart join the intellect in the praise and worship of God, and it matters little in what form that praise and worship may be rendered. Simplicity has its merits; forms and ceremonies have theirs. A happy blending of both may encourage, may strengthen, may edify, Christians; may give voice to heartfelt devotion, where the others might freeze, or might disgust. The cold, barren worship which chills and benumbs, is as much to be avoided as the gorgeous and unmeaning Ritualism, which detracts from the worship due to the Creator and leads poor humanity to forget Deity in candles and genuflexions.

The service, as rendered at the Sunday evening meetings, has been most enjoyable. Minister and people have heartily entered into its spirit. The choir, under the admirable training of Mrs. Halsted, has added much to its interest and impressiveness.

ORDER OF SERVICES.

Chant or Anthem : (By the choir.)

Gloria Patri, (All uniting; congregation standing.)

Glory be to the Father, and to the Son,
And to the Holy Ghost ;
As it was in the beginning, is now, and ever shall be,
World without end. Amen.

Invocation : (Congregation standing.)

Apostles' Creed : (Congregation standing and joining.)

I believe in God the Father Almighty, Maker of heaven and earth.

And in Jesus Christ his only Son our Lord ; who was conceived by the Holy Ghost ; born of the Virgin Mary ; suffered under Pontius Pilate, was crucified, dead and buried ; the third day He rose from the dead ; He ascended into heaven; and sitteth at the right hand of God the Father Almighty ; from thence he shall come to judge the living and the dead.

I believe in the Holy Ghost ; the holy Catholic church ; the communion of saints ; the forgiveness of sins ; the resurrection of the body ; and the life everlasting. Amen.

Scripture Lesson : Precepts.

Response : (By the Choir.)

I

Lord, have mercy upon us, and write all these thy laws in our hearts, we beseech Thee. Amen.

OR THIS II.

The law of the Lord is perfect, converting the soul ;
The testimony of the Lord is sure, making wise the simple. Amen.

OR THIS III.

Let the words of my mouth and the meditation of my heart, be acceptable in Thy sight,
O Lord, my Strength, and my Redeemer. Amen.

OR THIS IV.

Who shall ascend into the hill of the Lord?
Or who shall stand in his holy place ?

He that hath clean hands, and a pure heart;
Who hath not lifted up his soul unto vanity, nor sworn deceitfully. Amen.

Prayer of Confession.

Scripture Sentences of Forgiveness and Promise.

Gloria in Excelsis: (Congregation standing and joining.)

Glory be to God on high, and on earth peace, good will towards men.

We praise Thee, we bless Thee, we worship Thee, we glorify Thee, we give thanks to Thee for Thy great glory.

O Lord God, heavenly King, God the Father Almighty!

O Lord, the only begotten Son, Jesus Christ; O Lord God, Lamb of God, Son of the Father,

That takest away the sins of the world, have mercy upon us.

Thou that takest away the sins of the world, have mercy upon us.

Thou that takest away the sins of the world, receive our prayer.

Thou that sittest at the right hand of God the Father, have mercy upon us.

For thou only art holy; Thou only art the Lord;

Thou only, O Christ, with the Holy Ghost, art most high in the glory of God the Father. Amen.

Scripture Lesson ; Gospel.

Prayer of Thanksgiving and supplication; (Concluding with the Lord's Prayer, in which all are invited to unite audibly.)

Hymn : (Congregation standing and joining.)

Sermon.

Response : (By the Choir.)

Hymn: (Congregation standing and joining.)

Prayer of intercession.

Benediction : (Congregation seated and bowing in silent prayer.)

CALENDAR FOR FEBRUARY AND MARCH, 1883.

The Lord's Day Services.

Morning Service, at 10:30 A. M.

Evening Service, at 7 30 P. M.

School of the Church, at 3 P. M.

Young People's Prayer Service, at 6:45 P. M.

OFFERINGS.

For Foreign Missions, Sunday morning, March 4th.

For Home Missions and Sustentation, Sunday Morning, April 1st.

MID-WEEK SERVICE OF PRAYER.

Thursday Evenings, at 7:30.

Feb. 8.—The Unity and Trinity of God— I Cor. viii.: 4; Matthew xxviii., 19.

" 15.—The Creation of the World—Gen. i.: 1 ; John i.: 3 ; Heb. xi.; 3.

" 22.—Preservation and Providence—Ps. cxlv.: 15, 16 ; Matt. vi.: 26 ; Rom. viii.: 28.

Mar. 1.—The Creation of Man—Gen. ii.: 7 ; James iii.: 9.

" 8.—The Genesis of Sin—Rom. v.: 12.

" 15.—The Nature and Extent of Sin—I John iii.: 4 ; Rom. iii.: 4 ; Matt. xv.: 19 ; James iv.: 17 ; 1 John i.: 8 ; Matt. xii.: 31.

" 22.—The Punishment of Sin—Rom. i.: 8 ; Jno. iii.: 36 ; Luke xii.: 47, 48 ; Mark ix.: 44.

SPECIAL SERVICES.

Baptism of Infants.—Sunday Morning Service, March 4th.

Children's Missionary Society Quarterly Meeting, Sunday, Mar. 25th.

Preparatory Lecture.—Friday, at 4 o'clock P. M., March 30th.

The Lord's Supper.—Sunday Morning Service, April 1st.

OTHER MEETINGS.

Teacher's Meeting, at close of Mid-Week Service, Thursdays.

Sewing Circle, Wednesdays, at 3 P. M.

Annual Parish Meeting, Tuesday, 3 1-2 P. M., March 13th.

The Pastor will be found at his residence, on Franklin Place, Tuesdays; and on Fridays, from 5 to 6 P. M., in the Study of the Chapel.

It must not be forgotten that the spelling of names and of other words is retained in the RECORD as they appear in the original registry. All other peculiarities, as far as possible, are also retained.

This is done so as to exhibit to the readers of the paper the original records of the church as they actually exist.

Our ancestors, if they did not spell correctly, generally did what was better, acted right. Let us imitate their virtues if we do not follow their orthography.

THE NEW YORK GAZETTE AND AMERI-CAN ADVERTISER

Is a venerable looking affair. A bound volume of a portion of its issues, although in a moderately good state of preservation, in some respects, presents, as it lies before us, a weather stained appearance, and is a dilapidated representative of the Public Press of the last century. The initial number of the first volume was published January 4, 1776, and was *printed for Samuel Loudon, 10 Water Street, between the Coffee House and the Old Slip.*" It appeared weekly. In the centre, at the top of the first page, is the picture of a packet-ship, with all sails set, as if either ready to sail, or actually on the Ocean. The Declaration of Independence had not yet been proclaimed, and an examination of any editorial utterances do not give evidence as to the course the editor had determined to pursue in the conflict, which had been precipitated upon the country in the preceeding year, by the gun fired at Lexington. Of course Mr. Loudon could not anticipate the magnitude which that conflict afterwards assumed. The publisher of a newspaper in those days and for many years afterwards never assumed the position of an editor ; he was simply the printer, and in looking over the pages of the *Gazette* it is noticeable that all communications are addressed " *Mr. Printer.*"

In his address to the public, the publisher, among other things, says : " He will be extremely happy to have it in his power to convey, thro' the channel of this paper, together with useful intelligence, foreign and domestic, any considerations, that may illustrate and animate the glorious cause of constitutional liberty and at the same time pour medicine into the bleeding wounds of the Extended Empire. For this purpose he most earnestly invites the Friends of America and the British Constitution, to favor him with their kind assistance. Much has been said on the important controversy, that now engages the attention of all Europe ; but the subject is not yet exhausted ; there is sufficient scope for new discussion."

William Tryon was then Governor of New York, and in the first number of this paper, a proclamation from this loyal officer of the Crown appears, dissolving the Gene-

ral Assembly of New York, which had before been prorogued to the first of February then next. This proclamation is attested " in the sixteenth year of our Sovereign Lord, George the Third, by the grace of God of Great Britain, France and Ireland, King, Defender of the faith and so forth." At its close appears the usual formula, " GOD SAVE THE KING."

In the same number is to be found an advertisement, offering for sale " a valuable NEGRO MAN, by trade a blacksmith, about 25 or 26 years old. He will be sold on moderate terms."

Although the editor does not openly express his views on the all absorbing question of the day, it is quite easy to determine in what direction his real sentiments tend. He must have been a Whig, for his leanings are very decidedly manifested in many ways towards the cause of the colonies. But it was a time when prudence seemed to be the better course for men, situated as he was, to follow, so, at first, he ventured no decided expression of opinion. There were a large number of Tories in the city, although the Whigs were very largely in the majority. Tryon was still in command for the King as Governor, but he was soon obliged to leave the city and take refuge on board of an English ship in the harbor. It was about this time that Isaac Sears, who had before removed to New Haven, came to the city with a hundred men or more, moved at the head of his troops, in perfect order, down Broadway to the foot of Wall street, where was the printing office of Rivington's Gazetteer, which had so excited the wrath of Morris county Whigs. Sears sacked the office, captured the type and carried it off to be cast into bullets. Lord Dunmore, the Royal Governor, of Virginia, had just before that confiscated a Whig newspaper in Norfolk. Sears with a grim humor quite characteristic of the man, gave Rivington an order on the Virginia Governor for a new supply of type. The draft was never honored. The true name of this Tory paper was " *Rivington's New York Gazetteer,* or the Connecticut, Hudson's River, New Jersey and Quebec *Weekly Advertiser.*" It had been outspoken in its loyal utterances and had, really, laid itself open to the attack made upon it, as it had gone beyond the bounds of moderation and had been bold, violent and aggressive.

The New York *Packet*, whatever may have been its political sentiments, impartially reported the debates in Parliament and the proceedings of the Continental Congress.

Unfortunately the bound volume of the *Packet* to which access has been had, is imperfect, ending with the issue of the first volume which appeared August 29, 1776. The rest of the volume is made up of that part of Vol. 7 which began with No. 321 and ended with No. 450, which last number was issued December 30, 1784. Numbers 321 to 332 inclusive were published at Fishkill, but from No. 333 to No. 450 the issues are dated in New York from No. 5 Water street "between the Coffee House and the Old Slip." With No. 333 began a semiweekly publication, the paper appearing on Mondays and Thursdays.

Some of the advertisements are curious, and exhibit a method of conducting affairs then, quite unknown to business men of the present day. Richard Edsall, the 3d, confined in *gaol*, in Orange County, for debt, "take this method to notify his creditors that he intends to apply to the Legislature at their next meeting for an act to discharge him from his confinement." Comfort and Joshua Sands inform their friends that they have at their store in the house formerly occupied by Isaac Sears, Esquire, for sale on the lowest terms, among other goods, the following queer assortment: "Brimstone, Wool, Hats, Frying pans, Shovels and Spades, Bohea Tea."

Occasionally a notice is made of New Jersey and of some localities in the State. A sermon, preached by the Rev. John Witherspoon, the President of the College of New Jersey, is advertised for sale by this Printer; a robbery at New Brunswick is noticed, and the capture of the thief is stated with great satisfaction. In the issue of December 6th, 1784, a letter from Trenton, N. J., dated December 1, is published, which speaks of the meeting, at that town, of the Congress of the United States on the Monday preceding. The delegates from this State were William Churchill Houston and John Beatty. At this meeting Richard Henry Lee was elected President. The next number announces this, "his excellency P. I. Van Berckel, Minister Plenipotentiary from the United Netherlands, has arrived at Trenton." This gentleman built a house at Newark, afterwards occupied by the Pennington family, at least, so runs the tradition. It was a quaint frame building, with a large wide hall, capacious rooms, and with an appearance differing materially from other buildings in Newark. It was situate on the west side of Broad street, just north of South Park Presbyterian Church. It has long since given place to a more modern built edifice with modern improvements.

There are many advertisements and matters of interest in this venerable relic of the last century, to which reference may hereafter be made.

———

The South street Presbyterian church have initiated a movement which will, undoubtedly, commend itself to all teachers in the schools of the church. This movement really begins with the Sunday school and is undoubtedly due to the suggestion of its superintendent, Mr. J. F. Randolph. A series of five lectures, upon subjects, in which all Sunday schools are directly interested, has been begun. The first in the course was delivered Wednesday evening, February 7th, on Christian Biography, by the Rev. Kinsley Twining and was of course, admirable. The second on Church History will be delivered March 7, and will be succeeded by the others, as follows: Christian doctrine, by F. G. Burnham, Esq., April 4th; Christian Duty, A. F. West, A. M., May 2d; and Christian Devotion, by Rev. Albert Erdman, D.D., pastor of the church, June 6; the programme published calls them "Conferences on Sunday Reading," and states that they are to be held in the Bible class room, at 8 P. M. The object is to afford information to teachers and others on these various subjects and especially to instruct in a course of reading from which that information can be obtained. The plan is an admirable one and worthy of imitation by all Sunday schools.

———

The promised sketch of the life of Dr. James Richards must be postponed until the next issue. Want of time prevents full justice being done to the subject.

Sunday schools have assumed such proportions and struck their roots so deep into the soil of the church that they must now be considered permanent institutions. Their importance is an established fact. They deserve and should receive all the care which the church can possibly afford them. The title of "School of the Church" is an admirable one and should not merely in name, but in the whole spirit and meaning of the title, be applied to them. They should be *schools of the Church* in real earnest, subject to the supervision and under the control of the proper authorities of the several churches with which they are connected. This supervision, this control should not be merely nominal but subsisting and substantial.

The tendency in Americans, of all classes, toward the expenditure of great energy, sometimes at the utmost possible expense of mind and body, in any direction which, for the time, seizes upon the public, either by way of fashion or taste, is so marked and often so detrimental as to require repression. Religion does not, perhaps unfortunately, suffer too often nor too much from the expression of this tendency. But it may, and great care is needed to preserve it and its adjuncts from this apparent tendency of the times. This tendency has exhibited itself, in a measure, in this matter of Sunday schools.

Much may be said in favor of conventions and something may be said against them. Ought not a fear to be indulged and a warning given that undue efforts in this direction may exhaust the energies of teachers and of the friends of Sunday schools in the multiplicity of conventions?

This suggestion is made with some hesitation, but with the hope that it may be received in the same spirit in which it is given.

A proposition has been made to divide the State into districts and hold conventions in these districts, instead of having a great State convention as heretofore. A meeting of some of the pastors and superintendents in town was held last Friday evening to discuss this subject. This district plan may be excellent; it is still untried. County conventions are exceedingly useful and perhaps all that are necessary for the main object. They bring neighbors and friends together face to face at a place, some quiet country village or town, where great good may be accomplished by introducing new thoughts, new methods of teaching, by waking up dormant faculties, by the attrition of mind with mind. What is needed in this undertaking, as in all others, when good is to be accomplished, is honest, sincere, persistent, loving action, here, in the school, among scholars, and if in conventions, among the teachers. A great State convention is unwieldy, burdensome upon teachers and their entertainers, expensive and really accomplishes nothing like what may be done at county conventions held at points where just such meetings are most desirable. A day spent at a small meeting such as would be gathered in the various counties, is worth the two or three days generally employed at the State conventions.

SOUTH ORANGE, Feb. 4th, 1883.
Mr. Editor :

Last evening marked a new era in the history of the South Orange Presbyterian Church. Its beautiful new brown stone edifice was dedicated to the service of Almighty God, with appropriate services. The exercises were conducted by the Rev. John Crowell, D. D. Several clergymen participated in the services. The prayer invocation was offered by the moderator of the meeting; Scripture lessons were read by the Rev. J. A. Ferguson, and the Rev. Samuel Sargent; the dedicating prayer was made by the Rev. Alfred Yeomans, D. D., and the other prayer by the Rev. Joseph A. Ely. The sermon was preached by the Rev. J. H. Worcester, Jr., the retiring pastor, from the text "*This is none other than the House of God.*" Delightful music, appropriate to the occasion, was rendered by the choir.

The new structure is beautiful and cheerful, has a commanding position and cost about $20,000. It lacks an element of success, however,—a settled pastor. With a true man of God, and the blessing of a descent of the Holy Spirit, the good people who gather to worship within its walls, may be assured of that success which must always attend those who have faith in Jesus.
                                        J. M. C. M.

PULPIT ECHOES. No. 2

Unfortunately we are all likely to overlook the moles on our own faces, unless a mirror from God's word is held before our eyes.

In some lights a cobweb looks like a curtain of steel wire, bright, flexible and airy, but stout and impenetrable. So many a one stays in the dark corner of doubt, refusing to come out into light and liberty, because he fancies that he cannot break through the barrier which separates him from Christ; when, in reality, that barrier is only the cobweb of his own wilful fancies.

The cause of religion suffers, but it will not perish, because of the doubting Thomases who stay away from meeting and the timid souls who, after touching the hem of our Lord's garment for blessing, mope in the secret tumult of hope and fear off on the edge of duty.

The church and cause of the Lord Jesus Christ goes on its knees to no man or woman for the purpose of begging the honor of his name or the weight of her influence.

Secret faith and all the good resolutions in the world, if brought out for airing only in the privacy of our innermost thoughts, will not have very much effect on our moral standing in the eyes of men or of God. So long as one's Sunday clothes are kept in a dark closet one does not mind how much mud there is in the streets.

It is no wonder that we have had to mourn over the coffins of many good resolutions. There was really no chance for the little things to live. How can we live up to our holiest aspirations, when we suffocate them at their birth?

Who is the meaner sort of hypocrite: the one who openly promises good and secretly laments his backslidings; or the one who makes secret vows to God and publicly sits on the fence?

There is good reason to suspect the man who knows himself so little as to start in the Christian life with the assertion, "It matters not what others may do, but I mean to hold out to the end." When that man stumbles he falls over his own feet, his chief prop is gone; he has put confidence in himself, and there is danger that he will conclude there can be no more religion for him, because he can no longer trust himself.

There were some spectators at the Saviour's cross who were deeply touched with compassion and roused to heroism, by the meekness of the Lamb of God in the shame of his crucifixion and the agonies of his torture. Two of them are particularly named, Joseph of Arimathea and Nicodemus. They appear only in what may be called flashes of light. But these brief flashes make their position and character stand out in striking vividness. Both are rich men, prominent in the councils of the Jews, earnest seekers after truth, and yet, like their class everywhere, cautious, conservative, slow to commit themselves and hazard either social standing or property to the uncertanties of a new movement, although this movement wins the sympathy of their hearts and receives their secret aid.

At the very beginning of his ministry Jesus was sought by Nicodemus; but at night, for fear of the Jews. Afterwards this rich ruler disappears from the page, enveloped in so prolonged a shadow that we might think him turned away sorrowful, unbelieving and unyielding, except for his appearance after the crucifixion as a bold and true mourner of the now lifeless Master.

Joseph of Arimathea, we are told, was a disciple of Jesus; but he, too, has given only secret adherence, for fear of the Jews. Not till he could no longer escape the avowal of his position, did he begin to show boldness in the cause of the Nazarene. It is said to his honor that he did not consent to the counsel and deed of the elders in sentencing Jesus to death. By that opposition he gave unmistakable evidence of his favorable disposition towards the despised Messiah. And now, as he watches in sorrow before the cross, from which his tardy courage and confession could not save the Master, he is perhaps the first to observe the last flicker of life and the drooping signal of death in the beloved form. At any rate, Joseph is the first to bring word to Pilate that "the king of the Jews" no longer lives.

No hesitation chills the zeal of these two now for the cause whose sun has set. For the lukewarm spirit they shewed when their enthusiasm might have given success, they now exhibit a tender ardor of devotion when apparent failure marks the end of the Nazarene's career. So it is to-day. It is not Christ the teacher; it is not Christ the miracle-worker; it is not Christ the model example; but Christ the suffering Son of God, dying upon the cross, that at last breaks down the opposition of the selfish human heart to his love, and draws those most absorbed in worldliness away from the world, to honor the precious name of him who loved them and gave himself to death for them.

What is the duty of Christian churches in answer to the question, what shall be done to stop the growth of intemperance? That this awful vice is growing, statistics unquestionably and fearfully prove. The teachings of the church of Christ are undoubtedly opposed to the habit which has destroyed so many lives and wrecked so many souls. The solving of the problem troubles thoughtful minds and oppresses the true lover of his kind.

But what shall be done? It is well to think and plan, but action is required. The pulpit utterances are fearless, but what shall be said about the action of individual Christians? The pastor may teach and preach but his hearers must act.

The State provides Alms Houses to receive the pauper, the Jail, Court House and State Prison, to hold secure, try and punish the criminal. The very great majority of crimes are committed under the influence of rum. But our municipal authorities license saloon and grog shop. Where is the responsibility for crime! With the poor soul, tempted at every corner by the licensed dram-shop; with the good citizen, who claims to be governed by the divine precepts of Christian morality, and who refuses or neglects to use his influence to elect the right kind of men to office; or with the authorities who license?

Christian! as you see the poor wretch, staggering away from the saloon, licensed by the men you selected for office, and follow him to his miserable home; as you hear of his arraignment for foul murder committed under the blinding, soul-destroying, conscience-blasting influence of rum, answer this question. Am I in no way responsible for all this?

ON TAKING DOWN THE CHRISTMAS GREENS.

Take down the fading wreaths,
  Untwine the garlands gay,
Though the glad time we hung them up,
  Seems but as yesterday.
And from their crumbling leaves
  We still can almost hear
The echoes of the Carols sweet,
  And greetings of New Year.

But ah! too well we know
  The festive season's o'er;
For treading in life's dusty paths
  We find ourselves once more.
Swifter than the wheels of steam
  The golden hours have rolled;
And while we deemed the year was young
  We wake to find it old.

Now clear above the din
  Of earthly toil and care,
We hear once more in solemn tone
  The Lenten call to prayer,
Bidding us turn from pleasure's sound,
  A higher joy to find
In fellowship with Him whose death
  Gave life to all mankind.

Thus do the years go on,
  And times and seasons glide;
Till soon the story of our life
  Is closed and laid aside.
Yes, since the New Year's dawn
  How many a soul has gone
From scenes of earth to realms unseen,
  Whose record here is done.

Ah! life's a mystic page!
  In vain we try to scan
The hidden thought between the lines,
  God's purposes to man.
Like children in the dark
  'Tis ours to meekly stand
And wait in hope the eternal morn,
  Clasping a father's hand.

Morristown, N. J.   E. F. R. C.

The Clyde Methodist Advocate is welcome. It is devoted to Temperance, the Home and the Church. It is outspoken in its utterances about intemperance, and gives no uncertain sound in its denunciations of that terrible evil. It is published at Clyde, N.Y., and is a neatly printed, well edited paper.

THE RECORD.

FIRST PRESBYTERIAN CHURCH, MORRISTOWN, N. J.

"This shall be Written for the Generation to Come."—Psalms 102 : 18.

VOLUME III.   APRIL, 1883.   NUMBER 4.

[Printed with the Approval of the Session.]

THE RECORD

Will be published monthly at Morristown, N. J. Terms $1.00 per annum, *in advance*: Subscriptions may be made at the book-stores of Messrs. Runyon and Emmell, or to Messrs. James R. Voorhees and William D. Johnson, or by letter addressed to the EDITOR OF THE RECORD, Morristown, N. J.

Entered at the Post Office at Morristown, N. J., as second class matter.

CALENDAR.

For April and May, 1883.

THE LORD'S DAY SERVICES.

Morning Service, at 10:30 A. M.
Evening Service, at 7:30 P. M.
School of the Church, at 3 P. M.
Young People's Prayer Service, at 6:45 P.M.

OFFERINGS:

For Bible Society, Sunday morning, May 6th.
For Freedmen, Sunday morning, June 3d.

MID-WEEK SERVICE OF PRAYER.

Thursday Evenings, at 7:30.

April   5.—MISSION CONCERT.—The Light of the world for India. Jno. 1 : 1-9.
"   12.—ORGANIZATION AND WORK OF THE PRESBYTERIAN CHURCH.
"   19.—UNANSWERED PRAYER. Deut. iii : 23-27.
"   26.—CHRISTIAN GIVING. 1 Cor. xvi : 2 ; 2 Cor. ix : 6-11.
May   3.—MISSION CONCERT—Siam. Josh. v : 13-15.
"   10.—EMBLEMS OF CHRIST IN THE BIBLE. Rev. v : 5, 6.
"   17.—INDWELLING OF THE SPIRIT. Rom. viii : 8-17.
"   24.—STAGES IN CHRISTIAN EXPERIENCE. Jno. ix : 1-38.

SPECIAL SERVICES.

BAPTISM OF INFANTS.—Sunday Morning Service, May 6th.
PREPARATORY LECTURE.—Friday, at 4 o'clock, P. M., June 1st.
THE LORD'S SUPPER.—Sunday Morning Service, June 3d.

OTHER MEETINGS.

TEACHER'S MEETING, at close of Mid-Week Service, Thursdays.
SEWING CIRCLE, Wednesdays, at 3 P. M.

The Pastor will be found at his residence, on Franklin Place, Tuesdays ; and on Fridays, from 5 to 6 P. M., in the Study of the Chapel.

THE ANNUAL PARISH MEETING.

The Parish meeting for 1883 was held in the chapel on the afternoon of March 13th last. Mr. John Whitehead acted as chairman and Mr. James R. Voorhees, the clerk of the parish, as secretary. The pastor was present and invoked the Divine blessing. The usual reports of the trustees and treasurer were read. That of the latter, being the more important, is printed in full.

The following named gentlemen were elected trustees :

Aurelius B. Hull, Henry C. Pitney, Edward Pierson, Thomas C. Bushnell, Joseph H. VanDoren, James R. Voorhees and Henry Cory.

James R. Voorhees was re-elected clerk of the parish and Henry Cory, treasurer. Mr. Hull, who for ten years has so worthily filled the position of treasurer, was obliged to resign. His declination was received with very great regret, and the following resolution passed on motion of Doctor Stephen Pierson.

Resolved, That we express to Mr. Hull our appreciation of his services in our behalf as treasurer, and our regret that he feels unable longer to serve us in that capacity.

TENTH ANNUAL REPORT OF A. B. HULL, TREASURER:

1882.   DR.

March 13. Cash in Bank, $345 61
1883.
March 12. Received from annual
pledges and voluntary contributions to this date, compris-
ing 12 monthly payments.   4,978 96
Proceeds of fair held Dec., 1882,   293 25
Two-thirds balance Sunday offerings,   849 50
Balance of advances by Treasurer,   500 00
                               _____
                              $6,967 32

1882.   PER CONTRA.
May 1. Paid for pulpit supplies to
this date, $370 00
1883.
Feb. 28. Paid Rev. W. Durant's sal-
ary and commutation for
parsonage for 10 months
to this date,   3,166 66
Mar. 12. Paid chorister to this date,   180 80
Organist do.,   231 02
Bass, do.,   90 40
Alto,   45 20
Sexton,   598 12
Blowing organ,   50 00
1882.
Sept. 30. Treasurer of the Sunday
School,   200 00
1883.
Mar. 12. Sundry expenses as per
schedules rendered quar-
terly to Trustees and
Session,   2,034 64
Balance Cash in Bank,   48
                               _____
                              $6,967 32
A. B. HULL, Treasurer.
Morristown, March 12th, 1883.

THE REGISTERY.

Asterisks will be found appended to some of the names appearing in the Registery. They need an explanation. The former editor of the RECORD, the Rev. Mr. Green, in his preparation of the paper, spared no pains to present as far as possible, a correct record. To secure this perfection with that persistent energy, which marked all his efforts in whatever he undertook, he examined with great care some files of old newspapers he found in the possession of Mr. Monroe Howell, then living at Troy in this county. An asterisk appended to a name in the Registery denotes that the name is taken from the files of the old newspapers thus examined and may not be in the Registery.

The name of William Goble appears twice in the list of marriages, on the same day, in this number of the RECORD, An asterisk is attached to one of these entries; which means that that marriage was taken from the newspaper; the other was taken from the church registery. Probably the bride may have been an adopted daughter, and in one case gave her own name, while in the other, her adopted father's name was taken. But this is mere suggestion.

REV'D. JAMES RICHARDS. D. D.

Dr. Richards was the third settled pastor of the First Presbyterian Church at Morristown. He succeeded the Rev. Aaron Collins, who was for a few years, the associate of Dr. Timothy Johnes. Mr. Collins was dismissed September 2, 1793, and Dr. Richards was settled 1795 and remained in charge of the church for fourteen years and until April 26, 1809.

The Richards family is of Welsh origin and emigrated early to this country. Branches of the family are to be found today in New England, New York and Pennsylvania, and doubtless in other parts of the United States. A German family who also early came to America have Anglicised their name, now calling themselves Richards. The original German is Reichert or Reichard. This must not be confounded with that from which Dr. Richards sprang. His ancestor, who came to New England in his early youth, was undoubtedly of Welsh origin. His name was Samuel Richards; he served in the British army in Canada against the French in the reign of Queen Anne, it is said. When his term of service expired he settled in Connecticut near Stamford. The exact date of this settlement cannot be ascertained, but it must have been very early in the 18th century or at the close of the 17th. It was probably as early as some date in the 17th century. Queen Anne succeeded William III. in 1702. War had been raging in North America between the English and French for several years prior to the accession of Anne. Samuel Richards was a youth of eighteen years when he emigrated from Wales. Dr. Richards was the fourth in descent from this Welsh soldier, the originator of the family in this country, and was born October 29, 1767, at New Canaan, in Connecticut. His father whose name was also James, became a captain in the Continental army during the Revolution. The father was a fair representative of New England yeomanry; when a demand was made upon his patriotism he responded with alacrity; when the necessity for action for his country ceased, he at once resumed his peaceful avocations and served her in another direction. He was a farmer, a man of sound, common sense and held in estimation by his neighbors for social and Christian virtues. The subject of this sketch was the eldest of nine children, four of whom survived him. His mother's name was Ruth Hanford, and to her he seems to have been much indebted for many of the prominent characteristics which so enriched his nature. She was a woman of uncommon merit. The idea prevalent among many, that much of great men's mental strength is due to their mothers, was fully proved in the case of Dr. Richards. His mother was of strong intellect, of ardent piety and was uncompromising in the performance of duty. At the time of the birth of her children, parental authority in the family was paramount, and implicit obedience was demanded from the younger members. They were expected to obey and did obey. Parents did not then love their children less, nor were the children less affectionate than now. The household looked up to father and mother as heads and directors, and no question could be made when command came from them.

James Richards was a very precocious boy, fond of study, but of such delicate constitution that it was feared that he would not be able to submit to the necessary privations and hardships then involved in a student's life. The advantages then within reach of a youth, even though possessed of sufficient means to enable him to pursue a course of study, however great those means might be, were very limited compared with those which may now be obtained by even the poorest. The parents of Dr. Richards did not seem to have had the pecuniary ability to afford their eldest born the means of availing himself of even the slender opportunities for intellectual improvement which the country then possessed. He was not daunted by these hindrances, but early resolved to avail himself of all the appliances for an education which could possibly be found. His industry and perseverance overcame every obstacle. His untiring energy must have been early developed, for it is reported of him, that at the early age of thirteen he had charge of a district school. He was so successful in discharging his duties as teacher that he secured the same school for a second winter. If this fact were not well authenticated it would seem almost incredible, but it is so well proved that it cannot well be disputed.

The ideas gained by his service as principal of a school, only strengthened his desire for an education. But his father could not afford him the means, so, at the early age of fifteen, he determined to select some occupation for future use. Accordingly he entered, as an apprentice, into the business of cabinet and chair making, and also as a house painter. But his plan for a future avocation was soon interrupted by a severe illness which obliged him to return to his father's house. After his recovery he again took up the occupation of cabinet making. This was, however, abandoned, and in his nineteenth year, with the full consent of his master, he made preparations to pursue a course of study with a view of entering the ministry.

Like all New England youth of his day he had been piously educated, had been taught the Catechism and to repeat hymns, texts from the Scriptures, and indeed, had, at one time in his early youth, memorized entire chapters of the Bible. But he had never considered himself a subject of the forgiving grace of Christ, until he had passed his eighteenth year. He then gave the most hopeful evidences of his having become a true Christian. Soon after this and on the 17th September, 1786, he united with the Congregational Church at Stamford, and by his earnest zeal and pious efforts to promote all Christian work, and to stimulate the Congregation to a higher interest in all religious matters, he very soon satisfied others that he should be aided in attaining the dearest object of his heart, that he might enter the Christian ministry. His pastor and many friends strongly advised his preparation for that office. Accordingly he proposed to enter College and studied for that purpose under the Rev. Justus Mitchell. In the fall of 1789 he entered Yale College, but was soon obliged to leave for the want of funds. In his preparation he was aided, in his studies, by Dr. Burnett, of Norwalk, and materially by two excellent ladies, who were relatives, Sarah and Phebe Comstock. These ladies never withdrew their helping hands so long as he needed their aid.

After being obliged to leave college he determined that it was impossible for him to pursue a regular collegiate course of study, so he abandoned that plan, but only to take advantage of the means which were within his reach. He pursued his studies with Dr. Burnett at Norwalk and with Dr. Dwight at the "Greenfield Hill," school. These difficulties and the still more depressing one, arising from frequent and prostrating illness, did not deter him from his purpose. Amid them all he persevered until in 1793 he was licensed to preach by the Association in the Western District of Fairfield County in Connecticut. His first sermon after his license to preach, was delivered in the pulpit of his old friend and preceptor, the Rev. Dr. Burnett, of Norwalk, in compliance with a special request made to the former pupil of the good Dr. Mr. Richards for a few Sabbaths preached at Wilton, near Norwalk, and then made a short engagement with the church at Ballston, in New York. He was at this last named place certainly in December, 1793. Soon after this he went to Long Island and there took charge of two small congregations, one at Sag Harbor and the other at Shelter Island. The Rev. N. S. Prime in his history of Long Island, pays a warm tribute to Mr. Richards for his ministery while at these two places. This tri-

bute is the more striking as the time which was employed by Mr. Richards on Long Island was very brief, for early in 1794, he was invited to visit the church and congregation at Morristown. This invitation was the result of the very strong recommendations of the young pastor given by the Rev'd Dr. Buel of East Hampton, and by the Rev. Aaron Woolworth of Bridgehamton, who was the son-in-law of Dr. Buel. These two clergymen, especially Dr. Buel, strongly commended Mr. Richards to Dr. Timothy Johnes. The Rev. Mr. Collins, the associate of Dr. Johnes, was dismissed in the preceding year, and the congregation had been in great difficulty arising from its relations with that gentleman. The position was one of great delicacy and involved great responsibility, but the young pastor was equal to the task. There seems to be some difficulty in establishing some dates relative to events in the life of Mr. Richards happening at this period. Mr. Gridley, in his biography, says that he was invited in May, 1794, to visit Morristown ; Louis Richards, Esq., whose notes, relative to the Richards family, are very full, states that he was called to the pastoral charge of the church in Morristown, in June, 1794. Both of these gentlemen agree that he was not installed until May, 1797. The RECORD, Vol. I., No. 1, gives the date of his settlement as May 1, 1795. Mr. Barnes, in his church manual, published in 1828, says he was installed "as pastor May 1, 1795," by the Presbytery of New York.

The church seems then to have been in ecclesiastical relations with what was called the Presbytery of New York, and the installation took place at a stated meeting of that body. In November, 1794, Mr. Richards married Miss Caroline Cowles, daughter of James Cowles, of Farmington, Connecticut.

At the time Mr. Richards assumed the pastorate Dr. Johnes was still living, but he died very soon after, in September, 1794. The young pastor, therefore, must have had the entire charge of the congregation, from the very beginning of his ministry here. It was a very difficult duty imposed upon him. The congregation was large, the parish extensive, and the state of feeling arising from the unfortunate position in which it had been left by the action of Mr. Collins, all combined to make the task of the new pastor a laborious and responsible one. But his wisdom and good, sound sense enabled him successfully to meet all the exigencies of the situation. He was untiring in the performance of all ministerial duties, but did not lose his interest in literature and scientific pursuits. His attainments in mental culture had been so great that in 1794 he received the degree of Bachelor of Arts from Yale College, and in 1801 the trustees of Princeton college conferred on him the honorary title of Master of Arts. In 1805 he became Moderator of the General Assembly of the Presbyterian church, a very great honor, when it is remembered that he was then but thirty-seven years of age.

While at Morristown three distinct and powerful revivals of religion marked his ministry. The first occurred in 1799, the second in 1803 and 1804, and the third in 1808. At the first more than a hundred were added to the church. Mr. Richards seemed to have regarded the last of these seasons with the most favor. In 1828 he wrote to Mr. Barnes, who was then pastor of the church, in which he referred to these three revivals, but spoke of the third " as the most precious."

In April, 1809, he received a call from the First Presbyterian Church at Newark, which he accepted, removing to his new field of labor in May of the same year. This action does not seem to have been the result of any dissatisfaction, either with pastor or people. There was mutual love between them. Mr. Richards never spoke, nor wrote of his people at Morristown, but in the very warmest and most affectionate terms. Just before his death he wrote to a member of the church here in these words : " Never was a minister more happy with his people than I with mine during the fifteen years I spent among you. With you I was willing to live and with you I expected to die." These sentiments he more than once repeated. But his expenses were increased, a growing family involved greater outlay, the health of Mrs. Richards was precarious, and he required additional salary. The people did not feel able to meet the additional burthen, and had declined to vote any increase

of salary, although, in anticipation of the proposed change of pastorate, they afterwards offered to do so. The refusal of the congregation, at first, to increase the salary, made no change whatever in the hearts of either people or pastor towards each other. Before it was known that the call from the Newark church had been accepted a memorial, signed by seventy-one ladies of the congregation, was presented to their pastor which closed with these words : " Whether you leave us or remain with us, you may rest assured of our prayers for a blessing on your labors, and our best wishes for the happiness and prosperity of yourself and family."

This memorial fully showed the feeling of love with which their pastor was regarded. The difficulties attending the discharge of his duties at Newark were of a different character from those which met him at Morristown, but they were of no ordinary kind. The Newark church contained within its membership some of the best minds in the State. Dr. Griffin, whom Mr. Richards succeeded, was one of the foremost men in the church. He was eloquent and accomplished and had been most successful. The membership, during his ministry, had doubled ; when he entered the pulpit he found two hundred communicants ; when he left, after eight year's service, it had increased to five hundred. All this Mr. Richards knew and fully appreciated. But he trusted in a mightier power than could be afforded by man.

In 1811, the second Presbyterian church was organized in Newark, the new congregation being mainly gathered from that to which Mr. Richards ministered. To this new organization Mr. Richards gave not only his full consent, but aided it with advice and counsel. An event happening in the subsequent history of this new church, evinced the wisdom and true Christian spirit of Mr. Richards. After an absence of six years from Newark, a call was extended to Dr. Griffin to become the pastor of this Second church. This call became the subject of correspondence between the two clergymen, and in all kindness and brotherly love these two men, differing so materially from each other, labored side by side in the two congregations for several years. While at Newark he was elected trustee of the College of New Jersey, and in 1812 in the very organization of the Theological Seminary at Princeton he was appointed a director. The position of trustee of the college he held until he removed from the State. In 1815 he received the degree of Doctor of Divinity from two colleges, Union and Yale. This was an honor which at the time it was conferred, was a certain evidence of moral and professional worth.

He remained in Newark fifteen years and during that period received many tokens of the respect and confidence with which he was regarded by the church, in addition to those already mentioned. He was for several years secretary of the Educational Society, and took a very deep interest in the American Bible Society, which, in fact, was largely indebted to him for its organization. Several revivals occurred during his ministry in Newark, and the addition of five hundred members to his church marked the faithfulness and fervor of his efforts for the salvation of sinners.

In 1819, Auburn Theological Seminary was organized, and Dr. Richards, as he must now be called, was regarded by its friends and founders as the proper person to fill one of its professorial chairs. One of them was tendered to him very early in the history of the seminary, but was declined. In 1823, however, after a unanimous re-election, he accepted the appointment, and removing there in October of that year, on October 29, 1823, his fifty-sixth birthday, he was duly inaugurated professor of Christian theology.

From this date to the time of his death he was engaged in the performance of his duties as professor. While connected with the Seminary, he took a prominent part in all of its various interests, aiding it materially, not only in his Professor's Chair by the tuition afforded to hundreds of students, but by his efforts in various parts of the country to place the seminary in such position with reference to finances, that there should be no fear for its future. In whatever he undertook, for the advantage of the institution, he was eminently successful. Before his death the seminary was placed in such a position that its usefulness in the church was assured beyond a question.

Dr. Richards was not at the head of the Seminary, but his sound judgment, his wise action, and his commanding talents secured him a pre-eminent position in the Faculty. Dr. Richards died at Auburn, Aug. 2nd, 1843, twenty years after his inauguration and in the 76th year of his age. His death was acknowledged as a public calamity by the citizens of Auburn, and by the church. Resolutions passed in different parts of the country and by many public bodies, fully attested the estimation in which this eminent clergyman was held by all classes.

The personal appearance of Dr. Richards was striking and commanded universal respect. In social life he was simple, dignified, but courteous withal. Not a stain was ever cast upon his irreproachable character as a man, a citizen, or minister of the Gospel. His name is a household word in the families of the church at Morristown. His former parishioners have perpetuated it by giving it to their children. One of the youngest ruling elders of the church to-day bears it, and doubtless it will be borne by many in future generations.

The debt of gratitude our church owes him is great. He found it divided, despondent; he left it strong, united, aggressive. He vivified it by his teachings, edified it by his Christian doctrine, increased its membership, and leading it by his example, incited it to every good work.

The memory of James Richards will ever abide with us, cherished as one of our dearest possessions.

INTEMPERANCE.

The problem connected with this subject is one which must be met by all patriots and Christian philanthopists. No citizen can avoid individual responsibility either by inattention or refusal to act. How shall the problem be solved? Of course all thinking men agree that intemperance is an evil and should be repressed. But how shall it be done? No question involves more difficulty than this. Perhaps one part of the difficulty arises from the want of courage. The number of those who are engaged in the business of selling liquors is small as compared with the rest of the community. Another part of the difficulty arises from the want of union among the friends of temperance. Plans for the remedy of the evil of intemperance are too numerous and the proposers of these plans are too strenuous in promoting their pet schemes to admit of that hearty co-operation always necessary for the success of any important measure. If any one plan could be adopted with unanimity and prosecuted with courage there is enough Christian sentiment and Christian ability in the land to accomplish all that is needed in this contest with evil. But indecision on the part of many and dis-union everywhere have paralyzed effort and prevented success.

The strict Prohibitionist proposes simple Prohibition. Refuse to license saloon and tavern; stop the traffic in liquor at once and entirely; make the sale of ardent spirits a crime; even destroy the very manufacture of alcohol, says the Radical. As a means to this end he proposes to carry this great moral question into politics, submit all candidates to strict inquiry as to their sentiments, and vote only for those who favor his peculiar views, or else to nominate only those who are pledged to the support of his plan. Another would introduce the growth and culture of the vine, manufacture cheap wines and present beverages comparatively innoxious, for common use, at such price that those who require them can easily procure the apparently needed stimulants. A third says, control, regulate the traffic, throw around it such safeguards that it may be deprived of its terrific power to brutalize men; keep it within such bounds that its ability to destroy soul and body may be lessened. Still another says the laws now in force are sufficient for every purpose; put them in operation, bring to bear upon the retailer of liquor, and all engaged in the traffic, every lawful means which the laws afford, to repress the evil; make saloon and tavern keeper amenable to every provision which is to be found in the Statute Book; there is enough there for all needed purposes; if the law cannot be enforced, then educate public opinion up to the point where the community will demand, imperatively, that the law shall have full force. Still another says, let the experiment of putting the present laws in force be fully tested before any other plan be attempted. If, after a fair trial be had, the statutes now in force prove unavailing, then pass other acts; but until this be done do not change the present status. And still another plan is proposed.— Throw open the traffic to all; abolish the license system: but impose a very heavy tax on the seller; oblige those who sell liquor to place their saloons in public places where they will be open to all, and be strictly under the surveillance of the police. And still another says: Trust alone to the teachings of the church; this is a great moral evil not to be reached by laws, but only by an enlightened Christian sentiment which the church of Christ can alone inculcate.

These various plans show the divergence of opinion on this most important subject. This evil is to be treated like all others in some practical method. Which method is the proper one is the question now before the Christian public and must be met.

EASTER

Sunday, March 25, 1883, was celebrated in most Christian churches as an anniversary of the day on which the Resurrection of the Savior took place. In many churches there were service of song and praise and gorgeous ritual. Flowers, rich and rare, decked pulpit and chancel; while, with ceremonies, grand and imposing, pious priest and devout worshipper marked their appreciation of the occasion.

The Resurrection of Christ was a grand event and worthy of our highest reverence. Without it the Christian system would be worthless and our hope of salvation vain. But there is no historical proof that the day, or even any day in the period, usually selected to commemorate the event, is an anniversary of the one on which it actually occurred, nor is there any historical evidence that the very early Christians ever celebrated any day in remembrance of the Resurrection. On the contrary, such testimony as may be gained from history is against the assumption that there was any such custom. In fact, some writers derive Easter from a festival, celebrated in the month of April by the Teutonic race, in honor of Eostre or Ostara, the Goddess of Spring. Easter, as a name, undoubtedly, is taken from the title of this

Divinity. Bede gives this derivation of the word and says that April was called the *Eostre-monath*. The French give to the festival the name of Pasque ; the Greek church call it Pascha ; and several branches of the Latin church know it by a similar appellation. Neither of these names is derived directly, either from the Greek or Latin language, but from the Hebrew in its Aramaic form, where it was used to denote the Passover. A difference of opinion arose very early in the Christian church on this subject among the learned Fathers ; some insisting that the word was derived from the Greek verb, Paschein, *to suffer*, while others asserted that it was from the Hebrew. The knowledge of this latter tongue among the Anti-Nicene Fathers, was very limited. The controversy is now at an end by the assent of all scholars to the Hebrew derivation.

Socrates, the Greek church historian, who continued the history of Eusebius, writing in the 5th century, uses this language with reference to this festival. "The Savior and His Apostles have enjoined us, by no law, to keep this feast, nor in the New Testament are we threatened with any penalty, punishment, or curse for the neglect of it, as the Mosaic law does the Jews. *   * The Apostles had no thought of appointing festival days, but of promoting a life of blamelessness and piety, and it seems to me that the feast of Easter has been introduced into the Church from some old usage, just as many other customs have been established."

These quotations are taken from Book V., chapter 22d of the history of Socrates, where he enters quite largely into his own views respecting the celebration of Easter.

Discussions arose, certainly as early as the 3d century, as to the proper time of Easter feasts. These discussions soon degenerated into controversies, which were characterized by great vehemence and acrimony, and assumed such importance that Constantine, the Great, in A. D. 325 submitted this vexed question, as well as some doctrinal disputes, which had divided the church, to the great council, known as the Nicene.

It certainly is a fair argument against the idea that the Easter festival is derived from Eostre or Ostara, the Teutonic Goddess ; to say that if Socrates be right, and the holy day had an existence in the Christian church at the period about which he wrote ; since the German had not then embraced Christianity, it is more probable that the Easter festival originated from the Jewish observance of the Passover. This conclusion is also confirmed by the Hebraic origin of the word. It may be added in this connection that the word Pascha is to be found in the Septuagint translation of Exodus, 12, 27, where it denotes the Passover. This translation was probably made 300 years B. C. It must not be forgotten that the Resurrection actually took place at the time of the Passover.

Let all this be as it may, no Christian, who loves his Savior, should hesitate to celebrate the Resurrection of that Savior, an event so full to him of hope and promise, even if there be doubt as to the day. Days and times are of no account. Events, such as the Resurrection of Jesus Christ, mark eras in the history of man which are not bounded by time, or divisions of time, but extend over Eternity.

Father ! in thy mercy, spare !
On the children of thy care,
Worthy only of thy frown,
Look in tender pity down !
   Miserere, Domine !

All the pleasures of the past,
Dead-Sea apples, in our grasp ;
Subject, by our passions base,
To the hidings of thy face,
   Miserere, Domine !

All our idols, made of clay,
Ever crumble, day by day ;
One by one, they all depart,
Soothe each sorrow-stricken heart !
   Miserere, Domine !

Joy, to every human soul !
Earth, rejoice from pole to pole !
Herald angels, on the wing,
Tell us of our risen king.
   Christ, the Lord, is risen to-day !

Weary mortal ! Sin-sick heart !
Jesus bids your fears depart.
Only keep your armor bright ;
He will make your burden light.
   Christ, the Lord, is risen to-day !

Cast your idols all away !
Lean on Him from day to day.
Mountain high your sins have seemed ;
Now, by precious blood redeemed !
   Christ, the Lord, is risen to-day !

THE RECORD.

·FIRST PRESBYTERIAN CHURCH, MORRISTOWN, N. J.

"This shall be Written for the Generation to Come."—Psalms 102 : 18.

VOLUME III. MAY, 1883. NUMBER 5.

[Printed with the Approval of the Session.]

THE RECORD

Will be published monthly at Morristown, N. J. Terms $1.00 per annum, *in advance*: Subscriptions may be made at the book-stores of Messrs. Runyon and Emmell, or to Messrs. James R. Voorhees and William D. Johnson, or by letter addressed to the EDITOR OF THE RECORD, Morristown, N. J.

Entered at the Post Office at Morristown, N. J., as second class matter.

MEMORANDA

OF THE FIRST PRESBYTERIAN CHURCH, MORRISTOWN, N. J.,

For the Year ending 31 *March,* 1883.

MEMBERSHIP.

Number of Communicants,	.	381
Added during year by Baptism,	.	4
" " " " Confirmation,		6
" " " on Examination,	.	10
" " " " Certificate,	.	11
Adult Baptisms, 4.	Infant Baptisms,	3

SUNDAY SCHOOL.

Number of Officers,	.	9	Number rec'd, into church, 6.	
" " Teachers,	.	47	Am't given to our Boards,$340	
" " Scholars,	.	348	" " " other objects,280	
Total Membership,	404	Total contributions,		$620
Average Attendance,	250	Number of Books in Library,		540

BENEFICENCE.—THE HOME FIELD.

HOME MISSIONS :

Annual Collection, .	$134 96	
" " for Church Extension Com. of Synod,	63 28	
Woman's Home Mission Soc. Boxes,	400.00	
Individual gifts,officially acknowledged,336.50		
Children's Mis. Society,various objects,115.00		
Stevenson Band, .	11.00	
		$1,060.74

EDUCATION OF CANDIDATES FOR MINISTRY

Annual Collection, .	.	50 45
Appropriated from Session Fund,for German Sem. at Bloomfield,	.	50.00
Children's Mis Soc. for Lincoln Univ.,	75.00	
Stevenson Band, for Sitka School,	25.00	
		200.00

PUBLICATION, or PRESBYTERIAN COLPORTAGE :

Annual Collection,	58.00	
		58.00

CHURCH ERECTION :

Annual Collection, .	.	81.45
Appropriated from Session Fund, for Lakewood Church,	.	50.00
Appro'd from Session Fund, for Building Fund of Synod's Com.,	.	50.00
		181.45

RELIEF OF AGED AND INVALID MINISTERS :

Annual Collection,	.	76.45
Special "	.	35.00
		111.45

MISSIONS TO FREEDMEN :

Annual Collection,	.	73.00
Individual gifts, officially acknowledged,55.00		
		128.00

SUSTENTATION OF FEEBLE CHURCHES :

Annual Collection,	.	45.59
		45 50

MISCELLANEOUS :

Annual Collection for Bible Society,	59.14	
Contributions to Tract Society,	230.00	
" " " Chn's Home, Parsippany,	.	774.00
Woman's Home Mis. Soc., for sufferers by Cyclone in Iowa,	.	300.00
Chn's Mis.Soc.for Seaman's Friend Soc.,50.00		
		1,413.14
Total for "The Home Field,"		$3,198.82

THE FOREIGN LAND.

FOREIGN MISSIONS :

Annual Collection,	.	$743.71
Zenana Society,	.	350.00
Individual gifts, officially acknowledged,	.	80 00
Children's Mis. Soc., for work in France,	.	50.00
Do. do. do. Gould Home,	150.00	
Do. do. do. Foreign Board,	200 00	
Total for "The Foreign Field,"		1,553.71
" "The Home Field,"		3,198.82
Total beneficence,		4,752.53

CONGREGATIONAL EXPENSES.

Assessment for Presbytery and General Assembly, 39.50

CONGREGATIONAL :

Current expenses of Church,	6,766.84	
" " " Sunday school,	200.00	
Care of Poor by Deacons,	.	133 04
Miscellaneous (mainly for additions to Chapel),	.	1,147.77
		8,247 65
Total contributions,		$13,059.68

PASTORAL.

From 1st May, 1882, to 31 March, 1883.

Sermons preached,	84
Prayer Meetings addressed,	39
Special Addresses,	18
Meetings with Catechism Class,	16
Missionary Sermons and Addresses,	7
Preparatory Lectures,	6
Communion Services,	6
Marriages solemnized,	5
Funeral Services,	19
Calls made,	523
No. of Families on list of Congregation	245

SOME EVENTS OF THE YEAR.

1882.

May 11. Pastor installed : the Rev Dr. A. Erdman presiding, assisted by Dr. T. F. White and Dr. R Aikman ; sermon by the Rev. T. B. McLeod, charge to Pastor by the Rev. J. H. McIlvaine, and charge to people by Dr. H. F. Hickok.

" 13. Fair in Lyceum for addition to Chapel and Gould Home.

" 28. Union service in evening, at the South Street Church, for Torbert Post, G. A. R

June 1 Anniversary of Sunday School, with address by Mr. Ralph Wells.

" 13 Delegates present at Anniversary of Bible Soc., Boonton.

" 15. First use of appointment cards for prayer service.

Sept. 22. Steeple struck by lightning, damage slight.

" 29. Adoption of new blanks for dismissal and recommendation of members.

Oct. 3. Delegates present at County Sunday School Convention.

" 13. Anniversary of the Children's Missionary Society, in Church ; followed by sociable in Chapel

" 15. Union service in evening, at South Street Church, addressed by Rev. Dr. R. Aikman, on Growth of the Church in South Jersey.

" 16. Death of Rev. Gavin Langmuir, at Florence, Italy : Pastor from July, 1866, to Sept. 1868.

" 22. Union service in evening, at First Church, addressed by the Rev. Dr. H. H. Jessup, " Bearing of recent Egyptian war on missions to Mahometans."

Nov 12. Infant Class occupied its new room, for first time.

" 12. Union service in evening at South Street Church, for Y. M. C. A

" 30. Union Thanksgiving service at Baptist Church, sermon by Rev Mr. Pannell.

Dec. 8. Fair and supper in Chapel, for furnishing addition.

" 24. Christmas service of School held Sunday evening

" 29. Christmas festival of Sunday School.

1883.

Jan. 8-13. Week of Prayer ; Union meetings held in South St Church, at 11 A. M. on Monday, Wednesday, Thursday and Saturday, and at 7:30 P. M. on Tuesday and Friday.

" 13. The Record resumed publication under editorial charge of Mr. John Whitehead.

" 16. Afternoon and evening meeting in chapel, with addresses on Home Missions, at invitation of Stevenson Band, by Mrs. Walker and the Rev. Dr. T. Hill.

" 21. Union service, at Methodist Church, addressed by the Rev. I. W. Brinkerhof, for Howard Mission.

Feb. 4. First use of order of evening service arranged on old Presbyterian models.

" 16. Supper of Zenana Society, in chapel.

Feb 19. "Temperance Voters' League," organized by delegates from all parts of the county, in Chapel.

Mar 11. Eleventh consecutive stormy Sunday.

" 13. Annual Parish Meeting Mr. A B, Hull declined re-election as Treasurer, after ten years of service.

HON. GEORGE K. DRAKE.

Col. Jacob Drake, the father of George K. Drake, was born at Piscataway, Middlesex county, April 21, 1732, and while yet a young man removed to Morris county, locating at Drakesville, then an unbroken wilderness. His nearest neighbor was Gen. Woodhull, who had made a settlement six miles distant in the direction of Chester. Indians were all about him. Here he built the hotel property, now owned by Jeremiah Baker and here he spent the most of his life. He was a very active and energetic man, of fine physique, six feet in height and very erect in his carriage, exceedingly neat in his person and habits, punctilious in meeting his engagements, generous and hospitable. In illustration of his character, it is said, he would discharge a workman who would strike a blow after the signal had sounded for dinner, and that when in his last sickness he noticed from the window some unsightly weeds growing by a fence, he sent word to his man "Jimmy" to cut them down at once. When told that Jimmy was away but that the work would be attended to in a few minutes, he replied, "I may be dead in a few minutes." When the difficulties between Great Britain and her colonies became serious, Capt. Jacob Drake, as he was then called, became at once one of the leaders in the popular movement. At the meeting of the Freeholders of Morris county, Jan. 9, 1775, presided over by Gen. Winds, and which approved "the association" of the Continental Congress, he was made one of the committee of correspondence. On Monday, May 1, 1775, the Freeholders of the county elected him one of the nine delegates who were "vested with the power of legislation" and directed "to raise men, money and arms for the common defence." These delegates in convention, Aug. 12, directed another election Sept. 21, for the choice of delegates to meet at Trenton, October 3, and Col. Drake was one of the five so chosen. Again in May, 1776, another general election was held by direction of the Provincial Congress to choose delegates to a new convention, and Col. Drake was again chosen one of the five from this county, receiving 491 votes, a larger number than was cast for any other of the candidates. These frequent re-elections were necessary in a body, ruling not under any constitution but proceeding directly from the people and thus receiving frequent endorsements for their acts. This last convention which assembled at Burlington, June 10, approved July 2, the first constitution of this State and directed the manner in which the first State Legislature should be chosen. In this Legislature and in the two succeeding ones, Col. Drake was one of the representatives from Morris. Meantime two battalions of Militia had been raised and organized. The Eastern commanded by Col. Jacob Ford, the Western by Col. Drake, but the appointment of the latter to the Legislature obliged him to resign his colonelcy in 1776. Col. Drake was married twice. By his first wife, Miss Charity Young, he had one daughter, Mrs. Howell. His second wife was Esther, daughter of Capt. Peter Dickerson and the widow of Mr. George King, of Morristown. To her he was married Dec. 13, 1781, by Dr. Timothy Johnes. They had six children, viz.: Clarissa H., born Aug. 23, 1783, who married Dr. Ebenezer Woodruff; Jacob B. Drake, born May 5, 1786; Silas Drake, born April 10, 1790; George King Drake, born Sept. 16, 1788; Peter Drake, born April 9, 1792, and Eliza Drake, born April, 4, 1794, who married Dr. Absalom Woodruff. After the war Col. Drake continued to reside at Drakesville, until about 1811, when he sold the hotel to Henry Mooney and removed to a house he had built at Succasunna, afterwards occupied by Dr. Ebenezer Woodruff, where he died in September, 1823.

George K. Drake was born at Drakesville and named after his mother's first husband, who was the brother of Henry King of Morristown and uncle of William L., Charles and Jacob King. In the absence of neighborhood schools he was placed by his father under the care of the celebrated Rev. Amzi Armstrong of Mendham. Here he undoubtedly received the strong religious bias which ever after manifested itself in his life. Under the tuition of Dr. Armstrong he fitted for Princeton college, from which he graduated in 1808, in the same class with the late Bishop Meade, of Va., George Wood and Judge Wayne of the U. S. Supreme Court. After graduation he begun at once the study of law in the office of Sylvester Russel, then one of the leading members of the Morris county bar. In 1812 he was licensed as attorney and began the practice of his profession at Morristown. In 1815 he was made Counselor and in 1834 Sergeant-at-Law. October 4, 1815, he was united in marriage to Mary Alling Halsey, daughter of Jacob Halsey of New York city, and set up his house. In January, 1816, he purchased from Israel Canfield a lot adjoining the Lewis Mills' property, where the Bates' stores are now in Washington street, and upon this he built his residence and had his office. He soon established himself in a fine practice, his well known integrity and ability securing for him the business of the leading men of the community. August 15, 1822, he united with the First Presbyterian Church, then under the pastoral care of Dr. McDowell, his wife having united in May previous; At a meeting of the church on Friday, the 1st of September, 1826, Mr. Drake and five others were elected ruling elders, and on Sabbath, the first day of October following, they were solemnly set apart to the office by prayer.

In 1823 he was elected a member of the House of Assembly and re-elected the three following years. The last two years of his membership he was Speaker of the House. In 1824, and again in 1825, he was appointed Prosecutor of the Pleas for Morris County. In December, 1826, while a member of the House, he was appointed in joint meeting one of the Justices of the Supreme Court, to succeed Judge Rossel. To accommodate the people of the judicial district to which he was assigned, he left Morristown in 1828 and removed with his family to Burlington, where he resided for five years, and then to Trenton where he remained two years.

During the last years of his term the celebrated case of Shotwell against Hendrickson and Decow, growing out of the division which had taken place in the Society of Friends, was referred to Chief Justice Ewing and Justice Drake for decision, the Chancellor having been engaged as counsel in the case. Hendrickson, in 1821, as Treasurer of the School Fund of the Preparative Meeting of the Society of Friends of Chesterfield, loaned $2,000 to Shotwell on mortgage. At this time there was no division in the Society, and until after the yearly meeting, held in Arch street meeting house on the third Monday of April, 1827, there was but one yearly meeting. At this memorable meeting the presence of a disturbing element was very apparent. The meeting nevertheless adjourned "to meet in the next year at the usual time." The "Hicksite" party were very much dissatisfied with the proceedings, and a convention of their party was called in October, which resulted in forming a new yearly meeting which held its first session in Green street, in Philadelphia, on the second Monday in April, 1828, the "Orthodox" party meeting on the third Monday of April in that year in Arch street meeting house as formerly. The division in the yearly meeting extended to all the branches of the Society. Each quarterly, monthly and preparative meeting separated into two. The Hicksite preparative meeting accounted to the Hicksite monthly meeting, that to the Hicksite quarterly meeting and that to the Green street yearly meeting. The Orthodox meetings were maintained as they had been. There were two Chesterfield preparative meetings and of these Decow was treasurer of that of the Hicksite party, while Hendrickson remained treasurer of that of the Orthodox party. Both claimed the money from Shotwell who sympathized with the Hicksite party and compelled the parties to interplead. Hendrickson in his bill of complaint stated among other things that there were three prominent points of doctrine always deemed fundamental in the Society on which they differed. That the Orthodox Friends believed in the divinity of the Saviour, the Atonement and the inspiration and certainty of the Scriptures, but that the Hicksites rejected these doctrines. Decow in his answer denied that these doctrines were fundamental, and that every individual member of the society might believe in regard to them what he pleased.

The Chief Justice decided the case against the Hicksite party in a very elaborate opinion, arguing quite conclusively that the preparative meeting represented by Decow and accountable through its respective monthly and quarterly meetings to the Green street yearly meeting was not the one to whom the money was payable. That the Orthodox preparative meeting was the original institution, not destroyed or legally affected by the separation of a portion of its membership. He did not discuss the differences of belief of the two parties.

Judge Drake, in his opinion, went further than the Chief Justice. To use his own phraseology the propriety as well as the legality of the courts noticing the doctrines of the preparative meeting, which was to superintend the expenditure of the fund in question, was too manifest to admit of doubt, and he declared that in his opinion the fund should be awarded to that meeting which had shown, at least to his satisfaction, that they agreed in doctrine with the society of Friends as it existed at the origin of the trust.

This decision gave great dissatisfaction to the losing party. They declared that while the Chief Justice took away their property Judge Drake had robbed them also of their religion. Accordingly their enmity to him was much deeper and took a practical form. By their votes the next fall they helped to elect a Democratic Legislature which appointed Thos. C. Ryerson, Esq., of the same political faith to succeed him. Judge Elmer, in his reminiscences, remarks that this was the only case where the reappointment of a generally accepted judge had been defeated by a single obnoxious decision. Judge Ryerson, with many other Democrats, stoutly opposed this unjustifiable proscription and warmly advocated his reappointment. His name was used to secure the votes of Sussex members, and "thus without his knowledge, he was made the instrument of defeating an excellent and irreproachable judge, his own warm and personal friend." That this would be the probable result of his opinion Judge Drake foreknew, but believing it to be his duty he did not hesitate to declare his convictions with the greatest freedom, and to put his decision on principles which, not being necessarily required to be assured, others would have deemed it wiser to avoid.

In 1835, after the expiration of his term, he returned to Morristown and again resumed the active practice of his profession. But severe trials waited upon his remaining years. While still living in Trenton he was afflicted with rheumatism which confined him for months to his house and troubled him ever after. He became financially much embarrassed in the settlement of his father's estate and by the impairment of his practice from his long absence from Morristown. On the 26th of March, 1836, he lost his only son, Edmund Burke Drake, a youth of great promise, who died of erysipelas in his nineteenth year. In the spring of the following year he rode on horseback from Morristown to Succasunna without a buckskin vest he had been in the habit of wearing during the past winter. He was taken with pleurisy at the house of his brother-in-law, Dr. Ebenezer Woodruff, and after an illness of only one week died May 6th, in the forty-eighth year of his age. He was buried at Morristown in the old church yard, but his remains were afterwards removed to the Evergreen Cemetery. His widow survived him many years and died at the house of her son-in-law in Newark, April 18, 1872.

Judge Drake left four children. Eliza Halsey, who married George R. Howell; Annie McKenzie, who married Henry G. Darcy; Mary L., who is the wife of Justice Scudder of the Supreme Court, and Marion McLean, who died in childhood.

A gentleman who remembers Judge Drake very well prior to 1821, says of him, "He was my father's counsel. I consequently saw more of him than most boys of my age, having occasion to go to his office frequently on errands, and his appearance, voice and manners are very strongly impressed on my mind. He was rather tall and had a slight bend or scholarly stoop in walking. But his height, with rather a long neck, gave him a commanding appearance when on his feet. His most striking feature was his voice which was an uncommonly deep bass, rich and sonorous. His utterance was slow and deliberate. It seemed as if not only every sentence but every word was weighed when he spoke. In conversation his manner was marked by extreme gravity. I don't recollect ever seeing him laugh but what I recollect of him with the greatest pleasure, was the winning charm and kindness of his manner in conversation, of this I have distinct recollection. It was just that manner which would impress a stranger with the idea, 'this is a man I can trust.' My father had the most exalted idea of him as a gentleman and a friend. I suppose no man ever stood higher in public estimation in Morristown, either socially or as a safe, and trusted counselor. I regret that I am unable to give a fuller sketch of this good man."

THE SOUTH STREET SUNDAY SCHOOL LECTURES

The second and third in this course have been delivered; the second on "Church History," March 9th, by Mr. John Whitehead, and the third on "Christian Doctrine," April 4th, by F. G. Burnham, Esq.

Before the delivery of the third lecture, a kind friend sent the communication which follows this notice. The maternity of the letter is strongly suspected. Praise is pleasant even to the most modest, and it could hardly be expected that human nature, especially that of an editor, could resist the temptation to publish so flattering a commendation, coming as it does from this suspected source.

These lectures are delivered in the church parlor, in the rear of the main building. The arrangement of the rooms connected with the parlor, is admirable and reflects great credit on the architect and building committee. The compactness and convenience which have been obtained is simply wonderful. It can hardly be credited that seven rooms are to be found in the rear of the one used for regular worship. Beside the parlor there are a pastor's study, two rooms for Sabbath school purposes, one for the older scholars and one for the infant classes—a ladies room, kitchen and library. The parlor is admirably adapted for lecture purposes; its acoustic properties are excellent; it brings speaker and audience close together and gives a home like feeling and appearance. This plan of instruction for Sunday schools is again commended.

Mr. Editor:

The second lecture of the course on "Sunday reading" was delivered in the Bible class room of the South street Presbyterian church, March 7th, by John Whitehead, Esq.

"Church History" was the subject selected for that evening, and a goodly number assembled to partake of the literary feast, for such, indeed, it proved to be. The lecturer gave a history of the Christian church to the era of the Reformation. The time subsequent to this period was not considered, as well from lack of time, as from the fact that it must be more familiar to the audience.

The history of the church was divided into three periods, Ancient, Medieval and Modern.

The Ancient period included the "Apostolic Era," the era of the "Persecuted Church," and the era of the "Church Triumphant."

The Medieval period included the time from Gregory the Great, to Gregory VII; from Gregory VII to Boniface VIII; from Boniface VIII to the Reformation. The modern period extends to the present time and is still in progress.

The treatment of the subject indicated deep research on the part of the lecturer and an ability to mould the facts into a form that could be readily grasped. At the close of the lecture a list of books, valuable to the student was cited, many of which are to be found on the shelves of the library.   B.

TEMPERANCE.

In the last number of the RECORD mention was made of several plans proposed for a check to intemperance. Each plan, of course, has its honest advocates. The views and prejudices of these advocates ought to be respected; but, where the common sentiment of all who favor these different plans, is in one direction and all are desirous of reaching one end, the mutual respect due to each other should permit and the common desire for the same great end should induce, a united effort in adopting one of the various plans proposed.

Is it possible to accomplish this union?

Why not? What is lacking is union. What will secure undoubted success is one common impulse of all opponents of intemperance in one direction.

Take a practical view of the subject. Morristown has nine Christian churches, into which gather statedly a very large majority of the people of that city. If the vote should be taken of the worshippers in these nine churches upon the simple question, temperance or intemperance, there could be no doubt as to the result. In all probability, every man, woman and child would vote for temperance.

But present the question to the same voters in this form; what practical plan is the best to adopt to stop the further progress of intemperance, and quite another result would be obtained.

This divergence of *opinion* cannot be avoided, but this can be done; When a question of *action* is submitted, then Christian men and women can surrender mere opinion and adopt a course of action which involves no surrender of principle, but by a united effort can be made successful.

Let every one who opposes intemperance and really desires to check it, put himself in such a position that he may honestly subscribe to this sentiment: My opinion favors one certain plan, but I am willing to do whatever is thought best by the majority provided I am not called upon to surrender a principle.

The Index, published at Brockport, N. Y., in the interest of the Baptist church there, is welcome. It is a bright paper, fully alive to the duties of a church of Christ and of individual Christians. We tender our congratulations to our brithren at Brockport on the good work. they have accomplished for their church édifice, but more especially for a higher and better work, which seems to have blessed the series of meetings they have been holding.

The next lecture in the course in South street church, in this city, will be delivered by Mr. Andrew F. West, May 2d next, on *Christian Duty.*

Why, cannot the old First Church imitate this excellent example?

HISTORY OF THE SUNDAY SCHOOL.

On the banner of the Sunday school of the church hanging every Sabbath in the chapel, is the date 1816. It is presumed that this date is intended to denote the year in which the Sunday school was organized. But is this correct?

Mr. Manning Rutan, in his 81st year, writes from Greenville, Michigan, that he thinks he attended Sunday school, in the gallery of the church, in 1814 or 1815. The superintendent was then a lady, and lived, so says Mr. Rutan, about one hundred yards from the church and carried on the millinery business. Two of the teachers were employed by the superintendent in her shop, one of whom was Miss Charity McCarty, who afterwards married a Mr. Johnston and also carried on the millinery business. This lady superintendent, says Mr. Rutan, afterwards married Col. Cobb, of Parsippany, but he does not remember her name. A friend says she was a widow and her name was Shaw.

Our former pastor, the Rev. Dr. Irving, in his sermon, published in the RECORD, Aug. 1882, say's that in 1816 a Sabbath school, in connection with this church was established. Before, a few active friends met on Sabbath to instruct the colored people. This school for colored folk, Dr. Irving supposed was the first movement in this part of the country in the direction of Sunday schools.

Dr. Irving's sermon was preached on Thanksgiving day, 1862. Undoubtedly the preacher made his statement after all possible research. But, if Mr. Rutan be correct, there must have been a Sunday school for white children prior to 1816.

In 1880, the Rev. D. E. Platter prepared a historical manual of the Rockaway church ; in the sketch of the history of the church contained in this manual, it is stated that in 1815, Mrs. Electa Jackson, wife of Col. Joseph Jackson, living at Rockaway, started the *first* Sunday school in Morris County, in the *"old red school house,"* near the church, at Rockaway. Mr. Platter adds to this the statement, that "Mrs. Jackson and her sister-in-law, Mrs. James Jackson, had previously gathered the neighboring children for religious instruction in their own homes."

All honor to these pious ladies and to the church which supported them.

A correct history of the Sunday school is very desirable. A kind friend, at one time, much interested in the school and occupying an important position in it, has given some interesting facts relative to it. But her acquaintance with the school began at a date subsequent to its early history. What, therefore, is now most needed for the present purpose, are the exact facts connected with that early history. Any such facts will be gladly received.

BIOGRAPHICAL

Sketches of the lives of former pastors, ruling elders and prominent men connected with the church, will be published from time to time. The June number of the RECORD will probably contain a notice of Hon. Ira C. Whitehead, a former elder. Persons in possession of facts, anecdotes, or circumstances connected with the lives of any of these persons thus designated, will confer a very great favor by forwarding them to the editor.

Information of any kind in reference to any of the former pastors or elders of the church is particularly requested.

During the week ending April 21, large temperance meetings have been held in Washington Hall, under the charge of the Y. M. C. A. These meetings have been addressed by Major Scott, whose labors as a temperance evangelist have been so successful elsewhere. The clergymen of the town have been present and added their influence to the efforts made to aid struggling humanity in its attempts to cast off the incubus·of intemperance. Maj. Scott is an eloquent speaker, well calculated to impress audiences, and knows whereof he speaks.

A large assemblage, notwithstanding the severe storm, gathered on Sunday evening, April 22d, in the First Presbyterian Church, at which Maj. Scott was present and spoke. The meetings have been continued during the week following. Great good is anticipated from these efforts, and it is hoped that many, who have been in the grasp of the enemy of human souls, may have been released.

OPEN COMMUNION.

The *Rector's Assistant* quotes, with commendation, the following, taken from one of its exchanges, which, the *Assistant* says, is not edited by a Low Churchman:

"Now as then, she "—the church—" welcomes to that Sacrament of the Lord's body * * * * all baptized and faithful Christians, whatever they may call themselves, and whatever opinions they may have added to the simple faith of the Apostles Creed which she holds to contain all the essential articles of the Christian faith. Though separate in their organizations from the historical church, such Christian people are by their baptism and by their faith members of the Church Catholic and universal—' the mystical body of Christ, which is the blessed company of all faithful people ;' and hence have the right to approach reverently the table of the Lord."

The sentiment is Catholic and Scriptural, and is in exact conformity with the teachings of the Presbyterian church : the communion table, when spread in our church, is not a Presbyterian table, but it is the Lord's table and all who love the Lord Jesus Christ are welcome to sit with us at the feast, let them be called by whatever name they may.

THANKS

To the *Rector's Assistant* for its kindly notice and fraternal words with reference to what it is pleased to call " The new departure of Presbyterianism." No quarrel can be had with any of its utterances on this subject, even if there were a disposition to do so, because of the true Christian spirit which pervade the whole article.

THANKS, too, to the *Hansom Place Quarterly* for its pleasant notice of the RECORD. Is the *Quarterly* quite sure of its orthography ? Does it spell its own name aright ? Ought it not to be *handsome ?*

Among the many good things which appear in the *Quarterly*, the article headed " *How to Encourage your Minister*," is specially commendable. It may be read and followed with profit by members of any congregation. The hints there made are practical, considerate, Christian, and ought to be carried out.

VERBAL INSPIRATION.

What is verbal inspiration ? It is the theory that the Bible is a work dictated word for word by the Holy Ghost. According to it, the writers of the Scriptures were simple amanuenses, reproducing what was communicated to them with the liberal accuracy of a short-hand reporter. This doctrine finds favor with a large number of orthodox readers of the Old and New Testament. Nevertheless, it is an hypothesis which is utterly unsupportable ; even the book itself, in whose behalf it is alleged, contradicting it. Christians who undertake to maintain it, place themselves thereby at a pitiable disadvantage in their efforts with infidelity.—*Rector's Assistant..*

THE WORLD A GAME,

This world a hunting is,
The prey, poor man, the Nimrod fierce is
　　death ;
His speedy greyhounds are
Lust, sickness, envy, care,
Strife that ne'er falls amiss
With all those ills which haunt us while we
　　breathe.
Now, if by chance we fly
Of these the eager chase,
Old age with stealing pace
Casts up his nets, and there we panting die
　　　　　　　DRUMMOND.

TO-MORROW.

Our yesterday's to-morrow now is gone,
And still a new to-morrow does come on ;
We by to-morrows draw up all our store,
Till the exhausted well can yield no more
To-morrow you will live, you always cry.
In what far country does this morrow lie,
That 'tis so mighty long 'ere it arrive ?
Beyond the Indies does this morrow live !
'Tis so far fetch'd this morrow, that I fear
'Twill be both very old and very dear.
To-morrow I will live, the fool does say :
To-day itself's too late ; the wise liv'd yesterday.
　　　　　　　COWLEY.

THE RECORD.

FIRST PRESBYTERIAN CHURCH, MORRISTOWN, N. J.

"THIS SHALL BE WRITTEN FOR THE GENERATION TO COME."—Psalms 102 : 18.

VOLUME III.   JUNE, 1883.   NUMBER 6.

[Printed with the Approval of the Session.]

THE RECORD

Will be published monthly at Morristown, N. J. Terms $1.00 per annum, *in advance.*

Subscriptions may be made at the book-stores of Messrs. Runyon and Emmell, or to Messrs. James R. Voorhees and William D. Johnson, or by letter addressed to the EDITOR OF THE RECORD, Morristown, N. J.

Entered at the Post Office at Morristown, N. J., as second class matter.

BENEVOLENCE.

True benevolence is not always manifested by munificent gifts. Too frequently ostentation directs the hand which showers gold. The small rills which feed the mighty river are always the sweetest and purest. The simple, humble Christian, whose life is a constant reflection of the goodness which shone in the Master, is surer of a welcome at that Master's coming than the millionaire, who, from display gives his thousands.

All over the land, in our churches, are to be found those silent witnesses of the true Christian life. They do what they can and leave the rest with their God. Women, whose names are never heard, go about on their mission, heavenly missions, of good. They feed the hungry, clothe the naked, visit the sick, comfort the widow and protect the fatherless. They found no hospitals, endow no colleges, make no great gifts of money, but they do what they can. From loving, willing hearts go out deeds of kindness and mercy. Their reward is not in the world's adulations; they seek no such reward. Their reward is found in the praises of conscience, in the sweet assurance that Christ, whose great heart went out in such paths of mercy, will at some time own and bless.

In our church are to be found some such souls and they deserve something more than a passing notice. Among some of the associations where these true workers for Christ and humanity are to be found exerting a blessed influence, is the Young Ladies' Missionary Society, which was organized October 4, 1882. They are few in number and are probably not known or recognized as very important factors in our church work, and probably they are not. But they are doing what they can, and that was the high praise which the Master gave while here on earth to another worker.

This association has met together twenty-seven, times since its organization; the average attendance has been eleven. They only make garments, so did Dorcas; but when that woman died, she was worthy of a mention in the sacred record, which has sent her name down the ages; and when she lay prepared for her burial, the widows for whom she made garments, with tears, showed the coats which she had made.

Silently and patiently this little association has been doing its work. Until January 24th last, the finished garments were taken to the house of one of the ladies and distributed among the poor of our church. But now, with strengthened hands and purpose, these young ladies essay to enlarge the bounds of the field of their labors; so, after providing in a measure, at least, for the wants of our own poor, they began work for the "Home of the Friendless" in New York. Nor content with this enlargement they propose now to work for Dr. Snowden's family, and have actually undertaken to clothe the three youngest children of that devoted missionary.

Listen to what this association has done

since its organization, October 4, 1882. Eighty garments have been finished, nearly one-half of which has been donated to the poor of our church. They are not disposed to intermit their labors, but are going on now to finish more garments. All this has been accomplished with only thirty-seven members.

But something else remains to be said about this young missionary society. They look after their own hearts and minds as well as caring for the material good of others.

At their meetings they discuss important subjects, have vocal and instrumental music and repeat quotations from the Bible and good authors. Neither do they forget their duty to the great head of the church, for prayer is always made as a preparation for their exercises. Finances do not form a strong part of their association but their treasury is in a healthy situation; they have a small balance to its credit.

This charming state of affairs ought not to be disturbed by naming names. The RECORD would like to speak out and tell who are the master spirits in the society, but it forbears. This, however, must be said, that while perhaps it would be invidious to point out one name more deserving of praise than others, still it is quite true that to one young lady more than any one else, very much is due for the success of the Young Ladies' Missionary Society of the First Presbyterian Church. The RECORD says God speed to the Association.

WHAT'S IN A NAME.

Some authors who have given great attention to the subject, insist that every patronymic had its origin in an attempt at the descriptive. That is to say, that every family name originated in some peculiarity of the person to whom it was first given. Every Bible name is of this character, except, perhaps, that the characteristics intended to be described, relate rather to external circumstances surrounding the individual named, than to the intrinsic attributes of the one bearing the name. Thus, all names into which enter the syllables, *ja*, *je*, *ah*, *el*, denote some connection with Deity. The Jews were very apt to give to their children some name, into which entered some part of the name Jehovah—the sacred word, by which in their holiest service, they denoted God.

Our German ancestors, with a grim humor, when naming their serfs, descended far below the standard adopted by the pious Hebrews in naming their sons and daughters. The patronymics, used by the people of the Teutonic race, denote other characteristics than are to be found connected with Divinity. Such names as Wolf, Fox, Bear, Lion, Cow, Sheep, Pumpkin Head, are to be found in the names of German families.

The Bible society is to meet at the First Presbyterian Church in Morristown, in this month of June, and an address is promised from the Rev. Dr. Schaf. Dr. Schaf is a representative of German thought and learning, one of the ablest men of the century and one of the most cultivated. His name *Schaf* is the German for *Sheep*.

In this issue of the RECORD is a sketch of the life of Judge Whitehead.

One legend, as to the manner in which the family name he bears originated, is this.

In the 12th century, Henry 2d of England attempted the conquest of Ireland, in which attempt he was partially successful. He found the people of the Island divided into septs or clans; each member of the clan bearing the same patronymic. Between these clans there existed strong animosities which led to constant civil war. The English were desirous of breaking up the terrible custom of war between the tribes, and adopted various means to accomplish their end.

One of their plans was the baptism of wild Irishmen, as they were captured, with a new name, different from the one by which they were known. These names, as may well be imagined, were generally descriptive. In the south part of Ireland, where this law mostly obtained, are to be found many of these descriptive names.

So, goes the story, a wild Irishman with a remarkable head of white hair, one day was brought to the font, and was baptized Whitehead. The story may not be accepted by all the members of that respectable family whose names appear so frequently, on the records of the church, and it may not be true, but it illustrates, very forcibly, how family names may arise.

HON. IRA CONDICT WHITEHEAD.

Judge Whitehead was directly connected with the interests of the church for nearly the whole of his life time. He was baptized in early childhood and thus according to the opinions of the great body of Presbyterians of that day, became entitled, on his arrival at maturer years, to the privileges of church ordinances. From his infancy to his death he was a constant attendant at the meetings on Sabbath and other days, and when, at a later time, wisdom and experience were added to his natural and other acquired qualities of mind and heart, he became trustee and ruling elder. His interest in the church was so great, his affection for its ordinances so manifest, and the part which he took in promoting its highest advantage, so prominent that it seems eminently proper that some sketch should be given of his life and character in the pages of the RECORD.

He was born in Morristown, April 8, 1798, and was descended by both parents from old Morris county families. One of the names he bore denoted his maternal ancestry. He came from the same stock which has given to New Jersey such men as Silas Condict of Revolutionary fame ; Lewis Condict who was a representative in Congress for so many years from Morris county ; John Condict of Essex county, who represented his part of the State also in the national Councils for so long a time, and which has given to the church such exemplary men of God as Ira Condict, D.D., for whom Judge Whitehead was named, and Jonathan B. Condict, D.D., who died after many years service, a professor of Auburn Theological Seminary.

His father's family were numbered, for several generations, among the yeomanry of the country.

From the ranks of this part of the community have ever come the sturdy, honest, intelligent thinkers, the strong men, the patriotic and honest statesmen, who count no sacrifice a loss, when the country demands.

Judge Whitehead's father was Ezekiel Whitehead, a sturdy, independent man, who feared nothing but sin and the anger of his God. His mother was Mary, the second child of Jabez Condict, who was the cousin of Silas Condict, of Revolutionary times. The strong bias of religious element, which entered into the life and character of Judge Whitehead, was found in his ancestry.

Philip Condict, his maternal great-grandfather, was a ruling elder in the First Presbyterian Church, and his grand-father, Jabez Condict and his wife, were life long members, ardent in their piety and most exemplary in their Christian devotion.

At the time of his birth his father's family lived upon the farm, at present owned and occupied by Mr. F. B. Betts, near Morristown.

Ezekiel Whitehead had five children, of whom Judge Whitehead was the third. The second, a son, Sylvester R., still surviving at the ripe old age of 88, lives at the homestead at Washington Valley, occupied by his father for so many years prior to his death.

Judge Whitehead when a youth manifested a taste for letters, and was destined by his parents to a professional life. He was prepared for college at the old academy, then standing where the present Library is erected. Mr. James Johnson, a name well known in the educational annals of Morristown as an able and most successful teacher, was his instructor and prepared him for college. He entered Princeton College November 9, 1814, in his seventeenth year, being admitted to the Junior Class. Very soon after entering college, Nov. 29, 1814, he became a member of the Nassau Bible Society. His connection with this society continued so long as he was a student in college.

During his collegiate course, in the winter of 1814-15, a powerful revival occurred among the students. It is not known whether Judge Whitehead received any religious impressions at this revival; but, it cannot be doubted that a young man with his strong bias towards religion and with the recollections of his home teachings, must have felt the influences of the hour. While at Princeton, Judge Whitehead, to use the words of one of his classmates, who afterwards became President of the college, was an irreproachable student. He graduated in 1816, having maintained during the first year of his course, a standing in scholarship at about the middle of his class, and rising somewhat above this in his second year. At the commencement exercises he took part in a debate, arguing the negative of the question, "Is it desirable that the patriots of South America should succeed in their present struggle for liberty and independence?" Of course, it will be understood that he was a debater in these exercises, and that he did not express the true sentiments of his mind when he argued the negative of the question. The wording of the resolution submitted for debate was of such a character as to leave but little chance for the debaters who opposed.

At that time the accommodations at the college, in the way of dormitories, was rather limited, and he roomed with two other students, the Rev. R. K. Rodgers, so long secretary of the Synod of New Jersey and pastor of a Presbyterian church at Bound Brook, and the Rev. Mr. Lowe.

His classmates numbered several students who afterward became distinguished as statesmen, jurists and divines. Among them were found the following: James McDowell, Governor of Virginia; Cornelius Ludlow, LL. D., Chester Butler, U. S. Senator; James S. Nevius, Associate Justice of the Supreme Court of New Jersey; John MacLean, D.D., President of Princeton College; Rev. William Jessup Armstrong, D.D., Charles Pettit McIlvaine, Bishop of Ohio and President of Kenyon College.

After graduation he taught school for about two years, one of them in the old Academy at Morristown, and then entered the office at Newark, of Joseph C. Hornblower, afterwards Chief Justice of the Supreme Court of New Jersey, as a student-at-law. At that time, his uncle, Silas Whitehead, was Clerk of the County of Essex, and Judge Whitehead employed his leisure hours in his uncle's office, so as to enable himself to pay his own way and not continue to be a burden on his father.

He was licensed as an Attorney by the Supreme Court of his native State about the year 1821 and immediately began the practice of his profession, opening an office at Schooley's Mountain, in the building known as the Heath House. He remained here for a short time only, perhaps for two or three years, when, at the request of

George K. Drake, afterwards associate Justice of the Supreme Court of New Jersey, he removed to Morristown and became a partner with Judge Drake. From this time he remained in this city until his death, in the full practice of his profession, except when engaged in the performance of his duties as an Associate Justice of the Supreme Court.

April 6, 1829, Judge Whitehead married Sarah Louisa Johnson, eldest child of Silas Johnson, of this city. One child, a daughter, was born to them. She lived to grow up but died early in womanhood. Being an only child she naturally became the object of the fondest, tenderest affections of her parents. She early became the subject of religious impressions and to the great joy of her friends and especially of her pious parents, she united with the church in early life. She gave promise of great usefulness in the church and in the community where she lived. Death came early and destroyed this promise. It can well be imagined how the loving heart of her father was wrung by this affliction. He went sorrowing for his daughter to the grave, but in all his sorrow he found true consolation in the solace of religion. The funeral sermon of this daughter, to whom had been given the name of Mary, from her grand-mother, the wife of Jabez Condict, was preached by the Rev. David Irving, D.D., who was then the pastor of the church, and between whom and Judge Whitehead and his family there always existed the truest affection. That sermon was preached January 30, 1858, and was subsequently printed. It was the heartfelt tribute of the pastor and of the friend to the virtue and the loveliness of the dead, and was evidently the work of one who deeply felt the loss of so young and so bright a spirit.

The text was this; "*She hath given up the ghost; her sun hath gone down while it was yet day.*" None but those who have gone through the like sorrow can appreciate the great affliction which the loss gave to the father. He never recovered fully from the blow.

On Nov. 3, 1841, Judge Whitehead was appointed an Associate Justice of the Supreme Court of New Jersey by the Governor of the State.

The County of Hudson had recently been

created and Judge Whitehead held his first circuit in the new county. There was no Court House then erected in Hudson and the courts were held at some public place in Jersey City. He held this position but for one term ; as the Governor who came into office, at the time his term expired, was of different politics, and he retired to private life. He practised his profession for a short time after this, but finally accepted, at the urgent request of the bar of Morris County, the position of Judge of the Court of Common Pleas, which position he held for one term. He then, practically, retired from public life, giving his attention, however, occasionally, to the charge of important estates. He was the leading and active executor of the late William Gbbons, whose large estate in his hands received a fostering care which enabled him to hand it over to the heirs, at their majority, largely increased in value.

Judge Whitehead, very early, manifested a deep interest in the affairs of the church. He would not have been true to himself nor to his ancestry,if he had not done so. In 1832, he was parish clerk ; in 1838 and 1839 he served as trustee. In 1841, at a time when the most careful and delicate conduct of the affairs of the church was needed : when prudence and wisdom were most especially necessary, he, with Lewis Condict, William Sayre, Jr., Abraham Tappen and John F. Voorhees, acted as agents for the parish and took the place of the trustees, who had resigned. This was at a period of the great excitement in the church, which resulted in its division and the withdrawal of the congregation now organized as the South Street Presbyterian Church. None but those familiar with the state of affairs as they then existed in the church, can fully appreciate the very great care and prudence which was necessary. The excitement was intense ; families were divided and a feeling existed which if fostered or not controlled and checked, would have led to the most disastrous results. Judge Whitehead was ardently attached to the old church, all his sympathies were with her in the contest. His strong nature was enlisted ; but, notwithstanding all this, he showed a prudence and exhibited a wisdom which guided the storm and brought about the peace which

has since continued and led, eventually, to the union and Christian feeling which now bind the two churches. In this he was aided by the gentlemen who were his fellows in the Board of Trustees, at that most trying time in the history of the church. During this period he was also parish clerk.

While thus aiding the church in its temporal affairs he was mindful of the claims which it had upon his higher and better nature. He made a public profession of his faith in Christ, and was received into the full communion of the church August 27, 1829. His brother, Sylvester R., united at the same time. He was the subject of one of the great revivals which occurred while Mr. Barnes was pastor. It cannot be doubted, but that Judge Whitehead would have been led by the instincts of his nature to this step. He was strongly inclined to a religious life and after his union with the church he devoted himself to the exercise of the ruling bias of his heart and convictions. His was no grudging service. He gave his whole life to the Master. That service was large hearted and sincere. His was not a nature to hold back when once he had set out in the path of duty.' He was earnest, sincere, generous, " instant in season and out of season." Never obtrusive, but always ardent in his piety, he never failed on proper occasions to give his testimony to the truth. But his exemplary life was the highest evidence of his faith. He preached Jesus by his daily walk and conversation.

May 3, 1846, he became a ruling elder, which office he held until his death, which occurred Aug. 27, 1867, when he was in his seventieth year.

For some time before his death Judge Whitehead had expected that event. He had received unmistakable warning. But he was undismayed at its near approach. He had much around him to bind him to life. The wife of his youth, whose gentle affection had gone with him, through the many years of their married life, still lived to bless and cheer. He was an honored and respected man ; the whole community, in which he lived, delighted to honor and bless him. Troops of strongly attached friends and relatives gathered about him. He had acquired independent competence, and was, therefore, not subject to the carking care of poverty, nor obliged to labor for the support of himself and his family. But, he knew in whom he trusted, and setting his face steadily heavenward, with an undying trust in the Rock of his salvation, he, calmly and patiently, awaited the end. It came at last and the honored man, the devout Christian, sank to his rest. His memory still lingers with us, and can not be lost for many generations. The good he did can never die, the wisdom he gave to the councils of the church guarded her safely though perils, the material aid afforded by him, manifested the true generosity of his nature.

In person Judge Whitehead was striking, being fully six feet in height, robust and commanding. He possessed a kindly, attractive manner, which always brought young persons lovingly to his presence. He was firm and decided in his utterances ; his convictions were strong and he never failed to speak the true sentiments of his mind and heart. Perhaps if he failed anywhere, it was in the abrupt and positive manner in which he declared his opinions. But those opinions very rarely failed in being correct

As a lawyer he was untiring in his devotion to the interests of his client ; as a counsellor he was correct, careful and wise; as a Judge he was most industrious, patient and considerate ; as a man of business he was of spotless integrity; as a husband and father he was loving, kind and affectionate; as a Christian he was humble, consistent and exemplary, and in all the relations of life he never failed in the discharge of duty. Of him it could well be said, " An honest man is the noblest work of God."

THE TEMPERANCE SPUR.

The temperance people of Boonton have done a good work, At their last municipal election they elected town officers pledged to give no license to saloons. This result is especially noticeable at this present moment, as in Boonton is to be found a large population of working people, who are, generally, supposed to favor the license system. But there seems to have been an influence at work in Boonton which was potent in obtaining so desirable a result.

This little paper, whose name heads this article, is published at Boonton, and gives an idea of what this potent influence was.

The good women of our neighbor city, evidently, took part in the contest and on the right side.

This sprightly paper is edited, so says its title page, by four young ladies. It is bright, sparkling with gems of thought, beautifully illustrated and altogether most creditable to its editors and friends. Its title page is an exquisite picture. We suspect the artist, whose genius produced the work, does not live many miles from Boonton. The decided teachings of the *Spur* are excellent, its testimony is all in favor of the right and it must wield a power in the community for good order, temperance and religion.

Success to the young ladies who are doing this good work.

SUNDAY SCHOOL ANNIVERSARY.

The 67th anniversary of the Sunday school was observed in the church, Sunday afternoon, May 27th. An address was made by Mr. S. W. Clark, the Secretary of the New Jersey Sunday School Association. The school occupied the body of the church and made a most creditable appearance. Judge W. E. Church, recently appointed Associate Justice of the territory of Dakota, was present and also addressed the audience.

The annual report was presented and read by Mr. W. D. Johnson, the superintendent of the school. Mr. Mahlon Pitney presented several of the pupils with Bibles for proficiency in the catechism, and for regular attendance upon school during the year.

The report gave some interesting particulars. It has been placed at the disposal of the RECORD and the permission kindly given by Mr. Johnson to take extracts from it, is accepted with thanks.

Number of officers,   9
    "   teachers,   47
    "   scholars in primary department,   90
Number of scholars in main school, 266

Total,   412
New scholars,   49
Scholars withdrawn or moved away,   46

Scholars died during last year, 2
Teachers, " " " " 1
One of the two scholars, who were reported as dying during the past year, was from the primary class and one from the main school. Of the officers seven are church members; all the teachers and one hundred and seven scholars are professors of religion.

Officers present at every service
during the year, 1
Teachers present at every service, 4
Scholars " " 9

These scholars all received a Bible as a reward for this punctual attendance. Six from the school have united with the church during the past year.

Average attendance, 260
Largest attendance, 299
Smallest attendance, 108
Average attendance of officers, 7
" " teachers, 38
" " scholars, 210
Number of volumes in the library
of the main school, 510
Number of books in the library of
primary department, 140
Value of library and piano belong-
ing to the school, $800 00

The parish has appropriated $200 for the expense of the school.

The Children's Missionary Society has contributed $590 06. Ten scholars have learned the catechism perfectly, and for this each received a Bible from Mr. Pitney. The report made honorable mention of several classes, whose record of attendance and other meritorious action deserved this particular mention.

It is most desirable that there should be an accurate and careful history of the school prepared and printed. Our good friend, J. D. Stevenson, Esq., former superintendent, and whose interest in the school is still unabated it is said, prepared such a history. Repeated and earnest requests for facts and dates relative to this history have been made in the RECORD. Strange to say these requests have been unanswered, except by one good friend who lives in Michigan. The information he gives would seem to indicate that the school had reached an older age than sixty-seven years. He cannot be definite. Will not some kind friend look up this matter and furnish the RECORD with full dates and facts. Those, who are in possession of such dates and facts are fast leaving us and soon the possibility of obtaining

the desired information will be gone. At a late meeting of the teachers held for the purpose of electing officers, the following were elected :

William D. Johnson, superintendent; Mahlon Pitney, assistant superintendent; P. B. Pierson, secretary and treasurer; O. F. Lozier, Librarian; William Leek, Henry Potts, assistant Librarians; Miss Emma Campbell and Miss Lottie Campbell, superintendents of primary department; Miss Laura Pierson, assistant superintendent of primary department.

TEMPERANCE.

This important subject is still occupying the attention of our community. At the last municipal election in this city, the issue of license or no license was presented to the town and decided in favor of the ticket which represented license. The majority was small, very small, in so large a vote as nine hundred and more. But it was sufficiently large to prove that the sentiment of the voters of Morristown is decidedly favorable to licensing beer saloons. This is a humiliating fact but it must be acknowledged. Let it be stated in all its full-ness. In this city there are opened places of business where nothing is sold except beer and other stimulants. They afford temptation on every hand to the idler, the vicious and the young. They lead the way to drunkenness, vice, the prison and often to the gallows. They are not a necessity ; that cannot be pleaded in their behalf. They are simply nuisances, open and undisguised in their trade of destroying souls and winning lives for sin and wickedness. The result of the last election demonstrates the terrible fact, that a majority of the citizens of Morristown is in favor of licensing these moral pests. It is useless to shut our eyes to this deplorable fact. It cannot be urged that the gentlemen, who were elected upon the license ticket, were elected as members of a political party and are entirely unpledged as to their future action on the subject. The question of politics did not enter into the contest. One of the great political parties did not present a ticket. The question was placed squarely before the citizens and it was well understood by every voter when he deposited his ballot, that he was expressing his views on this important subject.

How shall this terrible blot on the character of the voters of Morristown be removed? The answer is evident: The only way is for the friends of temperance to be earnest, faithful and diligent. The time is coming when public sentiment on this subject will be purified. To do this needs patience and work.

PULPIT ECHOES.

REV. J. LEONARD CORNING.

Charity is a problem of the head as well as of the heart, it is the fruit of intelligent judgment quite as much as affectionate sympathy.

There is not such a demonstration of the blundering moral philosophy of society under the heavens, as is found in the stereotype apparatus by which crime is punished. The highest providential mystery in the world to my mind is the divine permission of human penalty in its present forms.

Jails and gibbets may be allowable as bulwarks of self defense in society, but as indexes of various degrees of culpability they are the most monstrous monuments of human folly. Who but the all-seeing God himself, can trace the broad, deep river which goes under the name of sin through all its thousand tributaries to the far-off source? Uncounted generations in the past send down to the present the almost omnipotent forces which give shape and color to the human soul. The will is the eternal denier of fate and yet there is a divinity, kindred to fate, which sways her scepter over character.

The man who pronounces final judgment upon the merit and demerit of human conduct, with his present light, or rather I may say his present darkness on the subject, is simply a fool. Ten thousand antecedents of personal volition determine the ascendancy of appetite over reason and passion over conscience. Certainly, there is a residual fact in every individual soul, on which accountability rears itself, that most terribly solemn prerogative of human nature. But who hath eyes keen enough to take just measurement of this fact beside all the collateral facts which qualify it! In other words who can trace up the sinuous streams of heritage? Who can measure the force of temptation as it addresses itself from within and from without to each individual soul? Ah! What a labyrinth of undiscovered and at present undiscoverable history have we here! When a man has tracked out its thousand passages then, but never till then, let him sit in final judgment upon the frailties of his brother.

Do you remember the story which Clara Barton tells of that wounded soldier at Antietam whom she lifted up to give him drink, when a shot from the enemy passed through the sleeve of her dress and pierced him in the heart? Oh! have I not seen that horrible tragedy enacted again and again when some soul whom Satan had wounded was taking cheer at the ministering hand of pity and merciless calumny smote it down again into despair and death?

A man thinks he evidences the strength of his moral principle by withdrawing on the other side of the highway from a sin-maimed soul, but he only evidences the weakness of his moral principle. Is he afraid of his character? No he is afraid of his reputation. Does he tremble for his soul's safety? No, he trembles for his respectability. The very interest that is really most secure he is most anxious about. For I want to ask you if you ever knew one to set himself apart to labor for the restoration of the fallen that God did not take care both of character and reputation, both of the soul and respectability.

There is another realm than the asthetic, the realm of love where notes sweeter than angelic warble and tints brighter than vernal greet the eye. When a man is in that realm all the voices of sinful allurement are silent. Passion dare not lift its viper head in the presence of this divine charmer. And so the soul never gets such rapid growth in purity as when to the eye of sense its purity seems most imperilled by surrounding corruption. Love is a sunbeam and is no more defiled when stealing into some dark cavern reeking with filth than when nestling in the petal of a lily.

THE RECORD.

FIRST PRESBYTERIAN CHURCH, MORRISTOWN, N. J.

"This shall be Written for the Generation to Come."—Psalms 102 : 18.

VOLUME III. JULY, 1883. NUMBER 7.

[Printed with the Approval of the Session.]

THE RECORD

Will be published monthly at Morristown, N. J. Terms $1.00 per annum, *in advance.*

Subscriptions may be made at the bookstores of Messrs. Runyon and Emmell, or to Messrs. James R. Voorhees and William D. Johnson, or by letter addressed to the EDITOR OF THE RECORD, Morristown, N. J.

Entered at the Post Office at Morristown, N. J., as second class matter.

THE CHRISTIAN ERA.

The chronology of the Christian Era has never been accurately determined; that is to say, the true date of the birth of Christ has remained unknown. Many attempts have been made to ascertain it. These attempts have been based upon various methods of calculations, some erroneous, many fanciful, all difficult of solution. Until recently these have failed and it is very doubtful whether success can possibly be reached. It, certainly, remains, for further investigations, to learn whether accuracy has been attained. It may be deemed by some as not a subject of the importance commensurate with the pains which have been taken to solve the problem; but to the student of history, who desires entire accuracy, it is desirable to fix a certain date for the beginning of the Christian chronology.

At the birth of the Saviour, each nation, which had attained to any degree of civilization, had its own way of denoting time. The Romans counted their era from the building of the city; the Greeks by the Olympiads; the Egyptians, Assyrians, Chinese, and other races, had adopted their own peculiar eras. These methods obtained for several centuries after the crucifixion.

The mode of computing time from the birth of Christ was not introduced until the sixth century—the real date is said to be 527—and it did not then become universal, not even in Christendom. Its introduction was very gradual, and it was not fully recognized, even by Christian nations, until many centuries after.

So many eras are found adopted by historians, ancient and modern, that the student of history, even with all the light which modern investigation has thrown upon the subject of chronology, is necessarily confused. The want of accurate mathematical and, especially of astronomical, knowledge in ancient times, and the very vague methods so frequently used for computing time, give still more puzzling ideas to the reader. Generations, the lifetimes of monarchs, priests, priestesses, or of prominent men were frequently adopted to denote eras.

Even after the 6th century, when the Christian Era seems, in a measure, to have been received, as a mode of denoting chronology, the old methods still continued to be used.

A curious mode still in use by the Popes, called *Indictions,* was introduced about the 4th century. Its origin is unknown and many fanciful theories are advanced concerning it. The original meaning of the word, "the imposition of a tax," has aided several imaginative writers in displaying these fanciful theories, for which, however, there is no possible foundation. This mode was in use in France as late as the 15th century. Many charters and public deeds are still in existence, bearing the double date of the Indictions and the Christian Era. There is no certain way of learning why this peculiar mode of denoting time was originally used and it seems useless to speculate about it. It was first used by ecclesiastical writers in the time of Athanasius, who flourished in the 4th century. Why his name is associated with this first use is unknown. It was not employed exclusively by ecclesiastical authors, but was used by them in preference to other modes.

There is a difference of opinion as to the date from which it is reckoned; some holding that it was September 1st, 312, others, September 15th, 312.

The Popes date their Indictions from different times than those ordinarily received, but their use seems simply arbitrary, and not to be based upon any other foundation than the will of the Pope, who first ordered it. They reckon from January 1, 313. This is now the only one in vogue and is called the *Papal Indiction.* Each Indiction is a period or cycle of fifteen years. A rule is adopted by which a calculation can be made showing the exact cycle in which any given year of the Christian Era will fall.

It will be readily perceived that if there be any doubt as to the date of Christ's birth, as now denoted by the current chronology, the systems of computing time, which depend upon the ordinarily received year of that event, are also in doubt. For instance, the era adopted in fixing the date of the building of Rome, is said to be 752 or 753 B. C. But if the usual date employed to denote the birth of Christ, be incorrect, then there is uncertainty as to the time of the building of Rome. The chronology adopted by Christian nations is generally received and made the basis of most other chronologies. It is, therefore, important that the Christian Era should be entirely correct; that can only be so made by fixing precisely the true time of what is chronologically called the year one, A. D. It is doubtful whether this can be accurately accomplished, but it is worth the trial.

For a long time scholars have determined that a mistake has crept in the Christian Era; that the date of the birth of Christ has been erroneously postponed for four years; that is, that the present year should be 1887 and not 1883, By what method this supposed inaccuracy has been ascertained cannot now be stated.

German students, with their usual pertinacity, have devoted much time and patient labor to this subject. The result of the investigation of one of them is summed up in the following extract which appeared in the *Newark Evening Journal,* a political newspaper; which, however, devotes a large portion of one of its pages to excellent literary extracts, evincing a discriminating taste not often displayed by daily papers, whose declared utterances are generally and avowedly purely political. The extract is given for what it is worth and must be received by the readers of the RECORD, unindorsed in its statements as to dates and as to its conclusions.

The 25th of December is given as to the exact date of the birth of our Lord. This is by no means certain and is not received without very strong objections. December, it is claimed, was the month of the year, during which occurred the worst part of the rainy season, and that on the 25th of that month was the height of that season, and consequently shepherds would not be watching their flocks in the open air. Perhaps, however, the learned German scholar, the result of whose studies is given in this article, may have fully considered this objection, and disposed of it, at least, satisfactorily to himself. It does not appear in the quoted article that he has done so.

THE CHRISTIAN ERA.

Professor Sattler, of Munich, claims the distinction of having solved the problem as to the year in which Christ was born, and of having demonstrated the fact that the current year is probably 1888 instead of 1883. He bases his proofs mainly on the three coins which were struck in the reign of Herod Antipas, son of Herod the Great, and which date, consequently, from the first half of the first century of the current era. Madden admits the genuineness of these coins, and other numismatic writers do the same. The evidence they offer is said to coincide with the narrative of the gospels and with astronomical calculations. The following are the results at which Professor Sattler has arrived: Jesus was born on the 25th of December, 749 years after the founding of Rome, and commenced his public career on the 17th of November, 780 years after the founding of Rome. He was then thirty years, ten months and twenty-two days old. The date on which he commenced his career fell in the fifteenth year of the Emperor Tiberius, and in the forty-sixth year after the building of Herod's Temple. This is in accordance with St. Luke, iii., 1, and St. John, ii., 20. Jesus died on the 7th of April, 783 of the Roman era, that is to say, on the Friday before the Passover ; for it has been ascertained by exact calculation that Passover fell that year on the 7th of April, 783 ; and as the latter year was a Jewish leap year, and consisted, accordingly, of thirteen months, his public career lasted two years and seven months. According to Professor Sattler, the Christian reckoning is at fault by five years, and we are now, therefore, in 1888 and not in 1883.

DOES IT PAY?

At this moment's writing, a young mother lies dead, in a neighboring city, shot to her death by her husband. The woman was only twenty years old, comely, of pleasant manners, the light of her mother's eye, her father's joy and the mother of two children. Rum nerved the hand of the murderer and inspired the thought which contemplated the deed.

The rum was bought at a licensed saloon. For the license the city received a pittance. Strike the balance and learn what this murder will cost the government. Police officers, police magistrates, judges, prosecutors, sheriffs, constables and jurors must all be employed in trial and punishment. Police office, jail and court room must be provided in which to secure and try the felon.

When comes the dread day of punishment the hangman must be paid, the witnesses of the hanging and the coroner and coroner's jury must be compensated.

The cost of all this cannot well be calculated, but an approximate amount might be ascertained. It will not be less than several thousand dollars. To offset this the city has received fifteen or perhaps twenty dollars from the saloon where was sold the rum.

But is this all? A home desolate, two children are made orphans, a young life is destroyed ; another must be taken ; hope for the murderer is dead ; a mother and father go mourning all their days ; two children are disgraced for life. But why pursue the sad theme? DOES IT PAY?

JAMES RICHARDS, D. D.

The Rev. Mr. Green, from whom it would be very pleasant to hear oftener, sent a letter to the RECORD, which ought to have appeared in the last number, but was postponed, for lack of room. The communication cannot lose interest by lapse of time. It needs no explanation, as it speaks for itself. Mr. Green's letters will always be welcome, and, it is to be hoped, that he will write whenever he finds anything in the RECORD to correct or criticise.

BUFFALO, N. Y., May, 1883.
Editor of THE RECORD, *Morristown, N. J.:*
My Dear Sir :

The receipt to-day, of the May RECORD reminds me that I must not delay writing you regarding the article in the April No. on the Rev. James Richards, D.D. The article says, (see page 28, 2d column), "There seems to be some difficulty in establishing some dates relative to events in the life of Mr. Richards happening at this period. Mr. Gridley, in his biography, says that he was invited in May, 1794, to visit Morristown. Louis Richards, Esq., whose notes relative to the Richards family, are very full, states that he was called to the pastoral charge of the church in Morristown, in June, 1794. Both of these gentlemen agree that he was not installed until May, 1797. The RECORD Vol. I, No. 1, gives the date of his settlement as May 1, 1795. Mr. Barnes, in his church manual, published in 1818, says he was installed as pastor May 1, 1795, by the Presbytery of New York."

I have a much greater interest in the above paragraph than the mere verification of my own accuracy in the date quoted from Vol. I, of the RECORD. The history is important and the dates should be accurate. Permit me therefore to call your attention to a *third* pastor of the church, who has a word to say on this subject. I had the pleasure of printing in the RECORD two invaluable historical sermons by Rev. David Irving, D.D., now of the Board of Foreign Missions. I quote from him, " He (Dr. Richards) not only preached to the people with great satisfaction but also to the aged pastor in his own dwelling that he might judge of his fitness, and to both with such acceptance, that on the 21st of July, 1794, a call was made and put into his hands the same day ; in which he was to receive $440 salary in quarterly payments, the use of the parsonage and firewood. This was in due time accepted by him, and on the first of May, 1795,* he was ordained and installed pastor of the church by the Presbytery of New York. Dr. McWhorter of Newark, preached the ordination sermon from Acts 20 : 24. Dr. Rogers of New York, presided; Mr. Austin of Elizabeth, gave the charge to the people."

My remembrance is that the above account of the installation will be found either in the Sessional or Trustees' Record, or both. The same account is given in my history of Morristown in "the History of Morris County," published in 1882 by W.W. Munsell & Co., of New York—I should dislike to think without sufficient reason. Please examine the records.

Of one thing there is no doubt. There lies before me as I write a worn and yellow paper—the call of the First Presbyterian Church of Morristown to Rev. James Richards for his pastoral service.

It is dated July 21st, 1794.

It is signed by

Isaac Pruden,   Gilbert Allen,   )
Samuel Freeman, Jonas Phillips, } *Elders.*
Matthias Crane, Joseph Lindsly,)

Silas Condict,   John Mills,   )
Benj. Lindsly,   Rich'd Johnson, } *Trustees.*
Jona. Ford,   Jona'n Ogden,   )

The following is appended to the call :

" At a parish meeting of the first presbyterian Church and Congregation in Morris Town on Monday the 21st Day of July, A.D. 1794.

Resolved, That a call be preferred to Mr. James Richards to be the pastor of this congregation. One hundred and forty-two votes being taken for giving the call, and two votes for his being invited to preach a further time on trial.

---

*The two following facts are of interest in connection with this date : George O'Hara advertised that his stage would commence running from Morristown to Powles Hook, (Jersey City,) on first Monday of April, 1795, twice a week for 9 shillings, and one penny a pound for all baggage above 7 lbs., way passengers 4d. a mile. Morristown postoffice was the only one in the county in 1795. In it letters were advertised for persons at Bedminster, Mendham, Baskingridge, Bottle Hill, (Madison), New Market, Flanders, Hanover, Bound Brook, Franklin, Mt. Hope, Pompton, Ramapaugh. Record Vol. 2, p. 140.

Resolved, That the Elders and Trustees be a committee to sign the call in behalf of the Congregation to be given to Mr. Richards.

Extract from the minutes.
                    GILBERT ALLEN, Modt'r.
Mahlon Dickerson, Clerk."

I will simply add, THE RECORD, Vol. II. p. 149, indicates that Mr. Richards began the active duties of the pastorate as early as February, 1795. Can you imagine any reason for a delay of over two years in his installation ?
                    Cordially yours,
                        RUFUS S. GREEN.

REV, ALBERT BARNES.

It was fully expected that a sketch of the life of the Rev. Albert Barnes, the sixth pastor of our church, would have been prepared for this number of the RECORD. But, when the attempt to gather the materials necessary for the article was made, it was almost impossible to collect such facts, without which, even the barest sketch would be almost an insult to the readers of the RECORD ; certainly a pain to those venerable members of the church and congregation whose memories carry them back to his time.

Albert Barnes occupied too large a space in the Presbyterian church ; he was too prominent in his time, in the field of letters, especially, of biblical research ; and altogether too grand a man to permit even the briefest notice of his life to be made without the presentation of such incidents as would give present readers, who can only know him by report, some idea of him and his character. Few, very few of the congregation have personal recollections of him.

He was installed February 8, 1825, and was dismissed June 8, 1830. After his dismissal he played a prominent part in the history of the troubles of the church, and was even at one time tried for heresy before the Presbytery to which he was attached.

Nearly two generations have passed away since Mr. Barnes left this church, but there must be some who can give their personal reminiscences of him.

The intention, so long cherished, of preparing a sketch of his life must be postponed until the next issue. In the meantime will not some who must have known Mr. Barnes while he was here in Morristown, furnish the RECORD with such facts, anecdotes, and personal recollections of him as will aid.

Any printed matter, giving particulars about him, scraps from newspapers and other publications, will be valuable. Kind friends in other localities have cheerfully responded to calls made upon them in this direction. But they cannot give what can only come from those who knew Mr. Barnes personally.

In this connection, let it be added, that facts generally, about any of the former pastors of the church and prominent men of the congregation, will be most acceptable.

The following article taken from "*The Church Union*" of April 1, 1876, relating to a most interesting event in Mr. Barnes's life, will furnish some idea of the kind of printed matter needed. There must be persons in the congregation who have many such, in their possession, in which are to be found valuable notices. If placed in the possession of the RECORD, they can be used for occasions such as the present, and will be returned to the owner.

CONVERSION OF ALBERT BARNES.

BY PROFESSOR MEARS, OF HAMILTON COLLEGE.

While at Fairfield Academy, Mr. Barnes had been decidedly sceptical in his views; but before he left that institution he was roused from his unbelief by reading the article, "Christianity," by Dr. Chalmers, in the Edinburgh *Encyclopædia*. He was satisfied with the drift of the argument; he gave up his speculative scepticism, but had no intention of going a step further. He came to Hamilton College "resolved to be an honest, upright, moral, industrious man and to leave religion out of the question." His plans were laid for the study of law.

Thus matters stood until February of the following year, when occurred the first general revival the college (or the neighborhood since 1800) had enjoyed. My chief informant as to its character and influence is the Rev. H. H. Kellogg, of Guthrie, Iowa, whose class, two years behind that of Mr. Barnes, included such names as those of Judge Bacon, of Utica, and Secretary Woolworth, of Albany. He says:

" The revival of religion exerted a powerful influence upon every class in college, and upon the community by which we were surrounded. * * Several of our students had spent the previous vacation in places blessed with the visitation of the Divine Spirit, and returned to College with hearts glowing with love to Christ, and to the souls of their impenitent associates. * * The work commenced in college."

The narrator himself was, as he trusts, " the first of those who found Jesus, or rather who was found of Him."

The circumstances of his conversion are so closely connected with that of Mr. Barnes, that they belong properly to this narrative. He says:

" Mr. Barnes was my senior by two years in college grade, and much more than that in age, yet it was my privilege to enjoy a more than usual intimacy with him. During the second term of the year, about the middle of February, I went into his room to pass away a dull hour. Our tutor, the Rev. Salmon Strong, of blessed memory, (who died in Harrisburgh, Pa., July 14th, 1872,) had preached a sermon that morning of unusual earnestness—his heart warmed with love to our souls—from Matt. v. 25, 26, "Agree with thine adversary quickly." The sermon, however, had passed through my mind leaving no impresssion on my careless heart. Not so with Mr. Barnes. Soon after I was seated, he said to me—" Kellogg, what do you think of that idea of Strong's to-day?" " What idea?" said I. " This: that sinners in hell will continue to sin, and thus, in place of paying their debt, will increase it, and consequently can never come out of their prison." " I suppose it is true," I replied. To which he rejoined: " I do not believe a word of it. I know if I was in such a place as they represent hell to be, I would stop sinning.' "

In two weeks the prayers and pious counsels of classmates and friends were rewarded by Kellogg's conversion, thus unwittingly promoted by Barnes. Nor did the impression made upon the latter vanish away. According to Mr. Kellogg, the conflict was long and severe. For many weeks he struggled with his growing convictions,

His reservedness and his known skeptical tendencies, together with his admitted ability, prevented that near approach and those earnest christian efforts, on the part of pious students, which might have been blessed in his case, as they were in that of others, to an earlier conversion. Mr. Barnes himself mentioned, in the interview already referred to, that one of his classmates felt a deep interest in his condition. "Subsequently," says Mr. Barnes, "he told me he felt it his duty to talk to me on the subject as he did. He performed his duty. He produced no impression on my mind."

Mr. Kellogg says :—"His was a struggle in respect to his plans of life. He expected to enter upon the study of law. His place as a student, and as he fondly hoped, as a practitioner, was already engaged in Utica, in the office of his friend, Hiram Denio, late Judge of the Court of Appeals, N. Y. If he became a christian he must forsake all for Christ. He must sacrifice that more brilliant career which he and his friends had anticipated. The gains, the honors, the friendships of life would all, as he viewed it, be sacrificed by his choice of the christian life."

Mr. Barnes traces his conversion at last to the influence of another classmate. " It so happened that my friend Avery became converted, and in a few words stated his own feelings to me. It was the means, I trust, of my conversion, if I was ever converted to Christianity."

Charles Avery, LL. D., afterwards, 1834 —1869, Professor of Chemistry in Hamilton College, says he met Mr. Barnes on the hillside, and addressed him with the question, " What do you think is the cause of the great work which is now going on in College ?" and then left him to his own reflections. This brief interview he regards as the means of bringing his classmate to a decision. It would imply that skeptical difficulties were still in the way of Mr. Barnes' conversion.

Mr. Kellogg says:—"After his conversion, Mr. Barnes' stay in college was short. It was only on the last and short term of his senior year, that his avowal of discipleship was made. His life was consistent, but no special forwardness or activity distinguished it. He appeared like a babe in Christ, a lamb of the flock."—*Presbyterian.*

SUGGESTIONS.

That members of the congregation aid the RECORD in preserving history, by sending to the editor, old newspapers, magazines, or other printed matter, containing historical notices about the church, its pastors and prominent men ; or about the city or county. One of the main objects in the publication of this paper is the preservation of just such facts. It is hoped that there will be presented in the RECORD such a publication as will induce its subscribers to preserve it in a bound form.

In addition to this printed matter, facts, anecdotes, and incidents from personal recollection, of pastors and others, sketches of whose lives are worth preserving, are very desirable.

Apropos : since the above was written, the following letter was received from Mr. Durant, the pastor.

It is hoped that this letter will have the effect which the appeals heretofore made in the RECORD have failed of accomplishing.

Editor of The Record :

My Dear Sir :—How can we get the attention of those who possess items of interest respecting the past history of the First church, of its old members, of the town and its people ? There must be many whose memories could furnish us with material worthy to be preserved in the permanent type of THE RECORD. And there must be many more who have old diaries, old newspapers, old pamphlets, or clippings preserved in scrap-books, from which a large number of forgotten facts might be gathered. Then, too, there must be many old family Bibles which could correct or complete our Registers in the spelling of names, the dates of birth, marriage and death. The value of such material, especially of old newspapers, pamphlets and magazine articles, is strikingly apparent in the recently published volume of McMaster's " History of the People of the United States," the most popular history that has been published since the day of Macaulay, and which owes its popularity and thoroughness very largely to the fact that Mr. MacMaster has gone to just such out of the way sources to gather the news and opinions current in the days he describes.

The plan of making THE RECORD a store-house for material of this sort, collecting and reprinting whatever of value can be found that bears upon the history of the church and town and people of this region; it seems to me is a most admirable plan. For the bound volumes of THE RECORD will thus give permanence, as well as put within handy reference, this valuable material which is now buried in the dust of garrets.

I shall be glad to assist you in becoming responsible for the return of any old books or papers offered for publication; and also in examining and copying from any diaries, files of newspapers, or family Bibles, which the owners are willing to open in their houses, though preferring not to loan them out for the purpose.

How can we get the attention of those who possess this valuable material for history—material that, in all probability, will be lost forever in a few years, unless preserved now in the columns of THE RECORD? Doubtless those who have it are willing to furnish it. But how shall we know who have it, unless the readers of THE RECORD *take pains* to inform us.

Very truly yours,
WILLIAM DURANT.

THE OLD COURT HOUSE AND JAIL.

At the beginning of this century there stood on " *the Green*," opposite what is now the United States Hotel, a quaint, old and somewhat dilapidated frame building. It had been painted red, but had grown gray and lost its original color. It was built after no particular order of architecture, and was neither in its appearance, nor when the use to which it was put, was considered, a pleasant sight. It was an incumbrance and a blot on the public square, but the original deed for that part of the Green where it was located, was made with the condition that "if the Court House aforesaid should be removed to any other place, then this indenture and everything therein contained to be void, and title to the aforesaid lot of land to revert" to the grantors of the deed.

It would seem from this that this quaint building, which was used for a Court House and Jail, must have been in existence at the time of this deed; which was dated September 7, 1771.

In 1816, April 1, the trustees of the church conveyed to certain persons, subscribers to the fund, for the consideration of $1,600, that part of the land now used as a public square. The deed effecting this last conveyance, contained a condition, that no building should be erected on this last named lot, except a meeting house, a market house, a Court House and Jail. In 1868, however, means were taken to wipe out this condition and the title to the "Green" is now held free from any such incumbrance.

The object of this reference to the old Court House was not to refer to the history of the green nor its title. Mr. Green, in his admirable notice of Morristown, in the history of Morris County, has entered some what fully into this subject. What is desired is to call the attention of those, who can remember it, to this old structure and to ask some kind friends to give recollections about it for the RECORD.

It had apartments in it for the Jailor, or, as he was called, the Under Sheriff. The Sheriff, of later times, rarely occupied these apartments, as is now done in the present Court House.

What became of the old building? When was it destroyed? What was its history? Who can tell?

———

At the beginning of this century a library was in existence in Morristown. It was in connection with an association called the Morris County Agricultural Society. A collection of about fifteen hundred volumes were gathered; many of which, when the Morristown Library and Lyceum was formed, were transferred to the shelves of that institution. The history of this library as it existed in connection with the Agricultural Society and afterwards under the auspices of the Apprentices library, is given by Rev. R. S. Green in his history of Morristown.

———

Hamilton College, at its last commencement, did itself honor in conferring the title of D. D. on the Rev. R. S. Green, our former pastor. We congratulate the college and the Rev. R. S. Green, D.D., and hope we are the first in Morristown to annex the title to the name so deserving the honor.

CLIPPINGS.

I would rather believe all the fables in the Talmud or the Alcoran than to believe that this universal frame is without a mind. —*Lord Bacon.*

A holy life is a voice, it speaks when the tongue is silent, and is either a constant attraction or a perpetual reproof.—*Christian Advocate.*

It was believed that leap year had been caused by Joshua, when he made the sun stand still. A writer of the tenth century notices this as the opinion of some "unlearned priests."—*Wright Biog. Liter.*

Southey says that it was not till about the middle of the eighteenth century that a circulating library was first opened in London. It was set up by Samuel Fancourt, a dissenting minister.

Pamphilius, presbyter of Cæsarea, who flourished A. D. 294, erected a library at Cæsarea, which according to Isidore of Seville, contained 30,000 volumes. This collection seems to have been made merely for the good of the church, and to *lend out* to religiously disposed people. St. Jerome particularly mentions his collecting books for the purpose of *lending them* to be read ; and this is, if I mistake not, the first notice of a circulating library.—*Adam Clarke.*

Chamber's traditions of Edinburgh states that Allan Ramsay in 1725 set up a circulating library at Edinburgh, which was the first "known in Scotland." It was however only "for plays and other works of fiction."

The first Christian library was established by Hilary, Bishop of Rome. He was elected in 461.—*LeClerc.*

A library existed in the Whitby monastery "*about* 1180 A. D." It had eighty-seven volumes, sixty theological and twenty-seven grammatical or classical. In the theological department, most of the authors were of the fourth, fifth, sixth, seventh and eighth centuries. It had scarcely any of the early Greek and Latin fathers, except Origen ; none of Augustine, Jerome or Cyril. In the classical department were found Homer, Plato, Cicero, Juvenal, Persius, Statius and Boethius. Virgil's name does not appear, but he must have had a place in the library as a volume appears in the catalogue, called "The Bucolics."—*White's History of Whitby.*

[It must be remembered that these were manuscripts.—EDITOR.]

The "highest library" at Greenwich contained according to inventory, three hundred and twenty-nine volumes.—*Harleian Mis.*

At the beginning of the seventeenth century there were only three public libraries in Europe ; the Bodleian founded in 1612 ; the Bibliotheque Angelique, at Rome, founded in 1620, and the Bibliotheque Ambroisienne, at Milan, founded in 1608.—*Radel.*

Charles the Bold, Duke of Burgundy, was very fond of reading. He succeeded his father in 1467. It is quite remarkable that a man of such a stormy life and whose great ambition in war seemed to be constantly engaged in war, should have employed himself in so peaceful an occupation as reading. His library was quite extensive. In it were enumerated the Romances of King Arthur and Lancelot of the Lake and the Chronicles of Pisa, translated from the Italian, for the Duke. In 1405, before the reign of Charles the Bold, the work of John Mandeville, the traveller, was found in this library. This was in the lifetime of Philip, the Good, the father of Charles, a different man from his son, a gatherer of books, and who had collected some of the volumes in his library for the education of his son.—*Various.*

"I will and bequeth to the abbot and convent of Hales-Oweyn, a book of myn called Catholicon, to theyr own use forever ; and another book of myn wherein is contaigned the Constitutions Provincial and De Gestis Romanorum, and other treatis therein ; which I will be laid and bounded with an yron chain to some convenient parte, within saide church, at my costs, so that all preests and others may se and rede it when it pleaseth them."—*Will of Sir Thomas Lyttleton,* the famous lawyer, who died 1481.

[This will explain two subjects of interest to scholars—the value of books, at the time, and the custom of chaining them in churches. They were generally fastened to the altar and were read at stated times to audiences, by some one appointed for the purpose.—EDITOR.]

THE RECORD.

FIRST PRESBYTERIAN CHURCH, MORRISTOWN, N. J.

" This shall be Written for the Generation to Come."—Psalms 102 : 18.

VOLUME III. | AUGUST, 1883. | NUMBER 8.

[Printed with the Approval of the Session.]

THE RECORD

Will be published monthly at Morristown,
N. J. Terms $1.00 per annum, *in advance.*

Subscriptions may be made at the book-
stores of Messrs. Runyon and Emmell, or to
Messrs. James R. Voorhees and William D.
Johnson, or by letter addressed to the

EDITOR OF THE RECORD,
Morristown, N. J.

Entered at the Post Office at Morristown,
N. J., as second class matter.

DOES IT PAY.

For about twenty years, there has been
no place in Edwards county, in Illinois,
where intoxicating liquors could be obtained as a beverage. There is a satisfactory
condition of things in that county that is
one of the best of temperance sermons.
The taxes are 33 per cent. less than in any
other county in Illinois. The length of the
sessions of its court is from two to three
days. The justices of the peace are called
but little from their ordinary pursuits.
From one to two persons in five or six years
are imprisoned in the county jail. It has
sent one man to State's prison for killing
his wife while drunk on whisky obtained in
a neighboring county. Its expenses in providing for paupers are $500 per year, while
the county next to it, where licenses are issued, though only half as large, annually
pays for the same purpose $6,000. In
May, 1879, but two mortgages were on record in the county. A very large per cent.
of the inhabitants are religious. Such ex-
emptions in the midst of a people weighted
down with alcoholic burdens ought to have
the effect to open their eyes, and to cause
the universal banishment of the bottles and

barrels and beer kegs, under which they are
now staggering.

Will some one, who believes in licensing
saloon and grop shop, calculate the taxes
paid by the citizens of Morris county for the
various expenses of providing for county
poor house, police offices, Court House and
Jail ; paying for the fees and salaries of the
several officers of the law, where their expenses are the legitimate consequence of the
sale of rum by licensed saloon and groggery?
When the appalling result is reached, by an
honest inquiry, then continue the calculation, in all the ramifications of the subject
and record the misery and woe to wives and
children, to families and the community by
the traffic, licensed by those who were put
into office by the good tax paying citizens.

A series of meetings has been recently
held at Ocean Grove in this State, under the
auspices of a Temperance Association.
At one of these meetings Neal Dow, that
veteran in the Temperance movement, made
an address, in which he referred to the often
reiterated statement that prohibition in
Maine was a failure. He proved conclusively, however, by figures, that Maine financially, as well as morally and religiously,
was a gainer by the enforcement of the
Maine law.

Space does not permit a repetition of
his arguments and statements ; but they
were full and, convincing. Of course, as
society is now constituted, even in Maine, it
is an impossibility to stop entirely the use
of intoxicants. But, if the experiment of
prohibition be fairly tried with good results
to the taxpayers, the citizens and the family, so much at least, has been gained. Taking, then, the results in Maine and in the
small county of Edwards, Ill, would it not
pay to make trial of the same experiment
elsewhere ?

MORRISTOWN LIBRARIES.

When Mr. Spaulding had charge of the Morristown Academy, a school paper called the *Avalon*, was edited and published by his scholars. A very interesting history appeared in it [Feb.–April, 1879,] of Morristown Libraries, which, by permission of Mr. Oscar Babbitt, its young author, is transferred to the RECORD. The patient examination which Mr. Babbitt gave to his subject resulted in the production of an article which is worthy of reproduction in a form where it may be preserved for future reference.

There is nothing, perhaps, which awakens more vivid reminiscences of the old citizens of this county, than the sight of the present beautiful library whose magnificent building graces our street and the scholars of whose school win laurels at foot ball and the admiration of their friends at their studies.

The oldest man was but a small boy when the first library was organized in Morris County. This was in 1792. On the 21st of September of that year, eleven of the inhabitants of Morris County, met at the house of the venerable Benjamin Freeman, at Morris Town, and "advised and consulted" upon the propriety of organizing a society which should be called, "The Morris County Society for the Promotion of Agriculture and Domestic Manufactures." It was a great step for these ancient gentlemen, but they succeeded nobly.

Captain Pet Layton (a relic of the revolution) was chosen chairman, and Col. Russell, clerk. The constitution presented was rather defective. A committee was appointed to revise it. The meeting then adjourned to meet at Mr. Freeman's house, on September 25th, 1792.

Such was the first meeting of the kind ever held in Morris County, and so far as we know, in New Jersey. These noble patriots, scarce ten years after the great war, were now seated peacefully together advising a plan to help their less favored brethren from the slough of ignorance. These patriots realized the necessity of an education. They understood clearly that our infant republic could not be of "one mind" long, if her citizens remained uneducated. They could not organize schools, and if they did, there would be few who would be able to avail themselves of the advantage, since our forefathers had literally to work for a living. They had their long evenings, and these wise men conceived a plan by which all might obtain the desired knowledge without neglecting their families.

The eventful week rolled round. The committee had been busily engaged in revising the old constitution, informing their neighbors and friends of the great work contemplated, and requesting their attendance. When the hour for meeting came, there were one hundred people present.

Samuel Tuthill, was installed chairman, with Col. Russell again clerk. The constitution was read as revised, and was adopted. From it, we take (Art. VIII.) the following " * * * * upon the application of any member of the society for a book, he shall deliver him one, and at the same time, take a promissory note for the same, to be returned in one (1) month from the time, on paying one shilling for every week over time." On October 7th, 1793, this was amended, and the librarian was only to keep an account of the book taken. Article XI. informs us that the dues were one dollar a year, "to be paid on the first Monday in October, of each year," and that the stock was transferable. Ninety-seven of those present then signed the constitution, and a good portion of these paid several dollars over the assessment for the sake of encouragement. The total receipts were two hundred and twenty-seven dollars.

On October 1st, 1792, the election of officers came off. Samuel Tuthill was elected President. Joseph Lewis, Vice President. Dr. W. Campfield, Secretary. W. Canfield, Librarian and Israel Canfield, Treasurer. Six gentlemen were then elected a committee of correspondence.

It was resolved that the society purchase three books and a stamp for marking all books. "They then adjourned." The next meeting was April 1st 1795, at which the by-laws were read and adopted, and from which we learn that "the librarian was to be at the library to deliver books on all days, Sundays excepted, from six a. m. to nine p. m." and "that he shall collect all dues in specie." The society started with ninety-six volumes. At the end of the year. the treasurer reported $35.47 on hand, and an addition of twenty volumes to the library.

The society thus organized, went along swimmingly, until 1812, when a "Morris Library Association" was started, and the "Association for Promotion of Agriculture and Domestic Manufactures" merged into it.

February 3d, 1812, a party of gentlemen met at Bull's Hotel and agreed to the proper measures, necessary for the organization of a Library, and adjourned until February 24th, on which day G. H. Ford was elected President, and was to be Secretary as well. A seal was ordered to be engraved. At the next meeting April 6th, they elected Jabez Campfield, librarian. The seal was received, and was very unique. They received also a communication from the President of the "Society for the Promotion of Agriculture and Domestic Manufactures," who wished to sell out the old organization. It was duly accepted. The inventory showed 123 names, who were to be placed on the new company's books, together with 396 volumes, and other articles, amounting to $656.55. At this meeting, a code of laws was read and adopted, which was to govern the Library. It allowed a person holding a share, to have a book out not longer than one month, for which, each year, he was to pay fifty cents.

It also recognized strangers and non-possessors of shares, but charged them extravagant prices for allowing them the use of books. No subsequent meeting is recorded until February, 11th, 1815, but all this time the Library was in good running order. This meeting was of little importance. In 1820, an amendment was made to the code of laws that any person, paying one dollar, was entitled to all the privileges of a stockholder. From the report of the librarian for 1820, the first report since its organization, we gather the following. The amount of scrip taken, is $417.00. The first year (1812) 144 books were taken out, at a fee to the librarian of six cents each, and in 1820, 600 were taken out, at two cents each.

In 1823 a number of shares were confiscated by the association and advertised for public sale in the *Palladium of Liberty*. They were all sold, except four. In 1825, the trustees presented Rev. A. Barnes, pastor of the first Presbyterian Church, with one of these (No. 1) shares, " to be used by him so long as he may remain pastor of the said church," and not subjected to yearly annuity. Mr. Barnes accepted the share, and was elected a trustee.

The next library, for public benefit at Morristown, was instituted June 16th, 1848. The books and chattels of the former organization were purchased by the infant association, which started with the brightest prospects imaginable. This library was begun solely for the benefit of the apprentices of Morris County.

There were a great many in Morristown at the time who had none of the literary privileges which may be enjoyed now. This fact caused some of the best men in the town to get together and organize the needed society.

From the constitution, which is a finely written article, by Dr. R. W. Stevenson, we learn that " The capital stock of the Association was limited to fifteen hundred dollars, divided into shares of three dollars each, half of which was in three months subscribed."

This was a wise measure because the apprentice for whom the library was intended received no money for his work ;—what money he did manage to obtain he must either receive as a gift from his guardian or secure in small sums by work done "after hours."

Outsiders—that is, those people who were neither stock holders nor apprentices— could secure books only upon the payment of excessive charges which were not limited but were at the option of the librarian.

The library started with fifteen hundred volumes, ranging with many and frequent gaps, from Mother Goose to the English Encyclopedia, and was considered for the times a very good collection. The library rooms were in the building now used by James Douglas as a drug store.

The association with various vicissitudes lived from 1848 until 1851. This library did without doubt, a great deal of good. The Apprentices' Library, at closing, had some twenty-five hundred volumes including all from the ancient books of the "Society for the promotion of Agriculture and Domestic Manufacture" to the "latest edition of Shakespeare in eight volumes." By common consent the library was closed and literary mechanics were unable to read at reasonable cost for some time.

The Morris Institute succeeded the Apprentices' Library Association. It lived however but a short time. It was founded February 11th, 1854, with G. T. Cobb, Esq. as its president and J. R. Runyon, Esq. its secretary. They rented rooms in "Mr. Marsh's building" which is now called Washington Hall. They purchased or rented all the books of the Apprentices' Library and in addition had a reading room with some of the prominent weekly and monthly periodicals. But the enterprise was not a success, the books were old and the privilege of reading cost so much that but few availed themselves of it. The society dissolved in two years and all the books were stored away in the building on the corner of Court and Washington Streets. Soon after this took fire and about half of the books were destroyed. The rest were stored in a safer place where they remained until they were claimed for the "New Library."

If any of the Associations whose history we have endeavored to give, met with any success it was because there were some who were really interested in the welfare of that institution. When this person died or his zeal abated, then, unless there was some one to take his place at the helm, the society likewise perished. Such seems to be the law of human nature.

About 1860, a number of gentlemen began to be impressed with the need of a library which might support itself and be in no way dependent upon the personal efforts of one or even two gentlemen.

In 1863, the Morris Lyceum took the matter up and called a public meeting at Washington Hall, December 26th, 1865. At this meeting, a committee was chosen consisting of Messrs. J. Whitehead, J. F. Voorhees, W. C. Caskey, W. S. Babbitt, J. T. Crane, E. J. Cooper, G. T. Cobb, A. Mills and Rev. R. N. Merritt. They drew up a charter which they presented at a public meeting, January 6th, 1866. It passed the State legislature in March of the same year.

The present library was really organized in 1872, although, as we have said, the commissioners received the charter, several years prior.

The meeting for organizing the "Morristown Library and Lyceum" was held in the Grand Jury room, May 11th, 1872. At which meeting $3,700 was reported to be unconditionally subscribed while $9,500 more had been conditionally subscribed. The next meeting was held in the same place, May 25th, 1872, at which time, after some discussion, a board of directors was chosen. They immediately met and elected Mr. W. L. King, President, Mr. J. Whitehead, Vice President, Rev. W. G. Sumner, Secretary and Mr. E. F. Randolph, Treasurer. A committee was appointed to "further subscriptions" and another to "procure information as to a site." At the meeting November 30th, 1872, Mr. W. S. Babbitt was elected Secretary, having been the month previous elected a director, owing to the departure from town of Rev. W. G. Sumner. At the same meeting, a communication from a majority of the stock holders of the Morris Academy was received. They expressed a willingness to transfer the deed of the property to the Morristown Library and Lyceum, provided that in the intended building there should be a part set aside for a classical boys' school, and that they should receive stock in the new institution, in proportion to the value of the Morris Academy property. The board accepted this favorable offer and, the property having been appraised, they issued the necessary certificates.

A legacy of five thousand dollars had also been received during the year. This bequest was by Mr. M. Blatchley who had taken a generous interest in the library and now his executors paid over this amount solely for the purchase of books. At the meeting of the board of directors May 28th, 1873, Mr. J. E. Taylor was elected to fill the vacancy caused by the resignation of Mr. Randolph.

The board of directors had secured the majority of the stock of the old Morris Academy. Still there was some out which could only be bought. So, at their request, the old academy property was sold, October 13th, 1873, by G. W. Forsythe, Master in

Chancery. for the sum of six thousand dollars, to the Morristown Library and Lyceum. About this time a very pretty piece of poetry appeared in the *Morris Republican* written by "South Street," we clip one stanza.

" My heart seem'd standing still, Tom, my eyes were dim with tears,
" I thought o' their taking it away, where it's stood for many years;
" They're going to build a library, Tom, open'd to high and low, ,
" In the place of the old school-house of fifty years ago."

How true this appears, for the new library is indeed "open'd to high and low."

The resolutions presented at the meeting January 10th, 1874, were two, the first offering all architects an opportunity to submit plans for a proposed building ; the second " that immediate steps be taken to remove and store in a safe place, the old ' academy bell." The academy building was sold to Mr. Kelly for a small sum who removed it from the grounds. March 28th, 1874, a meeting was held at which it was decided to have the proposed building of stone ; and each architect was requested to change his plan accordingly. May 22nd Mr. G. B. Post was selected as the architect as his plans conformed most closely to the designs of the board. Stone was discovered of fine quality and attractive appearance on the land of the Morris Aqueduct near the Jockey Hollow road. On testing it, it proved. all that could be desired and as there seemed to be an abundance, the board accepted the friendly offer of the Aqueduct Company to give them the stone.

During the year 1875, the building had been entirely enclosed. A large number of governmental documents had been received from Washington and Trenton, as well as a complete file of the " Palladium of Liberty" from the daughters of the publisher, Mr. J. Mann; these have been added to the library.

During 1876 but little was done. Inside, the building had been partitioned off and the gas pipes had been laid, while without the walls had been pointed and the tile had been "set." But during the succeeding year much more was accomplished. The building was nearly completed. The hall was finished except the drapery and the drop curtain. A very brief sketch of this room may not here be amiss. The hall is

nearly square. It has three ways of admittance, by the front door, eight feet wide,. and by doors on either side of the building. The stage is 23x50 feet, with retiring room in the *entresol* beneath it. The gallery is made semicircular, conforming somewhat to the curve of the stage. Four furnaces throw their united heat, when desired, into the hall. There are four private boxes, two on either side of the stage, and they are very finely made. The whole room is fitted up with opera chairs. It has a seating capacity of about one thousand. The acoustical properties of the hall are pronounced perfect.

At this time the library and reading rooms were in a bare and unfinished condition. They had secured for it the books of the " Apprentices' Library." August 14th, 1878 was set apart by the directors for the opening of the Library and Lyceum and it was a splendid success. Almost everyone who had heard of the library came during the day and evening, and were shown over the building by the directors. The ladies of the city had trimmed the library and reading rooms with flowers, and secured a band for the evening. The library and reading rooms open together. The front room neatly covered with a fine double linoleum and furnished with elegant walnut tables and chairs, is used as a reading room. On the tables may be found all the latest periodicals of importance, as well as some German and French monthlies. These may be read by anyone gratuitously. The other room is a very large one and is used for the library. It is fitted up in alcoves with shelves ranged around the room. There are at present, exclusive of Public Documents, some 5207 vols. and constant additions are being made. The charge for the privilege of taking books from the library is very small. That 2245 vols. were taken from the building in six months, is pretty conclusive proof that the people of Morristown really appreciate the efforts of the gentlemen who have devoted so much time and money to the library. In the rear of Library and running the whole width of the building is the Morris Academy, now a very flourishing institution.

On the whole the Library and Lyceum, together with the School, may be said to be a grand success, much grander in fact than any of the directors, at the meeting in '72, ever expected. The library is the culminating point of all previous Morristown libraries.

What man in Benjamin Freeman's house in 1792, would have dared to prophesy such wide results from their feeble efforts? Still we, who may profit by the library have not only to thank and praise those venerable patriots, but also a gentleman of our day to whom we should be more than grateful for the great work he has done for the library. We refer to the President of the Board of Directors:

" I wander'd every where, Tom, till the time for us to part,
" Then I left the dear old place with a sad and heavy heart ;
" I thought of our dead playmates, Tom, and my tears began
    to flow
" As I bade fare-well to the school-house of fifty years ago."

HON. IRA CONDICT WHITEHEAD.

In the sketch of this gentleman's life, given in the last number of the RECORD, reference was mostly made to him, as connected with the church, and but little said about him as a Justice of the Supreme Court. There are some incidents in his life, as a Judge, which space would not permit to be given before.

When Judge Whitehead took his seat on the bench, no more able or brilliant array of Counsel was to be found anywhere than at the Bar of New Jersey. At the Capital of the State were Peter D. Vroom, Garret D. Wall, Wm. Halsted and Henry W. Green, afterwards Chief Justice and Chancellor, whose decisions in both those positions have been quoted by the English Courts with great approbation, and Mercer Beasley, now Chief Justice of the State. At this end of the State were Isaac H. Williamson, Theodore Freelinghuysen, Att'y Gen. and U. S. Senator, Wm. Pennington, for seven years Governor, Oliver S. Halsted, Senr., afterwards Chancellor, and Chancellor Asa Whitehead, Aaron S. Pennington. Henry A. Ford, Jacob W. Miller. Among the younger men were Benjamin Williamson, afterwards Chancellor for many years, Edward W. Whepley, afterwards Chief Justice, Amzi Armstrong, A. C. M. Pennington. In other parts of the State were Alexander Wurts, Abraham Browning, Abraham O. Zabriskie, Chancellor for one term, Wm. L. Dayton,

made Associate Justice of the Supreme Court at the early age of 29, afterwards U. S. Senator and minister to France, Peter Vredenburg, also Associate Justice of the Supreme Court. Joseph C. Hornblower was Chief Justice. These are but representative men.

Judge Whitehead's first experience, as a Judge in a murder trial, was most peculiar. It was an important case, interesting in all its aspects and it created the profoundest sensation in the county of Essex where it was tried.

A house, near the Market street depot, at Newark, had been burned between eight and nine o'clock at night, and two persons, a man and his wife, destroyed by the fire. Suspicion pointed at once to a man named Thomas Marsh, the former owner of the property. He had exchanged it with Gershom Cheddick for a farm near Rahway. Marsh was a shrewd, cunning man, but, this time, had been outwitted by Cheddick in making the exchange. After his arrest, Marsh was indicted. The theory of the State was that Marsh, finding himself cheated, determined that Cheddick should reap no advantage from his fraud, and resolved to burn the house down, before Cheddick could take possession. But Cheddick, fearing that he would not obtain possession of the house in Newark, removed his family thither before he was expected, and was sleeping soundly in the house on the fatal night.

Marsh lived in New York, and when the trial came on, it was necessary that his presence should be proved in Newark and near the house. The evidence of his guilt, entirely circumstantial, was dependent, in a large measure, upon the exact moment of time when the fire broke out. According to the theory of the State, Marsh came out from New York in the train leaving at eight o'clock, went to the house, only a few minutes walk from the depot, fired it and returned to the city in the train leaving Newark at nine o'clock. The evidence was strongly conclusive as to Marsh's guilt, but there was a lingering doubt in the minds of many as to its being sufficient to convict. He was, however, convicted. His counsel were a gentleman and his son ; the father, one of the leading men at the Bar of Essex County, an experienced and able advocate and who afterwards wa raised to the highest judicial position in the State. The son, then just licensed, was a young man of great ability and afterwards became prominent as a politician. The father and Judge Whitehead had been rival candidates for the position of associate Justice, in which contest Judge Whitehead had been successful. During the trial the elder counsel for the prisoner, an impulsive, quick tempered man, had been led away by his zeal for his client, and perhaps by other feelings, to a course of conduct, which no one regretted more than he, and Judge Whitehead was obliged to order him into arrest. It was a most trying ordeal for a Judge, especially under the circumstances. The forbearance, the dignity and Christian bearing of Judge Whitehead were most remarkable. But the most singular part of the whole transaction was this, that before the close of the trial and on the summing up of the testimony to the Jury, the leading counsel for the prisoner showed most unmistakable evidence of aberration of mind. This placed the presiding Judge in the most delicate position. The manner in which, through the whole trial, he had met the difficulties of the case, had elicited universal respect, but here was a new dilemma to meet which there could have been no possible preparation. It was met, however, and in a manner which only increased the admiration of those present.

After the verdict of guilty, Marsh employed Asa Whitehead and Gov. Pennington, and a motion for a new trial was made to Chief Justice Hornblower, who was called in to hear and decide the motion. The Chief Justice, it is said, after argument, decided to refuse the motion and had actually prepared an adverse opinion, but finally yielded to the arguments and persuasions of Judge Whitehead, and the motion was granted. Marsh was retried and acquitted.

The sound common sense mind of Judge Whitehead made him a valuable addition to the Bench. His opinions were always regarded with respect, and were the result of thorough research and the most patient investigation. One of the earliest delivered by him, in 1842, was in the celebrated case of Den. vs Allaire. This was an important case, involving many intricate and abstruse principles of law, and the opinion of Judge Whitehead, which was acceded to by all the members, showed immense amount of industrious labor and a thorough examination of the subject. The cause was argued by the first Counsel in the country, Henry W. Green and William L. Dayton for Plaintiff, and Peter D. Vroom and George Wood for Defendant.

All causes presented to Judge Whitehead, both at Circuit and at Bar, received the same patient, industrious investigation, and the record of his opinions left in the books of reports, only serve to enforce the respect that is due to a learned and laborious Jurist and impartial Judge, and a Christian gentleman.

CLIPPINGS.

There is a beautiful practice common throughout a portion of Mexico for little children to kneel before a stranger and pray that he may have a safe journey.

A Coptic church of the fifth century has recently been discovered among the ruins of Thebes. The way down to it is by five brick steps, the floor is tiled and the walls are of rough bricks, bearing inscriptions. On a stela, covered with a hard white substance, are 300 lines written in red ink in Theban, forming part of a sermon directed against heretics.

In Prussia the numeral Protestants are to the numeral Catholics almost exactly two to one. In Bavaria the position is more than reversed in favor of the Catholics, who are five to two ; in Elsass Lothringen they are more than four to one. On the other hand, Saxony, in spite of its Catholic king, counts less than 100,000 Catholics and not far from 3,000,000 Protestants. The Jews are about one-half of the population.

It is now claimed that Prof. Sattler of Munich, has solved the problem of the day of Christ's birth, and that he has demonstrated the fact that "Jesus was born on the 25th of December, 749 years after the founding of Rome :" so that the current year is properly 1888 of this era, rather than 1883. This claim is heralded widely by German, English and American periodicals. Yet the truth is, that the arguments as made by Professor Sattler, and the precise results reported by him, are identical with those given by the Rev'd Dr. S. J. Andrews, of Hartford, Connecticut, twenty years ago, in the Chronological Essays which precede his life of our Lord,—a work which has prominence in England as in America for its critical accuracy in chronological details. The only addition by Professor Sattler is the corroboratory evidence of certain Roman coins to which he refers.—Sunday School Times.

It has been claimed for German scholars that any statements made by them on biblical or scientific subjects are entitled to the highest respect because of the well known fact that they give to the examination of any subject most extended investigation with patient and profound research.

The contributions of American scholars are now received with almost equal respect. In fact, it may be said that on both sides of the Atlantic, in many instances the results of American scholarship are held in just as high estimation as are those of the German.

In the last issue of the RECORD reference was made to this subject of Christian Chronology in connection with Prof. Sattler's views; but, a doubt was expressed by the Editor, as to the date fixed by him of the birth. of Christ, that is the 25th of Dec. It is not known whether Dr. Andrews agreed with Prof. Sattler with regard to this. date, and the extracts just given from the Sunday School Times throw no light on that subject. Whether there is an agreement between these two learned scholars, or not, that doubt is still held. [EDITOR.]

The minutes of last Conference of the Methodists at Leeds, in Aug., 1806, represent the members of that society to be as follows:

In Great Britain,		110,803
Ireland,		23,773
Gibralter,		40
Nova Scotia, New Brunswick and New Foundland,		1,418
West India, whites,	1,775	14,940
Colored people,	13,165	
U. S. whites,	95,628	119,945
Colored people	24,317	
		270,919

Of these upwards of 109,000 are found in England and Wales, to which may be added 109,000 more, who have not ventured to have their names enrolled; and, to these may be added the younger branches of families, making about 218,000 more, forming in the whole nearly half a million of persons ! ! !—Monthly Magazine, April, 1808.

The exclamation points are not the RECORD'S. How many would the wondering editor of the Magazine have placed after his article, if he could have looked into the future and have learned into what proportions the Methodists have now grown ?—EDITOR.

The time may be delayed, the manner may be unexpected, but sooner or later, in some form or another, the answer is sure to come. Not a tear of sacred sorrow, not a breath of holy desire, poured out in prayer to God, will ever be lost ; but in God's own time and way it will be wafted back again in clouds of mercy, and fall in showers of blessings on you and those for whom you pray.—Prof. W. S. Tyler.

OVERDOING IN CHARITIES.

Laziness and intemperance are the two great crimes against society. And we have much reason for believing that they are increased by the pious zeal of good people to provide for the indolent and the victims of drink.

Society gives too much in mistaken charity.

If the lazy and the intemperate were made to work and restrained from drink, there would be very little need of providing for the poor. We would require hospitals for the sick and wounded. Providential misfortune must be cared for, and the deserving poor must be supported.

But it is a divine principle that he who will not work does not deserve to have anything to eat.

Therefore we would have laziness and intemperance treated as vices to be punished ; and certainly the want of food is a light penalty to impose on him who will drink what is evil and will not work for his daily bread.

"The worst enemy, therefore, of those engaged in real charitable work is the indiscriminate and reckless giver. He undoes whatever good work they do."—N. Y. Observer.

THE RECORD.

FIRST PRESBYTERIAN CHURCH, MORRISTOWN, N. J.

"This shall be Written for the Generation to Come."—Psalms 102 : 18.

| VOLUME III. | SEPTEMBER, 1883. | NUMBER 9. |

[Printed with the Approval of the Session.]

THE RECORD

Will be published monthly at Morristown, N. J. Terms $1.00 per annum, *in advance.*

Subscriptions may be made at the bookstores of Messrs. Runyon and Emmell, or to Messrs. James R. Voorhees and William D. Johnson, or by letter addressed to the

EDITOR OF THE RECORD,

Morristown, N. J.

Entered at the Post Office at Morristown, N. J., as second class matter.

The remains of George Whitefield are beneath the pulpit of the old Presbyterian Church in Newburyport, Mass.

The RECORD for next month will contain interesting extracts from Mr. Barnes's "Manual of Our Church."

Special attention is requested to the list begun in the next column. Doubtless most of our readers can furnish some information. It is very desirable that the facts should be had before publishing the roll of members received during the pastorates of Drs. Fisher and McDowell.

A private diary contains this entry, under date of Sept. 29, 1842 : "Attended the centenary celebration. Doct. Fisher preached the sermon, in place of Dr. Richards, who was sick. The house was pretty well filled." This was probably the centenary anniversary of the church, since Dr. Johnes came in 1742; but it seems to have passed very quickly out of memory. Dr. Irving writes, "When I was hunting facts, no one mentioned that celebration to me." Who can give an account of the occasion?

WHO CAN TELL?

Information is desired concerning the following members of the church. Did they unite with other churches, and if so, what churches? Did they remove from Morristown, if so, when? Are they dead? If so, the date of death? Are they living? If so, where? In case of the names of women, if married after joining the church, what was the date of marriage and name of husband? Our readers will confer a favor by sending a postal card, addressed to the "Pastor of First Presbyterian Church, Morristown, N. J.," with such information as they can furnish respecting any one or more of the names given below :

JOINED CHURCH.	NAMES AND MARKS.

1810.

Feb. 21. Phebe, wife of Peter Norris, from Mendham,

Apr. 19. Joseph Beers.

May 4. Rachel Crowell, from South Hanover.

" " Elias Byram, from Caldwell.

1811.

May 5. Nancy Fairchild, widow.

" " Mary Canfield.

1812.

Jan. 3. Charlotte, wife of Matthias Pierson, from South Hanover,

Feb. 28. Flora, servant of James James.

Apr. 27. Jerusha, wife of Jacob Mann: she is recorded as having died July 12, 1865, but one of the rolls marks her "dismissed ;" to what church and when was she dismissed?

May 1. Mehetable, wife of Timothy Fairchild.

July 3. Elizabeth Hatfield Fairchild, wife of Jacob Beers.

Oct. 30. Matthias Williams, from Orange.

" " Sally, wife of Samuel Roff,

Oct. 30. Rachel, wife of Martin DeHart.

Nov. 1. Mary A. Dickerson.

Dec. 25. Elizabeth Edwards, widow.

" " Tryphena, wife of Joshua Secor.

" " Henry P. Russel.

" " Isabel, wife of John Conplin; she is marked "dismissed to · New Vernon;" but when?

1813.

Jan. 1. Rebecca, wife of Roseter Lum; she is marked "Euclid. O." but when?

Apr. 26. Hugh Huston (or Dustan), from Associate Reform Church, N. Y., marked "to New Vernon;" but when?

June 29. Anna, wife of Robert Harrison, from South Hanover, marked "to Newark;" but what church and when?

" " Mrs. Jerusha Alsover, from Parsippany.

Aug. 27. Amelia Maria Smith.

Nov. 2. William Johnson.

" " Sarah, wife of Enos Egbert, from Elizabethtown. Did she join the Methodist Church here?

" " Jonathan Dayton, from Baskingridge.

" " Phebe, wife of Jonathan Dayton, from Baskingridge.

1814.

Mar. 4. Anna Lambert, widow.

" " James Martin.

Apr. 22. Silva, a free black-woman.

June 14. Joseph Garner.

" " Susan, servant of Andrew Ogden.

" " Henry Hardy, colored.

" 22. Sally Oliver. Did she marry Mahlon Bonnel and go to New Vernon? If so, when?

" " Hilah Mitchell.

" " Margaret, wife of Isaac Goble.

" " Elizabeth, wife of Joseph Still.

" " Mehetable, wife of David Wood.

Aug. 29. James D. Johnson.

" " Phebe Pierson.

" " Hannah Miller.

" " Sally Meeker.

" " Julia Ann Pierson.

" " Julia F. Hedges.

" " Abby Connet (later Mrs. Philip Cook.)

Aug. 29. Joanna Freeman (later Mrs Ashbel U. Guerin.)

" " Clarrisa Byram (later Mrs Thompson.)

Nov. 3. Philip Cook.

" " Dina Young, widow (later Mrs. Eph Cutler), marked "dismissed;" but when and to what church?

Dec. 22. Sarah Dickerson, marked "later Mrs. Lewis Brookfield," and "dismissed;" but when?

" " Benjamin Lindsly.

" " Hannah, wife of Benjamin Lindsly.

" " Miss Mary Cook.

" " Stephen Conklin.

Dec. 30. Mary Bonnel, wife of Nathaniel, from Bottle Hill; marked "to Green Village," and "dead;" but when?

1815.

Feb. 23. Ann, wife of Wm. Davison.

" " Nancy (or Mary?) wife of Wm. Wooley.

" " Sarah, wife of David Wooley; marked "dismissed to the Methodist church as wife of Lewis Brookfield." Is this correct? if so, when married and dismissed?

" " David Wooley.

" " Sarah, wife of Ezra Halsey, Jr., marked "to Hamburgh, Sussex Co.," but when?

" " Elijah P. son of John Oliver; marked "to New Vernon" and "died at N. V," but when?

" " Zenas, son of Luther Connet.

" " Stephen H. son of David Pierson; marked "dismissed," but when and where?

April 28. Susan, daughter of Abner Fairchild; marked "to New Vernon as wife of Ager Lindsly." Is this correct? if so, when married and dismissed?

" " Dorcas, wife of Thomas Mitchel.

" " Elizabeth, wife of John Finegar, marked "dismissed," but when and where?

" " Akaba, servant of Joseph Cutler, marked "wife of Sam. Canfield" and "dead." Is this correct? if so, when married and died?

April 28 Phebe Condict, marked "later wife of Moses L. Guerin," and "dead." Is this correct? If so, when married and died.

" " Jonas Willis, and Elizabeth his wife, from Orange.

June 22. Isaac Prudden and his wife Anna marked "dismissed," but when and where?

" " Deborah, wife of Chatfield Tuttle; marked "dead."

" " Susan, daughter of the widow Edwards.

Aug. 23. John, son of Ebenezer Stiles.

" " Dinah, servant of Thomas Morgan.

Oct. 26. Phebe, wife of Ebenezer Pierson, marked "dismissed," but when and where?

" " Mary Lawrence.

" " Marcus, son of James Ford, marked "ordained."

" " Sarah, wife of James Humes (or Holmes ?), from Mendham.

Dec. 28. Sarah, daughter of Joseph Lindsly, Jr., marked "dismissed 1818."

" " Phebe, daughter of Edward Condict ; marked "later Mrs. Peter Freeman" and "dead," but when married and died?

" " Eliza, wife of David Hurd.

" " Hannah, daughter of Moses Estey ; marked "dismissed."

" " Eliza, daughter of Jonathan Ogden.

1816.

Feb. 22. Halsey, son of Daniel Prudden.

" " Elia W., son of Noah Crane ; marked "ordained."

" " Sophronia, daughter of Jeremiah Day.

" " Harriet, wife of Jacob Canfield.

" " Sarah, daughter of Henry Benfield.

" " Ann C. Lindsly ; marked "dismissed," but when and where?

May 3. Delancy Newton and wife Sarah ; marked "dismissed," but when and where?

" " James Garrigues ; marked "dismissed," but when and where?

" " Jane, daughter of Joseph Marsh ; marked "later Mrs. Henry Thorp." and "dead," but when married and died?

May 3. Eliza, wife of John Millard.

" " Titus, servant of Dr. Hunt.

" " Rose, servant of Henry King.

Aug. 15. Jerry, son of John Caldwell ; marked "dismissed."

" " Franklin, son of Jonathan Cowdery ; marked "dismissed."

" " Hannah, wife of Samuel Pierson ; marked "dead," but when?

" " Jane, wife of Abraham Johnson.

" " Mary, daughter of Caleb Campbell ; marked "later Mrs. James Martin." and "dead," but when married and died?

" " Ruth, daughter of Stephen Turner.

Aug. 25. John M. Benedict, from New Haven.

1817.

Feb. 20. Louisa, daughter of Chas. Morrell ; marked "dismissed."

May 22. Maria, wife of Henry J. Browne.

" " Lucy, wife of Charles Comstock.

" " Elizabeth, widow of —— Fine.

" " John Wooley and Elizabeth his wife.

" " Susanna, wife of Henry Alwood, from Rockaway.

Aug. 28. Margaret, wife of Joshua De Hart, marked "dismissed," but when and where?

" " Mary, daughter of Moses Estey ; marked "dismissed."

" " Sarah, daughter of Demas Ford, from Newburgh.

" " Martha, wife of John Robinson, from Hanover.

Sept. 3. Margaret, "a free blackwoman," from Mendham.

1818.

Feb. 19. Benajah Burnet, from Jefferson.

May 28. Mahlon Ford ; marked "dismissed," but when and where?

" " Gabriel Green and his wife Mary ; marked "to Newark," but when and where?

Aug. 27. Joseph, son of John McCord.

1819.

May 6. James Davis, and his wife Nancy from Bloomfield.

Aug. 26. Aaron Bonnel, from Springfield.

" " Phebe, wife of Aaron Bonnel, from Elizabethtown.

1820.

Feb. 24. Eliza S. Johnes, daughter of Timothy Johnes.

June 15. Mary, wife of Jacob Shipman.

"   " Abigail, wife of Henry Vail from Hanover.

Aug. 24. Matilda, daughter of Moses Prudden ; marked to "New Vernon," but when?

"   " Sarah, wife of Silas Bowen.

"   " Bythinia, wife of Joseph Canfield.

Nov. 23. Phebe Babbit ; marked "later Mrs. Samuel Pierson" and "dead," but when married and died?

1821.

Feb. 22. James Shelley, "a free colored man."

May 28. Sarah, wife of John Munson.

Aug. 23. Elizabeth, widow of John Haines (or Harris).

Dec. 6. Cleopatra, wife of Daniel Prudden, from Succasunna.

1822.

Feb. 26. Susan, daughter of Mahlon Johnson, "later Mrs. Jon. E. Huntington, of Newark." Did she join a church in Newark?

May 16. Mary, wife of Geo. K. Drake, marked "dismissed;" but when and where?

"   " Hannah, wife of James Wilson.

"   " Anna and Hannah, daughters of Isaac Canfield, marked "dismissed;" but when and where?

"   " Mary, daughter of Stout Benjamin, marked "later Mrs. Stephen Tunis" and "dead;" but when married and died?

"   " Sarah, wife of Elisha J. Pierson.

"   " Henry Vail, Jr.

"   21. Abby, wife of Hiram Lindsly, marked "to New Vernon;" but when?

"   " Martha, wife of David Beers.

"   " Bernard McCormick.

"   " Stephen O. Guerin.

"   23. Urania, wife of Henry Minton.

"   " Phebe, wife of Lewis Johnson.

"   " Jonathan Thompson and his wife Harriet.

"   " Timothy H. Prudden, marked "to New Vernon;" but when?

"   " Ira Prudden.

May 23. Obadiah L. Woodruff.

Aug. 1. James Burnet.

"   " Elizabeth Trowbridge and Mary Ann B., daughters of Rev. Asa Lyman, marked "to Chatham;" but when?

"   " Phebe, wife of John Sparling.

"   " Eunice, widow of Mahlon Lindsly, marked "to New Vernon;" but when?

"   " Caty Lewis, servant of A. O. Pierson.

"   8. Gitty, wife of Ephraim Fairchild, marked "to New Vernon;" but when?

"   " Betsey, daughter of Caleb Howard.

"   " Jane, widow of David Carmichael, marked "now wife of Edward Condict."

"   " Sarah, daughter of Jonathan Baker.

"   " Jabez, son of Michael Edwards.

"   15. Julia, daughter of Wm. Beadle, marked "to New Vernon as wife of Lewis Armstrong;" but when married and dismissed?

"   " John, son of Daniel Tunis, marked "to New Vernon;" but when?

"   " Hannah, daughter of Uzal Munson, marked "gone west, wife of John Gillam;" but when married and dismissed?

"   " Eliza, wife of James Wood.

"   " William Cook, marked in pencil, "Newark,"

"   " Sarah, wife of Wm. A. Whelpley, marked "dismissed 1830;" but where?

"   " Louisa and Sarah, daughters of Jacob Mann, marked "dismissed;" but when and where?

"   22. Louisa, daughter of Chas. Carmichael.

"   " Hannah, wife of Chas. Wilson, marked "to New Vernon;" but when?

"   " Martha, wife of Jonathan Pierson, marked "to Newark."

"   " Ebenezer Pierson; two dates of his death are on roll, "Dec. 1, 1843" and "Dec. 19, 1851." Which is correct?

"   " Elizabeth, wife of James Conway.

ug. 22. Sidney D., son of Bethuel Pierson,
        marked " dismissed."
"   " Matthias Burnet, son of Stephen
        Freeman.
"   " Isaac, son of Isaac Canfield,
"   " Elias, son of Zophar Freeman.
ov. 12. John M., son of John Sparling,
        marked " gone to Ohio."
"   23, Adam Gilchrist.
  1823.
[ay 15. Hannah, wife of Wm. Goble,
        marked " to New Vernon ;" but
        when ?
"   " Martha, wife of John Lindsly,
        marked " to New Vernon ;" but
        when ?
    22. Elizabeth Coe.
"   " Sophia, wife of Elisha Cameron.
"   " Ruth, wife of Jonathan Miller,
        marked " to New Vernon ;"
        but when ?
"   " Huldah Ayers, marked "dis-
        missed ;" but when and where ?
"   " Nathanael Wilson, son of Jonathan
        Hathaway.
"   " Ann, widow of David Halliday,
        marked " to New Vernon ;"
        but when ?
"   " Susan R., daughter of Thomas
        Guerin.
"   26. Hannah Wooley, widow, from
        Spring Street Church, N. Y.
"   " Mary, daughter of Hannah
        Wooley, from same, and wife of
        James Van Fleet, Sr., marked
        " to Newark ;" but when and
        where !
  1824.
une 4. Hannah, wife of Francis Casterline.
Dec. 2. Phebe Canfield, widow, "from
        Hanover, daughter of Jacob,
        wife of Wm. Wisner, marked as
        having died "Aug. 1838" on
        one roll, and " Jan. 8, 1849, aet.
        '41," on another. Which is
        correct.

If we divide the known regions of this
world into thirty equal parts ; the Christian
part is as five ; the Mahometan's as six .
and the Idolaters as nineteen.—*Brerewood*
1674.

CLIPPINGS.

THE LAURENTIAN LIBRARY.

Passing up a staircase at one corner of
this cloister, I came out on its upper gallery,
close to the door of the vestibule to the
Laurentian Library. Entering at this door,
one finds one's self at the foot of the fine
triple staircase built by Vasari, whose ample and majestic lines form a fitting introduction to the chamber to which it conducts ; a
long, narrow hall, that at first sight reminds
you of a modern church. Rows of benches
and racks, resembling slips, stretch on either
hand throughout its length, with a central
aisle and a desk at its farther end. On examination you see that the eighty-eight
racks are bookcases, where each fastened
by a chain, the books are laid ready for the
occupant of the bench to turn their leaves.
This was the method adopted when this
hall was finished in 1571, and it has been
left unchanged to the present day. When
readers were few it was not an inconvenient
system, but now all books desired for reference are taken from their places and carried
to an adjoining room, fitted up with modern
conveniences for the student. The main
hall, therefore, presents no appearance of a
library, all the racks being covered with
curtains, and the clerks, with a few chance
visitors, being the only occupants of the
room. The dark ceiling and pavement, and
the racks of beautifully carved wood almost
black with time, the ancient stained windows, the work of a scholar of Raphael, John
of Udine, give it a solemn and impressive
magnificence. It seems a fitting home for
the relics of antiquity. A long, narrow
panel, inscribed with the names of the
books in that division, is attached to each
rack. The attendant lifts the green cloth
from these treasures with a reverent
hand. He shows you a Syrian Bible of the
sixth century, a Greek Gospel of the eighth,
and, earliest of all, a Virgil, with annota-
tions made in the year 494. Later manuscripts, many of them richly illuminated,
abound ; among the illustrations more interesting to ordinary eyes are the contemporary portraits of Dante, of Petrarch and
Laura.—*Springfield Republican.*

The Laurentian Library is at Florence, in

Italy, and is so called from Lorenzo de Medici, its real founder. It was begun by Cosmo de Medici, the grandfather of Lorenzo. Cosmo was a merchant who accumulated an immense fortune, but, notwithstanding his intense application to his business pursuits, gave great attention to letters. He instructed his friends and correspondents to procure for him ancient manuscripts in every language. The Eastern Empire was then falling to pieces, and this enabled him to obtain many inestimable works in Hebrew, Greek, Chaldaic, Arabic and in the Indian languages.

These books thus gathered were the nucleus of the great library. Lorenzo made many additions, donating his own library to it, and enriching it with books collected by him from every part of the earth. He employed every available means to procure the rarest volumes on every subject. Politian and Pico, two celebrated bibliophilists of his time, were, under his guidance, diligently engaged in purchasing, arranging and cataloguing books.

Lorenzo at last erected the present building occupied by this library, also using the talent and genius of Vasari, as the architect, in its erection.

During the troublous time attendant upon the ascendancy to power of Savonarola and his subsequent downfall, great loss to the library was feared from pillage by the populace. But, while the frenzy of the people was at its greatest height, some of the youth of the noblest families of Florence guarded it until the fury was over.

Prior to this many of the volumes had been distributed as presents by Savonarola to the cardinals and other eminent men, whose favor he desired to obtain.

Many of its volumes had been seized for the use of the State, which was afterwards obliged to sell these volumes to raise money for its needs.

Leo X. purchased all he could obtain—removed the library to Rome in 1508, where it was kept until the accession of Clement VII., who restored it to Florence where it has since remained.

Prior to this, in 1494, during the invasion of Italy by Charles VIII. of France, this invaluable library had been plundered by the French—aided, to their eternal disgrace be it written—by the Florentines themselves, who openly carried off or secretly purloined whatever they could lay their hands upon, that was interesting, or rare, or valuable. Manuscripts of inestimable worth, exquisite sculptures, vases and other works of art, shared in the general ruin, so that the vast storehouses, which Lorenzo and his ancestry had been able through their wealth and assiduity, to accumulate during half a century, were demolished in a day.

The present library contains 120,000 printed volumes and 6,000 manuscripts.

EDITOR.

FALSE MESSIAHS.
THREE REMARKABLE SPECIMENS.

Sabatai Sevi about the middle of the seventeenth century, appeared at Smyrna and proclaimed himself to the Jews as their Messiah. Evelyn says that "the report of Sabatai and his doctrine flew through those parts of Turkey which the Jews inhabited; they were so deeply possessed of their new kingdom and their promotion to honor, that none of them attended to business of any kind, except to prepare for a journey to Jerusalem." Unfortunately Sabatai was so zealous that he was locked up in the Castle of Abydos, where, we are told, "he composed a new mode of worship." He was carried to Adrianople and his divinity put to a singular test. The Grand Seignior ordered him to be stripped naked and set up as a target for the archers to shoot at. If his skin proved arrow-proof his pretensions were to be admitted. Upon this Sabatai, to save his life, turned Turk, declaring that he had long been desirous of making so glorious a profession. The Jews, who were all ready to start for Jerusalem, were much chagrined at this proceeding—the historian says that they "were overcome with confusion and dejection of spirit."

Richard Brothers was one of the last of the False Messiahs, and he made a good deal of noise and not a few converts in England toward the close of the last century. He undertook to restore the blind to sight; he saw visions; he emitted prophecies; he published a new gospel, entitled: "A Revealed Knowledge of the Prophecies and Times." Among his disciples was Sharpe, the celebrated engraver, together with a Mr. Halked, M. P., who is said to have been a man of considerable learning.

One last example of religious pretension will bring us nearer home. Robert Matthews, better known as Matthias, came to New York to work as a house carpenter. About 1829 he began to preach in the streets of Albany. He permitted his beard to grow; he wore grotesque clothing; he was repeatedly arrested for making a disturbance; he professed to be a Jew; he declaimed against Freemasonry; sometimes he mounted an old and half-starved horse. He declared to them that "He was the Spirit of Truth; that the Spirit of Truth had disappeared from the earth at the death of the Matthias mentioned in the New Testament; that the Spirit of Christ had entered into Matthias, and that he was the same Matthias, the Apostle of the New Testament, risen from the dead." Some of his dupes conveyed their property to him, and then went into insolvency. Ultimately he was found out and discarded. Of the subsequent career of the prophet nothing is known, except that he died in Arkansas.

THE CHURCH AND PROHIBITION.

The fact is that prohibitionists have crowded a question of civil policy back into the domain of ethical principles, and while sometimes, perhaps, right on the question of policy, they have generally gone wrong on the question of principle. It is true that human laws derive their binding force from their conformity with divine enactments, and the better the Catholic citizen understands his duties to the church the purer will be his conceptions of, and the readier will be his compliance with, his duties to the State. But farther than this it is scarcely prudent to combine their respective spheres of authority. While the State may well hesitate, under present circumstances, to enforce personal temperance by law, so the church acts wisely by confining her application of great moral principles to the private conscience rather than that of the general public. In short, the question of prohibition as it concerns whole communities, and properly understood, belongs to the domain of politics rather than theology, and it would be a grave mistake to assert that there was

dogmatic authority binding Catholics on any side of such question. What the State may do is to say that the liquor traffic is the prolific source of certain evils and inimical to the general welfare; and public authority being specially organized to preserve and not destroy, it cannot be a party to the destruction of its own existence by permitting the continuance of so destructive an agent. The State has the power to do any and all things needed to fulfil the end of organized society—viz., the preservation of the general welfare of the people. If the State comes to regard the liquor traffic as a disorganizing agent, or as destroying its members or otherwise rendering them unable to fulfil their part of that mutual relationship and obligation which exists between the citizen and the State, then the question of restriction or prohibition stands forth plain and simple as one for state settlement. Viewed thus, the church could find nothing in prohibition to oppose. For instance, from judicial statistics it is ascertained that a very large percentage of crime originates from frequenting liquor saloons; this fact alone is enough to place prohibition on the list of preventives to be used against crime—a basis which the church could not and would not oppose, since the State has a right to prevent as well as to punish crime. Again, equally as large a proportion of pauperism and lunacy, which demands State aid to provide for, is traceable to the convivial drinking commonly practised in liquor saloons; that may fairly place prohibition among the preventives of pauperism. Now, the church could not say it was otherwise than right for the State to seek relief from these burdens, which right might be extended to prohibition without infringing in the least upon the province of the church. It will thus be seen that prohibition, when it appears in politics, should be treated as a question of public policy, one of a variety of means for procuring the well-being of the State, the discussion of which by no means necessarily involves a conflict of religious principle between the parties for and against it.— *The Catholic World.*

At the recent ninth annual meeting of the Dakota Sunday School Association about

150 delegates were in attendance. "The most marked interest and enthusiasm characterized each session. The statistics of the past year were inspiring ; 464 schools were reported (an increase of over one-half from last year's report), having 20,579 members (an increase of 100 per cent). There are four missionaries of the American Sunday School Union at work in Southern Dakota, and the excellent reports are largely due to their efforts. Our work never looked so encouraging as now." So reports the Secretary.

It is part of the irony of fate that Voltaire's house is now occupied by the Geneva Bible Society. Similar coincidences are found in London. The Religious Tract Society's premises are where Bibles were at one time publicly burned, and the British Bible Society's house at Blackfriar stands where a council in 1378 forbade Wycliffe from circulating portions of the Scriptures, and where he uttered the famous words : "The truth shall prevail."

We picture death as coming to destroy ; let us rather picture Christ as coming to save. We think of death as ending ; let us rather think of life as beginning, and that more abundantly. We think of losing ; let us think of gaining. We think of parting ; let us think of meeting. We think of going away ; let us think of arriving. And as the voice of Death whispers : "You must go from earth," let us hear the voice of Christ saying, "You are but coming to Me."— *Norman McLeod.*

There is a scientific principle-called "the survival of the fittest" and we can study the growth of the church of God from his stand point. How grandly the religion of Jesus appears when we try it by this test. It has now stood two thousand years. and how many systems, during that time have come up, blossomed and died. How many of them are now on the brink of destruction, only waiting for some one to push them over.—*Rev. Mr. Vanalstyne, Mt. Tabor Record.*

BAPTISMS AND MARRIAGES.

The records of infant baptisms and marriages, from July, 1866, to June, 18 are at present inaccessible. Members the congregation during that time who children baptised, will confer a favor sending a note, or card, to the pastor, w the birthdays of such children, and probable year of baptism. Notices of m riages, with names and dates, during same period, are also requested, Fam Bibles probably contain the facts desired

DATE ON THE BANNER OF SUND SCHOOL.

In a former issue of THE RECORD, ref ence was made to this subject. To obta if possible, the true date of the organizati of the Sunday school, application was m to that true friend of the school, J. D. S venson, Esq., now at San Antonio, Tex He says in his answer, recently received " In regard to the history of the Sund school, I am not so well posted as y think. I tried, while Superintendent, to come so, but found it almost impossi The particular incident leading to my effo was the occasion of the grand Sunday sch rally at Mount Tabor under Mr. Page. had no fit Sunday school banner, and I int ested our teachers in procuring one. A raising the money—some $60—one of most active teachers, then Miss Mary Vo hees, afterwards Mrs. Stoutenburg, acco panied me to New York and bought materials.

Our next trouble was to get the true d of the organization of the school and to lect a motto. The only information I co find as to the date was from Miss Sa Johnson, who remembered that in 1816 and others took part in the establishm of the school. We, therefore, put that d upon our new banner, where I suppose i to-day. The motto we chose at the sa time, and, after a meeting of the teach interested, and making and putting our sign together, it was unfurled at the head our school August 6th, (I think that was date)—1870."

THE RECORD.

FIRST PRESBYTERIAN CHURCH, MORRISTOWN, N. J.

"This shall be Written for the Generation to Come."—Psalms 102 : 18.

| Volume III. | OCTOBER, 1883. | Number 10 |

[Printed with the Approval of the Session.]

THE RECORD

Will be published monthly at Morristown.
N. J. Terms $1.00 per annum, *in advance.*

Subscriptions may be made at the book-stores of Messrs. Runyon and Emmell, or to Messrs. James R. Voorhees and William D. Johnson, or by letter addressed to the

EDITOR OF THE RECORD,
Morristown, N. J.

Entered at the Post Office at Morristown, N. J., as second class matter.

MR. BARNES' MANUAL.

In 1828, Mr. Barnes, then pastor of the Church, published a Manual, part of which follows this. Its title page is this :—

"Church Manual, for the members of the Presbyterian Church, Morris-Town, N. J.

Compiled

By Albert Barnes, Pastor ; and published by order of the Session of said Church.

Morris-Town,

Printed by Jacob Mann,

1828."

This Manual is very scarce, and should be preserved. A copy has been kindly placed at the disposal of THE RECORD, and this method is taken to put it in the possession of every member of the congregation.

SKETCH OF THE HISTORY
OF THE
PRESBYTERIAN CHURCH,
MORRIS-TOWN.

At what time, or by whom, Morristown was first settled, is not certainly known. The records of the County of Morris contain no notices of its settlement, and there are no documents extant, as far as can be ascertained, which throw any light on the first organization of its civil and ecclesiastical society. It is probable, however, that it was settled in the early part of the last century and that the inhabitants were chiefly from Elizabeth-Town, Newark, and Long-Island. They were undoubtedly principally, or entirely, descendants of the settlers of New-England ; and may therefore be supposed to have brought with them habits of morality, and a disposition early to possess the ordinances of religion.

Among the regulations made by the Duke of York for settlers in the province, under which regulations Morristown was probably settled, we find the following, respecting the support of the Gospel :—" Every township is obliged to pay their own minister, according to such agreement as they shall make with him, and no man to refuse his own proportion ; the minister being elected by the major part of the householders and inhabitants of the town."

The charter of the Church and congregation was granted by Johnathan Belcher, Esq., Captain-General and Governor in chief over the Province of New Jersey, Sept. 18, 1756.

At what time the Presbyterian Church was organized is unknown ; but the Gospel was probably preached regularly soon after the settlement of the town. It is known that there was preaching here, before the installation of the first Pastor ;* but of the circumstances, and of the influence of those labours, there is no record. Neither is it known under what form of church government, whether Congregational or Presbyterian, the congregation was first organized. As Ruling Elders are mentioned, however, as early as the year 1747, it is probable that

*By the Rev. John Cleverly, who died Dec. 1776, aged 81 years.

the first organization of the Church, as it has continued since, was Presbyterian.

The authentic records of the church commence in 1742. The following is the title of the records of the Church, kept by its first pastor :—" The Record of the Church, in the town of Morris, from the first Erection and founding of it there :—and, under Christ, as Collected, and Setled, and Watered (in much weakness) by Timo. Johnes, Pastor; who first came, Aug. 13th, 1742, stayed 6 Sab., and then fetched my Family, and was ordained, Feb. 9, 1743," 42 till after equinox.

Dr. Johnes was pastor of the church more than half a century. He was a native of Southampton, on Long-Island, and was educated at Yale College, in Connecticut. From the catalogue of that college, it appears that he graduated in 1737. From the same college, he some years afterwards received the degree of Doctor of Divinity.

Dr. Johnes has left nothing, except the general impression of his labours on the minds of the church and congregation, by which the nature and value of his services can now be distinctly known. None of · his sermons were printed ; and few of his manuscripts are now remaining. The fact, however, that he received the highest honours of a college, deservedly ranking among the first in the United States, and that at a time when literary degrees were not conferred indiscriminately, and were therefore proof of merit, is a sufficient evidence that his standing in the ministry was of a very respectable order, and that he was well known in the American churches.

He was a man of respectable literary attainments ; but he was rather distinguished for his fidelity as a Pastor. As a preacher, he is said to have been clear, plain, practical, and persuasive. His discourses were rather an affectionate appeal to the heart, than profound and elaborate disquisitions on abstruse points of theology. He aimed rather to win men to the practice of holiness, than to terrify, and denounce them. Though faithful in reproving and warning, yet it was with mildness, and in the spirit of true Christian affection. He suffered no public vice to escape without reproof ; but the reproof was administered, in order that he might show them " a more excellent way." He seems to

have come to his people, particularly towards the latter part of his ministry, as an affectionate Christian pastor ; their father, counsellor and friend. No man could have had a better claim to the title of Father in the Gospel ; and no man probably would have used the influence thus derived, more to the practical benefit of the people.

Though not elaborate, or remarkably profound, or highly eloquent in the pulpit, yet Dr. Johnes had the faculty of instilling the principles of religion into the minds of the people. He was much with them. He visited much from house to house. He had become acquainted with the circumstances of every family. He had the moulding and training of the congregation. He had the power therefore of stamping his own sentiments on their minds. Beloved as their pastor, and venerated as their Spiritual Father, his sentiments on religion were received always with high respect, and almost uniformly with cordial approbation. He endeavoured to bring religion home to the business and bosoms of men—to associate it with their ordinary notions of living—of bargain and sale—of social, and political intercourse—with all their attachments and hopes and fears. By being much with the people, and by a faculty of adapting his instructions to their circumstances and capacities, he laboured successfully to instil into their minds pure sentiments ; to form them to good habits ; and to train them up to holy living. The consequence was that, at his death, there were probably few congregations, that were so thoroughly instructed in all that pertained to the practical duties of religion.

Dr. Johnes was eminently a peace-maker. His respectable standing, his high character, his long experience, his practical wisdom, and his undoubted integrity, secured the confidence of the people, and led them to listen with profound deference to him as the arbiter of their disputes. Without interfering, farther than became him as the venerable pastor of a people, in the controversies which arose in neighborhoods, he yet contrived, successfully, to suppress a spirit of litigation, and to produce an adjustment of difficulties in consistency with the laws of affection and concord. Habits of litigation he regarded as eminently inconsistent with the spirit of the Gospel, and he therefore laboured that his people might endeavour to " hold the unity of the spirit in the bond of peace." Nor did he labour in vain. He was regarded as the tried friend of his people, and they unhesitatingly reposed with confidence on his judgment.

Dr. Johnes was a warm and decided friend to revivals of religion. He received his education in the time of President Edwards, and Whitfield, and the Tennants. He came to this place, in the period of the greatest excitement on the subject of religion that this country has ever known. Many of the older inhabitants of this place, can still recollect the interest with which he read to his congregation, accounts of revivals in other parts of the country. He laboured, and prayed fervently that his own congregation might be brought also to a participation of the blessings that descended on other parts of the land. His sentiments on this subject are recorded in incidental notices attached to the names of those who were added to the church during these seasons of special mercy. In one place he says, "These the sweet fruites of yt wonderful effusion of God's adorable Grace began on our Sacrament Day, July 1, 1764." In another, "These yt follow the ingatherings of yt Divine harvest A.D. 1774.—Sweet drops of ye morning dew."

Few men have ever been more successful, as ministers of the Gospel, than Dr. Johnes. To have been the instrument of founding a large and flourishing church, to have been regarded as its affectionate Father and Guide; to have established the ordinances of the Gospel, and formed the people to respect its institutions; to have produced that outward order, and morality, and love of good institutions now observable in this congregation, was itself worthy of the toils of his life. In being permitted to regard himself as, under God, the originator of habits, and good institutions which are to run into coming generations, he could not but look upon his toils as amply recompensed. But he was permitted also to see higher fruit of the labour of his ministry. It pleased a gracious God, not only to grant a gradual increase of the church, but also at two different times to visit the congregation with a special revival of religion. The first

occurred in 1764. This commenced, as has been noted, on the sacrament day, July 1. The fruits of this revival, were the admission to the church, within the space of about a year, of ninety-four persons. Of the characteristics of this revival little is known, except that it is remembered by some of the members of the church now living, to have been a work of deep feeling, much anxiety, awful apprehensions of the nature of sin, and of the justice of God, impressive solemnity, and sound and thorough hopeful conversions to God. The second revival commenced in 1774. As the result of this revival, about fifty were added to the church. In 1790, there was another season of unusual excitement on the subject of religion, and about forty were united to the church.

Dr. Johnes died, of the dysentery, September 1794, aged 78 ; and was buried in the common burying ground—where a plain unostentatious monument marks his grave.

The following is a summary of the labours and results of his ministry :—

Those who composed the church when first organized, and received afterwards from other churches - - - - 176
Added by his ministry - - 424

	Total,	600
Baptisms - - - - -		2,827
Marriages - - - - -		948
Cases of Discipline - - -		170

The Rev. Aaron C. Collins, was ordained, and installed as Collegiate Pastor with Dr. Johnes, January 6, 1791 ; and was dismissed, by mutual consent, Sept. 2, 1793.

The Rev. James Richards, D. D. now Professor of Christian Theology in the Theological Seminary at Auburn, N. Y. was the next pastor of the congregation. He "preached his first sermon in Morristown, the latter part of June, 1794—received a call from the congregation to become their pastor, the last of August, or first of September following—was ordained and installed as pastor, May 1, 1795, at a stated meeting of what was then called the Presbytery of New-York, and was allowed to resign his pastoral charge of this people, by the Presbytery of Jersey, met at Elizabeth-Town, April 26, 1809 ; at which time he accepted a call from the first Presbyterian Church in Newark.

Dr. Richards's ministry, in this place, continued therefore, about fifteen years. During that time there were admitted to the communion of the church—

On examination   -   -   -   214
On certificate   -   -   -   29
Baptisms   -   -   -   -   444

Of those admitted to the church, a considerable part were the fruits of three revivals of religion. The first commenced in the spring of the year 1797; and as the result of it, more than one hundred persons connected themselves with the church. The second occurred in 1803, and 1804, and the number added to the church as the fruits of this work, was about forty. The third commenced in 1808, and about eighty were in consequence added to the church.

Of these revivals, Dr. Richards, in a letter to the present Pastor, dated January 9, 1828, says: "During my ministry at Morristown, there were three seasons of special attention to religion, the first and last of which were the most considerable. The first was remarkable chiefly from this circumstance, that it came upon the congregation by surprise. None of the church members, that ever I could learn, were specially stirred up to desire or expect it. Of course the church appeared full of unbelief, when it was announced that the Lord was in the midst of us, of a truth. Even those who from their exemplary character might have been expected to be waiting for the consolation of Israel, were manifestly unprepared for this sovereign act of divine mercy. But, prepared or unprepared, the windows of Heaven were opened, and the spiritual rain descended, and about one hundred souls were hopefully brought into the Kingdom as the fruit and effect of this refreshing. They did not all join the church at once, but principally in the course of that and the following year.

"The second revival in 1803, was much more local in its operations, and by no means characterized with the same power. It excited considerable attention in the congregation, and served to draw forth the prayers and exertions of Christians, but still it was confined chiefly to one or two neighbourhoods.

"The third and last of these interesting seasons, I always regarded as the most precious—not because it seemed to take a wider sweep, but because as far as it went, it appeared to be more deep and effective, and exerted a more benign influence on the church. This revival was evidently preceded by a spirit of prayer. To my latest breath, I shall remember, how some of the dear people of God appeared to feel, and agonize, in their supplications before the Lord, when imploring his gracious presence in the midst of us. Through the whole of the preceding winter, there had been some feeling and some expectancy in the church on this subject, occasioned perhaps by the revivals which had occurred, and were then occurring, in some of the neighbouring congregations. But the church seemed to calculate that this good work would go from congregation to congregation, as a matter of course. When, however, they saw that the cloud of God's presence had come to our very borders, on two sides of us, and was stayed, they began to tremble, to feel their dependence, and to cry mightily unto God, that he would not utterly refuse to bless us. The blessing came, and sealed, not a few, I trust, unto the day of redemption. Between seventy and eighty were added to the church in that and the subsequent year, who dated their conversion from this interesting period. I will only add, that on enquiring of my brethren, I was uniformly told that the members gathered during this revival, had been peculiarly circumspect, and very few of them subjected to any church censure.

"As to means employed, either in the commencement or progress of these revivals, I can say nothing—except that the Gospel was preached as plainly and faithfully as I was able, and that publicly, and from house to house. Prayer meetings, anxious meetings, or conferences, were found to be of special service in promoting the good work."

Dr. Richards was succeeded by the Rev. Samuel Fisher, D. D. now pastor of the Presbyterian Church in Paterson, N. J. Dr. Fisher was installed as pastor in 1809, by the Presbytery of New York, and dismissed by the mutual request of him and the people, April 27, 1814.

Dr. Fisher laboured in this congregation about four years. During the year in which he was settled more than twenty persons were received to the communion of the church. In the year 1813, about forty were received; and about forty in the year 1814

While, here, by a personal visit to every part of the congregation, he ascertained that there were five hundred and twenty families in its bounds who professed to be Presbyterians.

He was succeeded by the Rev. William A. McDowell, D. D. a native of Somerset County, in this State, and settled previous to his installation here in Bound-Brook, N. J., now of Charleston, S. C. Dr. McDowell was installed, Dec. 13th, 1814, and was dismissed, Oct. 21, 1823. He was here, therefore, about nine years. During the year succeeding his settlement fifty persons were added to the communion of the church. About the same number was received the following year. In 1822 the church was blessed with an extensive revival of religion. This revival commenced in the spring, and continued through the summer, and prevailed in all parts of the congregation. As the fruits of it, during that and the following year, not far from *one hundred and fifty* were added to the church. This was the most extensive revival with which the congregation has ever been visited.

The present pastor, a native of Rome, in the State of New York, was ordained and installed, Feb. 8, 1825.*

The following Miscellaneous Items are deemed of sufficient importance to be recorded.

The trustees of the congregation were "according to charter," elected by the session of the church, until 1788, when they were, under the laws of the State of New-Jersey, elected by the congregation.

January 23, 1791, it was resolved that the Elders, together with the minister, shall be a committee to examine all candidates for church membership. From which, as well as from the records of the session, it appears probable that the examination of candidates previously, were, as in Congregational churches, conducted by the members of the church.

At the same time it was resolved, that those persons who have covenanted with God, and [been] admitted members of the church, and have come to the ordinance of baptism, but not to the ordinance of the Lord's Supper, were not required to renew their covenant in order to come to that ordinance, but that they should be required to inform the minister that it is their desire to come to the Lord's Supper, previous to their coming, and that the minister publish the same to the church. From which it appears that it had been the practice to receive persons into covenant, and baptize them, who did not participate in all the privileges of the church. Baptized children also came forward and renewed their covenant, or took their baptismal vows upon themselves, who were not admitted to the communion. During the ministry of Dr. Johnes, no less than eighteen hundred and fifty thus " renewed their covenant."*

June 2, 1795, it was resolved, that whereas it had heretofore been the practice of this church to admit all persons having made profession of religion, and who were of good moral character, to the privilege of baptism for their children, and to a regular standing in the church, although they continued to neglect the ordinance of the Lord's Supper; the Session, upon mature deliberation, judging this, their former practice, to be anti-scriptural, and productive of evil to the church, resolved, that no person for the time to come, who shall be found to neglect the command of Christ, to show forth his death in the ordinance appointed for this purpose, shall be considered a member in good standing with this church, or entitled to the privilege of baptism for his children, that is, so long as he shall continue in the neglect of the above-mentioned duty. This rule is still acted on in the church.

June 27, 1808, it was resolved, that no person professing to belong to any sister church, shall hereafter be admitted to occasional communion in this church, for more than one year, without producing a certificate of regular standing in the church to which such person professedly belongs. This is still a rule of the Session of the church.†

[*Mr. Barnes's date is here correct; but on another page of the Manual, in his "List of Minutes," the year given is "1824," probably an oversight in printing, which has been widely copied. The error was corrected, with full proof, by the Rev. Dr. Green in THE RECORD for March and April, 1880, pp. 17 and 27.—EDITOR.]

[*This is an error. The correct number is 599. It is an interesting fact that Mr. Barnes's figures are on record and show a mistake in addition. He makes "1859" the sum of "37 x 140 x 130 x 67 x 76 x 78 x 71."—EDITOR.]

[†Of course, it is understood that reference is made to the rules in force in 1893.—EDITOR.]

According to the constitution of the Presbyterian church, members dismissed are always considered under the watch, and subject to the discipline of the church dismissing them, until they are actually received by the church to which they are dismissed. See Confession of Faith under the head of "Discipline," chap. x. sect. 1.

In the same book, under the same head, ch. xi. sect. 2, there is the following rule :— No certificate of church membership shall be considered as valid testimony of the good standing of the bearer, if it be more than one year old, except when there has been no opportunity of presenting it to the church.

It is regarded as the duty of members removing from our bounds, to apply for a dismission and recommendation to some other church. Incalculable disorder in the church, and great evil to the person neglecting it, have arisen from a forgetfulness or disregard of this duty.

The resolution to build the present place of worship was passed June 5, 1788 ; and it was built and completed between the years 1789, and the 26th day of November, 1795.

PRESENT OFFICERS OF THE CHURCH AND CONGREGATION.

MINISTER.
ALBERT BARNES.

RULING ELDERS.

EZRA HALSEY,	TIMOTHY TUCKER,
SAMUEL FREEMAN,	WILLIAM ENSLEE,
DAVID LINDSLY,	GEORGE K. DRAKE,
HENRY VAIL,	FREDERICK KING,
STEPHEN YOUNG,	JONATHAN THOMPSON,
PETER A. JOHNSON,	JONATHAN OLIVER,
LEWIS MILLS.	

DEACONS.
SAMUEL FREEMAN, DAVID LINDSLY.

TRUSTEES.
EZEKIEL WHITEHEAD, President,
STEPHEN A. PRUDDEN,
EDWARD CONDICT, CHARLES FORD,
JOSEPH CUTLER, LOAMMI MOORE.
LOAMMI MOORE, Treasurer.
MOSES CHERRY, Sexton.

THE FOLLOWING
FORM OF COVENANT,*
IS USED AT THE ADMISSION OF MEMBERS TO THE COMMUNION OF THE CHURCH.

You have presented yourselves in this public manner before God, to dedicate yourselves to his service, and to be incorporated with his visible people. You are about to profess supreme love to God ; sincere contrition for all your sins ; and faith unfeigned in the Lord Jesus Christ. You are about to enter into a solemn covenant to receive the Father, Son and Holy Ghost, as they are offered in the Gospel, and to walk in all the commandments and ordinances of the Lord blameless.

We trust you have considered the nature of these professions and engagements. The transaction is solemn, and will be attended with everlasting consequences. God and Holy Angels are witnesses. The eyes of the church and the world are, and will hereafter be upon you. Your vows will be recorded in Heaven, to be exhibited on your trial, at the last great day. Yet be not overwhelmed with these reflections. In the name of Christ you may come boldly to the God of grace ; and if you have sincere desires to be his, may venture thus unalterably to commit yourselves to Him, and trust in Him for strength to perform your vows.

Attend now to the
PROFESSION AND COVENANT.

I. You believe that there is one 1 God only,2 infinite in being,3 glory,4 and blessedness ;5 eternal,6 unchangeable,7 and Almighty ;8 most wise,9 most holy,10 most just,11 most merciful and gracious, long suffering, and abundant in goodness and truth.12

1 Deut. vi. 4 : 2 I Cor. viii. 4 : 3 Job xi. 7, 8, 9 : 4 Acts vii. 2 : 5 I Tim. vi. 15 : 6 Ps. xc. 2 : 7 Mal. iii. 6—James i. 17 : 8 Rev. iv. 8 : 9 Rom. xvi. 27 : 10 Isa. vi. 3 : 11 Deut. xxxii. 4 : 12 Exodus xxxiv. 6.

II. You believe that there are three persons in the Godhead, the Father, the Son and the Holy Ghost ;1 and that these three are one, true, eternal God, the same in substance, equal in power and glory.2

1 Matth. iii. 16, 17 ; and xxviii. 19—II Cor. xiii. 14 : 2John x. 30—Acts iv. 4, 5.

III. You believe that God governs the

[*It is not known when this covenant ceased to be used. Can any one inform us ?—EDITOR.]

universe ;1 that he doeth according to his will in the army of Heaven, and among the inhabitants of the earth ;2 that by his Providence he upholds, directs, disposes, and governs all creatures, actions, and things ;3 and that he confers grace and mercy according to his good pleasure.4

1 Ps. xciii. 1 : 2 Dan. iv. 35: 3 Mark x 29; Matth. v. 26, 30 ; Isa. x. 5, 6, 7 ; Rom. ix. 17, 18, 21, 22 ; Jude 4 : 4 Eph. i. 5—11 ; II. Tim. i. 9 ; Rom. viii. 30 ; II Thess. ii. 13 ; John iii. 5.

IV. You believe that man is a free agent, responsible to God for all his actions, thoughts, and plans ;1 that his sin, and indisposition to obey the law of God, are no excuse for transgression ;2 that every man is bound to repent ;3 and believe ;4 and that the Gospel is to be preached to all mankind.5

1 Rom. xiv. 12; II Cor. v. 10 ; 2 Matth. xxv. 14—30; Josh. xxiv. 15 ; Ezekiel xviii. especially the 31st and 32d verses ; 3 Acts xviii. 30 : 4 Mark xvi. 16 ; 5 Mark xvi. 15.

V. You believe that the Scriptures of the Old and New Testaments are a revelation from God, and are all given by inspiration of God, to be a rule of faith and life.

VI. You believe that God created man in his own image, in knowledge, righteousness, and true holiness ;1 that the first man sinned, 2 and that in consequence of his transgression all mankind are become sinners,3 and are, before generation, wholly destitute of holiness, and wholly disposed to evil,4 and on account of sin are justly liable to all the miseries of this life, to the agonies of death, and to the pains of hell forever.5

1 Gen. i. 26; Col. iii. 10 ; Eph. iv. 24: 2 Gen. iii. 6 : 3 Rom. v. 12—19 : 4 Gen. viii. 21 Ps. xiv. liii. v. cxl. x. xxxvi. and Isaiah lix. compared with Rom. iii. 10–-17 ; John iii. 1—7 ; Romans v. 12 : 5 Rom. vi. 23.

VII. You believe in the divinity of the Lord Jesus Christ,1 that he is truly and properly God ; that he assumed our nature ;2 that as mediator God gave him up to die for the sins of mankind ;3 that he suffered and died in the place of sinners, and thereby made atonement for transgression ;4 that it is only on account of his merits that men can be pronounced just before God ;5 that he rose from the dead, and ascended into Heaven, where he ever liveth to make intercession ;6 and that God can now be just, and yet the justifier of him that believeth.7

1 John i. 1—3 ; Heb. i. 10—12 ; Col. i. 15—17 ; Rom. ix. 5 ; John xx. 28 ; Phil. ii. 5—8 ; John v. 21—23 ; 2 John i. 14: 3 John iii. 16 ; Isa. liii. : 4 I Cor. xv. 3 ; Heb. ix. 26 ; Rom. iii. 25 ; II Cor. v. 21 : 5 Rom. iii. 24 ; Titus iii. 5, 7 ; Eph. i. 7 ; Phil. iii. 9 : 61 Cor. xv.; Mark xvi. 19 ; Acts i. 9 ; Heb. vii. 25 : 7 Rom. iii. 26.

VIII. You believe in the personality and divinity of the Holy Ghost ;1 that he renews and sanctifies the heart ;2 that he is given to the people of God to enlighten their minds, to guide them in the path of duty, to comfort them in affliction, and to sustain them in dying.3

1 Acts v. 4, 5 ; Matth. xii. 31, 32 ; Eph. iv. 30 ; Acts vii. 51 ; I Cor. ii. 9, 11 ; Heb. ix. 14; I Cor. xii. 11 ; II Cor. xiii. 14 : 2 John iii. 7, 8 ; I Cor. xi. 11 ; II Thess. ii. 13 : 3 John xv. 26; I Thess. l. 6 ; Rom. xiv. 17 ; Eph. iii. 14, 19 ; Luke xi. 9—13.

IX. You believe that the law of God is binding as a rule of life on all mankind ;1 that a holy life is necessary to honour God, to evidence and adorn the Christian profession, and to reap the rewards of Heaven ;2 and that those who are violators of that law will be excluded from his kingdom of righteousnsss.3

1 Rom. vii. 12; James ii. 10, 11 ; I Tim. i. 9, 10 ; Ps. xix. 7 ; Matth. xxii. 37—40 : 2 Heb. xii. 14; I John iii. 3 ; Phil. iv. 8 ; I John iii. 7, 8 ; II John 6 ; Matth. vii. 16 ; 3 Exod. xxxiv. 7 ; Rev. xxi. 27 ; I Cor. vi. 9, 10.

X. You believe that at the end of the world the Lord Jesus Christ will return with the glory of his Father and with the holy angels ;1 that there will be a resurrection of the dead, and a final judgment pronounced on all mankind.2

1 Acts i. 11 ; Matth. xvi. 27 : 2 I Cor. xv. : John v. 28 ; Matt. xxv. 31—56.

XI. You believe that the righteous shall be everlastingly rewarded in Heaven, and the wicked everlastingly punished in hell.1

1 Matth. xxv. 46.

[Here the candidates bow assent.]

In this public manner you do hereby confess and bewail the original and total depravity of your nature ; the past enmity of your hearts against God; the unbelief which has led you to reject a Saviour ; and the manifold transgressions of your lives ; all which sins you do condemn, and in your purpose forever renounce.

And now in the presence of God, his holy angels, and this assembly, you do solemnly avouch the Lord JEHOVAH to be your God and portion, and the object of your supreme delight; the Lord Jesus Christ to be your Saviour from sin and death—your Prophet to instruct you, your Priest to atone and intercede for you; and your king to rule, and protect, and enrich you : and the Holy Ghost to be your Sanctifier, Comforter, and Guide.

To this God, Father, Son, and Holy Ghost you do now, without reserve, give yourself away, in a covenant never to be revoked, to be his willing servants for ever; to observe all his commandments and ordinances in the sanctuary, in the family, and in the closet. You do also bind yourselves by covenant to this church, to watch over us in the Lord, to seek our peace and edification, and to submit to the government and discipline of Christ, as here administered.

This you profess and engage. [*Here again the candidates bow assent.*]

The candidates are then addressed by the minister in the following, or in a similar manner :

In consequence of these professions and promises, we affectionately receive you as members of this church, and in the name of Christ declare you entitled to all its visible privileges. We welcome you to this fellowship with us in the blessings of the Gospel, and on our part engage to watch over you, and seek your edification as long as you shall continue with us. Should you have occasion to remove, it will be your duty to seek, and ours to grant, a recommendation to some other church; for hereafter you cannot withdraw from the watch, and communion with the Saints without a breach of covenant.

And now, beloved in the Lord, let it be impressed on your minds that you have entered into solemn relations, which you can never renounce, and from which you can never escape. Wherever you are, these vows will remain. They will follow you to the bar of God; and in whatever world you may be fixed, they will abide on you to all eternity. You can never be again as you have been. You have unalterably committed yourselves, and henceforth you *must* be the servants of the Lord.

Hereafter the eye of the world will be upon you ; and as you conduct yourselves, so will religion be honoured or disgraced. If you walk worthy of your profession, you will be a credit and comfort to us; but if otherwise, you will be a grief of heart, and vexation ; and if there is a wo pronounced on him who offends one of Christ's little ones, wo, wo, to the person who offends a whole church.

But, beloved, we are persuaded better things of you, and things that accompany salvation, though we thus speak.

May the Lord support and guide you through this transitory life, and after this warfare is accomplished, receive you and us, to that blessed church, where our love shall be for ever perfect, and our joy for ever full.

A frequent and devout perusal of the above FORM OF ADMISSION TO THE CHURCH, *is recommended to all our Communicants; especially to read it with meditation and prayer, as a preparatory exercise before every Communion.*

(*To be continued.*)

A writer of the tenth century says that the opinion of some "unlearned priests" was that leap year had been caused by Joshua, when he made the sun stand still !

The history of the churches in Morristown must be full of interest. THE RECORD hopes to be able to present those histories in its pages. Will not the pastors of the various congregations aid in this good work ?

In the present day bishops form only about one-fourteenth of the numbers of the House of Lords in England. In the eighteenth century they composed about one-eighth, but in the twelfth they formed six-sevenths of the entire House. The reason of this is to be found in the fact that in olden times education was confined to the clergy.

A poem entitled "On the Creation and Paradyce Lost," was written in English metre before Milton was born. Its author was Sir Richard Maitland. It was first published by Ramsay in 1724. It is quite probable, therefore, that John Milton never saw this production. Certainly, no one who reads Maitland's poem will charge Milton with plagiarism.

THE RECORD.

FIRST PRESBYTERIAN CHURCH, MORRISTOWN, N. J.

"THIS SHALL BE WRITTEN FOR THE GENERATION TO COME."—Psalms 102 : 18.

VOLUME III.   NOVEMBER, 1883.   NUMBER 11

[Printed with the Approval of the Session.]

THE RECORD

Will be published monthly at Morristown, N. J. Terms $1.00 per annum, *in advance.*

Subscriptions may be made at the bookstores of Messrs. Runyon and Emmell, or to Messrs. James R. Voorhees and William D. Johnson, or by letter addressed to the

EDITOR OF THE RECORD,
Morristown, N. J.

Entered at the Post Office at Morristown, N. J., as second class matter.

[*Continued from page 80*]

MR. BARNES'S MANUAL.

FORM USED AT THE BAPTISM OF CHILDREN.

Children, one or both of whose parents are members of the church, only, are by a rule of the church to be baptized. It is regarded as the duty of parents to present them for baptism at as early an age as may be practicable.

The time for administering this ordinance to children is on the Friday previous to the Communion, *before the Sermon.* They are expected, therefore, to be present at the commencement of the service.

The Book of Discipline of the Church directs that a record be kept of the names of all who are baptized. A scrip of paper, therefore, containing the name of the child, and the *names of both the parents,* is indispensably necessary. When the time of the birth of the child is also communicated, it will be faithfully preserved on the records of the church.

Children are regarded as members of the church by right of their birth. The ordinance of baptism is not, therefore, strictly an initiating ordinance; but a public recogni-

tion of their relation to the Church. It is also the duty of parents, as well as an expression of pious feeling, to dedicate them thus to the Lord.

As members of the church they should be brought up in the nurture and admonition of the Lord. They are subject to the watch and counsel of those set over them in the church. They are to be taught that it is their privilege, as well as their duty, early to devote themselves personally to his purpose. See " Directory for Worship," ch. ix. § 1.

When baptism is administered, the parents are addressed in the following or similar words :

Baptism was instituted by the Lord Jesus Christ, the Great Head of the Church, to be a seal of the Covenant of Grace. The water in this ordinance implies guilt and pollution, and the necessity of the gracious operation of the Divine Spirit to cleanse us from sin. It represents to us regeneration, and sanctification by the Spirit of God. It is the public sign of admission to the privileges of the Church of God. But you are not to imagine that any external rite will cleanse from sin. A deeper, far deeper work, than can be accomplished by the use of any external ordinances, is requisite, to prepare the souls of these children for the Kingdom of Heaven.

The authority for administering this rite to children is based on the conduct of Christ and his Apostles, and on the privileges granted to the ancient people of God. In the time of our Saviour, the Jews regarded it as an inestimable privilege, to devote their offspring to the God who gave them, in the rite, which had been appointed to their fathers. That rite had been directed by the authority of God. There is no intimation in the New Testament of any purpose to deprive them of this privilege, in the new economy. If there had been any such design of exclusion—any such material change in the mode of administering the mercies of God to his church—it is fair to suppose that our Saviour would have been at pains to have satisfied the Jews of the intention. If it had been the design of the Founder of our Religion to abridge the privileges of those who should embrace his religion—of cutting off by one fell sweep all children from the communion of the faithful, and of overturning an economy that had been sanctioned by God, and endeared by long observance, they had a right to expect that there would have been some formal reason given of a proceeding so remarkable, and of an act that interfered so much with what they deemed their dearest rights, and the appropriate expression of parental feeling.

So far from it, however, there is not the most distant intimation in the New Testament, of any design of *excluding* children from a public dedication to God, or of *excluding* parents from devoting them to him. On those who deny the right to such a dedication, it is incumbent to allege the proof of any such purpose.

The contrary of any such design, is fairly gathered from the New Testament. Our Saviour encouraged parents to bring their children to him. He reproved those who would have prevented such a purpose, and who would have maintained that they were to be *excluded* from a public presentation to him. He said, " of such is the Kingdom of Heaven."

The Apostles acted as the Saviour did. They baptized households—that is, families —without any intimation that they were all adults—a thing that in itself is so improbable, that if it had been the case, we might have expected a formal statement of the fact. No allusion is made, however, to any such unusual state of things—nothing to lead us to believe that these families differed from others—or in others words, no intimation that there were *no children* in them. When men speak of *households*, without any qualifying or *limiting* expressions, we are to suppose that they do not differ essentially from other households. Such we may fairly suppose the households mentioned in the New Testament to have been

—that is, until the contrary is shown, we have a right to suppose that children and servants were baptized.

It is an indubitable fact, moreover, that very early in the Christian church the practice was universal. The first mention of the subject implied that it was common.* Such an early universal practice could have had no other origin than the practice of the Apostles.

You have a right, therefore, to offer those children to God in this ordinance. It is a proper expression of pious parental feeling. It is suitable to invoke the blessing of your and their Great Father on them, in the beginning of their years, and to commit them thus early to his guidance. Their souls are immortal. They have commenced an existence which can never end. None but God, can befriend them in the temptations and trials before them; and it is right, therefore, to seek for them the guidance of his hand.

They are committed to your care. On *your* conduct will depend much of their usefulness and respectability on earth. But they are doomed to an eternity of being; and on *you* also will, in a most tremendously responsible degree, depend their destiny beyond the grave. Be prepared, then, to resign their spirits into the hands of God who gave them, when he shall call for them.

If it shall please God to spare your lives, and the lives of your children, until they come to years capable of receiving instruction, it will be your duty to teach them, or to cause them to be taught, to read God's Holy Word; to instruct them in the principles of the true religion—the history of man—the creation and fall—the law of God —the economy of the ancient society of believers—the promises of a Saviour—his advent, life, instructions, sufferings, death, resurrection, and ascension—to teach them the necessity of the new birth, and a holy life—to remind them that they must die, and that after death will be the judgment, and to endeavour to direct their thoughts as the great, supreme object of their living, to the tremendous scenes of the eternal world—to pray *with* them, and *for* them; to set an example of piety before them ; to

---

*In the third century. See Milner, Ch. Hist. Vol. I. p. 320 ;

govern your temper, and speak the truth; to exercise a wholesome discipline, and to endeavour to show by your life the comparative worthlessness of wealth, and fashion, and amusement, and adorning, and the transcendant excellence and value of the things of religion; and to endeavour, by all the means in your power, and by all attainable aid, and direction from heaven, to train them up for a world of holiness. These duties, or whatever else you are convinced or shall 'be convinced, from the word of God, are binding on you as Christian parents, you do promise and covenant, in the presence of God and this church, that as God shall give you strength, you will endeavour faithfully to perform.—(*Here the parents bow assent.*)

It is reccommended to those who have offered children to God in baptism, frequently, and with careful self-examination, to persue the preceeding Form. The hopes of the church rest in the rising generation. These hopes can be expected to be realized only in the faithful discharge of duty on the part of parents.

CHURCH NOTICES.

1. The seasons of SACRAMENTAL COMMUNION occur in this church only in the months of March, June, September, and December, on the *first* Sabbath in each month.

2. A lecture, preparatory to the solemnity, is attended in the church, on the *Friday* previous to the Communion, in the afternoon, at half past two o'clock in December and March. and at half past three in June and September. The baptism of the children and servants of believers is administered in the *commencement* of the services.

3. A church meeting—that is, of the *communicants alone*, is held, by a resolution of the Session, in the months of January, April, July, and October, on Thursday afternoon, in the Session House, at such times in the month as the pastor may appoint. The object of this meeting is mutual prayer, exhortation, and praise. It is designed to promote Christian acquaintance; to make firm the bands of Christian fellowship; and to present the united wants of the church, *as such*, before the Throne of Grace. At this meeting, which, hom its nature, is one of special interest, and which has in other churches been followed with a

special blessing, it is *peculiarly* desirable that every member should be present.

4. The session of the church meet regularly on the first Tuesday of every month, at the house of the pastor, for united prayer, and consultation on the state of religion in their own hearts, and in the church.

Their other meetings are held in the Session House, agreeably to notice given previously from the pulpit. Their ordinary time of meeting is on Thursday afternoon, in the week but one next preceding each communion. Before the Session, at a regular meeting, must application be made *in person* for union to the church. The applicant is examined on his knowledge of religion, and personal piety, and his wishes in coming to the communion, and on his purposes of life; and if approved, is publicly propounded for admission to the communion of the church; and, if there are no valid objections offered, on the day of the next communion, publicly admitted as a member of the church in full and equal fellowship. The meetings of the session are properly public; and any person has the right of access to accompany any applicant, propose any business, enter any complaint, or claim any redress which may properly relate to the jurisdiction of the session.

5. It is proper that individuals should seek and cultivate acquaintance with the elders. They are appointed to guard the interests of the church, and to promote the welfare of religion. Persons thoughtful, or anxious about their condition, will always be welcome to the attentions and counsel of any of the elders, or of the pastor.

6. It is proper for persons who are sick, to send for any of the elders or the pastor to visit them at their own houses. (James v. 14)—Is any sick among you? let him CALL for the *Elders* of the church. It is at no time considered as any interruption of the appropiate business of the pastor to be invited to visit the sick in any part of the congregation. On the contrary, such invitations will be thankfully received, and promptly attended to. It is regarded as a *privilege* to be admitted as a friend and comforter, to the room of the sick, and the bed-side of the dying.

7. It is wished that FUNERALS should be

attended, when convenient, in the *afternoon*. The duties of a large charge require that the pastor should have a portion of his time in which he may be free from interruption. All that is wished or desired is, that he may not be liable to such interruption in the forenoon. Where distance of relations or peculiar circumstances in the family, make an earlier hour desirable, however, the funeral will be promptly attended. Exercises at funerals, and at all other services, commence *precisely* at the hour of appointment.

8. A collection for the aid of the poor members of the church is taken up at each communion.

9. The deacons of the church have the care and service of the table of communion; and the management of the poor fund, and its distribution. They are responsible for a just appropriation of this fund; and are required to make report at the end of each year, to the church, of the distribution that has been made of it, and of the wants of the poor members of the church. It is proper for any poor members of the church to apply to them for aid.

This important and deeply beneficial charity deserves the particular attention of the members of the church. We have not *many* members of the church in indigent circumstances, but "the poor" are "with" us —and they are worthy of aid. There is no danger that this charity will be abused. It is committed to the hands of respectable men, and it is a proper expression of our regard for our brethren, as well as to our Saviour, that we should give of our abundance to those who are poor and needy.

10. A weekly lecture is kept up regularly in the Session House on Thursday evenings; and preaching once a fortnight is expected in some other part of the congregation.

11. The monthly concert for prayer is attended on the evening of the first Monday in the month, in the Session House, and in other parts of the congregation. Addresses are made, missionary intelligence communicated, and a collection taken up in aid of *Domestic Missions*.

12. A Bible Class is attended in the Session House once in a fortnight, on Tuesday evenings; and every Sabbath afternoon in one of four neighbourhoods in some other part of the congregation. About five chapters constitute a lesson. Sacred geography, chronology, and biblical history are taught, and a doctrinal and practical exposition of the lesson given. The classes are composed of persons of both sexes, and spectators are admitted. Though designed principally for the young, no age is excluded.

13. It is the duty of the members of the church to watch over each other, to aid each other in the Christian life, and to give and receive faithful counsel "in the spirit of meekness." They should *never* unnecessarily publish delinquencies and faults; but when a brother goes astray, and private admonition and entreaties are found unavailing—*which should always be the first measures*—it is their *duty* to report the matter to the Pastor or Session. (See Matth. xviii. 15, 16, 17.) To this neglected, but incumbent duty, their solemn church compact, their covenant engagements, and the command of their common Lord, solemnly bind them. No church can flourish, nor will religion *live*, where its members do not "speak the truth in love"—and " provoke one another to love and good works"—and maintain a sacred regard for the purity of the Christian character—and " strive to adorn the doctrine of God their Saviour in all things."

14. A Sunday School for the benefit of both sexes, is kept in the church, on the afternoon of the Sabbath; and schools are also established in other parts of the congregation.

15. The following is a LIST of the BENEVOLENT SOCIETIES existing in the congregation:

1st. *Gentlemen's Association*—formed to aid the American Board of Commissioners for Foreign Mission. Officers—a President, Vice-President, Treasurer, Secretary, three Directors, and nine Collectors. Time of the Annual Meeting, fixed by the Morris County Auxiliary Society.

2d. *Ladies' Association*—formed for the same object, and with a similar organization.

3d. *Morristown Domestic Missionary Society*—auxiliary to the New-Jersey Missionary Society. Officers—President, Vice-President, Treasurer and Secretary, and

Board of Managers. Annual Meeting, in September. This Society, now on the decline, has been the means of establishing two churches, and supporting the school at Split-Rock for two years, and has accomplished much good.

4th. *Tract Society of Morristown.*

5th. *Sabbath School Association.* Officers —First and Second Directress, Secretary, Treasurer, and five Managers. Annual Meeting, first Monday in April.

6th. *Morristown Female Charitable Society* —designed to aid the poor. Officers—First and Second Directress, Secretary, Treasurer, and six Managers. The Managers meet monthly. Annual Meeting, second Monday in November.

7th. *Tract Society of Monroe.* Officers— President, V. President, Secretary, and Treasurer. Annual Meeting, first Monday in September.

8th. *Tract Society of New-Vernon.*

9th. *Society for the Promotion of Temperance*—Monroe. Officers—President, Treasurer, and Secretary, and Board of Managers. Annual Meeting, in April.

10th. *Female Cent Society*—for the use of the Theological Seminary at Princeton. [*]

PRESBYTERIANISM.

[The following sketch was prepared, by request, for another publication. In its reproduction here several paragraphs have been added, which are of more interest to Presbyterians than to the readers for whom the sketch was prepared.]

The Presbyterian Church rests its right to be on the need of emphasizing certain principles which it finds in the Bible, and particularly in the New Testament. These principles respect three classes of subjects, doctrine, government and Church-membership. In the space at hand only the barest outline of these subjects is possible, but this may be given largely in the words of the late Dr. Charles Hodge.

DOCTRINE.

The latest embodiment of doctrines is contained in the Confession of Faith, together with the Larger and the Shorter Catechisms, issued by the Westminster As-

[* In addition to what has been reprinted in THE RECORD, Mr. Barnes's Manual contains, "List of Ministers," "List of Ruling Elders," "List of Deacons," and "List of Trustees," from the earliest records down to Mr. Barnes's pastorate, together with "List of Present Communicants," for the year 1828, and fifteen "Questions for Self-Examination," taken from the Laight Street Presbyterian Church, New York. These will not now be reprinted.]

sembly in 1646 and 1647. All candidates for the diaconate, the eldership and the ministry are required sincerely to receive and adopt this Confession, as containing the system of doctrine taught in the Holy Scriptures. The definition of this subscription is the key to the creed of the Presbyterian Church, Dr. Hodge makes the following points. (1.) The Confession is not adopted for "substance of doctrine"; because this is obviously not the meaning of the phrase, it is contrary to the decisions of the Church, and, in short, "substance of doctrine" has no definite assignable meaning. (2.) Nor does the candidate profess to adopt every proposition contained in the Confession as a part of his own faith; because this, too, is contrary to the plain meaning of the phrase, to the decisions of the Church, and it is impracticable. But (3.) subscription is simply and only to the *system* of doctrine which the Confession contains. There can be no dispute as to what this system is. It includes three distinct classes of doctrines, First, those common to all Christians, which are summed up in the ancient creeds, the Apostles', the Nicene, and the Athanasian. Secondly, those common to all Protestants, and by which they are distinguished from Romanists. Thirdly, those peculiar to the Reformed Churches, by which they are distinguished from the Lutherans, Arminians and other sects of later origin. As opposed to the Lutherans, the system of the Confession affirms a real, but a spiritual rather than a physical, presence of Christ in the Sacraments. As opposed to Arminians and others, it affirms the five points of Augustinianism, which were assented to "at the Synod of Dort by all the Reformed Churches, namely, those of Switzerland, Germany, France, England and Scotland, as well as Holland." These five points are (1.) The imputation of the first sin in penal consequences to all the human race ; (2.) The innate sinfulness of human character, (so that there can be no self-conversion,) and consequently the efficacious grace of the Spirit ; (3.) The special reference of Christ's work to those who had been promised him by the Father, by which their salvation is rendered certain ; (4.) Gratuitous, personal election to eternal life ; and (5.) The perseverance of the saints. "It is a matter of history," says Dr. Hodge, "that these doctrines constitute the distinguishing doctrines of the Reformed Churches. And, therefore, any man who receives these several classes of doctrine, (viz.: those common to all Christians, those common to all Protestants, and those peculiar to the Reformed Churches,) holds in its integrity the system of doctrine contained in the Westminster Confession. This is all he professes to do when he adopts that Confession in the form prescribed by our Constitution." The Confession also contains deliverances on other topics, but assent to these deliverances is not required. (See Dr. Hodge's Church Polity, pp. 317 to 342.)

GOVERNMENT.

The principles of government were also enunciated by the Westminster Assembly, though their statement has been expanded and amended by different bodies of Presbyterians at various times down to very recent dates. Says Dr. Hodge: "There are fixed laws assigned by God according to which all healthful and normal action of the body is regulated. So it is with regard to the Church. There are fixed laws in the Bible, according to which all healthful development and action of the external Church are determined. But, as within the limits of the laws which control the development of the human body, there is endless diversity among different races, adapting them to different climes and modes of living, so also in the Church. It is not tied down to one particular mode of organization and action, at all times and under all circumstances, * * * The leading principles laid down in Scripture, regarding the organization and action of the Church, are the parity of the clergy, the right of the people and the unity of the Church."

As to the *parity of the clergy*. In the New Testament, connected with the ministry of the word and the oversight of the Church, three classes of officers are mentioned ; apostles, prophets and presbyters or bishops. By the scholarship of all Churches it is now conceded that, in the New Testament, the titles of presbyter and bishop designate but one office, or order of the clergy. The old claim, that the New Testament bishops were a distinct order from the presbyters, has been abandoned on account of the overwhelming array of facts against such a claim. And now-a-days the Churches which assert the divine right of bishops make them the successors, not of the New Testament bishops, but of the apostles. We hold, on the contrary, that the apostles and prophets were temporary offices and have had no true successors, for the following reasons : (1) There is no command in the New Testament to continue them ; (2) There is no specification of the qualifications to be required in those who seek these offices ; (3) There is no record in the New Testament, or in the first century afterwards, of any one recognized as a true successor of an apostle ; (4) An apostle, as Paul defined his right to the title, must have seen Jesus so as to be a witness from personal knowledge, must be able to work miracles, must be inspired ; and no one, since the New Testament times, has ever possessed these three essentials of an apostle.

On the other hand the gifts of teaching and ruling, which constituted a New Testament presbyter or bishop, are continued ; the command to ordain them, the authority of presbyterial as opposed to apostolic ordination, their qualifications, and the account of their appointment, are minutely recorded in the New Testament : and they continue in unbroken succession wherever the Church is found. Every pastor in the Presbyterian Church is a bishop, in the New Testament meaning of the title, as conceded by the ablest scholars of the Church of England, as well as by others. These presbyters, or bishops, says Dr. Hodge, "are the highest permanent officers of the Church for which we have any divine warrant. If the Church, for special reasons, sees fit to appoint any higher order, such as the bishops of the Lutheran Church and the superintendents, clothed with the powers of a presbytery, in the early Church of Scotland, this is merely a human arrangement. The parity of the clergy is a matter of divine right ; they all hold the same office, and have the same rights, so far as they depend on divine appointment."

"As to the *right of the people* to take part in the government of the Church, this also is a divine right. This follows because the Spirit of God, who is the source of all power, dwells in the people, and not exclusively in the clergy; because we are commanded to submit ourselves to our brethren in the Lord; because the people are commanded to exercise this power, and are upbraided when unfaithful or negligent in the discharge of this duty; and because, in the New Testament, we find the brethren in the actual recognized exercise of the authority in question, which was never disputed in the Church until the beginning of the dark ages. This right of the people must, of necessity, be exercised through representatives. Under the Old Testament, in the assembly or congregation of the people, this principle of representation was by divine appointment universally recognized. By like authority it was introduced into the Christian Church as a fundamental principle of its organization. This is the broad, scriptural *jure divino* foundation of the office of *Ruling Elder.*" Ruling elders are laymen, and, as representatives of the people, compose the Session, which exercises the spiritual government of a particular congregation, and of which the minister is, *ex officio,* the moderator or president. The other courts of the Church are composed of equal numbers of ministers and elders, and in these the elders have the same rights and powers possesed by ministers. Deacons, like those appointed for the Church in Jerusalem, are also laymen; and, for the most part, their duties are simply the care of the poor in the local congregation, though in some cases they also hold the trusteeship of the church property.

"The *unity of the Church* is not merely a union of faith and communion; not merely a fellowship in the Spirit, but also a union of subjection, so that one part is subject to a larger, and a larger to the whole.* This also is *jure divino,* because the whole Church is made one by the indwelling of the Spirit; because we are commanded to be subject to our brethren, not on the ground of proximity in space, nor of a mutual covenant or agreement, but by the fact of Christian brotherhood; because in the apostolic, as in the Old Testament Church, the whole body of the professors of the true religion were thus united as one body; because by

---

*In contrast with all Independents, like Congregationalists and Baptists, who deny a union of *subjection.*

the instinct of Christian feeling the Church in all ages, has striven after this union of subjection, and recognized its violation as inconsistent with the law of its constitution. This, again, by necessity and divine appointment, is a representative union, and hence the provincial, national and œcumenical councils which mark the whole history of the Church." These councils among us are known by the names of The Presbytery, embracing the Churches of a small district and meeting frequently; The Synod, including the Churches of a State, meeting annually; The General Assembly, in which all the Churches of the nation are represented, also meeting once a year; and The General Council, where Presbyterians of various names and all lands meet by delegates every three or four years. (See Dr. Hodge's Church Polity, pages 118 to 156, and page 242.)

CHURCH MEMBERSHIP.

While candidates for office in the Presbyterian Church are required to assent to the system of the Westminister Confession, *no such assent* is required of candidates for Church-membership. The rule of the Church is briefly as follows:

Those baptized in infancy are to receive Christian instruction, and when they come to years of discretion, if they be free from scandal, appear sober and steady, and to have sufficient knowledge to discern the Lord's body, they are to be informed that it is their duty and privilege to come to the Lord's Supper, and be examined as to their knowledge and piety by the Session. "When unbaptised persons apply for admission to the Church, they shall, in ordinary cases, after giving satisfaction with respect to their knowledge and piety, make a public profession of their faith in the presence of the congregation; and thereupon be baptized." (Chap. ix. Directory for Worship.) No prescribed formula is given, assent to which is to be accounted as evidence of repentance and faith. The qualifications for membership, which the Session may require in any candidate, are limited by the words "knowledge and piety," "free from scandal," "sober and steady,' "sufficient knowledge to discern the Lord's body." Says Dr. Hodge, "Nothing can be plainer than that our church requires nothing more than credible evidence of Christian character as the condition of Christian communion. Of that evidence the Church officers are to judge. Not one word is said of the adoption of the Confession of Faith, or of anything but the evidences of piety. Any man therefore, who gives evidence of being a Christian, we are bound by the rules of our Church to admit to our communion. And so far from there being the slightest intimation that the adoption of the whole system of our doctrine contained in our standards is necessary to a man's being a Christian, there is the strongest evidence to the contrary. This evidence is found in the omission of any mention of the standards in those passages which speak of the communion of saints; in the mention of other terms than those of subscription to a formula of doctrine, and in the admission that true Churches may be impure both as to doctrine and practice, that is, may reject what we hold to be the truth without forfeiting their Christian character." (See Dr. Hodge's Church Polity, page 218 to 241.)

It is to be observed, that these statements refer to membership, and not merely to occasional communion. For example, if a member of a Baptist or Methodist, or Roman or Greek, or any other Christian Church, should apply to be received as a member in the Presbyterian Church, our rules would not require him to be treated as if he were not a Church member and so oblige him to submit to be again baptized, or again confirmed; but, on the ground of his Christian character, would recognize his previous Church membership, and simply welcome him to all the privileges of that membership in the Presbyterian household of Christian faith. Conversely, our rules provide for the dismissal, with Christian recommendations, of any of our members to any other household of the faith.

It should also be said that the Presbyterian Church recognizes the ordination, as well as the baptism and the confirmation of other Christian bodies; and accords these bodies equal standing with itself as true *Churches* of the Lord Jesus Christ. The claim might perhaps be justly made, especially in view of this recognition and of its doctrine of membership, that the Presby-

terian Church is the broadest and most Catholic of all existing Christian bodies.

FIRST REFORMED CHURCH OF PATERSON.

This church was originally called the "First Reformed Dutch Church of Totawa." Its history is interesting. It was organized some time about 1750; perhaps, between that year and 1756. Its first minister, believed to be the Rev. David Marinus, had charge also of the churches at Acquackanonk and Pompton. His parish, if this be true, was much larger than any pastor of modern times would care to attempt to serve. In 1762 Rev. Cornelius Blanco became the next pastor, and he, too, ministered to the three churches. Rev. Dr. Meyer, who succeeded Mr. Blanco, preached until his death in 1791. In 1816 the Rev. Wilhelimas Eltinge gave half his time and services to the Totawa church, and this he continued to do until 1833, after which he ministered to the church at Paramas. In 1834 Rev. George C. Vandervoort became pastor and remained until 1837, when he was succeeded by the Rev. Dr. Wiggins, who continued pastor until 1856. In 1857 the Rev. Philip Peltz, D. D. became the pastor and he was succeeded, in 1860 by Rev. Alexander McKelway, who resigned in 1865. In 1865 the Rev. John Steele was called to be the pastor.

The history of the Reformed Dutch Church, or as the members of that denomination prefer now to call themselves, the Reformed Church, in New Jersey is a most interesting subject and should receive the attention of some historian who can do justice to the theme. That history is largely interwoven into the history of the State, especially of this part of the commonwealth. The first settlers in Bergen County were all of that sect of Christians, and they brought with them from Holland, that sturdy independence, inherited from their ancestors, who fought for their political and religious liberty with Philip II. and his blood thirsty lieutenants, the Duke of Alva and Alexander Farnese, which made them the strongest and most zealous supporters of the cause of American independence in the war of the Revolution.

THE RECORD.

FIRST PRESBYTERIAN CHURCH, MORRISTOWN, N. J.

"THIS SHALL BE WRITTEN FOR THE GENERATION TO COME."—Psalms 102 : 18.

VOLUME III.	DECEMBER, 1883.	NUMBER 12

[Printed with the Approval of the Session.]

THE RECORD

Will be published monthly at Morristown, N. J. Terms $1.00 per annum, *in advance.*

Subscriptions may be made at the bookstores of Messrs. Runyon and Emmell, or to Messrs. James R. Voorhees and William D. Johnson, or by letter addressed to the

EDITOR OF THE RECORD,
Morristown, N. J.

Entered at the Post Office at Morristown, N. J., as second class matter.

LEWIS CONDICT, M. D.

Dr. Condict, for many years, was deeply interested in the First Presbyterian church. He was, at one time, a physician of large practice in Morristown and was considered very skillful in his profession. His family was collaterally connected with Silas Condict, of Revolutionary fame, of whom a sketch has already appeared in the RECORD

Dr. Condict married, for his first wife, a daughter of the Rev. Nathan Woodhull; D. D., who preached for many years in Long Island, and whose memory is cherished in the churches, as a great preacher and one of the saintly men of the land.

Dr. Condict, for fifty years and more, lived in the house on South street, now occupied by the Rev. Twining and owned by Mrs. Brandagee of Utica, N. Y., the widow of the Rev. Dr. John Brandagee and Dr. Condict's youngest daughter.

Dr. Condict died at a very advanced age, more than eighty, and then his death was accelerated by a fall from the back stoop of his house; by which accident his hip bone was broken. This confined him to his room for a year and more before his death.

He took a deep interest not only in public affairs, but also in all matters appertain-

ing to the first church. For many years he occupied a place in the choir and, up to the time of the accident, which resulted in his death, he was constant in his attendance upon the services of the sanctuary.

When nearly eighty years of age he undertook a journey into Kentucky, where he had relatives. Early in life he entered into public office, for which his talents and tastes peculiarly fitted him. In 1805, he was elected to the State Legislature and was a member of that body for five successive years ; during two of those years he occupied the Speaker's chair. Subsequently and for several sessions he represented this State in the Lower House of Congress. Those were times when the faithful representative was rewarded by many returns to office, and Dr Condict must have been considered worthy of the confidence of his constituents, for he was renominated several times without opposition from his own party, which was then dominant in the State, and was re-elected with large majorities. He was an original temperance man, for, while in Congress, on several occasions, he presented a bill, the object of which was to prevent the manufacture and sale of distilled spirits.

He was, too, a man of more than ordinary ability. He delivered a speech at Morristown, in the old church, upon the Fourth of July 1828, which met with such decided approbation from his fellow citizens that a copy of it was requested for publication, and it was afterwards printed and no doubt has been preserved by some citizens who knew the author.

Dr. Condict was remarkable for his geniality of temperament, his great conversational powers, his kindly wit and gentle humor. His wit sparkled and enlivened, but never wounded ; he delighted in humor, but he never descended ; his jests were inimitable, but they never were uttered at the expense of another. His anecdotal treasury was filled to overflowing, and was always ready to respond to any draft upon it, but it was always bright and pointed, always new and never wearied nor disgusted.

He had several children, two of whom survive, Dr. Nathan W. Condict, named for his maternal grand-father and Mrs. Martina Brandagee, now living at Utica, N. Y. One of his daughters married the Rev. George Bush, the eminent scholar; another married a Mr. Hall, a successful lawyer in Washington, D. C.; another became the wife of Mr. James Cook, and his youngest is now the widow of the Rev. John Brandagee, formerly Rector of an Episcopal Church in Utica. Three of his sons were physicians, Silas L., Nathan W., and Lewis, Jr., a young man of great promise, who died in early manhood.

Dr. Condict was an ardent patriot and served his country, not from love of office, but from patriotic sentiments. It was in his time no easy task to be in public life, and especially a member of Congress. Washington was then much farther removed from Morristown than is St. Louis at the present. The position of Congressman then carried with it banishment from home and family for an indefinite time. Dr. Condict remained long in office and devoted to the performance of his duties as a public servant, the best energies of his nature as well as the best years of his life. His family was large, and while he was in office, needed a father's rule. But his excellent wife was equal to the task, and her sons and daughters, a goodly number they were, hardly felt the removal of the father's protection, for in the mother they found combined the love and tenderness of the mother, and the strict and guiding rule of the father. She was a slender, delicate woman, but one of those rare souls whose presence in any household was a blessing. Her sympathies were alert for all, her benefactions were not for home and family alone, but were for the poor and needy, and, though illy able from feeble health to take a very active part, she never failed at the call of duty, from whatever place it might come. The Church benefitted by her gentle ways, the poor were the recipients of her benefactions, and in all public matters where woman's aid was needed, either by the way of

counsel or action, she never failed to respond. She lived to see her children grow up around her and then died a Christian's death, loved by all. His second wife was a Miss Elmendorf, of Somerset County, a woman of marked ability. Mrs. Brandagee was her only child.

In person Dr. Condict was tall and commanding. His manners were simple and unpretending, his judgment excellent, his intellect cultivated; he was decided in his views in politics and on all other subjects which he was called upon to discuss, but he never obtruded his opinions offensively upon others. In times when party politics raged high and his fellow citizens sometimes indulged in acrimonious debates, too often verging upon anger and violence, he calmed passion by a pleasant word, a kindly remark or a jest which provoked laughter and cleared away the frown and quelled the threatened tumult. His oration, to which reference has been made, was not delivered at a union celebration, but was pronounced at the request of a political party, who that year celebrated the national anniversary separate from their political opponents. It was a time of the utmost rancor, when party lines were drawn to their utmost tension. But in his oration there is manifested no bitterness, no rancor; nothing was uttered by him which could possibly injure the feelings of the most wilful of political antagonists. It was calm, cool, but decided in its statement of his opinions on public affairs, and a dispassionate discussion of political matters to which any one, no matter what might have been his party sentiments, could have listened and been pleased. Dr. Condict was then a member of Congress, and his constituents had a right to ask from him a statement of his views upon the politics of the day and it may well be supposed that under the circumstances which surrounded him and his audience, he might have given voice to utterances which would have inflamed his hearers and stirred up to still worse demonstration, the demon of party strife. But he refrained from any such desecration of the day, and while not hesitating to speak firmly and boldly, yet through the whole speech ran that kindly feeling so dominant in his character and which so pervaded his whole life.

A letter written by Dr. Condit, has been placed in the possession of the editor of the RECORD by William L. King Esq., to whom it belongs, by whose permission it is here copied.

It is in an excellent state of preservation, every word is legible, the hand writing is beautiful, the paper is of the old fashioned, unglazed, rough, character, so common in those days.

It is presented to the readers of the RE-CORD for the purpose of calling their attention to several facts which it illustrates ;— The present facilities of the postal system of the country ; the enormous growth of the Republic in the eighty years and more which have elapsed since the letter was written, and the quaint, formal style adopted by the writer. The letter, to which this was an answer, reached Morristown, one month after it was dated. The north western Territory ! How few of the present day can appreciate what is meant by that designation, or the momentous part it played in the terrible struggle in the Republic over slavery, or the influence which the celebrated ordinance of 1787 had in determining that contest. Cincinnati was then but an outpost on the very outside of civilization ; it had less than a thousand inhabitants.

MORRIS TOWN, Dec. 30th, 1797.

DEAR SIR :—I rec'd your's of the 18th Sept. in about one month from its date, and at that time did not imagine I should have delayed answering it so long, but unavoidable circumstances have prevented till now.

It affords me infinite satisfaction to hear of your prosperity in that Country which though young and uncultivated is rendered by nature one of the finest in the world in points of fertility, and climate. With propriety it may be termed the "*Land of Canaan*," if not the "*garden of Eden*" or ancient paradise of which we read. Had I settled my affairs in Jersey before I set out on my journey, I am convinced, I should not have returned, but have remained there to this day. The distance is so great and my friends here were so opposed to my settling there, that I was induced to pitch my tent in Jersey, where perhaps I shall spend my days. I have compleated my house, and find my prospects flattering. I am yet free from matrimonial shackles, and at present do not see much prospect of being encumbered with them. The married folks tell me I want nothing but a *wife* to compleat my happiness, and I in return, remind them of the fox that lost his tail in a trap, and wished it to become fashionable to go without tails. Parson Richards and his family live in the house with me, and I board with him. I endeavor to enjoy myself as I pass through life, as well as circumstances will admit, remembering that we cannot take the world with us when we die. * * * No remarkable occurences have happened among your acquaintances here since your departure, except the marriage of Samual Arnold to Miss Jackson of Rockaway. They have moved to Albany and are doing very well. Sylvester Russell is now practising law and lives next door to me. * * * I saw Judge Symmes in the beginning of the fall or latter end of summer when passing through this Town on his way to Detroit. * * * As to news we have none worth communicating. Political parties and disputes run high and apprehensions have been entertained that we should be involved in war with France but I hope we shall avoid it by prudent measures. Insults are more easily pocketed than bloody noses, though neither of them are very desirable. Do you ever visit Judge Symmes and family? If you do, please to present my respects to Mrs. Symmes and Mrs. Harrison, with whom I had some acquaintance in Jersey and Miami. * * * With best wishes for your health and prosperity I remain Dear Sir your sincere friend and humble servant.

LEWIS CONDICT.

MR. DAN'L C. COOPER.

This letter is addressed, in the excellent hand writing of its writer, "Mr. Daniel C. Cooper. Cincinnati, North Western Territory." Mr. Cooper, the gentleman to whom it was written, had then recently removed from Morristown, to what was then a new and untried Country. He afterwards went to Dayton, Ohio, and was for many years identified with that City, and died at an advanced age, leaving a large property to be inherited by his heirs. The State of Ohio was not then known, nor was the name, Ohio, given distinctively, to any extent of country. The North Western Territory embraced an undefined extent of Country, which has since then given birth to many great western states. The Judge Symmes spoke of, in this letter, is best 'known as the author of the idea, hardly remembered, at the present, that the earth was hollow and that its centre could be reached, possibly through a hole at the North Pole called "*Symmes's hole.*" The Mrs. Harrison, also mentioned, was, probably, the wife of General William Henry Harrison, who was then Governor of the North West Territory and afterwards became President of the United States. He had married before that time the daughter of Judge Symmes. Judge Symmes, himself, was a Jerseyman, a native of Sussex County.

ALBERT BARNES.

The following interesting reminiscences of the Rev. Albert Barnes are from the pen of the venerable Rev. William Sterling, now living at Williamsport, Pa. Mr. Sterling was for ten years a co-presbyter with Mr. Barnes, and for thirty years a member of the same Synod.

The readers of the RECORD will feel much indebted to Mr. Sterling for his most interesting article. It presents Mr. Barnes in some lights, which would not, probably, appear in any ordinary biography.

The occasion of the trial to which Mr. Sterling refers, which resulted in the deposition of Mr. Barnes, was a sermon preached by him, entitled, "*The Way of Salvation.*" The sermon gave great offence to the branch of the Presbyterian Church, then called the Old School, of which the Rev. Dr. Junkin was a prominent supporter. At that time party spirit raged very high between the two branches of the Church. Mr. Barnes was considered as one of the leaders, if not *the* leader of the new school. Like Paul, before his conversion, his opponents deemed they were doing God service in bringing him to trial as a heretic.

The action was at first successful; Mr. Barnes was deposed from the ministry, but the finding of the Synod of Philadelphia was over-ruled by the General Assembly, and Mr. Barnes restored, never again to be molested.

Any person having a copy of the sermon referred to, or a paper containing a history of the trial, will confer a very great obligation by loaning them to the Editor of the RECORD. They will be carefully preserved and returned at once.

REMINISCENCES OF REV. ALBERT BARNES.

Rev. William Durant.

DEAR BRO.:—I am sorry to say that I can call to mind few reminiscences of Rev. Albert Barnes that would be of general interest. As a student, and a preacher, and a commentator on the Scriptures, his reputation is world-wide. But, in private life, he was a grave man, of few words, and rarely spoke of himself or his experiences.

The first time I ever saw Mr. Barnes was on a Sabbath evening in the fall of 1835. I had just graduated at Princeton Seminary, and had accepted a call from the Church of Reading. On my way to my field of future labor, I stopped a few days in Philadelphia that I might make the acquaintance of some of the members of the Third Presbytery with which my church was connected; and also that I might consult with them in regard to my ordination and installation at an early day as pastor of that church.

My stay in the city extended over the Sabbath. Now it so happened that on that very week the Synod of Philadelphia at its meeting in York had suspended Mr. Barnes "from all the functions of the Gospel ministry." The brethren of the 3d Presbytery had just returned from the meeting of Synod deeply troubled and sore at heart. Indeed, all the city was moved; and little else was thought about or talked about, but the proceedings of Synod in the case of Mr. Barnes. I learned that it had been arranged that Rev. Ezra Stiles Ely, D.D., was to officiate in the vacant pulpit on Sabbath evening, and make a full statement to the congregation of the action of Synod in the case of their deposed pastor. Of course I went to the church, though it was a very inclement night. The house was crowded to its utmost capacity. I got, with some difficulty, a seat in the aisle. Presently the friend, who had accompanied me to the church, drew my attention to a gentleman sitting in the pew with his family directly opposite me, and whispered, "That is Mr

Barnes." He was in a bent position, with his chin resting on the top of his umbrella. I watched him closely during the long and painful recital of the proceedings of Synod up to the last crowning act of the drama—his deposition from the gospel ministry. During the whole time, Mr. Barnes never changed his position, nor even raised his head. The whole audience were in an indescribable state of excitement, and many of them in tears. On almost every countenance around me were written indignation and sorrow and distress, too deep for utterance. The feeling was general that a great and most grievous wrong had been done to an able minister of the gospel and a righteous man; in whom they all trusted and whom they admired and loved as their faithful friend and pastor. But what I remarked and wondered at was the perfect control of Mr. Barnes over his own deep emotions. When the audience was dismissed, I got a glance at his face as he rose and prepared to retire. It was calm and peaceful and heavenly. He seemed to me to have been sustained that evening by the immediate presence of his God—to have been borne up by the assurance that the Master, whom he loved and served, would take care of him, and overrule the trial, through which his servant was passing, to his own great glory. That evening I learned to love Albert Barnes. The impression then made upon my mind and heart, by his demeanor and the holy light that I saw shining in his countenance, I never lost.

Rev. Gideon N. Judd, D.D., Corresponding Secretary of the American Home Missionary Society, afterwards told me that he boarded in the family of Mr. Barnes at the time of his trial, and through the entire winter of his suspension from the ministry; and that he never heard him utter one unkind word against any of those men who had caused him so much pain and humiliation; that he rarely, if ever, alluded to the action of Synod, by which he was set aside from his pastoral work. Mr. Judd added that when the General Assembly had reversed the action of Synod, and restored him to his standing in the ministry, Mr. Barnes quietly resumed his duties, making no reference to what he had suffered from the Synod; and that the only time he ever

heard him refer to the matter in public was near the close of a doctrinal sermon, which he preached some considerable time afterwards, when he simply said, "These are my views of these doctrines;—it was for holding these views that I was deposed from the ministry by the Synod of Philadelphia." That was all.

In the Autumn of 1839, Presbytery held its stated meeting at Allentown. After the adjournment, we returned in extra stages to Philadelphia.

I was so fortunate as to get a seat in the same coach with Mr. Barnes. In the course of the day, Rev. Anson Rood said, "Bro. Barnes, I have a question I would like to ask you. In closing your defence before the General Assembly at Pittsburgh, you said that nothing had taken place during the long trial in Presbytery, and again in Synod, nor yet in that General Assembly that had at all lessened your respect for Dr. Junkin, or weakened your confidence in his piety. Now what I want to know is this. Is your opinion of Dr. Junkin still unchanged, or have you had any reason to modify it?"

Mr. Barnes sat silent for a few moments, during which he seemed to be weighing carefully the answer he would put into words. At length he said "I owe a great deal to Dr. Junkin. I think he has added ten years to my life. I was laboring too hard, and must in a short time have broken down entirely. But that winter's rest from my pulpit duties has proved most beneficial so that I have felt like another man ever since." That was his answer. Of course it left us to our own conjectures as to whether his views of Dr. Junkin's character had not undergone some modification; but if they had, he did not say so. He would suffer no word to pass his lips, that could by any ingenuity be construed as implying a doubt in his mind in regard to the perfect honor, and integrity, and purity of motives of the man who had been so long his most determined, and persevering, and ruthless prosecutor. If any thing had come to the knowledge of Mr. Barnes since the trial, to cast a painful doubt over his mind as to the holy principles and ends of his opponent, he would hide the fact from all the world: he would not reveal even in confidence, and by a single hint to his warmest friends and brethren, the existence of that doubt, or the grounds he had for changing his opinion of the man in any degree.

In regard to Mr. Barnes's views of punctuality, I have some very distinct recollections. At all our meetings of Presbytery and Synod he would insist most strenuously that no business however pressing should interfere in the least degree with our appointments for devotional exercises. They must not be deferred on any account whatever, but commence at the precise moment specified in the notice that had been given to the people. Any proposal to defer these services for a short time, until the business on hand should be disposed of, would draw him to his feet at once; and he would press the point that the notice that the religious service would begin at that hour was equivalent to a promise made to God and to the congregation, which we had no right to break. Let business wait; but the people assembled for the devotional services must not be kept waiting after the appointed hour.

And this view of punctuality to appointments I have some reason to know he constantly carried out in his own congregation. On one occasion I was in the city on Wednesday, and he invited me to lecture for him that evening, stating the hour at which the meeting commenced. I was a few minutes late, owing to the tea arrangements of the family with which I was staying. The bell stopped ringing when I was a little more than a square from the church gate. When I entered the house I found that the services had already begun. At the close of the meeting I apologized to Mr. Barnes for my tardiness, and said I was afraid I had given him reason to fear that I was going to disappoint him. His reply was, "The meeting always begins at the last stroke of the bell. This my congregation understand and expect." And then he added, "If you had not come to-night it would have put me to no inconvenience. I never attend any services in my church without being fully prepared to conduct it myself, no matter who has engaged to conduct it for me."

As illustrative of the very peculiar scrupulousness of his conscience, let me give you an incident. Mr. Barnes had agreed to preach on a certain occasion at a place in Chester County, some twelve or fifteen miles from Philadelphia. He went out in his own carriage and found the road exceedingly bad—rough, stony and cut up into deep ruts. It was a long, tedious ride, and he arrived at the place of his appointment very sore and weary, his horse, his carriage and himself well bespattered with Chester County mud. Now, before leaving his study he had selected the 122 Psalm, 1st part C. M., to be sung at the opening of the service. But when he opened the book and turned to it, his eye fell upon the second verse, " I love her gates; *I love the road.*" No, no; that would not do. He had discovered nothing to love in the road he had travelled to Zion that day. He could not sing, "I love the road," neither could the congregation honestly and heartily sing it, covered as they were with the dirt it had cast upon them as they came over it. That Psalm, beautiful as it was, could never have been intended to be sung in that place, in such a state of the public road. So he made another selection to be sung that contained no allusion to the road.

I furnish you this just as I heard it from one of the Philadelphia brethren a short time after the incident occurred. The intention of the narrator was to show the almost painful delicacy of Mr. Barnes' conscience, even in little things. Perhaps it was only his sense of the incongruity.

In a somewhat intimate acquaintance with Mr. Barnes, extending over a period of thirty-five years, from 1835 to his death in 1870, I found only constantly increasing reasons to esteem and love him, as a kind brother, a conscientious man, a meek and humble servant of Jesus. I never heard a harsh or hasty or unkind word fall from his lips. I never saw him lose his temper, even for a moment. I never witnessed in him any indulgence in silly jesting or unseemly levity. He was "always an example to his brethren, in word, in conversation, in charity, in spirit, in faith, in purity." He never forgot his calling as an ambassador of God, nor lost sight of the example of his divine Master. As He who had called him was holy, so was he holy in all manner of conversation. He was at all times and in all places the same humble and meek and devout man of God, leaving upon all around him the deep and abiding impression of his heavenly temper and spirit. Even those who took the strongest ground against him on account of certain doctrinal views, acknowledged his deep and sincere piety. Let me give you a single example of such acknowledgment, and it is not the only one I could adduce.

Rev. Ashbel Green, D.D., was, as you know, one of his decided and conspicuous doctrinal opponents. But even he, when the whirlwind of excitement had not yet fully passed, bore the most earnest and emphatic testimony to the deep and fervent piety of Mr. Barnes. On one occasion,—I think shortly after the restoration of Mr. Barnes to the ministry,—Dr. Green was visiting a relative in the State of New York. One afternoon a young minister, who was also a visitor in the same house, was talking to the Doctor about the heresies of Mr. Barnes. Somewhat abruptly the young man asked him if he thought it possible that such a man as Barnes could get to Heaven—evidently expecting a negative answer. The Doctor was walking back and forth across the parlor floor. After the question was asked, he still kept on to and fro on the floor for a time without making any reply and seemed to be absorbed in solemn reflection. At length the old Doctor stopped before his interrogator, and said most solemnly,—" Young man, if you and I are permitted to sit at the feet of Mr. Barnes in Heaven, we will have reason to bless God to all eternity. I never for a moment doubted his piety. I believed him to be unsound on certain doctrines, and on that ground I have opposed him. But his honesty and sincerity, and deep piety before God I never for a moment doubted. On the contrary, I consider him one of the best men in my knowledge." I got this years ago from my own dear brother, who was present on the occasion and heard the whole conversaiton.

It seems from the above conversation that Dr. Green had two sets of opinions in regard to Mr. Barnes. On the one hand, he thought him good enough for heaven: but on the other, he was sure that such a man was not fit to be in the Presbyterian church. On the one hand he was sure that Mr. Barnes would occupy a very high seat in Heaven, so that to sit at his feet there would be a glorious privilege; but at the same time he regarded him as a very pestiferous man in the church, and worthy only to be rejected by his brethren and cast out as a heretic, not delaying even for " the first and second admonition ' required by the apostle. However, I have no doubt that Dr. Green most sincerely believed what he said ;—that he really believed Mr. Barnes to be a " man of deep piety before God." I only wonder that it never occurred to him, that the same kind of doctrine that had borne such holy, heavenly fruit in the life and character of Albert Barnes would have been excellent in church and state, for the upbuilding of Christian character in minister and people.

———

An apology is due to the readers of the RECORD for the delay in the issue of this month's number. That delay was due to imperative engagements, in another direction, which presented the performances of the editorial duties requisite to prepare this number.

———

AN OLD DEED

For the burying ground at Whippany has been placed in the hands of the editor of the RECORD. The original paper is in the possession of William Howell, Esq., the present Sheriff of the county of Morris, by whose kind permission a copy is presented to the readers of the RECORD. It is copied *verbatim, et literatim, et punctuatim.*

" To all Christian People to whom These Presents shall Come: Greeting &c. Know Yee that I John Richards of Whipanong in ye County of Hunterdon in ye Province of New Jersey Schoolmaster for and in consideration of ye Love Good will & affection which I have and do bear towards my Christian friends and Neighbours in Whipanong afores'd as also for ye desire & Regard I have to promote & advance ye Publick Interest Especially of those who shal| or may Mutually covenant by subscription to Erect Build and place (upon the Land by these Presents Granted) a Decent & Suitable Meeting house for the Publick Worship of God Have Given & Granted and by these Presents do fully, freely and absolutely,

Give, Grant, Alein, Convey & Confirm from me my heires Executors & adm'rs forever unto those persons of my Neighbours as afores'd who shall Covenant by subscription and to their heirs and successors forever one certain piece or Tract of Land Containing Three Acres and one half (be it more or Less) Scittuate lying and being in ye Township of Whipanong on that part commonly called Peccepanong on ye North Easterly side of Whipanong River beginning sixteen Rods & a half distance above my house I dwell in : at a white oak tree standing by ye path side near by River, mark'd on two sides from thence runing seven Chains northwesterly Butted and Bounded South Easterly and Northwesterly with my own Land Southwesterly with Whipanong River and North Easterly upon ye Highway Twenty Rods Distant from sd River. *To have and To Hold* the said Hereby Granted Land with the appurtenances : only for Publick use Benifit and improvement for a meeting house, Schoolhouse, Burying Yard, Training field, and such Like Publick uses to the said Covenantors by Subscription and their Heires and successors for ever furthermore it is the true intent & meaning of Grantor and Grantee in these Presents that ye sd Granted Primises is not to be Given, Granted, Bargained, Sold, Alinated, Exchanged, Leased to farm Lett or Converted to ye particular use or Improvement of any person or persons neither for Publick advantage or any other pretence whatsoever or by any way or means whatsoever Alinated or Reverted from the Publick use & Improvement as afores'd and I ye sd John Richards do for myself my heires, Executors and adm'rs Covenant Promise and Grant to and with ye sd Grantees who have made themselves so : or hereafter shall make themselves so by their subscribing, their heires and successors for ever shall and may from time to time and at all times forever hereafter Have hold use Occupie possess and enjoy ye above sd Land & primises to yuse above sd without any maner of Lett Hindrance Molestation Eviction Ejection or Deniall of me ye said John Richards my heires Executors administrators or assigns or by or from any other person or persons whatsoever by from or under in or by any of our means, Act, Privity Title

or Procurement. In Witness whereof I have hereto sett my hand and seal this second day of September Anno: 1718 and in the fifth year of ye Reign of our Sovereign Lord George by ye Grace of God of Great Britain ffrance & Ireland King Defender of ye faith &c.

Signed sealed & }
Delivered Inn } JOHN RICHARDS { L. S. }
ye presence of }
JEDIDIAH BUCKINGHAM
JOHN COOPER."

The history of this old deed is interesting. It was found, after his death, among the papers of the late Calvin Howell, the father of Sheriff Howell, who was a prominent citizen of that part of the county of Morris, and who died several years ago, quite an old man.

The paper originally belonged to the Presbyterian church at Whippany, and although the records and papers, belonging to that parish, were removed to Hanover, when the Presbyterian church at that place was built, this deed must have been retained, as, after the death of Mr. Calvin Howell, in searching through the drawers of an old desk, it was found in a sort of secret drawer.

The first church in Morris county, a Presbyterian, was built upon the lot conveyed by this deed in 1718. The edifice fell into decay, and the timbers were utilized in the erection of the church at Hanover. The lot is now used as a burial ground, and, in the inclosure is to be found the grave of John Richards, the grantor in this deed, marked by a head stone bearing Mr. Richards's name, the date of his birth and death. The stone is made from brown sandstone in the old-fashioned manner, subject to decay, but reverent hands have cared for it, removed the moss and preserved it from the operation of time and accident.

The congregation, worshipping in this church at Whippany, came from Morristown, Madison, Parsippany, Hanover and Chatham, and the church was the centre for many years, for all that region of country represented by these places. The church at Hanover was built in 1755, but in 1740 and 1748, other churches had been built in other parts of the county, one at Morristown and the other at what was then called Bottle Hill, now known as Madison.

THE RECORD.

FIRST PRESBYTERIAN CHURCH, MORRISTOWN, N. J.

"This shall be Written for the Generation to Come."—Psalms 102 : 18.

Volume IV.　　　　JANUARY, 1884.　　　　Number 13

[Printed with the Approval of the Session.]

THE RECORD

Will be published monthly at Morristown N. J. Terms $1.00 per annum, *in advance.*

Subscriptions may be made at the bookstores of Messrs. Runyon and Emmell, or to Messrs. James R. Voorhees and William D. Johnson, or by letter addressed to the

EDITOR OF THE RECORD,

Morristown, N. J.

Entered at the Post Office at Morristown, N. J., as second class matter.

THE ENLARGED SUPPLEMENT.

In the Supplement to this month's number of the RECORD, will begin the publication of the oldest records of the church. It is not the purpose to print these records in full, but matters of special importance and interest will be selected, so that the Supplements, from this date, may be bound in a separate volume, which will contain the salient facts in the history of the church, for the one hundred and fifty years of its existence. In order to make the volume complete in itself, a reprint of portions of the Trustee's book will be necessary. New matter, however, to the extent of 96 pages, or eight per month, for the twelve months of the year, will regularly appear; and all necessary reprint will be furnished to subscribers, gratuitously in addition. It is calculated that the publication, in this form, will be completed in two years. If sufficient encouragement be given, a full list of all the names upon the Registers of the church, arranged alphabetically and grouped by families will then be printed, which may be added to this separate volume and be bound with it. In the meantime, the publication of the chronological lists of Baptisms, Communicants, &c. will be continued.

This change will, materially, interfere in the future conduct of the paper, with some cherished plans connected with the histories of the churches of the City and County and, also, with notices of persons identified with the past of the church. But, as these old records seem more important and, so much time would be required to print them, if the present mode of publishing the paper were pursued, it has been thought best to make the proposed change. The plan, however, of giving sketches of the lives of pastors and prominent members of the congregation, and of presenting histories of the churches of Morristown and vicinity is, by no means, abandoned. Considerable material has been gathered for that purpose, which will be utilized from time to time, so far as practicable.

MR. BARNES'S SERMON ; "THE WAY OF SALVATION."

William L. King, Esq., has kindly placed a copy of this celebrated sermon at the disposal of the RECORD. It was preached, February 8, 1829, in the First Presbyterian Church, at Morristown, and was printed in 1830, by Jacob Mann, the proprietor of the *Palladium of Liberty.* At the time of its delivery, there was an extensive revival of religion in the congregation.

It was stated, in the December number of the RECORD, that this sermon was the occasion of the trial of Mr. Barnes for heresy. This, perhaps, was an error; it may not have been the immediate cause of that trial, for, at the time of the charge against him, Mr. Barnes was Pastor of the first Presbyterian Church, at Philadelphia, and consequently, a member of the Presbytery to which that church was attached, and before which body he was impeached by the Rev. Dr. Junkin,

But, if this sermon were not the immediate cause of the trial, the charges against Mr. Barnes were for holding sentiments, identical with those declared from his pulpit at Morristown, and it was for holding these opinions, that he was deposed by the Synod to which Dr. Junkin appealed from the judgment of the Presbytery.

It is impossible for Presbyterians of the present day to understand the fierceness of discussion which characterized the controversy between the two branches of the church. Dr. Junkin, Mr. Barnes's great antagonist, pursued his opponent with an acrimony, which seemed, at times, to be any thing but brotherly. It is well that those dark times of trouble and dissension, when good and holy men could not agree upon doctrines, have passed away. Perhaps there would have been no real differences, if those, who so varied in opinion, could have alike understood the meaning of words and phrases.

The sermon was evidently, prepared by its author, with the greatest care. He has added foot notes, quoting numerous texts of scriptures, by which he sustained his various positions.

The sermon will be printed so as to present to the readers of the RECORD the utterance of this great man, than whom no one was more competent to give voice to views upon the distinctive dogmas of the church to which he belonged. It will be necessary, for want of room, to omit the quotations, and possibly, the foot notes; but, it is hoped, that the space may be given to these notes, or at least to some of them, as they are suggestive, certainly, of one fact, that Mr. Barnes was aware. when writing the sermon, that he was not in accord with the standards of doctrine, as received by the Presbyterian Church.

THE WAY OF SALVATION.

"But after that the kindness and love of God our Saviour toward man appeared, not by works of righteousness which we have done, but according to his mercy he saved us. by the washing of regeneration, and renewing of the Holy Ghost, which he shed on us abundantly, through Jesus Christ our Saviour ; that being justified by his grace, we should be made heirs according to the hope of eternal life."—Titus, iii. 4, 5, 6, 7.

All men have some scheme of salvation. Except the very few cases where individuals are thrown into a state of despair, there are none who do not expect to be happy beyond the grave. The proof of this is found in the composure with which most men look at eternity, and in their indifference when warned of a coming judgment. It requires the utmost strength of human hardihood, when a criminal looks without trembling of limbs on the gibbet where he is soon to be executed; and we infer. that there is no hardihood so great, no courage so strong. as to look upon eternal sorrow with a belief that it will be *ours*, and be unmoved. When we see, therefore, so · many unconcerned about their eternal state ; so many professing to believe that they are exposed to endless suffering, and still unanxious about it ; the fair conclusion is, that not one syllable of the book that teaches this is truly believed. It is not, cannot be, human nature, to believe this, and still sit in indifference. Every man, therefore, has some secret scheme by which he expects to be saved. Yet it is perfectly clear that there can be but one scheme of Salvation that is true. If the christian plan is *true*, then all others are *false*. If others are true, then there was no need of the sacrifice on the cross, and the scheme is an imposition. The admission then—an admission which probably all the sinners that I address would readily make— the admission that the christian religion is true, is a condemnation of all other systems, and shuts out all who are not interested in the plan of the gospel, from all hope of heaven.

The text contains the substance of the whole christian scheme. It expresses, I believe, every point that is peculiar to Christianity. It may be regarded as one of those condensing paragraphs, or summaries of the scheme, expressing all that is original in the plan in few words, in which the sacred writers seem to delight. It brings together distant doctrines—scattered rays of light, to be surveyed in the near neighborhood of each other, and to set off each other by the reflected light thrown from one point of view to another.

It is not often that a subject so extensive as the whole Christian plan of saving men, is introduced into the pulpit, with a view of giving its great points in a single discourse. I endeavor, from week to week, to explain particular parts of it, and to press its prominent doctrines and duties on your attention. It has occurred, that in the state of things now existing in this congregation, there is demanded a full, single view of God's way of saving men. Such a view, according to the interpretation which we give to the Bible, I wish this morning to present. If a demand somewhat more than usual should be made on your attention, it will be remembered, I trust, that it is difficult to give even an outline of the christian religion in a single discourse; and perhaps it will be deemed hazardous to have attempted it. Let me further premise, that I shall be indebted very much to your own knowledge of the Sacred Scriptures for the proofs of the particular points which I shall consider. I foresee that it will demand no ordinary degree of attention on the part of my hearers to obtain, and do justice to the views which I shall present,—perhaps no ordinary candor to necessary obscurity of statement, and barrenness of illustration. *For the views themselves*, if fairly understood, I ask no indulgence. They are the views, if I mistake not, of God; and I am bound only to present them with fairness, and you to receive them into good and honest hearts.

What, then, is God's plan of saving men? What are the great leading points on which that plan is based, and to bring out which, is the design of the Bible? These are the questions which it is my wish, in few words, to answer. It will be seen at once, that the text ascribes all the honor to God, and none to men. It will be the design in this discourse, honestly, in this respect, to follow the representation of the text. Sinners and saints, people and preacher, may expect from this plan an unqualified condemnation, and a pressing claim to lay aside all their own honor, and to ascribe all glory to God.

I remark then, in the first place, that God's plan of saving men is based on the fact that the race is destitute of holiness. So says the text. Not by works of righteousness which *we* have done. If it were not so, there would have been no necessity for the scheme. Men would have possessed full capability of saving themselves. If men, before or since the promulgation of this plan

of mercy, had any of the elements of holiness; or any traits of character, which could, by culture, be wrought into a texture of righteousness, then the design of interposition in this manner would have been a work unnecessary, and would not have been done at all. The design of interposing to save mankind, supposed that in themselves they were lost and must be ruined, if left to their own guidance.

In the explanation of his position, it is important to be understood. It is not asserted by the friends of the christian religion that all men are as bad as they can be; or that one man is as bad as another; or that there is no morality—no parental or filial affection —no kindness or compassion in the world— no love of truth, and no honest dealing among men. The friends of religion are not blind to the existence of these qualities in a high degree; nor are they slow to value them, or to render them appropriate honors. They suppose that the Bible presents the fact, that all these things may exist, and diffuse a charm over society, and cement the body politic, and still there be an utter destitution of right feeling toward God. They suppose that natural amiableness is no proof that a man is not selfish; that because a child loves its parent, it is no evidence that the child has any regard to God; and that it is possible that a man may be very kind to the poor, and very just in his dealings, and still have a heart full of pride, and selfishness, and envy, and be an entire neglector of God in the feelings of his soul, and in regard to prayer, and to every act that expresses homage to the Deity. Christianity does not charge on men crimes of which they are not guilty. It does not say, as I suppose, that the sinner is held to be personally answerable for the transgressions of Adam, or of any other man;* or that

*It is not denied that this language varies from the statements which are often made on the subject, and from the opinion which has been entertained by many men. And it is admitted that it does not accord with that used on the same subject in the Confession of Faith, and in other standards of doctrine. The main difference is, that it is difficult to affix any clear and definite meaning to the expression, "we sinned *in* him, and fell *with* him." It is manifest, so far as it is capable of interpretation, that it is intended to convey the idea not that the sin, of Adam is *imputed* to us, or set over to our account; but that there was a *personal identity* constituted between Adam and his posterity, so that it was really *our act*, and *ours only*, after all that is chargeable on us. This was the idea of Edwards.—The notion of *imputing* sin, is an invention of modern times : it is not, it is believed, the doctrine of the confession of faith.—The Author of this discourse intended in the Sermon only to state what he conceived to be the doctrine of the Bible. Christianity affirms the fact, that in con-

God has given a law which man has no power to obey. Such a charge, and such a requirement, would be most clearly unjust. The law requiring love to God, supreme and unqualified, and love to man, is supposed to be equitable; fully within the reach of every mortal, if there was first a willing mind. Every man is supposed to be under obligation perfectly, and for ever, to obey that law; be he in heaven, earth, or hell,—be he a king on the throne, or a beggar in the streets,—be he a bondman or a freeman.

What then is *the fact* on which the plan of mercy is based? It is simply, that all men have failed to yield obedience to the requirements of this reasonable law—that there is not an individual that has given evidence that he has not been its violator. The violation of this pure law is held to be the first act of the child when he becomes a moral agent; the continued act of his life, unless he is renewed; and the last act on his dying pillow. His whole career is set down as one act of rebellion, because he neglects God, is selfish, is proud, is cherishing enmity against his Maker, is opposed to the acts of his government, and is unfriendly to all the efforts made to produce better feelings. In innumerable instances this want of holiness, this destitution of love to God and man, goes forth in acts of falsehood, impurity, blasphemy, theft, murder, unkind feelings, and implacable individual and national war.—In support of this presentation of the character of men, the sacred scriptures assert the naked fact, claiming to be the testimony of God. Christianity has moreover recorded the history of the world, under inspired guidance, for more than two-thirds of its continuance, and presents no exception to the melancholy account of men. Profane writers, with no reference to any theological debate, and nine-tenths of them with no expectation that their testimony would ever be adduced to settle questions in Divinity, have presented the same fact. Not one solitary historian, though coming from the midst of the people whose deeds are recorded, and designing to give the most favorable representation of their character, has exhibited a nation bearing any marks of holiness. The world, the wide world is presented as apostate; and he must be worse than blind that would attempt to set up a defence of the conduct of men.

Christianity appeals to individuals. All who have been converted by its power, have given their decided testimony, to the darkest representations of the human heart, in the sacred record. Men, before, of all characters, the moral, and the vicious, have concurred in the representation that they were by nature the children of wrath, and that their hearts were enmity against God.

On this broad fact—wide as the world, and prolonged as its history—the christian scheme is based. Here is an apostate province of God's empire. Rebellion invaded it, not as it did the ranks of heaven. There it cut off a fixed number; all mature in wisdom and knowledge. It would not spread; it could not be extended to successive tribes. Here, it poisoned a fountain. It was amidst God's works, at first but a little spring, pouring into a rill, but soon swelling to creeks, to rivers, to lakes, to oceans. An incalculable number would descend from that first pair of apostates; and with prophetic certainty it could be foretold that not one of all their descendants would escape the contagion to the end of time,—however long the apostate world might be suffered to roll amongst the orbs that preserved allegiance. To all ages it would be the same—rising, sinning, apostate, dying man. On each island, on each mountain, in each valley, in each cavern, wild or civilized, it would be the same. Crime would be heaped on crime;—whole nations would bleed;—whole soils be wet with gore;—whole tribes would wail;—and generation would tread on generation—and then themselves expire—and all die as enemies of the God that made them.

II. What could be done? What *was* done to arrest the evil?—I remark, secondly, that a plan of salvation was devised on the

(To be continued.)

---

nection with the sin of Adam, or as a result, all moral agents in this world will sin—and sinning, will die. Rom. v, 12—19. It does not affirm, however, any thing about the *mode* in which this would be done. There are many ways conceivable in which that sin might secure the result, as there are many ways in which all similar *facts* may be explained. The drunkard commonly secures as a result, the fact that his family will be beggared, illiterate, perhaps profane or intemperate. Both facts are evidently to be explained on the *same principle* as a part of moral Government. The Bible does not, it is believed, affirm that there is any principle of moral government in the one case that is not in the other. Neither the facts, nor any proper inferences from the facts, affirm that I am, in either case, *personally responsible* for what another man did before I had an existence.

THE RECORD.

FIRST PRESBYTERIAN CHURCH, MORRISTOWN, N. J.

" This Shall be Written for the Generation to Come."—Psalms 102 : 18.

VOLUME IV.   FEBRUARY 1884.   NUMBER 14

[Printed with the Approval of the Session.]

THE RECORD

Will be published monthly at Morristown, N. J. Terms $1.00 per annum, *in advance.*

Subscriptions may be made at the bookstores of Messrs. Runyon and Emmell, or to Messrs. James R. Voorhees and William D. Johnson, or by letter addressed to the

EDITOR OF THE RECORD,

Morristown, N. J.

Entered at the Post Office at Morristown, N. J., as second class matter.

(Mr. Barnes's Sermon Continued.)

ground of this, sufficient for all ;—a healing balm fitted to extend far as the spreading moral pestilence and death. This plan consisted in the selection and gift of the Son of God to die for the race, that a way of salvation might be opened for all. The Being thus selected was the co-equal of the Father—existing in intimate union with him, in perfect honor and happiness, without deviation and without change, from all eternity. He was God. This person of the Godhead became intimately and indissolubly united to human nature, in the person of Jesus the Son of Mary of Nazareth. This union was such as to constitute the acts of the Divinity, and those of the humanity those of a person ; in the same way as the acts of the mind, or the sufferings of our body, are the acts and sufferings of a person—of *ourselves.* Thus united, this being possessing the divine and human nature in one person, became the mediator between God and man. In our nature the Son of God preached the good tidings of peace ; exerted his power in healing the sick, and raising the dead ; gave comfort to the desponding ; supported the weak ; traversed the valleys and ascended

the mountains of Judea ; founded a church and appointed its officers ; predicted his own death, his resurrection, the destruction of the temple and holy city, and the certain universal spread of the Gospel. In human nature the Son of God expired on the cross. The divine nature suffered not, but it gave dignity and value to the sufferings of the man of Nazareth.

He died in the place of sinners. He did not endure indeed the *penalty of the law—*, for his sufferings were not eternal, nor did he endure remorse of conscience ; but he endured so much suffering, bore so much agony, that the Father was pleased to accept of it in the place of the eternal torments of all that should by him be saved. "The atonement, of itself, secured the salvation of no one." It made it consistent for God to *offer pardon to rebels.* It so evinced the hatred of God against sin—so vindicated his justice—so asserted the honor of his law, that all his perfections would shine forth illustriously, if sinners through this work should be saved. The atonement secured the salvation of no one, except as God had promised his Son that he should see of the travail of his soul, and except on the condition of repentance and faith.

In our nature the Son of God arose ; gave proofs of his identity ; and ascended to heaven to make intercession ; to give repentance and remission of sins ; and to conduct the affairs of the universe, with reference to the welfare of the church. He still lives to teach his people, to defend them in danger, to preserve his church from ruin.

This atonement was for all men. It was an offering made for the race. It had not respect so much to *individuals,* as to the *law* and *perfections of God.* It was an opening of the way for pardon—a making forgiveness consistent—a preserving of truth—a magnifying of the law; and had no particular reference to any class of men. We judge that he died for all. He tasted death for every man. He is the propitiation for the sins of the world. He came, that whosoever would believe on him should not perish, but have eternal life.

The full benefit of this atonement is offered to all men. In perfect sincerity God makes the offer. He has commissioned his servants to go and preach the Gospel—that is, the good news that salvation is provided for them—to every creature. He that does not this; that goes to offer the Gospel to a part only; to elect persons only; or that supposes that God offers the Gospel only to a certain portion of mankind, violates his commission, practically charges God with insincerity, makes himself " wise above what is written," and brings great reproach on the holy cause of redemption. The offer of salvation is not made by *man*, but by *God*. It is *his* commission; and it is his solemn charge, that the sincere offer of heaven should be made to every creature. That all creatures have not heard it; that every heathen-man, every Indian, African, and Islander, have not heard it, has been owing to the unfaithfulness of ministers—to the avarice of the church—to the want of proper zeal among christians, and not to the command of God, or of any want of fulness in the atonement.

I assume the free and full offer of the Gospel to all men, to be one of those cardinal points of the system by which I *guage* all my other views of truth. It is, in my view, a corner-stone of the whole edifice; that which makes it so glorious to God, and so full of good-will to men. I hold no doctrines —and by the grace of God never can hold any—which will be in *my* views inconsistent with the free and full offer of the Gospel to all men; or which will bind my hands, or palsy my tongue, or freeze my heart, when I stand before sinners to tell them of a dying Saviour. I stand as the messenger of God, with the assurance, that all that *will* may be saved; that the atonement was full and free; and that if any perish, it will be because they choose to die, and not because they are straitened in God. I have no fellow-feeling for any other Gospel; I have no right hand of fellowship to extend to any

scheme that does not say that God sincerely offers all the bliss of Heaven to every guilty wandering child of Adam,—be he a Caffrarian, a Hindoo, a man of China, or a Laplander;—a beggar or a king, a rich man, a learned man, a moral man, or an abandoned wretch of christian climes.

The scheme of salvation, I regard, as offered to the *world*, as free as the light of heaven, or the rains that burst on the mountains, or the full swelling of broad rivers and streams, or the heavings of the deep. And though millions do not receive it—though in regard to them the benefits of the plan are lost, and to them, in a certain sense, the plan may be said to be in vain, yet I see in this the hand of the same God that pours the rays of noon-day on barren sands, and genial showers on desert rocks, and gives life, bubbling springs, and flowers, where no man is, to *our* eyes, yet not to *his, in vain*. So is the offer of eternal life, to every man here, to every man every where, sincere and full—an offer that, though it may produce no emotions in the sinner's bosom *here*, would send a thrill of joy through all the panting bosoms of the suffering damned.

III. In the presentation of this scheme, I proceed to remark, in the *third* place, that while God thus sincerely offers the gospel to men, all mankind, while left to themselves, as sincerely and cordially reject it. It is not to any want of physical strength, that this rejection is owing; for men have power enough in themselves to *hate* both God and their fellow-men; and it requires *less* physical power to *love* God than to *hate* him; less power to love a kind and tender parent, than in the face of conscience, and motive, and law, to hate such a parent. And so with regard to a kind, and patient, and holy God. It is found that it is far easier to be reconciled to him, and love him, than to remain at war and oppose him.

It is supposed that it is an evident reflection on the Deity, of a most serious nature, to say that he has required under the penalty of eternal vengeance, that of man, which he has in no sense power to do.

The rejection of the gospel, then, is to be traced to some cause, where man will be to blame, not God.

It is impossible for the pure gospel to have any fellowship with a scheme, which in any sense charges God with wrong. The fact that the gospel is rejected, is then to be traced to the obstinacy of men; to a decided, deliberate purpose *not* to be saved in this way. All men are supposed, by nature, to be insensible of the need of salvation by another. They are held to be so much opposed to God, that they *will* not submit to him. They are charged with being so much in love with sin, that neither commands nor threatenings,—neither love, nor vengeance, neither the offer of heaven, nor the prospect of hell, will induce them to forsake it. They are so proud, that they will not stoop to receive even eternal joy as a gift. They have so high a conception of their own merit, that neither argument nor intreaty, nor the mild voice of persuasion, will induce them to come to the arms of a bleeding Saviour.

Their hearts are so hard, their minds are so blind, that the Saviour might have prolonged his groans to the end of time, and the rocks—the hard rocks of Jerusalem, might have burst; and the firm granite of the everlasting hills been dashed to powder, but still the sinner's heart would have been unmoved by all his groans; and the race would have been giddy in pleasure, and immersed in business, and grasping honor unmoved. And, had the darkness of that unnatural night when he died, been prolonged to the present time; and had it been still whispered in every breeze, and heard in every echo, that the Son of God was *yet* suffering for men, and crying in the bitterness of a dying soul, "My God! my God! why hast thou forsaken me?" still not one solitary human heart would, of itself, care that there was no sorrow like to this sorrow. From this scene the world turns in cool contempt. The plan is rejected. Man will not come to Christ that he may have life. The proof of this we need not adduce. It is found in the Saviour's personal ministry—in the fact that a nation conspired to put him to death,—in the wide, universal rejection of the gospel since,—in the humiliating unconcern with which men listen, when

"In strains as sweet
As Angels use, the Gospel whispers peace,"
in the open opposition, the profane jibe, the bitter sneer, with which the multitude turn from the sufferings of Jesus.

You, who are impenitent sinners in this house, are most favorable representations, in this respect, of your fellow-rebels against heaven, in other parts of the world. May I ask what has been your treatment of the plan of salvation? From year to year, it has been pressed on your attention. Argument, entreaty, and persuasion, have been exhausted in vain. Never has the smoothness of your self-complacency been ruffled by any remorse that you have trampled on the blood of the Son of God;—never has the highness of your look been brought down by the remembrance that you have practically joined in the cry, "Crucify him, Crucify him;" never have you breathed one solitary emotion of gratitude to heaven, that Judah's rocks heard his groans, and that her mountains echoed his sighs; never have you sought his aid or felt your need of his salvation, or desired an interest in his blood. With one consent, you have turned your backs on the gospel. So have all the race—so would you, and they, to the end of time. There is such a cool indifference to it in the sinner's bosom,—or such decided contempt,—or such fixed opposition, that if it were left to itself, not a man would be saved. As the cold and putrid carcasses of the dead do not of themselves seek life; as the turf would not move, nor the tomb-stones shake, nor the pale mouldering people open their eyes, *of themselves,* if I were to go and preach to yonder graves; even so it is, when I preach to sinners. Of themselves, they are all sightless, and motionless, and fixed. They cordially reject the gospel. So it is with all the race, so it has ever been, and ever will be. Men are so wicked, that they will not be saved by a holy Redeemer, and a holy scheme.—We are prepared, then, to remark, in the

IVth place—That those who are saved, will be saved because God does it by the renewing of the Holy Ghost. If the last point which I suggested be true, that all are disposed to reject the scheme, then it would seem to follow, that if any are saved, it will be by the special agency of God. To accomplish this, it is supposed he has sent down his Holy Spirit into the world. In the discharge of his great official work, he arrests the attention of heedless sinners. He does it by applying the preached gospel, by leading the thoughts in a proper manner in the dispensations of his Providence,—by blessing the example and conversation of parents, brothers, and friends, or by a secret, silent influence, known only to the individual, drawing the thoughts along to eternity, producing distaste to the ways and wages of sin, and a panting and breathing of the soul for enjoyments suited to its nature. The effect of this operation of the Spirit is not to produce inactivity or slumber. It is not compulsion. No man is compelled, against his will, to be saved. The work of salvation, and the work of damnation, are the two most deliberate and solemn acts *of choosing*, that mortal man ever performs:

The Spirit of God acts on the will. He goes *before* the convicted sinner to remove obstacles ; he pours light into the mind ; he impresses truth ; he urges to duty. He calls up the sinners own activity ; and the guilty man, sensible now of his danger, commences the most mighty and persevering struggle in which he ever engages, that to secure the salvation of his soul ; and under the guidance of this spirit, he goes willingly and cheerfully, where he would not of himself go, to pardon and peace. There is here supposed to be no violation of freedom. In all this the sinner chooses freely. The spirit compels no one: he shuts out no one—if the particular influence is not given to all—as no man can maintain that it is, and as the world is full of facts to show—it is thought, that no man is injured when salvation is freely and sincerely offered to him ; and when he as freely and sincerely rejects it. No being in heaven or earth, but himself, shuts him out of the blessings of redemption. The same heaven is offered,—the same Saviour died,—the same promises are made to him, and he has all the requisite power to comply. If he chooses to go to hell, after all this, no injustice will be done him : nor will he suffer beyond his deserts, if all other beings choose of themselves to be saved, or *if God chooses to save them*, and takes the glory to himself.

It is an essential part of the scheme which I am stating, that *God*, not *man*, begins the work. In the language of the Episcopal and Methodist articles of religion, the grace of Christ "*prevents*"—that is, goes *before* the

sinner in his efforts to be saved. God begins the work, disposes the sinner to act, and pray, and repent, and gives him pardon. God does not himself repent, but he gives grace to man to do it for himself. That this is the true statement is clear. Man himself, as we have seen, *will* not come to Christ, that he might have life. One man has no power to produce this change in another. The Devil surely will not do a work so unlike himself, and so injurious to his kingdom. It remains, then, that it is the work of God. In the distributions of these favors, he acts by a rule that he has not made known to us. There can be no doubt that it is wise, but he has not given us the reason of it. The *fact* he has stated, and the world, the nations past, and present, the distant tribes of men, and this place, are full of proofs that God changes, by his power, the hearts of many ; and that there are many whose hearts are not changed—who choose not to be saved, and whom God has not yet chosen to renew and pardon. No man has a right to conclude, that *he* is shut out from salvation, except *by the fact*. If he loves sin, and will not repent, and believe the gospel, he has no evidence that he will be saved ; and if he persist in this course, he will be among the reprobate and be damned, by his own choice. If *he* should repent and believe, he would be saved, and be among the elect, and give the glory to God.

This doctrine, that God by his spirit *prevents*, or goes before a sinner in his efforts, or commences and carries forward the work by his own power, I deem of cardinal value in the work of religion. If it be true, then it is of the utmost importance that it should be *seen* and *felt* to be true, and that the Holy Ghost should have the glory. I have no sympathy with any scheme that divides the honor with man. I have so deep a sense of the utter and total wickedness of the human heart,—of its entire opposition by nature to all that is good, and of the corruption of all its best efforts, even when aided, that I involuntarily shrink from every scheme that seems to mingle in merit the pure work of the Holy Ghost, with the crude and abortive energies of my own bosom. I seek to ascribe, in this work, simple and undivided praises to God ; to

(*To be continued.*)

THE RECORD.

FIRST PRESBYTERIAN CHURCH, MORRISTOWN, N. J.

" This shall be Written for the Generation to Come."—Psalms 102 : 18.

Volume IV.	MARCH. 1884.	Number 15.

[Printed with the Approval of the Session.]

THE RECORD

Will be published monthly at Morristown
N. J. Terms $1.oo per annum, *in advance.*

Subscriptions may be made at the book-
stores of Messrs. Runyon and Emmell, or to
Messrs. James R. Voorhees and William D.
Johnson, or by letter addressed to the

EDITOR OF THE RECORD,

Morristown, N. J.

Entered at the Post Office at Morristown,
N. J., as second class matter.

(Mr. Barnes's Sermon Continued.)

feel and proclaim to my expiring breath,
that God " is first, is midst, is last, is supre-
mest, best," in all the work of saving men ;
and that poor human nature, in all cases except in the person of Jesus, is to be regarded
as undeserving. polluted, and meriting only
death eternal.

What God *does*, he *intends* to do. There
is no chance—no hap-hazard. What it is
right for him to do, it is right for him to
purpose to do. What he does in my salvation or yours, he always meant to do. In him
is no change, no *shadow* of turning. He has
no new plan. We should have no security
of the salvation of an individual if he
changed—no security that an act of justice
would ever be done to any of the living or
the dead. The welfare of the universe demands that he should have one unchanging
plan, running from the beginning to the
end of years ; and if there is a God immu-
tably just and holy, there must be. In that
purpose, and not in *our* poor abortive plans,
lies your welfare and mine.

It is no part of this scheme, as you will
see, that God made men on purpose to damn
them. No man, from the beginning of the
world, to my knowledge, has ever professed
to maintain that opinion. It is certainly not
the sentiment of the Bible. and no man has
any right to charge it on any system of religion ; and I do not deem it too serious to
say, is guilty of gross slander if he does it.
God made men to glorify himself in their
holiness and felicity; and has made provision for their salvation, and if they do not
choose to be saved ; if they choose to hate
him, and rebel, and go to perdition, and HE
does not choose to save them against their
will, they cannot blame *him* for their self-
chosen condemnation. It is an act of justice which we claim, that it should be. remembered, that neither here, nor in any
christian church on the face of the earth is
it held, that God made men on purpose to
damn them. If, then, God renews the heart
by his Holy Spirit, if he begins and carries
forward the work in all that shall be saved,
and holds the power of doing this over all
men, and does *not* thus incline all to come
to him, and it be asked, as well it may be,
why he does not renew and save all—we
have only to say, that all do not *choose* to be
saved, and *will* not come to him. If it be
asked why the great sovereign of worlds
does not *constrain* them to come, and bring
all to heaven, I answer, my powers of reason here fail,—my understanding faints.
and is weary ; and I ask also, why he did not
keep by his power men and devils from
falling, and save the universe from sin and
sorrow altogether ?—Secret things belong
to God, and I can only say as God's only
Son said long since, " Even so, Father, so it
seemeth good in thy sight." The christian
scheme, then, claims that God, by his spirit,
renews all that will be saved. I remark,

V. That this is done by a change in the
affections and life of man. This change has
been usually called regeneration, or the new

birth, or conversion. It is that revolution of character, when a man ceases to be a sinner total and unqualified, and begins to be a man of holiness. It implies a change in his views and feelings towards God, and the Saviour,—towards the truths and duties of religion,—towards christians, and a revolution in his objects and pursuits. It is not merely a love of happiness in a new form, it is a love of God and divine things, because they are good and amiable in themselves. It is instantaneous—not always indeed known at the time or precise moment, but to be tested by the new views and feelings, and especially by a holy life. New objects are loved; new views are acted on; a new world opens to the view; and the man before selfish, becomes now benevolent; he that was vicious becomes virtuous; he that hated religion is now its friend; he that looked with cool contempt on all that could be said or done to win him, now enters heart and soul into the same work, and *wonders* that all does not see as he sees; he that sought only to live and enjoy himself here, now rises to higher objects, begins to feel that he is in the infancy of his being, and casts an eye of desire to the green fields in the skies, where he may for ever sweep the lyre in the praise of the Son of God, and unite with angels and archangels in lauding him that sitteth on the throne forever and ever. Never was a more appropriate name given by inspired or uninspired lips than to call such a man a new creature. He *begins* now to live. He has just awaked to the great purposes of his being, and treads with a light heart, and soft step, the earth where he shall soon sleep, and fixes the eye on the heavens that are soon to become his home. All this is done through the merits of the Son of God, in virtue alone of his death, and in connection with two acts made indispensable by the authority of God. These high feelings, these exalted hopes, are conferred on no one who repents not of his sins, and believes not on the Son of God. The former act implies deep sorrow that God has been offended; a deep sense of the intrinsic evil of sin, as well as of its consequences; and a solemn purpose to renounce all that opposes God. The latter implies a sense of the lost condition by nature; a conviction of helplessness, and unworthi-

ness, and a simple reliance on the merits of the Lord Jesus Christ, a willingness to be in the hands of a holy God, and an humble trust in the promises of aid. It is a solemn, deliberate rejection of self, and a giving up the soul to God, and a cordial hatred of sin in every form, and an embracing of the only Lord God, as the portion and Saviour of the soul. In connection with this act of believing, the sinner is pardoned and justified. A sweet sense of pardon, a peace that passeth all understanding flows into the wounded spirit. The storms subside,— the sky becomes clear and serene. A new beauty—the beauty of a new spring, where every flower and fountain, every rock and hill, every sun and star, have "found a tongue" to tell the praises of the all-present God of redemption, spreads over the works of creation and providence. And the soul redeemed and disenthralled goes forth for the first time to enjoy truly the works of creation, or the business of life, or the society of *new-found friends*. There is a charm around the duties of religion, unfelt in all other employments; and all tell of the height and depth, and length, and breadth, of the love of Christ that passeth knowledge.

The evidence of this great change is to be sought in the life. By their fruits they shall be known. They shall grow in grace. They shall be progressively sanctified. They, and they only, have evidence of this change who die unto sin, and live unto righteousness, who put on the Lord Jesus Christ,—are clothed with humility, crucify the flesh with the affections and lusts—who do justice, love mercy, walk humbly, and persevere unto the end.

VI. The only other remark which I shall make in explaining our views of this scheme, is, that this salvation is complete; and that God will watch over each renewed spirit till the day of judgment, and bring it infallibly to his kingdom. We should deem it strange, if God should be at all the expense of this plan,—if he should awaken and renew a soul,—if he should sprinkle on that soul the blood of Jesus, and freely pardon all its sins, and adopt it into his family, and make it a joint heir with Christ to an inheritance incorruptible and undefiled,—if angels should rejoice over it, and after all in vain, and it should fall away and die forever. Such a once-pardoned sinner would, we should think, claim a rank in hell by himself. Such a work would belie all God's other works. When has he begun a thing, and abandoned it? Why should this be begun, and then forsaken?—It is then in accordance, we suppose, with a scheme complete in all its parts, that the all-seeing and all-powerful Saviour said, My sheep hear my voice, and I know them, and they follow me: and I give unto them eternal life, and they shall never perish, neither shall any pluck them out of my hand: and in accordance with the same system he will say in the day of judgment to all hypocrites and apostates, with their pretences to experience and joy, I NEVER *knew you, depart from me.*

It is with peculiar interest that we are permitted to proclaim that *all* that will believe, ALL, not a part, shall infallibly be saved; that God is able to keep that which you have committed to him against that day; that HE will *never* leave you, nor forsake you; that if you will come to him he will *in no wise* cast you out; that he will keep you by his mighty power through faith unto salvation; and that though you fall, you shall not be utterly cast down. *To all,* I say, if you believe the gospel, *heaven is yours.* When you believe, you lay hold with no feeble grasp, on eternal life; and in every season of temptation and conflict, you shall find the Saviour, like the shadow of a great rock in a weary land, a covert from the tempest, a hiding-place from the storm, a strong tower into which the righteous may run and be safe. A heaven of boundless felicity shall be yours; and neither the marshalled hosts of hell, nor the devices of men, nor the ten thousand foes in your own bosom, and around you, shall be able to pluck you from him who holds you in the hollow of the hand, and guards you as the apple of the eye. The angels await your approach. They shall come forth with the glorious Son of God in the day of judgment, to welcome you to your, and their, eternal home. With them, you shall ascend, amidst songs and loud hallelujahs, rolling sweet music o'er the skies, to your, and their Father and God, to dwell where shall be no more sin, nor pain, nor death.

There, in the blessed bosom of the living God, the everlasting Father of his redeemed people, there, shall terminate the efforts to redeem man. There, shall be gathered a countless host from every nation and tongue to join in one song of universal praise, to "extol *him* first, *him* midst and *him* without end." There shall be humbled all human pride; and God only shall attract all eyes, and fill all hearts with the glories displayed in devising and executing the scheme, resulting in the ceaseless felicity of lost, ruined man.

I still ask your indulgence, while I deduce from this fruitful subject some important practical remarks.

1st. Permit me to ask of you, my hearers, are you prepared to commit the interests of your immortal souls to this plan of salvation? If I mistake not, the scheme which I have presented, is that of the Bible. If it is, it is the only way in which men can be saved. No scheme of morality, no religious device, if it has not the elements of this scheme in it, can be true or safe. The plan that humbles man, and exalts God; that presents the great Sovereign of worlds as originating and carrying forward the scheme, is that which is presented in the Sacred Scriptures. Unless I have read the Bible, and facts to no purpose, this which I have presented contains the outlines of the scheme of truth. This is the system of the Bible. This is the doctrine which, in all ages, has excited the opposition of the human heart. Herein is the offence of the cross. Here is the scheme that abases all human pride, and gives honor, where honor is due, to God only.—I may add, that this is Calvinism,—the scheme so often misrepresented,—so little understood,—so much hated by impenitent sinners—a scheme that has excited, probably, more opposition than any other system of doctrines since the foundation of the world. This scheme, if I understand it, contains nothing more than an enlargement of the principles which I have stated in this discourse. It neither asserts, that God made men to damn them,—nor that infants will be damned,—nor that sinners will be lost, do what they can,—nor that God is unwilling to save them,—nor that a poor penitent may not be saved;

but it claims that God is full of mercy, making ample provision for all that *will* come and inviting all freely ;—that all men are, full of evil, and of themselves *will* not come ; —that those that are saved, are saved by the grace of God, in which he bestows his favors according to infinite wisdom, and his sovereign pleasure :—that he has no new views about it, but has always intended to do what he actually does ;—and that he renews *no heart* in vain, but will keep all that are renewed, unto salvation. I appeal to your consciences, dying sinners, if this is not the scheme of the Bible ? I ask not whether this is such a plan as a proud, impenitent sinner would love, or such as your unsanctified feelings would approve, but I ask, is it not the evident scheme of the Word of God ? Is it not the plan on which, in fact, God governs the world ?—Who in this house can gainsay, or resist it ; or prove, or *believe*, that it is not ?—*Not one.* I ask then, again, fellow-sinners, are you prepared to commit your eternal interests to this plan ? Are you willing to be saved in this way ? Are you willing to abase yourselves at the feet of the Sovereign of worlds, and to give all the honor to God ? Do you feel safe in this plan ; do you feel that you are lost sinners—that you deserve eternal death—that you lie at the Sovereign mercy of God—that you have no claim ; and feeling this, are you willing to drop into the hands of Jesus, and to be saved by his merit alone ? Do you feel, that if you are saved, it will not be by might or power of yours, but by the spirit of the Lord ? And do you love this scheme ? Do you seek that God should be honored in it ; and do you pray and earnestly desire that it should spread wide as the world ? Do you pant that all may taste the grace of God— that every inhabitant of the lost world should join with you in the song of redeeming mercy ? If these are your feelings, then you are christians. I hesitate not to hold out to you, all the consolation that a minister of Jesus can afford, and to assure you, that you are treading the narrow path that leads to life. In that strait way, moving as God directs you, you shall find indeed, here and there a thorn, or a deep ravine, or a fen, or morass ; but all along the path flowers shall shed their fragrance, the ear shall listen to sweet harmony, green fields shall spread out before you, and the hope of heaven shall cheer you. To such I say, go on. Press forward. The prize, even the eternal crown, is near. Look not back ; but depending on the grace of God, fix the eye on heaven, and fight manfully the fight of faith, and lay hold on eternal life.

Of impenitent sinners, whether anxious or not, I say,

2dly, Are you prepared to reject this scheme ? To your *consciences*, not to your *feelings*, for you will not love it,—to your consciences, I put it, whether this is not the scheme of the Bible ? If it is, and what rebellious man here can deny it, if it is the plan of God, then you reject it at your peril. Then all your present plans, your morals, your formal prayers, your self-righteousness, your vain reliance on the unpromised mercy of God, are schemes that are abominable in the sight of your Maker ; and they and you, unless you forsake them, shall be driven away like chaff before the tempest. There is but one path that leads to life. It is a path where God is honored, and the sinner humbled In that path the sinner does not, will not tread.—Again I ask, are you prepared, fellow-mortal, to reject this scheme ? I do not ask, whether you will deny it in words, for not a man dare, or can do this. But will you reject it *in fact?* Man of the world, you that love riches and honors more than God, will you still love your riches ; and in seeking your own honors, refuse to honor God ? Guilty sinner, you whose profaneness, and sensuality, and envy, and pride, have rendered your heart black as hell, and miserable almost as the damned, are you prepared to reject this plan, and still love your sins ?—Trembling sinner, bent under the weight of your guilt, and almost on the verge of life—you that seek salvation and have not found it, are you prepared to reject this scheme, and trust to your own merits ? If you do, you do it, I repeat it, at your peril. It is your duty *now* to embrace it. Here is all your hope. If this scheme is rejected,—if you *will* not submit to God's plan of saving men, —if you do it not *now* from the heart, you tread a broad and crowded path down to the chambers of death. In that path you

(*To be continued.*)

THE RECORD.

FIRST PRESBYTERIAN CHURCH, MORRISTOWN, N. J.

"THIS SHALL BE WRITTEN FOR THE GENERATION TO COME."—Psalms 102 : 18.

VOLUME IV. APRIL, 1884. NUMBER 16.

[Printed with the Approval of the Session.]

THE RECORD

Will be published monthly at Morristown, N. J. Terms $1.00 per annum, *in advance.*

Subscriptions may be made at the book-stores of Messrs. Runyon and Emmell, or to Messrs. James R. Voorhees and William D. Johnson, or by letter addressed to the

EDITOR OF THE RECORD,

Morristown, N. J.

Entered at the Post Office at Morristown, N. J., as second class matter.

(*Mr. Barnes's Sermon Concluded.*)

---

now go. You may be charmed with sweet sounds, and revel with the wicked, and be unwilling to turn and live, you may walk amidst flowers, and wealth, and honor, but beyond you is a dreadful hell; and as a minister of the Son of God, I proclaim, that you will soon hear the groans of the damned, and see the right arm of the God of vengeance lifted on high to cut you down in eternal death.—To this scheme set before you now, trembling mortal fly. Fly before it is too late. Fly before the day of vengeance comes, and you perish—perish for ever.

3d. From this subject, we see what excludes men from Heaven. It is not a want of fulness, and freeness, in the plan of mercy. It is not that God is unwilling to save the sinner. It is simply because *you will not be saved.* You choose your own pride, your own vanity, your own lust, your own course in life—the path that leads to hell. Need I repeat the assurance so often made here, and in the Sacred Scriptures, that if you are lost, it will not be because God, or the Saviour, or the Angels, or Ministers, or Christians are to blame? It will be simply because you choose death rather than life. No other being will bear the guilt but yourselves. Forever and forever, you will welter in eternal woe, bearing your guilt unpitied and alone. No other being will bear the blame. No solitary mortal or immortal can be charged with the guilt of your destruction. Nor will it be a trifling *crime* to be damned. It is not a thing which you are at liberty to choose. You have *no right* to go down to hell and become the eternal enemy of God. You are under solemn *obligations* to be saved. Think what is implied in being lost. It implies the rejection of God's plan of saving the soul—the grieving of the spirit of God—trampling on the blood of Jesus—unbelief of what the God of truth has declared—contempt of his threatenings—the love of self, of sin, of destruction. Sinner, have you *a right* to travel in this wretched path? Have you a right thus to trifle with a holy God? Have you a right to reject all the means of mercy, and deliberately sin forever, against the God that made you? I appeal to your conscience. Let me also remind you, if you go from this place to woe, you will inherit no common damnation. Here this amazing plan of God's mercy, has been presented again and again. Here you have been entreated in every possible way to be saved. Here God's Spirit has striven. Many of you have been before awakened, and lived through revivals of religion. With great power he has, within the past three months, awed you. Others have pressed into the kingdom; and you have felt and known, that you must *repent* or *die.* You are now passing through the most solemn and interesting scenes that the earth witnesses, and listening to the most affecting appeals that he makes, unmoved. Who will be to blame, if you are lost—if others are taken, and you are left? Will God? Will

Christians? Will ministers? Will parents? Will friends? or will you yourselves? Let conscience answer. Go home this day, impenitent sinner, if God spares a rebel like you to get home—go home and reflect, that if you pass through this revival unmoved, if you resist all the appeals that are made to you, from day to day, and week to week, the probability is, that you will be damned, and the certainty is, that *you* only will be to blame if you are. I do not say that you will *certainly* be lost, I say that a most fearful probability "thunders perdition on your guilty path." What *should* move you hereafter, if you are not now moved? What more can be done for you than has been done? You have been warned, entreated, impressed. You *know* your duty, and your doom, if you do it not. You are in the hands of a Sovereign God. There I leave you. I have no other power than to spread out the scheme of mercy—to entreat you by the love of Jesus, and the mercy of God, and the value of the soul, to embrace the offer of life; and if you *will perish*, I must sit down and weep as I see you glide to the lake of death. Yet I cannot see you take that dread plunge—see you die, die forever, without once more assuring you that the offer of the gospel is freely made to you. While you linger this side the fatal verge, that shall close life and hope and happiness, I would once more lift up my voice and say, See, Sinner, see a God of love. He comes to you. He fills the heaven, the skies, the earth. Hear his voice as it breaks on the stillness of this house. Listen to the accents of the ever-living God—"As I live I have no pleasure in the death of the wicked, but rather that he turn and live: turn ye, turn ye, for why will ye die?" In the hands of that present God, that benignant Father, whose mercy breathes from every page of this book, I leave you. To him I commend you, with the deep feeling in my own bosom, that you are in his hands; that you are solemnly bound to repent *to-day*, and believe the gospel, and that if you perish, you only will be to blame. I feel, and know, that for not repenting, you have no excuse, and that God will forever hold you guilty.

I also feel, and know, that God is under no obligation to save you. That if you die, he will be guiltless. That if you are saved,

it will be by his sovereign mercy—in such a way, that he only will have the praise; and that the great secret, whether you will live or die, is lodged in his bosom, and that no mortal can compel or control him. That he holds over you the sceptre of life, or the sword of death; and that if you die, all creation will bow and say Amen, and Amen.

We also feel, and know, that God *can* save you—that he hears prayer. We will bear you, then, before the throne of grace, and say—Sovereign of worlds, Arbiter of life and death, spare this people, and save these dying sinners. "Oh, most holy, blessed, and merciful Saviour, deliver them not into the bitter pains of eternal death!" AMEN.

COMBINED REGISTERS, FOR PASTORATE OF THE REV. SAMUEL FISHER; JULY 1809 TO DEC. 1814.

It will be esteemed a great favor if the readers of THE RECORD *will send* CORRECTIONS, *or additional* INFORMATION, *to* Lock Box 90, Morristown, N. J.

[To facilitate reference, the Registers of Baptisms, Communicants, Marriages and Deaths, will hereafter be combined alphabetically for each pastorate. The significance of the abbreviations used is as follows:

aet.—aged.
b.—born.
B.—baptized.
B. f. h.— " on husband's account.
B. f. w.— " " wife's "
C.—became Communicant.
Ch.—Church.
d.—died or buried.
dg.—daughter.
dis.—dismissed by letter.
Exc.—excommunicated.
fr.—from.
L.—received by letter.
m.—married.
ord.—ordained.
s.—son.
serv.—servant.
susp.—suspended.
w.—wife.
wid.—widow.

Names of Communicants are printed in small capitals; those of children are indented under the names of their parents. The brace { connects names of husband and wife.
Remarks or additions made by the Editor are inclosed in brackets, thus [ ]; and doubtful conjectures are followed by the sign of interrogation.]

Polly Abers, wid.; m. 4 Dec., 1813, to Samuel Nestor.

Phebe Adamson, w. of Wm.; d. 27 Aug. 1813, aet. 19.

Jemima Allen, w. of Timothy; d. 28 Nov., 1810, aet 28.

DEACON ALLEN.
 Jabez Lindsly Allen, adopted; b. 24 Dec., 1805; B. f. Dea'n. 2 July, 1812.
 Keziah Layton, adopted; b. 7 Jan., 1809; B. f. Dea'n. 2 July, 1813.

MRS. JERUSHA ALSOVER, L. 29 June, 1813.

fr. Parsippany; [Jerusha Halsey, m. 14 Jan., 1804, to Frederick A. Alsover, both of Hanover.]

{ JOHN ALWOOD.
PHEBE ALWOOD, [dg. of Samuel ?]; m. 2 Dec. 1811.

Elizabeth; b. 13 Feb., 1813; B. f. w. 2 July 1813.

{ JONAS ALWOOD, [s. of Samuel].
[RACHEL ARNOLD, dg. of Ziba.]
Susan, b. 27 Dec., 1807; B. 2 July, 1813.
Mary Ann, b. 16 Dec., 1809; B. 2 July, 1813.
Matilda, b. 16 Mar., 1812; B. 2 July, 1813.

Mary Ann Apthorp, of Long Island; m. 24 Nov., 1810, to Moses Holloway, [s. of Capt. Benj'm ?], of Morris Plains.

John Armstrong, [s. of Nathanael and Rachel ?]; d. 8 April, 1812. aet 26.

POLLY ARMSTRONG, wid. [of Nathanel, Jr., who d. 26 May, 1803, aet. 34]; now Williams, [2d w. of Matthias Williams ?]; dis.

Phebe Armstrong, b. 24 April, 1794; B. f. w. 30 Jan., 1811.
David Armstrong, b. 17 Sept., 1796; B. f. w. 30 Jan., 1811.
Lewis Armstrong, b. 15 Sept., 1802; B. f. w. 30 Jan., 1811.

RACHEL ARMSTRONG, w. of Nathaniel; C., 28 Aug., 1812; d. Jan. 14, 1807. aet. 73.

Rhoda Armstrong, wid. [of John, s. of Nath'l ? & dg. of ―― Norris]; B. & C. 6 Nov., 1814; dis. as w. of Timothy Pierson, 26 Jan., 1841, to 2d Ch.

Esther Arnold, m. 1 Feb., 1812, to Isaac Whitehead [s. of Onesimus ?], of Chatham.

MARY ARNOLD, w. of Robert [dg. of Joseph & Patience Pierson]; C. 26 Apr., 1813; d. March 16, 1823, aet. 75.

Mary Pierson Arnold [dg. of Robert & Mary Pierson Arnold], m. 26 Oct., 1811, to Nathan Mills.

ABIGAIL AYRES, dg. of Silas and Mary [Byram]; d. 18 Feb., 1812, aet. 39.

{ STEPHEN COOPER AYERS.
COMFORT ―――――
Isaac; b. 1 Dec., 1809; B. 20 May, 1810.

Stephen Day, b. 6 April, 1811; B. 13 Oct., 1811.
Henry, b. 1 Sept., 1813; B. 2 July, 1814.

JANE PRUDDEN AYRES, w. of John [B.], [dg. of Joseph, Jr., & Esther Prudden]; C. 1 May, 1812; dis. Sept., 1817; [d. 1845 in Texas, leaving three sons, Joseph, Alfred A. & Silas B., with one daughter].

MARY AYRES, wid. of Isaac [dg. of ―― Cooper]; d. 30 June, 1809, aet. 63.

Henry Badgley, d. 13 Mar., 1814, aet. 50.

Mons. Jean Francis Barbateaux, d. 18 Aug., 1811, aet. 28.

MARIAH BARKINS; C. 3 July, 1812; dis. Oct., 1816.

Capt. Enoch Beach, d. at Hanover, 7 Mar., 1814, aet. 77.

Henry Beach [s. of Asa ?]; m. 12 Feb., 1812, to Abigail [Condit] Smith, [dg. of John & Sally], who d. 19 July, 1812, aet. 20 [or 25 ?].

Matthias Beach, of Newark, m. 20 Jan., 1810, to Mary Cobb, dg. of Thomas.

Joseph Bedell, m. 27 Feb., 1812, to Sally Mills, [dg. of Samuel ?].

{ William Bedell, m. 4 Nov., 1813, to [2d w.] Abigail Hill, [dg. of Peter ?].
HANNAH SUTTON, [dg. of John & Leah]; d. 4 Sept., 1812, aet 39.

William, b. 23 June, 1811; B. f. w. 14 July, 1811; d. 18 Sept., 1811.

Abigail Beers, [dg. Joseph]; m. 7 Feb., 1810, to Mathew G. Lindsley.

Catharine Beers, dg. of Nathanael; d. 14 Nov., 1811, aet. 11.

HULDAH BEERS [dg. of Joseph], m. 25 Nov., 1813, to Shubaal Trowbridge.

{ Jacob Beers [s. of Nathanael].
ELIZABETH HATFIELD WOODRUFF, wid.;m. 13 May, 1811; C. 3 July, 1812; d. 29 Jan., 1873, aet. 83.

Juliann, b. 8 July, 1812; B. f. w. 28 Aug., 1812.

JOSEPH BEERS, C. 4 March, 1810; d. July, 1817, [aet. 67 ?].

Samuel Beers [s. of Joseph], m. 20 Feb., 1814, to Hannah Lindsley.

Sarah Beers, w. of Samuel; d. 21 June, 1810, aet. 23.

Joanna Benjamin, w. of Herrick [& dg. of Woodruff ?]; d. 23 July, 1812, aet. 90.

Dr. Ebenezer Blachly, b. 6 Dec., 1760; d. 20 Aug., 1812, aet. 51.

Isaac Blackford, m. 1 Feb., 1812, to Elizabeth Mills, [dg. of Timothy ?].

FRANCES BLEEKER, w. of Alexander; C. 25 Dec., 1812; dis. 2 Jan., 1815, to N. Y. City.

Alexander Noel, b. 11 Aug., 1813; B. f. w. 29 May. 1814.

George Bockhoven, d. 8 June, 1814, aet. 79.

Elizabeth Bowen, m. 19 May, 1820, to Isaac Minton.

William Bowen, d. 18 April, 1810, aet. 66.

Jemima Bowers, wid.; m. 20 July, 1810, to James Nixon.

Hannah Boyd, m. 2 Sept., 1809, to George Phillips, of Somerset.

Eliza Boyle, of Chatham, m. 13 Oct., 1811, to Wm. Mills.

JOHN PIERSON BREESE, [What was his wife's name ?]; L. 26 April, 1813, fr. Basking-ridge; dis. 28 May, 1828, to N. Y. State.

Charles Pierson, b. 18 Feb., 1808; B. 3 July, 1812.

Henry Vail, b. 5 Feb., 1810; B. 3 July, 1812.

Margaret Ann, b. 11 April, 1812; B. 3 July, 1812.

HANNAH BROOKFIELD, w. John [& dg. of Gilbert Allen]; d. 28 Jan., 1810, aet. 35.

John Brown, d. 11 Dec, 1811, aet. 26.

DEBORAH BRUSH, w. of Jesse; L. 12 June, 1811, fr. N. Windsor, N. Y.; dis. 4 Dec., 1813.

Jesse Brush, of Troy, d. 12 Nov., 1812, aet. 47.

James Bryant, b. 3 Dec., 1782; d. 5 April, 1811, aet. 26.

Mary Bull, w. of Nathanael; d. 16 Sept., 1814, aet. 39.

SARAH BURD, w of Bartholomew; C. 22 June, 1814; dis. 9 May, 1827, to Han-over.

Anna Prudden, b. 23 Nov., 1802; B. 29 Sept., 1814.

George Washington, 27 Sept., 1803; B. 29 Sept., 1814.

Mary Caroline, b. 6 Mar., 1808; B. 29 Sept., 1814.

Lewis Alfred, b. 5. June, 1810; B. 29 Sept., 1814.

Esther Prudden, b. 21 Aug., 1812; B. 29 Sept., 1814.

Charles Burnet.

MARIAH HALSEY [dg. of Joseph ?], m. 12 Nov., 1811.

Joseph Halsey, B. f. w. 30 April, 1814.

CLARISSA BYRAM [dg. of Eleazer]; C. 29 Aug., 1814; m. Chas. Thompson.

ELEAZER BYRAM, [s. of Jeptha]; b. 7 Jan., 1765; d. 9 Mar., 1811, aet. 46.

Hariette Byram [dg. of Eleazer ?], m. 30 Sept., 1813, to Jonathan Thompson.

JOSEPH BYRAM; L. 4 May, 1810, fr. Cald-well; dis. 31 Mar., 1812.

HESTER ———, L. 4 May, 1810, fr. Cald-well; dis. 31 Mar., 1812.

BETSEY; L. 4 May, 1810, fr. Caldwell; dis. 31 Mar., 1812.

JOSEPH, JR.; L. 4 May, 1810, fr. Cald-well; dis. Sept., 1817.

ELIAS; L. 4 May, 1810, fr. Caldwell; "gone."

Joseph Byram [Jr. ?], m. 30 Mar., 1814. to Abigail Harris.

NAPHTHALI BYRAM [s. of Japhet], d. 23 Jan., 1812, aet. 63—3-8.

Phebe Byram [dg. of Eleazer ?], m. 26 Mar., 1812, to Ebenezer Lindsley.

Silas Byram, m. 30 Nov., 1813, to Sarah Lu-man [?.]

SILAS C. BYRAM [s. of Naphthali]; C. 3 Nov., 1814; dis. 26 May, 1828, to Bask-ingridge.

SUSANNA BYRAM, wid. of Jeptha; C. 1 May, 1812; d. 1 Nov., 1813, aet. 72 [?.]

Isaac Canfield [s. of Abraham].

MARGARET CALDWELL, dg. of Rev. James C. 21 Feb., 1810; d. 3 Jan., 1831, aet 67.

Hannah Maria, b. 1 Nov., 1803; B f. w. 15 June, 1810.

Josiah Flint, b. 22 Mar., 1808; B. f. w 15 June, 1810.

Israel Canfield [s. of Abraham.]

RACHEL [O. Wetmore]; C. 25 Dec., 1812 dis. 26 Jan., 1841, to 2d Ch.

Cornelia Laura, b. 29 July, 1812; B. f w. 4 Sept., 1813.

Kata, serv. b. 14 Mar., 1813; B, Sept., 1813.

James C. Canfield [s. of Isaac], m. 20 of Jan., 1812, to Eliza Vail.

EUNICE CANFIELD, w. of Jacob [& dg. of Moses Munson], d 3 April, 1810, aet 44.

(*To be Continued.*)

THE RECORD.

FIRST PRESBYTERIAN CHURCH, MORRISTOWN, N. J.

" THIS SHALL BE WRITTEN FOR THE GENERATION TO COME."—Psalms 102 : 18.

VOLUME IV.   MAY 1884.   NUMBER 17.

[Printed with the Approval of the Session.]

THE RECORD

Will be published monthly at Morristown, N. J. Terms $1.00 per annum *in advance*.

Subscriptions may be made at the bookstores of Messrs. Runyon and Emmell, or to Messrs. James R. Voorhees and William D. Johnson, or by letter addressed to the

EDITOR OF THE RECORD,
Morristown, N. J.

Entered at the Post Office at Morristown, N. J., as second class matter.

(Continued.)

COMBINED REGISTERS, for Pastorate of the Rev. Samuel Fisher; July, 1809, to Dec. 1814,

For meaning of abbreviations see second page of THE RECORD for April 1884.

It will be esteemed a great favor if the readers of THE RECORD *will send* CORRECTIONS, *or additional* INFORMATION, *to* Lock Box 90, Morristown, N. J.

MARY CANFIELD, [dg. of John ?]; C. 5 May 1811.

Mary Campfield, of Hanover, [same as above ?]; m. 13 Nov., 1811, to Wm. Sayre.

William Canfield, of New York; m. 7 Oct., 1809, to Eliza Ogden, dg. of John, of Malapardis.

David Carmichael [s. of Alexander]; b. 31 Dec., 1764; d. 19 Aug., 1810, aet. 46; styled " High Sheriff of Morris Co.," in Bill of Mortality.

Mary Carmichael, wid. of Alex. [& dg. of David Ogden ?]; d. 21 Aug., 1814, aet. 72.

ELIZABETH CASTERLINE, w. of Daniel; B. & C. 3 Jan., 1813; dis. 10 Sept., 1825, to Rockaway.

MARY CHAMBERLAIN, w. of Jacob; C. 29

Aug., 1814; susp. 17 July, 1832, [Mary, Concklin Halsey, m. 20 April, 1805, to Jacob Chamberlain.]

Abraham Clark, d. 5 Feb., 1810, aet. 32.

Polly Clark, m. 13 May, 1809, to Squier Tomkins.

George Clifton, d. 20 Oct., 1811, aet. 67.

Hannah Cobb, w. of Thomas; d. 1 April 1812, aet. 52.

Mary Cobb, dg. of Thomas ; m. 20 Jan., 1810, to Matthias Beach, of Newark.

David F. Cockran, m. 9 April, 1812, to Mary Mills.

John Cockran, d. 26 Mar. 1814, aet. 92.

Grover Coe, d. 14 Sept. 1813, aet 49.

Eleanor Cohill, m. 23 Jan. 1811, to Isaac Wort, of Pompton, Bergen Co.

MIRIAM COMESAU, wid. of Nicholas; d. 20 June 1809, aet. 80.

ANNA CONDICT, dg. of Abner; C. 5 March, 1813 ; d. 7 Jan. 1823, aet. 36, 3-11.

EDWARD CONDICT, [s. of Peter.]
    Mary Ann, b. 27 July, 1809 ; B. 22, Oct, 1809.
    Lewis Byram, d. 2 Aug. 1811, aet. 5.
    Edward Byram, b. 23 June 1812 ; B. 30, Oct. 1812.

Eliza Condict, [dg. of Edward ?] ; m. 26 Dec. 1813, to Daniel B. Hurd.

JEDUTHAN CONDICT, [s. of Joseph ?]
    Ezra, b. 7 Oct. 1809; B. 3 Dec. 1809.
    Hannah Maria, b. 4 Aug. 1813; B. 19 Sept. 1813.

Lewis Condict.
    Nathan Woodhull, b. 28 Nov. 1809; B. f. w. " Matsey," 29 June 1810.
    Ellen Louisa, b. 1 Dec. 1811; B. t. w; 3 July, 1812.
    Lewis ; B. f. w. 29 May 1814.

Phebe Condict, w. of Jabez ; d. 6 Mar. 1813, aet. 77.

Silas Condict, [s. of Ebenezer ?]

Edward Lewis, b. 4 Feb. 1812; B. f. w.
[Charlotte Ford?] 4 June 1812.

Silas H [aines?] Condict, [s. of Abner.]
Alfred Dickerson, b..4 Dec. 1809; B.
f. w. 25 Feb. 1810.
Martha Haines, b. 17 Aug. 1812; B. f.
w. 30 Oct. 1812.

Johnson Conklin, m. 12 April 1810, to Hannah Tuthill.

Stephen Conklin, Jr., [s. of Stephen, Jr. &
Rachel?]; m. 29 Oct. 1809, to Abigail
Cook.

ABIGAIL CONNET, w. of Luther; L. 30 Oct.
1812, fr. Mendham; dis. 26 Jan. 1841, to
2d Ch.
Rachel, b. 5 Sept. 1811; B. f. w. 28
Aug. 1812.

ABBY CONNET, [dg. of Luther?]; C. 29 Aug.
1814; dis. 8 June 1841, as Julia Ann
to 2nd Ch.; m. 4 Mar. 1818, to Philip
Cook.

ISABEL [WINFIELD] CONKLIN, w. of John;
B. & C. 3 Jan. 1813, dis. May, 1833, to
New Vernon, d. 2 Jan. 1854.
Jonathan Stiles, b. 10 Aug. 1806; B. f.
w. 7 Jan. 1814.
Henry Winfield, b. 25 Nov. 1807; B. f.
w. 7 Jan. 1814.
Samuel Fowler, b. 8 April, 1809; B. f.
w. 7 Jan. 1814.
Gilbert Allen, b. 23 Oct. 1811; B. f. w.
7 Jan. 1814.
Ann Eliza, b. 27 April, 1814; B. 1 Jan.
1815.

Abigail Cook, m. 29 Oct. 1809, to Stephen
Conklin, Jr.

PHILIP COOK, B. & C. 6 Nov. 1814, "gone
on 4."

ICHABOD COOPER, d. 29 Nov. 1809, aet. 68.

Mary Cory, [dg. Simeon], m. 31 Dec. 1811, to
Walter Sturges, [s. of Moses?]

SIMEON CORY.
Silas Day, b. 14 Aug. 1810; B. 4 Jan.
1811.
Uzal, b. 28 Sept. 1812; B. 1 Jan. 1813.
John Crane, d. 24 Aug. 1812, aet. 36.

RACHEL CROWELL; L. 4 May, 1810, fr. So.
Hanover.

Silas Crowell, [s. of Seth, Jr.?]; d. at Green
Village, 24 May, 1814.

Jonathan Cutler, [s. of Jesse?]; m. 30 Sept.
1813, to Anna Marsh, [dg. of Aaron?]

JOSEPH CUTLER, [s. of Abijah?]

James Perrine, b. 8 Jan. 1812; B. f. w.
3 July, 1812; d. 31 Dec. 1813, aet. 2.

Susan Dalrymple, w. of William; d. 17
Dec. 1814, aet. 25.

David Day [s. of David & Deborah?]
MARY HOPPOCK, [2d w?]; m. 30 Nov. 1811.
David Hallack, b. 12 Oct. 1800; B. f.
w. 5 Mar. 1813.
Charles, b. 23 Aug. 1802; B. f. w. 5
Mar. 1813.
Martha Ann, b, 29 June, 1804; B. f. w.
5 Mar. 1813.
Emily, b. 12 June, 1812; B. f. w. 5
Mar. 1813.
James Lawrence, b. 9 Jan. 1814; B. f.
w. 24 April, 1814.

Ezekiel Day, d. 17 Mar. 1812, aet. 30.

John Day, [s. of Ezekiel].
Jane, b. 2 June, 1809; B. f. w. [Mary
King Ayers], 30 Aug. 1810.
Ezekiel Reeve, b. 23 Aug. 1811; B. f.
w., 6 May, 1812.
Silas Condict Ayers, b. 29 July, 1813;
B. f. w., 5 Nov. 1813.

Sally Day, d. 15 of Feb. 1812, aet. 26.

JONATHAN DAYTON; L. 2 Nov. 1813, fr.
Baskingridge; dis. before 1845 to Mendham; d. 1849.
PHEBE ——— L. 2 Nov. 1813, fr. Baskingridge; dis. before 1845 to Mendham.
Amos Cooper, b. 4 Sept. 1813; B. 4
Mar. 1814.

JANE [HUGHES] DeCAMP, w. of Timothy; L.
4 May, 1810, fr. Hanover; dis. 29 June,
1813, to South Hanover.
Timothy, b. 1 April 1809; B. 1 Sept.
1809; d. 7 Aug. 1810, aet. 1.
Lewis [Allen], d. 8 Sept. 1811, aet. 6.
Ellis, d. 8 Sept. 1811, aet. 1.
John [James Hughes?] d. 11 Sept.
1811, at 5.
Eliza, d. 12 of Sept. 1811, aet. 8.

RACHEL DeHART, w. of Martin; b. 13 Feb.
1791; B. & C. 1 Nov. 1812.
Ann, b. 3 Mar. 1810; B. f. w. 1 May,
1813.
Frances, b. 30 Dec. 1811; B. f. w. 1 May,
1813.
Wm. Still, b. 6 Sept. 1813; B. f. w. 5
Nov. 1813.

PHILEMON DePOE, C. 3 July 1808; dis. 22
June, 1814, to Madison.
David, b. 10 Dec. 1809; B. 6 May, 1810.

Charles Wheeler, b. 15 Sept. 1811; B. 5 Jan. 1812.

Benjamin Dickerson, d. 9 June, 1809, aet. 27.

Jophenes Dickerson, m. 21 Feb, 1811, to Abraham Slaught, of Roxbury.

MARY A. DICKERSON, wid.; L., 1 Nov. 1812; [dis. to M. E. Ch., Succasunna; 15 March, 1854 ?]

William Dickerson,[s. of Capt. Peter ?]; d. 31 Oct. 1810, aet. 37.

George Dixon, d. 24 May, 1814, aet. 29.

John Dixon, d. 1 Jan. 1811, aet. 68–6; [*in Bill of Mortality, but name neither on roll of Communicants nor of Half-way members.]

Mary Dixon, wid. of John ; d. 16 April, 1814, aet. 72–7.

Gertrude LeBeaux Doughty, b. 23 Aug. 1726; wid. of Thomas ; d. 3 Aug. 1810, aet. 85 ; [*in Bill of Mortality, but name neither on roll of Communicants nor of Half-way members.]

ANNA DOUGLAS, w. of Timothy ; [Anna Peer, m 16 Aug. 1806 ?]; C. 5 May 1811 ; dis. [22] Nov. 1824, [to Rockaway.]

ELIZABETH EDWARDS, wid.; C. 25 Dec. 1812; d. 1827.

SARAH EGBERT, w. of Enos ; L. 2 Nov. 1813, fr. Elizabethtown ; dis. to Meth. Ch.

William Enslee. [What was the name of his wife ?]

Sally Ann, b. 28 June, 1810 ; B. f. w. 2 Sept. 1810.

Caroline, b. 17 June, 1812 ; B. f. w. 30 Aug. 1812.

Ann Estey, [2d ?] w. of Moses ; d. 11 Nov. 1811, [1809 ?] aet. 47.

John Jacob Faesch, d. 8 Nov. 1809, aet. 32.

Hannah Fairchild, d. 13 Oct. 1809, aet. 23.

Jane Fairchild, m. 11 Oct. 1811, to Tunis Hoppock.

Jonathan Fairchild, [s.of Matthew & Sarah?]; d. at Morris Plains, 5 Aug. 1813, aet. 63.

Joseph Fairchild, m. 20 Oct. 1811, to ELIZABETH HOPPOCK.

Squier Harrison, b. 17 Dec. 1813 ; B. f. w. 17 April, 1814.

MEHETABLE FAIRCHILD, [dg. of Thomas Tuttle ?], w. of Timothy [s. of Phineas ?] ; C. 1 May, 1812, d. May, 1843, [aet. 79 ?]

NANCY FAIRCHILD. [dg. of —— Loper, of Hanover ?]. wid. [of David, s. of David ?] ; C. 5 May, 1811.

Sarah Fairchild, wid. of Phineas; d. 2 Nov. 1811, aet. 82.

THEODOSIA FAIRCHILD, [dg. of —— Conger ?] w. of Abner ; B. & C. 4 July, 1813; d. at New Vernon, 3 Dec. 1814, aet. 50.

Sarah Ferguson, wid.; d. 17 Sept. 1811, aet.70.

ALICE FISHER, w. of Rev.Samuel; L. 29 June, 1813, fr. Consociated Ch., Wilton, Conn.; dis. 22 April, 1814, to 1st Ch. Paterson.

Catharine, b. 24 May, 1810 ; B. 1 July, 1810.

Harriet, b. 10 April, 1812 ; B. 31 May, 1812.

Samuel Ware, b. 5 April, 1814, B. 29 May, 1814. [Ord.;

Catharine Ford, of Hanover, [dg. of Jonathan ?]; m. 8 Sept. 1813, to Joshua Wiltz, of N. Y.

Elizabeth Ford, [dg. of Nathan Reeve ?], w. of Samuel [Moore, adopted s. and nephew of James Ford & Elizabeth (Odell) ?]: d. 15 Aug. 1809, aet. 39.

Sarah Ford, [dg. of —— Martin ?] w. of Wm. O [dell, s. of James Ford?] of South Hanover; d. 7 Jan.1813, aet. 26.

ELIZABETH FREEMAN [dg. of —— Carter], w. of Benjamin ; d. 3 Jan., 1812 [1813?], aet. 58.

Huldah Freeman [dg. of Samuel ?] ; m. 30 Mar., 1811, to Samuel Kork, of Hanover.

JOANNA FREEMAN [dg. of Zophar, Jr. ?]; C.; 29 Aug., 1814 ; m. Ashbel U. Guerin ; dis. 9 Nov., 1831, to New Foundland, N. J.

Wm. Freeman, m. 3 Feb., 1810, to Phebe Hinds, dg. of John, both of Morris Plains.

ZOPHAR FREEMAN [Sr. ?] ; d. 15 Dec., 1810, aet. 83.

ZOPHAR FREEMAN [Jr., the Elder, & his w. MARY ?].

Hannah, b. 14 June, 1809 ; B. 1 Sept., 1809.

Chatharine, b. 5 Nov., 1811 ; B. 28 Feb., 1812.

Phebe Frost, w. of Ezekiel ; d. 1 April, 1810, aet. 20.

Rhoda Gardiner, m. 8 Jan., 1814, to John Talmage.

Sarah Gardiner [Garner ?], w. of Joseph ; d, 27 June, 1810, aet. 34.

JOSEPH GARNER, C. 14 June., 1814; [dis. as "Joseph Gardiner," 8 Feb., 1815 ?].

James Garrigas, m. 12 Oct., 1811, to ELIZABETH GODEN [dg. of Joseph ?]; both of Hanover.

Mable Gregory, b. 8 July, 1812; B. f. w. 28 Aug., 1812.

Jacob Henry, b. 25 Dec., 1813; B. f. w. 17 April, 1814.

Ossy Gilman, wid.; m. 11 Nov., 1809, to Jacob Tingler.

ANNA GOBLE, B. & C. 6 Nov., 1814; m. Ezra Scott; dis. 8 June, 1841, to 2d Ch.

MARGARET GOBLE, w.of Isaac; B. & C. 3 July, 1814, [dis. to New Vernon ?].

ELIZABETH GODEN [dg. of Joseph ?]; m. 12 Oct., 1811, to James Garrigas, both of Hanover.

Joseph Godden [& w. EUNICE FAIRCHILD ?]. Henry Fritz, b. 5 Sept., 1809; B. f. w. 5 Jan., 1810.

Susan Gould, dg. of Joseph & Sarah; d. 7 June, 1810, aet. 29.

ASHBEL[U.] GUERIN; B.& C. 3 Sept.,1814; dis. 9 Nov., 1831, to New Foundland. N. J.

Jonas Guerin. [What was the name of his wife ?]
Jared Goble. b. 10 May, 1809; B. f. w. 3 Sept., 1809.
Charles, b. 28 Feb., 1812; B. f. w. 14 June, 1812.

Sary Guerin, m. 14 Mar., 1811, to Samuel Leonard; d, 9 Jan., 1813, aet. 23.

Thomas Guerin [s. of Joshua ?]
ELIZABETH LINDSLEY [dg. of Moses ?]; C. 27 Aug., 1813; d. 30 April, 1825, aet. 56.
Susan Raynor, b. 3 June, 1805; B. f. w. 7 Jan., 1814.
Francis Johnes, b. 19 July, 1811; B. f. w. 7 Jan., 1814.

Samuel Halliday [d. abt. 1840, in N. Y.]
AMY BYRAM [dg. of Naptali; d. abt. 1852, in Ithaca, N. Y.]
SARAH JANE, b. 10 June, 1810; B. 26 Aug., 1810; [m. 1834 to Charles Whitin, of Whitinsville, Mass.]
SAMUEL BYRAM, b. 8 June, 1812, B. 19 July, 1812; [C. 1825 in Spring St. Ch., N. Y.; after revival of 1830 & '31 began study for Ministry at Bloomfield; Gen. Agt. & 1st Missionary of N. Y. Tract Soc., 1833: Agt. Female Guardian Soc.; Agent for Providence Y. M. Tract Soc. 1844; ord,

& pastor Cong. Ch., Lodi, N. Y., 1 yr.; Agent and Superintendent Five Points House of Industry 12 yrs.; Assistant Pastor Plymouth Ch., Brooklyn, since 1869; m. to Mary W. Chapin. of Uxbridge, Mass.; celebrated golden wedding Jan., 1883.]

HENRY HEDGES, b. 7 Mar., 1814; B. 24 April, 1814; [C. 1825 in Spring St. Ch., N. Y.; grad. N. Y. Univ., 1833; studied for ministry, but d. spring of 1834.]

Henry Halsey [& 2d w. LYDIA. who d. 29 Jan., 1871, aet. 93.]
Eliza, b. 4 Oct., 1801; B. f. w. 30 April, 1811.
Amy Caroline, b. 19 Aug., 1803; B. f. w. 30 April, 1811.
James Melville, b. 16 June, 1805; B. f. w. 30 April, 1811.
Joshua Freeland Batchelor, b. 15 June. 1807; B. f. w. 30 April, 1811.
George Washington, b. 4 July, 1809; B. f. w. 30 April, 1811.
Henry Hyer, b. 29 July 1811; B. f. w. 1 Nov., 1811.

JOSEPH HALSEY, [s. of Benj. & Sarah Prudden ?[; d. 18 May, 1811, aet. 56.

MARIA HALSEY [dg. of Joseph], m. 12 Nov., 1811, to Charles N. Burnet.

MARILLA HALSEY; C. 22 June, 1882; dis. 15 Aug., 1825, to Spring St. Ch., N. Y.

HENRY HARDY, colored; B. & C. 3 July, 1814.

Hannah Harporee [dg. of John ?], m. 17 April, 1810, to Mahlon Whitehead, of Sussex.

ABIGAIL HARRIS, m. 31 Mar., 1812, to Stephen Loper [?].

Abigail Harris, m. 30 Mar., 1813, to Joseph Byram. [Or was this Abigail H., the communicant ?]

ANNA HARRISON, w of Robert; L. 29 June, 1813, fr. South Hanover; dis. to Newark.

JONATHAN HATHAWAY, d. 26 Aug., 1814, aet. 76-7-7.

Mabel Hathaway, w. of Josiah; d. 14 July, 1811, aet. 39.

Silas Hathaway, [s. of Benoni ?]; d. 23 July, 1811, aet. 39.

Phebe Hayt, wid.; m. 9 Oct., 1813, to John Nestor.

(To be Continued.)

THE RECORD.

FIRST PRESBYTERIAN CHURCH, MORRISTOWN, N. J.

"THIS SHALL BE WRITTEN FOR THE GENERATION TO COME."—Psalms 102 : 18.

VOLUME IV. JUNE, 1884. NUMBER 18.

[Printed with the Approval of the Session.]

THE RECORD

Will be published monthly at Morristown, N. J. Terms $1.00 per annum *in advance.*

Subscriptions may be made at the bookstores of Messrs. Runyon and Emmell, or to Messrs. James R. Voorhees and William D. Johnson, or by letter addressed to the

EDITOR OF THE RECORD,

Morristown, N. J.

Entered at the Post Office at Morristown, N. J., as second class matter.

————:o:————

(Continued.)

COMBINED REGISTERS, for Pastorate of the Rev. Samuel Fisher ; July. 1809, to Dec 1814

For meaning of abbreviations see second page of THE RECORD for April 1884.

It will be esteemed a great favor if the readers of THE RECORD *will send* CORRECTIONS. *or additional* INFORMATION, *to* Lock Box 90, Morristown, N. J.

————:o:————

——— Hedden. m. 14 Aug., 1813, to Phebe Taylor ; both of Orange.

Elias Hedges [s. of Elias ?] ; d. in Ohio, 1813, [aet. 43 ?].

JULIA FORD HEDGES, [dg. of Abra'm] ; C. 29 Aug., 1814 ; [m. 8 May, 1821, to Nathanael S. Crane ; dis. 5 Jan., 1823, to Caldwell ; d. 14 Dec., 1852.]

Abigail Hill, dg. of Samuel ; d. 29 Aug., 1812, aet. 11.

Abigail Hill, [dg. of Peter & Anne ?] ; m. 4 Nov., 1813, to Wm. Bedell.

Jonathan Hill, [s. of Samuel] ; d. 12 Feb., 1810, aet. 22.

Hannah Hinds, [dg. of Isaac?] ; m. 11 Nov., 1809, to Samuel Pierson.

Phebe Hinds, dg. of John ; m. 3 Feb., 1810, to Wm. Freeman, both of Morris Plains.

Esther Holbert [Hurlburt ?] ; m. 22 Feb., 1812, to Joseph Jaggers.

ELIJAH HOLLOWAY [(s. of Elijah) & w. Elizabeth (Gamble) ?.

 Caleb, b. 8 Dec., 1869 ; B. 2 Sept., 1810.

 Daniel, b. 17 July, 1813 ; B. 21 Nov., 1813.

Moses Holloway [s. of Benjamin ?], of Morris Plains ; m. 24 Nov., 1810. to Mary Ann Apthorp, of Long Island.

Mary Hopkins, m. 22 Oct., 1810, to SILAS MILLER.

AMY HOPPOCK, B. & C.6 Nov., 1814 ; dis. 1 July, 1837, to Newton.

ELIZABETH HOPPOCK. m. 20 Oct., 1811, to Joseph Fairchild ; [dis. 19 Jan., 1848, to Newark ?].

MARY HOPPOCK, m. 30 Nov., 1811, to David Day ; [dis. 1841, to 2d Ch. ?].

Tunis Hoppock, m. 11 Oct., 1811, to Jane Fairchild.

Elias Howell [& w. HANNAH PRUDDEN, dg. of Isaac & Sarah ?].

 Sally Reeve, b. 23 Jan., 1810 ; B. f. w. 2 Sept., 1810.

Elizabeth Howell [2d ?] w. of Elias P. ; d. at Chatham, 27 May, 1814, act. 24.

[Phebe ?] Howell, [wid ?] of John ; d. at Troy, 1814.

SARAH HOWELL, wid. of Nathan ; d. 7 Aug., 1813, aet. 81.

HEZEKIAH HULBURT, b. 28 Mar., 1778 B. ; & C. 3 May, 1812 ; dis. 6 May, 1819. to N. Y., & 1 April, 1828, to Geneva, N. Y.

ELIZABETH Martin, dg. of William, of Chatham] ; b. 14 Jan., 1790 ; B. & C., & dis. with husband.

William Martin, b. 8 Oct., 1809; B. 3 July, 1812.

Charles Goodrich, b. 27 Mar., 1811 ; B. 3 July, 1812.

David B. Hurd, m. 26 Dec., 1813, to Eliza Condit, [dg. of Edward ?].

HUGH HUSTON, [once "Houston," & w. MARTHA ?]; L. 26 April, 183, fr. Associate Ref.
    Ch., N. Y.; dis. with w. Martha, May 1833, to New Vernon. [No record of
    "Martha's" reception ; who was she ?]

    Eliza, b. 18 April, 1812 ; B. 1 May, 1813.

    John, b. 23 Aug., 1813 ; B. 29 Dec., 184.

Joseph Jaggers, m. 22 Feb., 1812, to Esther Holbert.

[Peter ?] Samuel Jerome, formerly from Northern N. Y ; d. 15 April, 1813, aet. 30.

Ann Johnes, m. 4 April, 1812, to Henry Tunis.

ELIZABETH JOHNES, w. of John S[utton, s. of Armstrong]; C. 4 Mar., 1810; d. 19 Oct.
    1815.

    Catharine ; b. 15 Aug., 1807 ; B. f. w. 29 June, 1810.

    Lewis Armstrong : b. 12 Feb. 1808 ; B. f. w. 29 June, 1810.

    Mary ; b. 4 Sept., 1811 ; B. f. w. 30 Oct., 1812.

JOAN[NA NITEL] JOHNES, [dg. Timothy, M. D., & Abigail ?] ; C. 26 April, 1813 ; dis. as Mrs.
    Joanna Woodruff 14 Jan., 1832, to Succasuna, [what was first name of her hus-
    band ? when married ?]

WILLIAM JOHNES, [(s. of Rev. Timothy,) with w. Charlotte ?]

    Harriet ; d. 3 Aug., 1813, aet. 10.

    Charlotte Catharine ; b. 8 Nov., 1809 ; B. 2 Mar. 1810. •

    Louisa Jane ; b. 22 April 1812 ; B. 3 July, 1812.

    Edward Rudolphus ; b. 16 Dec., 1813 ; B. 30 April, 1814.

    William ; d. 26 Dec., 1813, aet. 9 mos ?

Abigail Johnson ; m. 16 May, 1812, to Isaac Wychoff, both of Chatham.

Emma Johnson ; m. 3 Nov., 1811, to Silas Mills.

JAMES D. JOHNSON ; L. 29 Aug., 1814 ; dis. 14 Dec., 1824 ; Principal Morris Academy.

MAHLON JOHNSON, [of Hanover, & w. SARAH (BAKER.)]

    Thomas Vail ; b. 8 Oct., 1809 ; B, 25 Mar., 1810.

    Sarah ; b. 10 Mar., 1811 ; B. 14 April, 1811.

    Catharine Wheeler ; b. 5 July, 1812 ; B. 23 Aug., 1812.

    Mary ; b. 2 Aug., 1814 ; B. 30 Dec., 1814.

PETER A. JOHNSON, [(s. of Richard),with w. Elizabeth Mills.]

    John Mills, b. 14 June, 1810 ; B. 30 Aug., 1810 ; d. 28 Sept., 1811, aet. 1.

    Julia Ann ; d. 6 Jan., 1811, aet. 3.

SARAH CHETWOOD JOHNSON, [dg. of Major R. Stanbury, of Scotch Plains,] w. of SILAS [s.
    of Richard] ; B, & C. 4 July, 1813 ; d. 9 May, 1851, aet. 72.

    Sarah Louisa ; d. 2 Nov. 1809, aet. 1.

    Sarah Louisa ; b. 10 Oct., 1810 ; B. 27 Jan., 1811.

    Recompense Stanbury ; b. 19 Oct., 1813 ; B. 31 Dec., 1813 ; d. 18 Sept, 1814, aet. 10
        mos.

WILLIAM JOHNSON ; [s. of Thomas ?] C. 2 Nov., 1813.

Richard Kimble ; d. 21 Aug. 1813, aet. 81.

FREDERICK KING ; b. 11 Sept. 1792; L. 29 Aug., 1814 ; dis. 21 Nov. 1816, to N. Y. City
    returned with w. ABBEY LA RUE, fr. Millstone, June 1820; ordained Elder,
    1 Oct. 1826 ; dis. 29 Nov. 1828, to Rahway ; d. 13 Aug. 1874

CHARLOTTE KING, [dg. of ——Morrell], w. of Henry [s. Frederick & Mary (Ayers)] b. 19
    April, 1767 ; B. & C. 1 May 1813 ; d. 17 Mar. 1816, aet. 49.

    Sally Ann , b. 26 Feb., 1799; 1 May, 1813.

    Caroline Eliza ; b. 18 Mar., 1801 ; B. 1 May, 1813.

    Cornelia   b. 3 Sept., 1803 ; B.   "   "

    Wm. Lewis   b. 30 Jan., 1806 ; B.   "   "

    Hannah Morrell; b. 14 June, 1808; B.   "   "

Hannah Kirkland, w. of Joseph P.; d. 9 Jan., 1814, aet. 27.

Matilda Kitchell, w. of Ezekiel, d. 3 July, 1814, aet. 34.

Uzal Kitchell ; d. at South Hanover, 22 Jan., 1813, aet. 67.

Samuel Kirk, of Hanover ; m. 30 Mar., 1811, to Huldah Freeman, [dg. of. Sam'l ?]

ANNA LAMBERT, wid. [of Joshua, & dg. of ——Johnson ?] ; C. 4 Mar., 1814.

Samuel Lane, [of Hanover, with w. MARY (Decker)].

    Elizabeth Woodruff ; b. 8 Dec. 1810 ; B. 5 May, 1811.

    Samuel ; d. 10 May, 1810, aet. 2.

Wm. Lee, [what was his wife's name ?]

    John Lake ; D. 26 Jan., 1811 ; B. f. w. 14 April 1811.

    Henry ; d. 26 Oct., 1811, aet. 16.

    Edward Perrine ; b. 19 Jan., 1813 ; B. f. w. 13 June, 1813.

Abigail Leonard, w. of Samuel [& dg. of Joseph Pierson ?] ; d. 5 Jan., 1810, aet. 48.

Samuel Leonard, [Jr.] m. 24 Mar., 1811, to Sary Guerin, who d. 9 Jan., 1813, aet. 23.

ISAAC LEWIS ; d. 23 Feb., 1812, aet. 60.

JOSEPH LEWIS ; b. 23 Dec., 1748; d. 30 July 1814 ; ["my son-in-law," says Rev. Dr. Johnes.]

{ TIMOTHY JOHNES LEWIS, [s. of Joseph] ; d. 19 Jan., 1814, aet, 34.

  ABBEY L. PERRINE, [of Long Hill] ; L. 24 Oct. 1809, fr. Baskingridge ; dis. May 1816, to N. Y. City.

    Sophia Woodhull ; b. 12 Dec., 1809 ; B. 2 Mar., 1810 ; d. 13 Jan., 1814, aet. 4.

    Anne Maria ; b. 29 July, 1812 ; B. 30 Oct., 1812.

Abigail Lindsley, dg. of Ephraim & Martha [Goble] ; d. 8 Aug., 1814, aet. 13.

Ebenezer Lindsley ; [s. of Isaac ?] m. 26 Mar., 1812, to Phebe Byram, [dg. of Eliezer ?]

Elizabeth Lindsley, wid. of Elihu ; d. 23 April 1812, aet. 63.

Hannah Lindsley ; m. 20 Feb., 1814, to Samuel Beers, [s. of Joseph ?]

IRA LINDSLEY [s of Joseph & Mary ?], with w. Rachel [what was her maiden name ?]

    Henry Connet ; B. 2 July, 1814.

JANE LINDSLEY, [dg. of Benj'n & Sarah Lindsley ?] w. of Silas [s. of John ?] ; C. 29 Aug., 1814 ; dis. 8 June, 1841, to 2d Ch.

Mahlon Lindsley, [s. of David ?] m. 27 April, 1809, to EUNICE TOMKINS, who was dis. as widow. May, 1833, to New Vernon.

MATTHEW G. LINDSLEY, [s. of Joseph & Mary ?] m. 7 Feb., 1810, to Abigail Beers, [dg. of Joseph.]

    William Francis ; b. 17 April 1812 ; B. 31 May, 1812.

    Alfred Elmer ; b. 9 Jan., 1814 ; B. 10 July, 1814.

SARAH LINDSLEY, w. of Benj. ; b. 12 Aug., 1738 ; d. 16 Dec., 1811, aet. 74.

Stephen Lindsley, of Spring Valley ; [s. of John & Sarah (Rainer ?)] d. 21 Feb., 1813, aet. 49.

Lyon Loper ; d. 14 June, 1811 aet. 68.

Stepen Loper(?) ; m. 31 Mar., 1812, to Abigail Harris.

ELIZABETH LUDLOW, w. Jonas, d. 14 Jan., 1810, aet. 42. [what was her maiden name ? She is marked as a communicant in Bill of Mortality, but no " Elizabeth, w. of Jonas Ludlow" was received between 1793 and 1810. They probably married in 1793 or 1794 as oldest child, David W. was born 25 Dec., 1795.]

REBECCA LUM, [dg. of Abner Condit ?] w. of Rossiter ; C. 1 Jan., 1813 ; dis. to Euclid, O.

    Silas Condit ; b. 19 May 1808; B. f. w. 2 July, 1813.

    Mary Adaline ; b. 22 May, 1811 ; B. " "   "

SARAH Lum, [dg. of Matthew & Jemima ?] ; d. 10 July, 1809, aet. 64.

Sarah Luman [?] ; m. 30 Nov. 1813, to Silas Byram.

John McCord, [with w. MARY].

    John ; b. 11 Feb., 1811 ; B. 3 May, 1811.

    Elias ; b. May, 1813 ; B. 2 July 1813.

John McMurtry, m. 11 Jan., 1814, to Elizabeth Simpson, both of Baskingridge.

JACOB MANN ; C. 30 Oct., 1812 ; d. 17 Dec., 1843.
JERUSHA MILLER ; C. 27 April, 1812 ; dis. 13 Oct., 1860, to Succasunna ; d. 12 July, 1865,
aet. 88.
    Mary Louisa ; b. 18 Oct., 1803 ; B. 1 May, 1813.
    Sarah Maria ; b. 8 April, 1805 ; B.'" " "
Anna Marsh, [dg. of Aaron ?] ; m. 30 Sept., 1813, to Jonathan Cutler.
JAMES MARTIN ; B. & C. 6 Mar., 1814.
John Mattax ; d. 16 Mar., 1813, aet. 67.
SALLY MEEKER ; B. & C. 3 Sept. 1814.
    Daniel ; B. 18 Dec., 1814.   •

Dr. Gurdon J. Miller, m. 13 April 1810, to Henrietta Trezevant, formerly of Savannah.
HANNAH MILLER, [dg. of Samuel ?] ; B. & C. 3 Sept., 1814; m. Keen Prudden [s. of Isaac];
    dis. 11 Aug. 1819.
James Miller, d. 24 Feb., 1811, aet. 84.
Joanna Miller. wid. of Isaac [& dg. of Benj. Halsey] ; d. 31 Mar., 1811, aet. 60.
MARTHA MILLER, w. of Ichabod [s. of James ?]; L. 3 July, 1812, fr. Orange ; d. 9 April,
    1816, aet. 55.
SAMUEL MILLER, [with w. JANE.]
    Sally Wickham, adopted ; b. 23 Aug. 1801 ; B. 30 Jan., 1811.
Silas Miller, m. 22 Oct., 1810, to Mary Hopkins. [Silas M. was first undertaker in town to
    use a hearse ; previously coffins were carried in one horse wagon.]
Thomas Miller, d. 14 Oct., 1810, aet. 74.
Amy Miller, [dg. of Stephen Hedges,] w. of Nehemiah [s. of Timothy] ; d. 31 Mar. 1811,
    aet. 54.
CHLOE MILLS, [dg. of Isaiah Wines], w. of John [s. of Timothy] ; b. 13 Jan., 1748 ; d. 26
    Sept., 1813.
EDWARD MILLS ; C. 1 Jan., 1813 ; d. 13 Jan., 1827, aet. 78.
Elizabeth Mills [dg. of Timothy & Abigail ?] ; m. 1 Feb,. 1812, to Isaac Blackford.
Irene Mills [dg. of Moses & Irene Lindsley] w. of Silas [s of John & Cloe] ; d. 9 May
    1811, aet. 40.
JABEZ MILLS [(s. of Edward) with w. Hannah ?]
    Francis Augustus ; b. 27 Sept., 1810 ; B. 2 Dec. 1810.
    Charles Lewis ; b. 11 Aug. 1812 ; B. 30 Oct., 1812.
Jonas Mills [s. of John & Cloe] ; b. 13 Sept., 1781 ; d. 2 Nov., 1810, aet. 29.
Mary Mills ; m. 9 April, 1812, to David F. Cockran.
Nathan Mills ; m. 26 Oct., 1811, to Mary Pierson Arnold, [dg. of Robert & Mary].
Nehemiah Mills [s. of Timothy] ; d. 23 Mar., 1812, aet. 63.
Sally Mills [dg. of Sam'l and Phebe ?] ; m. 27 Feb., 1812, to Joseph Bedell.
Silas Mills ; [s. of John & Cloe ?] ; m. 3 Nov., 1811, to Emma Johnson.
William Mills ; m. 13 Oct., 1811, to Eliza Boyle, of Chatham ; d. 27 Dec,. 1813, aet. 29.
Elizabeth Minton, w. of Aaron ; d. 14 June, 1811, aet. 28.
Isaac Minton, m. 19 May, 1810, to Elizabeth Bowen.
HILAH MITCHELL ; B. & C. 3 July, 1814 ; dis. May, 1817.
LOAMMI MOORE [s. of David] with w. HULDAH BYRAM [dg. of Naptali].
    Henry [Southard] ; d. 31 Oct., 1809, aet. 1.
    Abby Elizabeth ; b. 29 April, 1810 ; B. 15 July, 1810.
    Amy Sophia ; b. 14 Aug., 1812 ; B. 20 Sept., 1812 ; d. 5 Oct. 1813.
    Henry Augustus ; B. 30 Dec., 1814 ; d. 1 No/., 1817.
    [Amy Sophia ; b. 14 Aug., 1814, d. 16 Nov. 1820].

THE RECORD.

FIRST PRESBYTERIAN CHURCH, MORRISTOWN, N. J.

"This Shall be Written for the Generation to Come."—Psalms 102 : 18.

| VOLUME IV. | JULY 1884. | NUMBER 19. |

[Printed with the Approval of the Session.]

THE RECORD

Will be published monthly at Morristown N. J. Terms $1.00 per annum, *in advance.*

Subscriptions may be made at the book-stores of Messrs. Runyon and Emmell, or to Messrs. James R. Voorhees and William D. Johnson, or by letter addressed to the

EDITOR OF THE RECORD,

Morristown, N. J.

Entered at the Post Office at Morristown, N. J., as second class matter.

————:0:————

(Continued.)

COMBINED REGISTERS, for Pastorate of the Rev. Samuel Fisher: July 1809, to Dec. 1814.

For meaning of abbreviations see second page of THE RECORD of April, 1884.

It will be esteemed a great favor if the readers of THE RECORD *will send* CORRECTIONS, *or additional* INFORMATION, *to* Lock Box 90, Morristown, N. J.

————:0:————

MARY MOORE, w. of Samuel [s. of Stephen, adopted by James Ford?]; C. 4 Mar., 1810; dis. 26 Jan., 1841, to 2d Ch.; d. 13 Mar., 1854, áet. 79.

    Stephen , b. 23 Aug., 1799 ; B. f. w. 29 June, 1810.

    Ira ; b. 12 May, 1801 ; B.   "   "   "   "   "

    Julia Ford ; b. 4 July, 1803 ; B.   "   "   "   "   "

    Mary Ann ; b. 5 Sept., 1805 ; B.   "   "   "   "   "

    Wm. Harrison ; b. 20 Dec., 1812 ; B. f. w. 24 May, 1813.

Zebulon Morris ; d. at New Gloster, 14 Jan., 1813, aet. 36.

ZIBA MUIR ; L. 1 Mar., 1813, fr. Rockaway ; d. 20 May, 1831, act. 66.

    Jesse ; B. 17 April, 1814.

Solomon Munson ; d. 20 May, 1812, aet. 27.

SILVA, free blackwoman ; B. & C. 1 May, 1814.

Abigail Nestor ; m. 20 April, 1811, to Freeman Sharp, both of Mendham.

John Nestor ; m. 9 Oct., 1813, to Phebe Hayt, wid.

John Nestor, Jr.; d. 28 Nov., 1814, aet. 25.

Samuel Nestor ; m. 4 Dec., 1813, to Polly Abers, wid.

CAROLINE Nichols, w. of Abimael ; C. 29 June, 1810; dis. 2 Nov. 1813, to Baskingridge.

    Caroline Mary Stites [Stiles ?] ; b. 9 June, 1813 ; B. f. w. 5 Nov. 1813.

James Nixon, m. 20 July, 1810, to Jemima Bowers, wid.

{ PETER NORRIS [s. of Peter & Mary (Mahurin)] ; L. 21 Feb., 1810 fr. Mendham ; d. 5 May, 1838, aet. 94.

{ PHEBE LUDLOW ; m. 1769 ; L. 21 Feb., 1810, fr. Mendham.

Rebecca Norris, w. of Stephen ; d. 30 May 1809, aet. 83.

Stephen Norris ; d. 25 Oct., 1811, act 86.

Thomas Norris, of Bottle Hill ; d. 19 April, 1812.

Henry Noyes, of N. Y. ; m. 25 June 1812, to Offa C. Pierson, of Chatham, [dg. of Benjamin, Jr ?]

Eliza Ogden, dg. of John. of Malapardis ; m. 7 Oct., 1809 to Wm. Canfield, of N. Y.

John Ogden, [s. of David & Ann] ; d. 7 Aug., 1810 aet. 70.

PHEBE OLIVER, dg. of John; C. 22 June, 1814; dis. 11 June, 1836, to New Vernon; d. 8 Sept., 1863, aet. 72.

SARAH [PRIMROSE?] OLIVER, dg. of John; C. 22 June, 1814; dis. as w. of Mahlon Bonsell, to New Vernon.

SAMUEL OLIVER, d. 16 Aug., 1811, aet. 79.

ELIPHALET OSBORN, L. 12 June, 1811, fr. Bloomfield; dis. 26 Jan., 1841, to 2d Ch.; d. 5 Oct., 1848, aet. 74.

MARY OSMUN ; L. 3 Jan., 1810 fr. Parsippany; d. Mar., 1820.

Ezra Owen; d. 83 April, 1812, aet. 39.

Huldah Parish, w. of Joel; d. 20 Nov., 1809, aet. 66.

Joel Parish ; d. 18 Sept., 1811, aet. 78.

Sarah Patterson; d. 1 May, 1811, aet. 90.

Sarah Patterson ; d. 2 May, 1812, aet. 89.

George Phillips, of Somerset; m. 2 Sept., 1809, to Hannah Boyd.

JONAS PHILLIPS; Elder; b. 12 Mar., 1735; d. 25 Dec., 1813, aet. 78. [Ordained 12 Sept., 1777, last met with Session, 26 Dec., 1810, present 81 times out of 99.]

MARY PHILLIPS ; dg. Jonas ; d. 2 July 1811, aet. 39.

ABIGAIL B. PIERSON [dg, of——Garthwaite, of Elizabethtown], w. of ALBERT OGDEN [s. of David, Jr. & Abigail]; C. 4 Mar., 1814; dis. 17 July, 1837, to 3d Ch., Newark.

Maria Smith ; b. 28 June, 1814; B. 3 Sept., 1814.

Benjamin Pierson, s. of Gabriel; d. 31 Oct., 1812, aet. 13.

CHARLOTTE PIERSON, w. of MATTHIAS [s. of Gabriel?]; L. 3 Jan., 1812, fr. South Hanover.

Julyet ; b. 26 Feb., 1812 ; B. 1 May, 1812.

Ambrose ; b. 12 Aug., 1813 ; B. 31 Dec., 1813.

DANIEL PIERSON [s. of Benj'n & Patience?] ; C. 3 July, 1812; dis. 22 Apr., 1814, to Ohio.

Eleazer Miller Pierson [s. of Isaac & Hannah?]; d. 6 Dec., 1814, aet. 29.

GABRIEL PIERSON ; d. 16 Sept., 1814, aet. 47.

Jacob Pierson [s. of Isaac & Hannah?] with w. [Jane Burnet.]

Rhoda ; b. 24 Sept., 1803 ; B. 2 July, 1812.

Sally ; b. 4 Sept., 1807 ; B. 2 July, 1812.

Jane , b. 6 Sept., 1810 ; B. 2 July, 1812.

Asa; b. 21 June, 1814: B. 3 Sept., 1814.

JULIANN PIERSON [dg. of Benj'n & Abigail?] ; C. 29 Aug., 1814 ; dis. May, 1834 [to Madison.]

MARY PIERSON w. of Isaac ; C. March, 1810 ; dis. 29 Mar., 1826, to 3d Ch., Newark.

George Seman : b. 11 May, 1797 ; B. f. w. 24 June, 1813.

Isaac Howell ; b. 16 June, 1800 ; B. " " " " "

Mary Pierson [dg. of——Howell], wid. of Aaron ; d. 13 May 1810, aet. 66.

MARY PIERSON [dg. of Joseph, Jr.? or Jacob & Jane?] ; C. 29 Aug., 1814 ; m. Amos Prudden ; dis. 1 June, 1836, to New Vernon; d. 22 Aug., 1873.

MEHETABLE PIERSON ; [dg. of Gabriel?] C. 22 June, 1814 ; dis. 26 Jan., 1841, to 2d Ch.

Offa C [aroline ?] Pierson, of Chatham [dg. of Benj'n, Jr.?] ; m. 25 June, 1812, to Henry Noyes, of N. Y.

PATIENCE PIERSON, wid. of Joseph ; d. 9 Dec., 1813, aet. 89.

PHEBE PIERSON [dg. of Elijah ?] ; C. 29 Aug., 1814 ; dis. 15 April, 1823, to Chatham.

Samuel Pierson [s. of Samuel & Rebecca (Garrigus)]; m. 11 Nov., 1809, to HANNAH HINDS, [who d. 25 July, 1825; he m. 7 Oct., 1826 PHEBE BABBITT, who d. 1862 ; he d. 3 May, 1853, aet. 68 ?]

Stephen Pierson, of Hanover, [s. of Samuel & Rebecca (Garrigus)], with w. [Phebe Beers, dg. of Joseph.]

Elizabeth Tuttle ; b. 8 Jan., 1811 ; B. 5 May, 1811 ; d. 21 April, 1812, aet. 1.

Edward ; b. 13 Mar., 1814 ; B. 1 May, 1813.

Charles ; b. 27 May, 1815 ; B. 31 Aug., 1815.

Joseph Post, with w. MARY.

William b. Aug., 1799 ; B. f. w. 2 Nov., 1809.

Margaret Cooper ; b. Nov., 1802 ; B. f. w. 2 Nov., 1809.

Mary Ann ; b. July, 1805 ; B. f. w. 2 Nov., 1809.

Sary Dickerson ; b. Nov., 1807 ; B. f. w. 2 Nov., 1809.

Phebe Vail ; b. 11 Oct. 1810 ; B. f. w. 9 June, 1811.

Esther Price. w. of Isaac, [s. of Philip ?] ; d. 10 July, 1811, aet. 69.

Daniel Prudden, [whose son ? & what his wife's name ?]

Harriet ; b. 23 July, 1811 ; B. 3 July, 1812.

John Prudden ; d. 4 Jan., 1813, aet. 36. [Son of whom ?]

JOSIAH PRUDDEN, [s. of Isaac & Sarah Keen] ; d. 4 Dec., 1809, aet 22.

Mihitabel Prudden, w. of Adoniram ; d. 3 Aug., 1811, aet. 63.

MOSES PRUDDEN [s. of Moses & Mary ?] [what was his wife's name ?)

Joanna ; b. 13 April, 1813 ; B. 2 July, 1813.

STEPHEN AYERS PRUDDEN, [s. of Deacon Joseph, Jr.] ; C. 3 Nov., 1814 ; Elder & Deacon, ord. 9 Sept., 1832, last met with session 1 April, 1865, present 25 times out of 267 ; d. 29 Dec., 1869, aet. 86.

NANCY PRUDDEN [dg. of ———Guerin] ; w. of Stephen A.; B. & C. 6 Nov., 1814 ; d. 17, Sept. 1830, aet. 45.

John Rodgers ; d. 18 Sept., 1811, aet. 79.

Robert Roff, Jr. [s. of Robert & Phebe (Cooper)] d. 7 Mar. 1813, aet. 27.

SALLY ROFF [dg. of Timothy & Abigail Mills], w. of Samuel [s. of Robert] ; L. 30 Oct., 1812, fr. Mendham ; d. 29 May, 1832,[or 1822 ?]

Phebe Cooper ; b. 12 Mar., 1812 ; B. f. w. 30 Aug., 1812.

Mary Rose ; m. 2 July 1809, to Ebenezer Strebbins.

SAMUEL ROSS [s. of Daniel ?] ; C. 3 Nov., 1809 ; dis. 19 April, 1810, to N. Y. State.

HENRY P[IERSON] RUSSELL, [s. of Caleb] ; C. 25 Dec., 1812, [dis. to N. Y. City ?]

SARAH P[EER, of Stratford,] C. 25 Dec., 1812 ; d. 14 Oct., 1816, aet. 37.

Lewis Henry ; b. 14 Dec., 1807 ; B. 5 Mar., 1813 ; [m. 1831, to Anna M. Benjamin, ot Strattord.]

LUCRETIA RUSSELL [dg. of ———Pierson ; b. 29 June, 1752 ; m. 10 Oct., 1771], wid. of Caleb; C. 26 Dec., 1810 ; dis. 28 July, 1828, to Laight st. Ch., N. Y.; d. 5 July 1837.

Sylvester D. Russell [s. of Caleb], with w. [ELIZABETH, dg. of Jon. Stiles.]

Mary Elizabeth ; b. 13 Sept., 1809 ; B. f. w. 5 Jan., 1810 ; [d. 1830.]

[Morgan Edwards] ; d. 28 Sept., 1812, aet. 1.

Amelia Smith ; b. 31 Aug., 1813 ; B. f. w. 5 Nov. 1813 ; [m. Wm. A. Tomlinson, of Mich.]

Eliza Pierson ; B. f. w. 31 Aug., 1815 ; [d. 1820.]

[Caroline Phoenix ; d. 1836.]

MOSES SAYRE, [what was his wife's name ?]

Margaret Elizabeth ; b. 12 Nov., 1810 ; B. 9 Jan., 1811.

William Sayre ; m. 13 Nov., 1811, to MARY CAMPFIELD, of Hanover, [dg. of John ?]

SETH CROWELL SCHENCK ; C. 2. Nov. 1813 ; dis. 18 April, 1815, to Georgia ; d. 3 July, 1863, aet. 70.

Samuel Scott, [what was his wife's name ?]

Harriet ; b. 14 Aug., 1808 ; B. 5 Jan., 1810.

PHEBE SCRIBNER, wid.; L. 27 Dec., 1809, fr. Cedar St. Ch. N. Y.; dis. 22 April 1814, to New Albany, Ind.

ANNA ; b. 16 Oct., 1785 ; C. 3. July 1812 ; d. 18 Jan., 1814.

ESTHER ; C. 3 July, 1812 ; dis. 22 April, 1814, to New Albany, Ind.

ELIZABETH ; C. 25 Dec., 1812 ; dis. 22 April, 1814, to New Albany, Ind.

TRYPHENA SECOR, w. of Joshua ; C. 25 Dec., 1812.

Sarah Ogden, wid. of Charles ; d. 3 April, 1810, aet. 32.

  Mary Ann Clarke ; b. 17 Nov , 1811 ; B. f. w. 27 Mar., 1814.

  Charles Raynor ; b. 12 Sept., 1813; B. " " " " "

Servants.

  CANDACE, serv. of Daniel Pierson ; B. & C. 30 Oct.. 1812 [or 1 May, 1813.]

  Charles Samuel, serv. of Phebe Scribner ; b. 10 June 1812 ; B. 18 Mar., 1813.

  FLORA, serv. James James ; B. & C. 1 Mar., 1812.

    Linda, dg. of Flora ; b. 4 Sept., 1810 ; B. 2 Aug., 1812.

  Lucy, serv. ch. of Clary Pierson ; b. 10 June, 1802 ; B. 12 Dec., 1809.

  MARIA, serv. of Gen. Doughty ; C. 30 Oct., 1812 ; dis. 8 June 1841, to 2d Ch.

  PHILLIS, serv. of James Wood , C. 1 May, 1812; dis. 28 Jan., 1828, to Brick Ch., N. Y.

    Lewis, s. of Phillis ; b. 12 Mar. 1809 ; B. 26 July, 1812.

  SUSAN, serv. of Andrew Ogden ; B. & C. 3 July, 1814.

    Hagar, dg. of Susan ; B. 3 Sept. 1814.

JESSE SEXTON ; C. 3 July, 1812 ; d. 2 Sept., 1813, aet. 55.

  Harriet Allen, adopted ; b. 11 Aug., 1807 ; B. f. w. 2 July; 1812.

Freeman Sharp ; m. 20 April, 1811, to Abigail Nestor, both of Mendham.

Elizabeth Simpson ; m. 20 April, 1814, to John McMurtry, both of Baskingridge.

Abraham Slaught, of Roxbury ; m. 21 Feb., 1811, to Jophener [or Tophenes ?] Dickerson.

ABIGAIL SMITH, m. 12 Feb., 1812, to Henry Beach, [s. of Asa ?] ; d. 19 July 1812, aet. 20 [or 25 ?]

AMELIA MARIAH SMITH ; C. 27 Aug., 1813 ; dis. June 1816.

JACOB SMITH, d. 1 May, 1811, aet. 43.

Mary Southard [dg. of Solomon] ; d. 3 Dec., 1811, aet. 40.

Mary Stagg, w. of Sam'l ; d. 15 July 1810, aet, 35.

SALLY STEVENS [dg. of——Tompkins?], w. of James, Jr.; B. & C. 6 Nov., 1814 ; dis. 8 June, 1841, to 2d Ch.: d. 1 May 1850, aet. 68.

ABIGAIL STILES [dg. of——Conger, & wid. of Simeon Goble] w. of Ebenezer ; d. 7 Dec., 1810, aet. 78.

EBENEZER STILES ; d. at Morris Plains, 22 Nov.; 1814, aet. 88.

Elizabeth Stiles, wid ; m. 14 Dec., 1810 ; to Rev. Wm. Woodbridge, of Greenwich, N. Y.

ELIZABETH STILL [2d ?] w of Joseph ; C. 22 June, 1814.

Rev. Richard S Storris [Storrs ?] of Mass ; m. 2 April, 1812, to Sally S Woodhull, of Long Island.

Ebenezer Strebbins, m. 2 July, 1809, to Mary Ross.

Phebe Sturges, w. of Nathanael ; d. 18 Dec., 1814.

REBECCA STURGES ; B & C. 3 July, 1814 ; m,——McIntyre ; dis. 26 Jan. 1841, to 2d Ch.

Walter Sturges [s. of Moses ?] : m. Dec., 1811, to Mary Cory [dg. of Simeon ?]

John Talmage [s. of Abraham ?] m. 8 Jan., 1814, to Rhoda Gardiner.

Mehitabel Talmage [dg. of Abraham] ; d 2 May, 1811, aet. 22.

Phebe Taylor ; m. 24 Aug., 1813, to——Hedden.

George Templeton, with w. SARAH [dg. of Matthias Ball].

  Useby Elvine : B. f. w. 3 Sept., 1814

Elizabeth Tharp ; m. 21 Oct , 1809, to Joshua Wilson.

Jonathan Thompson ; m. 30 Sept., 1813, to Harriet Byram, [dg. of Eliezer.]

Jacob Tingler, m. 11 Nov., 1809, to Ossy Gilman, wid.

Eunice Tomkins ; m. 27 April, 1809, to Mahlon Lindsley, [s. of David ?].

Squier Tomkins, m. 13 May, 1809, to Polly Clark.

Henrietta Trezevant, formerly of Savannah ; m. 13 April, 1810, to Dr. Gurdon Miller.

Shubal Trowbridge, m. 25 Nov., 1813, to HULDAH BEERS, [dg. of Joseph.]

Charles Tucker, d. 9 June, 1809, aet. 40.

George P. Tucker [s. of George & Anna (Arnold)] ; d. 22 Dec., 1811, aet. 23.

Henry Tunis, m. 4 April, 1812, to Ann Johnes.

Jane Tunis, of Hanover ; m 18 Sept., 1813, to Andrew White, of Monmouth Co.

THE RECORD.

FIRST PRESBYTERIAN CHURCH, MORRISTOWN, N. J

"This Shall be Written for the Generation to Come."—Psalms 102 : 18.

| VOLUME IV | AUGUST, 1884. | NUMBER 20 |

[Printed with the Approval of the Session.]

THE RECORD

It published monthly ; terms $1.00 a year, *in advance.*

It will probably be completed with Dec , 1885 : the Minutes being brought down to 1882, and the Registers to 1842.

Cash subscribers in advance for 1885 *will receive all issues* FREE *after Dec.* 1885, *if it should be necessary to continue the publication beyond that date in order to make it complete.*

Single numbers for any month, 10 cents each.

Subscriptions should be made to Mr, James R. Voorhees,

Matters pertaining to the publication should be addressed to the

EDITOR OF THE RECORD,

Entered at the Post Office at Morristown, N. J., as second class matter.

CORRECTIONS AND ADDITIONS.

Communications are earnestly solicited for this column. Address, Lock Box 90, Morristown, N. J.

Page 123 :

Stephen A. Prudden was present at 251 (not 25) meetings of the Session.

Page 122 :

Sarah P. Oliver was dis. as w. of Mahlon Bonnell, (not Bonsell).

Edward, s. of Stephen Pierson, was b. 1813 (not 1814.)

Page 120 :

Loammi Moore was s. of David Moore and Bathiah (Cutler, dg. Uriah) ; his w. Huldah Byram died at Easton. Pa., in 1860.

Henry Southard Moore, s. of Loammi, was b. 5 Sept. 1808.

Abby Elizabeth Moore, dg. of Loammi, married 18 May 1842, to Rev Andrew Young, of Mercersburgh, Pa.; he died 14 Feb. 1848 ; she was married in Mar., 1851, to James Henry Coffin, Prof. of Mathematics in La Fayette College, Easton, Pa.; he died Feb. 1873 ; she died 9 Dec., 1880, aet. 70.

DR. IRVING'S SERMON.

With the present number, THE RECORD begins the publication of a very valuable sermon by the Rev. David Irving D. D.; an historical sketch of the revivals in the First Church. It was written during a time unusually full of distractions and trying interruptions, and preached on the first Sabbath after the completion of the most extended and expensive renovation which the Church has ever received. This sermon has just now a special interest, owing to the fact that Dr. Irving is suffering from a painful accident, which he received while in attendance at the Presbyterian Council in Belfast. His friends will be glad to learn that the latest letters report him to be making good progress towards recovery.

—:O:—

REVIVALS IN THE CHURCH :

BY THE

REV. DAVID IRVING, D. D.

Preached on first Sabbath after the renovation of the Church, Sept. 18th, 1859.

Psalm 122, 5th part ; Anthem ; Psalm 132 2d Part.

But I will remember the years of the right hand of the Most High. I will remember the works of the Lord : surely I will remember thy wonders of old. I will meditate also of all thy work, and talk of thy doings.—*Psalm, lxxvii,* 10-12.

If it were good for the children of Israel to look back and remember all the way which the Lord their God led them ; if the Church in the text encouraged herself by the remembrance of former deliverances ; so does it become his covenant people now, at times, to talk of his wonders of old, and hover with the deepest gratitude over the years of the right hand of the Most High. Around these the fondest and the holiest memories of the few cluster; whilst the mass live rather in what they heard than in what they saw, able however to utter the language of the Church in the days of David, " we have heard with our ears, O God ; our fathers have told us what works thou didst in their days, in the time of old." And all of us in the survey can repeat the declaration and longing of Zion, "Lord, thou hast been favorable unto thy land; thou hast brought back the captivity of Jacob. Wilt thou not revive us again, that thy people may rejoice in thee ?" For such a survey of the Lord's work in the past will give us a fresh occasion to delight in our relation to God, and in the manifestation of his transforming and sanctifying power.

This disposition to look back to former times is instructive. Who of us does not cherish in thought our youthful deeds, and wonder—yea, oft linger—over the scenes of childhood. As a Nation we seek to perpetuate the story of our youth, and are aiming to hand down to coming ages, by commemorative signals, some of the prominent incidents and characters of the past. Shall we not, as a Congregation preserved and blessed of heaven, but for a holier purpose, endeavor to bring distant events near, when we meet for the first time in this renovated but dear old building, in which our fathers worshipped, since our present prosperity is so intimately and indissolubly connected with God's covenant dealings with those fathers ?

The expression "years of the right hand of the Most High" may have reference to times of special favor, in which he had wrought wonders for his people ; or, it may mean, as some interpret it, "the change of the right hand of the Most High," expressive of trouble, as the hand that had been displayed for them was now turned against them. With the latter interpretation, they are represented, in the midst of their present trials, as still clinging to God, and solacing themselves with the sweet recollections of his wonders of old. Whatever rendering is given, the conclusion is the same ; that God has oft appeared gloriously among his people, in deliverance and revival, the bare remembrance of which was enough to inspirit his Church when feeling the loss of his refreshing presence or groaning under afflictions.

Whatever was the nature and extent of the favors so munificently bestowed in the past, we find that they were regarded as proceeding wholly from the Most High. This truth underlies all gratitude, praise and love ; and on no other ground can the glory of the work be given to Him. God is a sovereign,—at liberty to act as he pleases and carry out unrestrained the purposes of his heart. He has, therefore, a right to accomplish those purposes in the way that shall seem best to him. He may come as the dew of Israel, silently and gently moving upon his Church ; or, he may come in Pentecostal showers, beautifying and enlarging the moral power of Zion. In both ways has he displayed his might in the earth,—as well as in hiding his face from those who forget his wonders,—teaching his people that He sits upon the throne, and giving the assurance that he will accomplish the transcendant issues promised in his word. In these majestic and compassionate movements of the Most High towards our race, he does not act capriciously but in harmony with his revealed will and the faithful improvement of the means of grace—the gifts of his wisdom and love ;—so that it may be laid down as a principle to govern us, that, according to the preparation of heart and the faithful employment of means, the Spirit is given. This is clearly revealed in the Scripture.

Now, coming under the influence of these truths, verified so oft in our history and experience as a Church, we can to-day sing of goodness and mercy,—we can meditate on his work and talk of his doings ;—for God, mighty to save, has oft appeared in the midst of us, filling this house with his glory, and more than once answering the cries of his awakened and longing people. And to some of God's wonders among us let me turn your thoughts.

Scarcely was this region of country surveyed before we find a Church organized. In 1718, three years after it became the legal property of the white man, and when there were but few farms cleared and few dwellings to be seen, a new Church was formed at Whippany, called at that time East Hanover; and a house of worship reared near,

(To be continued.)

(Continued from page 124.)

COMBINED REGISTERS, for Pastorate of the Rev. Samuel Fisher; July. 1809, to Dec. 1814

For meaning of abbreviations see second page of THE RECORD for April, 1884.

It will be esteemed a great favor if the readers of THE RECORD *will send* CORRECTIONS, *or additional* INFORMATION, *to* Lock Box 90, Morristown, N J.

————:0:————

Stephen Tunis, with w. [MEHITABLE BISHOP.]
 Eliza Ann ; b. 20 Sept., 1808 ; B 4 June, 1812.
Joseph Turner [s. of Stephen & Phebe (Peck)] ; d. 22 July, 1811, aet, 22.
Hannah Tuthill ; m. 12 April, 1810, to Johnson Conklin.
JANE (HANCOCK) TUTHILL, w. Theodorus, s. Dr. Sam'l ; d. 1 June, 1814, aet. 55.
Samuel Tuthill, M. D., d. 31 May, 1814, aet. 89.
SARAH TUTHILL ; [dg. of————Kinney], w. of Dr. Samu'l ; d 12 Nov , 1811, aet. 80
Barnabas Tuttle, d. 16 April, 1812, aet. 56.
Catharine Tuttle ; m, 11 May, 1814, to Joseph Youngs, both of Hanover.
Thomas Tuttle (once " Tuthill"); d. 8 March, 1810, aet 79.
BETHIAH (YOUNG) VAIL, w. Stephen ; C. 27 April, 1812 ; dis. 26 Jan., 1841, to 2d Ch.;
 d. 19 Sept. 1847, aet. 69.
 Harriet, b. 7 March, 1802 ; B. f. w. 3 July, 1812.
 Alfred Lewis, b. 25 Sept, 1807 ; B. f. w., 3 July, 1812.
 George, b. 21 July, 1809 ; B. " " " "
 Sarah Davis, b. 19 Feb,, 1811 ; B. " " " "
Eliza Vail ; m. 20 Jan,, 1812, to James C. Canfield [s. of Isaac ?] ; [dis. 1819, to Missouri
 Territory, as w. of Charles Tucker ?"
MARGARET [VAIL], serv. of Silas Johnson & w. of "black Jack Vail" ; B. & C. 1 May, 1814 ;
 dis. 1 Nov. 1827, to N. Y. City.
 Clarey; b. 12 Mar., 1806 ; B. f. w. 2 July, 1814.
 John ; b. 3 Aug., 1808 ; B. f. w. 2 July 1814.
 Harry ; b. 1 Dec., 1810 ; B. f. w. 2 July, 1814.
 Jane Frances ; b. 3 Dec., 1812 ; B. f. w. 2 July, 1814.
PHEBE VAIL, w. of Henry ; d. 28 Mar., 1814, aet. 56.
David Ward ; m. 18 Aug., 1811, to Phebe Ward, both of Bloomfield.
Phebe Ward ; m. 18 Aug., 1811, to David Ward, both of Bloomfield.
Thomas Watson ; d. 6 May, 1812, aet. 51.
Andrew White, of Monmouth Co.; m. 18 Sept., 1813, to Jane Tunis, of Hanover.
Abner Whitehead, with w. [ABIGAIL, dg, of Jabez Condit ?]
 "Child," d. 13 Feb., 1810, aet. 3.
 Isaac ; b. 16 Sept., 1809 ; B. f. w. 24 June, 1810.
 Lucinda ; b. 1 Jan., 1812 ; B. f. w. 14 June 1812.
 Asa Horace ; b. Dec., 1813 ; B. f. w. 30 June 1815.
Isaac Whitehead, of Chatham, [s. of Onesimus?] ; m. 1 Feb., 1812, to Esther Arnold.
Mahlon Whitehead, of Sussex ; m. 17 April, 1810, to Hannah Harporee.
ONESIMUS WHITEHEED, [s. of Isaac & Sarah ?] ; d. 4 July, 1814, aet. 72-10-21.
MATTHIAS WILLIAMS ; L. 30 Oct., 1812, fr. Orange ; m. Mary Armstrong, wid. [of
 Nath'l ?] ; d. 1832, aet. 79.
Sarah Williams, d. 1 May, 1810, aet. 48.
Joshua Wilson ; m. 21 Oct., 1809, to Elizabeth Tharp.
Sarah Wilson, w. of Joshua ; d. 12 July, 1809, aet. 56.
Joshua Wiltz, of N. Y.; m. 8 Sept., 1813, to Catharine Ford, of Hanover, [dg. of Jon ?]
MEHITABLE WOOD [dg. of————Fairchild], w. of David ; B. & C. 3 July, 1814.
Rev. Wm. Woodbridge, of Greenwich, N. Y.; m. 14 Dec., 1810, to Elizabeth Stiles, wid.
Sally S. Woodhull, of Long Island ; m. 2 April, 1812, to Rev. Richard S. Storris [Storrs ?]
 of Mass.

Elizabeth Hatfield Woodruff, [2d] m. 13 May, 1811, to Jacob Beers, [s. of Nath'l]

Isaac Wort, Pompton, Burgen Co.; m. 23 Jan., 1811, to Eleanor Cohill,

Isaac Wychoff; m. 16 May, 1812, to Abigail Johnson; both of Chatham.

DINAH YOUNG, wid.; C. 3 Nov., 1814; dis. Nov., 1821; m. to Ephraim Cutler; d. 1 Feb., 1839, aet. 84.

Isabella Young, [dg. of——Berry], wid. of Joseph; d. 27 July, 1814, "advanced."

Joseph Youngs; m. 11 May, 1814, to Catharine Tuttle, both of Hanover.

STEPHEN YOUNGS [s. of Ephraim ?], with w. [Abigail ?]

> Harriet Cook, b. 21 Feb., 1810; B. 6 May, 1810, [d. 6 Mar. 1812 ?]
>
> Stephen } b. 2 Jan., 1813, ; B. 4 July, 1813.
> James
>
> Irene ; b. 6 Mar., 1015; B. 30 June 1815.

COMBINED REGISTERS, from Jan. 1815 to Dec. 1840, through the Pastorates of Wm. A. McDowell, Albert Barnes, Charles Hoover, and Orlando L. Kirtland.

Adams, William ; d. 6 May, 1826, aet. 47.

Adamson, William, of Camden, So. Carolina ; m. 22 May, 1827, to Frances A. Carmichae

ADAMSON,——w. of William ; L. 28 Dec., 1815, fr. Hanover; d. 20 Feb., 1836, aet. 75.

{ ALLEN, GILBERT ; [elected elder and deacon, 31 July, 1777, last met with Session, 23 Feb., 1815, present 120 times out of 158] ; d. 6 Jan., 1816, aet, 80.

{ ELIZABETH,—— ; d. 10 Jan., 1816, aet. 79.

Allen, Harriet, [adopted dg. of Jesse Sexton] ; m. 20 Aug., 1825, to Timothy H. Prudden.

{ ALLEN, JABEZ [LINDSLEY], [adopted s. of deacon Allen] ; C. 22 Nov. 1827 ; dis. 8 Dec., 1828, to 1st. Ch., Newark ; returned fr. same 17 May, 1832 ; dis. again.

{ CAROLINE CONKLING MILLS, [dg. Jabez & Hannah (Coe)] ; m. 21 Mar., 1827 ; dis., returned & dis. again with her husband.

> Hannah Caroline, b. 23 July, 1828; B. 5 Sept., 1828 ; d. 29 Nov. 1831, aet. 3.
>
> Charles Mills, b. 11 June, 1833; B. 1 Sept. 1833.

Allen, Moses, deacon ; d. near Green Village, 9 Nov. 1823, aet. 70,

{ ALLEN, RODERICK ; B. & C. 7 Dec., 1834; dis.

{ SOPHRONIA, P.——, C. 18 Feb. 1836 ; dis.

Allen, Sally ; w. Moses, Jr.: d. at Green Village, 25 Nov. 1815, aet. 23.

ALLISON, MARIAN ; L. 20 Feb., 1834, fr. 1st. Ch., Southwark, Philadelphia.; gone.

ALWOOD, Elizabeth ; w. Samuel ; d. 25. Oct. 1820, aet. 81.

{ ALWOOD, JOHN.

{ PHEBE [ALWOOD.]

> Susan, [b. 1807 ; B. 1813] ; d. 24 Dec. 1824, aet. 17.
>
> John Henry, b. 3 Sept. 1820 ; B. 5 Sept. 1828,
>
> Emeline Parson, b. 10 Jan. 1823 ; B. 5 June 1829.
>
> ELIZABETH, dg. wid. Phebe ; [b. 13 Feb., 1813 ; B. f. w. 2 July, 1813] ; C. 26 Feb. 1830 ; d. 24 Jan., 1847, aet. 33.

{ ALWOOD, JONAS, [s. Samuel.]

{ NANCY,——[2d. w. ?]; C. 24 Aug., 1820 ; dis. 8 June, 1841, to 2d Ch. ; d. 11 Jan., 1862, aet. 73.

> MARY ANN, [b. 1809 ; B. 1813] ; C. 23 Feb. 1827.
>
> [Martha Whitehead ; B. 5 Dec., 1823] ; dg. d. 27 Jan., 1833, aet. 11.
>
> Helen Maria, b. 9 Nov., 1828 ; B. 27 Feb. 1829.
>
> ELIZABETH R., [b. 1800 ; B. 1803] ; C. 28 May, 1829 ; dis. 8 June 1841, to 2d Ch.; d. 5 Nov., 1861, aet. 61.

Allwood, Mary Ann; d. 30 Jan., 1835, aet. 35. [dg. Jonas and Nancy ?]

Alwood, Ruth ; w. Samuel [R ?] ; d. 1 June 1818, aet. 79.

Alwood, Samuel R. ; d. 24 June, 1818, aet. 86.

ALWOOD, SUSANNA ; w. Henry [s. Samuel & Elizabeth ?] ; L. 22 May 1817, fr. Rockaway.

Ames, Levi ; m. 19 Sept, 1833, to Ruth Goble.

THE RECORD.

FIRST PRESBYTERIAN CHURCH, MORRISTOWN, N J

"This shall be written for the Generation to Come."—Psalms 102 : 18.

VOLUME IV　　　　　SEPTEMBER, 1884.　　　　　NUMBER 21

[Printed with the Approval of the Session.]

THE RECORD

Is published monthly ; terms $1.00 a year, *in advance.*

It will probably be completed with Dec. 1885 ; the Minutes being brought down to 1882, and the Registers to 1842.

Cash subscribers in advance for 1885 will receive all issues FREE *after Dec. 1885, if it should be necessary to continue the publication beyond that date in order to make it complete.*

Single numbers for any month, 10 cents each.

Subscriptions should be made to Mr. James R. Voorhees.

Matters pertaining to the publication should be addressed to the

EDITOR OF THE RECORD.

Entered at the Post Office at Morristown, N. J., as second class matter.

CORRECTIONS AND ADDITIONS.

Communications are earnestly solicited for this column.　*Address,* Lock Box 90, Morristown, N. J.

Page 120.

Silas Mills was s. of John and Cleo(Wines,) not Cloe ; he was married to Eunice (not Emma) Johnson, a dg. of Richard. This correction and addition should also be made on page 118, opposite " Emma Johnson."

Page 118.

James D. Johnson was a s. of Richard.

Page 115.

Huldah Freeman was married to Samuel Kirk (not Kork.)

George W. Dixon (not George Dixon) was b. 2 June, 1784.

Page 114 :

Jane DeCamp, w. of Timothy, was a Humes (not Hughes.)

Supplement, page 65, Trustees and Parish, 2d column, 9th line from bottom ; read " meekness" (not " weekness.")

Page 211 of Sup., May, 1883 :

June 20, 1807 ; Aaron Boylan was married to Phebe Breese (not Breeze.)

(*Continued from page* 126.)

REVIVALS IN THE CHURCH :

BY THE

REV. DAVID IRVING, D. D.,

or on, the spot of land now occupied by the graveyard. This Church was attended by the scattered settlers of the township of Whippany, embracing the territory now included in the townships of Morris, Chatham and Hanover, until the year 1733, when the people of West Hanover formed a separate congregation, though not organized into a Church till 1738 or 9 on account of strenuous opposition on the part of the eastern portion of the congregation.

Religion, during this period, was at a low ebb throughout the whole country. In New England, one of the Mathers writes, "The glorious and precious religion of our heavenly Christ generally appears with quite another face, in the lives of Christians of this day, than what it had in the lives of the saints, into whose hands it was first delivered. The modern Christian is but too generally a very shadow of the ancient." Said one of our own ministers, of the state of things in Pennsylvania in 1734 : " True religion lay as it were a dying and ready to expire its last breath of life. The common notion seemed to be that if people were aiming to be in the way of duty as well as they could, they imagined there was no reason to be much afraid." In our own state we have this mournful picture : "The love of many had waxen cold. The savor of religion was lost ; family prayer was scarcely known ; ignorance of divine truth overshadowed their minds, while the practices of many were loose and profane." In view of such declension, the Synod of Philadelphia, which then comprised the whole of our Church, found it necessary to issue a series of most solemn admonitions to the Presbyteries.

But soon after the organization of this Church better days dawned upon Zion. The great awakening, as it has been styled, commenced. The earliest manifestation of this extraordinary presence of the divine Spirit in this country was in our own state, under the preaching of the Tennents, soon followed by that of Whitefield who traversed our land with a heart glowing with seraphic fire for the salvation of the perishing. Whether our Church, then in its infancy, received any of the great tidal flow of special spiritual influences that were permeating so many places, we have no means of knowing, though we find Whitefield and others preaching all around us. Still I can find no trace that he ever preached in this Church.

In 1742 Timothy Johnes visited the place, preached several Sabbaths, was invited to the pastorate, and a few months afterwards was ordained by New York Presbytery and duly installed over this people, among whom he died after a long settlement of nearly fifty-two years. His ministry was a happy one, and was abundantly blessed to many souls. Entering upon his charge in a reviving time, he ever took the deepest interest in the prosperity of Zion, and was often accustomed to rehearse to his people what was occuring in other portions of the Church. Still no instance of more than ordinary success is recorded of the first twenty years of his labors. After this his longings were met, and his heart gladdened, by an unusual turning of his people to divine realities. For more than a year there had been no additions to the Church. This filled his soul with sadness; and, as he dwelt upon the unmistakable evidences of declension and the necessity of a closer walk with God, as he administered the elements at the sacramental feast, tears began to flow over many a cheek, and prayers to arise for an outpouring of the Spirit. This was graciously answered, and at the next communion forty-four were added to the membership on profession of their faith ; and, during the year, ninety-four in all. Opposite to their names in the Session book I find the following entry: "These the sweet fruits of the wonderful effusion of God's adorable grace, began on our sacrament day, July 1, 1764." And in a letter afterwards published he says : "The Lord

Jehovah has rent the heavens and come down and the mountains are fleeing at his presence. There is something of this blessed work all around me." Again, in 1774, we find the Church enjoying a special manifestation of divine favor, and another record : "These are the ingathering of the divine harvest ; sweet drops of the morning dew ;" and, as the result of this awakening, fifty united themselves with the people of God.

Influences were at this time working which, in their developments, were unfavorable to the progress of true piety. Instead of rejoicing over the spoils of spiritual conquests, nothing was heard but the confused noise of battle. The struggle of the colonies for independence, and the formation of the general government, occupied the thoughts and efforts of the masses ; and as a consequence Zion languished. Then followed the French revolution, preceded and accompanied by much that was demoralizing and atheistic, and whose influence was greatly felt throughout this country.

But soon rays of light penetrated the deepening gloom ; here and there a Church arose from the dust and put on her beautiful garments. Among these was our own, which in 1790 enjoyed a fresh and cheering baptism of the Spirit, bringing into her fold some forty members. This was the last refreshing period that the aged pastor was permitted to see. Whilst Europe was being deluged with blood, whilst Christendom was rejoicing in the uprising of a missionary spirit and in its manifested power among the heathen, and whilst the first signs of a moral change appeared, that afterwards swept from a large portion of the Church its laxity of doctrine and discipline, the spirit of the devoted pastor took its flight, leaving behind him, for that day, a strong Church which was destined under his successors to experience fuller displays of the riches of sovereign and saving grace.

During the closing years of his life, the congregation had become so large and the old Church so crowded, that a new building was deemed expedient and necessary ; and, as the result of much prayer, deliberation and effort, the present structure in which we now worship was reared, which, says one, "for strength, solidity and sym-

(To be continued.)

(Continued from page 128.)

COMBINED REGISTERS, from Jan. 1815 to Dec. 1840, through the Pastorates of Wm. A. McDowell, Albert Barnes, Charles Hoover, and Orlando L. Kirtland.

For meaning of abbreviations see second page of THE RECORD for April, 1884.

It will be esteemed a great favor if the readers of THE RECORD *will send* CORRECTIONS, *or additional* INFORMATION, *to* Lock Box 90, Morristown, N. J.

———:0:———

Anderson, Eliakim ; m. 26 April, 1838, to Effy Dickerson, wid.

Anderson, William ; m. 24 July, 1828, to Sarah B. Douglas, eldest dg. James K., both of Camden, So. Carolina.

ANDRESS, JAMES ; m. 23 Sept. 1819, to Jane Bonnell, dg. Luther, of Springfield ; L. 2 ; May, 1821, fr. Springfield ; susp. 1 Jan. 1830.

ARMSTRONG, ANN ELIZA, [dg. Rhoda (Norris ?)] ; step-dg. Tim. Pierson ; C. 22 Aug. 1833 ; dis. 26 Jan., 1841, to 2d. Ch.

ARMSTRONG, HARRIET, [dg. Rhoda (Norris ?)] ; step-dg. Tim. Pierson ; C. 22 Aug., 1833, dis. 26 Jan, 1841, to 2d Ch.; mar. 1 May, 1853, to Wm. S. Townley.

{ Armstrong, Lewis [s. wid. Mary, who m. Matthias Williams ?]
{ JULIA BEADLE, [dg. William.]

　　Hariet Mills, b. 10 Jan. 1827 ; B. 14 July, 1829.

{ Armstrong, Nathaniel ; d. 23 Oct., 1822, aet. 80.
{ RACHEL LYON [dg. Samuel] ; d. 14 Jan., 1817, aet. 73.

ARMSTRONG, POLLY, wid. [of William ?] ; m. 19 Dec., 1827, to David Lindsley.

Armstrong,———Mr.; [Samuel, s. Nath'l ; b. Aug. 1779?] ; d. 17 Sept. 1832, aet. 52.

Arnold, Abraham ; m. 7 Nov., 1832, to Louise Goble.

Arnold, Betsey ; [dg. Robert & Mary (Pierson), b. May, 1782?] ; d. 23 Sept., 1834, aet. 52.

Arnold, Deborah M. ; m. 17 Sept., 1834, to John S. Johnson.

Arnold, Col. Jacob ; b. 14 Dec., 1749 ; d. 1 Mar., 1827.

ARNOLD, JOHN ; d. 14 Dec., 1830, aet. 87.

Arnold. Mary Ann ; m. 13 Nov., 1833, to Samuel A. Loree.

ARNOLD, [MARY (PIERSON)], wid. Robert ; d. 16 Mar., 1823, aet. 75.

ARNOLD, PHEBE PHILIPS, dg. wid. Sarah ; B. & C. 7 June 1829 ; m. 24 Feb., 1830, to Barnabas B. Thompson ; dis. "probably."

Arnold, Samuel ; d. ("lately," 13 Feb.,) 1817.

ARNOLD, SAMUEL, [s. John] ; d. 18 Jan., 1832, aet. 50.

ARNOLD, SARAH ; L. 28 April, 1815, fr. Newark ; dis. 26 Jan., 1841, to 2d. Ch.

Arnold Sarah, [2d w. &] wid. John ; d. 1 Sept., 1838, aet. 90.

ARNOLD, SILAS HOWELL ; s. Sarah ; B. & C. 7 June, 1829 ; m. 9 Oct., 1837, to Martha L. Pierson.

Ashback, George ; m. 22 Mar., 1832, to Susan Gillem.

Axtell, Amzi ; m. 3 April, 1830, to Mary Nixon.

{ AXTELL, HENRY ; L. 9 Nov., 1836 fr. Mendham ; dis. 26 Jan., 1841, to 2d Ch.
{ ABIGAIL———; L. "　"　"　"　"　dis. "　"　"　"　"　"

　　ELIZABETH L.; C. 24 Nov., 1836 ; dis. 26 Jan., 1841, to 2d Ch.

　　PHEBE ANN C.; C. 27 Feb., 1837 ; m. 16 Oct., 1839, to Ziba S. Smith ; dis. 8 June, 1841, to 2d Ch.

{ Axtell, Henry, "Major;" d. 6 April, 1818, aet. 80.
{ Axtell, Phebe ; d. July, 1829, aet. 89.

{ Axtell, Jacob T. [s. of Henry & Abigail ? or s. of Timothy ?]
{ RACHEL ENSLEE ; m. 22 Dec.; 1827 ; C. 5 Feb., 1829 ; dis. 8 June 1841 to 2d Ch.

　　Phebe Elizabeth ; B. 4 Sept., 1829,

　　Alfred Reeves, b. 10 April, 1830 ; B. 4 Aug. 1830 ?

　　Mary Louisa ; B. 1 June, 1832.

　　Caroline Louisa ; b. 16 Dec., 1833 ; B. 30 May, 1834.

Joanna Gardner ; B. 3 Dec., 1837.

William Enslee ; B. 29 Nov., 1839.

Axtell, Joanna, w. Jacob ; 18 Oct., 1826, aet. 18.

AXTELL, JONATHAN R.; C. 21 May, 1829 ; dis. 29 Sept. 1831, to Mendham.

Axtell, Melinda ; m. 18 Oct., 1817, to Ellis C. Morris, late of Morristown.

Axtell, Phebe ; m. 18 Oct., 1817, to Charles Roff.

AXTELL, RACHEL ; w. Timothy ; L. 26 Aug., 1830, fr. Orchard st. R. D. Ch., N. Y.

Axtell, Sarah Ann R.; m. 8 June, 1839, to James Henry Snook.

Axtell, Col. Silas, ; b. 5 April, 1769 ; d. 29 Sept., 1823, at Zanesville O., & buried there ;
    headstone here.

Ayres, John ; d. at Baskingridge, 4 Sept., 1815.

Ayres, Abigail, w. John ; dg. Ebenezer Coe ; d. at Flanders, 27 Dec., 1827, aet. 44.

Ayres, John
{ HULDAH AVERS, [dg. Silas & Mary (Byram) ?] ; C. 22 May, 1823 ; m. 26 Feb., 1829 ; dis.
    8 June, 1830.

AYRES, NANCY, dg. Samuel ; B. & C. 6 Sept., 1829 ; m. Oliver Hadden ; dis.

{ AYRES, SILAS ; d. 29 Dec., 1826, aet. 77.
{ MARY BYRAM ; d. 30 Oct., 1819, aet. 64.

Ayres, Tillah P.; m. 29 Nov., 1826, to Sidney D. Pierson.

Ayres, William, of Brooklyn ; m. 15 Feb., 1827, to Phebe Bedell.

BABBITT, ELKANAH ; d. Aug., 1822, (1821 ?)

BABBITT, PHEBE ; L. 23 Nov., 1820, fr. Mendham ; m. 7 Oct., 1826, to Samuel Pierson ; d.
    1862.

Babcock, John ; m. 8 Mar., 1821, to Eliza Humes, both of Solitude.

Badgeley, Catherine M.; m. 16 June 1830, to Cephas Holloway.

Badgeley, Elizah D.; m. 28 Sept. 1840, to John Ransley.

BADGELEY, FANNY, w. Timothy ; C. 7 April, 1823 ; dis. 8 June, 1841, to 2d. Ch.

Badgeley, Sally Ann, dg. Timothy ; d. 28 Aug., 1839, aet. 31.

BAIRD, ELISHA ; m. 10 Oct., 1827, to Eliza A. Shelley, dg. William ; B. & C., 6 Sept., 1829.

Bard [Baird ?], Elizabeth M.; m. 20 Feb. 1826, to Eli Carter, of New York.

Baker, Charles, lately of N. Y.; m. 9 Oct., 1819, to Elizabeth Casterline.

BAKER, CLARISSA, w. Albert A.; B. & C. 7 June, 1829 ; dis. 21 Nov., 1836, to Orange or
    Newark.

BAKER CLARISSA ; B. & C. 7 Sept., 1828 ; dis. 21 Nov., 1836.

Baker, Capt. David ; d. Mar. 1833, aet. 83.

Baker, Esther ; d. at Littleton, 24 May, 1828, aet. 67.

BAKER, SARAH, dg. Jonathan ; C. 8 Aug., 1822 ; m. 14 Jan. 1828, to Alfred Johnson.

Baker, Wickliffe G.; m. 1 Nov., 1826, to Louisa Smith.

BALL, MAGARET ; L. 27 Aug. 1828, fr. Indianapolis, Ind. : dis. 10 Dec. 1830.

BALL, MARY, wid. Jacob ; d. 14 May, 1833, aet. 81.

BALLARD, ELIZA, w.——— ; B. & C. 3 June, 1827 ; dis.

Bangheart, Eliza ; m. 15 Sept. 1822, to Edward C. May.

Banker, Christopher ; d. 10 Feb. 1817, aet. 45.

BARNES, ABBY ANN, w. Rev. Albert ; L. 17 Feb. 1825, fr. Fairfield, N. Y.; dis. 21 July,
    1831, to 1st. Ch., Philadelphia.

    Albert Henry, b. 11 Feb. 1826 ; B. 7 May, 1826.

    James Nathan, b. 1 Sept. 1827 ; B. 29 Feb. 1828.

    Charlotte Woodruff, b. 11 June, 1829 ; B. 2 Aug. 1829.

Barton, Hannah Mariah, w. Rev. Wm. H., & dg. Rev. Aaron Condict, of Hanover ; d. 20
    Jan., 1827, aet. about 27.

BASTEDO, MARY JANE, w.———L. 1 Sept., 1839, fr. Rockaway ; dis. 27 May, 1841.

BATES, MARY, wid. John ; b, 6 Feb. 1771 ; C. 8 Aug., 1822 ; d. 14 Jan. 1823.

THE RECORD.

FIRST PRESBYTERIAN CHURCH, MORRISTOWN, N. J.

"This shall be Written for the Generation to Come."—Psalms 102; 18.

| VOLUME IV. | OCTOBER, 1884. | NUMBER 22. |

[Printed with the Approval of the Session.]

THE RECORD

Is published monthly ; terms $1.00 a year, *in advance.*

It will probably be completed with Dec. 1885 : the Minutes being brought down to 1882, and the Registers to 1884.

Cash subscribers in advance for 1885 will receive all issues **free** *after Dec. 1885, if it should be necessary to continue the publication beyond that date in order to make it complete.*

Single numbers for any month, 10 cents each.

Subscriptions should be made to Mr. James R. Voorhees.

Matters pertaining to the publication should be addressed to the

EDITOR OF THE RECORD.

Entered at the Post Office at Morristown, N. J., as second class matter.

COMBINED REGISTERS ; 1742 to 1884.

We begin this month the publication of the complete alphabetical list from all the Church Registers. It covers a period of 142 years, from 1742 to 1884, and exhibits all the facts of record in connection with each name, except as provided below. The correction of errors is earnestly solicited. All requests from those who prefer that the dates of their birth, baptism, &c., should not be published will be welcomed and complied with. Address Lock Box 90, Morristown, N. J.

CORRECTONS AND ADDITIONS.

Communications are earnestly solicited for this column. Address, Lock Box 90, Morristown, N. J.

Sept. 11, 1806 ; Joseph Byly may possibly be Ryly, the writing is indistinct.

Page 210 of Sup. for May, 1883:

June 14, 1806 : Stephen Prudden should be Stephen A. Prudden.

Jan. 17, 1806 ; David Mann may possibly be Munn, the writing is indistinct.

Page 209 of Sup. for May 1883:

Sept. 5, 1804 ; Robert McCleanen should be Robert McClennen.

(*Continued from page* 130.)

REVIVALS IN THE CHURCH :

BY THE

REV. DAVID IRVING, D. D.,

metry of proportion was not excelled by any wooden building of that day in New Jersey." Ere its completion, and without being permitted to preach in it, the good old man was gathered to his fathers, after having been privileged to receive into communion with the Church 424 persons, baptize 2,827, and marry 948 couples.

The first sermon ever preached in this Church was by Mr. Richards, the successor of Dr. Johnes, on the last Sabbath* of Nov., 1795, and in the following years his arduous labors were crowned with a rich and lasting blessing. This came unexpectedly. In his account of it he says : "None of the Churchmembers, that ever I could learn, were specially stirred up to desire or expect it. Even those who, from their exemplary character, might have been expected to be waiting for the consolation of Israel, were manifestly unprepared for this sovereign act of divine mercy. But, prepared or unprepared, the windows of heaven were opened, and the spiritual rain descended; and one hundred souls were hopefully brought into the kingdom, as the fruit and effect of this refreshing."

In 1803, in two of the neighborhoods belonging to the congregation, there was more than the usual interest in the truths of religion, and which served to draw forth the prayers and exertions of the Church. Still conversions were limited almost wholly to these two localities, but during the year the Church was increased by some

* The Parish minutes of 18 Feb., 1796, say that worship began in the new building on the 26th Nov., 1795. In that year the 26th of Nov. fell on Thursday, so that if the note is correct the first service was probably the weekly lecture.—[Editor.]

forty members. From the narrative of the General Assembly, which referred to our Church along with some others, we learn that most interesting revivals had been enjoyed in very many portions of the Church. Through a great part of the South and West, North and North-west, the Spirit of God was remarkably poured out, and the whole Church greatly enlarged and encouraged.

Again did the Most High come down as rain upon the mown grass; again did the skies pour down righteousness, thereby communicating more life to the Church, and a capacity to the world to receive that life. The first indications of God's special power were seen in Newark, in connection with the sacrament of the Lord's Supper, which had been preceded by a day of fasting and prayer. "The work," says Dr. Griffin, "exceeds all that I have every seen, in point of power and stillness and numbers; between two and three hundred converts." In describing the revived state of the Church in Newark, Judge Boudinot says, in a letter to a friend, "It has extended to Elizabeth-town, Rahway, Springfield, North and South Hanover, Caldwell and Bloomfield. Yesterday I was informed that the same blessed work had begun in Morristown, where about fifty are under conviction." Of this movement Dr. Richards says, "It is deep and effective. To my latest breath I shall remember how some of the dear people of God appeared to feel and agonize in their supplications before the Lord, when imploring his gracious presence in the midst of us. Between seventy and eighty were added to the Church in that and the subsequent year, who dated their conversion from this interesting period." The Synod thus alludes to this gracious outpouring: "The revivals of religion have been most remarkable within the bounds of the Presbytery of New York. There the kingdom of Satan appears to have been greatly shaken; combinations against religion have been destroyed; prayer-meetings on the Sabbath, and religious societies on other days, have been established in many places and well attended. Many persons grossly immoral in their conduct, and some distinguished for their zeal in promoting deistical principles, have been ar-

rested by the influences of the Spirit, and hopefully converted. During the year past, within the bounds of the Presbytery, more than 1,100 have been added to the communion of the Church; the greater portion of whom are young persons."

Whilst thus alluding to these distinctive years of the right hand of the Most High, in which the stream of divine influences communicated greater fertilizing power to the moral waste, through which it ran, I wish in no way to overlook the gentle flowing of the water of life, that noiselessly imparted increased activities to the Church, that slaked the thirst of some wearied spirit, or removed here and there the feverish desire of the sin-burdened soul. In both ways has God wrought wonders in Zion; in each is his creative agency felt, and in each has he acted like himself. Scarcely a year passed by without souls being renovated and transformed by his sovereign love and power; and on several communions, besides the notable cases referred to, there were large and important accessions to the Church, revealing to us God's watchful care and loving remembrance of the vine under whose branches we have been privileged to sit, and thereby laying us under the deepest obligations to do everything for it that will increase its efficiency, beauty, growth and power. Oft did our fathers sing, "The Lord hath done great things for us, whereof we are glad;" oft did they say of this sanctuary, "Peace be within thy walls and prosperity within thy palaces. Because of the house of the Lord our God we will seek thy good."

This Church had by such means grown in strength and moral power, so that we hear the successor of Dr. Richards saying, "I have, indeed, a weighty charge; nearly as large as that of any two ministers within the bounds of the county." It then covered a region occupied by 520 families, and now supplied by eight evangelical Churches. Dr. Fisher, the third pastor, was installed in 1809, and during the first year of his ministry more than twenty persons were admitted to Church privileges. In 1813 forty were received, and about forty the succeeding year; the membership of the Church being at this time 360.

Soon after this Dr. Wm. A. McDowell en-

(To be continued.)

COMBINED REGISTERS ; 1742 to 1884.

It will be esteemed a great favor if the readers of THE RECORD *will send* CORRECTIONS, *or additional* INFORMATION, *to* Lock Box 90, Morristown, N. J.

————:o:————

[The significance of the abbreviations used is as follows :

aet.—aged.	L.—received by letter.
b.—born.	m.—married.
B.—baptized.	M. 1742.—Communicant at settlement of Dr. Johnes.
B. f. h.—Baptized on husband's account.	ord.—ordained
B. f. w.— ". " .wife's "	q. v.—Consult under last name.
C.—became Communicant.	R. C.—Renewed Covenant,
Ch.—Church.	R. L.—Reserved List, absent & unknown.
d.—died or buried.	s.—son.
dg.—daughter,	serv.—servant.
dis.—dismissed by letter.	susp.—suspended.
Exc.—excommunicated.	w.—wife of.
fr.—from.	wid.—widow.

Names of Communicants are printed in small capitals; those who Renewed Covenant, or became "Halfway Members," are in italics ; those of children are indented under the names of their parents. The brace { connects names of husband and wife.

Remarks or additions made by the Editor are inclosed in brackets, thus [ ] ; and doubtful conjectures are followed by the sign of interrogation ?]

A

Abeel, Joanna ; m. 12 Nov. 1783, to Major Leonard Bleeker.

{ Aber, Aaron
{ MARTHA EASTON ; m. Nov. 1 793 ; C. 18 Aug 1797 ; " moved away."

Hannah, b. 27 July, 1794 ; B. f. w. 4 May, 1798.

Timothy Johnes, b. 14 April, 1797 ; B. f. w., 4 May, 1798.

Aber, Christian ; m. 26 Feb. 1759, to Anne Margaret Battleren.

Aber, Elizabeth ; m. 9 June, 1790, to William Denman.

Aber, Israel ; m. 29 Feb. 1756, to Dorothea Leonard.

Aber, John ; m. 21 Jan., 1745, to Mary Hulbard.

Abers, Polly, wid. ; m. 4 Dec., 1813, to Samuel Nestor.

ABER, SUSAN LOUISA ; B. & C.'31 July, 1881.

{ Ackley. Erastus J., of Newark.
{ ELIZABETH D. MARVIN, dg. Dr. Jonathan ; m. 14 March, 1843; L. 1 Feb. 1862, fr. 1st Ref. D. Ch., Newark ; dis.5

ELIZABETH M.; L. 1 Feb. 1862, fr. 1st. Ref. D. Ch., Newark ; dis.5

HENRIETTA A.; L. " " fr. " " " " " dis.5

Adams, Aaron, of N. Y.; m. 10 Mar., 1880, to Mary Bell Hockenbery.

Adams, Joseph, (colored) ; d. 30 April, 1851, aet. 98.

Adams, William ; d. 6 May, 1826, aet. 47.

Adams, Chloe, wid. ; d. 18 July, 1800, aet. 42.

Adams, John, of Woodbridge ; m. 23 Sept., 1770, to Agnish Bloys, wid.

Adams, Lidia, wid. ; m. 29 Oct., 1769, to Matthew Rue, both of Hunterdon.

ADAMSON, MRS. WILLIAM ; L. 28 Dec., 1815, fr. Hanover ; d. 20 Feb. 1836, aet. 75.

Adamson, Phebe, w. [dg ?] William ; d. 27 Aug., 1813, aet. 19.

Adamson, William, of Camden,S. C. ; m. 22 May,1827,to Frances A. Carmichael,dg. David.

Adamson, William O.; m. 28 May, 1871, to Marietta A. Mills, dg. William Freeland.

Ader, Prince, (colored) ; d. 17 Nov. 1847, aet. 50.

{ ADDISON, WILLIAM ; C. 29 June, 1808; dis. 29 June, 1810; returned 1 Nov., 1811.
{ CATHERINE ——— C. " " dis. " " " returned " " "

Sally Ann, b. 17 Dec. 1804 ; B. 11 Jan. 1809.

John Montgomery, b. 15 March. 1808 ; B. 11 Jan. 1809.

Aikman, Alexander ; m. 8 Jan., 1764, to Elizabeth Lewis.

Akeman, Margaret ; m. 18 Jan., 1753, to John Brown, of Somerset.

{ *Akeman. William* ; R. C. 12 Aug., 1758.
{ *Letitia Bailes* ; m. 8 Dec. 1756 ; R. C. 12 Aug. 1758.

Jane ; B. 20 Aug. 1758; m. 13 April 1777, to John Beach.

Hannah ; B. 29 March, 1761.

Rebecca ; B. 14 Oct., 1770.

Albertson, Emma F., of Blairstown ; m. 22 Sept. 1874, to Charles M. Keepers.

{ ALEXANDER, THOMAS ; C. 30 March, 1860 ; dis. 1 Oct., 1865, to New Vernon.

{ MARGARET, MCALISTER ; m. 30 March, 1858 ;

Jane A.; B. 30 March, 1860.

Tryphena ; B. 2 Aug. 1862.

Allen, Aaron, of So. Hanover ; m. 28 Nov. 1750, to Abigail Bonel, of Turkey.

Allen, Aaron [s. John & Rebecca ?]

Phebe, b. 11 April, 1785 ; B. 26 June, 1785.

ALLEN, ANN, wid ; L. 1743—1756.

{ Allen, Charles ; d. 13 Sept', 1781, aet. 106.

{ ———— d. 27 Feb., 1781, aet. 90.

Allen, Elizabeth, of So. Hanover ; m. 28 Nov. 1750, to Nathaniel Bonel, of Turkey.

Allen, Eunice ; m. 23 April, 1758, to David Core.

{ ALLEN, GILBERT (usually "Gilbard"); B. 17 Aug., 1761 ; C. 4 March, 1763 ; [elected
deacon & elder 31 July, 1777, last met with Session 23 Feb., 1815, present 120 times out of 158 ;] d. 6 Jan., 1816, aet. 80.

{ ELIZABETH ———— ; B. 17 Aug., 1762 ; C. 4 March, 1763, d. 10 Jan., 1816, aet. 79.

ABIGAIL ; B. 17 Aug., 1761 ; m. 3 May, 1780, to Abraham Munson, q. v.

KEZIA ; B. 16 July, 1762; m. 30 Oct., 1783, to Jesse Sexton (" Saxon"), q. v.

Stephen ; B. 8 April, 1764 ; d. 19 Dec., 1778, aet. 15.

Elizabeth ; B. 15 June, 1766 ; d. 21 July, 1785, aet. 19.

Phebe ; B. 5 June, 1768 ; d. 30 March, 1786, aet. 18.

Silas ; b. 5 Feb., 1770 ; B. 8 April, 1770.

SARAH ; b. 1772 ; B. 5 July, 1772 ; m. 17 June, 1790, to Jeptha Wade, q. v.

HANNAH, b. 31 March 1774 ; B. 29 May. 1774 ; m. to John Brookfield, q. v.

Anne, b. 29 April, 1776 ; B. 23 June, 1776 ; [m. as "Nancy" to Charles Leyton, q. v.?]

Timothy, b. 26 Dec. 1778 ; B. 11 April, 1779 ; [m. to Jemima ———— ?]

Jemima, b. 18 March, 1781 ; B. 3 June, 1781 ; d. 16 Feb. 1786, aet. 5.

John Frase, adopted ; B. 15 Aug. 1790.

JABEZ LINDSLEY, adopted ;　b. 24 Dec., 1805 ; B, 2 July, 1812; see below.

Kezia Layton,　　"　b. 7 July, 1809 ; B. "　"　"

Allen, Harriet, [dg.　　　　　　　], adopted dg. Jesse Sexton, b. 11 Aug., 1807 ;
B. f. w. 2 July, 1812 ; m. 20 Aug., 1825, to Timothy H. Prudden.

Allen, Henry ; d. 4 June. 1803, aet. 71.

{ ALLEN, JABEZ LINDSLEY, adopted s. Gilbert ; C. 22 Nov., 1827 ; dis. 8 Dec., 1828, to
1st Ch., Newark; L. 17 May. 1832, fr. same ; dis.4

{ CAROLINE CONKLIN MILLS, dg. Jabez and Hannah (Coe) ; m. 14 March, 1827 ; L. &
dis. with her husband.

Hannah Caroline, b. 23 July, 1828 ; B. 5 Sept., 1828 ; d. 29 Nov. 1831, aet. 3.

Charles Mills, b. 11 June, 1833 ; B. 1 Sept. 1833.

Allen, Jacob, of So. Hanover ; m. 15 Jan. 1751, to wid. of George Day, "at River."

Allen, Jacob ; m. 8 May, 1802, to Polly Minton.

Allen, Jacob, of Caldwell ; m. 24 Sept., 1803, to Hannah Whitehead [dg. Onesimus ?],
of Mendham.

Allen, Jarzel ; m. 14 March, 1803, to Mary Pierson [dg. Samuel ?]

Allen, Jemima, w. Timothy [s. Gilbert ?]; d. 28 Nov., 1810, aet. 28.

ALLEN, JOB, of Rockaway ; M. 1742.

Elizabeth ; B. 18 Sept. 1743.

Deborah ; B., 17 Aug., 1746.

Lois ; B. 10 July, 1748 ; m. 21 Dec. 1766, to Daniel Talmadge, of Baskingridge.

Job ; B. f. w. 14 Aug., 1751 ; [m. 2 Jan., 1774, to Mary Minton, both of Rockaway.]

THE RECORD.

FIRST PRESBYTERIAN CHURCH, MORRISTOWN, N. J.

"THIS SHALL BE WRITTEN FOR THE GENERATION TO COME."—Psalms 102 : 18.

| VOLUME IV. | NOVEMBER, 1884. | NUMBER 23. |

[Printed with the Approval of the Session.]

THE RECORD

Is published monthly ; .terms $1.00 a year, *in advance*.

It will probably be completed with Dec., 1885 ; the Minutes being brought down to 1882, and the Registers to 1884.

Cash subscribers in advance for 1885 *will receive all issues* **FREE** *after Dec.* 1885, *if it should be necessary to continue the publication beyond that date in order to make it complete.*

Single numbers for any month, 10 cents each.

Subscriptions should be made to Mr. James R. Voorhees.

Matters pertaining to the publication should be addressed to the

EDITOR OF THE RECORD. .

Entered at the Post Office at Morristown, N. J., as second class matter.

CORRECTIONS AND ADDITIONS.

Communications are earnestly solicited for this column. Address, Lock Box 90, Morristown, N. J.

Page 208 of Sup. for April, 1883 :
Dec., 4, 1802; Timothy DeCamp to Jane Humes (not Hughes.)
Page 206 of Sup. for April, 1883 :
June 5, 1798; John F. Ellis to Maria Wilcocks (not Wilrocks.)
Page 205 of Sup. for April, 1883 :
Nov. 23, 1796; John Hinchman to Deborah Luker. should probably be " to Deborah Tucker."
" 16, 1796; Jonas Smith to Nancy Lorain (not Losier ?)
" 14, 1795; Andrew Charles to Sally Kelso? (the " Kelso" is indistinct.)
" 19, 1795 ; Ira (not Ara) Broadwell.
Sept. 6, " Joseph Lloyd (not Lord.)
May 5, 1809; Stout Benjamin, ch. Nathaniel Peck (not Tenk.)
Page 204 of Sup. for Mar., 1883 :
July 17, 1808 ; Rev. John Keyes (not Reyes.)
Page 203 of Sup. for Mar., 1883 :
Feb. 28, 1807 ; Abrm. Hedges, ch. James Harvey ? (not Henry ?)

Continued from page 134.)

REVIVALS IN THE CHURCH :
BY THE
REV. DAVID IRVING, D.D.,

'tered upon the pastoral office, which he filled for more than nine years ; being blessed in his work and proving a blessing to others. In the year following his settlement his own heart was gladdened, the graces of the people strengthened, and the number of the sacramental host of God's elect increased by an addition of fifty to the Church ; some of whom remain to this day, though the greater number have fallen asleep. From this period to 1822 there were yearly accessions to this Zion ranging from seven to thirteen ; then the Most High made bare his arm for the deliverance of his chosen from the dominion of Satan. This was the most extensive revival with which the congregation had ever been visited ; and yet, after the most diligent search and inquiry, I can find no prepared account of this special outpouring, and but little from living witnesses who can only recall the general impression made on them.

Previous to the spring of 1822, there were no hopeful signs of God's reviving power. But then, on a pastoral visit to a family of his charge in Littleton, Dr. McDowell found great tenderness and weeping on the part of its inmates, preceded, as he soon discovered, by great wrestling with God on the part of the parents in the night watches, for God's blessing on Zion. And here it is an interesting fact, that the parents of the head of this house were brought to Christ through the instrumentality of the first pastor of this Church ; the father caring for none of these things, and the mother attached to the Society of Friends; the husband was first converted and then the mother publicly confessed her faith in Christ in the old Church. The son never forgot the kindness and efforts of Dr. Johnes; he was brought to Christ under the ministry of Dr. Johnes' successor, and he was now permitted to see the Spirit striving with his own children, and to rejoice in it as the commencement of a remarkable work of grace. Among the fruits was a son who is now laboring as a missionary in the West. Of his family and descendants there are sixteen now in connection with this Church alone.

The much desired inquiry, What must I do to be saved? intensified the longings of the pastor and of the people of God. Means of grace were multiplied; neighboring pastors were called in, to proclaim saving truth and direct the anxious to the Lamb of God. Many impenitents were arrested by the gospel and awakened to concern for their souls. The drunkard was reclaimed, and is to-day a trophy of redeeming love. The profane saw new power in the names of God and of Christ. The worldling let go his hold upon earth, and, with streaming eyes and warm heart, rejoiced in heavenly riches. The careless professor was quickened; the yearning spirit felt a nearness to God never before experienced; estrangements were healed; past misconduct mourned over; and heaven was brought nearer to many souls. As a result of this gracious outpouring, there was an ingathering into Zion of nearly one hundred and fifty. Associated with this, we find, from the General Assembly's narrative, that the surrounding Churches shared largely in the work; Hanover, Rockaway, Chatham, Baskingridge, and Hackettstown.

Soon after this, partly on account of impaired health, Mr. McDowell resigned his charge, and in due time was succeeded by Mr. Barnes, who was frequently cheered and incited to diligence by finding that his labors were not in vain in the Lord. He had much to contend with; but firm, decided and resolute, he went forward in his work, dealing with sin in its varied forms, and showing its opposedness to God, whether committed by the believer or the unbeliever. During the winter of 1827 and the spring and summer of 1828, Mr. Barnes delivered a series of sermons on the great doctrines of the cross and the character of the Redeemer. The only marked effect of these discourses was, at first, an increased attention on the means of grace, a deepened interest in preaching, and a manifested seriousness among the people. This continued for some time, without anything more than the ordinary means of grace, until the quarterly meeting of the Church previous to the communion. Of this meeting says Mr. Barnes, in a letter to myself, "Personally I had feelings which I had never had before, and which I have never experienced since. I went to the meeting with no unusual emotions, and with no expectation of any special interest; but there was something about it which wholly overcame me. I spent a considerable part of the meeting in tears, and my emotions were shared by a considerable part of the congregation present, and all felt there was the presence of a higher power." A prayer was offered at that meeting by a member of this Church, (Mr. Enslee, an elder,) that "came nearer to *inspiration,*" says the pastor, "than anything that I ever heard from human lips; so fervent, so tender, so full of faith, so devoted, so much of the Spirit; which I then thought must belong to heaven, and never since have I heard such a prayer."

This meeting was the manifestation of the beginning of the revival. Soon the whole community was affected; town and country were alike awakened, and all bent upon one common object,—to give heed to the interests of eternity. To meet this state of feeling an increased number of religious services was deemed advisable. These were mostly conducted by the pastor, assisted by a neighboring minister or by the eldership of the Church. For a period of three months there were services of some kind nearly every evening, in which no other measures than the simple presentation of the truth were employed. So widespread and general was the feeling, that the farmer left his farm and the merchant his store, to attend upon the services of the sanctuary; and, when the hour for evening service arrived, nearly all, if not every, store was closed. The meetings were first held in the Lecture-room; but this soon became too strait for

(To be continued.)

(Continued from page 136.)

COMBINED REGISTERS ; 1742 to 1884.

For meaning of abbreviations see page 135 of THE RECORD for October, 1884.

It will be esteemed a great favor if the readers of THE RECORD *will send* CORRECTIONS, *or additional* INFORMATION, *to* Lock Box 90, Morristown, N. J.

———:o:———

{ ALLEN, JOHN ; B. & C. 2 July, 1767 ; "moved."
{ Tabitha Lyon, wid., of Mendham; m. 6 Aug., 1751.
{ REBECCA ——— L. 1766.
    Daniel ; B. 17 June, 1753.
    Aaron ; B. 1 Nov. 1767.
    Jehosheba, b. 31 Aug., 1769 ; B. 24 Sept., 1769.
    Phebe, b. 14 Dec, 1771 ; B. 23 Feb., 1772.
    Abigail, b. 13 Nov., 1773 ; B. 9 Jan., 1774.
    Silas, b. 26 June, 1776 ; B. 4 Aug., 1776.
    Hannah, b. 5 Feb., 1779 ; B. 21 March, 1779.
    Rachel, b. 12 March, 1781 ; B. 3 May, 1881.
{ Allen, Jonah
{ *Sarah Muir* ; m. 30 Jan., 1752 ; R. C. as wid., 19 March, 1758.
    Amos ; B. 19 March, 1758.
    Elizabeth ; B.   "   "
    Jonah ; B.   "   "
Allen, Mary ; m. 9 Oct.. 1745, to Samuel Munson.
Allen, Mrs. Mary, sister of Timothy Pierson ; d. 11 April, 1847, aet. 65.
Allen, Moses ; m. 8 Dec., 1772, to Elizabeth Turner [dg. Jarzel ?] who d. 25 July, 1784, aet. 29.
Allen, Moses, deacon of Bapt. Ch.; d. near Green Village, 9 Nov., 1823, aet. 70.
Allen, Moses ; m. 22 Dec., 1806, to Sarah Lindsley.
Allen, Naomi, wid. ; d. 9 March 1784, aet 70.
{ ALLEN, RODERICK ; B. & C. 7 Dec., 1834 ; dis.+
{ SOPHRONIA P. ——— C. 18 Feb. 1836 ; dis.+
Allen, Samuel ; m. 4 July, 1779, to Hannah Beach.
Allen, Samuel ; d. 21 March, 1855, aet. 78.
ALLEN, SARAH, wid. ; B. & C. 23 Aug., 1787 ; d. 28 Nov., 1789, aet. 92.
Allen, Sally, w. Moses, Jr. ; d. at Green Village, 25 Nov., 1815, aet. 23.
ALLEN, SUSANNA ; C. 1 Nov., 1764 ; confest 4 Jan., 1771.
    Jacob, b. 19 March, 1770 ; B. 4 Jan., 1771.
{ Allen, Uriah
{ *Rachel Coe*, dg. Benjamin & Rachel ; m. 21 Nov., 1773 ; R. C., 29 June, 1775.
    Aaron, b. 24 Feb., 1774 ; B. f. w. 29 June, 1775.
ALLERTON, JACOB ; C. 10 May, 1745 ; "moved away."
    Jacob ; B. 5 June, 1745.
Allerton, John ; m. 18 Dec., 1754, to Hannah Kent.
Allerton, John ; m. 15 Aug., 1786, to Rhoda Carter.
{ ALLERTON, THOMAS ; R. C. 26 Aug., 1744 ; C. 11 Jan., 1745 ; susp, 29 June, 1752 ;
           " moved away."
{ DEBORAH ——— R. C. 26 Aug., 1744 ; C. 2 Nov. 1744 ; " moved away."
    Sarah ; B. adult & R. C. 26 Aug., 1744.
    John ; B. 26 Aug., 1744.
    Charity ; B.   "   "
    David ; B.   "   "
    Benjamin ; B. 20 Sept. 1747.

Allison, John, m. 17 June, 1771, to Catherine Mitchell, both of Brookland Forge.
ALLISON,⸸MARIAN ; L. 20 Feb,, 1834, fr. 1st. Ch., Southwark, Phil.; gone.⁴
{ Alsover, Frederick A., of Hanover.
} JERUSHA HALSEY, of Hanover ; m. 14 Jan., 1804 ; L. 29 June, 1813, fr. Parsippany.
Alward, Hetty T. ; m. 1 April, 1854, to Cheodore Mrovzkowski.
{ ALWOOD, JOHN ; B. 4 Oct., 1789 ; C. 23 Oct., 1789; "moved away."
} PHEBE ALWOOD, dg. Samuel ; m. 2 Dec., 1811 ; d. 27 Jan., 1850, aet., 71.
    ELIZABETH, b. 13 Feb., 1813 ; B. f. w. 2 July, 1813 ; C. as dg. wid. Phebe, 26 Feb.,
        1830 ; d. 24 Jan., 1847, aet. 33.
    John Henry, b. 3 Sept., 1820 ; B. 5 Sept., 1828.
    Emmeline Parson, b. 10 Jan., 1823 ; B. 5 June, 1829.
{ ALWOOD, JONAS, s. Samuel ; dis. 8 June, 1841, to 2d Ch. ; d. 25 Dec., 1841, aet. 71.
{ RACHEL ARNOLD, dg. Ziba ; m. 12 Dec. 1798.
{ NANCY ———— C. 24 Aug., 1820 ; dis. 8 June, 1841, to 2d. Ch.; d. 11 Jan. 1862, aet. 73.
    ELIZABETH R., b. 1800 ; B. 21 Dec., 1803 , C. 28 May, 1828 ; dis. 8 June, 1841, to
        2d Ch.; d. 5 Nov., 1861, aet. 61.
    Susan, b. 27 Dec., 1807 : B. 2 July, 1813 ; d. 24 Dec., 1824, aet. 17.
    MARY ANN, b. 16 Dec., 1809 ; B. 2 July, 1813 ; C. 22 Feb., 1827 ; d. 30 Jan., 1835,
        aet. 35 [?]
    Matilda, b. 16 March, 1802 ; B. " " "
    Amzy Newton, b. 30 Sept., 1814 ; B. 3 March, 1815.
    Martha Whitehead ; B. 5 Dec., 1823.
    Helen Maria, b. 9 Nov., 1828 ; B. 27 Feb., 1829 ; d. 1 Jan.. 1850, aet. 21.
Alwald, Mary ; m. 2 June, 1860, to Robert McLaren.
Alward, Ruth, w. Samuel ; d. 1 June 1818, aet. 79.
{ Alwood, Samuel ; R. C. 14 April, 1764 ; [Samuel R. d. 24 June, 1818, aet. 86.]
} ELIZABETH ———— R. C. " " " C. 30 Sept., 1786 ; d. 25 Oct., 1820, aet. 81.
    Mary ; B. 14 April, 1764.
    Joseph ; B. "at yr. house," 8 Aug., 1766.
    Samuel ; B. 30 Aug., 1767.
    JONAS ; B. 4 June, 1769 ; C. 1 Nov., 1796 ; see above.
    Sarah, b. 7 Aug., 1771 : B. 14 Sept., 1771 ; m. 16 Feb., 1797, to Philip Easton.
    Joseph ; b. 16 Feb., 1773 ; B. 11 April, 1773 ; d. 11 July 1775, aet. 2.
    Henry, b. 11 Oct., 1775 ; B. 3 Mar., 1776 ; [m. to Susanna———— ? see below.]
    Elizabeth, b. 7 Oct.. 1777 ; B. 4 Dec. 1777 ; d. 20 Oct., 1800, aet., 22.
    PHEBE, b. 25 Oct.. 1779 ; B. 9 Dec., 1779 ; C. 10 May, 1797 ; m. to John Alwood,
        q. v.
    Stephen, b. 5 Jan. 1782 ; B. 5 May, 1783.
ALWOOD, SUSANNA ; w. Henry [s. Samuel ?] ; L. 22 May, 1817, fr. Rockaway.
AMBUHL, WALTER; C. 3 Dec., 1875 ; R. L., 1884.
Ames, Levi ; m. 19 Sept., 1833, to Ruth Goble.
ANCRUM, MARY ; C. 4 June, 1864 ; "went abroad;" "dead."
ANCRUM, MRS.— L. 31 July, 1875, tr. U. P. Ch., Glasgow. Scotland.
Anderson, Eliakim ; m. 26 April, 1838, to Mrs. Effy Dickerson.
{ ANDERSON, ELI ; L. about 1766 ; "moved away."
{ MARY ——— L. " " " "
{ ANDERSON, JAMES ; C. 31 March, 1870 ; dis. 4 April, 1879, to Dover ; d. 28 Jan., 1880,
{   aet. 60.
{ ELIZABETH ———— ; L. 1 June 1866, fr. Mendham ; dis. 4 April, 1879, to Dover ; L. 5
    May, 1880, fr. Dover.
    ALICE D. L. 3 Aug., 1872, fr. Mendham ; dis. 4 April, 1879, to Dover ; L. 5
    May, 1880, fr Dover.
ANDERSON, SUSANNA, w. Wm. H. ; L. 1 Dec. 1860, fr. Mendham ; d. 25 May, 1883.

THE RECORD.

FIRST PRESBYTERIAN CHURCH, MORRISTOWN, N. J.

"THIS SHALL BE WRITTEN FOR THE GENERATION TO COME."—Psalms 102 : 18.

VOLUME IV.   DECEMBER, 1884.   NUMBER 24.

[Printed with the Approval of the Session.]

THE RECORD

Is published monthly ; terms $1.00 a year, *in advance.*

It will probably be completed with Dec. 1885; the Minutes being brought down to 1882.

Cash subscribers in advance for 1885 will receive all issues **FREE** *after Dec. 1885, if it should be necessary to continue the publication beyond that date in order to make it complete.*

Single numbers for any month, 10 cents each.

Subscriptions should be made to Mr. James R. Voorhees.

Matters pertaining to the publication should be addressed to the

EDITOR OF THE RECORD.

Entered at the Post Office at Morristown, N. J., as second class matter.

SPECIAL NOTICE.

The offer of the RECORD *free* after Dec. 1885, (if continued beyond that date), to cash subscribers in advance for 1885, will be withdrawn at the close of the present month. To receive advantage of this offer, subscriptions for 1885 must be paid on or before 31 Dec. 1884.

Continued from page 138.
REVIVALS IN THE CHURCH:
BY THE
REV. DAVID IRVING, D. D.

the number attending, and they were removed to the Church. The number of anxious ones amounted frequently to three or four hundred, occupying nearly the whole of the central block of pews in the body of the church. The work was characterized by a long previous preparation, and by an earnest presentation of the truth pertaining to the work of the Redeemer. And yet it was sovereign on the part of God, for the same sermons delivered here were afterwards preached to another congregation without producing the least visible effect. There was little opposition to the work : all men felt that it was the power of God, and those who were not professors were deeply interested for others. All persons and classes in the community were affected ; the most wealthy and respectable of the congregation were the subjects of the work, the old man of eighty rejoiced in a new found Saviour, while the youth in his budding years consecrated himself to God. The irreligious, the Sabbath-breaker, and the infidel bowed alike before the same mercy-seat and sang the same song of praise, "O, to grace how great a debtor."

As a fruit of that astonishing display of divine love, over two hundred united at successive times with this Church, and a number with the Methodist Church, then in its infancy. And from this and the preceding work has been derived, for a long series of years, the strength of this Church in piety, liberality, and a maintenance of religious ordinances ; and not a little of the good order, sound morality, and religious power in this community is owing to these extraordinary displays of Jehovah's mercy.

"In Morristown," says a magazine of that day, "the work of grace is spreading rapidly from family to family." Says the New York Observer: "At Morristown God is doing great things. The town seems to be the radiating point from which the Spirit seems to be extending its divine influence in various directions. He has graciously visited Chester and Flanders." To which the General Assembly, in its notice of the work, adds : "In Morristown, a spot often visited by the outpouring of the Spirit, there has been a display of divine grace, more powerful and more wonderful than has ever before been known in that place. It commenced in November last and rapidly increased, until the whole town seemed to be shaken ; almost the entire population appeared bowed in the dust before the majesty of Jehovah. Opposition was hushed and every one seemed to say and feel, 'Truly this is the finger of God.'

In this allusion to by gone scenes, I have touched chords, no doubt, in many hearts ; brought before your minds vividly the past, when, in the presence of a thronged and interested Church and in the hearing of the blessed Saviour, you gave yourselves away in a convenant never to be revoked, to be willing servants forever;—when in this house you sat down at the Master's table for the first time, and in all the glow of first love, vowed to be only and wholly the Lord's. And have you ever regretted it, as you have oft sung, "Jesus, thy feast we celebrate," or "Why was I made to hear thy voice?" and "Enter while there's room."

"When thousands make a wretched choice,
And rather starve than come."

In view of God's constraining mercy and electing love; in view of the hallowed communions here enjoyed with heaven; in view of the spiritual strength received; in view of the good accomplished to your families and the community by this noble structure, reared with such munificence by your fathers, who were at the time impoverished by a long war; and in view of the sainted dead, your children, your parents and dearest friends, gathered into the heavenly home through the instrumentality and ordinances of this Church: will you murmur at the improvements placed by your liberality and that of others on this building, which has been consecrated so oft by the presence and the glory of the Lord of Hosts; or say that the feeling which animated the men who had it in charge was at war with the spirit of those who reared it; or complain of the sums given to beautify the temple of the Most High?

I should love to bring before you other doings of the Lord in these latter days, when, under Mr. Hoover's ministry, Morris Plains and part of the town were moved, and several before me rejoiced in the lovingkindness and in the smiles of a sin-for-giving God; or of the precious mercy-drops that descended during the pastorate of Dumont; or of the cheering fruits that accompanied the earnest and devoted efforts of the now sainted Townley; but time will not permit. Suffice it to say, that there are but few Churches in our land that have a more glorious past; few that can speak oftener of the years of the right hand of the Most High; but few that have a stronger warrant to cry; "Drop down, ye heavens, from above, and let the skies pour down righteousness;" and perhaps but few have more need to pray. "O Lord revive thy work."

Since the first pastor was installed, when the Church numbered 176, there have been added: under Dr. Johnes 424, Dr. Richards 243, Dr. Fisher 97, Dr. McDowell 302, Mr. Barnes 303, Mr. Hoover 109, Mr. Kirtland 103, Mr. Dumont 111, Mr. Thompson 31, Mr. Richards 59, Mr. Townley 85, and under the present pastorate to this date, 171; making nearly 2,000 admitted to Church privileges, and mostly from the kingdom of Satan; over 1,500 since the congregation commenced worshiping in this house.*

[*There are the names of 179 persons on the list in Dr.

Johnes' record which he entitled, "The Number and names of the Persons that were in full communion when the Church was first collected & founded, together with the number that came since from other churches." Neither marks nor dates are given to distinguish between the original members and those who were received from other Churches; but it is evident, both from this title and from the fifty years of Dr. Johnes' pastorate, that the original members constitute but a small part of this list. From other records, however, there is derived a strong probability that the roll of communicants contained between 52 and 55 names when the pastorate of Dr. Johnes began. For instance, the 52d name on this list is that of "Martha, wife of Cornelius Austin;" and as Cornelius Austin was one of the 21 who made "Publick Confession at the settlement of the Ch." for abandoning Hanover in disregard of "the lot," it is almost certain that his wife was a communicant in 1742. On the other hand, the name of "Elizabeth, wife of David More," is the 56th on the list: but, in the Marriage Register, it is recorded that "David More and Elizabeth Roff" (or Buff?) were married by Dr. Johnes on the 13th of April, 1743; it seems conclusive that she would appear under her maiden name on the list of members if she had been a communicant on Dr. Johnes' arrival in 1742. Other records confirm the conclusion that there were about 55 communicants enrolled at the end of 1742, but there is no need of reciting them.

We append a table, recently compiled with much care, to show the additions during each pastorate and vacancy for 140 years of the Church's history. Two items need explanation. The number of adults baptized by Mr. McDowell is evidently inaccurate; he left no record of Baptisms, except for the first year or two that he was here. Again, Dr. Irving should be credited with the additions in the Vacancy that followed his pastorate, since he resided here and conducted the services at the time; which would make his work the most fruitful, after that of Dr. Johnes; that is, 27 Adults Baptised, 178 Confirmed (or 205 on Examination,) and 161 by Certificate, —a total of 366.

The significance of the columns is as follows:
A. B. shows the number of Adults Baptized.
C. " " " " received to communion who were Baptized in infancy.
L. shows number of those received by Certificates from other Churches.
T. C. shows total number added to the roll of communicants.

Pastorates and Vacancies.	A. B.	C.	L.	T. C.
Dr. Johnes, 13 Aug., 1742 to 5 Jan., 1791.	40	385	124	549
Mr. Collins, as't, 6 Jan.,1791 to 2 Sept.,1792.2	22	0		94
No additions recorded, 3 Sept., 1792 to Feb., 1795.	0	0	0	0
Mr. Richards, to 26 April, 1809,	35	187	27	249
Vacancy to 9 Aug., 1809,	1	8	0	4
Mr. Fisher to 27 April, 1814,	18	44	29	86
Vacancy to 18 Dec., 1814,	15	19	2	36
Mr. McDowell to 28 Oct., 1823	? 9	257	51	317
Vacancy to 8 Feb., 1825,	2	1	5	8
Mr. Barnes to 3 June, 1830,	90	141	62	293
Vacancy to 8 Feb., 1832,	0	3	8	11
Mr. Hoover to 10 March, 1836,	36	86	54	176
Vacancy to 23 March, 1837,	1	12	15	28
Mr. Kirtland to 26 Aug., 1840,	8	25	72	105
Vacancy to 19 Jan., 1841,	0	2	0	2
Mr. Dumont to 9 July, 1845,	16	39	53	108
Vacancy to 14 Jan., 1846,	0	0	0	0
Mr. Thompson to 28 July, 1847,	0	10	21	31
Vacancy to 25 Nov., 1847,	0	0	0	0
Mr. J. R. Richards to 15 April, 1851,	1	13	49	63
Vacancy to 27 Dec., 1851,	0	4	6	10
Mr. Townley to 5 Feb., 1855,	4	32	50	86
Vacancy to 5 Nov., 1855,	0	0	5	5
Dr. Irving to 10 May, 1865,	19	149	143	311
Vacancy to 17 July, 1866,	8	29	18	55
Mr. Langmuir to 10 Sept., 1868,	4	10	31	45
Vacancy to 21 Dec., 1868,	0	0	4	4
Mr. French to 31 Jan., 1877,	60	146	131	337
Vacancy to 18 July, 1877,	0	0	1	1
Mr. Green to 19 Oct., 1881,	18	99	76	193
Vacancy to 11 May, 1882,	0	0	2	2
	382	1,658	1,039	3,079.
Original Roll, 1742,	-		55	
Added to 11 May, 1882 :				
By Baptism	-	382		
" Confirmation	-	1658		
On Examination -	-	2,040		
On Certificates -	-	1,089		
Total Communicants,		3,134		
Yearly Average on Examination	14.57			
" " " Certificates	7.42			
" " " added	21.99			D.]

(To be continued.)

(Continued from page 140.)

COMBINED REGISTERS ; 1742 to 1884

For meaning of abbreviations see page 135 of THE RECORD for October, 1884.
It will be esteemed a great favor if the readers of THE RECORD *will send* CORRECTIONS, *or additional* INFORMATION, *to* Lock Box 90, Morristown, N. J.

————:o:————

Anderson, William ; m. 24 July, 1828, to Sarah B. Douglas, eldest dg. James K., both of Camden, S. C.

ANDERSON, WILLIAM G., L. 31 March, 1870, fr. 2d Ch., Mendham ; ord. elder 31 Dec., 1871, last met with Session 20 Sept, 1874, present 3 times out of 53 ; resigned 13 Nov., 1879 ; went to P. E. Ch. ; name removed 1884.

MARY L. ——— L. 31 March, 1870, fr. 2nd Ch., Mendham : went to P. E. Ch. ; name removed 1884.

ANDRESS, JAMES ; L. 28 May, 1821, fr. Springfield ; susp. 1 June, 1830.
Jane Bonnell, dg. Luther, of Springfield ; m. 23 Sept., 1819.

Andrews, Elizabeth Adams, of Port Oram ; m. 9 June, 1873, to Charles Johnson.

Apthorp, Mary Ann, of Long Island ; m. 24 Nov., 1810, to Moses Holloway, of Morris Plains, [s. Capt. Benj. ?]

Archer, Benjamin
Charity ———
Philip Pain, b. 15 Aug., 1777 ; B. 14 Dec., 1777.
William, b. 21 March, 1779 ; B. 28 May, 1780.

ARDEN, CHAROLOTTE B., w. Thomas, and dg. Rev. Benjamin Woodruff, of Westfield ; L, 30 Dec., 1808, fr. U. P. Ch., N. Y. ; dis. May, 1817 ; returned ; dis. 26 Jan., 1841, to 2d Ch. ; d. 13 Nov., 1850, aet 81.

Armstrong, Mr. ; d. 17 Sept., 1832, aet., 52 ; [Samuel, s. Nathaniel ?]
Armstrong, Anne ; m. 10 Nov., 1768, to James Loree.
Armstrong, Hannah ; m. 1 Dec., 1757, to Daniel Morris, Jr.,
Armstrong, Jane ; m. 17 Jan., 1754, to Elijah Pierson.

ARMSTRONG, JOHN ; L. 1 Oct., 1871, fr. Madison ; R. L. 1884.
ELVIRA ——— L. " " fr. " R. L. "
MARGARET ; L. " " fr. " R. L. "

Armstrong, Lewis [s. wid. Mary ?]
JULIA BEADLE [dg. William ?] ; C. 15 Aug. 1822 ; dis. Dec., 1835, to New Vernon ; d. 16 April, 1873.
Harriet Mills, b. 10 Jan., 1827 ; B. 14 July, 1829.

ARMSTRONG, MARY, wid. John ; L. 1767 ; d. 31 Jan. 1788, aet. 84.

ARMSTRONG, MARY, wid. [Nath'l s. Nath'l ?] : C. 18 Aug., 1797, m. [Matthias ?] Williams ; dis.
Silas, b. 21 April, 1792 ; B. 6 Oct., 1797.
Phebe, b. 24 April, 1794 ; B. 30 Jan., 1811.
David, b. 17 Sept., 1796 ;, B. 30 Jan., 1811.
Lewis, b. 15 Sept., 1802 ; B. 30 Jan., 1811, [m. Julia Beadle, dg. William ?]

ARMSTRONG, MARY, w. William ; C. 27 June, 1808 ; [m. 19 Dec., 1827, to David Lindsley.]

Armstrong, Nathaniel ; d. 23 Oct., 1822, aet. 80.
RACHEL LYON , [dg. Samuel] ; m. 24 Dec., 1675 ; C. 28 Aug., 1812 ; d. 14 Jan., 1817, aet. 73.
Nathaniel, B. 2 April, 1769 ; d. 26 May. 1803, aet. 34.
Silas, b. 12 Jan., 1771 ; B. 17 March, 1771 ; d. 9 Jan., 1794, aet. 23.
Phebe, b. 9 Feb. 1773 ; B. 11 April, 1773 ; d. 27 Nov., 1775, aet. 2.
Isaac, b. 23 Feb., 1777 ; B. 3 July, 1777 ; d. 5 Jan., 1778, aet. 1.
Rhoda, b. 13 Dec., 1778 ; B. 31 Jan., 1779.

Samuel, b. 21 Aug., 1779; B. 13 Aug., 1780.

Hannah, b. 10 Mar., 1783; B. 18 May, 1783; [m. 30 Nov., 1801, to Elias Pierson, [s. David?]

John, b. 21 June, 1786: B. 30 July, 1786; [m. 10 Dec., 1807, to Rhoda Norris?], d. 8 April, 1812, aet., 26.

Armstrong, Phebe (or Hannah); m. 31 Jan., 1760, to Joseph Stiles.

Armstrong, Phebe; m. 29 March 1779, to Benjamin Conger.

ARMSTRONG, RHODA, [Norris], wid. [John s. Nath'l]; m. Timothy Pierson; B. & C. 6 Nov., 1814; dis. 26 Jan., 1841, to 2d Ch.

HARRIET E., B. 5 May, 1815; C; 22 Aug., 1833; dis. 26 Jan., 1841, to 2d Ch.; m. Wm. S. Townley.

[ANN] ELIZA. B. 5 May, 1815; C. 22 Aug. 1833; dis. 26 Jan., 1841, to 2d Ch.

Armstrong, Sarah; m. 19 Oct., 1752, to John O'Hara; m. 7 Nov., 1763, to Peter Dickerson.

Arnold, Abraham; m. 7 Nov., 1832, to Louise Goble; d. 30 Sept., 1842, aet. 35.

Arnold, Deborah M.; m. 17 Sept., 1834, to John S. Johnson.

Arnold, Elizabeth; m. 17 June, 1744, to Jonathan Reeve.

ARNOLD, EMMA ELIZABETH, dg. Silas Howell; B. & C. 5 Dec., 1880.

Arnold, Esther; m. 1 Feb., 1812, to Isaac Whitehead, of Chatham.

ARNOLD, FRANCES C., dg. Silas Howell; L. 31 May, 1876, fr, M. E. Ch.

ARNOLD, HARRIET J., dg, "   "   L.   "   "   "   "   "

{ Arnold, Col. Jacob, s. Samuel & Phebe (Ford); b. 14 Dec., 1749; d. 1 March, 1827.
ELIZABETH TUTHILL, dg. Samuel & Sarah; m. 1 Oct., 1770, R. C. 14 Dec., 1773; C. 3 May, 1782; d. 9 May, 1803, aet. 50.

[Sarah Nixon, b. 11 Oct., 1783; m. 26 Dec., 1807; d. "wid. Col. Jacob," 29 July, 1846.]

Hannah, b. 29 July, 1773; B. f. w. 14 Dec., 1773; [m. to Silas White Arnold?]

Samuel, b. 8 Aug., 1774; B. "   18 Sept. 1774.

Sarah, b. 7 Aug., 1776; B. "   6 Oct., 1776.

Gitty, b. 29 Nov., 1779; B. "   19 March, 1780; [m. to Jared Russell?]

Jacob, b. 21 Sept., 1781; B. "   29 Nov., 1781; d. 14 Jan., 1782.

Abraham Brasher, b. 29 March, 1783; B. f. w. 2 May, 1783; d. 1 Oct., 1801, aet. 18.

Jacob, b. 16 Sept., 1786; B. f. w. 5 April, 1787.

Charles, b. 29 Sept,, 1788; B. f. w. 19 June, 1789.

Eliza Maria, b. 2 Mar., 1792; B. "   3 July, 1792.

{ Arnold, John; R. C. 26 April, 1778; 12 Mar., 1790; d. 14 Dec., 1830, aet. 87.
{ Sarah ——   R. C. "   "   "   d. 1 Sept., 1838, aet. 90; [or 2d w. John d. this date?]

Cloe, b. 24 April, 1774; B. 26 April, 1778; [m. to Ebenezer Hathaway, of Hanover.]

SAMUEL, b. 6 Oct., 1782; B. 12 March, 1790; C. 21 Aug., 1803; d. 18 Jan., 1832, aet. 50.

Sarah, b. 5 Oct., 1785; B. "   "   "

Abigail, b. 30 Jan., 1789; B. "   "   "

Arnold, John; m. 21 June, 1795, to Hannah Eddy, [dg. James & Hannah?]

Arnold, John; m. 3 Nov. 1800, to Phebe Larey, of N. Y. State.

Arnold, Mary Ann; m. 13 Nov., 1833, to Samuel A. Loree.

ARNOLD, NANCY; C. 3 May, 1782; "moved away."

Arnold, Nathan [s. Robert]; m. 26 Feb., 1776, to Elizabeth Freeman, [dg. Daniel & Sarah]; d. 16 Aug., 1777, aet. 23.

Arnold, Phebe; m. 24 Dec., 1766, to Jonas Phillips.

ARNOLD, PHEBE PHILIPS, dg. wid. Sarah; B. & C. 7 June, 1829; m. 24 Feb., 1830, to Barnabas B. Thompson; "probably dis." 4

{ Arnold, Robard; d. 9 Dec., 1793, aet. 73.
{ Elizabeth —— d. 22 Dec., 1795, aet. 70.

Robard; B. f. w. 20 May, 1750; [m. to Mary Pierson, see below.]

REPORT*

OF THE

First Presbyterian Church, Morristown, N. J.,

FOR YEAR ENDING 7TH APRIL, 1884; TOGETHER WITH THE ROLL OF MEMBERS AND CONGREGATION.

THE REPORT.

Elders, 9.   Deacons, 2.

Communicants rec'd by Letter,		14
" " " Confirmation,	14	
" " " Baptism and Confirmation,	14	
" " on Examination,	28	
Total received in year,		42
Communicants on Roll, 7th April,		495
Baptisms of Adults,	14	
" " Infants,	14	
Total Baptisms,		28

Sunday school : Officers—15
"   "   Teachers—50
"   "   Scholars—395

" " Total,		460
" " Average Attendance,		270
" " Church Attend. of Scholars,		150
" " No. rec'd to Communion,		28
" " No. books in Library,		512
" " Am't. given to Boards,	$385.00	
" " Amt given to other objects,	195	
Total gifts,		580.00

Teacher's meetings are held; Shorter Catechism is taught; Westminster Helps are used ; 25 are members of the Bible Correspondence Class.

BENEFICENCE.

Home Missions,	-	$1,662.00
Ch. Col's. for Board,	$309.55	
" " " Miles City,	150.00	
" " " Synodical Extension,	100.00	
Woman's Mis. Soc.,	676.60	
Individual gifts,	310.00	
Children's Mis. Soc.,	115.85	

Education of Candidates for Ministry,		$391.54
Ch. Col. for Board,	$88.83	
" " " Bloomfield,	302.71	
Publication of Christian Literature,		590.54
Presbyterian Colportage,	$74.80	
Tract Society,	457.00	
Bible Society,	58.74	
Church Erection,	- -	190.59
Ch. Col. for Board,	95.59	
Ch. Col. for Morris Plains,	50.00	
Children's Miss. Soc.,	45.00	
Relief of Aged and Invalid Ministers,		137.90
Ch. Col. for Board,	77.90	
" " " Home,	50.00	
Individual gift,	10.00	
Missions to Freedmen,	- -	177.89
Ch. Col. for Board,	102.87	
Child'ns' Miss. Soc.,	75.00	
Sustentation : Ch. Col. for Board,	-	30.14
Miscellaneous,	- -	180.00
Total for Home Field,		3,360.58
Foreign Missions,	- -	1,694.50
Ch. Col. for Board,	$770.66	
Zenana Soc.,	405.00	
Children's Mis. Soc.,	510.00	
Stevenson Band,	8.84	
Total Beneficence,	-	5,055.08

EXPENSES.

General Assembly,	- -	59.50
Congregational,	- -	6,891.60
Current expenses,	$6,113.28	
Sunday school,	100.00	
Care of Poor,	224.03	
Miscellaneous,	454.29	
Total contributions,	-	12,006.18

THE ROLL.

It is scarcely to be hoped that this Roll is free from errors of omission and commission, altho much pains has been taken by the Session in order to make it as complete as possible. Grateful acknowledgment is made to the Rev. Dr. Green for the prodigious labor he gave, while pastor, in preparing the list of Communicants upon which the present Roll is based. So far as known

*[Supplement: Bind at end of volume IV.]

there has not been a publication of the living membership till now, since the Manual issued by Mr. Barnes in 1828. It is hoped that the present publication will provoke corrections, and so help to make the Roll complete.

As to *Communicants* the aim has been to present the names of all received from 1841 to the present time, who are not accounted for by dismission, death, or excommunication; together with those received before 1841 so far as they are known to be still living.

As to *Baptized members*, the Roll contains the names of all under the age of twenty-one, who appear upon the Register; the Christian names alone being printed in italics, and these indented, or set back from the margin, under those of their parents. It is the right of parents, received by letter, to have the names of their Baptized children put upon the Roll along with their own ; since Presbyterianism holds that the *family*, and not the individual, is the unit of the Church.

It will be esteemed a great favor if any one will send CORRECTIONS, OR INFORMATION, *especially concerning names upon the* RESERVED LIST *and those marked* "UNKNOWN" *among the absentees, to* Lock Box 90, Morristown, N. J.

Abbreviations used:
C.—became Communicant.
fr.—from.
L.—received by letter.
w.—wife of.
wid.—widow of.
{ —connects names of husband and
{ wife.

A

Aber, Susan Louise.	West. Ave.
Ancrum, Mrs.	Maple "
Anderson, Elizabeth, wid. Jas., Elm St.	
Anderson, Alice D.	" "
Arnold, Harriet J.	Wash. Val.
Arnold, Frances C.	" "
Arnold, Emma E.	" "
Axtel, Frances	Speedw'l Ave.

B

Babbitt, Caroline, wid. J. W., Wash. St.
Albert Albro
Babbitt, E. Emily, w. F. E., Morris St.
Joseph Woodman
Grace Amelia
Charles Andrews
Babbitt, Eliza, wid. Geo., Sussex Ave.
Babbitt, Gertrude D. " "
Babbitt, Ellen, wid. South St.
Babbitt, Sarah M.; w. L. D. " "
Baldwin, Wm. T. Speedw'l Ave.
Barmore, Annie S. " "

Beam, J. Maria, wid.
{ Becker, William, "Sr." Court St.
{ Becker, Susan M. " "
Becker, Fred. W. " "
Becker, Wm. H. " ".
Becker, Lily A. " "
{ Becker, William, "Jr." Church St.
{ Becker, Kate " "
Becker, Katrina " "
Beers, ——, w. Jno. H. Morris Plains
David S.
{ Beers, Wm. W. Wash. St.
{ Beers, Mary J. " "
Benjamin, Sarah J. Mill "
{ Berry, Joseph H. Wash. "
{ Berry, Elizabeth McDowell " "
John Henry
Anna Elizabeth
George Lindsley
Sadie Randolph
{ Bird, Charles S. Early St.
{ Bird, Maggie Woodhull " "
{ Bird, Joseph C. " "
{ Bird, Anna Doty " "
Blanchard, George W. Mt. Kemble
{ Blanchard, Joseph A., Olmsted's Mill
{ Blanchard, Anna Hays " "
Joseph Henry
Fred Anson
Minnie Catharine
Anna Briscoe
Bleything, Mary A. Maple Ave.
Bockhoven, Anna E. Sussex Ave.
Bockhoven, Joanna E. " "
Bockhoven, Sarah N. Mt. Kemble
{ Bohan, Richard Speedw'l Ave.
{ Bohan, Jane " "
{ Bonnell, John Y. Collinsville
{ Bonnell, Jane "
Bonnell, Lewis C. "
Born, Catharine L., w. B. F., Morris Pl's
Briant, Charles L. Wash. Val.
Briant, Elizabeth L. " "
{ Brink, David S. Wash. St.
{ Brink, Katy J. " "
Ella Melick
Brookfield, Cath. Acker, wid. M. A., South St.
Bunn, Anna Townley, wid. L. D., Speed'l Ave.
Burnett, Harriet A., wid. David Morris St.
Butterworth, S. A., w. Theron H., Sussex Ave.

C

Campbell, Charlotte T. DeHart St.
Campbell, Emma F. " "
Carithers, James New Vernon
Carpenter, Eliz'th Eakley, w. Wm., High St.
Caskey, Addie N. Early St.
{ Caskey, Enoch T. " "
{ Caskey, Mary Young " "
Mary Olivia
Jane Guild
Caskey, Robert C. " "

Caskey, Catharine Y.   Early St.
Caskey, Mary A.   "   "
Caskey, William C.   South St.
{ Cobbett, George   Mt. Kemble
{ Cobbett, Mary Potts   "   "
Coe, Penina, w. Oscar,   Wash. St.
Coe, Katy I.   "   "
Cole, Joanna Collins, w. F. P., Collins-
    ville
Cole, Phebe, w. Stephen   Collinsville
Colley, Eliz'th Nixon, w. Jno., Wash-
    ington St.
    John Frederick
    Mabel Pauline
Collins, Edward   Collinsville
Collins, Amelia Kranick, w. Sidney,
    Collinsville
Collins, Mary, w. Wm.   Collinsville
Collins, Hannah, w. Wm., Jr. Speed'lAve,
{ Combs, Charles B.   Water St.
{ Combs, Marian   "   "
Combs, Effie Lewis   "   "
Combs, Anna R.   "   "
Compton, David M.   Sussex Ave.
Conklin, Harriet Williams, wid., Olm-
    sted's Mill
Connett, Flora B.   Speed'l Ave.
Cook, Kate, w. Henry A.   Water St.
Cooper, Hester Prudden, wid. J. J.,
    High St.
Cooper, Myra   High St.
Cooper, Mary W., wid. Wm.   Ann St.
Cooper, Mary E.   "   "
Cory, AnnieFairchild, w. Henry, Early St.
{ Cory, Silas D.   Early St.
{ Cory, Sarah Freeman   "   "
Cory, Emma   "   "
{ Crane, Jacob   Speed'l Ave.
{ Crane, Helen Voorhees   "   "
Crane, Sarah P.   "   "
Crane, Clara Rosina   "   "
Cross, Lizzie   Court St.
Cutler, Adriana L.   Wash. St.

D

{ Dalrymple, Henry M.   Hill St.
{ Dalrymple, Frances Wheeler   "   "
    George Hull
Dalrymple, Emma H.   "   "
Dalrymple, Laura C.   "   "
Dana, E. Elizabeth   South St.
Darm, John   Green Village
Davenport, Charlotte T., w. Fred.,
Davis, Joel   Speed'l Ave.
Davis, Jacob J.   "   "
Davis, Horton J.   "   "
Ditmars, JessieVance, wid. J. R., Ridge-
    dale Ave.
Dix, Ophelia K., wid.   South St.
{ Doty, Joseph D.   Littleton.
{ Doty, Adaline Reynolds   "
Doty, Florence A.   "
Doty, Marietta A.   "
Drake, George W.   Morris St.
Drake, Mary A., w. Julius A., Wash. St.
Drake, Anna I.   "   "
Drake, George A.   "   "

Durant, Elizabeth S., w. Rev. Wm.,
    Franklin Pl.
    William Clark
{ Dustan, James C.   DeHart St.
{ Dustan, Sarah Lindsley   "   "
Dustan, Leonora   "   "

E

Eakley, Lucy   Ford Ave.
Eakley, Susan   "   "
Easton, Anna Dalrymple, w. Wm. J.,
    Court St.
Easton, Ella   Court St.
Easton, Fanny S.   "   "
Easton, Anna   "   "
Edwards, Lydia Roy, wid. Rev. Jas. C.,
    South St.
Eisenschmidt, Ida, w. Charles, Western
    Ave.
Eisenschmidt, Clara   West. Ave.
Emmell, Heyward G.   Speed'l Ave.

F

Fiske, Parnel C.   South St.
Fleury, Anna DeGroot, w. Geo. W.,
    Speed'l Ave.
Fleury, Edward A.   Speed'l Ave.
Fleury, Anna VanD.   "   "
{ Fleury, Victor   "   "
{ Fleury, Hannah Whitehead   "   "
Force, Eunice Hedges, wid. David,
    Kitchell Ave.
Force, Isabella   Kitchell Ave.
{ Forsyth, George W.   South St.
{ Forsyth, Catharine Brookfield "   "
    Alfred Brookfield
    Marian Isabel
Foy, Anna E.   Mt. Kemble
Fredericks, Charles T.   Water St.
    Martha Ann
    Charles Theodore
    Mahlon Pitney
Freeman, S. Jane   Early St.

G

Gibbs, Matilda L.   Sussex Ave.
Gillam, Edith Eisenschmidt, w. L. J.,
    Mt. Kemble
Goble, Margaret M.   Speed'l Ave.
Graham, Jane, wid.   Maple "
Green, Cassie Mills, w. Wm. H., Mt.
    Kemble
Guerin, Susan A., w. Jas.Ridgedale Ave.
Guild, Mary Jane   Early St.

H

{ Halliday, William S.   Convent Sta.
{ Halliday, Mary Pierson   "   "
{ Halsted, William A.   Maple Ave.
{ Halsted, Mary Freeman   "   "
Halsted, Charles F.   "   "
Hand, Hannah L.   Speed'l "
Headley, Helen T., wid. J. B., M'ple "
    Helen Thomas
Hegeman, Electa Talks, w. Jno., Cut-
    ler St.
    Augustus
    William Talks
Hockenbery, Mary Babbitt, wid. R. M.,
    Early St.

P

Parrott, Ruth Canfield, w. Jno. T., Morris Plains.
Peck, Sarah R., w. Dr. E. O., Morris St.
Jeannie Mary
Grace Emily
Peck, Theodore D. " "
Peppard, Laura A. Ann St.
Phelps, Mary Z., wid. Geo.W., Water St.
Phelps, Abigail, " "
} Pierson, Edward South St.
} Pierson, Anna Sayre " "
Pierson, Phil. B. " "
Pierson, Laura A. " "
} Pierson, Geo. W. Speed'l. Ave.
} Pierson, Ellen " "
} Pierson, James S. Mendham Ave.
} Pierson, Catharine H. " "
Pierson, Edith A. " "
Pierson, Milton J. " "
} Pierson, Lemel E. Wash. St.
} Pierson, Jane Quimby " "
Nettie Reeve
Stephen Ellsworth
Joseph Johnson
Floyd
} Pierson, Lewis South St.
} Pierson, Nancy Guerin " "
Pierson, Abby A. " "
Pierson, Julia E. " "
Pierson, Ella A. " "
} Pierson, Samuel F. Mendham Ave.
} Pierson, Mary " "
Pierson, Clara J. " "
Pierson, Anna L. " "
Pierson, Eugene " "
Pierson, Arthur S. " "
} Pierson, Dr. Stephen " "
} Pierson Amelia Cory " "
Pitney, Sarah Halsted, w. H. C., Maple Ave.
Frederic Vernon
Pitney, Henry C., Jr. Maple Ave.
Pitney, Mahlon " "
Pitney, John O. " "
Pitney Catharine J. " "
Pitney, Mary B. " "
Platt Anna M. wid. West. Ave.
} Platt, Prof. Charles D. " "
} Platt, Mary J. " "
} Polk, James K. Ann St.
} Polk, Mary A. " "
Irene Priscilla
James K., Jr.
Potts, Maria. wid. Ann St.
Potts, Ella V. " "
Potts, Henry " "
{ Powelson, Abraham C., Speed'l. Ave.
{ Powelson, Caroline Compton, "
Rosella " "
Powelson, Evalina " "
Powers, Irene A. " "
Price, Adelia Maple Ave.
Price, Rebecca " "
} Prudden, Cyrus Mt. Kemble.
} Prudden, Martha D. " "
Prudden, Laura H. " "

} Prudden Henry H. Mt. Kemble.
} Prudden Caroline C. " "
Prudden, Lydia A. " "
Prudden, David I. " "
Prudden Henry L. " "
Prudden. Mary C. " "
Prudden, Emma R. " "
Prudden, Lydia, wid. Stephen A., Mt. Kemble.
Prudden, William C. Morris St.

R

Reeve, Ella Johnson, w. Fred. South St.
Renegar, Annie Wash. Val.
Ritter, Annie Mills St.
Robinson Emma H. Maple Ave.
Robinson, Julia " "
Robinson, Phebe " "
Roelofson, A. Elizabeth " "
Roelofson, Mary A. " "
Roff, Phebe Speed'l Ave.
} Roff, Charles Wash. Val.
} Roff, Lovina " "
Rowe, Anna V. Speed'l Ave.
Roy, Elizabeth S. South St.
Roy, Mary E. " "
Runyon, John R. Maple Ave.

S

} Sayre, Theodore Wash. Val.
} Sayre, Mary Whitehead " "
Sayre, Anna P. " "
Sayre, Fanny L. " "
Schmidt, Maria, wid. Speed'l Ave.
Scott, Truman H. South St.
Shafer, Bertha Speed'l Ave.
} Shute, Bishop Morris St.
} Shute, Rhoda " "
Stevenson, Ellen D., wid. Dr. R. W., Maple Ave.
Stevenson, Louisa Maple Ave.
Stevenson, Mary G. " "
Stevenson, Kate S. " "
} Stiles, James E. B. Wash. St.
} Stiles, Ruhamah " "
} Stiles, James E. " "
} Stiles, Letitia K. " "
Leila Blanche
Stiles, Phebe E. Morris Plains.
Stites,Elizabeth C.,wid.Rich.W., ElmSt.
Stites, Maria L., w. Rich. M. " "
Stone, William W. Franklin Place.
Stone, Susan " "
Stone, Augusta " "
Stone, Frances " "
Stone, Cornelia " "
Stone, Isabel " "
Struble, Ida Earl, w. Wm. H., Flagler St.
Mary Elizabeth
Anna Augusta
William Henry
George Washington
Mildred Irene

T

} Tharp, Moses Morris St.
} Tharp, Eliza " "
Todd, Mary Roff, wid. Stephen, Speed'l Ave.

Trowbridge, Silas C.   James St·
} Trowbridge, Joseph   Lake Road.
} Trowbridge, Mary J.   "   "

U

} Udall, George   Ridgedale Ave.
} Udall, ——   "   "
    John
    Harrie
Udall, Fanny O.   "   "
Udall, George, Jr.   "   "
Udall, Minnie   "   "
Udall, Emma E.   "   "
} Uebelacker, Dr. A.   South St.
} Uebelacker, Mary C.   "   "
Uebelacker, Charles F.   "   "

V

Vail, Electa   Madison St.
} VanDoren, Joseph H.   Prospect St.
} VanDoren, Elizabeth Fleury, Prospect St.
VanDoren, William C.   Prospect St.
VanDoren, Mary   "   "
VanHouton, James C.   Morris Plains.
VanHouton, Elizabeth   "   "
VanPelt,SarahE.,wid.Isaac,Speed'l Ave.
VanPelt, S. Elizabeth   "   "
VanPelt, Amos F.   "   "
VanPelt, Emma H.   "   "
Voorhees, Frances Babbitt, w. A. E.,
    U. S. Hotel.
} Voorhees, George E.   Prospect St.
} Voorhees, Gertrude Ditmars, "   "
    George Emmell
    Gitty Remsen
    Mary Marguerite
Voorhees, James D.   Prospect St.
Voorhees, Cornelia E.   "   "
Voorhees, James R.   Wash. St.

W

} Ward, Lebbeus B.   Elm St.
} Ward, Elizabeth Starr,   "   "
Warnemunde, Henry   Speed'l Ave.
Weir, Emily Carland,w.Edw.,West.Ave.
Weir, Dora Smith, w. Wilmot D., Collinsville.
} Whitehead, Aaron D.   Wash. Val.
} Whitehead Harriet E.   "   "
    Mary H.
Whitehead, Charles   "   "
Whitehead, Sarah C.   "   "
Whitehead, Alphonse   Speed'l Ave.
Whitehead, Hannah F.   "   "
} Whitehead, Francis L.   Ann St.
} Whitehead, Caroline DeGroot, "   "
    Sarah Pierson
    Carrie Louisa
    Rufus Green
    William Fleury
Whitehead, M. Helen   "   "
} Whitehead, Isaac N.   Wash. Val.
} Whitehead, Mary L.   "   "
Whitehead, Abby L.   "   "
} Whitehead, John   High St.
} Whitehead, Catharine Mills "   "
Whitehead, Kate   "   "

Whitehead, Sylvester R.   Wash. Val.
Wilde, Eliza   "   "
Willis, Martha C., w. Ira C.   Hill St.
Willis, Elizabeth D.   "   "
Wilson,Jane Pierson, wid., Mechanic St.
    Lewis Pierson
Wilson, Mrs. L. H.   South St.
Woodhull, Maggie K.w. M. H., Court St.
Woodhull, Fanny E.   " . "

Y

Yawger, Evaline B. wid. Elias, South St.
Youngblood, Hattie C.   Perry St
Youngblood, James C.   "   "

ABSENTEES.

The following members are now absent, but frequent communication is had with most of them. Those who have taken permanent residence abroad are affectionately urged to apply for letters, that they may be enrolled in the churches where they reside. See the rules quoted below, under " Reserved List".

Baker, Looe ; Savannah, Ga.
Bennett, Miss S. E.; Ward's Island, N. Y.
Boss, Charles ; Stanhope.
} Burnett, S. Crane ; Harlem, N. Y.
} Burnett, Sarah N. ;   "   "
Burnett, Wm. H. ; 70 Passaic St., Newark.
Byram, Anna Guerin, w. Geo. ; Succasunna.
Castillon, Margaret S. ; Cognac,France.
Church, Wm. E. ; Deadwood, Dakota.
    Helen
Condict, Silas B.; Summit.
Conklin, Lydia Day, w. Jos. O. ; Chatham.
Conlon, Carrie Nixon, w. Rich.; Dover.
Conover,Hattie D.; Middleburgh, N. Y.
Cooper, Mary E.; Deadwood, Dakota ?
Cooper, Anna I.; Dover ?
Cooper, Silas B. ; New York City.
} Cooper, Wm. J. ; Ocean Grove.
} Cooper, Mary E.   "   "
    Agnes Jackson
Corkill, Ellen ; married, and lives here ?
Crane, Julia R. ; Newark.
DeCamp, Alfred ; Nova Scotia.
DeCamp, Edward ;   "   "
DeCamp, Clarence ; Powerville.
DeCamp, Mary A. ;   "
DeCamp, Susan ;   "
Dix, Walter S. ; Hoboken.
Drake, Ada A. ; unknown.
Drake Mary A.;   "
Duryea, Lillian ; New York City.
} Dwight, Jonathan ; unknown.
} Dwight, Julia H. ;   "   "
Field, Lillian Townley, w. Aug. K. ; Newark.
Finnblad, Clara C.; unknown.

Finnblad, Louisa A. ; unknown.
{ Guerin, Josephus S. ; Mendham.
{ Guerin, Pheba A. ;   "
   Elizabeth L.
Hankinson, Samantha ; unknown.
Hathaway, Delia A., w. Wm. ; New
   Vernon.
Hathaway, Martha ; married ? where ?
Hoagland, Lillian E. ; Gravesend, L. I.
Hopkins, George ; China.
Hopkins, Wm. B.;   "
Kofler, Leo ; Brooklyn.
Langmuir, Margaret B. ; unknown.
{ Lee, Joseph M. ; Summit.
{ Lee, Charlotte C. ;   "
Lee, Regnold ; Devils Lake, Dakota.
Marsh,Kate Yawger,w. Geo.; Brooklyn.
   Ellen Crater
{ Merritt, William ; Orange.
{ Merritt, Emma ;   "
Moore, Eliza J., wid. Wm. L. ; unknown.
Nixon, Susan V. ; Dover.
Norrie, Mary, wid. Wm.'; unknown.
Peer, Frances Bird, w. Solomon , Leo-
   nidas, Mich.
Renegar, Theresa ; Ocean Grove ?
Renegar, Victoria ;   "   "
Requa, Austin, Jr. ; San' Francisco.
Rickenbach, Sibelle ; unknown.
Shafer, Margaretta ;
{ Smith, George C. ; Columbia, Ga.
{ Smith, Elizabeth ;   "   "
{ Spaulding, Wayland ; New Haven,Ct.
{ Spaulding, Mary P. ;   "   "   "
   Leila Clement
Stevenson, Philippe ; San Antonio,
   Tex.
Thompson, John L. ; Wash., D. C.
{ Tompkins, Silas P. ; Dover.
{ Tompkins, Anna W.   "
{ Tunis, Wm. L. ; Raritan.
{ Tunis, Mary A. ;   "
Van Pelt, Marianne ; New Haven, Ct.
Yawger, Anna E., wid. Daniel ; Newark.
Yawger, Mary A., wid. ; Chester.
Resident, Bapt'd 73 ; Communic'ts, 423
Absent,   "   5 ;   "   72
Total,   "   78 ;   "   495

RESERVED LIST.

The General Assembly of 1872 recommended "each church to record, on a
separate list, the names of those who
have been absent for more than two
years from their church relations, and
whose residence is unknown ; and
names thus recorded may be omitted
in the statistical returns of the church."
In case the Revised Book of Discipline
shall be adopted by the Presbyteries
this year, the following rule will be in
force after June 1st : "If a communicant, not chargeable with immoral conduct, removes out of the bounds of his
Church, without asking for or receiving a regular certificate of dismission
to another Church, and his residence is
known, the Session may, within two
years, advise him to ,apply for such
certificate ; and, if he fails so to do,
without giving sufficient reason, his
name may be placed on the roll of suspended members, until he shall satisfy
the Session of the propriety of his restoration. But, if the Session has no
knowledge of him for the space of
three years, it may erase his name
from the roll of communicants, making
record of its action and the reasons
therefor. In either case, the member
shall be subject to the jurisdiction of
the Session. A separate roll of all such
names shall be kept, stating the relations of each to the Church."
Walter Ambuhl ; C. 1875.
John Armstrong ; L. 1871, fr. Madison.
Alvira Armstrong, w. Jno. ; L. 1871, fr.
   Madison.
Margaret Armstrong, dg. Jno. ; L. 1871,
   fr. Madison.
Susan Bayard ; C. 1856.
Mrs. S. C. Bartlett ; L. 1871, fr. Wysox,
   Pa.
Mrs. Jane Brant ; L. 1860, fr. Chatham.
E. V. Josephine Bunting ; L, 1881, fr.
   LaFayette, N. J.
Lydia Chamberlain, w. Henry ; L. 1852,
   fr. Newark.
Alice Crampton ; C. 1866.
Laura J. Crane (or Crone ?) ; C. 1856 ;
   married about 1867 to——Loree ?
Catharine W. Cree ; C. 1876.
Margaretta Davenport ; L. 1846, fr. New
   Foundland, N. J.
Margaret Doremus ; C. 1876.
Ann Louisa Fairchild ; C. 1842 ; did she
   marry John Taylor 1843 ?
Eva L. Fordyce ; L. 1876, fr. Rockaway.
Oliver S. Freeman ; L. 1869, fr. Dover.
Leila A. Gillam ; C. 1873.
Elizabeth Gustin, wid. ; L. 1841, fr.
   Hardwicke.
Anna Hammell ; C. 1874.
Thomas J. Harrison ; C. 1874.
Annie Heffern ; C. 1876.
Edward Irwin ; C. 1858.
Nancy Irwin, w. Edw. ; C. 1858.
Bridget Landon ; C. 1856.
Annie M. Lawrence ; C. 1873.
Louisa M. Leech ; L, 1864, fr. Orange.
Harriet E. Leonard ; C. 1862.
Elizabeth M. Lewis, w.Wm. L.; C. 1858.
Mrs. Eliza Lindsley ; L. 1876, fr. Chat-
   ham.

Sophia Mackid ; L. 1858, fr. Canada.
Jane Maria Martin, (colored) ; C. 1851.
Eliza Miller, L. 1872, fr. Newark.
Mary Miller, wid. ; L. 1845, fr. West Somers.
Elias Pierson Mount ; C. 1843.
Isabella McCord ; L. 1870, fr. N. Y. City.
Jenny E. McDermott ; C. 1875.
Margaret McDonald ; C. 1876.
Elizabeth Pemberton ; C. 1855.
Nelson A. Rankin ; L. 1865, fr. Mendham.
Frances Rittenhouse ; L. 1851, fr. Hackettstown.
Sarah Margaret Roy ; C. 1843.
Charles Stewart ; L. 1879, fr. Raritan.
John H. Tunison ; C. 1872.
Anna Van Doren (colored); L. 1863, fr. Hackettstown.
Luther G. Van Vliet ; L, 1879, fr. Washington, N. J.
Sarah Voorhees ; L. 1853, fr. Pleasant Grove.
Sarah Voorhees ; L. 1866, fr. Mendham.
Phebe A. Ward, wid. Wm. B.; L. 1858, fr. German Valley ; now wid. of Thos. F. Willoughby ?
George G. Wagner ; C. 1871.
Elizabeth Wilkins ; C. 1874.
Henry R. Williams ; C. 1861.

THE CONGREGATION.

In addition to the Baptized and Communicant members. the following have been attendants and contributors to this Church during the year ; many of them being enrolled as communicants in other churches :

Anderson, Wm. H.	Mendham Ave.
Anderson, Gitty	" "
Arnold, Silas H.	Wash. Val.
Arnold, William	" "
Arnold, Edward	" "
Babbitt, Fred. E.	Morris St.
Babbitt, L. D.	South "
Baird Maggie J.	Mt. Kemble.
Becker, W. Edward	North Side Park.
Bell, A. W.	Church St.
Bell, Mrs. A. W.	" "
Benjamin, Lewis	Mill "
Bockhoven, Harvey	Mt. Kemble.
Breese. Stephen	
Burroughs, L. C.	Wash. Val.
Burroughs, Mrs. L. C.	" "
Burroughs, Mary	" "
Burroughs, Ferman	" "
Bushnell, Joseph	Maple Ave.
Bushnell, Thomas C.	" "
Butterworth, Theron	Sussex Ave.
Butterworth, Addie	" "
Butterworth, Alexander	" "

Conklin, Rev. Nathaniel,	Convent Sta.
Conklin, Mrs. Nath'l	" "
Conklin, Wm. B.	Convent Sta.
Conklin, Edward	" "
Conklin, Archibald	" "
Conklin, Kate	" "
Conklin, Annie	" "
Cooper, Mrs. M. E.	Maple Ave.
Croll, Mrs. Eliz'th	"
Darcy, Mrs. Mary	Maple Ave.
Davis, Louis	Collinsville.
Davis, Mrs. Louis	"
Day, Henry	Sussex Ave.
Drake, Julius A.	Wash. St.
Drake, Mrs. Geo. W.	Morris St.
Erwin James	Mendham Ave.
Fairchild, Mrs. E. R.	Maple Ave.
Freeman, P. A.	Early St.
Freeman, Harrie	"
Freeman, John	"
Freeman, F. S.	Franklyn Pl.
Freeman, Robert	"
Freeman, Harrie A.	Maple Ave.
Gillespie, David	South St.
Gillespie, Mrs.	" "
Green, William H.	Mt. Kemble.
Hendershot, Maggie	Morris St.
Howell, Wm. H.	Wash.Ave.
Howell, Mrs. Wm. H.	" "
Hurlbut, F. M.	Franklin St.
Hurlbut, Martha S., w. F. M.	" "
Hyatt, J. Smith	Maple Ave.
Hyatt, Mrs. J. S.	" "
Hyatt, Viola	" "
Hyatt, Anna	" "
Hyatt, Bertha	" "
Hyatt, Nettie	" "
Jennings, Miss	Morris St.
Lane, Cornelius	Western Ave.
Leek, Daniel H.	Wash. St.
Leek, Mrs. D. H.	" "
Lockwood, Charles	
Lord, Mrs. J. Couper	Sussex Ave.
Lord, James B.	New York.
Lord, Scott	"
Loree, Mary E.	Early St.
Lyman, Mrs.	
Macknett, Theodore	Madison Ave.
Martelle. Celia	Phœnix Ave.
Marvin, Parmelia	Early St.
Miller, Phœnix,	West. Ave.
Muir, Charles	Monroe.
Muir, Miss	Morris St.
Mumby, Laura	James St.
Peck, Dr. E. O.	Morris St.
Pitney, Henry C.	Maple Ave.
Reasoner, Andrew	Elm St.
Sanborn, Mr.	Maple Ave.
Skellenger. Anna	Court St.
Smith, Fred.	Wash. Val.
Thompson, Wm. L.	Wash. Val.
VanGiesen, Albert	Mt. Kemble.
Voorhees, A. E.	U. S. Hotel.
Willis, Ira C.	Hill St.
Yawger, Fred.	Mt. Kemble Ave.
Yawger, Minnie	" "

THE RECORD.

FIRST PRESBYTERIAN CHURCH, MORRISTOWN, N. J.

"This Shall be Written for the Generation to Come."—Psalms 102 : 18.

| VOLUME V. | · | JANUARY, 1885. | NUMBER 25. |

[Printed with the Approval of the Session.]

THE RECORD

Is published monthly; terms $1 00 a·year, *in advance.*
— It will probably be completed with Dec., 1885; the Minutes being brought down to 1882.

Single numbers for any month, 10 cents each.

Subscriptions should be made to Mr. James R Voorhees.

Matters pertaining to the publication should be addressed to the

 EDITOR OF THE RECORD.

Entered at the Post Office at Morristown, N. J., as second class matter.

CORRECTIONS AND ADDITIONS.

Communications are earnestly solicited for this column. Address, Lock Box 90, Morristown, N. J.

Page 203 of Sup. for Mar. 1883:
July 5, 1806; Rev. James Richards, ch. Edward Cowles (not Coures.)
Page 202 of Sup. for Mar., 1883:
Feb. 24, 1805; Amos Ward's child is the only one in this column which was baptized " by Rev. Mr. Finley."
Oct. 21, 1804; John Day (not Dayton.)
" 7, " Loammi Moore's ch. Susan Mariah was born Jan. (not July.)
Page 201 of Sup. for Mar., 1883:
Mar. 4, 1802; omit "by Mr. Aaron Condict ;" he baptized only Mr. Richard's child, on 21st.
Dec. 2, 1802; Jeptha Wade's child was Kezia *Allen.*
Sept. 26, 1802 ; should be Oct. 11.
Page 200 of Sup. Feb., 1883:
Dec. 13, 1801 ; J. P. Bollin (not H. P. Bollin.)
Sept. 12, 1801 ; should be Oct. 12.
Page 199 of Sup. for Feb., 1883:
June 8, 1800 ; Benj. Holloway, dg. (not ch.) Julian.
Aug. 30, 1799 ; Wm. Lee, on wife's accts, Henry Perine (not Perin.)
July 28, 1799; Wm. Stiles' child Eliza was born Feb. 1st.
" 1, 1798 ; Benj. Holloway, ch Seth (not Lott.)

Continued from page 142.

REVIVALS IN THE CHURCH :
BY THE
REV. DAVID IRVING, D. D.,

I ask you, in view of this large number, and of a past teeming with mercies, could we justly do less than we have done for a building fragrant with covenant blessings, and to which are attached some of the tenderest associations. All that has been done was demanded by the taste of the times, and it is in harmony with the true grandeur and dignity of public worship. The first Church that was erected stood over fifty years, and in that time was enlarged. The present Church was completed 64 years ago and was repaired and altered, in the manner known to us all, some 19 years ago. But for some time the Church showed signs of neglect, which strangers especially noticed; and when they saw the neatness and beauty of our own dwellings, they justly said, "Is it for you, O ye, to dwell in your ceiled houses, and this house lie waste?" The necesssity of some improvement pressed with increasing weight upon us, so that five months ago repairs were commenced, which have occupied the thoughts, efforts and time of the committee to whom the work was entrusted, and in the completion of which we are this day permitted to rejoice. And herein their name and my own, we thank you for the cheerfulness with which you have contributed of your substance to carry on the undertaking ; for the encouragement extended ; and for the noble manner in which, as a society, you have come forward and extinguished the debt. Happy, very happy, am I to announce that, though more than double of the amount originally intended to be expended on the Church has been required, with a generosity worthy of all praise, and with a generous rivalry on the part of most to do what they could, you have either given or subscribed the sum needed ; so that

I am authorized to announce that no debt remains to disturb our devotions, to paralyze our efforts in behalf of a perishing world, or to restrain the outgoings of love to the Best of all beings. And, whilst we regard the past as a pledge of your readiness to do what is required, to maintain the ordinances of the Church ; let me tell you, for your encouragement, that no man will be haunted with terror, and troubled on his dying bed, for the sums contributed for the support of religious institutions.

And here let me thank those who, without my solicitation, have reared and furnished this beautiful pulpit; and those young men who by their own efforts have placed on it this massive and elegant Bible and hymn book,—may its truths find a lodgement in your souls, form principles that shall render your lives full of usefulness and happiness, gild your whole future, and introduce you at last into the presence of that Saviour, who gave himself and his word to save, illumine, and purify sinners like you, that being taught of Jesus here and hymning his praises, we may blend our voices in the sweetest harmony, in that temple not made with hands, singing the song of Moses and the Lamb.

The whole interior has been changed. We see it in a new dress,—alike comfortable without distinction to every worshipper, and yet it is the same dear old building still. "May the glory of the latter house be greater than the former." That glory has been shadowed forth to-day. It was not in any outward splendor, or any architectural display; but in the wonderous manifestation of Jehovah's converting and sanctifying power. Its glory has been, that in refreshing times every pew has been filled with a listening and interested audience ; and at other times the thoughtless have been awakened, and brought to the cross. Its glory has been, that in the past it has done more than everything else to mould public opinion, and to create a healthy moral tone in the community. Its glory has been to send forth her sons and daughters through the length and breadth of our land, to enrich and influence other places by the truths here inculcated and received. And its glory has been to stand up for Je-

sus, and to give due attention to the benevolent movements that are blessing our earth.

And, in closing, let me remind you that something more is wanting than a stately building and the impulsive utterances of admiration. All that is now seen and prized will in no way render our services acceptable, fill this Church with the presence of Jesus, and you with the graces of his Spirit, unless the glory of the Lord irradiates it ; its lofty spire, its decorated ceiling, and the varied displays of comfort and taste, will all be in vain. God must be here ; the Saviour must be here ; the Holy Ghost must be here, to make it the gate of heaven. Here oft repair ; here be regularly found as devout worshippers, and with hearts glowing with love rejoice in purchased blessings. And now, standing as a link between the past and the future, with the memories of other days crowding on us, with the rich legacy bequeathed by our fathers, and coming under the influence and prestige of scenes the most hallowed, and with hearts swelling with gratitude and praise, let us now make an offering of all that has been done and given to Jehovah Jesus, asking him to cause his face to shine upon us and to be gracious to us ; asking him to give us more of his Spirit, that we may oft sit with him in heavenly places, reflect in holy deportment the beauty of his holiness, the constraining power of his love and the transforming energy of his truth ; that the Spirit of Pentecost may sway and melt many future assemblies, and that through these aisles the loud triumph of Messiah's mighty conquests may be chanted in increasing volumes.

Whilst appreciating the solemnity of the occasion, let us now renew our prayers that God would fill this house with new and brighter glories, that it may be the birthplace of new born souls, and that from it an increasing moral power may go forth to make glad the city of our God ; so that when the house shall have disappeared, and time shall have consumed the labors of our hands, we shall be found in the heavenly sanctuary, forever adoring the hand that formed it, the grace that led us to it, and the Saviour who is the light and glory of it. Amen and amen.

(Continued from page 144.)

COMBINED REGISTERS ; 1742 to 1884.

For meaning of abbreviations see page 135 of THE RECORD for October, 1884.

It will be esteemed a great favor if the readers of THE RECORD *will send* CORRECTIONS, *or additional* INFORMATION, *to* Lock Box 90, Morristown, N. J,

————:o:————

Elizabeth ; B. f. w. 24 Sept., 1752 ; [m. to Jacob Whitehead.]

Nathan ; b. 17 Aug., 1754; B. 22 Sept., 1754 ; [m. to Elizabeth Freeman.]

Ziba, b. 12 Nov., 1756 ; B. 16 Jan., 1757 ; [m. Mary——? see below.]

Silvanus, b. 21 Sept., 1758 ; B. 29 Oct., 1758 ; [m. Phebe ———, see below.]

Betse, b. 1 April, 1761 ; B. 3 March, 1761.

Sarah, b. 24 Dec., 1763; B. 4   "   1764.

David, b. 18 March, 1766 ; B. 20 April, 1766.

Hannah, b. 24 Dec., 1767 ; B. 10 April, 1768.

Catherine, "g' child of Elizabeth"; b. 13 Jan., 1783 ; B. 20 Aug., 1786.

{ *Arnold, Robart,* [s. Robard & Elizabeth ;] R. C. 30 March, 1786.

{ MARY PIERSON [dg. Joseph ?]; m. 26 May, 1771 ; R. C. 30 March, 1786 ; C. 26 April, 1813 ; d. 16 Mar., 1823, aet. 75.

Hannah, b. 21 Nov. 1771 ; B. 30 March, 1786.

Abraham, b. 15 Oct., 1776 ; B. 30   "   "

Elizabeth. b. 2 May, 1782 ; B. 30   "   "   [d. 23 Sept., 1834, aet. 50.]

Nathan, b. 9 Sept., 1784 ; B. 30   "   "   [m. 20 July, 1806, to Huldah Mills.]

Phebe, b. 7 May, 1787 ; B. 10 June, 1787.

Mary Pierson, b. 15 Nov., 1789 ; B. 17 Jan., 1790 ; [m, to Nathan Mills, 26 Oct., 1811.]

{ *Arnold, Samuel*; B. adult, 24 Feb., 1754 ; d. 3 Oct., 1764, aet. 38.

{ *Phebe Ford*; m. 16 Oct., 1748 ; R. C. 24 Feb., 1754.

Jacob ; B. 24 Feb., 1754 ; [m. to Elizabeth Tuthill, see above.]

John, b. 19 Nov., 1752 ; B. 24 Feb., 1754 ; d. 14 Dec., 1756.

Hannah, b. 22 July, 1754 ; B. 25 Aug., 1754 ; d. 3 June, 1755.

Samuel, b. 8 July, 1757 ; B. 24 July, 1757 ; d. 23 Nov. 1760.

PHEBE; B. 24 Oct., 1760 , [m. to John Kenny, q. v.]

Anne ; B. 27 March, 1763 ; [m. to George Tucker, q. v.]

Arnold, Samuel ; d. 1817 ; [s. Col. Jacob ? Sam'l ? or Ziba ?]

Arnold, Sarah ; d. 2 Aug., 1778, aet. 33 ; [1st w. John ?]

Arnold, Sarah ; m. 9 Dec., 1800, to Abraham Richards, of N. Y.

ARNOLD, SARAH, w.   L. 28 April, 1815, fr. Newark ; dis. 26 Jan. 1841, to 2d Ch.

ARNOLD, SILAS HOWELL, s. wid. Sarah ; B. & C. 7 June, 1829; m. 9 Oct.. 1837, to Martha L. Pierson.

Arnold, Silas White ; m. 13 Nov., 1792, to Hannah Arnold.

{ Arnold, Silvanus, [s. Robard] ; d. 2 April, 1796, aet. 38.

{ PHEBE ——— L. about 1782.

Anne ; B. 29 Sept., 1782.

Joanna ; b. 17 May, 1784 ; B. f. w. 2 July, 1784 ; d. 26 Dec., 1785.

Lewis, b. 15 Feb., 1786 ; B. " 17 Sept., 1786.

Stephen Harrison, b. 4 Oct., 1788 ; B. f. w. 4 Jan., 1789.

Isaac, b. 5 April, 1791 ; B. f. w., 3 July, 1791.

Lydia, b. 9 Oct.. 1795 ; B. f. w. 10 March, 1796 ; d. 15 May, 1796.

{ Arnold, Stephen ; d. 1754, (letters of administration granted to his wife 16 Feb, 1754).

{ Rachel ——— d. 16 June, 1786, aet. 98.

{ ARNOLD, STEPHEN [s Stephen & Rachel]; C. 6 Jan., 1765 ; moved away."

{ PHEBE GUERIN; m. 24 Jan., 1770 ; B. & C. 3 May, 1771 ; "moved."

Ezekiel, b. 19 Dec., 1770; B. 3 May, 1771 ; d. 15 Jan., 1773. aet. 2.

Elizabeth, b. 14 Feb., 1772; B. 15 March, 1772; d. 14 Jan., 1773. aet. 1.

Naomi, b. 13 Oct., 1773 ; B. 21 Nov., 1773; [d. 17 June, 1777.]

Phebe, b. 24 Sept., 1775 ; B. 29 Oct., 1775 ; [d. 20 Dec., 1775.]

Jacob, b. 14 Jan., 1778 ; B. 3 May, 1778.

Thomas. b. 29 Nov., 1779 ; B. 30 Jan., 1780.

Sarah, b. 5 April, 1781 . B. 12 June, 1781.

Susanna. b. 15 April, 1783 ; B. 8 Feb., 1784.

Hannah, b. 26 March, 1785 . B. 26 June, 1785.

Stephen, b. 23 Sept., 1789 ; B. 23 Jan., 1791.

} Arnold, Ziba [s. Robard.]
} MARY ——— C 2 July, 1785; d. 30 April, 1791, aet. 38.

Elizabeth, b. 30 July, 1771 ; B. f. w. 2 July, 1785.

Samuel, b. 20 April, 1775 ; B. " " " "

Mary, b. 11 April, 1778 ; B. " " " " [m. to Joshua Guering, of Somerset Co.]

RACHEL. b. 18 Dec., 1780 ; B. f. w. 2 July, 1785 ; C. 16 Dec., 1796; [m. to Jonas Alwood, q. v.]

Robert
Jonathan Reeve } b. 2 July, 1787 ; B. f. w. 19 Aug., 1787.

Joanna } b. 13 Nov., 1790 ; B. f. w. 28 Feb., 1791.
Gitty

Ashback, George ; m. 22 March, 1832, to Susan Gillem.

} Austin ("Arstin"), Cornelius
} MARTHA ——— M. in 1742 ; "moved away."

Peter ; B. 15 April, 1744.

Austin, Deborah ; m. 1 April, 1756, to Benjamin Bailey, Jr.

} AUSTIN, JONAH ; M. in 1742 ; "moved.'
} ——— w. Jonah ; M. " " "

Moses ; B. 28 Aug., 1743.

Mary ; B. 7 Oct., 1744.

Jesse ; B. 12 July, 1747.

Axtell, in earlier records Extel.

Axtell, Amzi ; m. 3 April, 1830, to Mary Nixon.

Axtell, Bethany, [sister Major Henry] ; m. 21 Jan., 1767, to Artemas Day, of Mendham.

} *Axtell, Calvin* ; R. C. 18 July, 1773.
} *Mary Mills*, [dg. Timothy & Phebe], m. 7 Nov., 1771 ; R. C. 18 July, 1773,

TIMOTHY, b. 11 Sept., 1772; B 18 July, 1773 ; C. 19 Dec., 1803 ; "moved."

Ann, b. 29 Sept., 1774 ; B. 6 Nov., 1774.

Philip Lindsley, b. 3 Dec., 1779 ; B. 9 July, 1780.

Axtell, Daniel, of Mendham ; m. 8 Oct., 1770, to Ruth Tuttle.

AXTELL, FRANCES ; C. 6 March, 1858.

Axtell, Hannah ; m. 29 May, 1764, to Zepheniah Burt.

} Axtell, Henry ; " Major Henry" d. 6 April, 1818. aet. 80.
} Phebe Day, [dg. Capt. Samuel] ; m. 7 Jan.' 1767 ; d. 6 July, 1829. aet. 89.

{ AXTELL, HENRY ;L. 9 Nov., 1836, fr. Mendham ; dis. 26 Jan., 1841, to 2d. Ch. ; [d. at Newark, 28 July, 1863, aet. 69.]
{ ABIGAIL ——— L. 9 Nov., 1836, fr, Mendham, dis. 26 Jan., 1841 to 2d. Ch.

ELIZABETH, L. ; C. 24 Nov., 1836 ; dis. 26 Jan., 1841, to 2d Ch.

PHEBE ANN C. ; C. 27 Feb., 1837 ; m. 16 Oct., 1839. to Ziba S. Smith ; dis. 8 June, 1841, to 2d Ch.

{ Axtell, Jacob T. [s. Timothy ?]; d. 26 Oct., 1880, aet. 75.
{ Joanna ——— d. 18 Oct., 1826, aet. 18.
{ RACHEL ENSLEE ; m. 22 Dec., 1827 ; C. 5 Feb., 1829 ; dis. 8 June. 1841, to 2d Ch. ; d. 7 Oct., 1849. aet. 43.

Phebe Elizabeth ; B. 4 Sept., 1829.

THE RECORD.

FIRST PRESBYTERIAN CHURCH, MORRISTOWN, N. J.

"This Shall be Written for the Generation to Come."—Psalms 102 : 18.

VOLUME V.   FEBRUARY, 1885.   NUMBER 26.

[Printed with the Approval of the Session.]

THE RECORD

Is published monthly ; terms $1.00 a year, *in advance.*

Single numbers for any month, 10 cents each.

Subscriptions should be made to Mr. James R. Voorhees.

Matters pertaining to the publication should be addressed to the

EDITOR OF THE RECORD.

Entered at the Post Office at Morristown, N. J., as second class matter.

The regular edition for subscribers this month contains twenty pages instead of twelve.

This part of THE RECORD will hereafter be distributed in the pews of the Church on the Sunday after publication.

It is not designed, however, to force the publication upon the attention of any, or to make it exactly free. If not wanted, the paper can be left in the pew: if wanted, take it, and welcome to it.

Subscribers will continue to receive their copies through the mail. New subscribers will be gladly enrolled. From the first, the subscriptions have never paid the cost of publication, and the deficit has been made up by a few who appreciated THE RECORD as a means of preserving the valuable historical materials of our Church.

In this part of THE RECORD it is now proposed to publish some matters of present moment. A beginning is made this month on the last two pages. Besides recording items of passing interest, the various departments of Christian work will be given an opportunity to make known their aims and needs ; and subjects of importance can be brought to the attention of the Congregation in this way, which could not well be published in any other.

NEW HISTORICAL PAPERS.

In response to a large number of requests, we begin in this number the publication of the sermon delivered last spring by the Pastor.

Dr. Irving, in his historical sermons, which have been published in THE RECORD, touched but lightly upon the period from 1842 down to his own pastorate ; while from the beginning of the latter period no account has ever been published, or even written so far as is known. We are, therefore, happy to say that a gentleman, who has been an active member of the Church throughout these periods, promises a historical paper to bring the narrative down to 1882. The publication of this paper will probably begin some time during the summer.

EXTRA SUPPLEMENT.

In addition to the regular supplement, containing the Minutes of Session, Parish and Trustees, for the close of Dr. Irving's and the beginning of Mr. French's pastorates ; we issue with this number eight pages of the Combined Registers. The succeeding parts of the Combined Registers will be issued during the year, in the form here presented, the pages being numbered continuously; so that the parts may be bound in a volume by themselves, or with the Minutes. Although this puts extra expense upon the few who are interested in publishing these records—since the subscriptions fall considerably short of paying the cost of publication—it is adopted in order to make the valuable historical material more convenient for permanent preservation in book form. There will be a delay of three or four months before the issue of the next part of the Combined Registers.

A SUNDAY IN THE FIRST CHURCH,

BETWEEN 1800 AND 1825.

HISTORICAL SERMON BY THE PASTOR, PREACHED 13TH APRIL 1825.*

1 Cor. xii.: 5.—"Ther ar diferences of administration, but the same Lord."

The year of the Presbyterian Church thru-out the land closed with March. Our own Parish year came to an end only a few weeks ago. Last Sunday's was the third April communion in this Church at which I have officiated with a pastoral interest. Valuabl lessons miht be drawn from the twelv months thru which we hav just cum. Their course has bin impressivly markt by the Lord's diversities of ministrations. In worship and in charities, in activ labors and in patient endurance, in gladnes and in grief, in sweet surprises and in bitter disapointments, in songs over the repentant and tears over the bakslider, in helth and in siknes, in life and in deth;—in all our varied experiences the same Lord, our wise and loving Father in hevn, has souht to make us worthy of the blesednes to which another year brings his disipls nearer.

But why recall these experiences now? They ar yet fresh in memory; and too tender, perhaps, with joy or soro for public recital. We may well leav them in silence, til they bring forth, in good time, the fruits of chastend hope and consecrated endevor; while we spend this 'anniversary hour in noting sum of the contrasts between the old and the present life of our Church. A contrast of this sort wel illustrates our text, since it givs one, in a particular and familiar exampl, a vivid conception of the diferences of administration thru which the same Lord imparts those divine impulses that make for ritiusnes in sinful humanity.

During the year I hav becum much interested in THE RECORD of our Church; the litl pamflet that is hardly appreciated acording to its valu, in which ther ar publisht, once a month, original papers of historical importance, extracts from the Minutes of the Session, of the Parish, and of the Trustees, with long lists of names from the Registers of Baptisms, Comunicants, Marriages, and Deths. No dout this publication offers very dry reading, except to those who ar curious about odities in spelling and others who seek the names of ancestors. But to me it is a cool and crystal spring of history, which clearly reflects the scenes witnest by these walls in the oldn time; the rinkls of laufter, of soro and of age, that crost the faces of those who ust to sit in these pews long ago; their quaint costumes and their customs, now almost forgotn. As I hav red THE RECORD from month to month, altho neither engraving nor wood-cut has enlivend its pages, it has seemd full of pictures. And perhaps the diferences of administration, which have foloed one another in the history of this Church, can be set forth most plainly and from the tru historic point of view, if I attemt a ruf description,—what miht be cald a charcoal sketch,—of a Sunday in the oldn time. I do not mean a particular day of a particular year, but a typical day; for then slight anachronisms wil only giv our view a broader range without impairing its accuracy. Let us chooz a typical Sunday in the midl age of the Church, that is in the period between 1800 and 1825, for then we shal hav contrasts to note on both sides.

It is "a tedious day," the frozn ground and leafles trees swept by angry gusts of a piercing wind; a patch of snow only here and there in sum shelterd spot. The old bel,—not queen Anne's but king George II's gift, as tradition goes,—rings out its high, sharp, impatient call for the pepl to worship in the new Presbyterian Meeting house. The hand of William Cherry is not upon the rope this morning, for that hand has grown feebl with age, in the twenty years it has biu ringing the bel; digging graves, at from five shillings to a dollar each; and compiling his Bill of Mortality, in which he aimd to bestow as impartial immortality upon the child of poverty, that livd but an hour, as upon the patriarch who died amid honors and welth and widest affection. His son Moses pulls the rope today, having begun his long career as Sexton at the age of seventeen.

While the pepl gather we wil look about the town, to note the growth of half a cen-

---

*The spelling follows the rules of the Spelling Reform Association, which ar advocated by scolars like W. D. Whitney of Yale, and Max Muller of Oxford.

tury. And first, try to imagin the original setlment. A bilding down Water street is associated with those oldest times and wil help to recall the past. It is now a distillery of apl whisky, but once it formd part of the first Meeting house. When that was put up by ardent piety, in 1740, amid the hardships of the new setlment, it stood a litl east and north of the present Church;* a low, square structure with shingld sides, to which later elegance aded a steepl that remaind in the graveyard, doing duty as a scool-house, several years after the main bilding had bin removed. Water street, or rather a cuntry road running up a natural "gully," was the only approach to the Meeting house for more than a generation; and no bilding was in siht on the south, the primitiv forest cuming almost to the door. That old sanctuary, standing on the edge of the hil and looking down upon the river bank, saw a gradual and prosperous chanj during the fifty years of Dr. Johnes' pastorate; the three or four dwelings, an iron forj, a cuntry store, expand into a village of 250 inhabitants at the date of the Revolution. In that hard winter of 1777 & 8, when the pews wer beds for the smallpox patients from the Continental camp, the congregation gatherd under the shelter of the hil in Dr. Johnes' orchard.† It was at one of these services that Gen. Washington partook of the communion for the only recorded time in his official life; and there, on another day, he gave up his own campchair to a poor woman, who was trying to hear the sermon while she stood with a babe in her arms.

(*To be continued.*)

THINGS OF TO-DAY.

Baptism of Infants:

30 Jan., Lemel Ellsworth, son of Lemel E. and Jane E. Pierson; born 10 May, 1884.

Communicants Received:

21 Jan., by confirmation, Virginia, daughter of Dr. James C. Dustan.

30 Jan., by certificate from the 2d Mansfield Presbyterian Church, Melissa, wife of William C. Prudden.

---

*A litl back of the big butn-wood tree and nearer Morris St., tho ther was no street or road then.

†The peculiar hollow on the north of Morris St., between Mr. King's and Mrs. Ayers' houses.

1 Feb., by baptism, Georgiana, wife of J. Frederick Richter; and Georgian, daughter of William C. Prudden.

Certificates Granted:

2 Jan., to Martha C. Kneighton, to unite with the 1st Presbyterian Church of Ottumwa, Ia.

1 Feb., to Mr. and Mrs. Josephus S. Guerin, with their baptized daughter, Elizabeth L., to unite with the 1st Presbyterian Church of Mendham.

Marriage:

21 Jan., Frank Ellsworth Prudden to Almeda Conklin Walling.

The prayer meetings during January have been well attended, and have exhibited a very earnest spirit.

Why will people choose seats on the west wall of the Chapel? As respects both hearing and light the seats are better in any other part of the room.

Some one suggests that we all sing frequently at our homes from the new Spiritual Songs for Social Worship, saying that many very beautiful hymns and tunes are thus found. The book may be obtained thru Mr. H. G. Emmell.

One of the Divisions of the Children's Missionary Society has been very active during the past month. The special interest is connected with the Gould Home in Rome, Italy. Is this your Division? If not, do you propose to let another excell you in good works?

Two new Bible Classes have recently been formed in the Sunday-school; with Mr. Hastings and Prof. Platt as their respective teachers. These classes are for ladies. They are not yet full. Did you not say, and not very long ago, that you wished there was a class which you might join, because, for one reason or another, you could not be a teacher just now? Suppose you join one of these new classes; it may be just what you were wishing for.

The Young Ladies' Missionary Society— Oh! dear, what a long name!—would not have made a very long procession, if the regular attendants on Friday afternoons during December, had marched around the Green at the end of their hour of meeting.

But it is different now. They took a new departure the other Sunday, and followed it up on the following Friday with a roomfull. A good many new members are as eager as the former ones to lend a hand in doing something for the waifs of a mission school in New York City. Perhaps they will have to turn to the Primary room to find a place big enough for the many busy fingers that sew together on Friday afternoons. Even that would not be big enough, if every young lady in the Congregation would deny herself one entrance to the Rink a week, and bring the price, with ready fingers to work, for the needy.

Work on the Parsonage is nearing the end; the plastering will be done before the close of the month. It has been proposed to hold a general reception in the house as soon as it is completed, so that all the Congregation may inspect it. But why not call it the Manse, which is a good Presbyterian name, and would distinguish it from the Methodist Parsonage as well as from the Episcopal Rectory.

A Seal was agreed upon by the Trustees of our Church, on the 24th of April, 1788, "the device & impression of which is a Sheaf of Wheat," according to the Minutes of that date. This was chosen at the first meeting of the first Board of Trustees elected by the Congregation, when they "assumed the name of THE TRUSTEES OF THE FIRST PRESBYTERIAN CHURCH AT MORRISTOWN." Previously, under the Charter granted by George II, Sept., 8th, 1756, vacancies in the Board were filled by the appointment of "the Minister or Ministers, Elders, and Deacons for the time being." Apparently this original seal was never made, or at least became lost and forgotten before the sons of those who adopted it came into the active work of the Church; for in 1846, Nov. 14th, the Seal in present use was adopted. This is very commonplace, having the word "SEAL" in plain letters across the face, and the following around the margin, "1st PRES. CH. MT. N. J." There is a rumor that the Committee talk of having the original Seal of the Church appear in a prominent part of the window of colored glass, which the Sunday-school proposes to put in the Manse.

WOMEN'S FOREIGN MISSIONS.

The new year has already shown a good deal of very commendable energy in the work and the giving for missions among the women of heathen lands. At the popular meeting, held at Miss Dana's on Monday afternoon, Jan. 19th, the large room was nearly filled by the ladies of the Church. Dr. Ellinwood, one of the Secretaries of our Board of Foreign Missions, presented the scriptural grounds for the work in an exceedingly impressive and persuasive statement; and then took his hearers upon an imaginary journey around the world, to see the work for women, its needs and its results, as he had seen it in the schools and missions in Japan, in China, in India, in Syria, in Africa, and in Chili.

After the address, the ladies present were asked to pledge themselves to give what they could for this special work, and responded generously; many of them largely increasing their offerings over the amounts given in previous years.

It was also decided to hold monthly meetings of a popular character. At some of these meetings speakers from abroad will be present, and at others papers upon different fields and different phases of the work will be read by ladies of our Church. The first of these popular gatherings will be held in the Chapel on Monday afternoon, Feb. 9th, when papers will be read upon the new world opened in Africa by the recent discoveries of Livingstone and Stanley, and the providential opportunities there for our prayers and our gifts, to send the Light of the Gospel into that Dark Continent.

The managers of the Zenana Society are talking of abandoning their organization, in order to put their energies into this popular form of the work. The desire of all seems to be to effect two things principally: To carry on the work in a way that is most likely to inform and interest the largest number in the Congregation, so that each will see and feel that she has a part in it; and, To rely for gifts upon the free-will offerings of all who feel that it is a privilege and a joy to give what they can, to send the message of their Savior's love to their sisters who are now in heathen lands.

THE RECORD.

FIRST PRESBYTERIAN CHURCH, MORRISTOWN, N. J.

" This Shall be Written for the Generation to Come."—Psalms 102 : 18.

VOLUME V. MARCH, 1885. NUMBER 27.

[Printed with the Aproval of the Session.]

THE RECORD

Is published monthly ; terms $1.00 a year, *in advance.*

Single numbers for any month, 10 cents each.

Subscriptions should be made to Mr. James R. Voorhees.

Matters pertaining to the publication should be addressed to the

EDITOR OF THE RECORD.

Entered at the Post Office at Morristown, N. J., as second class matter.

The Supplement for this month contains the Minutes of the Session, during the pastorate of Mr. French, from 3d Aug., 1870, to 3d March, 1875.

Last month the types gave a wrong date for the preaching of the historical sermon. It was not preached in 1825, but in 1884. The Preacher may be taken for the father of one of the Elders, but hardly for his grandfather.

The extra Supplement, issued to subscribers last month, has a title page, which reads as follows : " History of the First Presbyterian Church, Morristown, N. J. Part II., The Combined Registers, From 1742 to 1885." This title page, and the new numbering of the pages, will allow the " Combined Registers" to be bound by itself, or with "The Minutes." A complete history of the Church should contain three parts : Part I, The Minutes of the Session, Trustees and Parish. The printing of this part is nearly completed. Part II, The Combined Registers, containing all the names on the books of the Church, with all the facts of record concerning each, arranged in alphabetical order. The printing of this part has just begun. Part III. The Historical Sermons of Dr. Irving, and such other papers as can be gathered. Whether the work shall reach this complete form, depends on the interest taken by the friends of the Church in providing means, in subscriptions and contributions, to meet the cost of publication.

A SUNDAY IN THE FIRST CHURCH.

BETWEEN 1800 AND 1825.

HISTORICAL SERMON BY THE PASTOR,.

PREACHED 13TH APRIL 1884.

(Continued.)

When the new Meeting house was proposed it met with strong opposition, under the lead of elders Phillips and Condict ; tho Dr. Johnes urgd the project, and preacht a special sermon in its favor one Friday afternoon in Dec., 1789. That sermon must hav bin a rousing one, for imediatly after the benediction the pepl appointed Joseph Lewis,—the Dr.'s son-in-law—with Moses Estey, and Daniel Phœnix, Jr., a comitee to bild the new house. But discussion delayed the undertaking, so that it was a year later before material began to be gatherd, and not til Sept., 1791, did the frame rise on the present foundations. The first service was held in the new house while it was still incomplete ; a weekly lecture, on the last Thursday of Nov., 1795.

Before examing the new Meeting house, note sum of the great improvements that hav takn place within the sixty years and more since the old one rose on the edge of the forest. At the date of our visit, the stores and mils and shops, stil cling to the river bank, and only there ar the dwelings clusterd together. Among them rises the spacious new hotel, a striking evidence of enterprise ; for it has just bin bilt, "in sixty days from the stump," imediatly after the fire which destroyd the old tavern : [and tho bilt so hastily, it stands to our day—the yellow bilding opposit the gas-works.] Alredy the tendency of growth is towards the hil, and especially along the lane which is soon to becum Bridge street. But now, near the corner of Water, it passes between two houses that stand so close together as to be almost grazed by any wagon going thru. Ther is talk, however, of widening, and, in the course of time, of throwing a bridge over the stream beyond. In confidence of this improvement, Abraham T. Schenck has just erected, half way to the brook, on the south side and overlooking his brik mil, a duble mansion, one of the most elegant in town. Just beyond is Mrs. Edwards' bakery where sum folks get their lunch between meetings ; one of the Deacons being always on hand, to see that the poor ar provided with cake and ale at the expense of the Church. Nearer at hand, the Baptist Church, on its present site, not yet enlarjd, its doors ofn shut for lak of a preacher, is still, in 1825, the only other Church in town, or for more than ten miles around. On the Green—which has hardly yet ernd this titl, for it is now a treeles and grassles comons, with wagon ruts runing from opposit corners,—in the angl near the Baptist Church stands the Court-house. As it was bilt in 1770, the shingls that cover its cupola and sides as wel as its roof, tho once glaring with red paint, ar now a dingy gray, and the bilding is forlorn with neglect. A few dwelings ar scaterd around the comons. Off to the left can be seen the Academy, on land bought in 1792 from this Parish for £30. Jersey money, equivalent to only £15. sterling. The long radius from the Meeting house to the Academy would make a circl inclosing nearly the hole town and its population of about 1,000. Beyond this circl, in all directions, ar farm and wood lands.

Now take several positions at a litl distance, and look more particularly at the new Meeting house. It has bin finisht, painted, and otherwise beutified, only a few years. Observ its fine proportions which modestly hide its larj size; its steepl rising 173 feet into the air; and the clok, with its three faces. Ther ar not six other Meetin houses in the hole State as larj and grand and perfectly appointed as this. The ball that crowns the spire looks like a Connecticut pumpkin, as if a symbol of the New England origin of the community ; and old William Cherry points out to us a hole in this ball, which sum vandal made by a rifl bullet before the spire had bin up six weeks.

The Meeting house and graveyard ar inclosed by a neat piket fence, with a rail on the outside where horses may be fasnd. As many as sixty teams hav alredy arived, bringing the wimen folks and children, for the men who do not cum on horseback ar acustomd to walk. Most of the wagons ar plain boxes, without springs ; and a bundl of straw on a board makes a good enuf seat. The larjer part of the congregation cum a long distance, sum of them six and eight miles. New Vernon and Green Village send forty or fifty families ; Prudden-town and Washington Valley, each as many more. Those that come from Washton Valley turn off thru Mills street and approach the Meeting house thru Spring and Water streets, as the Court-house hil of a later day, and the brook in Bridge street, hav not yet bin crost by good road or bridge. The largest number cum from Watnung or Morris Plains and Littleton, the latter being a prosperous and populous village on the direct stage line to the west. The arrival of an ox-cart, tho not an unusual siht, made "quite sum" sport for the young folks this morning. For its owner, who always oblijd his wife to walk the four miles to meeting, took her at her word to-day, when she begd to ride, "even like a load of stone in the ox-cart ;" and on reaching the Meeting house gate, before she knew what he was about, he tilted the cart and dumpt her to the ground.*

(*To be continued.*)

THINGS OF TO-DAY.

Standing Notices :

Sunday : Church Services, 10.30 A. M., and 7.30 P. M.

Sunday : Sunday-school, 3 P. M.

Sunday : Young People's prayer meeting, 6.45 P. M.

Tuesday : The Pastor may be found at his house from 4 to 5.30 P. M.

*It has since bin lernd that this insident did not occur here but at Mendham.

Thursday : Young Men's prayer meeting, 6.45 P. M.

Thursday : Church Service of Prayer, 7.45 P. M.; preceded by a Song Service at 7.30 P. M.

Friday : Young Ladies' Missionary Society, from 3 to 5 P. M.

Saturday : Bible-class and Teachers' meeting, led by the Rev. Dr. Erdman, 4 P. M.

Special Calendar :

March 1, *Sunday ;* Collection for Bloomfield Seminary.

" 5, *Thursday ;* "Keeping the Heart." Prov., iv. 23.

" 9, *Monday ;* Woman's Foreign Missionary Society.

" 11, *Wednesday ;* Literary and Social Union.

" 12, *Thursday ;* Mexico. "The Warning Voice." Mark xiii. 32-37.

" 17, *Tuesday ;* Annual Parish Meeting.

" 19, *Thursday ;* "Watching for Souls." Heb. xiii. 17.

" 25, *Wednesday ;* Session meeting, 4 P. M.; applications for Church membership.

" 26, *Thursday ;* "Joy in Heaven." Luke xv. 10.

" 29, *Sunday ;* Sunday-school. Mission Quarterly.

April 2, *Thursday ;* Preparatory prayer meeting.

" 3, *Friday ;* Preparatory Lecture, 3.30 P. M. Baptism of infants.

" 5, *Sunday ;* Communion. Collection for Sustentation.

The friends of Mr. William B. Hopkins, a member of our Church, will be saddened to learn, that he died in Shanghai, on the 7th of January, at the early age of twenty-two.

Parish Meeting on March 17th, will fall a week later than usual, in accordance with a resolution adopted last year. There should always be a good attendance ; but this year it may not be necessary to urge it, since many will be interested to hear the report of the Building Committee.

Judging from the remarks that have been heard, their number and favorable tone, there seems to be a pretty general opinion that our suggestion of last month to call the new building the Manse was a good one. If the inference is correct, it would be well to have the name regularly adopted at the Parish meeting.

The exercises of the Literary and Social Union last month were very entertaining. Whoever suggested the novel device to mystify the audience is a genius. And the device gave us the privilege of hearing several who have not heretofore appeared on the programs of the Union. It is to be hoped that this new talent, and more of the same good sort, will not hide in shadows any longer. Those who realized too late what they lost by not attending the last meeting, should be sure to be present at the next.

WOMEN'S MISSIONS.

The meeting of the Woman's Missionary Society, which was announced in the last RECORD for the second Monday in February, was held at that time, but with a change of program. Instead of the popular exercises intended, a reorganization of the Society was effected, and other necessary business transacted preparatory to future effort. Altho a very stormy day, about fifty ladies were present, and much interest was manifested. It is hoped that both branches of Woman's work in our Church, Home and Foreign, have taken a new departure, and will henceforth work upon a broader basis, extending their sympathies and increasing their offerings. Meetings are to be held monthly, in the interest alternately of the Home and Foreign Societies. The next one will be held the second Monday of March, (the 9th,) by the Foreign Society ; subject; "Africa." The arrangements are in the hands of a very efficient committee, and an interesting program may be expected. Let every woman in the Church count it her duty and privilege to be present.

EVENING SERVICE.

Practically the sittings at our evening Service on Sunday are free. Strangers and members of the Congregation, who find it difficult to obtain such sittings at the morning Service as they would like, will be cheerfully accommodated in the evening. The evening attendance has been frequently remarked, as " good, if not large, considering the customs of the place, and the traditions of the Church." It does not, however, seem to be generally appreciated by those who attend, that the grouping of a congregation has much to do both with their enjoyment of the Service and with the ease and effectiveness of most preachers. To sit off under the galleries, or back by the door, while there are empty pews in the centre and near the pulpit, is to do as much as possible to make the Service cold, to discourage the preacher, and to render the sermon dull and uninteresting. Let the ushers give you a sitting in the middle aisle, and well up towards the pulpit.

WHY NOT ?

Would it not add to the interest of our weekly prayer meeting, if those who think they cannot otherwise take part, would read a short extract from some good book or paper, bearing on the subject of the evening if possible; or, if not relating to the evening's subject, something helpful to spiritual life? The weekly religious papers, one of which every family in the Church is supposed to take, always contain stirring appeals or vivid illustrations of truth, which come home forcibly to the heart of the reader, and might be equally impressive to the hearers, if read in the social prayer meeting. The Bible at any rate is always at hand for reading at such a meeting, and there is no law against anyone's reading from it. A short passage, or even a single verse, read aloud after a prayer or hymn, would often drive a truth home, and bring encouragement, comfort, or new impulse for the Christian life. Don't wait for somebody else to begin, if you think the suggestion a good one; but set the good example yourself.

BLOOMFIELD SEMINARY.

This German Theological School of our Church makes the following report :

Number of graduates,	35
German Churches and Missions under their care,	37
Number of Church-members,	3,704

Of these there are 31 organized Churches with an average membership of 119. There are also 5,718 Sunday-school members under their care, with an average of 178 in each school.

The additions to the Churches for last year were :

On Examination,	449
On Certificates,	46
In all	495

Financial results in contributions :

Benevolent objects,	$1,345
General Assembly. &c.,	181
Congregational objects,	40,533
Miscellaneous,	1,274
Total,	$43,333

The Churches under the care of the first two classes (1874 and 1875,) contributed, during the past year, for the above objects, $23,005.

These same German Churches, since these graduates assumed their care in 1874 and 1875, have contributed to all the above objects $132,075.—a sum much larger than the total cost of the current expense of the institution since it was founded.

At its meeting in October last, our Synod of New Jersey adopted the following : "That we endeavor, so far as opportunity offers, to induce competent young men of German parentage and of unquestioned piety, to consider the claims of the Gospel ministry, and to turn their attention towards the German Theological School.

"That we endeavor to make up the deficit of last year and to increase contributions for the current expenses."

Our Church has also a German Seminary at Dubuque, Iowa ; and the graduates of these two schools now supply some sixty-five German Churches with pastors.

The necessary expenses at Bloomfield so far this year have been much in excess of the income. The School is in urgent need of an increase in its ordinary current contributions ; and also of funds to pay the deficit of last year. And this need is a present one. Nine months of the School year have passed.

THE RECORD.

FIRST PRESBYTERIAN CHURCH, MORRISTOWN, N. J.

"THIS SHALL BE WRITTEN FOR THE GENERATION TO COME."—Psalms 102 : 18.

VOLUME V.   APRIL, 1885.   NUMBER 28.

[Printed with the Approval of the Session.]

THE RECORD

Is published monthly ; terms $1.00 a year, *in advance.*

Single numbers for any month, 10 cents each.

Subscriptions should be made to Mr. James R. Voorhees.

Matters pertaining to the publication should be addressed to the

EDITOR OF THE RECORD.

Entered at the Post Office at Morristown, N. J., as second class matter.

CALENDAR FOR APRIL.

2. *Thursday:* Preparatory prayer meeting.

3. *Friday:* Preparatory Lecture, 3.30 P. M., Baptism of Infants.

5. *Sunday:* Communion. Collection for Sustentation. S. S. Lesson : Paul's Voyage, Acts. xxvii. 1, 2, 14-26.

9. *Thursday:* "Test of Love to Christ," I Jno. iii. 14 ; and India.

12. *Sunday:* S. S. Lesson. Paul's Shipwreck, Acts. xxvii. 27-44.

16. *Thursday:* " Symmetry of Christian Character," Ps. cxix, 6

19. *Sunday:* S. S. Lesson. Paul going to Rome, Acts xxviii, 1-15.

22. *Wednesday:* 7.30 P. M., Session meeting.

23. *Thursday:* "The Two Ways," Matt. vii. 13, 14.

26. *Sunday:* S. S. Lesson : Paul at Rome, Acts xxviii. 16-31.

30. *Thursday:* "The Blessedness of Giving." Acts xx. 35.

EVERY WEEK.

Sunday: Church Services, 10.30 A. M., and 7.30 P. M.

Sunday: Sunday-school, 3 P. M.

"   Young People's prayer meeting, 6.45 P. M.

Thursday: Young Men's prayer meeting, 7.00 P. M.

Thursday: Church Service of Prayer, 7.45 P. M.; preceded by a Song Service at 7.30 P. M.

Friday: Young Ladies' Missionary Society, from 3 to 5 P. M.

Saturday: Bible-class and Teachers' meeting, led by the Rev. Dr. Erdman, 4 P. M.

SUPPLEMENT.

The Supplement for this month completes the Minutes of the Session for the pastorate of Mr. French ; and brings the Minutes of the Trustees and Parish down to March 25, 1872.

PARISH MEETING.

REPORT ON THE MANSE.

The Annual Parish Meeting was held on the 17th of March, at 3.30 P. M.; Mr. John Whitehead, Chairman. The Trustees reported an unusually good condition of the finances, and recommended an appropriation of $6,750. for the coming year. The following were elected :—Trustees : Isaac N. Whitehead, H. C. Pitney, A. B. Hull, J. H. Van Doren, Henry Cory, James R. Voorhees, Edward Pierson ; Treasurer, Henry Cory ; Parish Clerk, James R. Voorhees.

The Committee appointed to build a Parsonage reported as follows : "Having been appointed, at an adjourned meeting held May 13th, 1884, to erect a stone building for a Parsonage, at a cost not to exceed $15,000.; your Committee accepted the plans offered by Mr. Louis R. Hazeltine, Architect.

"We were assured that the cost of construction would not exceed $15,000., but when the bids were opened, it was found that the cost of the building as planned would not be far from $18,000. The season was already well advanced when the bids were received, and as it was evident a smalter building would be unsuitable for our needs, we concluded not to call for new plans, which would delay the commencement of work a full month. We proceeded at once to cut off all ornamental work, inside and outside, which was not absolutely necessary to the safety and security of the building. By abandoning all the Ohio stone trimmings, the bay window in the dining-room, the laundry conveniences, various other bits of ornamental work outside, all the hard-wood flooring and trim inside, excepting in the hall and stair case where we left the cherry floor and stairs, all the double floors, &c., &c., leaving the finish throughout of white pine; we found that we could construct the building for about $15,000., or a few dollars less. We adopted this plan with great reluctance. It left us with a commodious and substantial, but very plain and unornamental building. Nevertheless it would be of stone, and would not cost more than $15,000.; and so we separated with saddened hearts.

"Shortly afterwards word was sent to us, that an aged member of the Parish, who had already contributed very liberally, was so much interested in the project, and so desirous that we should have a beautiful building according to the original design, that he was willing to make a special contribution of $500. towards the $1,000. needed to restore the original exterior. The remaining $500. necessary was at once made up, as a special gift for this purpose, by three other gentlemen who also had previously contributed liberally. With this encouragement, the work of construction was immediately begun.

"As already stated, the reductions found to be necessary, left us with a pine finish inside, except the main staircase and hall floor. When the outside was completed, we felt that to trim a stone-building, of its pretensions, in these times, with pine, would be an offence against good taste, for which the Parish would not excuse us; and, after careful deliberation, we concluded to restore the hard-wood trim on the first story. We were at once met with the liberal offer, from another member of the Parish, to fit up the dining-room in oak at his own expense, in accordance with designs to be approved by the Pastor. This offer reduced the expense

to the Committee by $350., as it was intended to be a special contribution for that purpose. The double floors were also restored, and yellow pine floors laid in the second story at very little additional expense.

"The requisite amount of stained glass had been included in the Committee's estimates, but the Sunday-school, in response to a suggestion from us, have offered to erect the triple window in the hall at a cost of $160., to be their special contribution. The design, by Miss M. Van Pelt, is heartily approved by Slack & Co., of Orange, who are to do the work.

"The whole estimated cost of the building is $16,743.64, and deducting from this amount $1,510. of special contributions, the net cost to the Parish is $15,233.64. Of this amount there remains to be raised but $4,679.07.

"Your Committee have labored together cheerfully and harmoniously from the beginning of the work until the present day; but by far the major portion of the work has been done by two members, Messrs. Voorhees and Whitehead. These gentlemen have urgently requested that this report should not particularly refer to them, but the remaining members of the Committee insist that the Parish shall hereby learn a little of what it owes to them. By request of the Committee, Mr. Whitehead assumed special charge of the construction of the building, in addition to the overseeing to be done by the Architect. He has been present at the building almost every day; and it is safe to say that his labors have saved the Parish a great many dollars, and secured a building well and faithfully constructed from cellar to roof. Mr. Voorhees, as Chairman and Treasurer, has had entire charge of the financial part of the work, has attended to all the correspondence, kept the accounts, paid the bills, &c., &c., in addition to his other work as a member of the Committee. And we, the three remaining members, H. C. Pitney, W. D. Johnson and Stephen Pierson, desire to place upon record here our testimony concerning the faithful and efficient labors of the two gentlemen above named.

"We recommend: 1st, That the new

building be designated formally as the 'Manse.'

"2d, That the necessary funds to complete the building be obtained by the Board of Trustees, by temporary loans upon the credit of the Parish, and not by a mortgage upon the property.

"3d, That, in the opinion of this meeting, it is possible as well as desirable to pay off the whole of the debt during the year ; and that the Building Committee be instructed to make an appeal to this effect to the congregation."

The report, with its recommendations, was adopted, after remarks in approval of the work ; and the Committee was continued to complete the Manse, a vote of thanks to them being carried unanimously and heartily.

A SUNDAY IN THE FIRST CHURCH.

BETWEEN 1800 AND 1825.

HISTORICAL SERMON BY THE PASTOR, PREACHED 13TH APRIL 1884.

(*Continued.*)

Behind the Meeting house a litl group listens while John Mills, President of the Trustees, points out where the Session house ouht to stand, with its corners to the points of the compass and its entrance facing the northwest angl of the Meeting house. He declares that it should be bilt of brik and at once, offering, in his generous enthusiasm, to advance the money, if the subscriptions ar not sufficient to begin work with the opening of spring.* Near by, another group is discussing the recent action of the Parish in conveying the Green to the town for a perpetual comon, in consideration of $1,600., most of which was given by members of the Church. Edward Condict reminds them of the attemt to defraud the Parish of its rihts in the property, and of his jurney, not long since, to Amboy for the purpose of securing the titl in the Green from the Board of Proprietors. And Richard Johnson explains the connection between that attemted fraud and the remonstrance of the Trustees agenst the erection

*This was bilt, and stood til the present Chapel was erected in 1869.

of Moses Estey's bilding adjoining the Court house.

An excited crowd surrounds the doors, talking loudly about the stoves that wer put in the Meeting house last week for the first, and ar now to do away with the hot bricks and litl foot-stoves which sum of the wimen hav bin accustomd to bring. One venerabl old man, with emfatic gestures, says : "It is sacrelegious to desecrate the house of God with the devices and inventions of man. Providence has kept us and our fathers warm enuf without stoves in the coldest winters, for eighty years in the old Meeting house and in this, and Providence wil keep us warm in the future, if we wil only put our trust in it. But that is just the trubl ; this generation has n't any faith. Mark my words : before the year is out, on sum tedious day like this, you'l find that Providence has let your stoves burn the Meeting house to the ground, as a punishment for your sin. It is all of a peece with this new-fangld proposal of an assurance on the Meeting house, another invention of Satan to tempt the Lord. But no wonder ; for when you lose faith in Providence to keep you warm in his worship, of course you must get the devil's help to protect you from fire. I praise the Lord that the Parish has defeated this last ' device of the grand Adversary' to ensnare us. But can we expect the word to profit us withal, when, in the very house of God, we put our confidence in the sinful devices of man ?" Then elder M.—— speaks up. " I quite agree with you, brother Benoni, and let me tel these youngsters, ther is another very practical objection agenst their hot stoves. It wil be simply impossibl to keep the fires low enuf, and their heat, aded to that generated from the the bodies of the great congregation, wil suffocate us." With that, he goes to the porch, takes the big bar, used on the inside to hold the door shut, and with it braces the door wide open ; determind that ther shal be as much circulation of air in the Meeting house as he can secure on this windy day. Miss O., in passing, thanks elder M. and remarks on the "dredful hot blast" he has let out ; saying that she fears, even with the doors open, she "cannot stand the heat thru all the meeting time."

In order to view the interior we enter early by the commanding porch that opens thru the front of the steepl, facing the Green. Ther ar no steps from the porch up to the floor of the Church, and a glance within shows the archt ceiling rising to a majestic hight.* Here in the porch a man is "affixt," who receivs six-pence a Sabbath for keeping dogs out of the Meeting house. He explains to us a paper takt to the door: saying that it is an old notice of a vendue by the Trustees, which was held last week to dispose of two sadls and sum other property takn for pew rent; and that one of the sadls sold for ten dollars and ten cents, while the other broht ten dollars and four cents, the purchasers giving their notes payabl with interest in three months. As we pass the gallery stairs, we observ the stalwart forms of Jeduthan and Usual Condict, who stand as sentinels, one on each side, "to take charge of, and prevent as much as may be, disorderly and ill behaved boys siting on the stares, from playing and making disturbance in time of public service."

Now stand for a moment in the shadow of the gallery, and catch the pleasing effect of color and arrangement. The interior is painted a "light sky blue." Tall, substantial pillars of oak support the lofty gallery that sweeps around the house except at the end opposit to the entrance, where the pulpit towers alone. At that end, on either side of the pulpit, ar three square pews; ten similar pews line each side wall, separated by ampl iles from two bloks of slip-pews that ar themselvs separated by a broad ile down the midl of the Meeting house. All of the pews ar partitiond by high baks, reaching wel up the shoulders of those who sit in them. They sold originally at from $600. down to $100. and now pay a rent equal to seven and a half per cent of their valuation, or from $50. down to $7., according to location, those nearest the pulpit being most valuabl. In No. 1, the square pew next the pulpit, on the riht as we look from the entrance, sits the pastor's family, in plain siht of the congregation. Dr. Wm. Campfield occupies the square pew in the

cortner, whose high floor, which givs him a commanding view of the house, has bin a bone of contention for sixteen years: at last the Parish has orderd the Trustees to remove it at their expense. In another corner ar benches, where sit the negroe slaves of consequential families. In the gallery ar benches for the volunteer choir, a band of singers wel traind by Mr. Dunham, "the chorrister," who receives $40. a year for his services: all ar under the direction of the singing comitee, Lewis Condict, Joseph Cutler, Loammi Moore, Ezekiel Whitehead and Zophar Freeman, who "ar authorized to appoint chorristers, point out proper tunes to be sung, and generally do all things necessary for the promotion of harmony in the singing and with the singers." No "ritualistic organ" has yet bin introduced to despoil the praise of God with its "bag o' whustles.' The Sabbath School is up here in the gallery, holding its session before meeting begins. No men ar to be seen, the superintendent and the half dozn teachers are all wimen; for the scool is an innovation, introduced only a few years ago (1816), and thot by many to bode more harm than good: quiet horse-talk and gossip, about the Meeting house door, ar better for both men and wimen, elders and deacons, their wives and dauhters. Consequently only a score or so of very litl children ar on the benches to-day, studying A. B. C. Primers, reciting Scripture verses and the Shorter Catechism. Among them is a golden-haird descendant of John Alden and Priscilla Mullens, sitting between the first Fanny and the first George Washington in the community, whose names sound very stranj mingld with the many Naomi's and Phebe's, the Ebenezer's and Timothy's and other good old patriarchs and saints who hav stept out of the Pulpit Bible to becum agen restiv litl ones on these benches.

Descending to the floor, we notice the disturbing element of the day, the two stoves; plain affairs, iron boxes to burn long stiks of wood; together they cost but $37. Their long pipes, however, ar formidabl, and cost nearly $80. Another innovation broht in along with the stoves, at elevn lamps, each costing $6.25; great evils, according to sum, sure to drip oil, and

*In 1844, the floor was raised to its present level, and a flat ceiling thrown under the old arch.

(To be continued.)

THE RECORD.

FIRST PRESBYTERIAN CHURCH, MORRISTOWN, N. J.

"THIS SHALL BE WRITTEN FOR THE GENERATION TO COME."—Psalms 102: 18.

VOLUME V.   MAY, 1885.   NUMBER 29.

[Printed with the Approval of the Session.]

THE RECORD

Is published monthly; terms $1.00 a year, *in advance*.

Single numbers for any month, 10 cents each.

Subscriptions should be made to Mr. James R. Voorhees.

Matters pertaining to the publication should be addressed to the

EDITOR OF THE RECORD.

Entered at the Post Office at Morristown, N. J., as second class matter.

SUPPLEMENT.

The Supplement for this month continues the Minutes of the Trustees and Parish thru the Pastorate of Mr. French, from March 25th, 1872 to March 17, 1874.

CALENDAR FOR MAY.

3. *Sunday:* Collection for Bible Society. S. S. Lesson : Obedience, Eph. vi. 1–13.

7. *Thursday:* Religion in Business. Rom. xii. 11.

10. *Sunday:* S. S. Lesson : Christ our Example, Phil. ii. 5–16.

11. *Monday:* Woman's Foreign Mission Society.

14. *Thursday:* Compelling them to come in, Luke xiv. 32. Missions in Siam.

17. *Sunday:* S. S. Lesson : Christian Contentment, Phil iv. 4–13.

21. *Thursday:* Free Salvation, Rev. xxii. 17.

24. *Sunday:* S. S. Lesson : The Faithful Saying. I. Tim. i. 15–ii. 6.

27. *Wednesday:* 4 P. M. Session meets to receive candidates for the Communion.

28. *Thursday;* Final Separation, Matt. xiii. 40–50.

31. *Sunday:* S. S. Lesson : Paul's Charge to Timothy. II. Tim. iii. 14–iv. 8.

EVERY WEEK.

Sunday: Church Services, 10.30 A. M. and 7.30 P. M.

Sunday: Sunday-school, 3 P. M.

" Young People's prayer meeting, 6.45 P. M.

Thursday: Young Men's prayer meeting, 7:00 P. M.

Thursday: Church Mid-week Service of Prayer, 8 P. M.

Friday: Young Ladies' Missionary Society, from 3 to 5 P. M.

Saturday: Bible-class and Teacher's meeting, led by the Rev. Dr. Erdman, 4 P. M.

Strangers are cordially welcomed to all of these services.

IN MEMORIAM.

At a special meeting of the Woman's Foreign Missionary Society of the First Presbyterian Church, held on March 25th, 1885, the following resolutions were adopted in relation to the death of its late President, which occurred March 18th, 1885 :

WHEREAS, It has pleased the Heavenly Father to take to Himself so unexpectedly our beloved President and Pastor's wife, Mrs. Elisabeth S. Durant, thus giving to our Society, in its infancy, a baptism of sorrow; therefore,

Resolved, That while we bow submissively beneath the hand thus heavily laid upon us, believing that it is in love and not in wrath, we keenly feel our loss and deeply mourn that we shall have the cheering light of her sunny smile and helpful presence no more among us; yet rejoice that the grief is ours alone— for her there is only joy.

Resolved, That we cherish most tenderly the memory of her pure and lovely Christian character, her sweet resignation under trial, her ready obedience to every call of duty, her devotion to the Master's work as shown particularly by her earnest interest in the purpose and aim of this Society; and that we strive to emulate her example, praying that the inspiration of her beautiful life and peaceful death among us may lift each of us to a higher plane of consecration to the cause she so dearly loved.

Resolved, That in gratitude to God for the blessed hope of eternal life, through Jesus Christ His Son, and as a memorial of her who has entered into that life, we will make a special offering to the cause of Foreign Missions, devoting it to some object hereafter to be designated.

Resolved, That we tender to our bereaved pastor our heartfelt sympathy, commending him and his motherless little ones to the gracious care and comfort of Him who is infinite compassion, and whose loving presence alone can fill the vacant place in his heart and home.

HAVE YOUR ANSWER READY.

If you have hope in Christ, extraordinary talents and opportunities are not required in order "to give an answer to every one that asketh you a reason concerning the hope that is in you." (1 Peter iii, 15). The Bible itself supplies you with nearly every one of these reasons. It says, over and over again, what the Christian hope is, how it rests on Christ and his work, how it looks for divine support in this life and eternal blessedness in heaven.

If a man never studies for himself, or thru the law, a will which puts him in possession of a large property, so as to discover his title, and be able to defend it; you would say that he deserves to lose the property. But the Bible is God's will and testament, bequeathing to the believer the priceless legacy of salvation and eternal life; therefore, search the Scriptures.

Then, as to the influence of the Christian hope upon your own life, which must always be a large part of your answer to those who ask a reason "concerning the hope that is *in you*;" your daily experience gives material for a ready answer. Surely you can tell some troubled soul that is seeking peace, how your Christian hope is helping you to overcome sin and the world, to bear disappointment and sorrow, to strive after more purity, and love both to God and to man; and how it gives you a peace and joy which the world cannot take away, and more sweet than any it can give.

Some persons act as if this answer could be ready only after long Christian experience, and superlative Christian attainments. It ought, indeed, to grow fuller and clearer as you get nearer to the grave and nearer to the throne. But you do not need to wait till noon in order to give a convincing reason for believing that day has followed the night. He is worse than blind, who cannot tell why he hopes the day will come, just as soon as the first glow of dawn appears in the east. So the Christian is able to give this answer upon the first glimmer of gospel hope in his soul: he has no excuse for not *being ready always* after that.

REPORT TO PRESBYTERY,

FOR YEAR ENDING 31 MARCH, 1885.

OFFICERS.

No. Elders, of whom 8 are active,	11
No. Deacons,	2
No. Trustees,	7

COMMUNICANTS.

Added on examination,	7
Added on certificates,	12
Total number on roll 31st March, 1885,	473

BAPTISMS.

Adults Baptized,	5
Infants Baptized,	10
Baptized Infants added to Roll on Cert.,	6
Total No. Infants on Roll,	92

SUNDAY-SCHOOL.

No. Officers,	11
No. Teachers,	61
No. Scholars,	388
Total Membership,	460
Average Attendance,	290
No. received to Communion,	5
No. Books in Library,	428
Am't of Gifts to Boards of Church,	$305
Am't of Gifts to other objects,	$451
Total Gifts of Sunday-school,	$756

Westminster Helps are used; Catechism is taught; and Teachers' meetings are held.

BENEFICENCE.

Home Field:

Home Missions,	$1,668
Education,	136
Publication of Christian Literature,	513
Church Erection,	116
Relief of Disabled Ministers,	128
Missions to Freedmen,	760

Sustentation of Feeble Churches,	48
Aid for Colleges, . . .	100
Miscellaneous Objects, . .	3,482

Total for Home Field, . . 6,951

Foreign Field:

Total for Foreign Field, . . 4,830

Total Beneficence, . . . $11,781

CONGREGATIONAL.

Assessment for General Assembly, &c., $52
Support of Church services and payments on Manse, ... 18,010

Total Contributions and Support, $29,843

A SUNDAY IN THE FIRST CHURCH.

BETWEEN 1800 AND 1825.

HISTORICAL SERMON BY THE PASTOR,
PREACHED 13TH APRIL 1884.

(*Continued.*)

likely to explode,—nobody knows when.
But the old " two-branch candle sticks " ar
stil in place, at " each window below, two
for the desk in front of the pulpit, and one
for each pillar." Last and best of all the
objects in the Meeting house, take a real-
izing view of the pulpit ; the pride of the
congregation and the "great admiration of
travelers from abroad." This, too, is new ;
the old one, probably broht from the
original Meeting house, having bin uzd in
this til 1818, and then givn to the neighboring Church at New Foundland. The splendid work of art upon which we now gaze
was bilt by Joseph Cutler, at a cost of
$224.74. It is a box with high sides, having
three mahogany panels archt outward in
front, and is reacht by winding stairs, for the
platform rests on the top of pillars nine or
ten feet abov the Meeting house floor.
Overhed hangs the larj and shel-like sound-
ing board.*

It has takn les time to see all these things
than to describe them, and the first hym is
not finisht when we ar startled by a commotion : the singing sudnly stops, every-
body is looking, sum ar hastening, towards
one particular pew. It is that of Miss O.,

*The remains may now be seen in the loft of the steepl,
whither the pulpit was removed about 1860, to giv place to a
more modern and much cheaper desk, which in its turn gave
way to the present one about 1870.

who thankt elder M. for bracing the door
open. She has bin gasping with the heat
ever since she enterd, and now her fears
ar realizd ; she lies in a ded faint. Two or
three sympathizers carry her to the breezy
porch, and then return with rathful faces,
determined to put out the fires in the sinful stoves ; when the discovery is made
that ther has not bin a spark of fire in them ;
the temperature is down to freezing ; and
it was nuthing but prejudice and imagination that sent Miss O. off in her faint.

After quiet is restored, the minister rises
to giv out the notices. He is a man of sliht
bild, rather under than over the average
hight, but looking larjer than he really is
by reason of the flowing blak silk gown he
wears,—a gift from the ladies of the congregation. His face and manner at once show
spritual unction and win unusual regard
even from strangers.* He reads the foloing :

(1). It is my painful duty to inform the
congregation, that Mr. H., agenst whom
ther hav bin reports in circulation for sum
time, charging him with gross dishonesty,
is after all not a member of this Church, as
appears from his own assertion when cited
before the Session, and upon an examination of the Sessional Records. "After sum
deliberation, the Session Resolved that
they hav no authority to proceed in this
business, and therefore that it be dismissed.
Resolved further, that inasmuch as Mr. H.
has for many years been looked upon as a
member of this Church, entitled to its
privileges and subject to its discipline, and
in view of the Church and of the world, the
Session are responsible for their faithfulness to him as a member, Therefore they
feel bound, in justice to themselves and to
the cause of religion, to make a full and
candid statement of his case to the Church ;
that it may be known that we are not responsible."

(2). A meeting for special prayer, instituted by the Session, wil be held at Jonathan Ford's, Tuesday next at 2 o'clok in
the afternoon ; in which the ministers and
Churches of Hanover and South Hanover
hav bin invited to join, as the place is con-
tiguous to those congregations.

*Dr. Wm. A. McDowell, Pastor from 1814 to 1823. The
only record of a gown is one given to the elder Dr. Richards,

(3). A meeting wil be held at John Mills' this evening at erly candl liht.

(4). I wil make my quarterly visitation on Watnung (Morris) Plains, Thursday next; and in the evening a meeting for special prayer wil be held at Mr. Turner's, when children may be presented for baptism. [None this morning; hardly a Sunday without infant Baptisms in Dr. Johnes' pastorate of fifty years; he baptized 2,800 and more.]

(5). The Trustees hav voted that the money collected last Sabbath be applied to the support of missionaries on the frontiers.

(6). The foloing resolutions hav bin adopted by the Session: Whereas it is the duty of the Session to assist the Pastor in catechising and instructing the children, resolved, That, in addition to the stated catechetical instruction givn by the pastor, the Session wil catechise the children in the several districts of the congregation at least twice a year; and for the accomplishment of this important object, that they be classified in the foloing manner, Viz. Messrs. Vail, Cutler and Youngs be one class to catechise the children in the district on Watnung plain, at Littleton, and near Demas Ford's; That Z. Freeman, Mr. Pierson, and Mr. D. Lindsley be one class to catechise the children in Green Village, Mulbery and New Vernon districts: That Mr. S. Freeman and Halsey be one class to catechise the children in the district near Jacob Goble's in Jockey Hollow and near Mr. Vincent Guering's: That Messrs. Johnson and Mills be one class to catechise the children in Morristown. Resolved, That the above classes attend to the catechising of the children in their respectiv districts, in the months of March and October; and, if providentially prevented, as soon thereafter as Providence permits." [This is a measure of Dr. Fisher's pastorate, adopted a few years before the Sunday-school originated.]

(7). The Rev. Samuel Whelpley has presented a certificate of membership and ordination in the Baptist denomination, and after examination by the Session he has bin received and wil enter into covenant with this Church Sabbath next.

(8). The foloing persons appeard before the Session Thursday last, desiring to be received to the full communion of the Church. After conversing with them individually, and being satisfied with their nolej, the evidence of their piety, and their views in desiring to cum to the holy ordinance of the Supper, The Session agreed to propound them to the congregation; and they wil be publicly receivd to full communion Sabbath next, unles sufficient reason to the contrary shal be made known to the Session in the meantime: Silas Johnson, Abigail, widow of Joseph Prudden; Amos, son of Joseph Prudden, deceased; Deborah Tuttle, widow; and Anna, wife of Silas Byram. [This is an innovation. No examinations by Session til 1791. Only 38 adults Baptized by Dr. Johnes, and only 3 of these on Sunday; the 400 and odd admitted to communion in first 50 years wer granted the privilege, in virtue of their baptism in infancy, upon his approval. *Propounding* candidates as above appears only in records of Dr. McDowell's pastorate.]

(9). The holy ordinance of the Lord's Supper wil be administerd Sabbath next, and the Preparatory Lecture wil be held in the Meeting house Friday afternoon at 2 o'clok. [Another innovation. Previously there had bin 6 communions every year from 1743 down: the 1st Sunday in Jan. and 1st of every alternate month. After 1817 only 4 a year wer observd, falling on the 1st Sunday in each quarter: this continued until after Sept., 1858, in the pastorate of Dr. Irving; when the present custom began, which gives 6 a year, on the 1st Sunday in Feb. and 1st of every alternate month.]

(10). No person professing to belong to any sister church, can be admitted to occasional communion in this Church, for more than one year, without producing a certificat of regular standing in the Church to which such person professedly belongs. [This last notice marks an innovation of 1808, and seems to hav bin red annually for nearly twenty-five years. While its aim is good, it is one to be souht by persuasion and not by command, to be decided by the conscience of the communicant, not by any ecclesiastical authority in this off-hand manner. Ther is no such rule in force here today; ther never has bin any warrant in the constitution of our Church for such a rule;

(*To be continued.*)

THE RECORD.

FIRST PRESBYTERIAN CHURCH, MORRISTOWN, N. J.

"THIS SHALL BE WRITTEN FOR THE GENERATION TO COME."—Psalms 102 : 18.

VOLUME V.   JUNE, 1885.   NUMBER 30.

[Printed with the A pproval of the Session.]

THE RECORD

Is published monthly ; terms $1.00 a year, *in advance.*

Single numbers for any month,10 cents each.

Subscriptions should be made to Mr. James R. Voorhees.

Matters pertaining to the publication should be addressed to the

EDITOR OF THE RECORD.

Entered at the Post Office at Morristown, N. J., as second class matter.

SUPPLEMENT.

The Supplement for this month completes the Minutes of the Trustees and Parish for the pastorate of Mr. French ; covers all the Minutes for the period of the vacancy that followed; and brings the Minutes of the Session during Mr. Green's pastorate down to Nov. 7, 1878.

CALENDAR FOR JUNE.

4. *Thursday :* Prayer Service, 7:45 P. M.

5. *Friday :* Preparatory Service, 3:30 P. M. Baptism of Infants.

7. *Sunday :* Communion. Collection for Missions among Freedmen.

11. *Thursday :* " Indifference to Distress," Matt. xxv. 42, 48—Missions in Africa.

14. *Sunday :* Children's Day and Anniversary.

18. *Thursday :* "The Great Change," II. Cor. v. 17.

24. *Wednesday :* Session Meeting, 7:30 P. M.

25. *Thursday :* " How to hear the Word," Heb. iv. 2.

EVERY WEEK.

Sunday : Church Services, 10:30 A. M. and 7.30 P. M. School of the Church, 3 P. M. Young People's prayer meeting. 6.45 P. M.

Tuesday : Pastor at home afternoon and evening.

Thursday : Young Men's prayer meeting,

7:15 P. M. Church Mid-week service of Prayer, 7:45 P. M.

Saturday : Bible-class and Teacher's meeting, led by the Rev. Dr. Erdman, 4 P. M.

WOMAN'S HOME MISSIONS.

The regular meeting of the Home Miss'y Society will be held in the Chapel on the afternoon of Monday, June 8th, at 4 o'clock.

It is pleasant to see the increasing interest in this Society manifested in various ways, especially by increased contributions, thus enabling its work to be more extended and efficient.

NOTEWORTHY VERSIONS OF THE BIBLE IN ENGLISH.

CAEDMON, monk of Whitby, made metrical *parafrases* of historical portions about 680.

VENERABLE BEDE (672-735) completed a translation (some say a *commentary* only,) of St. John's Gospel on the day of his deth. May 26, 735.

ALFRED THE GREAT (849-901) prefixt a version of the Ten Commandments to his Code of Laws : and began, but did not live to finish, a version of the Psalms.

THE ORMULUM, by Orme, or Ormin, a *parafrase* of the Gospels and Acts, in the latter half of 12th century,

JOHN WICLIF (1324-1384) laid the foundation of liberty of conscience, by appealing to the Bible as the sole standard of truth, and began the Reformation in England, 1360. Translated Apocalypse, 1356; completed N. T., 1380 ; and O. T., 1384. *First English version of whole Bible,* but made from the Latin. Price of a copy equivalent to about 200 dollars in our money ; yet very many sold, at least 170 being still in existencs.

(Important connecting events : *Invention*

of Printing with cast metal types, 1452; *Revival of Learning*, on dispersion of Greek refugees thru-out Europe, after capture of Constantinople by the Turks in 1453; and beginning of *Luther's Reformation* in Germany, 1517.)

WM. TYNDALE (1484-1536). the father of the Bible in present use, strangld and burnt at the stake, by order of Henry VIII., near Brussels, Oct. 6, 1536. Publisht, at various places in Europe, translations of Matt. and Mark, 1524; of complete N. T., 1525 or 6; of Pentateuch, 1531; and before deth had translated O. T. as far as II Chron., with Book of Jonah. *First printed portions of Bible in English and first versions made from the original Hebrew and Greek.* By order of Henry and Cardinal Wolsey copies, and some who possest them, wer burnt when found in England.

MILES COVERDALE, in 1535, publisht *first version of whole Bible*, using Tyndale's work as far as printed, and, for the remainder, translating from Luther's and other recent versions; dedicated to Henry VIII., and freely admitted into England.

THOMAS MATTHEWS, pseudonym of John Rogers, a friend and assistant of Tyndale, martyrd in 1555, under Mary. Publisht revision of Tyndale's and Coverdale's work in 1537, the *first complete publication* of Tyndale's translation, having on title-page, " set forth by the King's most gracious licence." A copy ordered to be placed in every parish Church.

GREAT BIBLE, so called from large size of book, sometimes called *Cranmer's Bible ;* edited by Coverdale at the direction of the government, on the basis of the Matthew's version. *Source of Psalter* in present Book of Common Prayer. First version to print, *in different type,* words needed for English sense, but not found in the originals.

GENEVAN BIBLE, undertaken by English exiles at Geneva, Wm. Whittingham (brother-in-law of John Calvin), being chief editor; with Tyndale's work as its basis. N. T. publisht June 10, 1557, and whole Bible in 1560. The best version with the exception of King James', and for more than half a century continued to dispute with latter the right to popular favor. *First version* in size small enuf to meet the want of a *family Bible,* to be printed *in Roman type*

instod of the usual black letter, and to hav *the chapters divided into verses.* Sometimes called the *Breeches Bible,* because of the word "breeches" instead of "aprons" in Gen. iii. 7. Puritan and republican tone of marginal comments made it offensiv in certain quarters.

BISHOPS' BIBLE, also known as *Parker's Bible,* published in 1568, and so called because Archbishop Parker engaged 15 learned men, 8 of whom wer Bishops, to prepare the work. A revision of the Great Bible. Disappointed expectations as to scholarship, and never came into general favor. By appointment of King James made *basis of version now in use.*

CATHOLIC BIBLE : N. T. publisht at Rheims in 1528 ; O. T., at Douay in 1609. *Translated from the Latin,* in some instances so blindly as to be unintelligible ; but has many felicitous words and expressions, some of which wer adopted into King James' version.

KING JAMES' BIBLE, first publisht in 1611 ; *our present version.* Undertaken in 1604, on the informal order of James I., by 47 eminent scholars, divided into 6 classes, two sitting at Westminister, two at Oxford, and two at Cambridge ; with oversight by "three or four most ancient and grave divines not employ'd in translating," and finally revisd by two delegates from each class and six others. It was *never formally or truly "Authorized ;"* but gradually won its way to general favor. Aside from the Bishops' Bible, of the previous versions in English, "that of Geneva most influenct the *renderings* of our Bible, and that of Rheims and Douay the *vocabulary.*" Changes in spelling, punctuation, italics, marginal readings and references hav been made from time to time ; but otherwise the Bible in common use to-day is the same as that publisht in 1611.

THE ANGLO-AMERICAN REVISION, now completed, has for its object "to adapt King James' version to the present state of the English language, without changing the idiom and vocabulary, and to the present standard of Biblical scholarship, which has made very great advances since 1611." It originated in the Convocation of Canterbury, May 6, 1870. The American Committee was organized in 1871, by invitation and approval of the British Revisers. The two committees have numbered 101 names. In Jan. 1879, ther wer 79 active members, 52 in England and 27 in America. It is the first "*inter-national* and *inter-domi-national* effort in the history of the transla- tion of the Bible." N. T. publisht 1881 ; O. T., 21 May 1885.

NOTES OF THE PAST.

SUPPLIED BY WILLIAM KELBY, ESQ., OF THE NEW YORK HIST. SOC.

THESE ARE TO GIVE NOTICE.—That on the third Wednesday of May next there will be Sold at publick Vendue to the high- est Bidder, the House and Plantation of *John* Hayward situate in *Whippany*, now called *Hanover* in the Province of *New Jersey.* The Conditions of Sale are to pay one third Part at the Time of making the Deed of Conveyance and the two thirds of the consideration Money, to give good Se- curity to *Jonathan Crane* & *Nathaniel Whee- ler* of *Newark* and *John Haywood* of *Han- over.* The Premises to be put up to Sale being about two hundred Acres of wood- land part thereof cleared, and about one hundred Acres of rich Meadow, ditched and drained, most part thereof now in English Grass for mowing, and made fit for Corn, Hemp Flax and other Things with a good bearing Orchard, Dwelling-House and Barn, and other improvements. Whoever are in- clined to purchase the same, may repair to the said *Crane, Wheeler* or Hayward, and be further informed of the Premises and of the Clearness of the Title.

The New-York Gazette, April 3, 1732.

New Jersey and County of Hunterdon, in Hanover Township, May 1, 1732.

John Haywood, of full Age, deposeth, That on or about the 22d Day of April last past, in the Forks of the North Branches of Raritan River in said County, one Ben- jamin Hillyard, late from Potowmack River in Maryland, or Virginia but formerly of Piscattaway in New Jersey, Black-Smith, Took this Deponent aside, and there spoke to this Deponent as follows, viz : That one Timothy Burcham, and others were d——ned fools, that they would not be per- suaded to go with him, with whom they might get Money as fast as Heart could wish. Then added, D——n it, I'll show you (pointing to some Horses) he said, such would sell down in Maryland for 14 or 15 Pounds a piece, and that at this Season of the year they were plenty in the Woods, being turned out to get Flesh against ploughing time ; and that he would take them, and go back of the Inhabitants to Maryland, to sell them ; and if they did not sell amongst the English, he would sell them to the Indians, and there they would sell for Skins at a better Value. And that many new Plantations were settling to- wards the Head of the Potowmack River, where a great Number of Negroes was to be had, Ten or a Dozen at a Time, and take them back to the French Indian Traders to sell them. And that he would assure any one that would join with him in this Pro- ject, more than One Hundred Pounds in Three Months time ; and that it should be so nicely wrought (or carried on) that none should be suspected, of doing any wrong ; And he also proposed to take this Depo- nent, as a Partner in this wicked Design who absolutely refused. And this Depo- nent further saith, That the said Burcham and Fitzrandolph, are absent from their Wives and Children, and suspected to have been persuaded to undertake the above said Project with the said Hillyard, and fur- ther saith not.

Sworn before me John Budd, *Justice.* Note. In other Depositions, it was proposed to carry Horses and bring Negroes and sell them in New-York Colony, or New-Eng- land, and that he stole a Negro and sold him on Long Island. and had several times of 2 or 3 Horses, at first setting out, made 10 or 14 of them, before he came to Mary- land or Virginia, to sell them. He particu- larly mentioned Powtowmack for stealing Negroes from the new Plantations, where abundance of them are under Overseers. Its well known that Burcham is gone with Hillyard, and believed Fitzrandolph also.

The New-York Gazette, June 26, 1732.

A SUNDAY IN THE FIRST CHURCH.

BETWEEN 1800 AND 1825.

HISTORICAL SERMON BY THE PASTOR, PREACHED 13TH APRIL 1884.

(Concluded.)

and I wonder at the temerity which thus

undertook to fence the Lord's tabl, for logically it is a usurpation over privat judgment of the same sort as the Romish denial of the cup to the laity.]

I would urge upon you all a more general interest in the classes for the instruction of the young, which are held on every Sabbath morning before meeting. [Under date of 30 Jan. 1816, in the pastorate of Dr. Mc-Dowell, the Minutes of the Session contain the following : "The order of the Synod in regard to the formation of societies for the instruction of the young in the Scriptures was red, & the Moderator was appointed to draw a plan for the establishment and regulation of such societies or classes." This was probably the outgrowth of the idea suggested by the Rev. Robert Finley, of Baskingridge, which received the endorsement of the General Assembly in 1815 : and undoutedly the origin of the Sunday-school of this Church.]

The "long prayer" foloes the notices, occupying about twenty-five minutes, during which the congregation stands. Then the minister takes up Watts' Psalms and Hymns, the only collection ever yet allowed in the Meeting house, and announces " Psalm 51st, 2d part, long metre." On opening to the place, we find that the title reads : " Original and actual sin confessed." We sit to sing the Psalm, and at its close, the pepermints and sweet-flag having bin unrold from the corners of handkerchiefs, we are prepared to listen to the sermon. This does not impress us very much at first, since the exordium contains many generalities and much labord interpretation ; but as the preacher gets into his subject, and especially when he has warmd up to the improvement of his theme, we feel his power more and more. The tears stream copiously down his own face in the fervor of his appeals, and nearly every one in the congregation is weeping. We jot down a few of the closing sentences, but cannot copy their eloquence and power of pathos and persuasion. The preacher says : " From this subject, we see what excludes men from Heaven. It is not a want of fulness and freeness in the plan of mercy. It is not that God is unwilling to save the sinner. It is simply because yon will not be saved. You choose your own pride, your own vanity, your own lust, your own course in life—the path that leads to hell—No other being will bear the guilt but yourselves—forever and forever, you will welter in eternal woe, bearing your guilt unpitied

and alone—Nor will it be a trifling crime to be damned. It is not a thing which you are at liberty to choose. You have no right to go down to hell and become the eternal enemy of God. You are under solemn obligations to be saved. Let me also remind you, if you go from this place to woe, you will inherit no common damnation. Here this amazing plan of God's mercy has been presented again and again. Here God's Spirit has striven. Many of you have been before awakened and lived through revivals of religion. Others have pressed into the Kingdom ; and you have felt and known, that you must repent or die. Go home this day, impenitent sinner, if God spares a rebel like you to get home—go home and reflect, that if you pass through this revival unmoved, the probability is that you will be damned, and the certainty is, that *you* only will be to blame if you are. I do not say that you will *certainly* be lost, I say that a most fearful *probability* thunders perdition on your guilty path. What *should* move you hereafter if you are not moved now ? You *know* your duty, and your doom if you do it not. You are in the hands of a Sovereign God. There I leave you. I have no other power than to spread out the scheme of mercy—to entreat you by the love of Jesus, and the mercy of God, and the value of the soul, to embrace the offer of life ; and if you *will perish*, I must sit down and weep as I see you glide to the lake of death. Yet I cannot see you take that dread plunge—see you die, die forever, without once more assuring you that the offer of the Gospel is freely made to you. While you linger this side the fatal verge, that shall close life and hope and happiness, I would once more lift up my voice and say ; see, sinner, see a God of love. He comes to you. He fills the Heaven, the skies, the earth. Hear his voice as it breaks on the stillness of this house. Listen to the accents of the everliving God—" As I live I have no pleasure in the death of the wicked, but rather that he turn and live: turn ye, turn ye, for why will ye die ?" Then in an earnest, heartfelt prayer, he bears the congregation to the throne of grace ; imploring the Lord to spare this people, and save these dying sinners. "Oh, most holy, blessed and merciful Saviour, deliver them not into the bitter pains of eternal death ! Amen."[1]

Another Psalm is sung, the benediction is pronounced, and we pass out with the husht and awed assembly, to ponder what we have herd, while we eat our lunch, in a sheltered spot, during the intermission before the second services at 2 o'clock.[2]

[1. From close of Mr. Barnes' sermon on " Way of Salvation."

2. At service when this Historical sermon was preacht, the Scripture lessons were red from Pulpit Bible presented by Col. Jacob Ford before 1777, and the hymns from the Pulpit copy of Watts in use by Mr. Barnes.]

THE RECORD.

FIRST PRESBYTERIAN CHURCH, MORRISTOWN, N. J.

"This Shall be Written for the Generation to Come."—Psalms 102 : 18.

VOLUME V.   JULY, 1885.   NUMBER 31.

[Printed with the Approval of the Session.]

THE RECORD

Is published monthly ; terms $1.00 a year, *in advance*.

Single numbers for any month, 10 cents each.

Subscriptions should be made to Mr. James R. Voorhees.

Matters pertaining to the publication should be addressed to the

EDITOR OF THE RECORD.

Entered at the Post Office at Morristown, N' J., as second class matter.

AN UNSIGNED PLEDGE.

On March 28th, 1884, a pledge was sent to the Treasurer of the Manse Building Fund, for $18., but the sender neglected to sign it. Will the person who sent the pledge please give the name, and also oblige the Committee by an early payment ?

J. R. VOORHEES,

Treasurer,

WOMAN'S FOREIGN MISSIONS.

The regular meeting of the Woman's Foreign Missionary Society will be held on Monday afternoon, July 13th, in the Chapel, at 4 o'clock. An interesting program is in progress, and a full attendance is hoped for.

WOMAN'S HOME MISSION.

The meeting of the Home Missionary Society, held on June 8th, was well attended, and an increasing interest in the cause of missions was manifested.

The question of assuming the support of a teacher was freely discussed, and finally decided by the selection of Mrs. R. W. D. Bryan, of Albuquerque, New Mexico, as our teacher.

It was considered advisable to appropriate the remainder of the funds to mission work among the Mormons.

SUPPLEMENT.

Publication of the Minutes will be discontinued for a few months. In the meantime the "Combined Registers, 1742 to 1885," of which the first eight pages were published in Feb., will be continued ; the Supplement for this month beginning with "Phebe, daughter of Nathaniel and Rachel Armstrong," and extending to "Anne Ayres, dismissed 19 April, 1815 to N. Y."

This list in the Combined Registers is intended to contain all the names, with all the facts of record opposite each name, from all the Registers of the Church, arranged in alphabetical order. Great pains have been taken to make the list complete and accurate, but it is beyond hope that the list is free from errors ; corrections will be thankfully received.

Requests from any persons who prefer not to have dates of birth, baptism, &c., printed after their own names or those of their ancestors, will be cheerfully complied with.

EVERY WEEK.

Sunday : Church Services, 10:30 A. M. and 7:30 P. M. School of the Church, 3 P. M. Young People's prayer meeting, 6:45 P. M.

Tuesday : Pastor at home afternoon and evening.

Thursday : Church Mid-week service of Prayer, 7:45 P. M.

CALENDAR FOR JULY.

2. *Thursday :* Good Counsel and Bad, 1 Kings, xii. 6-17.

5. *Sunday :* 10:30 A. M.; Collection for debt of Foreign Missions ; 6:45 P. M.; Joy, Ps. cxxvi.

9. *Thursday :* An easy Religion and its

Motive, 1 Kings xii. 25–33 ; *Missions :* American Indians.

12. *Sunday :* 6:45 P. M. ; Praise, Ps. cxlviii.

16. *Thursday :* A Father's bad Influence extending to his Children and his grandchildren, 1 Kings xvi. 23–34.

19. *Sunday :* 6:45 P. M. ; Watching, Matt. 24, 42, 51.

22. *Wednesday :* 4 P. M. ; Session Meeting.

23. *Thursday :* The Riches of Poverty, 1 Kings xvii. 1–16.

26. *Sunday :* 6:45 P. M. ; Confessing Christ, Rom. x. 6–10.

30. *Thursday :* A Time for Boldness, I Kings xviii. 1–18.

31. *Friday :* 3:30 P. M. ; Preparatory Lecture ; Baptism of Infants.

THE SCHOOL OF THE CHURCH—REPORT FOR THE 69th YEAR.

Number of Officers, 7 ; of Teachers, 48 ; of Scholars in Primary Class, 90 ; of Scholars in Main room, 267 ; total membership, 412.

Changes : New scholars, 40 ; scholars withdrawn or moved away, 36 ; died, 1.

Contributions : For School window in Manse, $190. ; for Missions, $569.89.

Church-members : 7 officers ; 48 teachers ; 86 scholars ; total, 141 ; scholars received to Communion during the year, 7.

Attendance : Present at every service ; 1 officer, 9 scholars. Average attendance, 245 ; largest, 273 ; smallest, 108 ; of officers, 7 ; of teachers, 38 ; of scholars, 200. The following are the names of those who have been present at every service during the year : Sadie Whitehead and Nettie Pierson, of Miss C. J. Pierson's class ; John Berry, of Mr. Wm. B. Conklin's class ; Eva Powelson, of Mr. Geo. E. Voorhees' class ; Fred. Guerin, of Mr. Geo. A. Drake's class ; Ella Potts, of Miss Lizzie VanPelt's class ; Lizzie Struble, of Miss Rosa Crane's class ; Eugene Struble, of Mr. A. W. Conklin's class ; Mr. Edward Fleury and Mr. Frank Whitehead.

Volumes in Library, 485.

Appropriated by the Parish for the expenses of the school, $200.

The following scholars have committed to memory the Shorter Catechism during the year : Anna Hall and Alice Hall, of Miss Abby Pierson's class ; Edgar Martin, of Miss Emma VanPelt's class ; Charles Smith, of Mr. A. W. Conklin's class ; Hattie A. Boyd, of Miss Cornie Stone's class ; and Anna G. Bonnell, of Mrs. VanDoren's class.

Banner Classes. To be a Banner Class all the members must be present and all must contribute to the mission cause. The classes of Miss Augusta Stone and Mr. E. T. Caskey have fulfilled these requirements 23 Sundays, and therefore divide the honor of Banner Class for the year. Other classes have fulfilled the conditions and been Banner Classes, as follows :

Miss Minnie Mills' class, for 18 Sundays.
Mrs. Sadie Johnson's " " 17 "
Mr. Wm. B. Conklin's " " 17 "
Miss Lucy Johnson's " " 15 "
" Fanny Easton's " " 12 "
" Willis' " " 11 "
" C. Stone's " " 11 "
" Lizzie VanPelt's " " 10 "
Mr. Geo. E. Voorhees' " " 10 "

New Classes : Three have been formed in the Main room from the Primary ; and two important Bible Classes have been formed, during the year.

Officers for the ensuing year : Charles D. Platt, Superintendent ; Phil. B. Pierson, Secretary and Treasurer ; and Charles Bird, Librarian.

CHILDREN'S MISSIONARY SOCIETY.

Report of the Treasurer of the Children's Missionary Society of the First Presbyterian Church of Morristown, N. J., from March 29th, 1885, to June 28th, 1885 :

RECEIPTS.

Balance cash in bank,	$66.51
March 29, Collection,	10.93
Collections taken in April,	46.61
" " " May,	54.48
" " " June,	30.35
	—$208.88

DISBURSEMENTS.

April 7. Printing Treasurer's Cards,	$ 1.50
April 26. Board of Foreign Missions,	75.00

May 29. Lincoln University for
half support of James P.
Adams, 75.00
Balance cash in bank, 57.38
———$208.88

WILL. C. VAN DOREN,
Treasurer.

Appropriations made by the Society at the commencement of the year, amounting to $585.70, have been paid in full.

Mr. James P. Adams, toward whose support we contribute annually, finished his course in the Collegiate Department of Lincoln University, June 4th, 1885, and will immediately enter the Theological Department.

ELDER LEBBEUS B. WARD.

Lebbeus B. Ward, who died on Monday, June 15th, at the house of his son, No. 605 Madison avenue, New York, was born in Chatham, N. J., on April 7, 1801. His father was a farmer and manufacturer and his mother was from the Dod family of Newark. His grandfather was a captain in the Revolutionary Army. After receiving a common school education Mr. Ward went at the age of nineteen to Montreal, where his brothers John and Samuel had already started one of the first machine shops in Canada. He remained in business with them until 1839, when he went to England to study heavy iron forgings. Later he established the Hammersley Forge Works at Fifty-ninth street and the North River, New York city, which were then the only works in the city capable of handling large forgings. He also built a large stone house in the English style near the works and there his sons were born and reared. He remained in this business until 1851, when he retired, becoming director in the Broadway Bank, and later one of the founders of the Importers' and Traders' Bank and a stockholder in many other financial enterprises. In the same year he was elected a member of the New York Assembly, where he was Chairman of the Committee on Banking and Education. While there he secured a charter for the New York Juvenile Asylum, of which he was a corporator. He was also a member of the Presbyterian Board of

Foreign Missions and gave largely to other charities. In the early years of the present Metropolitan Police Board he was one of the Commissioners.

Mr. Ward was married three times. His first wife, Miss Diminis Dickinson, of Montreal, lived only one year after her marriage. By his second wife, Mrs. Abby Partridge Pratt, of Hatfield, Mass., he had three sons, one of whom died in his infancy, the other two being Dr. Samuel B. Ward, of Albany, and Willard P. Ward, of New York City. In 1848, three years after the death of his second wife he married Miss Elizabeth Starr, of New York City, who died a year ago.

Mr. Ward removed to Morristown, N. J., in 1867, and was installed Elder in our Church on the 17th of Dec., 1871. The Session adopted the following minute, June 18th: "In view of the death of Mr. Lebbeus B. Ward, on the 15th inst., in the 85th year of his age, Session would record their sincere appreciation of his Christian character, and of the faithful discharge of his duties, as a member of Session for many years past, and until incapacitated by his advanced age and increasing infirmities."

"A LIST OF CAPT. JOSEPH HALSEY'S COMPANY MILITIA.

Morristown, 7 June 1791."

(Contributed by E. D. Halsey, Esq.)

Cap't. Jos. Halsey, Sirus Condict,
Lieut. William Johnes, David Humphrevil,
Ens'n. Dan'l Lindsly, Ebenezer Humphrevil,
Samuel Ford,
SERJ'TS. George F. Fenery,
Jesse Cutler, Silvanus Tuttle,
Seth Gregory, Josiah Hathaway,
Abijah Sherman, Silas Baldwin,
Zenas Lindsly. Samuel Ayres,
Absalom Trowbridge,
CORP'LS. John Hathaway,
John Kirkpatrick, David Trowbridge,
Isaac Hathaway, Abraham Beers,
Timothy Fairchild. John (?) Hathaway,
Joseph Trowbridge,
Silas D. Hayward, John Woodruff,
William Marsh, Daniel Mills,
Timothy Force, Jobe Mills,

Jacob Meeker,
Isaac Walker,
Shadrach Hayward,
Timothy Extill,
Daniel Coleman,
David Mills,
Jabez Guiness,
Dave D. Budd,
Thadeus Mills,
James Vance,
William Burnet,
Matthias Crane,
Uzal Pierson,
Joseph Coleman,
Isaac Woolley,
Abraham Rutan,
George Oharrow.

Trune Goble,
William Marshel,
Hezekiah Mitchel,
David Y. Wheeler,
Daniel Spenser,
John Bollen,
Elijah Holleway,
Henry Feter,
Joshua Gorden,
John McDannels,
George Mills,
Michael Conner,
Silas Hathaway,
Ichabod· Crane,
John Still,
George Marsh,
Thomas Jean.

NOTES OF THE PAST.

CONTRIBUTED BY WILLIAM NELBY, ESQ., OF THE NEW YORK HIST. SOC.

To be sold by *John Budd*, of the County of *Morris*, and Township of *Hanover* in *New Jersey*.

The present Farm whereon he is now seated, consisting of near Three Hundred Acres of Up Land, about 600 Acres of Meadow and good Swamp; with a good Dwelling House, orchard and every kind of Fruit Trees; a large Piece of the Meadow drained, and in English Grass, fit for Hemp, Flax, or Planting ; and the same may be divided and sold in Three Parts; the Meadow and Swamp hath a suitable Fall, and may be all drained and be made as good as Maiden-Head Meadow. Also to be sold, The Place called *Pine Hammock*, in the same Township, consisting of about 600 Acres, on which is a good Orchard ; about 150 Acres of which is Up-Land, and 450 Acres of good Meadow and Swamp, ten Acres of which is cleared and brought to English grass; with other Improvements; and may be sold in two Parts, with Up-Land Meadow and Swamp joining to each Part. The title is indisputable.

—*N. Y. Gazette, revived in the Weekly Post-Boy, Aug.* 28, 1749

TO BE SOLD. A Tract of good Land, divided by *Whippany* River, containing Twelve Hundred and Eighty Acres, besides Allowances for Highways, bounded S. E. with *John Kay's* Land and N. W. with *William Biddles ;* it is a square Tract and good Cripple on both Sides the River for Meadow and lies within half a mile of the Iron-works : Those that incline to purchase may apply to *Peter Sonmans* near *Amboy*, or to *Hannah Hodges*, of *Philadelphia*, for Condition of Sail, with an indisputable Title.

—*The New York Gazette, April* 26, 1734.

This is to give Notice, That on Thursday last was brought to Cornelius Vanhorne, Esq. : A Negro Man who calls himself *Bristow*, was taken up at or near King's Bridge, and says he belongs to *Thomas Freeman* of *Whippany :* The Owner by applying may have him on Demand, paying the charges.

—*N. Y. Gazette, revived in the Weekly Post-Boy, April* 16, 1750.

To be Sold, A small Plantation in the Township of *Mendum* in *Morris* County, *West New-Jersey*, containing 95 Acres of choice Land, well water'd, timber'd, and meadow'd : There is on it, a good new Dwelling House, also a Saw Mill and a Grist Mill, both under one Roof, on a good Stream, which falls into the *North Branch* of Raritan. Any Person inclining to purchase, may apply to *David Allen*, jun. living on the Premises; who will give an indisputable Title to the same.

—*N. Y. Gazette, revived in the Weekly Post-Boy Aug.* 6, 1750.

RUNAWAY on the 5th Day of August instant from *Jacob Ford*, of *Morris-Town* and County, *East New-Jersey*, a Negro Boy, named *Ishmael*, aged about 16 years, short and thick, full Faced, has a very large Foot, born in the Country, and has a sly Look Had on when he went away, a Flannel Jacket, dyed with Logwood of a purple Colour, two woollen Shirts, one Tow Shirt, and a Dowlas Shirt, a new Felt Hat, Leather Breeches, and Oznabrigs Trowsers.

Whoever takes up and secures the said Boy, so that his Master may have him again shall have Three Pounds Reward, and all reasonable charges paid by me.

JACOB FORD.

N. B.—He went away with a Negro Fellow already advertised by *Shadrech Hathaway*.

THE RECORD.

FIRST PRESBYTERIAN CHURCH, MORRISTOWN, N. J.

"THIS SHALL BE WRITTEN FOR THE GENERATION TO COME."—Psalms 102 : 18.

VOLUME V.   AUGUST, 1885.   NUMBER 32.

[Printed with the Approval of the Session.]

THE RECORD

Is published monthly ; terms $1.00 a year, *in advance.*

Single numbers for any month, 10 cents each.

Subscriptions should be made to Mr. James R. Voorhees.

Matters pertaining to the publication should be addressed to the

EDITOR OF THE RECORD.

Entered at the Post Office at Morristown, N. J., as second class matter.

SUPPLEMENT.

The Supplement for this month continues the publication of the Combined Registers, beginning with, Capt. Jabez Beach, and extending to Lindsly, son of Nathaniel Broadwell.

CALENDAR FOR AUGUST.

2. *Sunday:* 10.30 A. M., Communion. 6.45 P. M., Brevity of Life, Ps. 39 ; 4-7.

6. *Thursday:* The Prophets of Baal, 1 Kings 18: 19-29.

9. *Sunday:* 6.45 P. M., No Other Name. 1 Tim. 5: 6; Acts 4: 12.

13. *Thursday:* The Prophet of the Lord, I Kings 18· 30-46.

16. *Sunday:* 6.45 P. M., Responsibility for Others, Ezek. 33: 1-11.

20. *Thursday:* Elijah at Horeb, I Kings 19: 1-18.

23. *Sunday:* 6.45 P. M., Liberty, Rom. 8: 8-22.

27. *Thursday:* The Story of Naboth, I Kings 21: 4-19.

30, *Sunday:* 6.45 P. M., From Darkness to Light, John 9.

EVERY WEEK.

Sunday: Church Services, 10:30 A. M. and 7:30 P. M. School of the Church, 3 P. M. Young People's prayer meeting, 6.45 P. M.

Thursday: Church Mid-week service of Prayer, 7.45 P. M.

Friday: Pastor at home afternoon and evening.

THE OLD CEMETERY.

BY LU LIGHT.

[The following sketch is reprinted from a newspaper clipping found among the papers of the late Mrs. J. F. Voorhees. On the scrap there is no mark to determine its source or author.—EDITOR.]

Long ago, in my childhood days, when I first began to listen to the stories of the American Revolution, and hung enchanted upon the lips of my loved grand-mother as she talked of the days of '76, and when I read for the first time the history, familiar to every American, of the lofty courage and heroic endurance of Washington and his little army, at that early period a wish arose in my heart to visit the places and view the scenes consecrated by their valor or their sufferings, and, as a pilgrim approaches with a reverential joy and holy boldness the shrine endeared to him by the recollections of the past, thus I hoped to wander among those old battle-fields and camping-grounds, where the hand of Time has almost obliterated the black and heavy marks that War, the stern historian, writes with iron pen upon the tablet of the earth.

Among those places most intimately connected with our Revolutionary history, Morristown, a beautiful and flourishing village in the northern part of New Jersey, occupies an important position. Twice during our war for independence Washington chose Morristown as the winter-quarters of his weary little band of heroes, and his troops were encamped here during the memorable winter of 1779-80, which was the coldest ever known in this locality, and which became somewhat celebrated in the historical records of the time under the name of the "hard winter."

As a body of troops were frequently stationed at Morristown, it seems to have been considered an important strategic position by our commanders; and although the British sent out several expeditions to capture it, they were never successful in their endeavors.

Here sat the court-martial that condemned the subsequent traitor Arnold to be reprimanded by the commander-in-chief for his excesses. Here Lafayette—the heroic youth who left his native land and beautiful bride and crossed the ocean to battle for freedom—hastened to meet his beloved Washington, on his second arrival from France, where he had exerted his powerful influence to procure aid of men and money for the young Republic.

Many of the buildings that were built before or during the time of the Revolution still remain standing, and some have changed but little in appearance since they were occupied by Washington and his compatriots. Of the latter class is the old "Ford Mansion," better known as "Washington's head-quarters," where may be seen many relics of "ye ancient time."

At a short distance from the village, and upon an eminence commanding the town, are the remains of an old fort erected during the Revolution; and as the visitor walks along upon the sunken ramparts, or climbs the broken wall that formed a part of the enclosure, he can almost imagine that he sees

"The old Continentals
In their ragged regimentals,"

throwing up dirt for the entrenchments, or rolling along the stones that are to strengthen the fortifications.

But it is in the old cemetery that we find the most interesting mementoes of the past and the clearest proofs of the antiquity of the town, for there we can find tombstones, green with the moss of age, with inscriptions worn away by the storms of years till they are almost illegible—which were placed there early in the eighteenth century, or over one hundred and fifty years ago. When my long-cherished desire to visit the ancient burial-place had been gratified, and I found myself wandering among the marble monuments and hoary headstones rich with the history of the past, I could not resist the temptation to linger for a time in a spot consecrated by so many sacred memories, and pencil in hand, to note a few of the inscriptions that I found there, and that are interesting or instructive to the student or curiosity-seeker.

Upon the rough notes thus hurriedly taken the sketch before you has its origin.

A complete history of all the extraordinary events that have happened in a neighborhood may frequently be gathered from a diligent study of its tombstones, and therefore this burial place at Morristown acquires new and stronger interest as it grows older, and will ever continue to be a favorite resort with the antiquary and the student of history.

The old Cemetery occupies a central position in the village of Morristown, immediately in the rear of the Presbyterian Church. This Church is built upon the spot where the meeting-house in which Washington worshipped and engaged in communion service once stood, and has lately been repaired and greatly improved in its appearance.

After entering the burial-ground I took the path to the right, and my attention was soon arrested by a large, flat tombstone inscribed as follows :—

"In memory of Peter Dickinson, member of the first Provincial Congress of New Jersey in 1775, afterwards captain of the second Company, third Regiment of the New Jersey Brigade of the Revolutionary army of 1776. Died 1785. Came to Morris Co. with his family 1724."

Then the path led me to the grave of the Rev. Dr. Johnes, who was pastor of the Presbyterian Church during the Revolution and concerning whom I find the following anecdote in Lossing's "Illustrated Field Book of the Revolution."

"It is related that he (Washington) called upon the Rev. Dr. Jones, the pastor of the Presbyterian Church of Morristown, or learning that the communion service was to be observed in his Church on the following Sabbath, and inquired whether communicants of another denomination were permitted to join with them. The doctor replied :—

"Most certainly. Ours is not the Presbyterian's table, General, but the Lord's ; and hence we give the Lord's invitation to all his followers of whatever name."

"'I am glad of it,' said the general ; "that is as it ought to be ; but as I was not quite sure of the fact, I thought I would ascertain it from yourself, as I propose to join you on that occasion. Though a member of the, Church of England, I have no exclusive partialties."

"Washington was at the communion table on the following Sabbath."

There appear to have been several clergymen of the name of Johnes (Lossing and several other historians spell the name Jones, but I prefer to follow the orthography of the old headstone), and the pulpit of this church may have been filled by the same family for several generations.

A little further on I saw the tombs of a number of the Ford family ; it was one of the most distinguished in the county in the days of '76. These tombs are surmounted by large stones raised some two feet from the ground, and supported by brickwork. The bricks, however, are crumbling rapidly, and in some places are tumbling down. One of the stones is inscribed as follows :—

"In memory of Colonel Chillion Ford, who departed this life on the nineteenth of October, 1800, aged forty-two years, nine months and twenty-three days. He early showed his attachment to his country by entering into her service at the commencement of her struggle with Great Britain, and continued during the war an able and active officer in the artillery. He was a warme friend, a tender husband, a kind father, and an honest man."

I will quote here two other inscriptions, the first of which shows that the Baptist Church of Morristown must have been established at a very early date in the history of our country.

"In memory of the Rev. John Walton, who was minister of the Baptist Church in Morristown, and who died October the first, 1770, aged thirty-five years."

"In memory of Captain Job Brookfield, an officer of the Revolution, who died in the year 1833, aged 83 years."

When the small pox was raging so fearfully in the little army of patriots stationed at Morristown, many of the soldiers who died of this loathsome disease—a more dreaded foe than the British rifle—were buried in this cemetery ; but although some of the inhabitants of the village know in what part of the ground they were interred, I could find no marks to indicate their final resting-place.

So after this war in which we are now engaged is concluded ; when relatives or friends search over the battle fields and grave yards to find some mark or trace of the dear ones who died in the service of their country, they will find as they wander upon the banks of the Potomac or Mississippi, or on the plains of Kentucky, that—

"No monument or lettered stone
Marks the lone resting of the brave."

but far from the scenes of his childhood and the loved ones at home sleeps the brave volunteer, where no willow shall weep, no flower bloom, no mother or sister come to mourn over the little spot of earth that covers their lost soldier-boy.

Many of the inscriptions found in this old cemetery, especially those written upon the oldest stones, are very eccentric, and often excite a smile by the quaintness and even humor that they exhibit. The poetry—if it should be thus designated— is in an especial manner remarkable for the poetic license and the new and often startling similes and figures of rhetoric that are used by the epitaph writers. I copied several inscriptions of this character, and will give them to you, although the quaint carving with which the headstones are decorated, and the curious manner in which the letters are engraved upon them cannot be described by type.

"Come see ye place where I do ly
As you are now so once was I
As I Be now soon You will be
PrePare for Death and Follow me."

Another :—

"Beauty and wit with virtue joined
Did grace the Body here confined
Weep not Kind reader but Rejoyce
In Heaven is heard here tunefull voice
However weep yt Faith has taken more
Than Nature can to Friends Restore."

The following curious epitaph seems to

be addressed pointedly and particularly to the wife of the deceased—

"Farewell dear wife my life is past
My love to you till death did last
Now after me no sorrow take
But love my orphans for my sake."

Most of those old epitaphs begin thus :—
"Here lyes ye Body of—"

The annexed is another of these super-scriptions :—

"In memory of Benjamin Hathaway Esqr
Aged 63 years Dec'd April 21 1762

"Here's ye Remains of him that was a Esqr
may Rest with Kings & Princes In ye
Dust
Until ye world Desolves In flaming Fire
At ye Last Resurrection of ye Dust
When ye arch Angels trump'h sound
Arise ye Dead appear before ye Lord
When Christ will meet Ye Righteous in
cloud."

The tombstone from which the above was copied had settled so much in the ground that I was unable, even after putting away the grass and leaves from its base, to make out the whole of the inscription, which appears to have been quite lengthy. What I have given, however, will doubtless furnish an idea of the whole.

"In memory of Susannah, consort of Uzal Tompkins. Aged 69 years. Died Jan. 25, 1817, and was attended with eight children and nineteen grand-children at her funeral."

Many of the epitaphs are elegant and very touching. The following verses, inscribed upon the tombstone of "Our little Willie" are truly beautiful :—

"There is another little hand
To heaven's sweet harpstrings given
Another gentle seraph's voice
Another star in heaven."

As no quotation marks were used I suppose the poetry to be original.

One handsome stone bore only the words, "Gone to Rest." One handsome monument was surmounted by a tastefully sculp-tured dove—

". . . just on the wing for heaven."

A little stone upon which was carved a rosebud just ready to burst with bloom was inscribed, "Our little Laura." A similar one in another part of the ground read, "Our Lizzie." Near the latter was a marble slab bearing only the words, "The Orphan Boy," and farther on was another, inscribed "Margaret, the Orphan." Upon one large gravestone was sculptured a sailor, clad in a short jacket and broad-brimmed straw hat with a wide ribbon, weeping at a tomb almost hid from view by a weeping willow. This stone was inscribed "My Mother's Grave," and we can imagine that from time to time the gallant tar who would erect so beautiful and costly a memorial above the ashes of his departed mother, will often re-call the pleasant little nook where she re-poses, when he is "rocked in the cradle of the deep," far from his native land and child-hood home ; and will recall the blessed moments when he sat, a happy child upon his mother's knee, and never dreamed of sorrow or death or ocean storms.

A number of slaves, as I believe, have been buried here, but few of their resting-places have been honored with headstones . The following is engraved upon a handsome block of marble :—

"Cato. Died Oct. 1831. He was, for nearly forty years, a faithful servant in the family of D. Phœnix."

Some of the tombstones are in the form of a cross, the letters I. H. S. being written above the epitaph. Many of the old stones have sunk so far in the ground that they are almost invisible; others have been broken off and disfigured, and others still have been worn away by the storms of a century until their inscriptions are no longer legible. Beneath one stone were placed the bodies of a husband and wife who were mur-dered, a short distance from Morristown, on the same day, by a French servant whom they had procured from the city only a short time previous, and had selected on account of his honest and prepossessing appearance. Upon a majority of the old stones are wretchedly carved a death's head and cross-bones. "Ye" for "the" and the old-fash-ioned long "s" are often used. One stone is inscribed as follows :—

"Sacred to the memory of Elizabeth Ica-eclo, wife of Moses Esty, who made her exit Feb. 11, A. D. 1793. Erected by her son, William, the Rover."

This inscription, like that written by the sailor is one very suggestive of thought. When we remember at what an exciting period in the history of our country and of the world "The Rover" lived, we cannot but suppose that his history was an event-ful and an exciting one.

The oldest date that I could discover upon a tombstone was 1722, but a friend informed me that he found a stone dated 1713, so it appears that this ground was used as a bur-ial-place more than half a century before the time of the Revolutionary War, and at least a hundred and fifty years before the present day.

Here beneath a handsome monument re-poses the dust of the celebrated William Alexander Duer, who was member of the New York Legislature, Judge of the Su-preme Court of the United States, author of a treatise on the Constitutional Jurispru-dence of the United States, and President of Columbia College. He was born at Rhine-beck, Dutchess County, New York, prac-tised law for some time at New Orleans, and died at Morristown, having been forced to return North for the benefit of his health.

THE RECORD.

FIRST PRESBYTERIAN CHURCH, MORRISTOWN, N. J.

"This Shall be Written for the Generation to Come."—Psalms 102 : 18.

Volume V. SEPTEMBER, 1885. Number 33.

[Printed with the Approval of the Session.]

THE RECORD

Is published monthly, terms $1.00 a year, *in advance.*

Single numbers for any month,10 cents each

Subscriptions should be made to Mr. James R Voorhees.

Matters pertaining to the publication should be addressed to the

EDITOR OF THE RECORD

Entered at the Post Office at Morristown, N. J., as second class matter.

SUPPLEMENT.

The Supplement for this month continues the publication of the Combined Registers, beginning with Mary, daughter of Nathaniel Broadwell. and extending to Hannah Campfield who was married to John McEwen, of Hanover, on the 5th of February, 1818.

EVERY WEEK.

Sunday: Church Services, 10:30 A. M. and 7:30 P. M. School of the Church, 3 P. M. Young People's prayer meeting, 6.45 P. M.

Tuesday: Pastor at home afternoon and evening.

Thursday: Church Mid-week service of Prayer, 7.45 P. M.

WOMAN'S FOREIGN MISSIONS.

The next meeting of the Woman's Foreign Missionary Society will be held in the Chapel on Friday afternoon, September 4th, 1885, at half past three.

This change of date has been made so that the ladies may have the pleasure of meeting Mrs. Dr. Dennis, of Beyroot, who will talk informally about the interests of the Tripoli School, and other mission work in Syria.

The meetings of this society are increasing in interest. A cordial invitation is extended to all the ladies of the congregation to be present at these meetings, and to become members of the society.

The question is frequently asked, "What are the conditions of membership in this society?" In answer we quote from Article VI of the Constitution, which reads :

"Every woman of the Church shall be considered a member of this society, who by signing this Constitution or giving her name to be affixed thereto, agrees to enter into the work by attending as far as possible each meeting, and giving according to her ability to promote its object."

OUR MANSE

BY E. F. R. C.

It stands in finished beauty ; broad and firm
Are its foundations, strong its stately walls,
As fitted to endure through coming years.
A monument of Christian faith and zeal.
Within, the tinted light falls cheerily
O'er graceful arch and polished floor, and
   through.
The well-appointed rooms, like rainbow
   hues
Of promise, betokening peace and joy ;
A fitting resting place for him who serves
This ancient Church of God.
       But ah ! to us,
Who hopefully have watched its rise and
   end,
Above it rests a cloud, bright-edged, 'tis
   true,
For all God's hidden ways are just and kind,
But dark with disappointment, and sur-
   charged
With bitter grief. The gentle presence,which
We fondly hoped would grace the finished
   home.
Is missing there ; the *heart* of home is gone.
Gone to a better dwelling, this we know,
A mansion far more fair ; 'tis not for her

We mourn, 'tis for ourselves alone. But now
The shadow deepens, as again the wing
Of the death-angel broods, this time above
The cradle of the home, the household
    shrine,
Where stricken hearts find hope and com-
    fort sweet
In loving homage. Soon the baby-tones
Are hushed, the shrine is broken, and fond
    arms
Are empty, as the happy little soul
Leaps to the new-found mother's clinging
    clasp,
And the sweet waxen form is laid to sleep
Among the summer flowers. And once
    more
Alone, the smitten one gives meekly back
To God the precious legacy of love,
And mutely bows beneath the added stroke.
Oh mystery supreme! We vainly ask
" What does it mean ?" then make reply,
    " God knows."
Thus has our beauteous Manse been sancti-
    fied.
'Twill ever be a consecrated place,
Hallowed by tender memories, baptized
In sacred tears, and linked in holiest thought
With Heaven and white-robed angelhood
    above.
                    August 17, 1885.

THE OLD CEMETERY.

SOME CORRECTIONS.

There was not room in our last number
to note and correct the errors in the article
entitled, " The Old Cemetery," which was
reprinted from an old newspaper clipping,
and it was thought best to give the article
entire, as it originally appeared.

Some of these corrections are here noted :
General Washington did not commune in
the old Church, which was used as a hospital at the time ; but in the hollow, shaped
somewhat like a half bowl, a little to the
east and rear of the house now occupied by
Mrs. Eugene Ayers, on Morris street. This
was then part of the parsonage property,
which included nearly all the land now
bounded by the Green, South street, Pine
street, and the river. The present Church
was begun in 1791.

Peter Dickinson, or as the name was then
commonly written, Dickerson, was born in
the year 1724. He came to Morristown with
three brothers, Thomas, Joshua and Daniel
and a sister Elizabeth, according to the
headstone. He was married to Ruth Coe,
20th Oct., 1745. He died on the 10th of May,
1780, in his 56th year.

The Church has had but one pastor by
the name of Johnes. This was the Rev.
Timothy Johnes, pastor from 1742 till his
death in 1794. Several of Dr. Johnes' descendants have been physicians here.

The soldiers that died with the small-pox
were buried in the Graveyard in trenches,
where the Lindsley vault now stands. When
this vault was out a great many brass
buttons were thrown out, and pieces of blue
cloth, parts of the uniform, have been turned up at even later dates.

The first wife of Moses Estey was Elizabeth Fearclo (not Icaeclo), who died 10th
Feb., 1783, aet. 23. His second wife was
Ann, who died 11th Nov., 1809, aet. 47 ; and
the stone bearing her name has the inscription, " erected by her son, William the
Rover."

It is a flat slab that marks the grave of
William Alexander Duer, in a lot surrounded by a thick hedge.

DR. WILLIAM A. McDOWELL,

PASTOR FIRST CHURCH, FROM 13 DEC., 1814,
TO 23 OCT., 1823.

[The following sketch is taken from one
entitled, " Sketch of an Eminent Jerseyman—Rev. Dr. McDowell, The Revivalist—
by an old Journalist," which appeared in the
Jerseyman, 23 Feb., 1883.—EDITOR.]

In writing a sketch of any eminent man,
it should be the aim of the biographer to
direct attention to the obstacles he had to
overcome in his youth in the pursuit of distinction, for sometimes young men are de-
terred from making any great effort at success because of some physical weakness
which they fancy may prove a bar to their
advancement ; but when they are told how
this or that distinguished person rose to
fortune and position despite his frail constitution or serious bodily ailments, they pluck
up courage and determine to do their best
to win the prize set before them.

We have written these introductory remarks to the biographical sketch of a reverend gentleman whose career was a very

remarkable one, because of their especial fitness to him. He was not gifted with a robust physique, his health was never very good, and his voice was far from oratorical, but, notwithstanding every drawback, he was enabled by his spirit, will and energy to place himself in the front rank of preachers, and become noted as a great revivalist.

It is true that the generation to which he addressed himself has mostly passed away, but the descendants of those who were wont to listen to him with such close attention still recur with interest to the period when he held sway over the religious communities to which he preached. Many good fathers and mothers were converted to the cause of Christ during his memorable ministry, and hence his name will ever be held in reverence and respect.

William Anderson McDowell was born in Lamington, N. J., on the 15th of May 1789. Up to the age of thirteen he was employed on a farm, attending at intervals the grammar school in the vicinity. About three years later he entered the college of New Jersey, from which he graduated in 1809. In 1811, while a tutor in Princeton College, his health became so poor that he was advised to visit Savannah, Ga., with a view of testing the experiment of a change of climate. In that city he was the guest of the Rev. Dr. Kollock, and it was at this time that young McDowell's gift for leading revivals was developed. Though a mere boy compared with Dr. Kollock, he took an active part in the services at the latter's Church, and such was the power of his appeals to the crowded audiences in attendance that, in a short time, a revival took place, second to none in the Church annals of Savannah.

In 1812 Mr. McDowell returned to his native State. Resuming his studies at Princeton, he remained there until 1813, when he accepted a call to Bound Brook, N. J. It was about this time that he was married to Miss Jane Kollock, daughter of Shepard Kollock, Esq., of Elizabethtown. While at Bound Brook, such was the popularity he had already achieved, he was called to Morristown and Flemington. He chose Morristown, where he preached with the greatest success until 1822, when his health gave way, and he was advised to visit the South. He journeyed as far as Charleston, S. C., and derived so much benefit from its mild climate, that in a little while he felt strong enough to return to Morristown.

But fate had willed that the North should no longer have the benefit of his ministerial labors, for his health soon again broke down, and when he received a most pressing call from a leading Presbyterian Church in Charleston, where he had made hosts of admirers and friends, he felt constrained to accept it, though parting from his congregation in Morristown with great regret.

He was installed in Charleston in 1823, and from that time, for years afterwards, was distinguished for the numerous and spirit-stirring revivals in which he was the leader. But his fame was not limited to a single city or State. Having occasion to visit Georgia, his exhortations while there were so effective that revivals took place wherever he preached. In truth he was known all through that portion of the South as "the great revivalist."

In 1827, Franklin College, Ga., honored him with the degree of Doctor of Divinity, and in 1832, he was elected Moderator of the General Assembly, and in the same year was chosen professor in the Theological Seminary at Columbia, S. C. But Dr. McDowell was averse to occupying so retired a position; he required a wider field of usefulness, and therefore he declined the very flattering honor.

It was about this period that, in the language of Dr. McDowell, "an awful cloud hung" over the South, and particularly over South Carolina. "Nullification," or opposition to certain Federal laws deemed oppressive, was the prevailing sentiment, and the Doctor being a Northern man, was placed in an embarrassing situation; but such was his attachment to the people of his Church, and such his devotion to the cause of religion, that he remained steadfastly at his post, secure in the confidence and affection of those who had been so frequently witnesses of his power as a revivalist. When he did leave Charleston, to accept the position of Secretary of the Board of Domestic Missions of the Presbyterian Church, he did so chiefly on account of his failing health.

Passing over the intervening years, we come to the year 1850, when Dr. McDowell resigned the Secretaryship of the Board of Missions and again visited Charleston, where he was received with literally "open arms," all eager to hear him once more in the pulpit which he had filled with so much ability and success.

In both public and private circles he was the recipient of the most hospitable attentions, and his sojourn in Charleston was protracted far beyond the time fixed upon for his stay. On his way back to the North, he was cordially greeted in every place where he tarried, showing that his fame as a revivalist had not abated one whit.

Dr. McDowell, on his arrival home, consulted his former physician concerning his health, but little could be done for him, and so the subject of this biography gradually succubmed to the approaches of the great destroyer and died from exhaustion on the 17th of September 1851. He was buried in the town in which he was born.

It is related of Dr. McDowell that during the summer preceding his death, notwithstanding his feeble health, he preached with much of his old-time vigor and earnestness, and that his voice was clearer and louder than it had been for some time before. How grand those sermons were we can readily imagine.

The success of Dr. McDowell shows to every youth in the land what may be accomplished by those who are filled with the same ambition—an ambition that nothing could check, not even ill health, and that finally won for him the marked distinction of "the great revivalist."

MASTERING CIRCUMSTANCES.

"His example teaches," said Lincoln, in his eulogy on Henry Clay, "that one can scarcely be too poor but that if he will he can acquire sufficient education to get through the world respectably." Lincoln himself illustrated the truth of his opinion. He was the son of a poor pioneer, who had a hard struggle to make a home in the wilderness. There were no common schools' but at intervals an itinerant teacher would stray into a settlement, and announce that he had come to teach "readin', writin' and cipherin'" as far as the "rule of three."

Young Lincoln sat at the feet of several of these "itinerants," until he had received twelve months' schooling, and then he was thrown upon his own resources. He used to walk four or five miles to school, taking "corn dodgers" with him for his dinner, and wearing a coonskin cap, cowhide-shoes, and linsey-woolsey shirt and buckskin breeches.

The boy was intensely fond of reading, and would walk miles to borrow a book. He was on the alert while reading to lay hold of any passage that was worth retaining. He would write it down on a shingle, and keep it until he had secured a sheet of paper. Then he would copy it, and repeat it, until it was lodged in his memory. Once there, it remained, and in his manhood he could quote Burns' poems from end to end, having learned them when a youth.

Having borrowed Weem's "Life of Washington" from a neighbor, he took it with him to bed in the cabin-loft. Reading until his nubbin of candle had burned out, he placed the book between the cabin-logs, that it might be on hand at daylight. During the night it rained, and the boy on waking found the book wet through. Drying it as well as he could, he went to the neighbor's house, told him of the mishap, and as he had no money, offered to work out the book's value. Three days of corn-pulling was the price agreed upon, and the boy became the owner of the volume. The book fascinated the youth; he read it over and over again, and mused over Washington's career while following the plow. It stirred his ambition, and he brooded over the question. "Can I not become a doer of great deeds?" The brooding brought forth this resolution: "I will go to the bottom of everything I read or study." He carried out that resolution until his death. His manuscript "Book of Examples in Arithmetic" illustrates this habit of learning thoroughly. On one page, headed "Discount," is written, "A Definition of Discount," "Rules for its Computation," and "Proofs and Various Examples."

After he had been admitted to the Bar, he studied in the same thorough fashion Euclid's geometry, in order that he might learn how to prove a thing, and see when it was proved. He practised writing until he wrote a clear, neat, legible hand, and studied the theory of surveying. "He was always reading, writing, ciphering, and writing poetry," says one of the companions of his boyhood.

Once, while a boy, he attended court, where a Kentucky lawyer made an eloquent speech in defending a man charged with murder. The boy went home and dreamed of courts. He got up mock trials, and defended imaginary prisoners. That court scene made him a lawyer, and he began making speeches on political and other topics. He would practice at all times, and his father had to forbid speech-making during working-hours. "For," said he, "when Abe begins to speak, all the hands leave off work, and flock to hear him."

Lincoln's life contradicts the common remark that circumstances make the man. He rose to eminence, yet his opportunities were few and meagre. He rose by mastering circumstances, and by gratifying his intense desire for learning and his habit of learning thoroughly. To faith all things are possible. Right purpose in youth is destiny.— *Youth's Companion.*

THE RECORD.

FIRST PRESBYTERIAN CHURCH, MORRISTOWN, N. J.

"THIS SHALL BE WRITTEN FOR THE GENERATION TO COME."—Psalms 102 : 18.

VOLUME V. | OCTOBER, 1885. | NUMBER 34.

[Printed with the Approval of the Session.]

THE RECORD

Is published monthly ; terms $1.00 a year, *in advance.*

Single numbers for any month, 10 cents each.

Subscriptions should be made to Mr. James R. Voorhees.

Matters pertaining to the publication should be addressed to the

EDITOR OF THE RECORD.

Entered at the Post Office at Morristown, N. J., as second class matter.

SUPPLEMENT.

The Supplement for this month continues the Combined Registers, extending the names from Matilda Campfield [dg. of John & Mary,] to Mabel Pauline, dg. of John and Elizabeth Colley. Among about 450 names in these eight pages, there are 44 Carmichaels, 33 Carters, 24 Casterlines, 55 Clarks, 68 Coes and 31 Coles.

LETTER OF LAFAYETTE.

A letter written by General La Fayette, which has never before appeared in print, will be published in next month's installment of the interesting and valuable sketch of Major Joseph Morris, begun in this number.

WOMEN'S HOME MISSIONS.

The next meeting of the Home Missionary Society will be held in the Chapel on Tuesday afternoon, the 13th of Oct., at half-past three o'clock. All are invited to attend, and to take an interest in the meeting.

MEMORIAL OFFERING.

The memorial offering of the Woman's Foreign Missionary Society, now amounting to $173., has been appropriated to furnishing a library for the Girl's Seminary at Tripoli, Syria, to be called "The Mrs. Elisabeth S. Durant Library." The object is warmly commended by missionaries from that country with whom the Society has conferred.

BENEFICENCE FOR SIX MONTHS :

MARCH 13, 1885 TO SEPTEMBER 14, 1885.

1885. COLLECTIONS.

M'ch 13.	To Special, Foreign Missions from box in Chapel,	$2.38
15.	To offerings,	26.16
22.	" "	29.54
29.	" "	29.53
		—— $87.61.
Apl. 5.	"Special, Home Missions,	37.00
5.	" Special, Sustentation,	69.12
10.	" Special, Foreign Missions from box in Chapel,	3.57
12.	" offerings,	27.85
19.	" "	36.85
26.	" "	21.05
		—— 195.44
May 3.	" Special, Bible Society,	69.58
10.	" offerings,	29.22
17.	" "	33.04
24.	" "	39.68
31.	" "	35.98
		—— 207.50
June 7.	" Special, Freedmen,	77.10
"	" " Foreign Missions for debt,	5.00
14.	" offerings,	34.52
21.	" "	42.96
28.	" "	39.90
		—— 199.48
July 5.	" Special, Foreign Miss. for debt,	202.85
10.	" Special, Foreign from box in Chapel,	1.88
12.	" offerings,	45.39
19.	" "	43.22
26.	" "	30.51
		—— 323.85

Aug, 2. " Special, Church
           Erection,   86.60
        9. " offerings,   33.12
       16. "   "   39.92
       " " Special, Foreign
           Missions   5.00
       23. " offerings.   36.96
       30, "   "   44.20
                                ——— 245.80
Sept. 3. " Special, Foreign
           Missions from box
           in Chapel,   4.25
        6. " Special, Foreign
           Missions,   151.13
       13. " offerings,   49.02
                                ——— 204.40

                                    $1,464.08

DISBURSEMENTS.

By cash remitted to Treasurer of the
Boards as follows, viz. :
1885.
Mar. 13. Foreign Missions, $ 2.37
Apl. 6. Home   "   37.00
      " Sustentation,   69.12
     10. Foreign Missions,   3.57
May 6. Bible Society,   69.58
June 10. Freedmen,   77.10
      " Foreign Missions,   5.00
July "   do.   do.   202.85
      "   do.   do.   1.88
Aug. 4. Church erection,   86.60
Sept. 7. Foreign Missions,   160.38
                                ——— 715.46
    " 14. One   third   balance
         transferred to Ses-
         sions fund,   249.53
         Two   thirds   balance
         transferred to Parish
         for Home Work,   499.09
                                ——— 748.62
                                    $1,464.08

1885.   SESSION'S FUND.
Mar. 13. Balance cash in bank, 139.08
Sept. 14. One-third Sunday of-
         ferings,   249.53
                                ——— 388.61
1885. PAYMENTS BY ORDER OF
         SESSION :
Apr. 4. D. M. Stiger, Treas.,
         Permanent Com-
         mittee on Temper-
         ance, $ 25.00

        Gen'l Assembly as-
        sessment,   52.03
May 6. Paid printing last
        statement,   5.00
June 2. American Tract So-
        ciety,   50.00
July 26. Deacons for poor of
        Church,   50.00   .
Sept. 14. Balance cash in bank, 206.58
                                ——— 388.61
No payments or contributions in sup-
port of our Public Worship are included in
the foregoing account.
        Morristown, Sept. 14, 1885,
                        HENRY CORY,
                             Treasurer.

CHILDREN'S MISSIONARY SOCIETY.

Report of the Treasurer of the Children's
Missionary Society of the First Presbyterian
Church of Morristown, N. J., from June
28th, 1885, to September 27th, 1885 :

RECEIPTS.

Balance cash in bank, $57.38
June 28. Collection,   10.94
Collections taken in July,   33.75
   "   "   " August,   44.90
   "   "   " September, 33.01
Birthday box from Infant Class, 1.89
Special—County and State Sun-
        day-school Work,   7.88
                                ——$189.75

DISBURSEMENTS.

June 19. Printing Treasurer's
        Cards, $1.50
July 6. Home Mission Board—
        six month's proceeds from
        Birthday box,   1.89
August 3. Treasurer's enve-
        lopes,   3.30
August 17. County and State
        Sunday-school Work,   7.88
September 21. Lincoln Uni-
        versity,   75.00
Balance cash in bank,   100.18
                                ——$189.75
        WILL C. VAN DOREN,
                             Treasurer.

A SKETCH OF MAJOR JOSEPH MORRIS.

BY SAMUEL HAYS, ST. LOUIS, MO.

Somewhere in the burial ground of the
First Presbyterian Church, Morristown,

New Jersey, lie the remains of Major Joseph Morris, who greatly distinguished himself in the Revolutionary War, and who is known to have been actively engaged in the French and Indian Wars of the Colonial period. Not much is known of his origin, but the belief has always been entertained in the family that his original ancestor in this country, was John Morris, who, it is asserted, was a captain under Oliver Cromwell. Investigation shows one of that name, as having that rank, in the army of the great Protector.

The line of descent so far as is claimed to be known by the family is John, Daniel and Stephen : the latter the father of Joseph. We are strongly inclined to believe, after a very careful scrutiny of all attainable evidence, that Capt. John Morris who came from New Haven, Conn., to Newark, and who was High Sheriff of Essex County in 1700, was one of Major Morris' progenitors. He is mentioned in the Connecticut records as "possibly from England." He died Oct. 22nd, 1749, aged 83 years. Of this stock Daniel and Stephen were known to be contemporaries in 1742 in Baskinridge, N. J. We are careful not to claim these as ancestors but the identity of names and residence with what is known by the family of Joseph Morris' immediate ancestors makes the probabilities very great. This reference may be the means of eliciting such facts as will determine the question. We find in the course of our inquiries that Daniel Morris was one of several who conveyed by deed a piece of land for Church purposes upon which a meeting house was then standing, February 8, 1731, in Baskinridge. He was an elder of that Church ; and in 1758 was received by letter by the Church at Morristown of which he was an elder from 1761 until 1767. From that year we lose all trace of him. Stephen Morris, the son of Daniel had four sons (including the subject of our sketch) and five daughters. Through the daughters' marriage the family became connected with the Southards, Kitchells, Lewis, Daytons and Predmores, all well known families.

The Morris' had their home near Morristown. Maj. Joseph Morris was born in 1732. Nothing whatever is known of his early history, except that he was fond of adventure, showing undaunted courage and unwavering determination, in the midst of dangers that would cause others to shrink. He had a fair education, and in disposition was unassuming and reticent in speech. He was a man of herculean frame, over six feet in height, and such facial charateristics, as would indicate clearly, the iron will that was the motor to all his actions. He had a double row of teeth, noted for their size and strength ; and stories have been handed down, through his associates and decendants, of some marvelous performances with these, which, while possibly exaggerations, sufficiently attest the great physical strength with which nature had endowed him.

On April 12, 1759, he was married to Hannah Ford by the Rev. Dr. Johnes, as appears by the valuable records left by the latter. Hannah Ford was the daughter of Samuel Ford, a brother of Colonel Jacob Ford, Senior. She had as brothers and sisters Jonathan, father of the late Rev. Jno. Ford, of Parsippany ; Samuel, who married Grace Kitchel ; Demas, whose lands were about a mile from Morristown on the Whippany road ; Charity, who married Abraham Kitchel ; and Eunice, who married, first, Stephen More, and second, [John] Scott. Her mother Sarah was left a widow, and died April 22, 1789, aged 80.

Several of the military commissions of Major Morris, which the writer has seen have been in possession, until within a few years, of one of his immediate descendants, but they cannot now be found. These commissions were stained with his blood, from the wound received in the battle which terminated his life. When he fell they were found in a small worsted bag, which, suspended from his neck, lay on his breast. They showed his official rank in both the Colonial and Revolutionary wars. In the former, but little knowledge is had of his exploits. We find in the Pennsylvania Colonial Records his deposition, sworn to before David Biddle, Notary, dated Philadelphia, August 22, 1771, in which, at length, (describing himself as from Morris County, N. J.,) he relates the history of an expedition made from Easton, with a company of men for the relief of some settlers "near Wyoming" (now Wilkesbarre), who were besieged in a block house by the Connecticut people during what was known as the Pennanite war. This is the only authentic record of him that we can discover during that period.'

It is well established that in 1775, he raised the first company in New Jersey for the Revolutionary war in the village of Whippany. His son Jonathan Ford Morris, who was born March 21, 1760, was made ensign of the Company. His selection because of his youth, being not quite 16 years old, caused considerable dissatisfaction in the Company. The record of this son through the war, fully justified the selection.

The Company being assigned to Col. Winds' Regiment, spent the winter of '75 and '76 in New York, and when the river was free from ice, sailed in sloops for Albany. From thence they marched to Lake George, crossing it and Lake Champlain. in boats to join the Canada expedition. We have discovered some mention of both father and son at Ticonderoga, in the records of that period, but not sufficient to enable us to give the history of their connection with that ill-starred expedition which terminated in the defeat of the American army, after almost unparalled suffering and great loss of life, including the death in battle of its gallant leader, General Montgomery.

We can discover no trace of Major Morris from this time until November 5, 1776, when he and his command were ordered by General Sullivan to New Jersey for discharge, the Company he had raised and commanded having enlisted but for one year. Washington during the Winter had secured, by special solicitation from Congress, the promotion of Captain Daniel Morgan to a Colonelcy. Morgan reached Morristown about the middle of April, in obedience to a summons from Washington, and was received by the Commander-in-Chief with marked kindness and consideration. The early military career of the latter, had taught him the value which might properly attach to a select corp of sharp shooters composed of active, hardy men, accustomed to the woods and skilful in the use of the rifle. The preceding campaign had presented many occasions, forcibly suggesting the want of such a corp, when its presence might have turned the tide of battle. Colonel Morgan was informed of this great want, and in pursuance of orders, a body of five hundred picked men was accordingly formed from the different Regiments composing the army.

The command of this corp was given to Colonel Morgan, the Lieutenant Colonelcy to Captain Richard Butler, while Captain Joseph Morris was made its Major. There are few readers of the history of the Revolutionary war, who properly estimate the very great service of this corp of select men in the prosecution of that momentous struggle. Washington, in his official reports and correspondence, repeatedly bore testimony to its value and expressed the utmost confidence in its efficiency. There seemed to be no other branch of the service upon which he relied so much. And justly so, for all of the officers named had already achieved distinction, while those in command of each of the eight companies were selected, by Morgan himself, from the army at large, because of their peculiar fitness for the positions assigned them. The same remark will apply to the privates. The whole force was composed of carefully selected men, as was desired in its conception. Washington under date of June 13, 1777, writes to Morgan :—"The corp of Rangers newly formed and under your command, are to be considered as a body of Light Infantry, and are to act as such, for which reason they will be exempted from the common duties of the line." From the time of its organization until about the middle of August 1777, this corp was actively engaged in a number of battles and skirmishes in New Jersey, in all of which it acquitted itself with great credit. Washington, in reporting one of these to Congress, says of them, " they constantly advanced upon an enemy far superior to them in numbers and well secured behind strong redoubts." On August 16, 1777, they were ordered to the north to join General Gates' army. Washington, in so advising General Gates, observes :—"From various representations made to me of the disadvantages the army lay under, particularly the Militia, from an apprehension of the Indian mode of fighting, I have despatched Colonel Morgan with his corp of riflemen to give assistance, etc. This corp I have great dependence on, and have no doubt they will be exceedingly useful to you as a check given to the savages, and keeping them within proper bounds, will prevent General Burgoyne from getting intelligence as formerly, and animate your other troops, etc."

(*To be Continued.*)

THE RECORD.

FIRST PRESBYTERIAN CHURCH, MORRISTOWN, N. J.

"This Shall be Written for the Generation to Come."—Psalms 102 : 18.

VOLUME V.	NOVEMBER, 1885.	NUMBER 35.

[Printed with the Approval of the Session.]

THE RECORD

Is published monthly ; terms $1.00 a year, *in advance*.

Single numbers for any month, 10 cents each.

Subscriptions should be made to Mr. James R. Voorhees.

Matters pertaining to the publication should be addressed to the

EDITOR OF THE RECORD.

Entered at the Post Office at Morristown, N. J., as second class matter.

MINUTE IN MEMORIAL

OF THE

REV. DAVID IRVING, D. D.

In view of the death on Monday, the 12th of October instant, of Rev. David Irving, D.D., for twenty years one of the Secretaries of the Board of Foreign Missions, and previously for ten years Pastor of this Church ; Session discharges a sad but grateful duty, in entering on their minutes their appreciation of his personal worth and his uniformly dignified ministerial bearing and Christian courtesy.

No page of the history of this venerable Church, which has been blessed with so many faithful and earnest ministers, records a more successful pastorate, so far as success is to be measured by additions to the Church, and especially by the development and cultivation of a spirit of beneficence. The record of his pastorate here will ever constitute a living testimony to his zeal and faithfulness in the Master's service.

Of him it may be truly said that he obeyed the exhortation of the apostle, in feeding the flock of God, taking " the oversight thereof not by constraint but willingly, not for filthy lucre, but of a ready mind, neither as being lord over God's heritage, but being an ensample to the flock," and we rejoice in the assurance that " when the Chief Shepherd shall appear" he " shall receive a crown of glory that fadeth not away."

CHILDREN'S MISSIONARY SOCIETY.

At the annual meeting on Friday, October 16th, the Treasurer reported as follows, for the year ending Oct. 1st, 1885 :

RECEIPTS.

Balance received from H. T. Hull, late Treasurer,	$277.94
Regular Sunday Collections,	528.61
Special Collections,	44.45
	$851.00

DISBURSEMENTS.

Expenses during the year,	$32.38
Special,	57.25
Home Missions,	390.00
Foreign Missions,	335.00
Balance cash in bank,	36.37
	$851.00

WILL C. VAN DOREN,
Treasurer.

A SKETCH OF MAJOR JOSEPH MORRIS.

BY SAMUEL HAYS, ST. LOUIS, MO.

(Continued from page 184.)

Washington also wrote to General Putnam on the 16 :—" The people in the Northern army seem so intimidated by the Indians, that I have determined to send up Colonel Morgan's corps of riflemen who will fight them in their own way."

In a letter to Governor Clinton of the same date, he says, speaking of the forwarding of Morgan's corps :—"They are all chosen men, selected from the army at large, well acquainted with the use of rifles, and with that mode of fighting which is necessary to make them a good counterpoise to the Indians, and they have distinguished themselves on a variety of occasions.

" I expect the most eminent services from them, and I shall be mistaken if their presence does not go far toward producing a general desertion among the savages." It would require great space to detail the part borne by this wonderful body of men in the several battles that culminated in the surrender of Burgoyne and his army.

Numerous histories, with song and story, give ample evidence of its prowess at Saratoga.

In Wilkinson's memoirs, we find special mention of Major Morris. Wilkinson was Adjutant to General Gates, and speaks as an eye witness. He says:—" Major Morris with characteristic impetuosity being forward in the pursuit." " He gallantly dashed his horse through their ranks, riding over the men, and succeeded amid a shower of balls in effecting his escape." " I passed on and met Major Morris, who was never so sprightly as when under a hot fire." In the battle to which these statements refer, the corps was formed in two lines, one being led by Colonel Morgan, and the other by Major Morris. Morgan's corps, in the events immediately preceding Burgoyne's surrender, lost 40 per cent. of its number in killed and wounded.

On General Burgoyne's introduction to Morgan after the capitulation he took him warmly by the hand, and said, " Sir, you command the finest regiment in the world." Under date of September 24, 1777, Washington wrote to Gates, that " if certain conditions are favorable," Morgan's corps be returned to him, to which Gates replied October 5th, describing the situation, " under which," he says, " your excellency would not wish me to part with the corps, the army of General Burgoyne are most afraid of." On November 1, 1777, Colonel Morgan received from Gates instructions to march southward to join Washington, in compliance with the express orders of the latter. It started immediately. Washington in his letter of instructions to Colonel Alexander Hamilton says, " I expect you will meet Colonel Morgan and his corps upon the way down. If you do, let them know how essential their services are to us, and desire the Colonel or commanding officer to hasten his march as much as is consistent with the health of his men after their late fatigues." Morgan reached Whitemarsh, near Philadelphia, the headquarters of the Commander-in-Chief, November 18th, about 170 of his corps being left in New Jersey, temporarily, under Major Morris, to aid Lafayette in some operations about Haddonfield. Under

date of November 26, Lafayette writes to Washington from Haddonfield, a few miles from Philadelphia, of a skirmish near that place, each party numbering 350 men. He says that on the preceding day " in an engagement with the Hessians the brave Major Morris with a part of his riflemen sent them back and pushed them very fast. I never saw men so merry, so spirited, so desirous to go on to the enemy, whatever forces they could have, as that small party was in this little fight. I found the riflemen above even their reputation."

In a report to Congress, Washington writes from Whitemarsh, under date December 10, 1777, referring to an engagement on the 6th between that place and Chestnut Hill :—" We lost 27 men in Morgan's corps, killed and wounded, besides Major Morris, a brave and gallant officer who was among the latter.

He fell, shot in the mouth by a bullet which lodged in the back of his neck. This bullet was in the possession of the family for a number of years and bore the impress of his teeth.

In Graham's life of General Daniel Morgan, this event is alluded to as follows :— " Among the wounded but beyond all hope of recovery, was the noble hearted and intrepid Major Morris. This officer from the soldier-like qualities displayed by him on a variety of occasions has attracted the attention and favor of the Commander-in-Chief, and upon the organization of the corps he was appointed its Major. He possessed a disposition the most kind and generous and a courage which no danger could shake, no misfortunes could diminish. He enjoyed the confidence and regard of all who knew him, and by the officers and men of the corps with whom he had shared the glories and dangers of the war, he was deeply beloved. His death which occurred a short time after this encounter, excited universal sorrow throughout the camp." He was conveyed to Morristown, where he died January 5, 1778, aged 46 years. His sufferings for thirty days, and especially during his removal from the battle field to his old home, over a rough country, a distance of about sixty miles, with a total lack of those comforts so available in more recent times, unable to speak or to take other than liquid nourishment, may be imagined if not described.

The following letter, never before published, was written by Lafayette to Lieutenant Jonathan Ford Morris (the son of the Major), at Morristown :

"At Camp, Dec. 10, 1777.

Sir :

It is with the greatest concern that I have heard that Major Morris went from camp to Morristown without surgeon to attend him. I will be much obliged to you to let me know immediately if he is well provided for at this time, because I should send to him a very good French surgeon belonging to Count de Pulaski, whom the Count has promised to me. I shall send at the same time a servant of mine, very attentive, to take care of the Major as long as you will think him of some use. Be so good, sir, as to let me know as soon as possible, if these measures are to be taken and if I can serve your father in some other ways. I hope you will give me a very particular account of his present state.

I have the honor to be, Sir,
Your most obedient,
The Marquis de Lafayette.
To Lieutenant Jonathan Ford Morris of the Artillery at Morristown."

In Graham's life of General Daniel Morgan, (to which we are greatly indebted), we find another letter from Lafayette to Morgan. This letter is dated 1777, and as it refers to the Major's death, it must either have been in confident anticipation of that event or the year given is an error. He certainly died January 5, 1778. It is more likely that Lafayette made the common mistake in naming the old year, the new year being but a few days old when Morris died. 1777.

"*Dear Sir :*—I just now received your favor concerning our late friend, Major Morris, and I need not repeat to you how much I am concerned in the interests of his family. I spoke the other day to his Excellency on the subject, and I shall write to Congress a very particular letter, where you will be mentioned. I intend to speak as in your name, and that of all your corps, and as being myself honored with their confidence. It is my opinion that a decent estate might be given to the family as mark of gratefulness

from their country, and that his son must be promoted as soon as possible. But, my dear sir, you know how long Congress waive any matter whatsoever before a decision, and, as Mrs. Morris may be in some want before that time, I am going to trouble you with a commission which I beg you will execute with the greatest secrecy. If she wanted to borrow any sum of money in expecting the arrangements of Congress, it would not become a stranger, unknown to her, to offer himself for that purpose. But you could (as from yourself) tell her that you had friends, who, being in the army, don't know what to do with their money, and as they are not in the mercantile or husbandry way, would willingly let her have one or many thousand dollars, which she might give again in three or four years, etc., etc.

One other way could be to let her believe that you have got or borrowed the money from any town or body you will be pleased to mention, or it would be needless to mention where it comes from.

In a word, my dear sir, if with the greatest secrecy, and the most minute regard for that lady's delicacy, you may find a manner of being useful to her. I beg you would communicate to me immediately.

I shall, as soon as possible, let you know the answer of Congress, whenever an answer will be got, and in expecting the pleasure to hear from you, I have the honor to be, very sincerely,

Your most obedient servant,
The Marquis de Lafayette.
Col. Morgan, of the Rifle Corps."

Major Morris' widow (Hannah Ford) survived him five years, dying at Morristown, Oct. 12, 1783, of consumption. She was buried by the side of her husband.

In the proceedings of the New Jersey Council, March 1, 1780, it was "ordered that a warrant do issue in favor of the said Hannah Morris for the sum of twenty-five dollars per month, being the amount of the half-pay of her deceased husband during her widerhood."

We have attempted no more in this sketch than to give without embellishment such facts in the history of Major Morris as have been discovered in a very desultory though protracted search, excluding many traditions which may be exaggerations and which are certainly wanting in the verities essential to our purpose.

It is our hope that we shall have attained one result at least. That of provoking additional interest with those inclined to such researches, and especially with those who are directly or collaterally related to. the subject of our sketch. We will be thankful for further information, promising that it shall be used, giving proper credit, in a more extended effort at some future time.

* * * * * *

Since writing the foregoing narrative, we have thought it appropriate to add a brief notice of Dr. Jonathan Ford Morris, the son of Major Joseph Morris. He was born in Hanover, Morris County, New Jersey, March 21, 1760. In his sixteenth year he was made ensign in his father's Revolutionary company. He is spoken of as tall and large, distinguished for his talent and energy even at that early age. We get traces of him at Ticonderoga early in 1776. On March 1, 1777 he was made Lieutenant in Proctor's Artillery, and was during the war also attached to Col. Stevens' Artillery. While with Proctor's Artillery he was in the battles of Brandywine and Germantown, and in the latter was conspicuous in the assault upon Chew's House. He was also in the battles of Princeton and Monmouth. In the Summer of 1779 he was with a body of Americans who intercepted the enemy under the command of Col. Simcoe of the Queen's Rangers, who made a raid for the purpose of burning some boats on the Raritan River. When near New Brunswick, Simcoe was attacked by the Americans, who had concealed themselves behind logs and bushes. Simcoe was taken prisoner, his horse being killed and himself stunned by the fall. Simcoe's life was saved by Morris, " who adroitly averted a deadly blow aimed at him by one of the soldiers." Simcoe in his journal records the fact, and mentions the further fact of his having been bled by Morris and receiving from him other necessary assistance. Long after the war, when Simcoe was Governor of Upper Canada, Morris received a letter from him inviting him to visit him at Toronto, and acknowledging the kindness which he experienced at his hands. He had resigned his commission in the army on Nov. 28, 1778, at the solicitation of his widowed mother. It appears from the proceedings of Congress that a letter of that date had been received from him tendering his resignation as Lieutenant of Proctor's Artillery. Early in 1779 he entered upon the study of medicine under the instructions of Dr. Moses Scott, of New Brunswick. He afterward studied under Dr. Shippen, of Philadelphia, who was so impressed with his abilities that upon the completion of his studies he suggested a partnership. Dr. Morris declined, but ever afterward regretted his decision. March 1st, 1784, he married Margaret Smith Euen, of Elizabeth. She was a decendant of Rev. Jno. Harriman, of the 1st Presbyterian Church Elizabeth, whose daughter married John Hendricks, whose daughter married David Smith whose daughter married a Euen : the latter being the parents of the wife of Dr. Jonathan Ford Morris. They had nine children :

Joseph Euen Morris, born Nov. 10, 1785. He died May 5, 1830, leaving a widow and six children in Steuben County, N. Y.

Wm. Cullen Morris, died an infant.

Wm. Cullen Morris (second), born Aug. 17, 1787. He died May 20, 1870. He was a highly respected lawyer in Belvidere for many years ; subsequently living in Jersey City where he died, leaving four sons and one daughter.

David Euen Morris, the fourth son, was born April 22, 1791. He died Sept. 24, 1870, leaving a widow (his second wife), six sons and three daughters in Michigan.

Edward Young Morris was born Sept. 5, 1793. He died April 6, 1819, leaving a widow without children in New Jersey.

Wm. Patterson Morris was born Oct. 9, 1795. He died Sept. 21, 1842, leaving a widow and two children in New York. His son Edward now lives in Rahway, N. J.

Alexander Melville Morris was born Aug. 11, 1797. He died May 7, 1837, leaving a widow and three children in Michigan

Hannah Mary Margaretta Morris was born April 24, 1799. She married Dr. Byington of Belvidere, N. J., and was left a widow without children. She now lives with her only surviving brother.

Rev. Jonathan Ford Morris, in Bushnell, Ills., who lived for many years in Mendham, N. J., and who is well-known as a retired clergyman of the Dutch Reformed denomination, whose talents and high character are recognized by all who know him. He was born June 7, 1801, and has had nine children, five daughters and four sons—all living but one son.

Dr. Jonathan Ford Morris practised medicine with great success in the region about Somerville for a number of years. It is recorded of him that, "As a citizen he was philanthropic and public spirited. In company reticent, but as a writer forcible and direct." He died April 13, 1810, aged 50 years. His widow died February 12, 1844, aged 86 years. They were buried in the old church yard in Boundbrook and over their remains a suitable memorial was erected.

In conclusion we find in a standard English authority (Burke) that the name of Morris is of very great antiquity and is known under various orthographies, among others occur Morys, Moris, Morris, Morriss. Mores, Morrice, Maurice, etc., compounded with Fitz Clan, Mount, De, and various other initial expressions. It is composed of the Welsh words Mawr-ryce meaning "warlike," " powerful in war." To this one of the mottoes borne by the family of Morris seems to have reference,

" MARTE EN MARI FAVENTIBUS."

THE RECORD.

FIRST PRESBYTERIAN CHURCH, MORRISTOWN, N. J.

"This Shall be Written for the Generation to Come."—Psalms 102 : 18.

| VOLUME V. | DECEMBER, 1885. | NUMBER 36. |

[Printed with the Approval of the Session.]

THE RECORD

Is published monthly: terms $1.00 a year, in advance.

Single numbers for any month, 10 cents each.

Subscriptions should be made to Mr. James R. Voorhees.

Matters pertaining to the publication should be addressed to the

EDITOR OF THE RECORD.

Entered at the Post Office at Morristown, N. J., as second class matter.

PUBLICATION OF THE RECORD TO BE STOPPED.

With this number the publication of THE RECORD will be discontinued, at least for the present. At no time have the subscriptions been sufficient to pay the cost of publication, and a point has now been reached in the total arrearage at which it is wiser to stop than to go on. No debt will be left and no call for help will be made, as contributions, mainly from two persons, have already been received sufficient to cover all deficiencies.

Subscribers who appreciate the amount of genealogical and historical matter contained in the RECORD as thus far published, aside from the labor which has been required to gather and prepare it, will be satisfied with the result attained. This result may be briefly stated as follows: 1st, Historical narratives of the Church and Town from 1742 to 1840; 2d, Biographical narratives concerning some of the pastors and leading men of former generations; 3d, Reprints of rare and valuable publications respecting the Church; 4th, A continuous copy of all the matters of importance recorded in the Minutes of the Parish, of the Trustees, and of the Session, from 1742 down to 1883; 5th, Complete lists of all the names recorded in the various Registers of the Church, viz., those of Baptisms, of Communicants, of Marriages and of Deaths, from 1742 down to

1815; together with the beginning of an alphabetical arrangement, printed nearly through the C's, which includes all names down to 1885.

It is hoped that it may be possible, before long, to complete the printing of the Combined Registers, and some other matters. In this case the monthly form will not be resumed, but all additional pages will be issued at one time, and supplied free to old subscribers, who may take the trouble to send us their names and addresses before Jan. 31, 1886.

DIRECTIONS FOR BINDING.

To those who desire to bind their RECORDS at once, and do not wish to take the risk and delay of waiting indefinitely for the possible issue of additional pages, the following order is suggested as best calculated to group parts that belong together. It should be remembered that no numbers were issued during the year 1882:

1st. All the numbers of Vols. I. and II. pages 1 to 192.

2d. All the four-paged Supplements of Vol. III., pages 193 to 240.

3d. Report and Roll for the year ending 7th April, 1884, pages 145 to 152, and issued as a Supplement with May number of 1884.

4th. All the parts of Vols. III., IV. and V, that bear the Title, each part containing eight pages in Vol. III., and only four pages in Vols. IV. and V.; running continuously from page 1 to page 192.

5th. All the Supplements containing the Minutes of the Session, the Trustees and the Parish for successive pastorates. The first issue of these was with the number for January, 1884; from which time they were issued every month until and including the number for June, 1885; the last and completing part, for the present, being sent out this month. Each part contains eight pages, and the paging runs continuously from 1 to 168.

6th. The parts of the Combined Registers. The first of these was issued, as an extra Supplement, with the number for February, 1885, the next issue was with the July number, from which time it appeared every month, closing, for the present, with the number for November. The paging is continuous, from 1 to 48.

Particular ATTENTION is called to the fact, that some of the Supplements have been *incorrectly folded;* care should be taken to have these folded properly before binding. In the set examined, this mistake was discovered in the Supplements for May and June, 1883, July, 1884, June and November, 1885.

WHO CAN TELL?

Diligent but futile inquiry has been made to learn whether any of the persons named below are now living, and, if so, what their present address may be. If the reader can give any information concerning any one here named, a great favor will be conferred by sending word to the Pastor of the Church. Once before, after a similar list had been published, it was casually discovered that several could have given the information desired; but they supposed that "somebody else would give it," and never troubled themselves any further about the matter. Please do not wait for "somebody else." If it is too much trouble for you to write out the information, the Pastor or Clerk will call on you, *if you will only somehow let him know* that you can help to clear up the Church Roll.

Susan Bayard, received in 1856.

Mrs. S. C. Bartlett, received in 1871, from Wysox, Pa.

Charles Boss, received in 1853, from Sparta, N. J.

Jane Brant, received in 1860, from Chatham.

Ellen Corkhill, received in 1858.

Laura J. Crane (or Crone,) received in 1856; did she marry a Loree in 1859?

Alice Crampton, received in 1856.

Catharine W. Cree, received in 1876.

Margaretta Davenport, rec'd in 1846, from Newfoundland, N. J.

Margaret Doremus, rec'd in 1876.

Ann Louisa Fairchild, rec'd in 1842; did she marry a Taylor?

Mary B. Freeman, rec'd in 1864.

Oliver S. Freeman, rec'd in 1869, from Dover.

Elizabeth Gustin, rec'd in 1841, from Hardwick.

Thomas J. Harrison, rec'd in 1874.

Anna Hammell, received in 1874.

Annie Heffern, received in 1876.

Edward Irwin, received in 1858.

Nancy Irwin, " " "

Sarah Maria Johnson, colored, received in 1851.

Leo Kofler, received in 1872, from Cincinnati.

Bridget Landon, received in 1856;

Annie M. Lawrence, rec'd in 1873.

Elizabeth Ann Marsh, wife of Wm. L. Lewis, rec'd in 1858.

Harriet E. Leonard, rec'd in 1862.

Louisa Matilda Leech, rec'd in 1864, from South Orange.

Mrs. Eliza Lindsley, rec'd in 1876, from Chatham.

Sophia Mackid, a servant of W. C. Baker, rec'd in 1858, from Canada.

Jane Maria Martin, colored, rec'd in 1851.

Mary Miller, rec'd in 1845, from West Somers.

Eliza Miller, rec'd in 1872, from Newark.

Eliza Jane Moore, widow of Wm. L., received in 1876.

Elias Pruden Mount, rec'd in 1843.

Isabella McCord, rec'd in 1870, from New York City.

Jenny Elizabeth McDermott, received in 1875.

Margaret McDonald, rec'd in 1876.

Elizabeth Pemberton, rec'd in 1855.

Nelson A. Rankin, received in 1865, from Mendham.

Austin Requa, Jr., rec'd in 1866.

Frances Rittenhouse, rec'd in 1851, from Hackettstown.

Sarah Margaret Roy, rec'd in 1843.

Margaretta Louisa Shafer, rec'd in 1843.

Charles Stewart, rec'd in 1879, from Raritan.

John L. Thompson, rec'd in 1876.

Wm. L. Tunis, and his wife Mary A., received in 1869, from Baskingridge.

John H. Tunison, rec'd in 1872.

Ann VanDoren, colored, rec'd in 1863, from Hackettstown.

Luther G. VanVliet, rec'd in 1879, from Washington, N. J.

Sarah Voorhees, rec'd in 1853, from Pleasant Grove.

Mrs. Sarah Voorhees, rec'd in 1866, from Mendham.

Phebe A. Ward, widow of Wm. B., rec'd in 1858, from German Valley.

George G. Wagner, rec'd in 1871.

Elizabeth Wilkins, rec'd in 1874.

Henry R. Williams, rec'd in 1861.

THE MANSE.

(From the Banner of May 21st, 1885.)

All the past winter and early spring we have been watching with great interest the building of the "Manse" for the First Presbyterian Church, and now that it has just been finished and is in every way such a perfect and complete house, a short description of it will be read with interest.

The beauty and quaintness of the exterior reflects great credit upon the architect. It is after the "Renaissance" style of architecture, but with a great deal of originality. The grey stone was quarried in Mendham, and the buff trimming stone is from Berea, Ohio. The whole effect of the building is picturesque on account of its long sweeping outline and sharp angles of roof and rough stone work, relieved by graceful gothic arches.

To enter the house we cross a broad entrance porch to the hall door, which is of the old Dutch style, being cut in two in the centre, allowing the upper half to open while the lower half is closed, giving good ventilation to the large reception hall. The vestibule is finished in cherry and has a large closet at one side for hats, umbrellas, etc.

The reception hall is also finished in natural cherry. The stairs at one end are broad and of beautiful design, winding up to the third story. The fire place in the hall is built of pressed brick, and opposite this in the recess of the stairs is an old-fashioned seat built in, and upholstered with red leather. The size of the hall is 9 feet 6 inches x 23 feet 6 inches.

The stair case and halls are lighted by an immense stained glass window of beautiful design, the central figure of which is the old seal of the Church, adopted by the Trustees in 1788—a sheaf of wheat within a maltese cross, around which is lettered "First Presbyterian Church, Morristown, N. J., MDCCXXXIII." This window was built with money raised by the Sabbath school, and bears under it the legend, "By the School of the Church, MDCCCLXXXV."

On the first floor to the left is a drawing room. It has a hard wood floor of oak, but all the rest of the wood work, including the mantel is of polished mahogany. This room is lighted in front by an immense window, partly of stained glass. The fire place cutting off one corner of the room is very handsome with its elaborate mantel especially designed for the room. All the mantels on this floor, including that over the hall fire place are ornamented with mirrors of heavy bevelled plate glass, and they are specially designed by the architect. This room is 15 feet x 18 feet 4 inches.

The dining room is large and bright. It is all finished in "quartered oak" with a high wainscoting. The bay window has a screen of wood-work over the upper part. The mantel of this room is hand-carved in fruit and floral pieces. Its size is 15 x 20 feet 6 inches.

The library is treated in Louis Quatoze style. The floor is of maple, but the remainder of the wood-work is painted a creamy white. The corner mantel is white to correspond, and has seats at each side of the fire-place. The impression that this room gives at first is quaintness, making a pleasing relief and contrast to the rooms connected with it. Its size is 12 feet 6 inches x 13 feet 6 inches.

All the rooms on the first floor open into the reception hall by large double rolling doors so that the whole floor can be thrown open when occasion requires.

The kitchen is large and light and has several roomy closets. A fully equipped butler's pantry connects the kitchen with the dining room, so that the kitchen is really isolated from the living rooms of the house, yet entirely convenient to them. The size of the kitchen is 13 x 15.

In the rear of the kitchen is the laundry, a fine large room thoroughly furnished for the business intended.

In a brief description we cannot do justice to the work. The wood-work of this floor is really a cabinet finish, the large amount of panel, spool and other work blending superbly. The door knobs and hinges are of brass, and altogether the work is harmonious and pleasing.

On the second floor, over the drawing room, is a large convenient study, the walls lined with book shelves. This room, as well as all the bed rooms in the house, has a roomy comfortable closet. Besides this room there are three large bed rooms, a dressing room and bath room on this floor. Two bed rooms and the dressing room connect, making a very handsome suite.

The wood-work in the bath room is oak, and all the plumbing work is particularly fine, every trap being ventilated and the work is sanitary in every respect. All the bed rooms on the second floor are provided with open fire places and originally designed mantels, a plaster-work feature forming panels and richly colored, being something new.

There are four fine bed rooms and a trunk room on the third floor. All the bed rooms are finished in pine, oiled, and all have large closets. The three halls are large and roomy, and yet there is no lost space in the building. The thickness of the walls form deep recesses for the windows and admirable space for inside blinds. The house is heated by furnace, as well as open fire places.

In no part of the building can it be said that convenience has been sacrificed to beauty, yet there is nothing to mar its architectural perfection, whether we consider the interior or exterior. Mr. Louis R. Hazeltine, the architect, has received many deserved compliments on his work, as a whole, as well as for the care and attention he has paid to every little detail, and the work certainly does him an honor that will prove lasting.

Messrs. Schenck & Young, the carpenters, Sturges Brothers, who did the stone and mason work, T. B. Pierson, the plumber, and Thatcher, the decorator, have all done their work well, as a critical examination will prove, all having aided in the erection of a building that will prove an ornament to Morristown as well as a graceful and substantial addition to the First Church property. The cost of the Manse is about $18,000.

" Ebenezer, hitherto the Lord hath helped us."

(HYMN SUNG AT THE CENTENARY ANNIVERSARY, 29th SEPT., 1842. BY WHOM WAS IT COMPOSED?)

Almighty God, great King, draw near,
Where Thou, with love, hast often heard
Our Fathers' voice of praise and prayer,
And blest, with power, Thy gracious word.

A hundred years have roll'd away,
Since here, in faith, they first did raise
An altar to the Lord. To-day,
Their sons would lift their voice in praise—

And tell of wonders God hath done,
To magnify His gracious name
In saving souls, who else had gone
To everlasting grief and shame.

Here Thou hast made the listening throng,
Imbibe Thy saving truth and love—
Here pardoned rebels joined the song
Of sinless seraphim above.

Still, let Thy word melodious sound,
And spread celestial bliss around,
'Till all shall humbly seek Thy face,
And joy in Thine abounding grace.

MINISTERS WHO HAVE BEEN MEMBERS OF THIS CHURCH.

(This list is but a partial one. We shall be glad to receive information by which the list may be enlarged and made complete.)

Philip Lindsley.
John Ford, son of Jas.
Marcus Ford, son of Jas.
Samuel Whelpley.
Melancthon Whelpley, son of Samuel.
Jared D. Filer.
Henry Ford, son of Jonathan.
Elias Winans Crane.
David Moffat Halliday, son of Samuel.
Samuel Byram Halliday, "   "   "
John Ray.
Charles L. Mills.
Isaac Todd, son of Robert.
Baker Johnson, son of Mahlon.
Arthur Granger.
Levi Hunt Christian.
Joseph Vance.
James Perrine Cutler, son of Joseph.
John Mills Johnson, son of Peter A.
Edward William Condict, son of Edward B.
James Douglass Robertson.
Calvin M. Parks.
Thomas E. Souper.
Walter Condict, son of Silas B.
Arthur Johnson, son of J. Henry.
Allan F. DeCamp.
David Maricnat Davenport.
David Olyphant Irving, son of Rev. David.